CHINA TODAY

China.

CHINA TODAY

AN ENCYCLOPEDIA OF LIFE IN THE PEOPLE'S REPUBLIC

VOLUME I: A–L

Edited by Jing Luo

Aimin Chen, Associate Editor, Economics
Shunfeng Song, Associate Editor, Economics
Baogang Guo, Associate Editor, Labor Relations
Ronghua Ouyang, Associate Editor, Education

GREENWOOD PRESS
Westport, Connecticut • London

Library of Congress Cataloging-in-Publication Data

Encyclopedia of contemporary Chinese civilization / edited by Jing Luo ; Aimin Chen, associate editor, economics ; Shunfeng Song, associate editor, economics ; Baogang Guo, associate editor, labor relations ; Ronghua Ouyang, associate editor, education.

    p. cm.

  Includes bibliographical references and index.

  ISBN 0-313-32170-1 (set : alk. paper)—ISBN 0-313-32768-8 (v.1: alk. paper)—ISBN 0-313-32769-6 (v.2 : alk. paper) 1. China—Civilization—1949—Encyclopedias.   I. Luo, Jing, 1960-
  DS777.6.E52   2005
  951.05'03—dc22   2004022532

British Library Cataloguing in Publication Data is available.

Library of Congress Catalog Card Number: 2004022532
ISBN: 0-313-32170-1 (set code)
        0-313-32768-8 (vol. I)
        0-313-32769-6 (vol. II)

First published in 2005

Greenwood Press, 88 Post Road West, Westport, CT 06881
An imprint of Greenwood Publishing Group, Inc.
www.greenwood.com

Printed in the United States of America

∞™

The paper used in this book complies with the Permanent Paper Standard issued by the National Information Standards Organization (Z39.48-1984).

10 9 8 7 6 5 4 3 2 1

CONTENTS

PREFACE

China Today: An Encyclopedia of Life in the People's Republic provides information on the main aspects of communist China. Its goal is to present an analytical view of Chinese communism in transition. The entries are generally comparative in approach, highlighting the broad-based economic reforms and social changes that have occurred in the People's Republic of China (PRC) since 1949, and especially since Deng Xiaoping's pivotal economic reforms launched in 1978. *China Today* contains 239 entries covering the following broad themes and topics: agriculture and rural China; arts and literature; diplomacy and foreign relations; economy, trade, and business culture; education; ethnic groups and issues; government, law, and administration; individuals; intellectuals; labor and human resource management; media; medicine and health; military, criminal justice, and human rights; political campaigns and leaders; population issues; regions; religion and spiritual life; social issues; Taiwan; United States and China; urban China; and women. A "Guide to Related Topics" breaks down the entries by these broad categories and allows the reader to trace main themes across related entries.

The section of economy, trade, and business culture is of high current interest. It is covered by more than fifty entries, including, among many others, those on banking, corporate governance, China's entry into the World Trade Organization (WTO), trade relations, credit spending, and the tobacco industry. Religion and spiritual life are explored in five entries—"Confucian Tradition and Christianity," "Islam," "Jews," "Religion and Freedom of Religious Belief," and "Spiritual Life in the Post-Mao Era." Although this topic is addressed in fewer entries, it reveals an important dimension of modern Chinese life. All other topics are similarly covered by an appropriate number of entries.

The average entry is approximately 1,000 to 1,500 words in length. Each entry is followed by a selected bibliography that directs the reader to further studies and sources. The entries are extensively cross-referenced, with in-text mentions of other entries highlighted in boldface type and other related entries listed in a *See also* section at the end of the text. A general bibliography and a chronology of important events since 1949 are also included. Additionally, many of *China Today*'s entries are illustrated. A detailed subject index provides further access to the wealth of information offered in the entries.

Most of the entries were contributed by well-established scholars in many related fields. Although most of the contributors have teaching careers in the United States or Europe, many were born in the New China and have personally witnessed its historical transition. Some have had opportunities to immerse themselves, one way or another, in the political campaigns of the 1950s through the 1970s and in the economic booms of the 1980s and 1990s. Their experience adds greatly to the wealth of accurate and current information provided by *China Today*.

China Today is designed with pedagogical needs in mind. It will directly benefit courses on modern Chinese civilization, including those on the modern Chinese economy and the state and government. This reference could also be adapted as a textbook for seminar-type courses, given that the articles provide not only reference information but, more important, views and perspectives that lead students to further research.

ACKNOWLEDGMENTS

The publication of *China Today: An Encyclopedia of Life in the People's Republic*, results from the generous support of many people. First, I am thankful to Cynthia Harris, formerly senior editor at Greenwood Press, who enthusiastically helped me format the proposal for submission early in 2001. Her patient and professional guidance was a key factor in getting the project on its feet.

Once the *China Today* project entered the writing phase early in 2002, soliciting articles and encouraging timely submission proved to be exciting challenges. In meeting these challenges, I feel privileged to have worked with the four associate editors—Dr. Aimin Chen, professor of economics at Indiana State University; Dr. Shunfeng Song, professor of economics at the University of Nevada; Dr. Baogang Guo, assistant professor of political science at Dalton State College; and Dr. Ronghua Ouyang, associate professor of education at Kennesaw State University. Their hard work secured more than one-third of the total entries.

During the writing phase, John Wagner, senior development editor at Greenwood, provided tremendous support. In addition to his detailed and timely feedback with respect to editing, I often found myself impressed with John's insights on many content-related matters. I feel fortunate to have worked with John through the most challenging phase of the project.

China Today represents a collaborative dedication in many ways. Hence my special thanks go to the contributors. Without their quality writing and timely submissions, this project would not have been completed within a remarkably short period of time. At the same time, the Internet enabled me to maintain communication with contributors and Greenwood. Consequently, I owe a debt of gratitude to Bloomsburg University for its stable computing facilities.

Finally, I would like to thank my family for their support. Cong was willing to read some of the entries and may have learned a great deal to supplement her college education at MIT. Jon and Janice enjoyed stapling papers. My wife, Yun, was always a strong supporter, though puzzled from time to time seeing me back from the office at 3:00 A.M. It was their support that made me feel the work was all the more meaningful.

INTRODUCTION

When Mao Zedong declared the founding of the People's Republic of China (PRC) on October 1, 1949, he achieved a China freed from warlords and cleared, for the most part, of foreign concessions. From the perspective of the nation's history, this was truly a day of great pride. A vast, ancient, weak, and long-divided China finally stood up as an independent country. But the new system, in its deeper nature, was hardly new. Mao fully intended that he and the Communist Party be in complete and unchallenged control of China. Democracy, rule of law, industrialization, and commercialization were tailored to serve the regime, and the subsequent procedures and processes of the government were all readily inherited from Chinese history. Indeed, the new regime ran the country in a way that resembled the system of the Qin dynasty (221–206 B.C.). To guarantee stability, the PRC rooted out overt enemies and potential "bad elements" through endless waves of political campaigns. To guarantee the economic foundation of communism, the source of all evil—the private sector—was eradicated. Factories were confiscated or bought out by the government, and farmlands were communized. To guarantee loyalty, Communist education was enforced; arts and literature had no purpose but to serve politics, functioning as the Communist Party's propaganda machine. By the late 1960s, the new system reached its nadir; the ongoing Great Cultural Revolution made people into enemies, and the economy was on the brink of collapse.

But the Great Cultural Revolution had a silver lining. When Mao Zedong died in 1976, his eventual successor was seventy-two-year-old Deng Xiaoping. The excesses of Mao's last years left a legacy that allowed the experienced Deng to initiate important economic reforms in the late 1970s. Deng reversed Mao's policies; his "reform" was a process of undoing what Mao had done wrong. For example, Mao's economic failure resulted largely from his policy of "revolution first, production second." Deng shifted the Communist Party's focus to the "Four Modernizations," that is, in industry, agriculture, science and technology, and national defense. Mao deprivatized the economy, while Deng reprivatized the land in its usage rights and initiated reforms of state-owned enterprises. Mao made the nation worship Marxism as "eternal" and "universal" truth, while Deng encouraged the nation to contest this "universal truth" by checking it against China's reality. Mao equated profit with evil, while Deng announced that "to be rich is glorious." Under Mao's rule, the market economy was taboo, while Deng endorsed a "socialist market economy." Mao isolated China from the rest of the world, while Deng opened the door to foreign investment. Mao advocated the simple life and hard struggle; Deng said that "poor communism is nonsense." Mao urged population growth; Deng firmly implemented family planning. Mao forced arts and literature to comply with and serve the state; Deng gave rise to a literary flowering. Mao vowed, "Let the Cultural Revolution happen once every few years"; Deng declared, "Stability is of primary importance." Mao's Communist Party was exclusively for the elite of the working class; Deng's successor, Jiang Zemin, opened Party membership to entrepreneurs.

Under Deng's rule, from 1978 to 1999, household incomes increased by 473 percent and 361 percent in rural and urban households, respectively, allowing China to reach the goal of becoming an "affluent society." Moreover, China joined the World Trade Organization (WTO) in 2001 and became firmly integrated into the world economy. By 2002, China had received $52.7 billion of foreign direct investment (FDI) inflows, surpassing the United States and becoming the largest FDI host country in the world. The Chinese Communist Party is also learning to do business. The Party's goal today is to represent the "majority of the people" rather than the working class alone. Deng's legacy is now being carried out by the fourth generation of leadership, headed by Hu Jintao and Wen Jiabao, who have shown no sign of slowing down their implementation of Deng's policies.

On the other hand, certain fundamental principles laid down by Mao and inherited by Deng are being carried forward by the post-Deng leadership. China's chief political principle remains adherence to socialism and to single-party government. The number one item on the national agenda remains reuniting Taiwan with the motherland. These principles have been upheld by every post-Mao government.

In retrospect, Mao's legacy served as a reference system for the reformists. It was the reason reform happened. However, undoing the damage that occurred under Mao is only the start of this profound reform process. As China moves ahead into a modern economy, it faces new challenges. For example, the urban-rural divide has widened, regional disparity has grown, reform of state-owned enterprises has resulted in tens of millions of lay-offs, the urban unemployment rate has risen sharply, and WTO entry will likely bring about a new set of challenges never encountered before. To meet future challenges, China's political and economic structures will need to adapt accordingly. Whether China will be able to realize further democratization and to implement the rule of law is critical for the country's future.

The past two decades of transition are widely applauded as a solid start and have laid the foundation for an optimistic economic and cultural revolution ahead. *China Today* is intended to be an early witness of that future.

CHRONOLOGY OF THE PEOPLE'S REPUBLIC OF CHINA

1949 The People's Republic of China (PRC) is founded on October 1 in Beijing. The Nationalist government withdraws to Taiwan. Mao Zedong declares the "People's Democratic Dictatorship." Mao is appointed chairman of the Central People's Government; Zhou Enlai is named premier; and Zhu De becomes general commander of the People's Liberation Army (PLA).

1950 The Sino-Soviet Treaty of Friendship, Alliance, and Mutual Assistance is signed in Moscow by Mao Zedong and Joseph Stalin. In June, Mao denounces American aggression in Korea. In October, the Army of the Chinese People's Volunteers publicly enters Korea in support of North Korea. Also in this year, the Marriage Law is promulgated by the central government, together with the Trade Union Law and the Agrarian Reform Law of the PRC.

1951 The Korean War progresses, with Chinese troops taking Seoul. Mao Zedong's son, Mao Anying, is killed in Korea. Domestically, the Agreement of the Central People's Government and the Local Government of Tibet on Measures for the Liberation of Tibet is signed in Beijing; the agreement recognizes Tibet as part of China and grants the region autonomous status.

1952 The Three-Antis Campaign is launched in January; it targets corruption, waste, and bureaucratism. In February, the Five-Antis Campaign is started; it targets business operations and is commonly viewed as the precursor to a looming deprivatization campaign. Deng Xiaoping becomes deputy premier.

1953 The armistice ending the Korean War is signed on July 27. The First Five-Year Plan (1953–1957) starts. Deng Xiaoping becomes finance minister for one year.

1954   Zhou Enlai and Indian prime minister Jawaharlal Nehru sign a joint communiqué that becomes the first international declaration to include the PRC's "Five Principles of Peaceful Coexistence." The first National People's Congress (NPC) convenes. Deng Xiaoping becomes deputy chairman of the National Defense Council.

1955   Zhou Enlai attends the Asian-African Conference (Bandung Conference) in Bandung, Indonesia; the conference seeks to build a united front of Asian and African nations against colonialism and racism. Deng Xiaoping is elected to the Politburo. The Chinese Language Reform Committee releases the first batch of simplified Chinese characters, which are first used in newspapers in Beijing and Tianjin.

1956   In April, Mao Zedong delivers his influential speech "On the Ten Major Relationships." In September, the Eighth Party Congress elects Mao Party chairman; Liu Shaoqi, Zhou Enlai, Zhu De, and Chen Yun are elected deputy chairmen; and Deng Xiaoping is elected as secretary-general of the Chinese Communist Party (CCP). In May, Mao Zedong calls for greater artistic and academic freedom with the slogan "let a hundred flowers bloom, and a hundred schools of thought contend."

1957   Mao Zedong delivers his speech "On the Correct Handling of Contradictions among the People." In June, the *People's Daily* states that rightists are trying to overthrow the Communist Party, and an Anti-Rightist Campaign is launched.

1958   In May, the Great Leap Forward is launched with the phrase "more, faster, better, and more economically soundly" as its general guiding principle. In August, at the Politburo's Beidaihe Conference, the people's communes plan is endorsed; the plan results in the organization of 26,000 communes in less than two months.

1959   In March, the State Council appoints the Panchen Lama to chair the Preparatory Committee for the Tibetan Autonomous Region. Democratic reforms start in April in Tibet. In April, Liu Shaoqi replaces Mao Zedong as president of the PRC, with Song Qingling and Dong Biwu as deputies. During July and August, an extremely serious drought hits vast areas of China, affecting 30 percent of production from the land. Rebellion erupts in Tibet. Lin Biao replaces Peng Dehuai as defense minister.

1960   In July, the Soviets notify China of their withdrawal of technological support. With the exception of Xinjiang and Tibet, serious famine occurs across China, causing tens of millions of deaths.

1961   Wu Han's controversial play *Hai Rui's Dismissal* is published in January. The Twenty-sixth World Table Tennis Championships takes place in Beijing, with the Chinese winning both the men's and women's singles titles.

1962   In October, Chinese troops launch major offensives on the Sino-Indian border. A cease-fire is declared in November. Mao Zedong steps up emphasis on class struggle.

1963   In May, Mao Zedong launches the socialist education movement in rural areas.

1964 In January, Zhou Enlai launches an extensive tour of Africa. In August, the United States bombs North Vietnam. In October, China carries out its first nuclear test.

1965 In May, China carries out its second nuclear test. In June, the *Wenhuibao* newspaper denounces Wu Han's drama *Hai Rui's Dismissal* as an anti-Party poisonous weed, thereby signaling the coming of the Great Cultural Revolution. The Tibetan Autonomous Region is formally inaugurated in September.

1966 In May, the Politburo sets up the Cultural Revolution Group and calls for attacks on all representatives of the bourgeoisie who have infiltrated the Party, government, army, and cultural world. In July, Mao Zedong swims in the Yangzi River at Wuhan, refuting the rumor that he is sick. In August, Mao Zedong, Lin Biao, and Zhou Enlai preside at a Cultural Revolution rally in Tiananmen Square at which Red Guards make their first appearance. The Guards subsequently begin destroying historical relics. *Chairman Mao's Quotations* are first published in the form of the "Little Red Book." Deng Xiaoping is ousted from his offices.

1967 In June, China tests its first hydrogen bomb. By December 25, China has distributed 350 million copies of Mao's Little Red Book.

1968 The army takes control of government offices, schools, and factories. Millions of young people are sent to the countryside to receive re-education from peasants.

1969 In March, Chinese and Soviet forces clash at Zhenbaodao Island in the Ussuri River. More clashes occur in the following months. In July, the United States lifts restrictions on travel to China; the United States lifts its partial trade embargo of China in December. Liu Shaoqi dies.

1970 In April, China launches its first satellite.

1971 In April, the U.S. Ping-Pong team visits China and is followed by U.S. secretary of state Henry Kissinger, who comes to Beijing in July. In October, China is admitted to the United Nations.

1972 In February, President Richard Nixon visits China, where he signs the joint Shanghai Communiqué admitting that there is but one China and that Taiwan is a part of China. In September, China purchases ten Boeing 707 civilian jet airliners from the United States.

1973 Deng Xiaoping becomes vice premier in August. The United States and China announce their intention to establish liaison offices in each other's capital.

1974 In April, Deng Xiaoping addresses the United Nations and denounces the world hegemony of the two superpowers, the United States and the Soviet Union.

1975 In January, Deng Xiaoping is elected deputy chairman of the Chinese Communist Party Central Committee (CCPCC).

1976 A huge earthquake in Tangshan, a city near Beijing, kills more than 250,000 people. Premier Zhou Enlai dies in January, and Mao Zedong dies in September at age eighty-two. Mao's death ends the Great

Cultural Revolution. The radical group called the "Gang of Four," led by Mao's widow Jiang Qing, is arrested by Hua Guofeng, Mao's hand-picked successor.

1977   University admissions based on college entrance examinations start. Enrollment based on recommendations ends. Deng Xiaoping is politically rehabilitated.

1978   The "Deng era" begins. Deng Xiaoping emerges as a key leader and sets about repairing the damage caused during the last years of Mao Zedong's rule. Deng's market-oriented reforms, embodied in the maxim "to get rich is glorious," spark more than two decades of phenomenal growth that lifts hundreds of millions of people out of abject poverty. In December, the Coca-Cola Company reaches an agreement with China to sell its soft drinks in the country and open up bottling plants. In the same month, the Third Plenum of the Eleventh Chinese Communist Party Central Committee (CCPCC) shifts the Party's focus to modernization, which is also seen as the onset of the economic reforms.

1979   In January, Deng Xiaoping visits the United States and resumes the Sino-American diplomatic relationship. From January to February, Chinese troops invade Vietnamese territory and destroy logistics facilities. In July, the Fifth National People's Congress (NPC) announces the Criminal Law and the Organic Law of the Local People's Congresses and Local People's Governments. Special economic zones are opened, including Shenzhen, Zhuhai, Shantou, and Xiamen. In September, the Party criticizes Mao Zedong's Cultural Revolution as ill judged and calamitous. In October, political dissident Wei Jingsheng is sentenced to fifteen years in prison.

1980   In February, the NPC Standing Committee declares regulations on issuance of academic degrees. In December, the *People's Daily* declares that Mao Zedong made great mistakes during his last years and that his Great Cultural Revolution was a disaster.

1981   Deng Xiaoping is elected chairman of the Military Commission, and Hu Yaobang replaces Hua Guofeng as chairman of the Chinese Communist Party Central Committee (CCPCC). Both Zhao Ziyang and Hua Guofeng are appointed deputy chairmen. The trial of the Gang of Four is held.

1982   In September, British prime minister Margaret Thatcher arrives in Beijing to start discussions with regard to the future of Hong Kong.

1983   The *Selected Works* of Deng Xiaoping is published in July. Sino-British talks over Hong Kong's future begin.

1984   In October, the Third Plenum of the Twelfth Chinese Communist Party Central Committee (CCPCC) adopts a decision on reform of the economic structure, shifting the focus to urban enterprises. Measures are taken to strengthen the Tibetan economy. Fourteen coastal cities and the island of Hainan are opened to foreign investment. A Sino-British declaration on Hong Kong's return is signed.

1985   In May, the Chinese Communist Party Central Committee (CCPCC) releases its Decision on the Reform of the Educational System.

1986 In September, Deng Xiaoping, during a *60 Minutes* interview with Mike Wallace of CBS, endorses Mikhail Gorbachev's reforms in the Soviet Union and indicates that China's economic reforms are not in conflict with communism. In September, the Shanghai Stock Market reopens for the first time since 1949. The Bankruptcy Law is issued in December. In May and December, students in large cities stage demonstrations demanding more rapid reforms and more democracy.

1987 Faced with rising democratic pressures, the Chinese Communist Party (CCP) reiterates its determination to stick to the "Four Cardinal Principles." Hu Yaobang resigns in January. Writer Liu Bingyan is expelled from the Party. Zhao Ziyang is appointed general secretary of the CCP, replacing Hu Yaobang. Student unrest occurs in twenty-two Chinese cities. In November, Deng Xiaoping remains in control of the Central Military Commission. In December, Zhao Ziyang resigns as premier and is replaced by hard-liner Li Peng. In October, 2,000 Tibetan monks demonstrate in Lhasa in favor of Tibetan independence; the demonstrations lead to clashes with Chinese authorities.

1988 China slides into economic chaos triggered by rising inflation that peaks at more than 30 percent in the cities. Public discontent sets the stage for prodemocracy demonstrations in 1989. Hainan is approved for provincial status. The first nude paintings exposition is opened in Beijing in December.

1989 On May 16, Deng Xiaoping and Mikhail Gorbachev meet and announce the normalization of Sino-Soviet relations. On June 4, after weeks of protests by students in Beijing's Tiananmen Square, troops backed by tanks crush the demonstrations, allegedly killing hundreds of people. The event once again isolates China on the world stage. On June 5, President George Bush suspends high-level relations with Beijing in protest against the massacre. On December 10, U.S. national security adviser Brent Scowcroft meets Deng Xiaoping in Beijing. After the crackdown, Deng plucks Jiang Zemin from relative obscurity in Shanghai to be the new Communist Party chief. Jiang replaces Zhao Ziyang.

1990 In January, almost 500 students who participated in the demonstrations of the previous year are released from detention. In April, President Yang Shangkun promulgates the Basic Law of the Hong Kong Special Administrative Region (SAR) adopted by the Seventh National People's Congress (NPC). The law is scheduled to take effect on July 1, 1997. Campaigns that aim at strengthening patriotism and discipline are launched at educational institutions.

1991 The first partial direct elections are held in Hong Kong.

1992 During his tour to Hainan and coastal cities, Deng Xiaoping reiterates his determination to continue China's economic reforms. Beijing establishes diplomatic relations with South Korea.

1993 Chinese President Jiang Zemin meets with U.S. President Bill Clinton in Seattle, Washington, during an informal meeting of APEC leaders.

1994 The Three Gorges Dam project starts.

1995 Hong Kong holds legislative elections.

1996 Dong Jianhua (Tung Cheehua) is selected chief executive of Hong Kong.

1997 Deng Xiaoping (1904–1997) dies at age 93. Deng's successor, Jiang Zemin, visits Washington. The British formally hand Hong Kong back to China on July 1.

1998 The Asian financial crisis negatively affects many of China's coastal businesses and causes severe deflation. The Chinese government maintains the yuan's value. U.S. president Bill Clinton visits Beijing.

1999 NATO's accidental bombing of the Chinese embassy in Belgrade, Yugoslavia, sparks a crisis in Sino-American relations. China and the United States reach an accord on the terms of China's entry to the World Trade Organization (WTO). China recovers sovereignty over Macao.

2000 Chen Shuibian of the Democratic Progressive Party is elected president of Taiwan, while Li Denghui (Lee Teng-hui) of the Kuomintang Party (KMT) resigns. The 9th National People's Congress (NPC) is held in Beijing in March; the Congress stresses anticorruption efforts and economic cooldown.

2001 Hijacked civilian planes hit the World Trade Center in New York City on September 11. An Asian-Pacific Economic Cooperation (APEC) meeting held in Shanghai in October is attended by American president George W. Bush. Jiang Zemin pledges to support the American war on terrorism. China joins the World Trade Organization (WTO) in December. China wins a bid to host the 2008 Olympic Games.

2002 The Sixteenth Congress of the Chinese Communist Party (CCP) is held in November. The Party completes a sweeping leadership reshuffle. Jiang Zemin and other aging leaders give way to a younger generation headed by Hu Jintao and Wen Jiabao. Jiang Zemin remains chairman of the Central Military Commission. The SARS outbreak is detected in November; attempts to cover up the spread of the SARS infection cause scandal.

2003 The Tenth National People's Conress (NPC) is held in March. Hu Jintao and Wen Jiabao are elected president and premier, respectively, of the PRC. Jiang Zemin and Zhu Rongji step down.

2004 Hu Jintao quietly consolidates power while both he and Premier Wen Jiabao reveal populist agendas in their first year in office. Chen Shuibian is reelected president of Taiwan in March, taking advantage of the popularity generated by an unsuccessful attempt to assassinate him. The growing belief that the assassination attempt was contrived sparks suspicion of Chen Shuibian's campaign strategy. In September, Jiang Zemin steps down from his last position as Chairman of the Central Military Commission. In December, President Bush meets with Hu Jintao at the Twelfth APEC meeting. Both sides express a commitment to a stronger Sino-U.S. relationship.

LIST OF ENTRIES

GUIDE TO RELATED TOPICS

Agriculture and Rural China

Agricultural Reform
Agriculture, Impact of WTO Accession on
Environmental Protection, Policies and
    Practices
Family Collectivism
Hukou System
Migrant Population
People's Communes/Household
    Responsibility System
Rural Administrative Organizations
Rural Credit Cooperatives (RCCs)
Rural Industrialization
Rural-Urban Divide, Regional Disparity, and
    Income Inequality
Tobacco Industry
Township and Village Enterprises (TVEs)

Arts and Literature

Ai Qing (1910–1996)
Anticorruption Literature and Television
    Dramas
Avant-garde Literature
Chang, Iris (1968–2004)
Experimental Fiction
Film Production
Film Production during the Seventeen Years
    (1949–1966)

Films of the 1980s
Films of the 1990s
Folk Music and Songs of New China
Great Cultural Revolution, Literature during
He Jingzhi (1924–   )
Li Zhun (1928–2000)
Literary Policy for the New China
Literature of the Wounded
Liu Qing (1916–1978)
Misty Poetry
Modern Pop-Satire
Neorealist Fiction and Modernism
Pre–Cultural Revolution Literature
Revolutionary Realism and Revolutionary
    Romanticism
Root-Searching Literature
Ru Zhijuan (1925–1998)
Sexual Freedom in Literature
Sun Li (1913–   )
Theater in Contemporary China
"Three Prominences," Principle of
Wei Wei (1920–   )
Yang Mo (1914–1995)
Yang Shuo (1913–1968)

Diplomacy and Foreign Relations

Bandung Conference of 1955
Cold War and China

Five Principles of Peaceful Coexistence
Independent Foreign Policy (1982)
Jiang Zemin (1926–), Diplomacy of
Korean War (1950–1953)
Nixon's Visit to China/Shanghai
    Communiqué (1972)
Ping-Pong Diplomacy
Rhetoric in China's Foreign Relations
Sino-American Relations, Conflicts and
    Common Interests
Sino-American Relations since 1949
Sino-Japanese Relations since 1949
Sino-Russian Relations since 1991
Sino-Soviet Alliance
Taiwan Strait Crisis, Evolution of
United Nations (UN) and China
U.S. Legislation on China-Related Issues
Vietnam War
Zhou Enlai (1898–1976)

Economy, Trade, and Business Culture

Agriculture, Impact of WTO Accession on
Agricultural Reform
Auto Industry Development
Banking and Financial System Reform
Brand-Building Phenomenon
Business Decision Making in the Public and
    Private Sectors
Central Planning
Coca-Cola in China
Commercial Advertising, Policies and
    Practices of
Consumption Patterns and Statistics of
    Living Conditions
Corporate Governance
Credit Spending, Development of
Domestic Government Debt
Economic Policies and Development
    (1949–Present)
Economic Structure
Energy Industries
Fiscal Policy and Tax Reforms
Foreign Debt
Foreign Direct Investment (FDI)
Foreign Trade
Growth and Development, Trade-offs of
Housing Reform

Industrial Structure
Land Policy
Land Reform
People's Communes/Household
    Responsibility System
Pharmaceutical Industry, Administrative and
    Regulatory Structures of
Pharmaceutical Products, Sales and
    Marketing of
Privately Owned Enterprises (POEs)
Reemployment of Laid-off Workers
Regions of China, Uneven Development of
Renminbi (RMB)
Rural Credit Cooperatives (RCCs)
Rural Industrialization
Savings, Pattern of
Special Administrative Region (SAR)
State-Owned Enterprises (SOEs)
Sustainable Growth and Development
Taiwan, Trade Relations with
Tobacco Industry
Township and Village Enterprises (TVEs)
Trade Relations with the United States
Western Region Development Project
World Trade Organization (WTO), China's
    Accession to
World Trade Organization (WTO), Impact of
    on Service Industries

Education

Character Education in Primary and
    Secondary Schools
Chinese Script, Reform of
Education Media and Technology
Educational Administration
Educational System
English Proficiency Levels
Entrance Examination System for Colleges
    and Universities
Foreign-Language Teaching Methodology
Foreign-Language Training
Fulbright Scholars in China (1979–1989)
Higher-Education Reform
Libraries and Development
Library and Information Science (LIS)
    Education
Management Education

Primary Education
Private Education
Putonghua, Promotion of
School Enrollment and Employment
Secondary Education
Special Education
Taiwan, Education Reform in
Teacher Education
Television Institute and Self-Learning
United States, Chinese Education in
Vocational and Technical Training

Ethnic Groups and Issues

Drinking in Ethnic Cultures
Ethnic Burial Customs
Ethnic Kinships
Ethnic Marriage Customs
Ethnic Minorities, Political Systems of
Ethnicity and Ethnic Policies
Minority Women in Xinjiang and Taiwan
Mosuo People, Matriarchal Tradition of
Taiwan, Ethnicity and Ethnic Policies of

Government, Law, and Administration

Administrative Reforms (1949–1978)
Administrative Reforms after 1978
Administrative Structure of Government
Correction System
Corruption and Fraud, Control of
Crime Prevention
Democratic Parties, Political Functions of
Environmental Protection, Policies and
    Practices
Grassroots Democracy
Hong Kong, Return of
Hukou System
Human Rights Debate
Illegal Drugs, Control of
Judicial Reform
Legal Infrastructure Development and
    Economic Development
National People's Congress (NPC), Structure
    and Functions of
New Party (NP) (Taiwan)
Patent Protection
Rural Administrative Organizations

Individuals

Ai Qing (1910–1996)
Chang, Iris
Chen Shuibian (1950–   )
Deng Xiaoping (1904–1997), Politics of
Deng Xiaoping (1904–1997), Reforms of
He Jingzhi (1924–   )
Hua Guofeng (1921–   )
Jiang Zemin (1926–   ), Diplomacy of
Jiang Zemin (1926–   ), Populism of
Li Zhun (1928–2000)
Liu Qing (1916–1978)
Liu Shaoqi (1898–1969)
Mao Zedong (1893–1976)
Ru Zhijuan (1925–1998)
Sun Li (1913–   )
Wei Wei (1920–   )
Yang Mo (1914–1995)
Yang Shuo (1913–1968)
Zhou Enlai (1898–1976)
Zhu Rongji (1928–   )

Intellectuals

Fulbright Scholars in China (1979–1989)
Higher-Education Reform
Intellectual Work, Changing Dynamics of
Intellectuals
Intellectuals, Political Engagement of
    (1949–1978)
Intellectuals, Political Engagement of
    (1978–Present)
United States, Chinese Education in

Labor and Human Resource Management

Human Resource Management (HRM)
Labor Market
Labor-Market Development
Labor Policy
Labor Policy, Employment, and
    Unemployment
Labor Relations
Labor Rights
Migrant Population
Reemployment of Laid-off
    Workers

CHINA TODAY

A

Administrative Reforms, 1949–1978

Administrative reform is a process of making deliberate changes in decision-making institutions with respect to their structure, process, attitudes, and the behavior of decision makers for the purpose of improving organizational performance (Caiden 1969). The goals typically include combating bureaucracy through streamlining, downsizing, reorganizing, decentralizing, and privatizing corruption- and inefficiency-stricken units. By bringing changes to administrative structure and resource-allocation priorities, the quality and competence of management is expected to be improved. Employment-related recruiting and training are important parts of the review process. New reward/punishment measures and new design, budgeting, and auditing programs are set up to optimize the value of money and fiscal capacity of the administrative apparatus in the delivery of services (Burns 1993). To facilitate economic development and political control, the People's Republic of China has undergone a series of administrative reforms since 1949.

The year 1951 marked China's first self-conscious administrative reform. **Zhou Enlai**, China's first premier, identified the need for reform in his report to the Third Plenary Session of the First National Political Consultation Committee. He recognized that due to the fact that the state had an overwhelming amount of work at its inception and that there was a serious lack of experience, many governmental organizations were overstaffed and inefficient, but there was a severe shortage of personnel in areas such as economic construction, culture, and education. Therefore, the State Department (predecessor of the State Council) decided to compress the personnel quota, adjust organizational structure, reduce levels of hierarchy, and downsize the number of government employees. Bo Yibo, then the chairman of the National Personnel Quota Committee, enumerated the problems with bureaucracy by noting that under a division of a ministerial-level department, there could be as many as

2,000 subdivisions, and a document could carry as many as thirty-six seals before it got out of a ministerial department. Also, every five to six cadres used a service assistant. Nannies and gardeners were also widely employed. The increases of nannies on the governmental payroll in one province were in the thousands. Also, as many as one-third of the employees had no work to do. It was estimated that 20 percent of them worked, 30 percent worked somewhat, and 50 percent worked at nothing (*Selected Archives of the People's Republic of China, 1949–1952*, 1990, 617). The major themes of this reform were anticorruption, antibureaucratization, and antiwaste movements. Many cadres from the central government were transferred to work in regional governments. The central government cut its personnel quota by between 20 and 25 percent. Provincial governments cut their personnel by between 10 and 15 percent.

In 1954, power struggles between the Northeast and the East Bureaus on one side and the central government on the other side led to the abolishment of six large district regional governments (Northwest, North, Northeast, East, South Central, and West Central Bureaus). Power was consolidated into the hands of the central government.

In 1955, the State Council established a formal Salary/Personnel Quota Commission, which was responsible for streamlining the central government. Between March and June, the central government reduced its size by 47 percent. Governments throughout the country were reduced by as much as 40 percent.

The administrative reform in 1956 deserves particular attention. That reform raised a set of issues that have been troubling Chinese leaders ever since, including central/regional government relations, Communist Party/government relations, government/business relations, and downsizing the existing governmental bureaucracy. The 1956 reform was China's largest effort to overhaul its administrative system. Between late 1957 and June 1958, 80 percent of the industries and enterprises that were managed by the ministries of the central government were decentralized into the hands of the provincial, municipal, and county governments. Unfortunately, the great plans proposed in the 1956 reform were interrupted by a mass movement known as the **Great Leap Forward**, which was brought forth at the Second Plenary Session of the Eighth National Congress of the Communist Party under the influence of **Mao Zedong**'s drastic plan of economic revival. The movement set astronomical standards for productivity growth and expected the main industrial and agricultural products to increase dozens of times. Chaos, lies, and exaggerations followed because Mao demanded to "see the results." He wanted China to catch up with England in fifteen years.

By 1964, China had recovered from the aftermath of the 1958 Great Leap Forward movement. A new round of industrialization began. In the same year, a central government survey group found that in one major industrial city, 463 **state-owned enterprises** (102 owned by the central government, fifty-four owned by the provincial governments, and the rest owned by municipalities) were managed by as many as thirty-eight bureaus in seventeen central government ministries, twenty bureaus in eighteen provincial-level departments, and many other offices (Ren 1998). Overlapping jurisdiction, redundant management, complex relationships, and red tape had become overwhelming. The battleground of competition for production was not in the marketplace, but inside the bureaucracy. This phenomenon was typical throughout China.

National leaders were forced to reexamine their administrative system. Toward the end of 1963, a central government document "On Industrial Development" urged that industries and enterprises be managed by economic means instead of bureaucratic means. Premier Zhou Enlai pointed out that after trust had been established, the scale of the ministries should be downsized and there should be fewer people working in the administrative units. He asserted that specialized ministries, such as the Ministry of Fossil Fuels, could be absorbed into larger enterprises. On August 17, 1964, the Party Central Committee and the State Council approved "The Report of Opinions on Experimenting with Industrial and Communication Trusts." Twelve trusts were established and achieved commendable successes in a short period of time. However, these conglomerates quickly started running into conflict with regional governments' interests when they attempted to take over less efficiently run but regionally owned enterprises. Again, had it not been for the **Great Cultural Revolution**, which interrupted these experiments, China would have gathered more experience in this respect, which would have made similar efforts by the end of the 1990s easier.

During the period of experimentation with building trust organizations, bureaucracy continued to grow. For instance, the central government cabinet-level departments grew from sixty-two in 1961 to seventy-nine in 1965. The improved economic situation opened the door for more bureaucratic expansion.

Meanwhile, Mao made efforts to tighten his political control. In January 1964, Mao called upon industries throughout the country to model the People's Liberation Army by establishing a political department, under the assumption that this was the only way to stimulate the revolutionary spirit of the millions of workers. Mao's call led to the Central Party Committee's Resolution on Establishing Political Departments in the Industrial and Transportation Department throughout the Country. In no time, almost all administrative units in China started to have their own political departments.

Unhappy about his loss of control over the bureaucracy, Mao started the Great Cultural Revolution. The old bureaucracy was pushed aside by the Red Guards. For a few years, the country was in chaos. Mao ordered the military, selected workers, and peasants to take charge of the situation by sending their representatives to each work unit. From 1969 on, many revolutionary committees were set up at every level of the hierarchy in various ways. These committees consisted of military personnel, workers, peasant representatives, and chosen members of the older bureaucracy. They formed the de facto governments. The new leaders were mostly poorly educated and could not handle the complexity of the old-type bureaucratic work. The radical and unstable political atmosphere made China's neighbors nervous. Border tensions with the Soviet Union intensified, and China's leaders prepared for war with foreign countries. Enterprises were decentralized to regional and local levels. The central government and its ministerial-level bureaucracy were downsized. The State Council was reduced to thirty-two cabinet-level departments, thirteen of which were under the direct leadership of either the Central

Military Committee or the Central Revolutionary Group. After the reform, the government was simple, small, and politically dynamic but economically insensitive and incompetent. The seeds were sown for a major system rejuvenation and bureaucratic restoration. When Deng Xiaoping came back to power in 1978, he started the modern reform.

See also Administrative Reforms after 1978; Administrative Structure of Government; Deng Xiaoping (1904–1997), Reforms of; Industrial Structure; Rural Administrative Organizations; Special Administrative Region (SAR).

Bibliography

Burns, John P., "China's Administrative Reform for a Market Economy," *Public Administration and Development* 13 (1993): 345–360; Caiden, Gerald E., *Administrative Reform* (Chicago: Aldine Publishing Co., 1969); "1960's Documents on the Creation of Industrial and Communication Trust," *Party Documents* 2 (1993); Ren, Xiao, *China's Administrative Reform* (Zhejian, China: Zhejian People's Press, 1998); *Selected Archives of the People's Republic of China, 1949–1952* (Beijing: China Urban Society Economic Press, 1990); Su, Shanxiao, *The Government Structure of the People's Republic of China, 1949–1990* (Beijing: China Economics Press, 1993); Xu, Dashen, *Factual Records of the People's Republic of China* (Changchun, China: Heilongjiang People's Press, 1994).

Zhiyong Lan

Administrative Reforms after 1978

Deng Xiaoping was China's first leader after **Mao Zedong**. As soon as Deng assumed a position of power, he launched a full-scale economic reform. For obvious reasons, the issue of administrative reform once again topped China's political agenda. A series of administrative reforms was launched immediately.

Between 1977 and 1981, many of China's veteran bureaucrats who had been pushed aside during the **Great Cultural Revolution** had their positions restored. In 1978, the State Council alone housed forty-eight administrative units; some were restored and others were newly formulated. By 1981, it expanded to 100 ministerial-level units. Deputy positions flooded the government. The Ministry of the Metallic Industry led by having nineteen vice ministers. Indignant with the extensive bureaucracy, Deng made a speech in the Political Bureau in January 1982 titled "Streamlining Governmental Departments Is a Revolution." Deng pointed out that the inefficiency and irresponsibility that resulted from bureaucracy had reached an intolerable point and must be corrected. Deng declared that the nation and the people wanted the situation improved.

In March 1982, the Twenty-second Plenary of the Standing Committee of the Fifth People's Congress approved "The Report on Organizational Reform of the State Council," which aimed at (1) clarifying the job responsibilities of various units and personnel, (2) selecting talented and competent leaders (revolutionary, young, knowledgeable, and specialized), (3) establishing a systematic retirement system for the veterans, (4) strengthening cadre training, and (5) reducing the ministerial cabinet departments from 100 to 61. Within a year, more than 30,000 veteran cadres throughout the country retired from their nominal functions. Among them were 145 ministerial-level cadres. An age limit was also imposed on governmental positions at every level. Later, in 1993, this system was formalized through the passage of China's civil service reform document titled "Provisional Rules and Regulations." Over the years, it has proven to be the most significant reform achievement. The bulk of reform policies took effect in 1983. However, the reform only shuffled around departments and failed to affect the root structure of the organizations. Despite downsizing at the time of reform, everything grew back quickly afterward.

China's second large administrative reform under Deng occurred in 1988. Leaders of the 1988 reform attributed the failure of the 1983 reform to the lack of change in the government's structural deficiencies. Therefore, the focus of the 1988 reform was to change the function of the government in order to make the administrative structure more commensurate with the political and economic reform. The reform aimed at divorcing governmental agencies from running profit-making enterprises and separating the Communist Party functions from the administrative functions. However, the reform did not structurally remove the direct governmental control over business enterprises. Instead, through a series of ordinances and regulations, supervising governmental agencies were allowed to enjoy more freedom and decision-making power at the enterprise level. The reform met with strong resistance, particularly from the bureaucrats who had a stake in running profit-making enterprises and from many party organizations who viewed removing the Party's role in day-to-day organizational management as an erosion of the Party's control. The tug-of-war between the reformers who wanted to remove Party control and conservatives who wanted to maintain Party control continued and created many administrative loopholes in the process. Corruption became rampant. Dissatisfaction with the slow pace of reform and anger at the rampant corruption in government led to the 1989 Tiananmen student movement.

After two years of stagnation in reform, Deng broke the ice again. Though he had already retired from his official capacity as China's paramount leader, he made a forceful speech during his visit to southern China in 1992 in which he indirectly criticized the incumbent leaders for not continuing to push for reform and stated that China would have no future without furthering its reform. Under Deng's influence, the reform resumed its course, and even more serious cases of corruption were exposed. The masses, however, were unwilling to participate. In 1993, the State Council initiated another round of reform. The main emphasis was on reducing the size of the government, but goals such as changing the function of the government were also mentioned. In this wave of reform, the number of cabinet ministries, agencies, and independent offices was reduced from eighty-six to fifty-nine, and central government employees were reduced by 20 percent.

However, not long afterward, it became clear that another administrative reform was necessary. Before the 1982–1983 reform, there were 15 million employees on the government's payroll. After three rounds of reform in 1982–1983, 1988, and 1993, the number of governmental personnel reached 34 million. With those who also drew partial salaries or supplemental pay from the government, the number of employees on the governmental payroll was 40 million. The compounded growth rate of governmental personnel was 9.5 percent annually, faster than the growth rate of governmental revenue during the same period, which was only 7 percent a year, adjusted for inflation. The bureaucracy was once again a heavy burden on the nation's economic development. As a result, the 1998 reform was launched. It aimed at reducing the role of the government in enterprise management and, at the same time, served as a vehicle to streamline the government.

On March 10, 1998, the First Plenary of the Ninth **National People's Congress** approved the State Council's plan to streamline the central government bureaucracy by cutting cabinet ministries from forty to twenty-nine, to reduce the size of the civil service, and to change some of the major functions of the government. Many of the ministries that directly managed industries were abolished. The **state-owned enterprises**, which had been managed by the governmental ministries, were mainly placed under the supervision of the State Economic and Trade Commission on a temporary basis. Furthermore, assorted other arrangements were also made temporarily to handle the transition of the state-owned enterprises. For example, the government established specialized committees chaired by a vice premier to manage the state-owned enterprises. Some ministries (e.g., the Ministry of Personnel) were asked to temporarily manage some state-owned enterprises on behalf of the State Council. Eventually, these state-owned enterprises would become independent legal entities managed by professional business managers and fully operating under market forces. It was planned that in a few years, all the streamlined staff members would be adequately placed, the state-owned enterprises would be restructured, and commensurate reforms at the state and local levels would be accomplished. At the National Conference on Regional Government Reform held in the spring of 2000, Premier **Zhu Rongji** reemphasized his reform objectives. His goals were to separate the management of the government and enterprises and to establish a diligent, practical, efficient, and corruption-free government for promoting regional economic development and social stability. Twelve provinces, including large municipalities such as Beijing and Shanghai, have already announced the beginning of their reforms. Both Beijing and Shanghai plan to downsize their governmental employees by 50 percent. Shandong and Zhejiang Provinces have managed to downsize their governments by 48 percent. Currently, the number of employees working for regional/local governments throughout China exceeds 5 million. It is planned that the number of these employees will be cut by one-half in a very short term.

The trajectory of China's administrative reforms shows that China has traveled a tortuous and difficult road during the past fifty years. Its reform practices have always been top-down. They have often repeated a cycle of downsizing, expansion, downsizing again, and expanding again. These reforms kept China's system of governance as well as its economy alive. China's bureaucracy has proven to be extremely buoyant. While all bureaucracies have a natural tendency to grow, on Chinese soil, where officialdom has been historically highly valued, the bureaucracy has even more potency. Whenever China directed its attention to economic development and management efficiency, the issue of reforming the bureaucracy became urgent. Reform was called for to allow for more grassroots autonomy to accommodate economic vitality. When this was done, the economy was enlivened, and the government's financial situation was improved, but then the bureaucracy would crawl back, quietly but forcefully and in a more expanded version. Time and again, reform leaders had to face the familiar problem of a large, bloated, and corrupted bureaucracy. The 1998 reform still did not go beyond the reform objectives originally proposed in 1956. However, due to the significantly changed global environment and China's new open-door policies, the reform achieved a level of significance in a much more open, privatized, and decentralized environment.

In 2002, China's leadership shifted hands to its new Party secretary, Hu Jintao, and new premier, Wen Jiabao. Their immediate challenge when taking over the gavel was to combat SARS (severe acute respiratory syndrome). In the process, they worked hard to address the deficiencies in the administrative system's ability to respond to emergency situations. They also made it a priority in their agenda to fight corruption and help China meet the new challenges of joining the World Trade Organization (WTO). It is conceivable that continued reform initiatives will move China in the direction of the rule of law.

See also Administrative Reforms (1949–1978); Administrative Structure of Government; Deng Xiaoping (1904–1997), Reforms of; Rural Administrative Organizations; Special Administrative Region (SAR); World Trade Organization (WTO), China's Accession to.

Bibliography

Deng, Xiaoping, *Selected Works of Deng Xiaoping*, vol. 3 (Beijing: People's Publishing House, 1993); Lan, Zhiyong, "China's 1998 Administrative Reform," *Asian Journal of Public Administration* 21, no. 1 (June 1999): 29–54; Ren, Xiao, *China's Administrative Reform* (Zhejian, China: Zhejian People's Press, 1998); Zhao, Libo, *The Administrative Reform of the Government* (Jinan, China: Shangdong People's Press, 1998).

Zhiyong Lan

Administrative Structure of Government

In the administrative structure of the government of the People's Republic of China, the **National People's Congress** is in theory the highest decision-making body (the legislature) (see Figure 1). Operationally, since China emphasizes the leadership of the Communist Party, the Political Bureau of the Party is the de facto highest-level decision-making body in that it has the ability to affect the choices of the candidates elected to the National People's Congress, the vital policies made by the Congress, and, in special cases, the verdict made or actions taken by the Supreme People's Court or lower-level legal entities. The National People's Congress of Political Consultation is an organization through which voices of representatives from other parties (non-Communist parties) can be heard by the nation's highest decision makers. The State Council is the executive branch of the government. It has twenty-nine ministerial cabinet departments and commissions after the 1998 administrative reform (see Figure 2).

At the subnational level, there are twenty-two provinces; four large municipalities enjoying provincial-level administrative privileges (Beijing, population 12.6 million; Shanghai, population 14.7 million; Tianjin, population 9.6 million; and Chongqing, population 30.8 million); five provincial-level autonomous re-

FIGURE 1
Administrative Structure

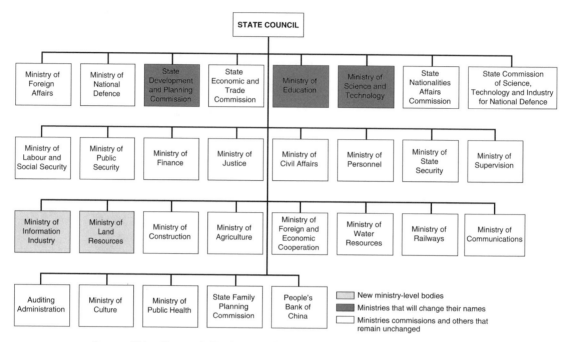

Source: China Economic Review, April 1998.

gions, **Xinjiang**, Ningxia, Inner Mongolia, **Tibet**, and Guangxi, which are respectively inhabited mostly by people of Uygur, Hui, Mongolian, Tibetian, Zhuang, and many other ethnicities; two **special administrative regions**, Hong Kong and Macao; and one out-of-control province that formally claims itself a "political entity" and informally considers itself a country, Taiwan.

Beneath the provincial level, there are administrative prefectures and administrative prefecture–level municipalities (medium-sized cities with supervising authority over three to five counties), counties, and townships. The central government does not have a direct working relationship with the governments at or below the level of prefecture governments. It can only reach them through provincial authorities. National laws and central government policies and directives are also enforced through provincial governments. Likewise, if a provincial government official needs to work with a city or township, he/she has to go through the prefecture or municipal government that has jurisdiction over that area. Officials of the provincial level are appointed by the central government, and similarly, the provincial governments appoint the lower-level officials within their jurisdictions. Since the late 1980s, efforts have been made to have the township-level officials elected locally by the citizens. While this practice is not yet a norm, it has been readily observable in many different localities in recent years. There are also a number of cities that are designated as special economic zone cities (fourteen coastal cities, including Zhu Hai, Shengzhen, and Dalian belong to this category).

Interestingly, within China's central-local relationship is the relationship between the central government and its autonomous regions in which a large pro-

FIGURE 2
China's Streamlined Ministerial Structure

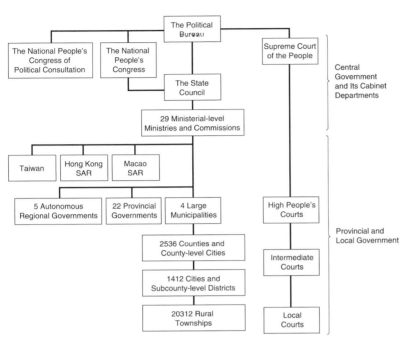

Source: China Statistical Yearbook (Beijing: China Statistics Press, 2001).

portion of their residents are ethnic minorities. Other than the five provincial-level autonomous regions, there are autonomous prefectures or counties in other provinces such as the Qinghai Province, Yunnan Province, and Guizhou where there are significant numbers of ethnic-minority regions (China has more than fifty ethnic groups). The Constitution stipulates that the principal governmental leaders, such as the chairman of the autonomous region (at the provincial, prefecture, or county level), should be from ethnic minorities. The People's Congress at the corresponding levels has the authority to make local laws that are suitable for the regional culture, customs, and political heritage. The Constitution even allows the regional governments to have local public security troops for the purpose of maintaining local stability (Section 5, Constitution of the People's Republic of China). All these privileges of the autonomous regions are subject to the approval of the appropriate authorities in the central government.

Hong Kong (which reverted to China from Great Britain on July 1, 1997, after a ninety-nine-year lease of Kowloon, a large and vital part of Hong Kong, expired) and Macao (which was returned to China on December 20, 1999, by the Portuguese government after its occupation and rule of Macao for more than 450 years since 1553) are two Special Administrative Regions that enjoy an even higher level of autonomy than the autonomous regions. The Basic Law of Hong Kong and the Basic Law of Macao gave these two regions authority to have their own independent legislature, supreme-court-equivalent power of final verdict, currency, and different social and political system. Except the right to keep an army and enjoy diplomatic prerogatives, these special administrative regions are given assurance that they can keep their political, social, and economic system for at least another fifty years. This is known as **"one country, two systems,"** a pragmatic solution proposed by Deng Xiaoping, China's late leader, to the problem created during China's history.

Taiwan is a special case. It had a long history of being part of China until 1895, when the Sino-Japanese War led to Japan's occupation of Taiwan. Taiwan was returned to China in 1945 at the end of World War II. Then the civil war started between the Kuomintang (KMT, otherwise known as the Nationalist Party) regime and the Communist Party. The war ended in 1949 with the KMT losing the war and moving its army and a large amount of movable assets to Taiwan. The KMT transformed Taiwan into the base of the Republic of China and promoted its economic and political development with the vast amount of monetary and human resources it had brought over; later Taiwan became an active international trading partner. In late 1987, when Jiang Jingguo, son of China's former KMT dictator Jiang Jieshi (Chiang Kai-shek), announced the abolishment of the one-party policy, Taiwan started to move to political openness. Until the last decade, the regime had regarded itself as part of China with a mission to regain the lost mainland territory.

However, as leadership changed hands, Taiwan's opposition party's (the Democratic Progressive Party) underground push for independence has gradually become official, and it intensified in 1999 when Li Denghui, the then president of Taiwan (a KMT president with strong Democratic Progressive Party sentiments), announced the abandonment of Taiwan's long-standing "One China" policy. In 2000, **Chen Shuibian**, Taiwan's Progressive Party candidate, won Taiwan's presidential election with the help of Li Denghui. More aggressive moves were made in the direction of achieving independence. At the beginning of 2002, the Progressive Party became the majority party in Taiwan's legislature as well. While Chinese leaders have expressed willingness to give Taiwan even more autonomy than they gave Hong Kong and Macao, Taiwan's regime clearly wants more.

As China keeps moving forward along its developmental agenda, more changes are expected. Recent developments have shown that China is growing rapidly to become the new manufacturing center in the world's economy. The rapid expansion and vitality of its private-sector businesses are constantly generating new pressures for change in its governmental administrative structure. The new leaders are already talking about possible political reform and have launched administrative training of China's younger cadres on a massive scale. More fundamental changes in its administrative structure are already in the making.

See also Administrative Reforms (1949–1978); Administrative Reforms after 1978; Deng Xiaoping (1904–1997), Reforms of; Hong Kong, Return of; Rural Administrative Organizations.

Bibliography

Lan, Zhiyong, "Federalism and the Central-Local Relations in the People's Republic of China," *Journal of Public Budgeting, Accounting, and Financial Management* 15, no. 3 (2003): 426–454.

Zhiyong Lan

Adoption, American Families and

Adoption of Chinese children by foreigners gained momentum with the start of the reforms started by Deng Xiaoping in 1978 and as exchanges at nonofficial levels increased. In 1989, the Chinese government formally gave permission for international adoption. In 1996, with the approval of the State Council, the Chinese Ministry of Civil Affairs established the Chinese Center for Adoption Affairs (CCAA) as the executive organ for international adoption. The Chinese government has attached much importance to international adoption, especially adoption by American citizens.

To guarantee a solid development of international adoption and to provide legal guidance in conducting international affairs in this regard, the Chinese government promulgated the Adoption Law of the People's Republic of China and Registration Procedures for Foreigners to Adopt Children in the People's Republic of China. In 1998, the two laws were revised to provide legal protection for the rights of adopted children and for maintaining legal adoptive relationships.

There are approximately 200 welfare institutions that provide international adoption services in provinces and cities such as Guangdong, Guangxi, Jiangxi, Hunan, Hubei, and Chongqing. In Guangdong alone, there are thirty-seven such services.

Statistics have shown that foreign families had adopted more than 50,000 Chinese children by the end of 2002. The authoritative Chinese statistics demonstrate that American families adopted more than 80 percent of these children. American official statistics also indicate that for several years in a row China has been the country that generated the highest number of American international adoption cases. This number is still growing.

In 1991, only sixty-one Chinese adopted children obtained American visas. In 2002, this number skyrocketed to 5,053. According to statistics provided by the American Immigration Bureau, by the end of 2002, American families had adopted more than 35,000 Chinese children.

The history of American international adoption dates back to the end of World War II, when Americans adopted postwar orphans such as children from South Korea and Vietnam. Many believe that American families are more willing to adopt Chinese children because Chinese adoption agencies follow legal procedures strictly, deal with the process in a serious and cautious manner, and charge minimally for the services. That adoptive Chinese children are healthy and intelligent is one important reason for the popularity of American adoptions.

The American government encourages international adoption by providing tax relief to adoptive families. To facilitate adoption, many professional adoption agencies have been established. Among the American international adoption agencies, ninety-six are recognized by CCAA. These institutions are required to be charity-based nonprofit organizations. This requirement is based on concern for protecting the legal rights of the adopted children. Responsibilities of adoption agencies include background checking of applying American families, including verification of the conditions for adoption stipulated by the Chinese laws. The agencies are also responsible for handling governmental documents, making arrangements for adoptive families with respect to travel, and reporting on the life and education of adopted children in the United States.

There are strict stipulations in Chinese laws regarding adoption of Chinese children by non-Chinese citizens. The adoption procedures are strictly monitored. The entire process begins with submitting an application to CCAA. In most cases, it takes about one and a half years from consulting with an American adoption agency to meeting with the child.

In its practice, CCAA customarily gives the priority of adopting one-year-old children to international adoptees younger than forty-five years of age and lets international adoptees who are fifty to fifty-five years old adopt children of approximately three years of age. It is reported that one reason for American international adoption is the high infertility rate of American families. The infertility rate among Chinese married couples is 2 to 4 percent, and this figure is 9 to 12 percent among American married couples. Adopted Chinese children satisfy the need of infertile American parents who aspire to raise children.

China has adopted the family-planning policy of "one child only per couple," but many Chinese families still prefer boys to girls. Many American families have learned about abandoned female infants in China, which is another motivation to adopt Chinese children. Many American families care greatly about disabled Chinese children in social welfare institutions. In general, these families are willing to adopt children with disabilities that can be cured through medical treatments such as surgery. Their most common request is that the adoptive children not have mental deficiency.

During the first year of adoption, the American family is required to submit written reports on the adopted child's life and development. After that, the adoption procedure is complete. Adoption also eases the pressure on social welfare institutions for children in China. Adopters' donations are used to improve the facilities in social welfare institutions. For example, each American family that adopts one Chinese child donates U.S. $3,000 to the social welfare institution the child came from. The donations that American adopters have paid for adopting 35,000 Chinese children have exceeded $1 billion.

The Chinese children adopted by American families are gradually assimilated into American society. The date of adoption becomes a special day of commemoration for the family. Many adoptive families provide Chinese learning opportunities to their children as a way to maintain a link to Chinese culture and history. Many adoptive parents study Chinese themselves in order to communicate better with their children. In addition, these adopted Chinese children are educated in an American way and are naturalized in their American families.

The biggest challenge that American families will be likely to encounter in adopting Chinese children is that after the children grow up, they may grapple with the issue of their own identities, an issue common in transracial adoptions. Most adopted children would like to know why they were adopted and to see their biological parents. To address this potential challenge that may adversely affect the growth of these children, in most cases, the American families tell them the facts about the adoption and Sino-American differences in history and culture. As these children grow up, their parents tell them that they are both American and Chinese.

The adoption of Chinese children by American families has contributed to a better understanding and a better relationship between the two countries. Because of their children's cultural heritage, the adoptive parents have a special attachment to China. On January 16, 2002, Chinese president Jiang Zemin met with the American Congressional Coalition on Adoption, led by Senator Maria Landrieu. He spoke highly of Sino-American collaboration in international adoption and commented that international adoption has helped Chinese and American people better understand each other and promote world peace and development.

See also Adoption, Reform and Practice of; Sino-American Relations, Conflicts and Common Interests; Sino-American Relations since 1949; United States, Chinese in; U.S. Legislation on China-Related Issues.

Bibliography

Ji, Minhua, "International Adoption: The New Life of Abandoned Chinese Children," *Nanfang Daily*, December 2, 2003; *Registration Procedures for Foreigners to Adopt Children in People's Republic of China*, May 12, 1999.

Youde Zhang and Lu Liu

Adoption, Reform and Practice of

Adoption involves creating new parent-child relationships that must be recognized by law. Since the reform of 1978, family planning has been forcefully implemented in China, and adoption has become a hot issue.

In 1949, after the founding of the People's Republic of China, the Chinese Marital Law made some stipulations to adjust adoptive relationships in order to protect legal relationships created by adoption, but there were no special legal standards, standardized procedures, or effective protection of legal rights of adopters and adoptees. On December 29, 1991, the Twenty-third Meeting of the Standing Committee of the Seventh **National People's Congress** passed the Adoption Law of the People's Republic of China, which went into effect on April 1 the following year. Since then, adoptive relationships have been regulated by law, marking the formal establishment of an adoption system in China.

During the years after it was put into practice, the Adoption Law was perfected through amendments. On November 4, 1998, the Standing Committee of the National People's Congress issued the first amendment. The new Adoption Law went into effect on April 1, 1999. In May 1999, with the approval of the State Council, the Ministry of Civil Affairs issued the Registration Procedures for Chinese Citizens to Adopt Children and Registration Procedures for Foreigners to Adopt Children in the People's Republic of China, and thus established a more systematic adoptive legal framework in this area.

The Adoption Law includes six chapters and thirty-four clauses, including "General Provisions," "Establishment of an Adoptive Relationship," "Validity of Adoption," "Termination of an Adoptive Relationship," "Legal Responsibility," and "Supplementary Provisions." The revised Adoption Law loosened restrictions on adopters. Specifically, the minimum age of the adopter was lowered from thirty-five to thirty, and those who adopt orphans, disabled children, and children under the care of social welfare institutions do not have to be childless or to be limited by the one-child adoption rule. The new rules resulted from revision of the old law to address long-standing problems in adoption practice. The amendments are aimed at providing much better protection for adoptees' legal rights and interests.

Citizens who meet the conditions set forth by the Adoption Law and Registration Procedures for Chinese Citizens to Adopt Children are allowed to adopt orphans and disabled children in local social welfare institutions for children. In order to encourage foreigners to adopt Chinese minors, the Chinese government promulgated Registration Procedures for Foreigners to Adopt Children in the People's Republic of China to standardize adoption by foreigners.

Every year about 30,000 adoptive relationships are established through adoption registration. Orphans under the age of fourteen, abandoned infants or children whose parents cannot be identified or found, and children whose parents are unable to rear them due to unusual difficulties can all be put up for adoption.

The Adoption Law has strict stipulations regarding adopters, adoptees, and those who place their children for adoption. To be valid, the adoptive relationship must meet the essential and formal requirements stipulated by law. Otherwise the relationship is considered invalid. Once the adoption is legalized, a dual effect takes place: (1) the relationship between adoptive parents and adopted children is established; and (2) the relationships between the adopted child and his/her original parents and pertinent kinships are terminated. The termination procedure must follow a certain legal process in order to be valid.

In the practice of adoption, social welfare institutions for children in China play an important role. In accordance with the United Nations' Children's Rights Treaty and China's Protection of Minors Act of the People's Republic of China, Chinese social welfare institutions treat children who have no income, no support, or no guardians in a humanitarian manner and provide special services for them.

To help adopted children grow in a wholesome manner, local departments of civil affairs have been trying to create more suitable adoption procedures. For example, the city of Shanghai has carried out an adoption evaluation system. Since August 2003, social workers have been involved in the whole adoption process. Adopters are evaluated before adoption rights are granted. After the adoption, there are follow-up interviews and house visits to make sure that adopted children's legal rights and interests are best protected. The city of Shanghai has set up local service centers for this purpose. At each center there are two certified social workers who have received special training and specialize in adoption evaluation.

To enable disabled children and older children (three years old and above) to enjoy life in a permanent home like other children, the Chinese Adoption Center under the Ministry of Civil Affairs has formulated more effective ways to assist adoption organizations to find suitable families for these children. Many social welfare institutions have launched plans to find foster homes to enable more children to participate in community life and meanwhile enjoy the warmth of the family. These institutions provide guidance and training for foster families so that children under foster care can grow in a healthy manner.

See also Adoption, American Families and; United States, Chinese in.

Bibliography

Adoption Law, December 29, 1991; *Registration Procedures for Chinese Citizens to Adopt Children*, December 1995.

Youde Zhang and Lu Liu

Agricultural Reform

Since the founding of the People's Republic of China (PRC) in 1949, there have been three major structural reforms in the agricultural sector that occurred in the 1950s, 1960s, and 1980s. The latest reform has had a profound impact on China's fast-growing economy today, because its successful experience commenced the overall reform that is transforming China's planned economy into a market-oriented one in every sector.

To deal with the concerns of land aggregation, rural income equality, and food security, the then newly established central government launched its first major economic policy, known as **"land reform,"** in the early 1950s. This policy redistributed the land among the rural population. Families were categorized into several classes from rich to poor based on the acreage they owned relative to the average in their area. Land and other capital such as livestock and tools from rich families were confiscated and reallocated to poor families at no cost. After the reform, rural residents on a per capita basis owned land equally, and the production unit was the household. Peasants owned all the outputs and sold the residual outputs, after saving for self-consumption and seeds, to government-operated agencies at a government-specified price.

In 1956, a collective farming system was formed. Initially, several rural households pooled their resources together voluntarily to complement each other and achieve economies of scale. At the early stage, the output was distributed among group members based on both labor and nonlabor resources, so that the landownership was still honored. These groups were promoted by the government and made larger and larger, until in the People's Communization movement in the early 1960s, rural communes usually consisted of all residents from several villages. The land was then owned collectively. Production decisions were made at the top governance of a commune and administered at the level of the production team (village). Output was first sent to the government in exchange for preallocated industrial inputs (machinery, chemicals, and so on) and cash, and the residuals were then distributed to members for consumption based on their labor inputs only. Ideally, the commune system could achieve higher economies of scale by intensified specialization and infrastructure construction through aggregated resources. However, productivity and output both decreased because of the inadequate management techniques in administering this scale of production.

The recent economic reforms have brought new practices and new technologies to Chinese agriculture.

In 1978, idealism was replaced by pragmatism within the central government. Long-dissatisfied peasants started to secretly redistribute the land to households on the condition that each household would submit a certain amount of output to the government. This practice achieved great success immediately because once again individual households gained complete control of their inputs and outputs. The practice was also officially accepted nationwide after a short pioneer experiment in some areas and promoted as the "household production responsibility system" (HPRS) in 1979. Communes were dissolved. Under the HPRS, landownership still belongs to the village collectively, but individual households have the use right. Although households own all the outputs from the land, they need to have contracts with the government that specify for what and how much acreage to produce. In 1985, a quota output was specified in each contract that needs to be sold to the government, and output beyond the quota can be consumed directly or sold to markets. These markets for agricultural products were the first free markets in the latest economic reform that eventually freed up almost all markets in China.

Total output and productivity were increased by a great deal in the early 1980s because peasants had more motivation in production. The annual growth rates of agriculture were 2.9 percent from 1952 to 1978, 7.7 percent between 1978 and 1984, and down to 4 percent in the late 1980s. The fast growth in the early 1980s was credited to the HPRS primarily through improved field management and increased labor inputs. However, the landownership entitled the rural residents to redistribute the land periodically due to natural changes in household size. The redistribution or the fear of redistribution prevented peasants from long-term investment in land, resulting in deterioration of soil fertility and irrigation structure.

Many efforts were made in the 1990s to ensure peasants their land-use right and discourage land redistribution. In 2001, the government legalized the promise of the households' land-use right for the following thirty years. This policy encourages long-term investment in land. Meanwhile, land can be leased to other households in exchange for rent.

Along with the land reform, the food-distribution system has also undergone a substantial reform. Beginning in 1953, the unified procurement and distribution policy excluded all nongovernment traders from dealing with agricultural outputs. Similarly, under the collective farming system, the central government monopolized the procurement and marketing of agricultural outputs. The outputs were collected and rationed to industries and urban residents at a fixed (planned) price. This consumer retail price was subsidized and lower than the producer procurement price in many years. The ration, the fixed-price system, and the consumer price subsidy existed until 1993. During the early years of HPRS, the free market emerged on a small scale. Peasants could sell their extra output to the free market at a market price after they have fulfilled the quota contracts at the planned price. The market price was usually higher than the planned price. Consumers could substitute and supplement the rationed food by the food available in free markets.

The dual-price system was not abolished until the late 1990s. Currently, although the distribution of major food grains, rice and wheat, is still controlled by the government, the prices are largely reflected by the market supply and demand situation. The emergence of agricultural commodity wholesale markets and futures exchange markets in 1993 further improved the institutional and informational efficiency of the market. Agricultural outputs other than major food grains are circulated through market channels.

Meanwhile, the agricultural factor market in China has been opened up. In the 1950s, agricultural production was in a low-input, low-output state, in which industrial inputs were rarely used. During the collective farming period, there was no market for agricultural inputs, and the government allocated industrial inputs such as fertilizers and machinery to communes. All peasants were working in the communes at their residence. In the latest reform, markets for industrial inputs emerged. The markets for these inputs also went through the dual-price stage together with the output market, when the in-plan price was lower than the beyond-plan price, and eventually became normal. Labor is also mobile today because more people are migrating to urban areas or to rural nonfarming sectors as more employment opportunities emerge.

See also Agriculture, Impact of WTO Accession on; Family Collectivism; People's Communes/Household Responsibility System.

Bibliography

Lin, Justin Yifu, "Rural Reforms and Agricultural Growth in China," *American Economic Review* 82, no.1 (1992): 34–51.

H. Holly Wang

Agriculture, Impact of WTO Accession on

Agriculture is one of the sectors in China since its accession to the World Trade Organization (WTO) that many believe is most vulnerable, because China has promised to lower its tariffs on main agricultural imports. Pessimists predicted that China's agriculture would face increasing external pressure, tens of millions, if not hundreds of millions, of peasants could be displaced as a result of a decline in agricultural production, and the income gap between rural and urban residents would get worse. Some even thought it likely that China would face social riots if the displaced peasants failed to earn a living in urban and coastal areas. The fear of this scenario was reflected in China's last-minute efforts to try to strike a better deal with the WTO on the issues of agricultural subsidies and protection.

However, the first-year performance of China's agriculture surprised not only pessimists but also optimists. Instead of being flooded by a large amount of agricultural imports, China enjoyed a surplus in its agricultural trade. According to China's official statistics, in 2002 China imported $8.74 billion and exported $12.62 billion in agricultural products, representing −0.4 percent and 11.5 percent changes, respectively, from 2001. As a result, the surplus in China's agricultural trade enjoyed a 52.3 percent jump over that of 2001. Even optimists expected to see widening deficits in agricultural trade in the short run.

However, the good news should not blur one's view of the tough situation that China has to face in the future. First, China's agriculture needs to be restructured

Rice paddies surround a rural farming village. The impact of China's accession to the WTO has been most strongly felt in places like this.

before it becomes more competitive internationally. Second, China needs to modernize rural areas. Third, China needs to raise its peasants' income. In China, these three issues are called "three agricultural issues" (*sannong wenti*).

To be fair, it must be pointed out that these three issues have existed for centuries. Therefore, they are not caused by China's WTO accession. However, many fear that they will become more complicated in a post-WTO world. According to the critics, WTO accession may bring benefits to urban sectors, but it is doomed to bring a mostly negative impact on China's agriculture. Optimists dispute this view. Therefore, views on how to evaluate the impact of the WTO accession on China's agriculture remain controversial, if not polarized.

However, the performance of China's agriculture in 2001 showed that the concerns on the first issue, the fragility of China's agriculture, are not well grounded. Given its huge rural labor pool, China has a strong comparative advantage in products that use labor intensively relative to other factors. Most vegetables, herbs and flowers, and meat and fish products are labor-intensive products, while most grain products other than paddy rice, such as wheat, corn, and soybeans, are land intensive. Paddy rice is labor intensive and happens to be China's staple grain crop.

Since the mid-1990s, in expectation of the WTO accession, the Chinese government has been encouraging peasants to restructure their product mix. As a result, peasants are moving away from land-intensive products quite rapidly. Meanwhile, the areas sown with vegetables, herbs, and flowers have significantly increased. The production of meat and fish also has been rapidly expanding. However, before China becomes a major exporter of agricultural products, it needs to learn how to improve packaging and how to reduce chemical residues in its products in order to meet international sanitary and phytosanitary standards.

Overall, Chinese peasants are responding well to market signals and are preparing themselves for the post-WTO era. When China completes its agricultural restructuring, it will become one of the major players in agricultural trade. China's growing confidence is reflected in its decision to put the Framework Agreement on China-ASEAN Comprehensive Economic Cooperation on a fast lane. In this agreement, signed at the end of 2001, China promises to liberalize agricultural imports from the Association of Southeast Asian Nations (ASEAN) within ten years. China is poised to be a leader in promoting liberalization in agricultural trade at a time when most developed nations are still offering high protection and subsidies to their farmers.

The remaining two issues, modernizing China's rural areas and raising Chinese peasants' income, are much more difficult to deal with. They are rooted fundamentally in a dilemma that China has long been facing, that is, a huge and still growing population that is endowed with limited arable land and that has been locked into a very isolated environment for most of the last several centuries.

China has more than 20 percent of the world's population, but depending on which number one believes, only 7 to 9 percent of the world's arable land. Even if one accepts 9 percent as the most correct figure, per capita arable land in China is among the lowest in the world, only about 25 percent of the world average. For this reason, the average farm scale in China is among the smallest in the world. In terms of per capita possession of other resources, China is also poor. For example, China's per capita water resources, a factor crucial for agriculture, are only one-third of the world average. Worse, 81 percent of national water resources are concentrated in areas (mostly in the Southeast and Southwest) where the arable land accounts for only 36 percent of China's total. The areas that have 64 percent of China's arable land and populations of hundreds of millions have only 19 percent of China's water resources. The enormous population pressure on China's land for the last several centuries has led to rapid deforestation, desertization, salinization, frequent sandstorms, and rampant water shortage.

Obviously, if China continued to live in autarky, the situation of Chinese peasants would become only worse as a result of growing population pressure on the land, decreasing farm scales, and degrading ecology. Therefore, without joining the WTO, it is hard to imagine that by its own resources, China alone can modernize its rural areas and significantly raise its peasants' income on a sustainable basis. It is exactly in this sense that WTO accession provides China a golden opportunity to resolve the remaining two agricultural issues, because the WTO accession will help China secure and expand its overseas markets. This will lead to the expansion of its labor-intensive manufacturing sector, the acceleration of urbanization, and an increase in nonfarming jobs in urban areas. As peasants move out of the farming sector, leaving the arable land and other resources behind, the remaining peasants will be in a position to expand their production scale and raise their per capita income. As the per capita income in rural areas rises, rural residents will have more financial resources to modernize rural areas.

There are some uncertainties, the biggest of which is whether or not China can create nonfarming job opportunities quickly enough. It is true that the WTO accession provides China more secure overseas markets for its labor-intensive exports. However, the surplus labor in rural areas is enormous. It may take many decades for China to completely absorb this pool, and during this period, the income gap between peasants and urban residents can further widen. In areas where the traditional product mix has been based on comparative disadvantage, the need for major production restructuring is most urgent. It is exactly this group of peasants that many think will be hit most heavily in post-WTO China.

A more careful look into this scenario leads one to believe that even in these areas, peasants at least can feed themselves, although they will not be rich. They will be protected by China's market power, underdeveloped social infrastructures, and geographic distance. First, China's huge population share in the world total means that any significant changes in China's self-sufficiency rate, say from 100 percent down to 85 percent, will sharply raise food grain prices in the international market. Consequently, it will become profitable again to grow these crops in China. For this reason, China will continue to produce most of its food grains, including wheat, corn, and soybeans. Its imports of these products will represent only a part of its total needs.

Second, most Chinese farmers will also be protected by China's backward infrastructures and geographic remoteness. It is simply too costly to ship a large amount of foreign grain to China's vast and remote inland, given that the grain price is very cheap relative to transportation cost. To residents living in China's inland, a markup to cover the shipping and handling cost cannot be too high; or the imported grain will immediately lose its price edge over the domestically produced one. In case of a sudden surge in the influx of foreign grain imports, China is entitled to raise its tariffs on imports according to the WTO rule.

In summary, while the WTO accession will not make many centuries-long thorny problems in China disappear overnight, it will help China gradually get out of the population-resources trap that it has been locked in for the last several hundred years. The WTO accession is a great opportunity for China as long as China is willing and able to pay the short-term costs of restructuring its agriculture.

See also Agricultural Reform; World Trade Organization (WTO), China's Accession to; World Trade Organization (WTO), Impact of on Service Industries.

Bibliography

Economic Research Service, USDA, "China's Fruit and Vegetable Sector: A Changing Market Environment," *Agricultural Outlook*, June–July 2001, 10–13; Johnson, D. Gale, "The Future of the Agricultural Sector," in *The Globalization of the Chinese Economy*, ed. S. Wei, G. J. Wen, and H. Zhou (Cheltenham, UK: Edward Elgar, 2002); The U.S.-China Business Council, "Summary of U.S.-China Bilateral WTO Agreement," 2000, http://www.uschina.org/public/wto/ustr/generalfacts.html, accessed November 9, 2004.

James Wen

Ai Qing (1910–1996)

Ai Qing was one of the most important poets and most prolific writers in modern China. His original name was Jiang Zhenghan. He was born in a landowner's family on March 27, 1910, in a village in Jinhua County, Zhejiang Province. Because he was sent to a farmer's family to be raised, Ai showed deep solicitude and sympathy for the peasantry throughout his life. In 1929, he went to France to study painting. Shortly after he returned to China in 1932, he was arrested by the Nationalist Party (Kuomintang) and was sentenced to six years' imprisonment for his attempt to "subvert the government." While in prison, he wrote many poems, including "Da Yanhe" ("My Maid"), in which he used the pen name of Ai Qing for the first time. After being released from prison in 1935, Ai decided to focus on poetry writing, and his first anthology, *Da Yanhe*, was published in 1936. Ai went to Yanan in 1941 and became a chief editor of the journal *Poetry* there. After 1949, he served as the deputy chief editor of *The People's Literature*, one of the most influential literary journals in China during the Mao era. In early 1957, he became a member of the editorial board of *Poetry* and *Harvest*.

In 1958, Ai was labeled a "rightist" and was forced to leave Beijing to do manual labor, which was a punishment. He first settled in a state-operated farm in the northeastern Heilongjiang Province. Later he was transferred to a reclamation farm in Xinjiang Uygur Autonomous Region. During the **Great Cultural**

Revolution (1966–1976), Ai was reprimanded for his political tendency. Although he did not stop writing during the years of confinement, most of his works could not be published.

Ai did not regain the right to write freely until October 1976. In February 1979, the grievous charges that he had suffered from since the 1950s were finally revoked, and he was rehabilitated. After that, he was entrusted with many important posts. The publication of Ai's short poem "Red Flag" (1978) not only signified his official return to the literary circle after his twenty-one years of disappearance, but also marked the beginning of a new stage in his writing career. His anthology *Songs of Coming Back* (1980) won the National Prize of Best Free-Verse Poems in 1983. In 1985, France awarded Ai a medal of literature and art for his contributions to literature. Ai was also a prolific author of theoretical articles on poetry in modern Chinese literature.

Ai paid close attention to society and reality of his time. In his early works, he created vivid depictions of the sorrows and joys of the Chinese people, their efforts to improve the country, and their optimistic and high-spirited will to fight for national liberation. In his post-1978 works, although Ai described his personal sufferings during his exile, his loving care for the nation was even stronger. He repeatedly used such images as the sun, light, spring, daybreak, and flame to express his inner feelings and his confidence in the country. He sought for the true, the good, and the beautiful with great enthusiasm and optimism, even after his traumatic persecution. His poems and theoretical works on poetry have exerted a profound and lasting impact on modern Chinese literature. Since the 1930s, a large number of Chinese poets have been inspired by Ai directly or indirectly. Ai's works have been translated into more than thirty foreign languages.

See also Anticorruption Literature and Television Dramas; Avant-garde Literature; Experimental Fiction; Great Cultural Revolution, Literature during; Intellectuals, Political Engagement of (1949–1978); Intellectuals, Political Engagement of (1978–Present); Literary Policy for the New China; Literature of the Wounded; Misty Poetry; Modern Pop-Satire; Neorealist Fiction and Modernism; Pre–Cultural Revolution Literature; Root-Searching Literature; Sexual Freedom in Literature.

Bibliography

Luo, Hanchao, *On Ai Qing* (Hangzhou, China: Zhejiang People's Publishing House, 1982); Yang, Kuanghan, and Kuangman Yang, *Biography of Ai Qing* (Shanghai: Shanghai Literature and Art Press, 1984).

Dela X. Jiao

AIDS, Prevention of

The Chinese government is becoming increasingly alarmed about the rapid growth of AIDS incidence and HIV infection, along with a steady surge of sexually transmitted diseases. The government estimates that the country currently has 600,000 HIV carriers with an annual growth of 30 percent, while the United Nations (UN) believes that the number of HIV carriers presently exceeds 1 million.

According to a report issued in June 2004 by the Ministry of Health, 840,000 people were infected with HIV as of 2003 and 80,000 had developed full-blown AIDS. Since 2001, the government has launched multiple programs to curb the spread of infection. The government annually invests 270 million yuan in preventive programs and allocates 120 million yuan in government bonds to improve the conditions of the 459 blood reserves in central and western China. Hundred million yuan of matching funds is also collected each year from local governments to develop local programs. Efforts have been increased, for example, in controlling prostitution and drug trafficking, particularly in coastal regions. The government has also stepped up propaganda and education on AIDS and HIV.

Local press reports have cited unidentified experts who say that as many as 100,000 of the 600,000 people in China who are believed to have the virus might be gay. Officials are usually reluctant to acknowledge homosexuality in Chinese society. As a result, health experts worry that many homosexuals lack the information needed to avoid being exposed through sex.

Prevention

Local and international health experts have been warning the Chinese government that China faces the choice of either undertaking bold efforts to head off a potential AIDS catastrophe or seeing the disease spread widely. In response to the growing incidence of HIV infection and increasing criticism and warnings, the central government has stepped up its efforts in recent years to fight the deadly infectious disease. It has formulated long-term strategies and increased its funding to control the spread of HIV/AIDS. The Ministry of Health has improved its venereal diseases and HIV/AIDS surveillance network, upgraded laboratory-testing techniques, and carried out extensive publicity to increase public awareness of the risks since the late 1990s. HIV-testing laboratories were set up in each of China's provinces in the 1990s.

The Ministry of Health also set up a national center for HIV/AIDS in the late 1990s to implement state HIV/AIDS policies. In October 2002, relevant departments of the Chinese central government reached an agreement to exempt imported AIDS drugs from customs duties and value-added taxes in an attempt to reduce treatment costs for AIDS patients. China also encouraged production of off-patent AIDS drugs by Chinese companies in order to reduce treatment costs further.

It was hoped that the annual treatment costs for AIDS patients would soon fall to a level of RMB 10,000 yuan from presently between RMB 30,000 yuan and 50,000 yuan as a result of these measures. In addition, the government increased its fiscal budget for AIDS prevention to RMB 100 million from only RMB 15 million as of 2002. In the same year, the central and local governments invested RMB 2,250 million in upgrading 459 blood stations and blood banks in order to secure the quality of blood. The government will also provide financial assistance to AIDS patients in poor areas.

International Cooperation

With the support of the World Bank, China launched a five-year health program to control noninfectious diseases and prevent the spread of HIV/AIDS in China in 1996. Pilot work of the program was targeted at Yunnan Province, which has the highest rate of HIV/AIDS infection, and seven major and medium-sized Chinese cities, including Beijing, Tianjin, and Shanghai. Another collaborative project between the British and Chinese governments on the control of sexually transmitted diseases and AIDS was launched in early 2000 in Sichuan Province. In 2002, China and the U.S. government agreed to collaborate on prevention of AIDS.

In August 2001, China announced a new anti-AIDS campaign, promising additional spending on health care and education. Foreign health experts have warned that without a dramatic increase in public awareness and preventive measures, the virus could spread to the general population. UN experts say that without effective measures, as many as 20 million Chinese could be infected by 2010.

In June 2002, the Chinese minister of health and the U.S. secretary of health and human services signed a memorandum of understanding on cooperation in the AIDS field. The areas of cooperation between the two countries specified by the memorandum include the following:

- New prevention strategies and measures
- Research on an AIDS vaccine, diagnostics, and therapeutic drugs, as well as therapy and nursing of AIDS patients
- AIDS epidemiological monitoring and data analysis
- Safety in blood testing
- Blocking the spread of AIDS through medical sources

The memorandum calls for a long-term partnership in AIDS research institutions between the two countries and mutual visits and information exchanges between scientists. Two specific cooperation projects were raised by the memorandum:

- The U.S. National Institutes of Health's "general international AIDS cooperative research" project will inject $15 million in research funding into China's AIDS prevention program, and this cooperation will be supported by AIDS experts from many well-known universities in the United States.
- The U.S. Department of Health and Human Services will send two experts from its Centers for Disease Control to China for long-term technical assistance in helping China develop AIDS monitoring measures, strengthen laboratory appraisal and quality control, and provide consultations and training.

China has set goals to limit the growth of HIV infections to within 10 percent by 2005 and to ensure that the total number of HIV infections does not exceed 1.5 million by 2010, a figure many think will be difficult to achieve.

Demand for Affordable AIDS Drugs

China was criticized by international organizations for lack of action in providing treatment for its AIDS patients. The Chinese government, however, responded by saying that it is trying to protect the intellectual property rights of foreign companies under the present laws and regulations, which comply with World Trade Organization (WTO) requirements.

China's AIDS problem has exploded in recent years. Despite the explosive growth in the number of HIV patients, the number of patients who are receiving AIDS medicines remains miniscule because of the high costs of these drugs that are patented and cost at least $10,000 a year. The estimated 1 million Chinese HIV carriers are currently left with almost no treatment for the disease.

Two Chinese companies were granted approval in 2002 to make generic versions of off-patent AIDS drugs to take advantage of the urgent demands for affordable HIV/AIDS treatment medications, and more are attempting to make such drugs. Meanwhile, physicians in China are frustrated by the lack of medications for their HIV/AIDS patients and often have to refrain from encouraging the potentially high-risk population to test for AIDS, fearing the lack of affordable treatment.

See also Disease and Death Rates; Health Care Reform; Medical Provision, Structure of; Pharmaceutical Industry, Administrative and Regulatory Structures of; Pharmaceutical Products, Sales and Marketing of; United Nations (UN) and China; World Trade Organization (WTO), Impact of on Service Industries.

Bibliography

Editorial Committee of the China Health Yearbook, *China Health Yearbook* (Beijing: People's Health Publishing House, 2002 and 2003); Editorial Committee of the China Pharmaceutical Yearbook, *China Pharmaceutical Yearbook* (Beijing: China Publishing House, 2001, 2002, and 2003); Editorial Committee, State Drug Administration, *State Drug Administration Yearbook 2002* (Beijing: State Drug Administration Yearbook Press, 2003); Ministry of Health, "Report on Current Situation of the Control over AIDS and Other Contagious Diseases," June 29, 2004, http://www.moh.gov.cn/public/open.aspx?n_id=8787&seq=0, accessed November 9, 2004; Shen, James, *Marketing Pharmaceuticals in China* (Whippany, NJ: Wicon International, 2001).

Jian Shen

Anticorruption Literature and Television Dramas

Since the mid-1990s, it has been admitted officially that corruption-related crimes in China are pandemic. Although the media frequently report on petty cases of corruption, such reports only touch the tip of the iceberg. In this situation, literature, in particular, folk poetry, turned more social issues-driven than ever. In addition, various other genres have joined in as well, with anticorruption literature and **television** dramas being well established by the late 1990s.

Since the late 1970s, journalistic literature (*baogao wenxue*) has achieved a prominence equal to that of fiction and poetry. Liu Bingyan (1925–   ), a leading journalist, was preeminent in this genre until the late 1980s. In 1956, the publication of "Zai Qiaoliang Gongdi Shang" (At the bridge-building site) and "Benbao Neibu Xiaoxi" (Our news office's inside story) led to his banishment to the countryside for twenty-two years. In 1979, the year Liu was politically rehabilitated, his long reportage *Ren-Yao Zhijian* (People or monster) created a sensation, arguably constituting a predecessor to anticorruption literature. This work depicts Wang Shouxin, a female cadre in a county of Heilongjiang Province, and her abuse of power within the bureaucratic maze. Liu concluded this work by asking, "Although the case of Wang Shouxin's corruption has been cracked, to what extent has the environment that gave rise to this case been really changed?" The answer is obvious: Liu himself was expelled from the Communist Party again in 1987 for his outspokenness and went into exile in the United States, where he lives today. While Liu's merciless denunciation touched the nerves of many high-ranking officials, the common people praised him for being the public conscience. For his perception and artistry, Liu won several prizes, including one for *People or Monster*.

Alongside the powerful weapon of reportage, the 1980s saw the rise of short stories and novellas that exposed official malfeasance. "Suolian, Shi Rouruan de" (Soft is the chain) by Dai Houying (1938–1996) and "Dayu de he Diaoyu de" (Those who fish with a net and those who fish with a hook) by Jin He (1943–) are noteworthy. Wen Ruixia, Dai's protagonist, was blind to the "soft chain" that willingly enslaved her to a public security bureau chief's benevolent oppression for decades. Similarly, in his short story, Jin depicts the behavior of lower-level cadres who troll with a net on behalf of a county deputy magistrate while simultaneously fining workers who fish with a hook. Both works reveal how officials up to the county level tactfully seek personal gain and angle for fame and power at the public's expense.

Faced with the increasingly high-profile official corruption exposed during the 1990s, literature responded with genres from reportage, folk poetry, satire, short stories, and novellas to novels. Among them, acclaimed writer Mo Yan's (1955–) *Tiantang Suantai Zhi Ge* (The garlic ballads) and *Jiuguo* (Liquorland) stand out. The former lays bare official manipulation of power in rural areas, the latter that in cities. *Liquorland* is named for the huge amount of alcohol produced and consumed in this hallucinatory world filled with corruption from the mayor down to the disabled residents. By the late 1990s, anticorruption literature was established as a genre named for its serious subject matter, and multiepisode anticorruption television dramas adapted from books were numerous. *Jiaru Wo Shi Zhende* (If I were for real), a satirical play on bureaucratic corruption and deception, is but one example of the early 1980s.

Some of the best-known literary writings with television dramas are Chen Fang's *Tiannu* (Heaven's wrath), quickly banned yet having wide underground circulation, and its three-volume sequel *Dushi Weiqing* (Municipal crisis), Chen Xinhao's *Hongse Kangnaixin* (The red carnation), winner of an award for its television drama; Lu Tianming's *Cangtian Zai Shang* (Heavens above), *Daxue Wuhen* (Heavy snow without traces), recipient of the Golden Eagle Award for its televised version, and *Shengwei Shuji: K Sheng Jishi* (The provincial Party secretary: Records of K Province), which sold nearly half a million copies and whose teleplay was dedicated to the Sixteenth Party Congress in 2002; Zhang Ping's *Jueze* (Choice), winner of three major literary awards, followed by a teleplay and a radio play of the same title as well as a film renamed *Shengsi Jueze* (Fatal decision); and Zhou Meisen's *Zhigao Liyi* (Supreme interests) and *Zhongguo Zhizao* (Made in China), the television version being renamed *Zhongcheng* (Loyalty). Some works are better known as award-winning books, including He Jianming's *Genben Liyi* (Fundamental interests) and Yan Zhen's *Canglang Zhi Shui* (The water of Canglang). Other works, though based on novels, are better known as television dramas, including *Jingjiexian* (Cordon). The corruption described in these works can be institutional, legal, moral, or sociocultural. However, all corruption is associated with officials in the Party, the state, or its enterprises, including provincial deputy Party secretaries, deputy governors, and Politburo member and Beijing Party secretary Chen Xitong. Corruption in the private sector is also included when characters are dependents and hangers-on of officials.

In some instances, when a major official corruption case is exposed, one or more writings follow. The case of the female Hunan provincial departmental official who took bribes of nearly 9 million yuan (more than U.S. $1 million) and used sex to bribe male officials, even when detained, brought about eighteen serial writings in *Shenzhen Weekly* (nos. 33–50, 2001). These later formed part of the book-length reportage *Hongyan Tanguan—Nü Jutan Jiang Yanping Chenfu Lu* (A beautiful but corrupt official: The rise and fall of the huge-scale female corrupt official Jiang Yanping) by Yang Yuanxin. Reportages about this and other cases usually use real names in order that readers may clearly identify the events in question. The case involving Chen Xitong and Wang Baosen, former deputy mayor of Beijing, produced not only reportage but also two novels, Chen Fang's *Heaven's Wrath* and *Municipal Crisis*. The fictionalized characters are so vividly depicted that readers can easily identify the parties involved. Despite their format, works that focus on topical official corruption frequently make best-seller lists, particularly when they are adapted as television dramas broadcast in prime time.

Interestingly, many authors seem reluctant to be recognized, as though the genre were stigmatized. Classifying anticorruption literature (*fanfu wenxue*) as critical realism seems plausible, since well-known writers of the genre often reject the label "literature," insisting upon the realism of their writings. While many works sell very well and their teleplays attract enthusiastic viewers nationwide, few have entered critics' circles. Some writers feature corruption in a naturalistic way but fail to give specific commentary. Others write in detail about political tricks and administrative schemes, satisfying the curiosity of many people in and outside of official circles. Finally, to insiders, certain novels may serve as textbooks in the art of manipulating power. It may be more accurate to regard some works as "corruption literature and television dramas" rather than anticorruption works. On the other hand, many serious writers try to examine the sources of official corruption. Of course, they do not call the Party an oppressive ruling class outright, but their frequent warnings addressed to the Party do contain such a subtext. Indeed, they have advanced the frontiers of political debate in the mass media, which has led to some of their works being banned. Banned or not, anticorruption writings all make obvious political compromises and often push limits. The truth is that official corruption is greater in life than can be revealed in literature or on screen, where a more delicate handling—one in which poignant text may be replaced by gesture or deleted entirely—is necessary. For example, Zhang Ping's *Choice* explores officials' motivation in risking embezzling money when they already enjoy very many privileges: arguably, they are preparing for the demise of Chinese communism.

The artistic value of anticorruption works varies, like that of any serious or popular literary genre. Writers in general wish to use literature as a tool for political awareness instead of writing a more artistic yet ideologically innocuous variety. That said, politically sensitive anticorruption literature and television dramas are not necessarily artistically inferior sensational works. While only a small part of the anticorruption oeuvre is highly regarded and wins prestigious awards (e.g., the Mao Dun Literary Award for Zhang Ping's *Choice* and *People's Literature* Special Award for Reportage for He Jianming's *Fundamental Interests*), the serious sociopolitical themes dealt with set most works well apart from popular literature, such as "literature by or about beautiful women" (*meinü wenxue*), another major genre in present-day China.

China has a literary tradition of exposing officialdom, notably the "literature about officialdom" (*guanchang wenxue*) of the late Qing dynasty. As ongoing anticorruption campaigns are a Party monopoly, most such works in literature and art are no longer severely criticized by authorities, who take a cautiously welcome attitude. Like their predecessors, contemporary writers express the fundamental concerns of the people. That this genre exists at all attests to the coexistence of pandemic official corruption and relaxed government policy toward literature and art.

See also Avant-garde Literature; Experimental Fiction; Great Cultural Revolution, Literature during; Intellectuals, Political Engagement of (1949–1978); Intellectuals, Political Engagement of (1978–Present); Journalism Reform; Literary Policy for the New China; Literature of the Wounded; Misty Poetry; Modern Pop-Satire; Neorealist Fiction and Modernism; Pre–Cultural Revolution Literature; Root-Searching Literature; Sexual Freedom in Literature.

Bibliography

Chen, Xinhao, *Hongse Kangnaixin* (The red carnation) (Shanghai: Shanghai Wenyi, 2001); Dai, Houying, "Suolian Shi Rouruan De" (Soft is the chain), in *Zhongguo Xin Shiqi Mingzuo Xuandu* (A reader in post–Cultural Revolution Chinese literature), ed. Vivian Ling Hsu (Hong Kong: Chinese University Press, 1988); Fang, Wei, *Shengzhang de Jiamen* (The provincial governor's home) (Beijing: Zhongguo Dianying, 2002); Jin, He, "Dayu de he Diaoyu de" (Those who fish with a net and those who fish with a hook), in *Zhongguo Xin Shiqi Mingzuo Xuandu* (A reader in post–Cultural Revolution Chinese literature), ed. Vivian Ling Hsu (Hong Kong: Chinese University Press, 1988); Kinkley, Jeffrey C., *Chinese Justice, the Fiction: Law and Literature in Modern China* (Stanford, CA: Stanford University Press, 2000); Liu Bingyan, *People or Monsters? And Other Stories and Reportage from China after Mao*, ed. Perry Link, Chinese Literature in Translation

(Bloomington: Indiana University Press, 1983); Lu, Tianming, *Shengwei Shuji: K Sheng Jishi* (The Provincial Party secretary: Records of K Province) (Shenyang, Liaoning: Chunfeng, 2002); Mo, Yan, *The Garlic Ballads*, translated from the Chinese by Howard Goldblatt (New York: Viking, 1995); Mo, *The Republic of Wine*, translated from the Chinese by Howard Goldblatt (New York: Arcade, 2000); Tian, Dongzhao, *Paoguan* (Jockeying for officialdom) (Beijing: Zhongguo Dianying, 2000); Wang, Fanghua, "Dianshiju Yishu de Yi Ba Lijian—Xi Jinnian de Xianshi Ticai Fan-fuju Chuangzuo" (A sharp sword in the art of television dramas: An analysis of creating dramas with the theme of anticorruption realism in recent years), *Renmin Ribao* (*People's Daily*), overseas ed., November 22, 2001; Yang, Su, Yan Hong, Jin Lin, and Huang Shuai, *Si Dayuan* (Four large courtyards) (Beijing: Dazhong Wenyi, 2000); Yang, Yuanxin, *Hongyan Tanguan: Nü Jutan Jiang Yanping Chenfu Lu* (A beautiful but corrupt official: The rise and decline of the huge-scale female official Jiang Yanping) (Guangzhou, Guangdong: Huacheng, 2002); Yu, Kai, "Against Corruption," *China Daily*, January 7, 2004; Zhang, Ping, *Jueze* (Choice) (Beijing: Qunzhong, 1997).

Helen Xiaoyan Wu

Anti-Western Nationalism in China (1989–1999)

A revival of nationalism in many parts of the world has characterized the post–Cold War era. The post–Cold War international situation, especially the rise of intense ethnic and nationalist conflicts around the world, helped increase Chinese awareness of the importance of nationalism. The new Chinese nationalism, which stressed China's role as a victim of modern history, was based on frustration over China's inability to overcome political and economic barriers set up by Western countries. In an effort to define an identity separate from the rest of the world, Chinese nationalists demanded a change in the international order, which was dominated by the West after the end of the Cold War.

Anti-Western nationalism increased in China in the 1990s. From official media to the frontiers of popular culture, from Beijing to Guangzhou, there was a mixture of rising pride and lingering insecurity. Many Chinese believed that they were reclaiming their rightful place as an international powerhouse in the world, a position they had lost decades before. As part of the return to prominence, nationalists were explaining the profound sense of humiliation among Chinese who suffered at the hands of Western powers during the nineteenth and twentieth centuries. They increasingly criticized U.S.-led Western countries. They excoriated Western governments for selling arms to Taiwan, for preventing China from entering the World Trade Organization (WTO), for promoting independence of **Tibet**, and for interfering with China's internal affairs in the name of human rights.

The first anti-Western book that appeared after the Tiananmen Square incident in 1989 was Yuan Hongbing's *Huangyuan Feng* (Winds over the plain). Yuan claimed that the Chinese race would survive in the modern world and condemned attempts to achieve freedom by fleeing China as a betrayal of the Chinese race. In addressing Western ideas and values, he criticized those who had tried to find Western solutions to Chinese problems. His book became popular with many college students in 1990.

In 1991, another anti-U.S. book titled *Yibi Xuelinlinde Renquan Zhai* (The bloody debt of human rights) became a best-seller in several of China's cities. General He Ming, author of the book, had been a political commissar of the Nineteenth Army of the Chinese People's Volunteers during the **Korean War** and had participated in negotiations with the U.S. government on repatriating POWs. He tried to convince the Chinese of the evil U.S. history by showing criminal activities of the U.S. Army.

Many Chinese were intrigued by a book, *Manhadun de Zhongguo Nuren* (Chinese woman in Manhattan) by Zhou Li, that described a Chinese woman moving to New York City and making a quick fortune. The book implied that American society was dishonest, that being dishonest was the only way to succeed in making money, and that if one did not make money, one was a loser. About 200,000 copies of the book were sold in 1993.

Another example of anti-Western artistic works was the television series *Beijingren Zai Niuyue* (A Beijing man in New York), which attracted a record viewing audience in China in 1993. The series involved a Chinese hero's trip to the United States, where he overcame adversity and made a fortune, but had to surrender all of his Chinese values to succeed in the United States. While emphasizing the conflicts between Chinese and American cultures, the series vilified American society, showing that there was no morality in the United States, where the strong destroyed the weak and money dominated everything. Successful people were ruffians, and good men always had bad luck.

Based on a semiautobiographical novel by Wang Zhoushen, who spent four years in the United States, the play *The Student's Wife* attracted hundreds of thousands of Shanghai natives in 1995. The play's message was that feeling did not matter in American marriages. Women married for money and men married for sex. Women had to keep an eye on their weight because if they were fat, they would not marry rich men.

In 1996, *Zhongmei Jiaoliang Daxiezhen* (A history of the rivalries between China and the United States) became one of the best-sellers in China. It reviewed Sino-American relations from the Korean War of 1950–1953 to Taiwan president Li Denghui's visit to the United States in 1996. The authors stated that Washington's policies contributed to a series of Sino-American confrontations in Korea and Vietnam, especially the **Vietnam War**, and conflicts over such issues as Tibet, Taiwan, human rights, and arms sales. They claimed that American containment of China would fail because China was more powerful than ever before.

In 1996, a popular book written by five young Chinese authors in their thirties, *Zhongguo Keyi Shuobu* (China can say no), unexpectedly attracted great attention in China and abroad. The 50,000 copies of the first edition sold out immediately, and the book drew hundreds of letters of support from all over China. The book attacked Western cultural, political, and economic imperialism and denounced Western opposition to China on issues such as human rights, population, most-favored-nation status, and Taiwan. It warned that the U.S. government had no right to tell China what was right or wrong, and said that China, being capable of confronting the United States in all spheres of international activities, should be prepared to go to war with America.

After Beijing and Washington reached a trade agreement in November 1999 that would enable China to join the World Trade Organization (WTO), a new anti-Western book, *Quanqiuhua Yinying Xiade Zhongguo Zhilu* (China's road in the shade of globalization), was published before the end of the year. This book, which soon became popular in Beijing, was written by Wang Xiaodong, a researcher at the Youth Research Center of China, Fang Nin, a professor at Beijing Teachers' University, and Song Qiang, one of the authors of the book *China Can Say No*. The book claimed that China would become a member of the WTO, but that Western powers would not stop their aggressive policies against the Chinese through ideological penetration, political control, and economic domination. Therefore, the Chinese had to see clearly the West's plots. The authors promoted cultural nationalism and advocated a native value system to maintain China's sovereignty and independence.

After the Tiananmen crisis, sports became a national obsession and a source of anti-Western nationalism; pride in China's athletes seemed to unify the Chinese. In 1993, the Beijing government, with the support of Deng Xiaoping, began to campaign to hold the 2000 Olympic Games in China. Hoping that the Olympics would boost China's economy and world standing, as the 1988 games had done for South Korea and the 1964 Olympics had done for Japan, many Chinese felt that Beijing should have an opportunity to host the 2000 Olympic Games. But Western countries refused Beijing its hoped-for propaganda victory. On July 26, 1993, the U.S. Congress adopted a resolution against China's bid. On September 23, Sydney edged out Beijing by two votes, forty-five to forty-three. The International Olympic Committee's (IOC) decision was a serious blow to Chinese pride and ambition.

Most Chinese believed that America was responsible for China's failure to win the games. Demonstrations were prohibited and security was increased in Beijing in case protests broke out. Before the IOC's announcement, the U.S. embassy had notified the Chinese Foreign Ministry that it needed official protection for American institutions in Beijing because many Chinese had indicated that if Beijing failed in its Olympic bid, they would blame America first. Anti-U.S. sentiment with regard to sports was surging among Chinese in Beijing in October 1993 and continued to develop during the 1996 Olympics.

During the live broadcast of the opening ceremony of the Olympics in Atlanta, Georgia, in 1996, NBC correspondent Bob Costas criticized China's human rights record and attacked Chinese women swimmers for using banned performance-enhancing drugs. Angered by Costas's reports, many Chinese protested against NBC. Some Chinese scorned the poor organization of the Olympic Games, took pleasure in America's misfortune when they heard of the bombing at the Olympic Park in Atlanta, and looked down on American athletes even though they had won many medals in the games. Some attributed the failure of Chinese athletes to an American plot, claiming that Americans sounded false alarms at night in the hotels where Chinese sportsmen were sleeping to disrupt their sleep and affect their performance the next day. They claimed that organizers of the games did not provide enough transportation to the Chinese athletes, so they did not arrive at the gymnasium on time and therefore lost their events. Local newspapers complained of unfair arbitration of American judges and a conspiracy by American organizers. The protest movement against NBC both in mainland China and in the United States continued until the end of 1996 when NBC apologized to Chinese students in the United States.

In 1999, China was ripe for an explosion of patriotic fervor about its women's soccer team. The U.S. women's team won the first Women's World Cup, which was held in China in 1991, and defeated China again for the Olympic gold medal in 1996. The Women's World Cup of 1999 attracted national attention in China. For the Chinese, the final between the United States and China on July 10 came to represent more than just a soccer match between two longtime rivals. Coming on the heels of the NATO bombing of the Chinese embassy in Yugoslavia in May, the face-off at the Rose Bowl became a matter of national pride and patriotism, with Chinese fans eager for a decisive victory. Many Chinese believed that they could not defeat the United States economically and militarily, but they could use soccer to beat it to vent their spite and to teach Americans a good lesson.

One **Internet** bulletin-board participant in Beijing implored Chinese ticket holders at the Rose Bowl to shout loudly and sing China's national anthem. Another strongly urged the Chinese women to wipe out the American she-wolves. During a meeting on July 5, in Shandong Province, when State Councilor Wu Yi, China's highest-ranking woman, interrupted the discussion to announce that China had beaten Norway 5–0 in the semifinal and that Chinese women would go head-to-head against the United States at the Rose Bowl, conference participants erupted in cheers and applause.

During the live broadcast of the Women's World Cup final, millions of Chinese were shaking off sleep and staggering to their television sets, hoping to see their women's soccer team beat the Americans for the world title. China's media tried to stir nationalist sentiment in their coverage and reported that President Jiang Zemin was watching the team's progress and had telephoned its members with encouragement before the game.

The team's 5–4 loss to the United States on overtime penalty kicks chagrined Chinese fans. For many Chinese, the defeat rankled even more because local resentment against the United States still simmered in the wake of NATO's bombing of the Chinese embassy in Belgrade. The *Beijing Morning Post* and other newspapers raised doubts about the impartiality of the referees. To many Chinese, the defeat was a result of Western conspiracy. They expressed their irritation at the Western athletes, judges, organizers of the games, and even Western governments.

Anti-Western sentiment in China reached a high in May 1999. Hundreds of protesters took to the streets in major cities to protest NATO's bombing of China's embassy in Belgrade, Yugoslavia, which killed three and wounded twenty Chinese. Protesters clashed with police at the U.S. embassy in Beijing, smashing cars and windows. Some of the protesters sang the Chinese national anthem, and others shouted, "Protect sovereignty, protect peace" and "We don't want war." Signs hung on a bus that brought students to the embassy said, "NATO Nazis." Some Chinese shouted obscenities or cast angry looks at westerners walking along the street. In Beijing, many Americans simply stayed inside.

More than 170,000 people massed in front of the U.S. consulate in Chengdu for several days following the bombing, and protesters set fire to the U.S. consul's residence in that city. Police in Guangzhou in southern China warned Western residents to stay indoors. The U.S. and British governments issued travel advisories for their citizens in China, urging them to remain in their hotels or homes. Protests in front of the U.S. and British embassies were the largest anti-Western demonstrations since the **Great Cultural Revolution** in the 1960s. The protests heightened the traditional feeling of humiliation of a weak China, bullied by the West during the past 150 years, but resisting in periodic outbursts of Chinese nationalism.

Today, anti-Western nationalist demonstrations occasionally happen, triggered by such events as an American warplane's accidental bombing of the Chinese embassy in Yugoslavia (1999) and the Hainan Spy Plane Event (2001), which caused the death of a Chinese pilot. Apparently, historical experience is revisited under circumstances like these.

See also Cold War and China; Nationalism in Modern China; Rhetoric in China's Foreign Relations; Sino-American Relations, Conflicts and Common Interests; Sino-American Relations since 1949; United Nations (UN) and China; World Trade Organization (WTO), China's Accession to.

Bibliography

Friedman, Edward, *New National Identities in Post-Leninist Transformations: The Implications for China* (Hong Kong: Chinese University of Hong Kong Press, 1992); Unger, J., ed., *Chinese Nationalism* (Armonk, NY: M. E. Sharpe, 1996); Xu, Guangqiu, "Anti-Western Nationalism in China, 1989–1999," *World Affairs* 163 (spring 2001), 151–162; Zhou, Li, *Chinese Woman in Manhatten* (Beijing: Beijing Chuban She, 1992).

Guangqiu Xu

Armed Forces, Reforms of

The Chinese Communist armed forces are collectively known as the People's Liberation Army (PLA), which is composed of an army, an air force, a navy, and a strategic missile force. The Chinese Communist Party (CCP) reorganized its armed forces into the PLA when it won the Chinese civil war and founded the People's Republic of China (PRC) in October 1949. Since then, the CCP's Central Military Commission (CMC) has conducted a series of military reforms for the PLA's modernization and professionalization.

After the **Korean War** ended in 1953, Marshal Peng Dehuai, vice chairman of the CMC, launched the PLA's first reform. The 1950s military reform extensively copied the Soviet military model to deal with inevitable conflicts against the international imperialists and achieve a victory in the next "people's war." From 1954 to 1959, Soviet military advisers were invited to China and assigned to various levels of the Chinese armed forces. In September 1954, the First **National People's Congress** promulgated a new constitution. According to the PRC Constitution, a new National Defense Commission was established under the central government, and a new Ministry of National Defense was created under the State Council. Peng became the first PRC defense minister. The

Chinese naval cadets in Shanghai in 2002. © Dave Bartruff/Corbis.

Soviet Union greatly influenced the 1950s reform by providing massive amounts of weapons systems and training for all the services and helping organize the defense industry. The 1950s military reform ended when **Mao Zedong**, chairman of the CCP and CMC, accused Peng of forming a "right opportunist clique" and conducting "unprincipled factional activity," charges that often meant pro-Soviet political positions, and removed him from his post as minister of defense in 1959.

After the fall of Peng, Marshal Lin Biao became the PRC defense minister. During the 1960s, when China and the Soviet Union split, Lin terminated most of Peng's reforming programs by criticizing them as part of the "Soviet revisionist military system." Lin was killed in a plane crash in Mongolia after his anti-Mao plot, or "counterrevolutionary clique," failed in September 1971. A purge of the top commanders of the PLA followed Lin's death.

Deng Xiaoping, chief of the PLA General Staff, announced a new military reform at an enlarged CMC meeting in June–July 1975 after his return from the **Great Cultural Revolution (1966–1976)**, in which he had been dismissed from all of his positions in the Communist Party, government, and military in 1966–1975. Having criticized the PLA for being "weak, lazy, and loose leading bodies" at the meeting, Deng began a new reforming effort by demobilizing 600,000 men and emphasizing a strategic transition from Mao's "people's war" doctrine to a new "people's war under modern conditions" doctrine. Deng was purged again in 1976. The military reform continued under the leadership of Marshal Ye Jianying.

After Deng staged his third comeback in 1977, he made a historic speech, "Emancipate the Mind," at the Third Plenary Session of the CCP Eleventh Party Central Committee in 1978. His speech declared an unprecedented seismic reform and an opening to the outside world in order to bring the Four Modernizations to China, including industry, agriculture, science and technology, and military modernization. Deng continued the reforming process of PLA modernization and professionalism in the wake of the 1979 Vietnam incursion. By 1982, Deng uprooted **Hua Guofeng**'s role as chairman of the CMC and reinstalled himself as the chief of the PLA General Staff. To oversee the downsizing and reform, a Military System Reform Leading Group was established in the CMC in February 1982.

From May 23 to June 6, 1985, the CMC held a landmark expanded conference that became the starting point of another PLA reform. Deng, chairman of the CMC, made an important speech at the conference, "Strategic Changes to the Guiding Principles on National Defense Construction and Army Building." He believed that a new world war was not inevitable, and a major nuclear war no longer seemed imminent. The PLA needed to contemplate a new and different international environment and take part in China's ongoing reforms. Later that year, Deng further explained his new strategic thoughts: The Chinese armed forces should expect a "local war" or a "limited war" rather than a "total war" or a "nuclear war" in the future. The military reforming movement then followed Deng's new doctrine of fighting "limited, local war" and emphasized the development and employment of new technology and improvement of PLA weaponry. Deng further downsized the PLA forces by another million troops during the next two years. Although he retired from official posts, Deng remained in the center of China's reform in the 1980s. The reform was, in his own words, to "cross the river by feeling the stones." Unable to solve the economic and social problems and unwilling to carry the reform into political aspects, Deng and other Chinese leaders in the summer of 1989 were challenged by prodemocracy student demonstrations. It was agreed by Deng that PLA soldiers were ordered to open fire on the protesting students in Tiananmen Square in Beijing on June 4, 1989.

After the Tiananmen incident, Jiang Zemin became the chairman of both the CCP and CMC in 1989. In the 1990s, Jiang launched a new military reform known as the "two transformations." Jiang stated that the PLA should be transformed from an army preparing to fight "local wars under ordinary conditions" to an army prepared to fight and win "local wars under modern high-tech conditions"; from an army based on quantity to an army based on quality. This recent effort at comprehensive reform and modernization appears to be cutting across every facet of PLA activity, affecting such areas as doctrine, operational concepts, and war-fighting techniques; the acquisition of modern weapons systems and the integration of new technologies; and reforms to weapons research, development, and acquisition processes. Jiang's doctrine of fighting "local wars under modern high-tech conditions" has become a new guideline for the PLA's institutional reform.

In the late 1990s and early 2000s, the PLA's institutional reform included some major changes in the personnel system, organization, and the sustainability system. The personnel reforms were the cornerstone of the PLA's transformation from an army based on quantity to an army based on quality. In 1997, at the CCP Fifteenth National Congress, Jiang announced and executed China's plan to reduce the PLA by 500,000 men. On July 28, 1998, the PLA stated that it had accomplished its goal of reduction, and that it would maintain the current 2.5 million troops. In December 1998, the Chinese government revised its Military Service Law. The previous law had required Chinese citizens to be drafted into the PLA and serve three years in the army or four years in the navy and air force. The new law reduced the service time to only two years for all military branches. The organizational reform has resulted in changes in the structure of headquarters organizations at all levels. Overall, the administrative reforms of the past decade have been focused on reducing headquarters personnel by 20 to 50 percent. The sustainability reforms encompass both logistics and the defense industry. With regard to logistics, a high priority is being accorded to modernizing and improving combat service support functions that comport with the new operational concepts. Since the PLA emphasizes joint operations, which ensure victory in local wars under modern high-tech conditions, joint logistics, rather than service-focused logistics, are now viewed as essential. Despite a decade of extensive reform, the Chinese armed forces today still face some problems and difficulties in their modernization, like other sectors of Chinese society, among which bureaucracy and intricacy in rankings and promotion are notorious.

See also Deng Xiaoping (1904–1997), Reforms of; Jiang Zemin (1926–   ), Populism of; June 4 Movement; Populism of; Military Ranking and Promotion; Military Service System; Vietnam War.

Bibliography

Allen, Kenneth, Dean Cheng, David Finkelstein, and Maryanne Kivlehan, *Institutional Reforms of the Chinese People's Liberation Army: Overview and Challenges* (Alexandria, VA: CNA Corporation, 2002); Deng, Xiaoping, *Selected Works of Deng Xiaoping*, vols. 2 and 3 (Beijing: Foreign Languages Press, 1994 and 1995); Li, Xiaobing, *Peasant Soldiers: Chinese Military in the Changing World* (Lexington: University Press of Kentucky, 2004); Shambaugh, David, *Modernizing China's Military: Progress, Problems, and Prospects* (Berkeley: University of California Press, 2002); Xinhua News Agency, *China's National Defense*, China's Defense White Papers (Beijing, 1998, 1999, 2000, and 2001).

Xiaobing Li

Asian-African Conference of 1955

See Bandung Conference of 1955.

Auto Industry Development

China's auto industry has experienced its most rapid development in the past two decades. The industry was characterized before the economic reform of 1978 by low technology, high cost, and heavy government interference. Cars before 1978 were driven only by cadres of certain high rank classified by the government, and there was no private auto ownership. The very few models of low-quality domestic cars were produced by a few state-owned automakers, such as the First and Second Auto Works. Few foreign cars were imported, and almost all came from the Soviet Union. The transportation mode was predominantly public or by bicycles, which constituted an important possession of wealth by private citizens.

After 1978, when economic reforms started and before China's World Trade Organization (WTO) entry, taxicabs, foreign cars, and domestic models grew steadily. The auto industry experienced a rapid growth in the number of domestic auto makers because of three major factors. First, economic reforms returned the production decision power to firms many industries became deregulated, and entry barriers were broken. Second, the auto industry was more profitable than many other industries and attracted especially **state-owned enterprises** that had formerly been munitions producers but that later changed to civilian goods production in order to survive. They became producers of agricultural vehicles, such as tractors, that turned unprofitable when agricultural production became family based and smaller scaled. Third, in the 1990s, local protectionism emerged while central planning weakened, leading to the production of autos by almost every province and protection of their local markets. This combination of high import tariffs and free entry into the domestic market resulted in low standards, low-quality cars, and severely underscaled production. The relatively larger producers, who were most likely also on an optimal scale, suffered from the additional costs of functioning as enterprise societies that provided services such as schools, hospitals, housing

This street scene from Chen Du City, Sichuan Province, shows the increasing prevalence of automobiles on Chinese streets.

management, and day-care centers. Thus, despite China's low labor cost, production of automobiles was costly because of low scales, inefficiencies, and outdated technologies. However, the producers survived well in the absence of foreign competition.

In the late 1990s, more foreign cars entered the domestic market as newly emerged domestic entrepreneurs demanded foreign luxuries at high tariffs. Meanwhile, joint ventures with foreign auto giants, such as Volkswagen, GM, Nissan, and Chrysler, started to be formed, which gradually improved the technological capabilities of domestic producers. Reforms within firms also sped up. Nonetheless, the auto industry was still considered the most vulnerable to foreign competition. Meanwhile, given China's high population density and the potential side effects of traffic jams, pollution, and other problems arising from auto industry development, policy makers and academicians debated whether to let the auto industry become a pivotal industry or to develop it cautiously at a controlled rate. The concern then seemed to fade in the midst of fears about the impact of China's WTO entry. On the market, most models of cars were of simple design, little comfort, and low quality. In 1998, the city of Chengdu, the provincial capital of Sichuan Province, had its first Buick sedan displayed, which was considered luxurious and of high quality. China's auto industry, therefore, was expected to bear the heaviest crush of foreign competition following China's WTO entry.

Imports have indeed grown rapidly following China's WTO entry. In 2002, China imported 120,000 automobiles worth U.S. $6 billion. Of the total imported vehicles, 70,000 were sedans, accounting for 6 percent of the total domestic market, which had expanded during the year. Meanwhile, prices had declined rapidly. There was a 35 percent increase in auto consumption and more than a 35 percent increase in auto production in 2002. In the first seven months of 2003, China imported 105,000 vehicles, and of that amount, 58 percent, or 61,400, were sedans. The imports of autos and auto-related products grew by 110 percent, compared to the same time the previous year, to reach U.S. $8.2 billion. Of this increase, 90 percent was from Japan, Germany, the Republic of Korea, the United States, and Sweden. However, these imports still accounted for a small percentage (around 5 percent) of total domestic production, which reached 2.0766 million in the first half of 2003, reducing the anticipated disadvantage.

In 2002, China produced a total of 3.251 million vehicles and became the fifth-largest auto-producing country in the world after the United States, Japan, Germany, and France (CCTV, February 14, 2003). In 2003, it surpassed France to become the fourth-largest auto producer. With the production of 2.0766 million cars in the first seven months, the production in 2003 was estimated to surpass 4 million. Prices have decreased annually by an average of 20 percent in the last two years. More profitable in the domestic market and less competitive in international markets, current auto production is supplied primarily to the domestic market, but this situation is unlikely to last. Michael J. Dunne, president of Automotive Resources Asia, predicts that within five years cars made in China will appear in European and North American markets.

Structurally, the major producers are First Auto Works in Changchun, Shanghai Auto Industry Group, Wuhan Dongfeng Motors, Changan Auto, and another two in Guangzhou and Beijing. The first three automakers have a market concentration rate of greater than 50 percent. Almost all large producers have formed joint ventures with foreign auto giants. Foreign cars in China have also become more diversified. In the 1990s, Volkswagen had a dominant position among foreign cars, comprising 60 percent of the market at one point, but its market shares have been severely diluted since China's WTO entry because Toyota, Honda, GM, and other foreign makers are rapidly expanding their market shares. The Chinese auto industry has been undergoing rapid consolidation among firms.

Despite its consolidation and development from a controlled industry to one much more sensitive to market forces, China's auto industry continues to be characterized by low economies of scale and dispersed production sites, with an average production per firm of fewer than 5,000 cars. Out of China's thirty-two provinces, autonomous regions, and municipalities, twenty-three have car producers, totaling 123. Of the 123 producers, only 2 have the capacity of producing more than 500,000 cars; 8 producers are capable of producing more than 100,000 cars; 95 others make fewer than 10,000 cars; and 70 percent of the producers produce only 1,000 cars a year. Fat profit margins continue to keep afloat many producers who started the business under earlier local protectionism. On the supply side, the producers of fewer than 1,000 vehicles are mostly making specialty trucks and buses fit for special needs in China at prices as low as $5,000 that are unmatchable by foreign producers. On the demand side, Chinese consumers are still at the stage where a basic car that can symbolize their proud ownership and carry them from one point to another is sufficient. Better brands of foreign cars are only affordable by entrepreneurs and executives.

The government has decided that domestic automakers are too small to realize economies of scale and is intending to steer the market toward consolidating into only a handful of producers. The rapid development of the auto industry has also raised concerns about overheating in the market. Beijing now has a total of 2 million cars and is predicted to have 3.5 million by 2005. Although Beijing has been continuously expanding its beltway system, this rapid expansion has made traffic jams a common phenomenon. Nationwide, it was estimated that there was a severe shortage of parking spaces in comparison to the growing number of cars. Some cities have started to restrict the number of cars on the road. Shanghai, for example, has set a quota for the annual amount of cars to be owned through auctions of car licenses. Guangzhou has adopted similar measures, but Beijing has stayed put.

Will China become an automobile-dominant society? Beijing is said to have said good-bye to the bicycle age and hello to the automobile age with the total of 2 million cars, or 19 cars per 100 households, surpassing the world average of 10 cars per 100 households. Regarding the long-term development of the auto industry, China still needs to address the issue of whether to adopt the mode of transportation by private cars, as does the United States, or to rely more on the public transit system, as do European countries. The two basic models have led to different modes of urbanization. In the United States, highways and private cars have been criticized as leading to the social problem of decaying central cities and the massive urban sprawl that has created more environmental problems. China's rapid development of private cars will also directly affect its mode of urban development, in addition to the resources required for building highways and parking facilities, as well as creating environmental problems. With a population density much higher than in the United States and even the European nations, is China going to adopt the European model? While the answer remains to be seen, the Chinese leadership must prevent itself from overemphasizing the current benefits of the auto industry as a pivotal sector for growth and consider seriously the longer-term interest of the country.

See also Energy Industries; Industrial Structure; World Trade Organization (WTO), China's Accession to.

Bibliography

CCTV, *60-minute News*, 12/2/03, 2/14/03, 8/26/03, 8/27/03; Chen, Aimin, "The Impact of China's WTO Entry: An Analysis *ex ante* and *ex post*," *American Review of China Studies* 4, no. 2 (fall 2003): 1–15; Chen, "The Structure of Chinese Industry and the Impact from China's WTO Entry," *Comparative Economic Studies*, spring 2002, 72–98.

Aimin Chen

Avant-garde Literature

Characterized by the introduction of Western concepts and styles into Chinese literature, the avant-garde literary movement (*xian feng pai*) began in China after 1979, when a change in governmental policy opened the country to Western influences. The movement included both younger writers eager to adopt new forms and ideas and more open-minded older writers willing to break out of the literary isolation long imposed by the government.

During the so-called **Great Cultural Revolution (1966–1976)** led by **Mao Zedong**, literature and art were expected to support political goals. Members of the Red Guards ransacked public and private libraries and burned most classical and imported books. Except for a few novels of the Russian Revolution, all Western literatures and their writing styles were considered bourgeois and antirevolutionary. Chinese literary creations were totally isolated from the outside world until 1979, when Deng Xiaoping's **Open Door policy** suddenly opened the country to Western influences in many areas.

Well-known pioneers of the Chinese avant-garde movement in literature include Wang Meng, Zong Pu, Zhan Rong, Zhang Jie, Li Luen, and Gao Xingjian. These writers were among the first to introduce contemporary Western concepts and writing styles into Chinese literature. In the beginning, they tried to bring Western stylistic seasoning into the realistic novels and short stories that had dominated Chinese literary activity for more than half a century. Gao Xingjian revolutionized modern Chinese dramas, which he both wrote and directed. Wang Meng and Zong Pu, both well-known literary figures, absorbed or borrowed some modern writing styles from Western novels, but otherwise continued writing mainly traditional realistic novels.

In the 1980s, the most important periodical publication in Chinese literature, *Dangdai* (Contemporary age), promoted the avant-garde movement in China.

In 1985, the movement entered its prime period. *Ni Bie Wu Xuanze* (No other choice for you) by Liu Sola and *Wu Zhuti Bianzouqu* (Variations without title) by Xu Xing were the first two important avant-garde works in China. They were characterized by modern concepts of reality, abstraction, existentialism, expressionism, and absurdism. Liu Sola graduated from the Central Conservatory of China's Department of Music Composition. However, she became more famous as a writer than as a composer. Her mother, Liu Jiantong, wrote a famous novel about a well-known Chinese revolutionary martyr named Liu Zhidan. Since Mao Zedong was at odds with Liu Zhidan, Mao reprimanded Liu Jiantong and accused her of creating an anti–Communist Party literature.

The main characters in Liu Sola's *No Other Choice for You* are a group of students at the conservatory who seek every opportunity to challenge the old methodology used to train musicians. Despite refusing to follow tradition and accept musical conventions, the students become the country's best composers and win international recognition for their music. Thus, contrary to most Western absurdist literature, the conclusion of this novel is full of happiness and idealism.

Xu Xing's *Variations without Title* goes even further into describing the young generation's rebellious lifeway. Its main character is a young man who drops out of the university to become a "common" person devoid of any ambitions. He self-confidently rejects all traditionally endorsed "positive" endeavors. In another important avant-garde work, Chen Cun's *Shao Nan, Shao Nu, Yigong Qi Ge* (Totally seven boys and girls), the nihilism and spiritual emptiness of a group of high-school students is vividly described.

One of the most influential avant-garde novels published in China is Mo Yan's *Hong Gaoliang* (Red sorghum). Mo Yan is a native of Shandong Province, where Confucius was born and Confucianism is still influential. In his previous literary works, Mo Yan's realistic tendency was obvious. However, with *Red Sorghum*, he changed his writing style and joined the avant-garde school even though the semantic contents of his works remained rooted in his traditional agricultural homeland. After the success of *Red Sorghum*, a series of novels and short stories that included *Gaoliang Jiu* (Sorghum liquor), *Gaoliang Bin* (Sorghum funeral), *Gou Dao* (Doctrine of dog), *Gou Pi* (Dog skin), and *Qi Si* (Strange death) were published as part of the Red Sorghum Series. The novel *Red Sorghum* was made into a film that, in its English-dubbed version, became well known to American audiences. In the Red Sorghum Series, the barbarian and civilization always found an acceptable balance in their ways of life. In Mo Yan's most recent works, this balance has disappeared, and the novels have as a consequence been heavily criticized by the public.

Can Xue, whose real name is Deng Xiaohua (1953–   ), is a famous avant-garde woman writer. Her most influential works are *Tiantang li de Duihua* (Dialogues on the heaven), *Shan Shang de Xiao Wu* (A small mountain house), *Huang Ni Jie* (Muddy street), and *Kuang Ye Li* (Wilderness). Full of dark themes, her novels intentionally exaggerate the ugly side of human life to an absurd level to show her love of illusion and the hope and beauty that she finds to be invisibly present in real life.

In the late 1980s and early 1990s, a new generation of avant-garde writers arose. Represented by Ma Yuan, Zhaxidawa, Hong Feng, Yu Hua, Su Tong, and Ge Fei, among others, this new group is now known as the "New Novelist Current." Ma Yuan began his career by writing personal experiences derived from his college life. The mysticism of **Tibet**, where he had worked for an extended period of time, provided him with a new vision of the world and pushed him from realism to superrealism in his literary works. His avant-garde stories are set in Tibet. Ma Yuan himself appears as Da Yuan, an image of the author in his childhood, or as Yao Liang, the author in his conscious status, or as Lu Gao, a depiction of the author's strength and genius. All these images of Ma Yuan are combined into a real, spiritual, material, unrestrained, and natural Ma Yuan in the narrative. Almost all Ma Yuan's Tibetan characters have a personality that is indeterminate, inexact, confusing, perplexed, and ambiguous. He does not care about the moral and philosophical value of the semantic content of his novels, but focuses instead on the narration itself. Ma Yuan's most influential works are *Lasa He Nu Shen* (Goddess on the river Lassa), *Ximalaya Gu Ge* (Ancient song of Himalaya), *Lasa Shenghuo de San Zhong Shijian* (Three times in the Lassa's life), *Xu Gou* (A made-up story), *Cuowu* (An error), and *Dashi* (Great master).

Zhaxidawa is a Tibetan woman writer who blends contemporary mythology with Tibetan folklore, as in her well-known work *Xizang, Ji Zai Pisheng Kou Shang De Hun* (Tibet—soul fastened onto Quipu). Hong Fen's *Shengming Zhi Liu* (Life current), *Ben Sang* (Funeral), *Yanmo* (Wrecking), *Han Hai* (Immense sea), and *Bai Wu* (White fog) describe the relationship between nature and human beings and between human beings and animals. These novels exhibit a strong longing for the primitive life and depict the rebellion of contemporary people against the modern lifestyle. An extremely absurd story titled *Wrecking* describes a young man so deeply in love that he intentionally pushes his girlfriend into the river and then jumps into the water to save her life. Such absurdity constitutes a profound reflection of the reality of human existence.

In 2000, Gao Xingjian, one of the leaders of the avant-garde movement, became the first Chinese writer to win the Nobel Prize in literature. He is today a French citizen and received the French title of Chevalier de l'Ordre des Artes et des Lettres in 1992, the Prix Communauté française de Belgique in 1994, and the Prix du Nouvel an Chinois in 1997. Gao Xingjian was born in Jiangxi Province in eastern China on January 4, 1940. His father was a bank employee. He received his basic education in Nanjing, the capital of Jiangsu Province, and in 1959 began the study of French at the Beijing Foreign Studies University, previously named the Beijing Foreign Language Institute. Upon graduation in 1964, he was sent to work as a Chinese-French translator for the National Foreign Language Press of China. While working as translator and editor of the magazine *China Reconstructs* during the daytime, he spent nights writing novels, short stories, plays, and poems. Because of his interest in writing, he was sent in 1965 to participate in a training program for young writers organized by the Chinese Writers Association. When the Cultural Revolution started in 1966, he participated actively in the political activities and became the leader of a political faction at the National Foreign Language Press. Because of his active participation in the Cultural Revolution, he was admitted to the Communist Party of China.

To be politically correct, he had to burn or hide much of his previous work. After working in a rural reeducation camp with other editors, photographers, and translators at the press, Gao became the coordinator of the French edition of *China Reconstructs*, but his main dream was to write literature and become a famous novelist. He continued to write plays and short stories at midnight when his roommate was sleeping.

At the end of the Cultural Revolution, in particular, after the April 5 Movement and the 1976 massacre in Tiananmen Square, he became tired of Chinese politics and extremely frustrated with Deng Xiaoping's opportunist attitude toward the democratic movement in China. Gao therefore decided to concentrate on his writing. He published his first work in 1979 and from 1980 to 1987 published several essays, short stories, and dramas in Chinese literary magazines. In 1981, because of his interest and success in writing plays, and with the strong support of Cao Yu, a famous Chinese dramatist, Gao started working as a professional playwright with the People's Arts Theatre. Profoundly inspired by such Western writers as Antonin Artaud, Bertolt Brecht, and Samuel Beckett, Gao wrote *Signal Alarm* in 1982, *Bus Stop* in 1983, and *Wild Man* in 1985. The three pioneering plays, which were said to be absurd, fantastic, dreamlike, and surrealistic, were performed by the Beijing People's Arts Theatre and were great successes. By the early 1980s, he was also writing short stories and a novel titled *Soul Mountain*.

Gao received a political reprimand for his work during Deng Xiaoping's campaign against "bourgeois intellectual pollution." In a newspaper controlled by the Communist Party, the play *Bus Stop* was described as the most pernicious piece of writing since the foundation of the People's Republic of China. His last play, *Wild Man*, was only on the stage for a short time before being banned because it gave rise to a heated domestic polemic. However, Gao's experimental dramas attracted favorable attention from both the international and Beijing literary communities. He became well known nationwide when he published his first book on literary theory, *Preliminary Exploration into the Techniques of Modern Fiction*, which provoked a major debate between pro-modernist writers and those who followed Maoist literary principles of socialist realism. In this book, Gao publicly and openly expressed his disagreement with Mao's principles of "art for the blue-collar workers, peasants, and solders" and promoted the principle of "art for art's own sake." This viewpoint was criticized in China as reactionary and antirevolutionary, and Gao was placed under surveillance. In 1986, he finished writing *The Other Shore* and presented it to the leading figures of the People's Art Theatre for performance, but it and all his plays were banned by the Chinese government, which in 1987 also prohibited publication of all his other works.

When the Chinese Communist Party began another antiliberalism campaign in 1987, Gao went to France as a political refugee and settled in Paris. During the 1989 Tiananmen Square massacre, he renounced his Communist Party membership. That same year, he published *Fugitives*, which constituted his declaration against this massacre and is one of the few works published in France to carry a political theme. With his play *Summer Rain in Beijing*, *Fugitives* was performed at the Royal Dramatic Theatre in Stockholm, Sweden. Gao also published two important novels, *Soul Mountain* and *One Man's Bible*.

The former is a kind of odyssey expressing the author's individual search for inner space, peace, liberty, and his roots during fifty years under a Communist regime, and the latter is an autobiographical narrative expressing the suffering and experience of a Chinese intellectual.

Gao also published several surrealistic plays, which were produced in Taiwan, Sweden, France, and other countries. In these works, he criticized both the Chinese authorities and the fugitives from government oppression. In France, he is regarded as being at the front of avant-garde Chinese-French literature. A number of his works have been translated into English, French, Spanish, German, Japanese, Swedish, and other languages. In recent years, he has also become known as a Chinese painter. His Chinese ink and watercolor paintings have been exhibited in Europe and the United States.

While Gao Xingjian is considered the top Chinese avant-garde writer, new generations of writers are becoming more popular among the Chinese community both within and outside China. Although the Association of Chinese Writers, guided by the Chinese Communist Party, still insists on encouraging social-political topics in literary creation, many young writers have tried to explore their inner space in their writing. Since 1978, Gao Xingjian and other writers have viewed literature as a purely artistic form that can exist independently from any social context. Instead of social reality, the younger generation of avant-garde writers enjoys dreams and fantasies. The art-for-the-art ideal brought some excitement to Chinese literary society after the 1980s.

Besides novels, short stories, and dramas, avant-garde poetry appeared in China in 1982 and introduced new vitality and diversity into contemporary Chinese poetry in the 1980s. Important works that were translated into English include Mo Fei's *Words and Objects*, Mo Mo's *Betraying Fingers* and *Sold Out*, and Liu Manliu's *Mayfly's Journal*. The freshness of this poetry contrasted sharply with the staleness of **misty poetry**'s symbolism and created the possibility for more radical experiments in Chinese poetry. Liu Manliu's *Autograph Book* and Y Jian's *Fence and Mouse* indicate a further step in the maturing of Chinese avant-garde poetry. Some other equally significant avant-garde experimental poetry groups, such as the "Original" poets based in Suzhou City and the "Feifei" poets based in Sichuan Province, reveal other new elements and directions in contemporary Chinese poetry.

See also Anticorruption Literature and Television Dramas; Experimental Fiction; Great Cultural Revolution, Literature during; Intellectuals, Political Engagement of (1949–1978); Intellectuals, Political Engagement of (1978–Present); Literary Policy for the New China; Literature of the Wounded; Modern Pop-Satire; Neorealist Fiction and Modernism; Pre–Cultural Revolution Literature; Revolutionary Realism and Revolutionary Romanticism; Root-Searching Literature; Sexual Freedom in Literature.

Bibliography

Guo, Zhigang, and Sun Zhongtian, eds., *Contemporary Chinese Literature—Second Part* (Beijing: Higher Education Press, 1993); Jin, Han, *Modern Chinese Novels* (Zhejiang, China: Zhejiang University Press, 1997); Zhang, Rongjian, ed., *Contemporary Chinese Literature* (Anhui, China: University of Sciences and Technology of Central China

Press, 2001); Zhang, ed., *Contemporary Chinese Literature—Reference Materials* (Anhui, China: University of Sciences and Technology of Central China Press, 2001); Zhang, Weizhong, *Transformations in the New Age Novels and the Chinese Traditional Culture* (Beijing: Xuelin Press, 2002).

Zhiyuan Chen

B

Bandung Conference of 1955

The Bandung Conference is a better-known name for the Asian-African Conference, which was held in Bandung, Indonesia, from April 18 to April 24, 1955. It was an effort of Asian and African nations and peoples after World War II to build up a front of cooperation to oppose colonialism and racism, to safeguard national independence, and to promote world peace.

The idea of cooperation among Asian and African nations was initiated by Indonesia. It reflected many new independent Asian nations' concerns over the international situation after World War II. The **Korean War** broke out in 1950. Though it ended in 1953, the tensions in Indochina increased. The nationalist movement in Vietnam made considerable advances in the early 1950s. The Geneva Conference of 1954 signified the withdrawal of France from Indochina. However, the United States began to move in. In particular, a U.S.-led military alliance, the Southeast Asia Treaty Organization (SEATO), took form in 1954. In the Taiwan Strait, the confrontation between Communist China on one side and the United States and Taiwan on the other side led the two sides to the brink of war.

From April 28 to May 2, 1954, five Asian nations, Burma (now Myanmar), Ceylon (now Sri Lanka), India, Indonesia, and Pakistan, met at Colombo, Ceylon, to discuss their shared concerns over issues caused by the Cold War in Asia. Indonesian prime minister Ali Sastroamidjojo suggested expanding the Colombo Conference to the other countries of Asia and Africa. In December 1954, the five nations met again in Bogor, Indonesia, and made a joint proposal for an Asian-African conference.

In April 1955, twenty-nine nations attended the Asian-African Conference in Bandung, Indonesia: Afghanistan, Burma, Cambodia, Ceylon, China, Egypt, Ethiopia, Gold Coast (now Ghana), India, Indonesia, Iran, Iraq, Japan, Jordan, Laos, Lebanon, Liberia, Libya, Nepal, Pakistan, the Philippines, Saudi Arabia,

On April 23, 1955, Chinese Premier Zhou Enlai *(right)* walks through
the streets of Bandung, Indonesia, shortly after his arrival for the Afro-
Asian Conference in Bandung. © Bettmann/Corbis.

the Sudan, Syria, Thailand, Turkey, North Vietnam, South Vietnam, and Yemen.
Nearly all of the Asian nations and most of the independent and nearly independent African nations were represented. Major topics discussed at the conference included economic and cultural cooperation among Asia and Africa,
human rights and self-determination, the countries still under colonialism, and
world peace and cooperation.

The most important achievement of the conference was the Declaration on
Promotion of World Peace and Cooperation, which put forth the following ten
principles:

1. Respect for fundamental human rights and for the purposes and principles of the Charter of the United Nations

2. Respect for the sovereignty and territorial integrity of all nations

3. Recognition of the equality of all races and of the equality of all
   nations large and small

4. Abstention from intervention or interference in the internal affairs of
   another country

5. Respect for the right of each nation to defend itself singly or collectively in conformity with the Charter of the United Nations

6. A. Abstention from the use of arrangements of collective defense to
   serve the particular interests of any of the big powers; B. Abstention
   by any country from exerting pressures on other countries

7. Refraining from acts or threats of aggression or the use of force against
   the territorial integrity or political independence of any country

8. Settlement of all international disputes by peaceful means, such as negotiation, conciliation, arbitration, or judicial settlement, as well as other peaceful means of the parties' own choice, in conformity with the Charter of the United Nations

9. Promotion of mutual interests and cooperation

10. Respect for justice and international obligations

The ten principles, often known as "the Bandung Spirit," inspired the newly independent nations and the movements for independence in Asia and Africa. It was a milestone in the growth of the Third World. The significance of "the Bandung Spirit" also went beyond Asia and Africa. It was accepted by many other nations later as a principle in solving bilateral and multilateral issues in the international world.

China was not among the five sponsors, but its participation and role assured the success of the conference. China's foreign policy toward the Third World countries in the 1950s underwent marked changes. During the initial phase of the People's Republic of China, China's foreign policy was to "lean to one side," the side of the Communist camp led by the Soviet Union, and to oppose any third road between the two camps. China had decided to "put the house in order before inviting guests." A major factor that contributed to its policy change was the rapid growth of new independent Third World nations. Burma was the first nonsocialist nation to recognize China, followed by India. In particular, India displayed a cooperative attitude by recognizing the legality of China's claim to **Tibet** and showed its sympathy to China in mediating the Korean War.

Its ideological commitment notwithstanding, China was anxious to break its diplomatic isolation in the world. The modification of its policy became evident in the Geneva Conference of 1954, where Chinese premier and foreign minister **Zhou Enlai** persuaded the Democratic Republic of Vietnam to accept a compromise with France. In June 1954, Zhou Enlai visited India and signed a joint statement with Indian prime minister Jawaharlal Nehru that formulated the **Five Principles of Peaceful Coexistence**. During his visit, Zhou Enlai seized the opportunity to express China's interest in participating in the Asian-African Conference then under consideration. In the subsequent meetings with the leaders of India and Burma, Zhou Enlai reiterated China's support. China's moderating gestures helped win an invitation from the sponsors of the conference.

The Chinese delegation to the Bandung Conference, which was headed by Premier Zhou Enlai, included Vice Premier Chen Yi, Minister of Foreign Trade Ye Jizhuang, Vice Minister of Foreign Affairs Zhang Hanfu, and Chinese ambassador to Indonesia Huang Zhen as the principal members. It proved to be a risk-taking mission. In an attempt to assassinate Zhou Enlai, the Taiwan Kuomintang authorities staged the incident of the plane *Kashmir Princesses* on April 11, 1955. A time bomb brought down the plane chartered by the Chinese delegation in the sea near the Natuna island group and killed all eleven people on board. Zhou Enlai and others survived because he changed his route to go to Burma first.

The Chinese delegation encountered a hostile atmosphere at the meeting. Among the twenty-nine participating nations, twelve were anti-Communist. During the general debate, while some suspected China of support for subversive activities within its neighboring countries, several others openly attacked communism. Neutral nations were concerned, afraid of the drift of discussion and even the possible collapse of the conference.

Faced with criticism and suspicions, Zhou Enlai took a conciliatory approach. Instead of responding to his critics with Communist rhetoric, he stated that China came to Bandung "to seek unity" and "not to quarrel," and "to seek common ground, and not to create divergence." The common ground, he pointed out, was their shared experience of "the calamities of colonialism." He assured the delegates that China did not intend to subvert the governments of its neighboring countries and would not bring up the issue of Taiwan for discussion to avoid divisions. Zhou's surprisingly mild speech impressed most of the delegates and received overwhelmingly favorable response. Throughout the meeting, Zhou Enlai's friendly attitude, as well as his artful diplomatic skills, convinced the delegates of his sincerity. He eventually became a mediator among the delegates and played a leading role in finalizing the Ten Principles. In fact, the Five Principles of peaceful coexistence formulated by China and India in 1954 served as the basis of the Ten Principles.

The Bandung Conference provided a springboard for China to approach Third World nations. The Chinese delegation made extensive contacts with both those delegates that were friendly to and those that were suspicious of China. China's diplomacy in Bandung paved the way for the formation of diplomatic relations with Nepal, Egypt, Syria, Yemen, and Ceylon and prepared Zhou Enlai's goodwill visits to South and Southeast Asia and Africa in the following years.

The Bandung Conference marked a new direction in China's foreign policy. Confronted with U.S.-led military alliances in Asia, China shifted from its early principle of "putting the house in order before inviting guests." It sought to cement bonds with the newly independent nations to safeguard its national security. It intended to foster cooperation among Asian and African nations to create a peaceful neighboring region free of American intervention. It strove to build a new image to strengthen its presence in the Third World. China strongly endorsed "the Bandung Spirit" because it well served its national interest. In doing so, China also demonstrated its independence from the Soviet Union, since it would eventually depart from the line of the Soviet Union. It must be noted that the principle of peaceful coexistence in the 1950s was not yet an end in China's view of international relations. For China, it was a means to form a broad base of the world revolution movement against the capitalist world led by the United States. Because of this conviction, China's foreign policy in the following decades would adopt both conciliatory and militant approaches.

See also Rhetoric in China's Foreign Relations; Sino-American Relations, Conflicts and Common Interests; Sino-American Relations since 1949; Sino-Soviet Alliance; Taiwan Strait Crisis, Evolution of.

Bibliography

Abdulgani, Roeslan, *The Bandung Connection: The Asia-Africa Conference in Bandung in 1955* (Singapore: Gunung Agung, 1981); Kahin, George McTurnan, *The Asian-African Conference: Bandung, Indonesia, April 1955* (Ithaca, NY: Cornell University Press, 1956); Xiong, Huayuan, *Zhou Enlai wanlong zhi xing* (Zhou Enlai attended the Bandung Conference) (Beijing: Zhongyang Wenxian Chubanshe, 2002); Zhou, Enlai, *China and the Asian-African Conference (Documents)* (Beijing: Foreign Languages Press, 1955).

Jinxing Chen

Banking and Financial System Reform

Even after China's economic reforms began in 1978, the People's Bank of China continued to function not only as a central bank but also as a loan-issuing bank. There was no real banking system in place outside the People's Bank and no established markets for bonds or stocks. Although government bond issuance resumed in 1981, these bonds were initially paid for by payroll deduction and represented little more than an alternative form of taxation. A first step toward a true central banking system occurred in September 1983 when the People's Bank was reconstituted in its modern form. The People's Bank has since gradually moved to exercise monetary control through such Western mechanisms as setting reserve requirements and managing credit

Most Chinese banks are open six days a week and offer foreign currency exchange services.

funds. Newly separated specialized banks began directing lending activities in their particular spheres of influence: the Industrial and Commercial Bank of China, the China Construction Bank, and the Agricultural Bank of China handle domestic transactions, while the Bank of China specializes in international transactions.

Commercialization of the four specialized banks was fostered by the creation of three new policy banks in 1994: the State Development Bank of China, the Import-Export Bank of China, and the Agricultural Development Bank of China. Policy loans were transferred to these new institutions, with the four specialized banks becoming responsible for their own profits and losses. Various other, much smaller commercial banks have been established subject to People's Bank approval. A 1994 Budget Law enhanced central-bank autonomy by prohibiting the government from borrowing from the People's Bank of China. Stock-market trading began in both Shanghai and Shenzhen in 1990, and a secondary market for government bonds gradually developed during the late 1980s, with over-the-counter trading first started by the Shenyang Trust and Investment Company on August 5, 1986. The rising importance of the bond market was such that when the Shanghai Securities Exchange opened in December 1990, it was dominated by the trading of government securities.

Fiscal strains developed in the 1990s, however, as the government launched a fiscal stimulus program aimed at combating slowing economic growth. As direct finance from the People's Bank started to be replaced by heavy borrowing from state banks, the burden of supporting the largely loss-making state enterprises sector fueled a buildup of bad debts in the banking system. In the second half of the 1990s, the government finally took steps to address the growing losses in the state enterprises sector and the bad-debt problem in the nation's banks. At the 1997 Fifteenth Party Congress, Chinese president Jiang Zemin announced a bold initiative that provided for the sale (or bankruptcy) of most of China's **state-owned enterprises**. At the same time, the government issued $32.5 billion in bonds to help recapitalize the four big state-owned banks and, in 1999, established four financial asset management companies to purchase and manage bad loans from the state banks. For the first time, a regional commercial bank, the Hainan Development Bank, was actually closed down in June 1998 following a payments crisis.

The first asset management company, China Cinda, was founded in Beijing on April 20, 1999. Three more asset management companies, China Oriental, China Great Wall, and China Huarong, were established later that same year, on October 15, October 18, and October 19, respectively. These institutions are state owned but nevertheless enjoy independent legal status. When an asset management company takes over a loan, the enterprise in question is to pay dividends to the asset management company instead of paying interest to the bank. The asset management company will then seek to recover the principal either by an initial public offering or by transferring the ownership. In September 1999, Cinda undertook China's first-ever debt-for-equity swap. The system of asset management companies is intended to strengthen the banks' balance sheets while also reducing the state enterprises' debt burden. The four asset management companies had disposed of 509.4 billion yuan's worth of nonperforming loans at the end of 2003, with a cash recovery rate of 19.5 percent.

The financial weakness of the state enterprises prior to the 1997 initiative was reflected in an officially reported ratio of liabilities to assets that reached 85 percent in 1995. Vast levels of nonrecoverable loans remained outstanding even after the 1999 bailout. At the end of 2003, total nonperforming loans at China's major banks were still estimated to be 2.44 trillion yuan, an amount equal to nearly 30 percent of China's GDP. The specialized commercial banks reported their ratio of nonperforming loans for the first time in 2001. The lowest ratio was 18.14 percent for the China Construction Bank, whereas the Industrial and Commercial Bank of China reported the highest ratio, 29.78 percent, together with a capital adequacy rate of just 5.76 percent as compared with the international standard of 8 percent. All four banks reported profit increases and lower ratios of nonperforming loans in 2002, however, with the aggregate ratio of nonperforming loans down to 15.59 percent of total loans in June 2004.

The reforms aimed at gradually eliminating the burden of the loss-making state enterprises and employing the system of financial management companies to address the bad-debt problem are clearly steps in the right direction, but these reforms cannot be pursued without continuing economic costs associated with layoffs and rising unemployment, on the one hand, and a rising debt burden, on the other. At the November 2002 Sixteenth Party Congress, Labor Minister Zhang Zuoyi acknowledged that 7 percent of Chinese workers were jobless and that more than 25 million jobs in the state-run enterprises had been lost since 1998. Unemployment and job losses are projected to increase as the government accelerates bankruptcies of loss-making state enterprises.

By 2002, private-sector firms' share of China's gross domestic product had risen above thirty percent. Private firms' access to commercial loans and to domestic stock markets still lags far behind that of the state-owned enterprises, however. The World Trade Organization (WTO) granted China a five-year "buffer period" before foreign banks will be allowed to compete directly with domestic banks, thereby delaying their scope for serving as an alternative source of capital for China's growing private sector, but foreign financial institutions like Merrill Lynch have made some inroads already, and foreign banks have been allowed to purchase minority stakes in local banks such as the Bank of Shanghai. There are ambitious plans to transform China's banking system by 2006. Interest-rate liberalization is being implemented as China seeks to move away from the current situation where deposit and loan rates are simply set by the central bank. Although it remains to be seen how successfully China's large state banks can be reborn as internationally competitive financial institutions, initial public offerings have already been planned for each of the big four. Bank of China may lead the way in 2005 and, in preparation for this step, aims to raise its capital adequacy ratio above 8 percent by the end of 2004.

See also Central Planning; Credit Spending, Development of; Economic Policies and Development (1949–Present); Economic Structure; Fiscal Policy and Tax Reforms; Foreign Debt; Foreign Direct Investment (FDI); Rural Credit Cooperatives (RCCs); World Trade Organization (WTO), China's Accession to.

Bibliography

Burdekin, Richard C. K., "Ending Inflation in China: From Mao to the 21st Century," *Cato Journal* 20 (fall 2000): 223–235; Chen, Baizhu, J. Kimball Dietrich, and Yi Feng, eds., *Financial Market Reform in China: Progress, Problems, and Prospects* (Boulder, CO: Westview Press, 2000); Lardy, Nicholas R., *China's Unfinished Economic Revolution* (Washington, DC: Brookings Institution Press, 1998); Nanto, Dick K., and Radha Sinha, "China's Banking Reform," *Post-Communist Economics* 14 (December 2002): 469–493; Tong, Donald D., *The Heart of Economic Reform: China's Banking Reform and State Enterprise Restructuring* (Aldershot, England: Ashgate, 2002). World Bank, *China: Weathering the Storm and Learning the Lessons* (Washington, DC: World Bank, 1999).

Richard C. K. Burdekin

Brand-Building Phenomenon

After a half century of communism, China more than ever is experiencing the many benefits of capitalism. The country is still in a transitional phase between communism and capitalism. However, the market economy that is characteristic of a country with democracy at the center of its government is now nearly as prevalent in China, a country with communism at its core. The place for capitalism in a Communist society is continually becoming more evident. **State-owned enterprises (SOEs)** have been fading with the rise in numbers of private businesses, and wealth in China is no longer an uncommon commodity. Competition and incentive have found their place in Chinese society, much to the benefit of the country's growing economy. One example of a positive advance in China's increasingly market-based economy is the evolution of brands and the concept of brand building. This has recently become a very popular way to advance the nation's economy, as well as its place in the world market.

Prior to the reform of 1978, China's place in the world market was not as well defined or as prominent as it is today. China simply did not have a market economy. Few products were traded on the market; these came from the few private businesses that were allowed to exist. China had no or few major brands that were strikingly positive assets to the country's economy. In the 1980s and 1990s, popular Chinese brands were still rare. Today, the idea is blossoming and taking hold. In a Communist country without a market economy, there is never a need for big-name brands, which is why this concept has not become nationally embraced until now. In the past, the government has always been responsible for having all goods and products put on the market. Supply and demand did not determine production; the government did. Individuals were not inspired to start their own businesses, and those who did were never allowed to be outstandingly productive and accumulate wealth. If a business got too large, the government would cut it back and prohibit any further growth to ensure that the goal of communism was upheld—equality for the county's entire population. By doing this, and by having SOEs in place, there was never an incentive for anyone to do great, quality work or to strike out on his or her own. Competition against SOEs was highly discouraged, and brands simply did not have a place in the still meager market of the time.

After the reform, there were plenty of overwhelming foreign brands that were firmly in place in China. It was difficult for other companies to compete with such big names as **Coca-Cola** and McDonald's. The majority of women in China take into consideration brands when they buy products. People of China have admitted to buying Coca-Cola over other brands simply because it is a big-name brand. To say that brands do not play a role in what consumers buy would not be true. It is seems safe to say that attitudes toward popular brands have not changed much in the past few decades. People have bought and will probably always buy products because of the brand names on them. In China, quality-control issues were still prevalent after the reform, and even the new brand-name items were usually not able to compare with foreign products. After nearly forty years without competition and little incentive, people were not used to turning out top-notch goods, so when Chinese brands first came into the market, they were not readily adopted, and the foreign products became what consumers sought.

In spite of the popularity of many foreign brands in China today, Chinese brands are likewise becoming well known worldwide. Unlike brands from other Asian countries such as Japan and Korea, Chinese brands have been able to expose themselves and become quickly successful in the world market. Companies like Haier, which supplies goods to Wal-Mart, Best Buy, and Home Depot, to name just a few, have definitely become worldwide names. By relying on cheap labor and resources, Haier is able to sell for much less than a similar supplier in America or Europe, for instance. In addition to low wages, government subsidies help allow companies like these to become very prosperous. Wages and subsidies alone, however, are not enough to bring a company from nothing to becoming a major player in the world market. Managers have been known to crack down severely when quality of products is in question. In fact, Haier's CEO, Zhang Ruimin, is known to have smashed seventy-six refrigerators that did not meet the company's quality standards with a sledgehammer. This type of behavior would have been unheard of prior to the reform of 1978. Aside from improving quality-control standards, the booming companies in China have focused heavily on specific customer demands, not only on what the market dictates should be produced. For instance, it has been found that many women wash vegetables, as well as clothes, in the washing machine. Therefore, companies like Haier have altered washing machines to better accommodate the washing of more than just clothes.

The Guangdong Kelon Electrical Holdings Company Limited, otherwise known as Kelon, is another success story in regard to brands in China. Today, Kelon is a leader in the refrigerator industry in China. The employees of Kelon staked out new distribution networks all across the country and catered to consumers, and unlike many SOEs, the company has stayed relatively small. The range of consumers of their products is, in reality, fairly limited, even within the borders of China. This might at first seem to hinder the success of the company, but it has actually had the opposite effect. Whirlpool, one of the major foreign brands in China, has enjoyed much success selling home appliances worldwide. However, Whirlpool never imagined the extent of competition it would be up against in China. Whirlpool believed that it would be competing with other foreigners, and the company was shocked to find that its main competitors were Chinese manufacturers of appliances such as Haier and Kelon. Each company sold quality appliances for lower prices than Whirlpool did. The people of China had recognized the value of their nation's new companies and, in the case of Kelon, taken advantage of the cheap, but reliable, products offered. This is not always the case in China, though. More often than not, a foreign company dominates over a Chinese brand, but that has been changing in recent years.

Today, China's market economy is still maturing. The process of change from a planned economy to a market economy is still under way and may yet take several decades to be complete. Despite the growth of brands in China, many aspects of brands are still in need of development. Advertising still remains a weakness of even the largest Chinese companies. For a brand to be as profitable and well known as it possibly can be, advertising is key. This is one of the major reasons why, even many years after the reform, foreign companies that sell products for more than a Chinese company still have the upper hand in China's market. Overall, brand building in China has come a long way in the past twenty-five years, and the growth of brands is not going to stop. China is moving to become one of the leaders, if not the top leader, in the world market. It is amazing how quickly the Chinese market has grown during the past few decades; it seems as if there is no end to what the nation can accomplish with the right direction and motivation.

See also Commercial Advertising, Policies and Practices of; Deng Xiaoping (1904–1997), Reforms of; Economic Policies and Development (1949–Present); Fast Food (Western Style), Integration of; Industrial Structure; World Trade Organization (WTO), China's Accession to.

Bibliography

Huang, Yasheng, *Selling China* (Cambridge: Cambridge University Press, 2003); Kirkpatrick, David, "A Global Legend in the Making," February 27, 2003, http://www.cnn.com/2003/TECH/ptech/02/27/fortune.ff.legend.pc/index.html, accessed on November 12, 2004; Schlevogt, Kai-Alexander, "The Branding Revolution in China," *China Business Review*, May–June 2000, 52–60; Wreden, Nick, "The Emerging Branding Threat from China," PRWeb, February 24, 2004, http://www.prweb.com/releases/2004/2/prweb103489.php, accessed on November 12, 2004.

Jennifer Kessler

Burial Customs

See Ethnic Burial Customs.

Business Decision Making in the Public and Private Sectors

From 1949 to 1978, that is, from the establishment of the People's Republic of China to Deng Xiaoping's declaration of the **Open Door policy**, there was no business of a private nature in China. The economy and industry with all their aspects were centrally planned and coordinated by the government. Resources and goods were rationed and distributed according to the national plan. The

Chinese Communist Party was the sole decision maker in China. Party policies and regulations and frequently **Mao Zedong**'s words served as the single guidance and command for actions and practices in the nation.

Since China's Open Door policy went into effect, significant changes have occurred in the economic and business landscape of China. The Chinese have long since learned how to work within a centrally planned economy. **State-owned enterprises** and collective enterprises have been existing alongside other types of businesses such as joint ventures, foreign-owned businesses, and individual enterprises. Despite the 43 percent of gross value of industrial output that comes from state-owned enterprises, the free-market economy is playing an indispensable role in the high level of development and performance of China's economy.

The mentality and practices behind decision making have also been undergoing tremendous changes. Elements of a new modern Chinese enterprising thinking are burgeoning: autonomous decision making, market-oriented thinking, collection and incorporation of internal and external information, and integration of proven concepts and practices of Western management with the Chinese traditional practices. However, the prediction may still be immature that the old Communist paradigms are dying and being replaced by completely new principles and practices of modern business decision making.

There still exists a fundamental difference between China and the West in terms of collection and usage of information in business decision making. In the West, sound information is the essential basis for sound decision making. In China, however, many factors come into play and affect decision making: hierarchical structures, face-saving, traditional protocols of behavior, and leaders' private agendas. The most important factor that affects business decision making, however, is the policies and regulations of the Communist Party. This is clearly emphasized in China's Constitution. Therefore, despite rapidly changing realities in China's economy and business decision making, predictions on business conditions should be based more on government policies than on microinformation gathering.

A fundamental difference also exists in organizational structure between the state-owned, collective, and joint-venture enterprises, on the one hand, and the individual, private, and foreign-owned enterprises, on the other hand. The Party committee is present in the former, but not in the latter.

The state-owned and collective enterprises are probably still the most typical enterprises in China. In a state-owned or collective enterprise, and even in a joint-venture enterprise, the Communist Party committee and its secretary are frequently able to exert more power than the general manager of that enterprise. This may be largely attributable to the fact that business decisions have to be in accordance with and even based on the Party's policies and the government's viewpoints. Holistically, the Party's polices have been the highest principles by which business decisions were made in China. Many believe that this is a fundamental fact that must be taken into account fully and must not be overlooked by any Western businessperson. Questions have been contesting the nature of the legal environment, such as, "Are the Party policies under the laws?" or "Are the laws under the Party policies?" Chinese reality probably represents a "yes" answer to the first question. The **Four Cardinal Principles**, which are affirmed in the Constitution and are probably the principles with the greatest force in China, guarantee that the Chinese Communist Party is the sole legal ruling party. Any Chinese law, including the interpretation and practice of the Constitution, must not go against Party policies, which, if changed, must accordingly cause changes to related Chinese laws. Judicature has not been independent yet in China, according to some analysts.

Since business decision making is based more on the Party's policies than on established laws, such decision making is plagued with dichotomies and oxymora such as flexibility versus inflexibility, predictability versus unpredictability, complexity versus simplicity, and radical extremities versus the moderate golden mean. Changeability in decision making, to some extent, may have been reflected in and encouraged by slogans by Deng Xiaoping, the helmsman of China's reform: "Fumble for stones to ford the river," and "A cat, white or black, is a good one so long as it catches the rat." The cultural and even administrative foundation for decision making is not legality and established procedures but more often the mentality and practice of benevolence and expediency. Rule by law emphasizes adherence to carefully established procedures. Rule by benevolence and expediency, however, emphasizes attention to contingencies, "reasonableness," and "face-saving." This emphasis easily leads to volatility. In addition, changing Party policies in China is not as complicated as changing a law in a society ruled by laws. Either the Political Bureau or its Standing Committee can decide to change the Party's policies, which in turn are often significantly maneuvered by powerful individuals like the president.

On the other hand, business decision making is also characterized by inflexibility. Since Party policies rather than factual information are the major guidance for decision making, many Chinese managers make a decision before collecting and analyzing information. Many scholars argue that if a decision maker ignores the importance of factual information and feedback analysis, he or she is likely to fail, give up a chance, or miss the last opportunity to change his or her decision. This may boil down to the decision maker's effort to stick to his or her decision until irretrievable failure. The obdurate personality of the "powerful man" with overly strong authority is another factor that contributes to inflexibility of decision making. Commonly used terms include "ironclad cases" to refer to the situation where the "powerful man's" (the official in control) final decision becomes a taboo and forbidden zone that no one dares to touch until this man loses his power. One Chinese phenomenon familiar to many is that the phraseology of official documents never seems to change.

Chinese people's accentuation of tradition and the Party's attention to certainty and maintenance of power tend to lead to the practice of moderation and the golden mean. This factor contributes to the simplicity and predictability of Chinese business decision making. Ironically, however, the short history of the New China has been cataclysmic—fraught with tumultuous changes and mass movements. The **Great Leap Forward** and the **Great Cultural Revolution** epitomize frantic and radical extremes. Lack of market economic experience and, perhaps more fundamentally, lack of balance of power tend to breed radical decision making.

The list of dichotomies and oxymora of business decision making in China should not end here. The characteristics of complexity and subtlety must be taken into consideration. The basic paradigm in Western decision making is collection and analysis of information, then making a decision, studying feedback after implementation of the decision and possibly revising the decision, and finally instituting guidelines for long-term practices. Decision making in China, however, is a synthetic result of numerous factors: reverence to power, sensitivity to face-saving, adherence to tradition, tiptoeing around taboos, and, as widely reported, widespread corruption involving decision makers. Poor continuity is another characteristic of business decision making of Chinese firms. The basic reason, again, is rule of the ruler's personal will rather than rule of law. Hence one barometer of business changes in China is the change of the ruler and, as a result, the transition of power.

In comparison with state-owned and collective enterprises, foreign-owned, individual, and private companies seem to enjoy more autonomy in their business decision making. No affiliation of the Chinese Communist Party is present in these enterprises. Decision making in these enterprises is largely similar to business decision making in the Western world, which is more pragmatic and oriented to facts, results, and profits. Owners and managers of individual companies tend to be open, flexible, and dynamic and are believed to be good candidates as potential business partners by Western businesspeople. However, all things considered, the presence and power of the Chinese Communist Party should by no means be ignored. Foreign-owned and individual companies cannot operate in a void isolated from the Party's policies. As a result, a frequent conflict exists between the Party's universal principles and the local business reality. Efforts to alleviate this conflict lead to the phenomenon "Where there is a policy from above, there is a countertactic from below." Local businesses learn to operate in a manner that is tailored to the local business reality without appearing to defy the Party's policies. In return, the Party's response to countertactics from the grass roots has led to another phenomenon: "Where there is a countertactic from below, there will be a policy from above." The game between universal regulations and local realities and practices seems to become an endless tug-of-war or a game of hide-and-seek.

See also Brand-Building Phenomenon; Central Planning; Commercial Advertising, Policies and Practices of; Deng Xiaoping (1904–1997), Reforms of; Economic Policies and Development (1949–Present); Economic Structure; Management Education; Privately Owned Enterprises (POEs).

Bibliography

Huang, Quanyu, R. Andrulis, and Chen Tong, *A Guide to Successful Business Relations with the Chinese: Opening the Great Wall's Gate* (Binghamton, NY: Haworth Press, 1994); Huang, Quanyu, Joseph Leonard, and Chen Tong, *Business Decision Making in China* (New York: International Business Press, 1997).

Xinan Lu

C

Central Media Bodies

See Media Bodies, Central and Local.

Central Planning

As a result of a massive economic reform that started during the late 1970s, privatization has bloomed in the urban and rural areas of China, rendering the term "central planning" almost an anachronism. However, it is from central planning that the current Chinese economic system, under the rubric of socialism with Chinese characteristics or market economy with Chinese characteristics, has evolved.

As a concept, central planning is defined in various ways. While Lyons (1987) produces a precise definition of central planning, Byrd (1991) delineates the Chinese characteristics in central planning. Lyons defines a planned economy as one "in which the activities of individual agents are controlled, to a large extent, by addressed directives emanating from representatives of government" and economic planning as "the process of formulating sets of addressed directives and of overseeing their implementation" (Lyons 1987, 186). Typically, central planning involves the submission of information regarding production, such as resources and instructions, to the agents by the government or central authorities with respect to what is to be produced and exchanged at predetermined prices (Lyons 1987).

In all centrally planned economies, production planning is linked to mandatory procurement of output at prices administratively fixed and distribution of output through the government's material supply and commercial systems (Byrd 1991). Historically, in the People's Republic of China hierarchical planning organizations were in charge of the administration of the central economy. Below the State Planning Commission, which reported to the State

Council, were two lines of subplanning: sectors (e.g., heavy industries, light industries, energy) and regional entities (provinces, municipalities, prefectures, and counties).

Before the economic reform, China pursued a centrally planned economy largely based upon the Soviet model, emphasizing industry over agriculture and heavy industry over light industry. However, Chinese central planning noticeably differed from the Soviet Union's model in several aspects. Byrd (1991) summarizes some interrelated features of Chinese central planning as identified in the literature. First, central planning was not comprehensive in China, because substantial amounts of goods were produced and allocated outside the central plan and there was relative autonomy of local governments and enterprises. The challenge that faces central planning is the impossibility of a perfect match between producers and consumers in terms of supplies and demands. Ironically, a government in favor of central planning may benefit from the coexistence of planned and unplanned economies so that the latter may help remedy the problems caused by shortage or excess in the production and consumption of the former system (Lyons 1987). Second, many industrial goods were not subject to the planning of the central government, and the agricultural sector in China was significantly less centralized than that in the Soviet Union. Third, central planning in China covered a relatively small number of products, though for these products, central planning was highly aggregated. Fourth, the Chinese planned economy involved bargaining and negotiation. Fifth, some input allocations were made before production plans were set, and therefore, these controlled allocations of inputs had power over production and distribution.

In China, typically, the degree to which the economy was centralized was lower than that in the Soviet Union. For example, in the former economy, transactions outside the plan were produced outside the plan, whereas in the Soviet Union, the goods originally produced in the plan were channeled into the extraplan sectors (Byrd 1991). It is also noted that **Mao Zedong** felt that the Soviet model was excessively centralized; as a result, the central government delegated some decision-making power to provincial and other local governments. Mass movements were also emphasized as a way to overcome natural and political difficulties, with the **Great Leap Forward** as one example (Pyle 1997). These differences between China and the Soviet Union may have accounted for the rapid privatization that occurred in the Soviet Union in the early 1990s and the gradual approach in China's experimentation with privatization. In Russia, the opportunity cost of central planning was significantly higher than that in the Chinese economy, where the extraplan economy was relatively strong.

The other aspect of central planning involves wealth distribution. Because central planning mandates the availability of products at fixed low prices, some groups of agents are potentially better off than others. Consequently, egalitarian allocations emerge as the easiest and often the only viable method for planners to deal with competing claims (Byrd 1991), which further decreases economic efficiency. One quintessential example is the Shengyang Smelter and Shengyang Cable Factory case (Byrd 1991). The Shengyang Smelter, which produced copper, was located next to the Shengyang Cable Factory, which used copper as an input. Nonetheless, under central planning, the Shengyang Cable Factory received copper not from the Shengyang Smelter, but from Yunnan Province thousands of miles away. Meanwhile, the copper produced at the Shengyang Smelter was shipped to Heilongjiang and other more distant provinces. What central planning tried to achieve was "fair distribution of transport costs among major copper users" (Byrd 1991).

In October 1984, the Third Plenary Session of the Twelfth Party Central Committee declared that the socialist economy was a planned commodity economy based on public ownership, which rewrote the concept of economic planning in China. As noted by Gao, "The socialist commodity economy established on the basis of public ownership is a unity of plan and market" (Gao 1996, 101). Though all the economic activities should be subject to planned regulation in varying degrees, "the market system can serve the function of coordinating and balancing the national economy through various economic mechanisms—price, competition, supply and demand, credit, interest rate, and so on" (Gao 1996, 98). Any working and successful economy requires planning and regulation. In China's "planned commodity economy," the balance between central planning and free market has been tilting toward the latter as more and more private enterprises have established and thrived riding the waves of the market forces.

See also Administrative Reforms (1949–1978); Administrative Reforms since 1978; Banking and Financial System Reform; Business Decision Making in the Public and Private Sectors; Economic Policies and Development (1949–Present); Economic Structure; Industrial Structure; Privately Owned Enterprises (POEs); State-Owned Enterprises (SOEs).

Bibliography

Byrd, William A., *The Market Mechanism and Economic Reform in China* (Armonk, NY: M. E. Sharpe, 1991); Gao, Shangquan, *China's Economic Reform* (London: Macmillan, 1996); Lyons, Thomas P., *Economic Integration and Planning in Maoist China* (New York: Columbia University Press, 1987); Pyle, David J., *China's Economy: From Revolution to Reform* (London: Macmillan, 1997).

Yi Feng

Chang, Iris (1968–2004)

Iris Chang was a Chinese-American journalist and independent writer best known for her award-winning but controversial books on modern Chinese and Chinese American history. Chang's English-language works stirred scholarly and political debate not only in the United States, but also in the People's Republic and Japan. Chang received numerous awards for her books, including the 1992 Program on Peace and International Cooperation Award from the John T. and Catherine D. MacArthur Foundation.

Born into a Chinese immigrant family in Princeton, New Jersey, Chang grew up in Illinois. Her father, Shaojin Chang, and her mother, Yingying Chang, held doctorates from Harvard University, and both were faculty members at the University of Illinois, where Iris earned a bachelor's degree in journalism in 1989. Chang then worked briefly as a reporter at the *Chicago Tribune*. She enjoyed the work for a while, covering a wide range of stories, but was frustrated by her inability to focus on what she called "in-depth and long-term issues." After winning a graduate fellowship to the writing seminars program at Johns Hopkins University, Chang earned a master's degree in writing in 1991 and soon after launched a career as an independent writer.

Chang's first "in-depth" project was *Thread of the Silkworm* (1995), a book about Tsien Hsue-shen, the scientist known as the father of China's missile program. The book was highly successful and quickly received worldwide critical acclaim. The Chinese-born Tsien helped pioneer the American space age, but returned to China to direct missile development for the People's Republic after he was accused of being a Communist during the McCarthy Era. His loss to American science has been called one of the most "monumental blunder[s] the United States ever committed." To accomplish her research on Tsien, Chang traveled to Washington, DC, California, and China. Her fluent Mandarin Chinese helped her gain access to Tsien's family, friends, former classmates, and students.

The success of *Thread of the Silkworm* encouraged Chang to undertake a more ambitious project, *The Rape of Nanking: The Forgotten Holocaust of World War II*, an immediate bestseller that came out in 1997 after two years of research. Based on extensive interviews with survivors of the Sino-Japanese War (1937–1945) and on volumes of newly discovered documents in four languages (English, German, Japanese, and Chinese), the book described one of the most horrifying episodes of World War II—the systematic rape, torture, and murder of more than 300,000 Chinese committed by the Japanese army in the city of Nanking in 1937 and 1938. Since her childhood, Chang had heard stories of Nanking from her grandfather, who had barely escaped the massacre. However, she could find little about the event in libraries and her teachers were "completely ignorant" of it. When she saw an exhibit of photographs on the subject in 1994, Chang was inspired to write on Nanking.

Ironically, one of Chang's most important sources was the diary of John Rabe, the Nazi representative in Nanking, whom Chang called the "Oskar Schindler of China." Shocked by Japanese actions in Nanking, Rabe helped establish an "International Safety Zone" in the city that saved many Chinese lives. Rabe's diaries recorded more than 500 massacres and rapes perpetrated by the Japanese and helped Chang convince Western readers of the scope and brutality of the Nanking atrocities.

In *The Rape of Nanking*, Chang also tried to trace the origins of a government-promoted militarism that she believed fostered "a total disregard" for human life in Japanese soldiers. Chang also pointed out that the violence in Nanking has been continually denied by the Japanese government and is little known in the rest of the world. She argued that the Cold War led to a concerted effort on the part of the United States and its Western allies, and even by both the Nationalist and Communist governments of post-war China, to "court the loyalty" of Japan and thus stifle open discussion of the Nanking atrocities. She labeled this persistent silence "a second rape."

In 2003, Chang published her third bestseller, *The Chinese in America: A Narrative History*. Jonathan Spence, a well known Yale historian, called the book a "broad historical panorama of Chinese migration with fascinating case studies of individual Chinese immigrants and the lives they made for themselves" in the United States. The book traced the experience of Chinese immigrants from the anti-Chinese racism of the mid-nineteenth century to such present-day success stories as architect Maya Lin, author Amy Tan, TV journalist Connie Chung, scientist Wen Ho Lee, and Yahoo founder Jerry Yang. Chang declared the experience of Chinese immigrants to be an American story common to all immigrants to this country, who sought to overcome "the loss of a place once called home" and who tried simply "to make a living and provide their children with food, shelter, and a good education."

Although all three of Chang's books were successful, *The Rape of Nanking* was the most controversial. In Japan, many right-wing intellectuals and even some government officials denounced the book as "one-sided," "erroneous," and filled with "historical inaccuracies." Faced with this criticism, Chang challenged the Japanese government to open all its World War II archives and commended those Japanese veterans who publicly confessed to war crimes. She also insisted that the Japanese government issue an official apology to the victims of Nanking, pay reparations to the people whose lives were destroyed by the invasion of China, and, most importantly, educate future generations of Japanese citizens about the true facts of the massacre. Chang's book and her contentions are endorsed by many historians, including William Kirby, chairman of the History Department at Harvard University, and Frederic Wakeman, head of the Institute of East Asian Studies at the University of California, Berkeley. Columnist George Will has declared that because of "Chang's book, the second rape of Nanking is ending."

Chang's tireless research and writing, especially on topics that uncovered the darker side of human nature, eventually took their toll on her. While on a research trip for her fourth book in early 2004, Chang had a mental breakdown. The new project focused on the experience of American troops who fought in tank battalions on the Bataan Peninsula and their subsequent imprisonment and torture by the Japanese during World War II. After her release from the hospital, Chang continued to battle depression. On November 11, 2004, she committed suicide, leaving behind her husband and a two-year-old son. In a note to her family, Chang asked people to remember her as the woman she had been before her illness, "engaged with life, committed to her causes, her writing and her family."

See also Cold War and China; Nationalism in Modern China; Sino-American Relations since 1949; Sino-Japanese Relations since 1949; United States, Chinese in.

Bibliography

Chang, Iris, *The Chinese in America: A Narrative History* (Middlesex, UK: Penguin Books; reprint 2004); Chang, *The Rape of Nanking: The Foreign Holocaust of World War II* (Middlesex, UK: Penguin Books; reprint, 1998); Chang, *Thread of the Silkworm* (New York: Basic Books; reprint 1996).

Xiansheng Tian

Character Education in Primary and Secondary Schools

In general, character education is intended to bring up students as ideal members of their community in addition to training in work skills and other knowledge. Character education, hence, is viewed as strategic instruction that promotes social and personal responsibility and is aimed at the development of good character traits and moral virtues. The Chinese definition is a broad one that includes morality, culture, and fitness, as well as skills. Morality is considered as the foundation, culture as the basis, skill as the necessity, and health as the investment for one's growth, living, and success.

In 1999, the Chinese government declared that character education should be carried out in schools at all levels. After a few years of experiment, character education has formed its own model that can be classified as (1) setting up a moral example and encouraging students' self-motivation, (2) creating extracurricular learning activities and developing students' self-recognition, (3) providing training opportunities and promoting students' self-support, (4) monitoring daily performance and nurturing students' self-regulation, and (5) integrating character education into curricula teaching and facilitating students' self-growth.

Setting Up Moral Examples and Encouraging Student Self-Motivation

To set up moral examples for the students, school buildings are usually symbolically named after well-known scholars, national heroes, and great thinkers and inventors in history. The names of Lu Shuxiang (a well-known linguist), Hua Luogeng (a famous mathematician), Zu Chongzhi (a mathematician of the Qi dynasty, A.D. 429–500, who discovered pi), and Gong Zizhen (a Qing dynasty, 1644–1911, patriot poet) typically figure on campus constructions. Pictures, sculptures, and achievements of these selected role models are displayed on campus to symbolically provide students with moral examples. These symbolic moral examples can be seen at the entrance of the school, on campus bulletin boards, and in the classroom. Their hardworking attitude, selfless contribution, and noble characteristics are to be modeled by the youngsters; their scholarly success, cultural influences, and unyielding spirit in pursuit of knowledge are constantly emphasized to students as a way of motivation. Students are encouraged to follow these models and mold their behavior in the right direction.

Creating Extracurricular Activities and Developing Student Self-Recognition

Extracurricular activities are designed to help students understand the value in their own lives and encourage students to acquire learning skills and to be creative. These activities typically motivate students to cherish their time and make good use of it. Inviting guest speakers and taking students off campus into the real world are among the many ways to let students develop their self-recognition. Outdoor activities often include visiting factories, hospitals, and sometimes farming communities. In the classroom, the values of patriotism, collaboration, mutual respect, and forgiveness are topics of discussion in the first ten minutes of the morning agenda. A variety of interest-based teams, groups, or clubs attract a great number of students after school. The extracurricular activities in Chinese schools usually include musical instrument playing, singing, dancing, drawing, chess, martial arts, and other sports. Computer technology has recently offered more diverse choices.

Providing Training Opportunities and Promoting Student Self-Support

The traditional concept favors book learning. In modern character education, it is believed that hands-on experience is an important part of learning because it bridges school knowledge to the real-world application. Facing the challenge of developing students' self-support skills, most schools offer work-skill classes (*lao dong ke*). Most schools have their workshops equipped with utilities for a variety of projects ranging from cooking to manufacturing. Moreover, physical labor is believed to help students learn how to take care of themselves. For example, students are required to do a weekly duty of cleaning the classroom, sweeping the floor, dusting the desks, and cleaning the chalkboard. Boarding students are even trained to make their own beds, clean the bedrooms, and take turns on bedroom duty. Students learn how to get along with each other, how to help each other, and how to manage their classrooms and bedrooms at school and are encouraged to catch up on chores at home. Students' hands-on participation in work-skill training obviously benefits them in developing their self-support skills.

Monitoring Daily Performance and Nurturing Student Self-Regulation

For promoting self-regulation, there usually is a student daily performance-monitoring and evaluation system, particularly in elementary schools. Schools keep a daily performance logbook for each student. A student's daily performance is monitored by the homeroom teacher and evaluated and recorded weekly by a team that consists of administrators, teachers, and students. Based on the daily rating score, the student receives weekly evaluation reports on his or her performance at school. The student's record, with both strong and weak points listed, is shared with parents to keep them informed.

See also Education Media and Technology; Educational Administration; Educational System; Higher-Education Reform; Primary Education; Private Education; School Enrollment and Employment; Secondary Education; Teacher Education.

Bibliography

Education Information Center (EIC), *What Is Character Education, and Does It Work?* 1998, http://www.osba-ohio.org/Research/CharterEducation.html, accessed on April 1, 2003; Zhou, Y., "Perfecting Characters, the Basis of Education," *People's Daily*, May 25, 1999, 9.

Ronghua Ouyang and Dan Ouyang

Chen Shuibian (1950–   )

Unlike most of his political opponents in Taiwan, Chen Shuibian came from a very humble background. He was born to an impoverished tenant-farming family in Kuantien Township of Tainan County in late 1950, but his identification certificate shows his date of birth as February 18, 1951. Because he was very weak as an infant, the family did not register his birth with the local census bureau until 1951. Chen was an excellent student, ranking at the top of his class from elementary school through college. In June 1969, he earned the second-highest score in the nationwide College Entrance Examination and was admitted to the prestigious National Taiwan University, where he passed the bar exams with the highest score and earned the distinction of being Taiwan's youngest lawyer before the completion of his junior year. In 1975, he married Wu Shujen, the daughter of a wealthy doctor, and became an ambitious young full-time lawyer.

In 1979, a human rights rally turned violent when government troops clashed with the demonstrators. The episode, which was known as the Kaohsiung incident, resulted in the arrest of many democratic activists. The defendants were sent for trial under martial law, which drew world attention to the political situation in Taiwan. The incident also inspired Chen's sense of righteousness. Chen became a member of the defense team, acting as the lawyer for Huang Hsin-chieh, who was the chairman of the Democratic Progressive Party (DPP). This was the beginning of his dedication to politics and democratization. Along with other leaders of the opposition, Chen carried on the work of the older generation in seeking freedom, human rights, and democracy for the people of Taiwan by acting as a vigorous defense attorney in the "court of the Taiwan people's conscience."

In 1981, Chen first ran for public office and made "democracy, balance of power, and progress" his campaign theme. He was elected as a member of the Taipei City Council with the highest number of votes. Adhering to his conscience and sense of righteousness, Chen became well known for exposing injustice and fearlessly criticizing the authoritarian government. In 1984, as publisher of a magazine critical of the government, Chen was accused of libel. On November 18, 1985, his wife, Wu Shujen, was hit by a truck and was left paralyzed from the waist down. Some in Taiwan believed that this was part of a government campaign to intimidate him. The pain of the accident has since all the more strengthened Chen's determination to support and assist the weak, challenge unfairness, and ensure social justice. The following year, Chen was sentenced to eight months in prison for libel for criticizing the government and began serving in the Tucheng Penitentiary along with Huang Tienfu and Lee Yiyang, two other defendants in the same case. While he was in prison, his wife campaigned and was elected to the Legislative Yuan. Upon his release in 1987, he joined the DPP and served as her legislative assistant while continuing to practice law.

After 1986, the Kuomintang's hold on power was challenged by the emergence of competing political parties. Before 1986, candidates who opposed the KMT ran in elections as independents or "nonpartisans." Before the 1986 islandwide elections, many "nonpartisans" grouped together to create Taiwan's first new political party, the DPP. Despite the official ban on forming new political parties, the Taiwanese authorities did not prohibit the DPP from operating, and in the 1986 islandwide elections DPP and independent candidates captured more than 20 percent of the vote.

In December 1989, Chen was elected to the Legislative Yuan and served as the executive director of the Democratic Progressive Party Congress. With the support of some KMT colleagues, he was also elected convener of the National Defense Committee. He was instrumental in laying out and moderating many of the DPP's positions on Taiwanese independence. He was reelected to another three-year term in 1992. During his terms as a legislator, Chen made an appeal to replace political struggle with policy debate, transforming the way in which ruling and opposition parties interacted with one another and opening additional opportunities for political participation.

In 1991, there was a move in the DPP to set the establishment of a Taiwan nation as a policy goal of the party. Chen suggested adding to the procedures the premise "Based on the principle that sovereignty belongs to the people, the issue should be decided by all the residents of Taiwan through a plebiscite." Thus the DPP independence platform was revised to accommodate discussion among different ideological groups in an open and pluralistic spirit. Chen was nominated by the DPP to run for Taipei mayor. He campaigned on the slogan "Happy Citizens in a City of Hope," emphasizing citizenship, direct participation, and the integration of the four ethnic groups. His vision was to recreate Taipei as the "New Hometown" for each and every citizen. His victory made him the first popularly elected Taipei mayor since the city was elevated to the status of a special municipality in 1967. This was the first time the position of Taipei mayor was held by an opposition political party.

During Chen's term as Taipei mayor, he allowed no reduction in the quality of public services and forbade government officials and staff from taking commissions. Taipei citizens generally praised his achievements and efforts. Significant progress was made in such areas as supervising the schedules of large-scale construction works, improving Taipei's traffic, and putting the Taipei Rapid Transit System (TRTS) into service. He further expanded the city's sewage system, promoted the Taipei Art Festival and Lantern Festival, and eliminated electronic game arcades and other specially licensed businesses. The improvement of Taipei's civil administration and the quality services provided by the Mucha line of the TRTS were awarded the ISO 9002 certificate by the International Organization for Standardization. Taipei City was ranked as the fifth-best city in Asia (it had formerly ranked below ten) for quality of life in 1998 by *Asiaweek* magazine. Chen was selected as one of the 100 top world leaders of the new century by *Time* magazine and one of the top fifty future Asian leaders by *Asiaweek* magazine.

As part of his drive to expand Taipei's city diplomacy and enhance Taiwan's international presence, Chen promoted the concept "let Taipei go out and the world come in." During his term as mayor, Taipei established fourteen sister-city relationships and one partner-city relationship. In 1998, Taipei hosted the first World Capitals Forum. With sixty-seven cities from fifty-eight countries participating, this event was an important milestone in expanding Taiwan's city-level diplomacy and garnering greater global visibility. Despite the hard work of Chen's city administration team and a high public approval rating close to 80 percent, in December 1998 Chen Shuibian lost his reelection bid for a second term. Shocked and disappointed by the outcome, his supporters urged him to run for the presidency instead.

During the months following his departure from the mayoral office, Chen engaged in quiet study and sought advice from leaders in different sectors of society. In 1999, he began a fact-finding journey throughout the island, listening to the views of the people while conceptualizing a blueprint for the nation's future. He also traveled to the United States and held talks with prestigious research institutes and leading policy makers, promoting the idea that the security of Taiwan was essential to international stability. Chen vigorously accumulated knowledge and experience in cross-strait relations and international affairs, gradually developing a well-rounded vision that incorporates both domestic and international agendas. In view of Taiwan's many differences in ethnic identity and ideology, during his campaign for the presidency, Chen advocated the "New Middle Way," with a focus on national security.

In July 1999, Chen accepted the nomination of the DPP as its candidate for the 2000 presidential election. In his speech "New Politics Is the Best Foundation for Taiwan in the Next Century," he urged the people to cooperate in terminating "black and gold" (money politics) and to enable a change of ruling parties. Subsequently, he campaigned on the slogan "Young Taiwan and Lively Government," vowing to sustain Taiwan's vitality and maximize the momentum for development. Throughout the campaign, Chen asserted that both sides of the Taiwan Strait should uphold the principles of "goodwill reconciliation, active cooperation, and permanent peace," thereby initiating the normalization of their bilateral relationship.

On March 18, 2000, with much international attention, Chen Shuibian and Lu Hsiulien were elected as the tenth-term president and vice president of the Republic of China. Initial intentions were to create a new era of economic development, politics, and cross-strait relations. Maintaining stability, peace, and national security has been the most important objective of President Chen's administration. In order to carry out his pledge that "Taiwan must not only stand up, but also reach out," he made two trips abroad to eleven diplomatic partners. These trips were labeled "Democracy, Diplomacy, and Friendship" and "Friendship and Cooperation for Mutual Prosperity," and they successfully consolidated diplomatic relations and promoted Taiwan's presence in the world. He has also directed relevant authorities to aggressively campaign for Taiwan's participation in international organizations such as the World Health Organization (WHO) and the World Trade Organization (WTO). In December 2001, Taiwan's accession to the WTO was formally approved by the WTO, paving the way for Taiwan's formal participation in this internationally significant trade regime in January 2002.

Today, Taiwan's political stage is dominated primarily by two forces: the Pan-Blue and the Pan-Green. The Pan-Blue Coalition, or Pan-Blue Force, is a political coalition consisting of the Kuomintang (KMT), the People First Party (PFP), and the tiny New Party (CNP). The name comes from the flag colors of the Kuomintang. This coalition tends to favor a Chinese nationalist identity over Taiwanese separatism and greater economic linkage with the People's Republic of China. It is opposed to the Pan-Green Coalition, which is an informal political alliance of the Democratic Progressive Party (DPP), Taiwan Solidarity Union (TSU), and the Taiwan Independence Party (TAIP). The name comes from the colors of the Democratic Progressive Party, which originally adopted green in part because of its association with the environmental movement.

In late 2003, Chen signed a controversial referendum bill, which he had supported, but had been heavily watered down by the Pan-Blue majority legislature. Within a day of the passage of the referendum bill, Chen stated his intention to invoke this provision, citing People's Republic of China (PRC) missiles aimed at Taiwan. Chen was shot in the stomach while campaigning in the city of Tainan on March 19, 2004, the day before the polls opened. Since the incident, numerous rumors, conspiracy theories, claims, and counterclaims have been generated and propagated both on the **Internet** and in the Taiwanese media. The following day, he narrowly won the election by less than 30,000 votes out of 12.9 million votes counted. Both of his referendum proposals were invalidated due to low turnout. On May 20, 2004, Chen was sworn in for his second term as president.

Taiwan clearly needs a new constitution. A constitution written for a dictatorship of half a billion people in 1947 does not work for a democracy of 23 million people in the twenty-first century. Some two-thirds of the Constitution's articles require revision or excision. In addition, the new constitution will need to account for changes in institutions as Taiwan adapts its government to its new democratic climate. Chen restated that the new constitution would not change Taiwan's national sovereignty or territory or touch on issues of unification and independence, in part because Taiwan itself has not reached consensus on these issues. Chen noted that the future of the relationship with China remained undetermined and there could even be unification between the two sides. However, he stressed that any decision about Taiwan's future must have "the consent of the 23 million people of Taiwan."

See also Taiwan, Constitutional Reform in; Taiwan, Development of Democracy in.

Bibliography

Government Information Office, *Chen Shui-bian* (Taipei: Government Information Office, Republic of China, 2004).

Janet Yun Wei Kuo

China Television Institute.

See Television Institute and Self-Learning.

Chinese Script, Reform of

The Chinese written language uses ideographs, better known as Chinese characters. These characters are primarily associated with concepts. Their representation of sounds has long vanished. Thus one can not read out unknown words as easily as in English, French, or other languages that are recorded in a phonetic script. There are as many as 150 dialects spoken in China that share the same writing system. Therefore, a newspaper published in one part of the country can be visually understood in any other part, although the pronunciation might be quite different. While people of different cities and regions might not understand one another's speech, they are able to understand written text. Further, newspapers published in China can be read in overseas Chinese communities. This is why traditional Chinese education tends to regard the written ideographs as the primary means of communication, rather than speech.

China is a country with a diverse population in fifty-six ethnic groups. The official language is **Putonghua**, also known as Hanyu (the language of the Han), Modern Standard Chinese (Putonghua), or Mandarin (the official language). The Han are the majority ethnic group, constituting 95 percent of the population. In Taiwan, the official language for the Han ethnic group is called Guoyu (National Language).

After the founding of the People's Republic of China (PRC) in 1949, the Chinese government launched a movement to eradicate illiteracy. At the same time, a language reform campaign was started to simplify many of the more complicated Chinese characters. The new Chinese government made great efforts to reduce the nation's illiteracy rate. The simplification of the complicated traditional Chinese script, an important component of the Language Reform, was a process implemented in several stages starting in the early 1950s. Many of the newly introduced characters are not new, but had already been simplified in the past. As a result of this reform, the simplified writing system has become the standard system in the PRC, whereas in Taiwan and most overseas Chinese communities the traditional script remains in use. As the names of the two systems suggest, the traditional version (*fantizi* or complicated

Chinese calligraphy.

characters) consists of more strokes and components. In the simplified writing (*jiantizi* or simplified characters), the strokes and components are dramatically reduced, contributing to easy legibility but—according to critics of the script reform—minimizing structural aesthetics.

In 1951, the government issued a directive that inaugurated language reform planning with three foci. First, Putonghua must be established as the standardized common language to be introduced as the language of instruction in schools and in the national media. Second, language reform would aim at reducing the number of strokes of a character. Hence the simplified writing system differs in two ways from the traditional writing system: (1) a reduction of the number of strokes per character and (2) the reduction of the number of characters in common use by collapsing two or more different traditional Chinese characters (under the same pronunciation) into one simplified character, which introduced a multimapping phenomenon between the traditional and simplified scripts. The third area of language reform involved the phonetic transcription of Chinese through the Hanyu Pinyin romanization (for short usually called Pinyin, which means "phonetic spelling"), using the Roman alphabet with diacritical marks for the tones of Chinese syllables.

Featuring fewer strokes and less composition effort, the simplified characters have been successfully established, accepted, and widely used in the People's Republic of China and Singapore, but not in Taiwan and most overseas Chinese communities that are adhering to the traditional script. During the past few decades, all books and newspapers in the PRC have been printed in simplified script, with only certain exceptions such as historical and classical publications being printed in traditional characters. Schools in mainland China have been teaching only simplified Chinese characters to students since the 1950s. Most teaching of modern Chinese outside China is conducted in simplified Chinese characters. In general, a knowledge of around 600 to 2,000 characters is necessary to be literate. By 1964, China had simplified more than 2,000 characters that were published by the Committee on Writing System Reform in a *General Table of Simplified Characters*, which also described the rules for deriving the simplified characters from their traditional forms and soon became the standard in schools and government offices. This table is updated once every few years.

Pinyin is a phonetic transcription based on the twenty-six Latin letters. It is used as a teaching aid in the instruction of characters, as well as an indexing system in reference books. Pinyin is now in widespread use, both in China and internationally. For example, in the 1970s a new map of China was published using the Pinyin romanization, and a list of standard Pinyin spellings for Chinese place names was compiled. The Pinyin standard was adapted to such diverse uses as telegraphy, flag signals, Braille, and deaf finger spelling.

In 1981, the International Standardization Organization (ISO) decided to use Pinyin as the official system to transcribe Chinese proper names and phrases. Finally, the Library of Congress announced its plan to adopt Pinyin as the standard romanization scheme for cataloging Chinese-language materials, a major step toward the international standardization of Modern Standard Chinese that was implemented in 1999. However, Pinyin does not replace the Chinese character script. In addition to its educational function, Pinyin is used on packaging labels, in the creation of writing systems of minority languages, and in transcribing road signs and geographic names.

The language reform at its earlier stage also drew criticism. Conservative opinions hold that Chinese culture and history would risk being destroyed by the language reform. Some criticize the simplified characters for collapsing components of the character structure and leading to loss of traditional elegance. The simplification movement dashed ahead in the 1970s with a more radical Second Plan for Character Simplification. This plan was drafted in 1977, immediately after the **Great Cultural Revolution**, but the changes proposed in this version proved to be too drastic and had to be rescinded in 1986.

The language reform caused numerous debates among scholars, who disagree on how far the reform should go. For example, some overseas scholars advocated the replacement of Chinese characters with Pinyin. This proposal was generally deemed to be going too far and was strongly rejected by sinologists and other scholars because of linguistic and sociocultural considerations. Although Pinyin today is heavily used for a range of specialized functions, for Chinese native speakers the ideographic Chinese character script remains the main communication medium within the written language, due to its visual information contents and its historical and cultural values. Any idea of replacing the Chinese characters with Pinyin was soon abandoned by the leadership in government and education in China. The reality is that the impact has been made: in mainland China, people use simplified characters, though they can also read, but not write, classical characters; in Taiwan, Hong Kong, and other overseas areas, most people are capable of reading simplified characters, but not writing them. Obviously, the promotion of simplified script is far from complete.

See also Putonghua, Promotion of; Taiwan, Education Reform in.

Bibliography

"Adult Education," http://www.countrystudies.us/china/71.htm, accessed on November 12, 2004; Li, Yue E., and Christopher Upward, *Review of the Process of Reform in the Simplification of Chinese Characters*, http://www.spellingsociety.org/journals/j13/chinese.html, accessed on November 12, 2004.

Senquan Zhang

Christianity

See Confucian Tradition and Christianity.

Cities

China has a large, dynamic, and complex city system that is divided into three levels based on their administrative statuses: county-level cities, prefecture-level cities, and central municipalities. In 1993, for example, China had 371 county-level cities, 196 prefecture-level cities, and 3 central municipalities. These numbers changed to 400, 259, and 4, respectively, in 2000. Among the 259 prefecture-level cities, 15 have an administrative status higher than the prefecture level but lower than the central level. Chongqing became the fourth central municipality in July 1997. Cities at different statuses are given different levels of authority, such as investment decision making and foreign-funded project approvals. The higher the level, the more directly the city reports to Beijing and the greater is its autonomy and influence.

The definition of a Chinese city is not straightforward. Chinese cities are administrative entities and must be officially designated, with designation criteria being a function of political-administrative status, economic development, openness, and total population of an urban place. Since an upgrade of status in the administrative hierarchy is usually accompanied by greater autonomy, political power, and access to resources, local authorities are eager to pursue the upgrading of their settlements to higher statuses. Such efforts, together with relaxation of designation criteria, have brought a significant growth in China's urban sector in the past two decades. Many county seats (*xian cheng*) were reclassified as cities (*shi*), resulting in a sharp increase in the total number of cities, from 223 in 1980 to 663 in 2000. Some county seats earned city status even though they had a relatively small population. During the past two decades, many existing cities were upgraded by expanding their territories or merging two adjacent cities or combining a city with its surrounding counties.

China also classifies its cities into five categories according to their sizes: superlarge for cities with a nonagricultural population of 2 million or over, very large (1–2 million), large (0.5–1 million), medium (0.2–0.5 million), and small (less than 0.2 million). In 1980, China had 7 superlarge cities, 8 very large

Shanghai's television tower, shown here, is the tallest in Asia.

cities, 30 large cities, 72 medium cities, and 106 small cities. In 2000, these numbers changed to 13, 27, 53, 218, and 352, respectively. Most Chinese cities are small cities. In fact, the primacy and intercity concentration are relatively low in China. For example, the primacy measured by the share of the largest city's population to the total urban population was only 4.08 percent in 1998, compared to the primacy of 10.14 percent for the United States in 1990. The urban population share of the ten largest cities for China was 19.37 percent in 1998, compared to 36.66 percent for the United States in 1990. Some empirical studies have shown that the city-size distribution of Chinese cities became more even in the late twentieth century because of the dynamic changes of existing cities and the inclusion of new cities into China's urban system.

Geographically, most Chinese cities are located in eastern and central China. In 1985, the number of cities in eastern, central, and western China was 113, 133, and 78, respectively. In 2000, the distribution became 295, 247, and 121 for the three regions. Less than 35 percent of all Chinese cities were in the coastal region in 1985. In 2000, 44.5 percent of all cities were in the east. More than 50 percent of China's urban population resides in the coastal cities. Furthermore, most superlarge and very large cities are in the coastal region. No doubt, China's economic reform and opening-up have promoted urbanization faster in the coastal region than in the inland areas.

Recently, three megalopolises, clusters of cities, have emerged in China. The Beijing-Tianjin megalopolis consists of Beijing, Tianjin, Tangshan, Baoding, Langfang, and five county-level cities. It covers an area of 70,000 square kilometers and has a total population of 45 million. The Yangtze Delta megalopolis includes 2 superlarge cities (Shanghai and Nanjing), 1 very large city (Hangzhou), 4 large cities, 14 medium cities, and 33 small cities. All cities are within 300 kilometers of Shanghai. The Zhujiang Delta megalopolis, located in southern China, includes Guangzhou, Shenzhen, Zhuhai, Dongguan, and 24 other cities and districts. It covers 41,698 square kilometers and has a total population of 23 million. The three megalopolises together account for about 80 percent of China's total GDP, 90 percent of national industrial output, and 95 percent of total exports.

The Chinese city system exhibits profound impacts of China's urban development strategies. Before the economic reform, Chinese urban policy emphasized the growth of heavy industries. Cities were narrowly viewed as potential sites of industrial plants, and favored cities were assigned a number of large state-owned heavy industrial enterprises. The government discouraged the growth of light and service industries, thus unnecessarily restricting urban economic diversity and limiting urban employment growth. In addition, the Chinese government was very concerned with coastal security, and it carried out the "three-front" project in the 1950s and 1960s. Many strategic manufacturing plants were moved from the coastal region to the interior. Industrial cities were built far from the coastal line, and the government sent many workers and technical personnel to these new cities. This practice affected both the geographic and city-size distributions of Chinese cities.

Since 1978, China has been speeding up its urbanization. As a result, its urban population increased from 172 million in 1978 to 458 million in 2000, and the urban population share increased from 18 percent to 36 percent. China's urban policy, however, favors the development of small cities. The slogan is "to control large cities, promote medium-sized cities rationally, and actively develop small cities." This policy has been challenged by many Chinese scholars in recent years. Some have argued that a certain consumption scale and population size are necessary for promoting service industries and markets. Some have shown that there is a high positive correlation between city efficiency and city size. Some have found that small cities are at a disadvantage with respect to the provision of urban infrastructure. Some have proved that larger cities tend to have lower unemployment rates.

China's city system has also been affected by migration policy. Until the late 1990s, China strictly limited rural-to-urban migration, especially to large cities. Thus the antimigration policy not only slowed down the pace of China's urbanization, but also affected the structure of China's city system because China limited migration to larger cities more strictly than to smaller cities. However, the concept of expanding big cities is becoming more acceptable among policy makers. In the future, China's city system will be largely determined by market forces rather than by government intervention.

See also Migrant Population; Rural-Urban Divide, Regional Disparity, and Income Inequality; Urban Households; Urban Housing Privatization; Urbanization and Migration.

Bibliography

Bureau of the Census, *1990 Census of Population and Housing* (Washington, DC: Bureau of the Census, 1993), 728–732; Fan, C. C., "The Vertical and Horizontal Expansions of China's City System," *Urban Geography* 20 (1999): 493–515; National Bureau of Statistics of the PRC, *China Statistical Yearbook* (various issues, 1981–2003) (Beijing: China Statistics Press); National Bureau, *Urban Statistical Yearbook of China* (various issues) (Beijing: China Statistics Press); Song, Shunfeng, and Kevin Honglin Zhang, "Urbanization and City Size Distribution in China," *Urban Studies* 39, no. 12 (2002): 2317–2327.

Shunfeng Song

Coca-Cola in China

Deng Xiaoping's economic reforms have opened the door to a steady flow of foreign capital. Since the economic reforms were initiated in 1978, China has become the largest recipient of **foreign direct investment (FDI)** among developing countries and globally the second largest (next only to the United States) since 1993. In 2002, China received $52.7 billion of FDI inflows, surpassing the United States and becoming the largest FDI host country in the world. By the end of 2002, the cumulated FDI received in China reached $446 billion. The contributions of inward FDI to the Chinese economy have burgeoned in ways that no one anticipated. In 2001, FDI inflows constituted more than 10 percent of gross fixed capital formation; 28.5 percent of industrial output was produced by the foreign-invested enterprises (FIEs); and half of China's exports were created by FIEs.

Arriving in 1979 when Deng Xiaoping launched the **Open Door policy**, Coca-Cola was the first U.S. company to open business in China. Currently, the company runs twenty-four bottling joint ventures, mostly through Swire Beverages and Kerry Group, two Hong Kong–based companies that it partly owns. A successful FDI, Coca-Cola holds 35 percent of China's carbonated beverage market. A 2000 study conducted by Beijing University, Qinghua University, and the University of South Carolina found that the company supported 14,000 employees in addition to 400,000 hired by distributors, wholesalers, and retailers. In addition, Coca-Cola has been an important contributor to reform of **state-owned enterprises (SOEs)**.

In the early 1980s, Coca-Cola started by importing its products, which were sold only to foreigners at the time. Soon the company built bottling plants in Beijing, Xiamen, and Guangzhou, giving away ownership of these plants to the Chinese government in exchange for distribution rights. In 1985, the company was granted rights to sell its products to ordinary Chinese consumers. Subsequently, twenty-four bottling facilities and two concentrate plants were built in twenty-one cities. Coca-Cola's operations in Hong Kong serve forty-three countries in the Asia-Pacific region.

Several successful strategies demonstrate the ingenuity of the management. One of them is the creative plan of working with China's bureaucracy-plagued SOEs to utilize their gigantic distribution infrastructure to promote Coca-Cola products. Some of the company's partners were large state-owned sugar, tobacco, and wine enterprises with an operating history of more than fifty years. Others were former SOEs in the process of privatization. In the early years, Maoist doctrine had encouraged each province and city to be self-reliant, resulting in considerable industrial overcapacity, few logistical synergies, and a vast bureaucracy. First-tier distributors were located in Beijing, Shanghai, Tianjin, and Guangzhou. The second tier was located at provincial levels. The third tier was at the town and city levels. These organizations rigidly followed vertical command and control lines. Each level of the network simply passed products to state retailers and enterprises at its own level or to wholesalers at the next level; distributors provided basic logistics services such as transportation and warehousing, but were not allowed to import products, which was part of the reason why Coca-Cola established bottling services in China. To work with this distribution environment was by no means easy.

Moreover, Coca-Cola was able to contract with neighborhood committees that are typically formed by retirees to take charge of neighborhood crime watch and to help the needy and elderly. The large distribution force, though inefficient in many ways, turned out to be in itself a large base of consumers of the company's products. However, the company soon realized that the virtual nonexistence of a market economy in the past decades had taken its toll on the quality of the sales force: the Chinese wholesalers and retailers lacked business expertise, despite the fact that they were willing to work hard and sweat. The company offered a training program called Partnership 101 to provide training and management assistance. It firmly believed that given the nature of the business, a sales force that had close ties with the grassroots people was exactly what the company needed. In this regard, Coca-Cola was ingenious in exploring mass-line, a political tradition held to heart by the Chinese Communist Party. This strategy proved to work effectively.

Another successful strategy is to advertise to the taste of Chinese consumers. In 1984, Coca-Cola was the first foreign company to advertise on Chinese Central Television (CCTV), the government-owned **television** station. Chinese viewers enjoyed the commercials for six consecutive years. The culturally appropriate, vivid, and colorful commercials were aired in prime times such as national and world soccer games and the Olympic Games and left a deep impression on viewers. These commercials not only promoted the classic Coca-Cola as the "real thing," but also showed a lifestyle that was deemed fashionable by young people. Hence Coca-Cola became a fashionable drink. The red umbrellas soon dotted every street corner of most large cities.

The third successful strategy is "thinking locally and acting locally." The Chinese tradition values health-strengthening foods and drinks. Such drinks typically include herb- or fruit-enriched liquors, tea, and countless medicinal drinks. To appeal to the culture, Coca-Cola developed several local brands, of which the best known is Tian Yu Di (Heaven and Earth), a line of noncarbonated drinks that features mango- and lychee-flavored drinks, oolong and jasmine teas, and bottled water. Xingmu (Smart) is a line of carbonated fruit drinks in green apple, watermelon, and coconut flavors that was introduced in 1997 and quickly became the top brand.

Nevertheless, in addition to financial constraints, the Chinese are by far less enthusiastic than westerners for sugar drinks. The price tag in 2000 for a can of Coca-Cola was 1.9 yuan or 23 U.S. cents in Beijing and 2.3 yuan or 28 U.S. cents in Shanghai. The joint study by the three Chinese and American universities showed that while Coca-Cola reached 80 percent of the Chinese population, Chinese people drank, on average, only eight 250 ml servings of Coca-Cola in 2000. The figure pales when compared with the 400 servings that Americans drank in the same year. The size of the Chinese population, 1.29 billion, is more than four times that of the United States, promising an almost infinitely expandable future market. Currently, China occupies seventh place in the largest markets served by Coca-Cola.

Breaking into new markets may present many challenges. Just because China joined the World Trade Organization (WTO) does not mean that foreign firms have immediate access equal to that of their Chinese competitors. Analysts believe that for the distribution industry as a whole, the more likely outcome will resemble the historical pattern of evolutionary opening rather than immediate, revolutionary change. For example, the Chinese logistics industry, transportation in particular, is notoriously underdeveloped and historically prone to local protectionism. Unfair competition, an excessive number of government-related operators who enjoy the privileges of monopolistic regulations at provincial or national levels, and the broader-context government fiscal policy changes add to the difficulties. Hope for improvement may lie with China's gradual compliance with WTO standards. Such changes will not typically be swift.

Faced with increasing competition from domestic brands, Coca-Cola stays on track in supplying, producing, and selling its products within China's borders. The company continues to creatively explore new opportunities to serve its seventh-largest market and to remain in the rank of the most successful FDIs in China.

See also Commercial Advertising, Policies and Practices of; Deng Xiaoping (1904–1997), Reforms of; Fast Food (Western Style), Integration of.

Bibliography

National Bureau of Statistics of the PRC, *China Statistical Yearbook* (various issues), (Beijing: China Statistics Press, 1992–1999); Powers, Patrick, "Distributing in China: The End of the Beginning," *China Business Review* 28, no. 4 (July–August 2001): 8–13; Weisert, Drake, "Coca-Cola in China: Quenching the Thirst of a Billion," *China Business Review* 28, no. 4 (July–August 2001): 52–55.

Jing Luo

Cold War and China

The Cold War is regarded as a state of relations between the United States and its allies, on one side, and the Soviet Union and its allies, on the other side, after World War II. The Cold War was marked by international tension and hostility that arose from various military, diplomatic, social, propagandistic, and economic pressures short of war that were employed by one side against the other to gain advantage economically, in terms of security, or in terms of world opinion. The Cold War, a competition to demonstrate which side was superior, was primarily a political and ideological conflict between communism and liberal capitalism, but it also had profound economic, social, and cultural ramifications, and it affected the lives of almost everyone in the world in some way. The end of the Cold War did not result from economic failure of the Soviet Union or from military defeat of the Soviet Communists by the United States and its allies. On the contrary, the Cold War ended due to a revolt of the leaders and people of the Soviet Union and Eastern European Communist countries and surrender to the superiority of free-market economies, Judeo-Christian values, and parliamentary democracy of the United States and the Western powers.

During the Cold War, neither the United States nor the Soviet Union ignored China, a giant with the world's largest population occupying the third-largest territory in the world. China's gigantic mass determined its influence in the course of the Cold War. In 1949, the Cold War was at a turning point because of two major events. First, after concluding that the Berlin blockade, the first major Cold War crisis, was being counterproductive in that the success of the American airlift was having highly positive psychological effects on the people of Berlin, the Soviet Union lifted the blockade in May. After this crisis, a dividing line between the two contending camps had been drawn in a definitive manner. Second, the Soviet Union successfully tested its first atomic bomb in August of this year. These two events posed a grave challenge to the United States and the Soviet Union because if one superpower tried to achieve a strategic upper hand against the other by the use of nuclear weapons, a showdown would occur in Europe, a third world war would be unavoidable, and the Cold War could evolve into a global disaster.

In this situation, the Soviet Union had to turn to China, which had been involved in a civil war for more than three years. The Chinese Communists under the leadership of **Mao Zedong**, without doubt, would soon completely defeat the Nationalists, who were supported by the United States. In August 1949, on the eve of the victory of the Chinese Communist revolution, the number two leader of the Chinese Communist Party, **Liu Shaoqi**, secretly went to Moscow to meet with Joseph Stalin. The two leaders concluded that the situation was favorable to communism and to revolutionary people in Asia. In an agreement on division of the role between the Chinese and Russian Communists for launching a Communist revolution all over the world, they decided that while the Soviet Union would remain the center of international proletarian revolution, China would play a major role in facilitating Communist revolution in Asia. The Soviet Union identified a new, large ally in Asia to confront its competitor.

At the beginning of the Cold War, a shared belief in Marxist-Leninist ideology served as a vital force to bring together Communist states and parties in the world. The ideology played an important role in China's foreign policy. The Chinese Communist leaders implemented a "lean-to-side" policy, a strategy to seek the Soviet Union's military and economic aid while making China a loyal follower of the Soviet Communists, when they created the People's Republic of China in October. This policy, in a practical political sense, established an alliance between China and the Soviet Union, as well as other socialist countries, to confront the United States and its allies—the Western countries.

The implementation of the plan resulted in China's support for the Vietnamese Communists under the leadership of Ho Chi Minh in the first Indochina War against the French imperialists between 1950 and 1954. In June 1950, encouraged by the Soviet Union, the North Korean Communist forces under the leadership of Kim Il Sung launched military campaigns across the thirty-eighth parallel and captured Seoul. In October 1950, only one year after the Communists took over power in China, Mao decided to help the North Korean Communists fight Americans because, to Mao, if China did not get involved in the **Korean War**, North Korea would be defeated by the United States, and the Communist movement in Asia would suffer a heavy loss. Chinese Communist troops began to enter North Korea secretly in October, and massive intervention in the Korean War followed in the subsequent months. The Chinese involvement in the Korean War made China a frontline soldier fighting against the U.S. military forces. Finally, China and North Korea, on one side, and the United States and South Korea, on the other side, signed a truce to end this war, maintaining the thirty-eighth parallel as a dividing line between North and South Korea.

After the Korean War, the United States, replacing the French, who withdrew their troops from Vietnam in 1955, soon became involved in another conflict against communism, the **Vietnam War**. During this war, the Soviet Union and Eastern European Communist countries provided North Vietnam with large-scale military and economic aid. Beijing also provided substantial and much-needed aid to Hanoi, especially between 1965 and 1968 under the banner of fulfilling China's duties of so-called proletarian internationalism. China sent 320,000 Chinese engineering and antiaircraft troops to North Vietnam in

1965–1969. To justify China's involvement in the Vietnam War, Mao used highly ideological language in a series of internal discussions and correspondence with other Chinese leaders, arguing that if China failed to help North Vietnam, the Communist movement would fail in Southeast Asia.

In the late 1940s and early 1950s, when China established a strategic alliance with the Soviet Union, the United States instantly felt gravely endangered. Facing offensives by Communist states and powerful nationalist forces in East Asia, the U.S. government began to create and implement the NSC-68 program, one of the foundations of the Cold War defense and diplomacy designed by the U.S. National Security Council, which recommended that the United States stand up to the Soviet Union by imposing order in the non-Communist world, using military power to deter Soviet expansionism, and fighting limited wars if necessary. Washington also responded with the most extensive peacetime mobilization of national resources in American history in order to overcome the Soviet Union's threat. Thus the United States got involved in the Korean War from 1950 to 1953 and the Vietnam War from 1954 to 1975, overextending itself in a global confrontation with the Soviet Union and its allies.

In the late 1960s and early 1970s, the situation reversed complexly when China began to challenge the Soviet Union in terms of ideology. When the Soviet Union dispatched a large number of troops along the Chinese border and had conflicts with the Chinese troops on the boundary, Beijing sought to improve its relations with the United States. To confront the Soviet Union, the United States lifted its economic embargo on China and began to help the Chinese strengthen their military power. In order to challenge the United States and its allies as well as its new enemy, Communist China, at the same time, the Soviet Union exhausted its military and financial resources, which led to the final breakdown of the Soviet Union in the early 1990s.

China's influence in the Cold War not only changed the balance of power between the two superpowers but also shifted the focus of the Cold War from Central Europe to Asia from the 1950s to the 1970s. Although the Cold War remained "cold" in other parts of the world, it became very "hot" in East Asia and Southeast Asia because of the Korean War and the Vietnam War.

China was a major Cold War player, but its capacity and influence to affect global issues and international affairs were limited because it was backward in technology, military strength, and economic development in comparison with the United States and the Soviet Union. Besides, China's foreign behavior was deeply limited by Chinese ethnocentrism, which was intensely rooted in its history and culture. As a result, in the Cold War's global framework, China played a significant role only in certain aspects and during certain time periods. Only the two superpowers—the Soviet Union and the United States—really occupied the unquestionable central position. The Cold War's multipolarity and multidimensionality definitely determined its complexity and made China's role all the more significant.

After Mao's death, Deng Xiaoping, the new Chinese leader, began to change China's policy toward the United States by establishing better relations with Washington. Thus the Cold War in Asia was practically over in the late 1970s, almost thirteen years before the end of the global Cold War. The Chinese leaders, however, in the 1980s and 1990s repeatedly maintained that under no circumstance would the Beijing government allow any foreign powers to impose their values and cultures on China's external behavior or to use their standards to intervene in China's internal affairs. Since the Tiananmen movement in 1989, the United States has increasingly accused the Chinese government of abusing human rights in China and of taking a hard stand on **Tibet**. In the 1990s, U.S. policy makers and some scholars claimed that the economic and military growth of post-Deng China posed a threat to security in Asia and the Pacific. They regarded China as a strategic competitor. More recently, Washington, as well as other Western countries, have also strongly condemned Beijing for aiming its missiles toward Taiwan and refusing to abandon the use of military force to bring Taiwan back to Chinese Communist control. Washington's criticism further offended Beijing's leaders. The Chinese government has steadily rebutted such criticism, claiming that the United States has been interfering in the jurisdiction of Chinese sovereignty. Therefore a cold war of another kind has continued between China and the United States, as well as other Western countries, since the formal ending of the global Cold War in the late 1980s and early 1990s.

See also Deng Xiaoping (1904–1997), Politics of; Jiang Zemin (1926–   ), Diplomacy of; June 4 Movement; Rhetoric in China's Foreign Relations; Sino-American Relations, Conflicts and Common Interests; Sino-American Relations since 1949; Sino-Soviet Alliance; Taiwan Strait Crisis, Evolution of; United Nations (UN) and China.

Bibliography

Chen Jian, *Mao's China and the Cold War* (Chapel Hill: University of North Carolina Press, 2001); Gaddis, John Lewis, *We Now Know: Rethinking Cold War History* (New York: Oxford University Press, 1997).

Guangqiu Xu

Commercial Advertising, Policies and Practices of

Nowhere is the transformation of Chinese society more visible than in the marketization of public communication and advertising culture. Some claim that the forests of **Coca-Cola** billboards have replaced "Red Oceans" of Maoist slogans. Propaganda organs have become advertising firms. China's advertising market is the ninth largest in the world, with a growth potential second to none. Some forecasts estimate that China's advertising market will overtake the U.S. market by the year 2015. Advertising has actually become one of the most lucrative businesses in China.

The turning point for advertising was the year 1978, when the Chinese Communist Party (CCP) declared the **Open Door policy**. Since then, the development of the market has been benefiting from two factors: the rapid growth of the Chinese economy and Chinese consumer spending, and a government policy that has encouraged the growth of spending on advertising.

Although commercial advertising has a long history in China, with advertisements appearing in Chinese magazines, newspapers, and posters as early as the 1920s, the 1949 liberation and the **Great Cultural Revolution** of 1966 to

1976 saw commercial advertising virtually disappear. The 1949 liberation ushered in an era of increasing governmental regulation and state ownership of industry and commerce. All areas of the economy and commerce were centrally planned by the central government. The government exclusively managed the designing, production, distribution, and pricing of commodities. This economic configuration presented no need for commercial advertising since there was no competition in the market. The Great Cultural Revolution brought a total ban on advertising, branding it a tool of "bourgeois capitalism." Individual and private business and commerce were denounced, a factor that further contributed to the nonexistence of commercial advertising before 1978.

Since 1978, under the Open Door policy, the CCP has been focusing its attention on economic and commercial development in China. Individual and private businesses began to be allowed and encouraged. Competition in a free market quickly became intense. The value of advertising suddenly emerged and is becoming increasingly recognized. The Chinese advertising market expanded in the past decade at an average annual rate of more than 40 percent. The sustainability of such rapid growth could be ascribed to the new policies of the government toward advertising, new practices in advertising, and the changing attitudes of the public toward advertising.

In the initial phase from 1979 to 1991, the market was largely dominated by limited state-owned advertising agencies, and there was no direct foreign participation in the advertising industry. As the Chinese market opened to foreign firms, foreign consumer product manufacturers focused on the mass "horizontal" media

Lighted billboards along the Huangpu River in Shanghai advertise various products.

by placing advertisements in **television**, newspapers, radio, magazines, and bill-boards to acquaint the mass market with their brand names.

The approach to advertising in this phase essentially focused on informa-tiveness, and advertisements thus tended to be largely simple, factual, and unsophisticated. In spite of this, the media began to muckrake and criticize abuse and deception by advertisers. This muckraking and criticism led to the development of a regulatory framework to prevent deceit and ensure political conformity. As is well known, all media messages, commercial advertising included, must be congruent with the policies of the Chinese Communist Party, which is the sole legitimate ruling party of the nation. The government's position with respect to the general value of commercial advertising, however, did not change. Advertising was considered an essential tool for economic de-velopment. In a 1987 address given by the then top legislator in China to the World Advertising Congress in Beijing, Wan Li declared advertising an "indis-pensable element in the promotion of economic prosperity."

The years 1992 and 1993 saw dramatic increases in advertising spending, a 100 percent jump, as well as a 90 percent increase in the number of advertis-ing agencies. The government permitted foreign advertising agencies to set up joint ventures in China and allowed **state-owned enterprises** to choose advertis-ing agencies without its interference. This resulted in increased competition among agencies and a marked improvement in the quality of advertisements. In 1994, government regulation of entry into the industry increased, and some of the incentives that had been introduced to attract foreign investments in the advertising and other service industries were eliminated. Only qualified for-eign advertising agencies were now allowed to enter China.

Since 1978, the Chinese people's general attitude toward advertising has un-dergone great changes. More people are positive toward advertising. One contributing factor to this attitudinal change may be the exposure of con-sumers to the mass media, which have grown significantly during the past de-cade. In 1997, the number of color television sets owned by Chinese families was 100.5 per 100 urban households, compared with less than 40 in 1987. Radio ownership is almost universal, and the circulation of newspapers was 30 billion copies for 1997, compared with 18 billion in 1987. The prodigiously increased exposure of the populace to the media dovetails with and facilitates producers' new need to reach more consumers via advertising.

Studies by Pollay, Tse, and Wang in 1990 indicate that Chinese consumers were more positive about advertising than their counterparts in the West. Chi-nese consumers at this stage also expressed preferences for foreign advertise-ments compared with domestic advertisements. Pollay, Tse, and Wang attributed the positive attitude toward advertising to government encouragement and in-fluence through its propaganda machine.

However, some studies and analyses in 1995 found that close to three-quarters of the respondents thought that there were too many advertisements, while a mere 2 percent wanted more. Some 24 percent of respondents found advertising to be an insult to their intelligence. Others believed and found that information contained in some ads was misleading, inaccurate, and even deceptive. To some extent, this attitudinal modification from 1990 to 1995 may indicate further development of the advertising industry in that the quantity of advertising in the mass media has increased to be ad nauseam. Consequently, people's experience with advertising is changing from one of novelty and curiosity to one of surfeit and aversion.

The 1995 study shows that negative feedback about advertising, nevertheless, did not translate to an overwhelming endorsement of tighter government regulations. Only 35 percent agreed that there was a need for further government intervention, despite the fact that a minority (34 percent) felt that self-regulation by the industry would be preferred. Chinese consumers by this stage also appeared to have increased their confidence in domestic product advertising and advertised domestic products, compared with the advertising of foreign products and advertised foreign products.

Besides the historical change in attitude of the general populace toward commercial advertising, attitudinal differences also exist among different contemporary groups. Younger generations tend to be more positive toward commercial advertising, which may be attributed to the fact that the older generation grew up in a puritanical culture where orthodox ideology rejected materialistic luxuriance and private and "frivolous" consumption. The younger generation, however, grew up in a culture that replaced orthodoxy with pragmatism and propagated and legitimized consumption values. It is also possible that advertisers consciously target the younger generation and thus have produced advertising that accords with the tastes of the young. People with a higher educational level tend to perceive commercial advertising more positively, which could be attributed to the close relationship between educational levels and cosmopolitan attitudes. The rich and urban people tend to enjoy advertising more than the poor and rural people, which could be attributed to the fact that the former have the resources to afford luxury products. Some scholars claim that to foster positive attitudes, the entertainment value of advertising has to be increased, and that investment in improving the content and presentation of advertising is also warranted.

Since China still focuses its effort on further economic and commercial development, it is likely a safe prediction that advertising will be more prominent. Further development and maturity of the advertising industry may also lead to more comprehensive and elaborate legal regulations to assure the quality of advertising and to protect the rights of consumers.

See also Brand-Building Phenomenon; Business Decision Making in the Public and Private Sectors; Fast Food (Western Style), Integration of; Foreign Trade; Internet.

Bibliography

Pollay, R. W., D. K. Tse, and Z. Wang, "Advertising, Propaganda, and Value Change in Economic Development: The New Culture Revolution in China and Attitudes toward Advertising," *Journal of Business Research* 20, no. 2 (1990): 83–95; Tse, D. K., R. W. Belk, and N. Zhou, "Becoming a Consumer Society: A Longitudinal and Cross-Cultural Content Analysis of Print Ads from Hong Kong, the People's Republic of China, and Taiwan," *Journal of Consumer Research* 15, no. 4 (1989): 457–472; Zhang, Y., and B. D. Gelb, "Matching Advertising to Culture: The Influence of Products' Use Conditions," *Journal of Advertising* 25, no. 3 (1996): 29–46; Zhao, X., and F. Shen, "Audience Reaction to Commercial

Advertising in China in the 1980s," *International Journal of Advertising* 14 (1995): 374–390; Zhou, Dongsheng, Weijiong Zhang, and Ilan Vertinsky, "Advertising Trends in Urban China," *Journal of Advertising Research* 42, no. 3 (2002): 73–81.

Xinan Lu

Conflict Resolution

Conflict resolution is a component part of China's social control system. It concerns settlement of conflicts or disputes among individual citizens or groups over various social and economic issues such as marriage, inheritance, debts, economic contracts, copyrights, labor, and the like. Conflict resolution has been a persistent concern of the Chinese regime and has been deemed by the latter as critical for maintaining social order and stability and ultimately for consolidating its rule.

Conflict resolution involves the use of two major mechanisms or channels, mediation and litigation (or lawsuit). Mediation is a nonlegal process in which a dispute is tackled through negotiation by the two disputing parties with the participation or help of a neutral third party (mediator). The dispute is settled if the two parties reach an agreement. Such an agreement has no legal effect and is not compulsory. If no agreement is reached, which means that the mediation fails, either party has the option to resort to litigation. Mediation generally takes place at the local level, within the local community—a village or township in the countryside, a residential committee, an urban neighborhood, or a factory. Mediation is supposed to be based on the principle of voluntarism. It is free of charge. In theory, mediation is regarded as an instrument of self-government of local communities that allows citizens in a community to handle and settle their disputes on their own. In practice, however, it often involves governmental agencies.

The other major mechanism for conflict resolution is litigation or lawsuit. Litigation is a legal process in which a conflict or dispute is handled and settled by a court of law (the People's Court). A case is first tried by the lower-level (county or district) court. If the plaintiff or defendant feels unsatisfied with the court's verdict, he or she has the right to appeal to a higher-level (municipal or provincial) court, whose decision is final and must be executed. The court's decision or judgment is compulsory and binding on the parties concerned. Litigation entails the payment of legal fees by the plaintiff or the defendant or both.

Mediation and litigation have existed and functioned during the whole history of the People's Republic of China. During the prereform years (from the 1950s to the late 1970s), mediation was adopted as the primary or predominant mechanism for settling conflicts, while litigation played only a secondary role. Under the then prevailing command economic system, private property and individual economic activities were almost nonexistent. Accordingly, conflicts over private economic interests were minimal. Most disputes were related to family affairs, marriage, and neighborhood relations. Mediation seemed sufficient for settlement of such disputes. Besides, due to the Communist Party's persistent propaganda and educational campaigns, people cultivated, more or less, the so-called collective or socialist consciousness, which required people to be selfless and to refrain from pursuing personal gains. As a result, people appeared reluctant to get involved in conflicts over individual interests, and if they found themselves in conflicts, they preferred settlement via mediation to resolution through litigation. For them, mediation had some advantages compared to litigation: it was less public, less time-consuming, and cost-free and would not necessarily cause deep ill feelings between the two parties in the dispute. From the perspective of the government, mediation was flexible, relatively easy to manage, and less disruptive.

During the prereform era, mediation served more as a governmental instrument for social control than as a medium of self-government by the people. The government, omnipresent and omnipotent, maintained tight control over the whole society and people's social life, leaving almost no space for individual initiatives. Under these circumstances, mediation was naturally within the purview of the government: local Party cadres served as mediators and presided over mediation. The so-called agreements reached in the mediation virtually represented the decisions of these local leaders rather than the will of people involved in disputes. Disputing parties were often persuaded (or coerced) to accept these "agreements."

The use of litigation in conflict resolution was quite limited during the prereform era. China was then a nation with an official ideology that stressed the rule of man rather than the rule of law. The Communist Party's documents or top leaders' instructions were virtually taken to be laws or even above laws and served as criteria of everything. Legislation was neglected, with the legislative body, the **National People's Congress**, sinking into oblivion. The courts of law were understaffed, and judges were essentially state bureaucrats rather than legal professionals. Administrative interference with court trials was frequent and severe. Services of law offices and lawyers were unknown during most of this period. All these factors combined to undermine the quality of trials by a court of law. This lack of a sound legal system partly accounted for the reluctance of individual citizens to exploit litigation as a major means to settle their disputes. To most of them, the court was remote, and lodging a lawsuit was inconvenient. This reluctance was reinforced by traditional Chinese culture that generally values social harmony and discourages the use of litigation. Many people were convinced that litigation would cause animosity among friends or relatives or acquaintances and incur personal embarrassment, especially when one lost a lawsuit case.

The two mechanisms for conflict resolution, mediation and litigation, have continued to function in the reform era that began in the late 1970s. Mediation still has been emphasized and used in solving most civil disputes. For example, in the year 2001, mediation committees in China numbered 923,452 and handled 4.86 million civil disputes, surpassing the number (3.459 million) of civil disputes tackled by a court of law. Nevertheless, litigation has gained increasing popularity and has played a more and more important role, especially since the early 1990s. The ratio of civil lawsuit cases and mediation cases was 40:100 in the year 1990 and became 64:100 in 1998 and 70:100 in 2001. This growing popularity of litigation has to do with the profound socioeconomic changes brought about by the market-oriented economic reforms.

With the collapse of the command economic system, private businesses emerged and flourished; possessing private property and seeking individual economic interests eventually gained legitimacy. Meanwhile, the society became more sophisticated and volatile. The family was increasingly susceptible to disruption as divorce rates grew rapidly. These changes provided a fertile breeding ground for the rise of multitudinous conflicts. In addition, with the demise of the Communist ideology, people were subject to the influence of various ideas that stressed personal happiness and material pleasures. They became ever more sensitive to any encroachments on their personal interests and were ready to protect these interests, no longer shying away from getting involved in conflicts or disputes. Consequently, conflicts in the reform era have multiplied, diversified, and intensified, threatening social stability.

To cope with this problem, the regime, besides improving mediation, adopted the strategy of building the rule of law. Under this strategy, the role of the National People's Congress was strengthened, numerous laws were passed and put into effect, private law offices were allowed to operate, legal education was promoted, propaganda campaigns on the rule of law were periodically conducted, legal professionals were recruited as judges, and legal aid centers and legal service agencies were set up. Accordingly, more and more individual citizens developed the consciousness of the rule of law and proved willing to use litigation to settle disputes. Some even ventured to sue governmental agencies or officials.

Mediation and litigation experienced a major change in nature in the reform era. Less susceptible to administrative interference and no longer simply serving as governmental instruments, these two mechanisms were increasingly coming under the influence or supervision of societal forces such as interest groups and social organizations or the general public. For example, mediation committees in enterprises were headed by trade-union leaders, who were mostly elected by workers. Court trials gradually became transparent—they were made open to the public, which meant that citizens were allowed to sit in the courtroom to observe the trials.

The reform era also witnessed the emergence of another channel for conflict resolution—arbitration. Arbitration is conducted at the city or district level by the arbitration committee. It is essentially a legal procedure. Decisions made by the arbitration committee, although not final, have legal effect and are binding on parties involved in a dispute and can be executed compulsorily by a court of law. Arbitration was mostly used in solving business and labor disputes. Starting in the 1980s and becoming standard procedure in the 1990s, a regulation required that labor disputes had to go through arbitration before being presented to a court of law. A labor arbitration committee was composed of representatives from management, the trade union, and the government's labor agency (or department). It employed legal professionals and labor-issue experts as full-time or part-time arbitrators.

The record of mediation, arbitration, and litigation in conflict resolution is mixed. Generally, they have functioned efficiently and contributed to the maintenance of social order. However, they need improvements. This is especially true in the case of litigation. Entering a lawsuit is too costly and beyond many citizens' financial capability; judicial corruption is serious in certain localities and on certain occasions; judicial independence is not guaranteed; and legal services (e.g., lawyers) are inadequate.

See also Judicial Reform; Legal Infrastructure Development and Economic Development; Mediation Practices.

Bibliography

Han, Bo, Zhang Weiping, and Shi Ye, "How to Improve the People's Mediation System," *Law Science Magazine*, no. 12 (2002): 45-52; *Judicial Administration Yearbook of China, 1999* (Beijing: Publishing House of Law, 1999); *Law Yearbook of China, 2002* (Beijing: Law Yearbook of China Publishing House, 2002); Zhang, Yunqiu, "Law and Labor in Post-Mao China," paper presented at the annual conference of the Association of Chinese Professors of Social Sciences in the United States, San Jose State University, California, October 25-27, 2002.

Yunqiu Zhang

Confucian Tradition and Christianity

An assessment of the influence of Confucianism and Christianity in contemporary China requires a historical perspective. Confucianism derives its name from the cultural figure Kong Zi or Confucius, as he is widely known in the West. Confucius, who lived about 2,500 years ago in Shandong Province, is credited with a moral philosophy that has guided Chinese society in covert and overt forms. Confucianism is not a single theoretical system; it rather refers to an assortment of thoughts before and after Confucius, and many individuals, such as Mencius, Xun Zi, Dong Zhongshu, and Zhu Xi, to name a few, played a pivotal role in developing, modifying, and substantiating Confucianism.

As early as the Han dynasty (206 B.C.–A.D. 220), Confucianism became a state-sanctioned, canonized doctrine. Through dynasties after dynasties and emperors after emperors, the position of Confucianism has rarely been shaken or challenged, even during the periods when the Mongols and the Manchu, who represented a different cultural tradition, ruled China.

Unlike Confucianism, Christianity is not an indigenous concept and has its roots in the West. Since the Tang dynasty (A.D. 618–960), when Western missionaries first made major journeys to China, Christianity has more or less been a cultural element in the mosaic of Chinese society, but it always remains in the periphery, not the center, of Chinese culture and society.

The twentieth century was a different story for both Confucianism and Christianity, because neither was favored. China's encounters with the modern world and its humiliating experience with the Western powers led many of its intellectuals to the belief that a fundamental change was needed for China to survive as a nation among other nations. Intellectuals in the May 4 Movement (1919) promoted and upheld ideas such as science and democracy, concepts quite alien to the Chinese, and charged that Confucianism was irrational and undemocratic. These influential intellectuals also dealt a blow to Christianity, which had just gained some ground in China. In their view, Christianity, like any religion, was superstitious and ran counter to scientific principles. Moreover,

Christianity was an accomplice of the imperialists and a tool of the imperial culture.

Confucianism and Christianity suffered more setbacks after the founding of the People's Republic of China (PRC). Confucianism was on the verge of extinction during the **Great Cultural Revolution (1966–1976)**. In line with the radical ideology of the revolution, eradicating Confucianism's "lingering influence" became the buzzword. Ironically, Confucius was even reconstructed and tied to the purged marshal Lin Biao, who had once served as the vice chairman and a designated successor to **Mao Zedong**.

With the death of Mao and the downfall of the **Gang of Four**, the position of Confucianism has been gradually recovered. Many people have started to realize that without Confucianism, China would be a nation without its own cultural traditions. However, because of a hiatus of almost three decades (1949–1976), Confucianism has remained a mystery and too complicated for a generation of Chinese to grasp.

In contemporary China, Confucianism is more accepted as a tradition than as a living culture, and its important ideas and concepts are taken only as heritages. Thanks to the long denial of Confucianism from the 1920s to the 1970s, the morality and ethics represented in Confucianism can no longer play an important part, as they did in the ancient times. After the Chinese Communist Party came to power, first Marxism and then Maoism became state-sponsored ideology. During the 1950s to the 1970s, the state was successful in influencing the thinking of several generations of people with this ideology, and Maoism was taken almost as a kind of religion. When the New Period (since 1978) approached and Deng Xiaoping came to power, the country became more open to the outside, and a public sphere with different ideas and beliefs appeared to emerge in Chinese cultural life. However, the ideology had been unchanged in the past and remains the same. In the classrooms, there is no place for Confucianism; Marxism and communism still fill pages and pages of textbooks. Yet Confucianism is embedded in people's behavior and relational protocols. Its exclusion in education causes much confusion among the younger generation. They face huge discrepancies between what is taught and what they see in reality, so skepticism is running deep.

Christianity has also not seen good fortune. By 1949, the clashes between Christianity and Chinese culture had lasted for almost 1,400 years. The founding of the PRC left little room for Christianity, which was virtually outlawed, although no law was clearly issued. In a series of efforts to limit or even eliminate the influence of Christianity, the Chinese government expelled all Western missionaries and restructured Christian churches. For instance, the Three-self Patriotic Movement Committee of the Protestant Churches in China (Zhongguo Jidujiao Sanziai Aiguoyundong Weiyuanhui) was formed in this historical context. "Three-self" here means self-governing (*zizhi*), self-supportive (*ziyang*), and self-propagating (*zichuan*). The Three-Self Patriotic Movement was launched "to remove foreign influences from the Chinese church." It was a government-sanctioned church on the mainland. The establishment of this church indicated that the government required "patriotism" or loyalty from the religious sector and churchgoers. In order to break away from the West, bishops in China were not ordained or nominated by the Vatican, because the government held that

Western missionaries were the clients of the Western imperialists. Although the government's control over Christianity is not as severe as before, it has never been hesitant to mobilize its media and other propaganda tools to instill the conviction that religion is harmful and even a public disease, and only science and the correct worldview can provide the right remedy. In short, the Party urges Christian churches in China to follow the Party line, holding that this is "an important premise" of the Party's religious policy.

Presently there are about 10 million Christians in China. Many scholars argue that among the baptized Christians and those who are self-proclaimed Christians, a significant number of people do not seem really to understand Christian doctrines. The self-proclaimed Christians, in particular, tend to associate Christianity with Western cultures, and their faith in Christianity is only a reflection of their blind faith in Western civilization.

In contemporary China, however, scholars are very enthusiastic about Christian studies. Many books on Christian history, Christian theology, and Christian culture have been translated and published. Research centers devoted to Christian studies have been established in Fudan University, Zhejiang University, Fujian Normal University, and other institutions of higher learning. It is safe to say that in contemporary China, Christianity as a belief is not encouraged, but Christianity as a study is not controlled.

Chinese scholars like to make comparisons between Christianity and Confucianism. They think that the study of Christianity is a means to understand the West, and in intercultural communication between China and the West, Christianity is unavoidable. Although scholars show great enthusiasm in studying the relationship between Chinese culture and Christianity, their interest is mostly in the past, not the present. In other words, Christianity in contemporary China is seldom a goal by itself in their studies.

See also Deng Xiaoping (1904–1997), Reforms of; Islam; Jews; Religion and Freedom of Religious Belief; Spiritual Life in the Post-Mao Era.

Bibliography

Gernet, Jacques, *China and the Christian Impact: A Conflict of Cultures* (Cambridge: Cambridge University Press, 1990); *Journal for the Study of Christian Culture* 1–5 (Beijing: People's Daily Press, 2000–2004); Ren, Yanli, ed. *Basic Knowledge of Chinese Catholicism* (Beijing: Religious Culture Press, 2000); *Selected Documents of Religious Works* (Beijing: Religious Culture Press, 1995).

Yihai Chen

Consumption Patterns and Statistics of Living Conditions

Since the economic reform in the late 1970s, the standard of living of Chinese consumers has improved greatly. Shares of expenditures for necessities continue to decrease, while expenditure shares for normal and luxury consumer goods have increased substantially. The National Bureau of Statistics in China has proposed several indicators to measure the standard of living at various levels in urban and rural areas. One goal was to achieve the *xiao kang* (small wealth, or middle economic status) level at the end of the twentieth century. For urban areas, the *xiao kang* level includes that Engel coefficients (referring to the proportion of expenditures on food in the total consumption expenditures of households) range from 45 percent to 47 percent; per capita intake from food is 2,600 calories, eighty grams of protein, and seventy grams of fat; life expectancy is seventy years; every three literate persons subscribe to one newspaper; per capita living area is eight to ten square meters, a family of three lives in a two-bedroom house, and the rate of complete living suites is 60 percent; and per capita green public area is eight square meters. For rural areas, the *xiao kang* level includes that Engel coefficients range from 45 percent to 50 percent; protein intake is greater than seventy-five grams; reinforced concrete structured living areas account for 80 percent or more of living areas; household **television** possession rate is about 75 percent; the average educational level is eight years; life expectancy is seventy years; the rate of households using electricity is more than 95 percent; and the clean water usage rate is greater than 90 percent. According to the standards of the *xiao kang* level set by the National Bureau of Statistics and several other national agencies in 1995, 95 percent of the country achieved the goal in 2000—100 percent in the eastern region, 78 percent in the central region, and 56 percent in the western region.

The annual per capita disposable income of urban households was 7,703 yuan in 2002, a real increase of 13.4 percent with decline in prices taken into consideration, compared with the previous year. The per capita net income of rural households was 2,476 yuan, a real increase of 4.8 percent. From 1978 to 1999, household incomes increased by 473 percent and 361 percent in rural and urban households, respectively. The increase in disposable income has improved the consumption structure of Chinese consumers. Per capita disposable income is 8,472 yuan in urban areas and 2,622 yuan in rural areas in 2003.

The decrease of Engel coefficients indicates that the Chinese consumption structure has been improved. In 1978, the Engel coefficient was 57.5 percent for urban residents and 67.7 percent for rural residents. The coefficients have decreased continuously in the last two decades. In 2002, the coefficients became 37.7 percent and 46.2 percent for urban and rural residents, respectively. In terms of Engel coefficients, both urban and rural residents, on average, have achieved the *xiao kang* level. In addition, Chinese consumers pay more attention to the quality of food consumption. Expenditure shares for staple foods have gone down, while those for nonstaple foods have increased.

The expenditure shares for clothing have decreased among both urban and rural residents. For example, for urban residents, in 1981, the share was 14.8 percent, and in 1999, the share was 10.5 percent. For rural residents in 1980, the share was 12.3 percent, but in 1999, the share was 5.8 percent. The

The antiques street in Tianjin City.

decrease of clothing expenditure shares implies that basic needs for clothing have been met and consumers spend relatively more on other categories, such as products and services for education and entertainment.

For urban residents, the expenditure share for household products decreased from 10.7 percent in 1985 to 8.6 percent in 1999, but the expenditure share for entertainment products increased from 7.72 percent in 1985 to 12.3 percent in 1999. For rural residents, the expenditure share for household products was stable during these years, 5.1 percent in 1985 and 5.2 percent in 1999, but the expenditure share for entertainment products more than doubled, from 3.9 percent in 1985 to 10.7 percent in 1999. Among household products, different consumer durable goods were popular in different historical periods. In the 1950s to the 1970s, the hot durable goods were watches, bicycles, sewing machines, and radios. In the 1980s, the hot durable goods were television sets, tape recorders, electric fans, washing machines, refrigerators, and video viewers. In the 1990s, the hot durable goods were multifunction big-screen television sets, air conditioners, and telephones. In recent years, computers, home theaters, VCRs, and cars have become consumption foci for more and more Chinese consumers.

Housing reform has changed the housing consumption patterns of urban residents, but housing expenditure share is still low. In 1985, the housing rent share was .96 percent, while in 1994, the share was still 1.01 percent. Expenditure for housing decorating is greater than the housing expenditure share. For example, in 1999, the share for housing decorating was 9.8 percent, but the share for housing expenditure was only 4.2 percent. Housing consumption is becoming the new focus of consumption for two reasons. First, housing reform resulted in an increase of housing expenditure share. Second, along with the increase of income and consumption level, consumer needs for food, clothing, and other household products are met, but consumers have a long way to go to meet their housing needs that are specified by government as the *xiao kang* level.

For rural residents, housing expenditure is the second-largest expenditure share after food expenditure. Since 1978, rural housing expenditure shares have increased. In 1978, the housing expenditure share was 10.3 percent, but in 1999, the share increased to 14.8 percent. Rural housing expenditures have regional differences. Housing expenditures in the eastern region are much higher than those in the central or western regions. It will take time for consumers in the central and western regions to achieve the *xiao kang* level in terms of housing.

Service consumption has increased in recent years. For urban residents, the share for service expenditures, which includes health care, transportation and communication, and education and entertainment tripled from 7.99 percent in 1981 to 24.3 percent in 1999. The service expenditure share for rural residents also increased substantially, from 2.7 percent in 1978 to 19.5 percent in 1999. Along with economic growth, service expenditure shares are expected to increase more.

Since the economic reform, new markets have emerged and are growing that result in new consumer issues and complaints. The National Administration of Industry and Commerce and its branches at provincial, city, and county levels serve as major regulatory agencies that enforce laws and regulations, inspect and manage markets, and protect consumer interests. Another major agency that protects consumers is the China Consumer Association (CCA). CCA, a quasi-governmental agency founded in 1984, has more than 3,000 branches at provincial, county, and city levels. According to the National Consumer Protection Law, CCA and its branches have authority to provide consumer information, inspect market goods and services, handle consumer complaints, encourage consumer lawsuits, and expose scandals that hurt consumer interests through the media. CCA publishes a magazine, *China Consumer*, similar to *Consumer Reports* in the United States, which prints exclusively product-testing and other consumer-oriented information and does not accept commercial advertisements. Working with the China Central television station, several other government agencies, and business organizations, CCA cosponsors the annual Consumer Protection Week around March 15 (the International Consumer Rights Day), highlighting a current and important consumption topic, which always has national impacts.

See also Brand-Building Phenomenon; Business Decision Making in the Public and Private Sectors; Commercial Advertising, Policies and Practices of; Economic Policies and Development (1949–Present); Economic Structure.

Bibliography

Liao, Jiuru, "The Goal of Building Up 'Xiao-Kang' Levels Is to Achieve the Living Standard of Average Developed Countries," *Journal of Consumer Economics* 20, no. 1 (2004): 8–9; Lu, Jiarui, ed., *Zhongguo Xiaofei Jiegou Yanjiu* (Research on consumption structures of Chinese peasants) (Hebei, China: Hebei Educational Press, 1999); National Bureau of Statistics of China of the PRC, *China Statistical Yearbook, 2000*, http:// www .stats.gov.cn/, accessed on November 12, 2004; National Bureau, "Statistical Communiqué of the People's Republic of China on the 2002 National Economic and Social Development," http://www.stats.gov.cn/, accessed on November 12, 2004; National Bureau, "Statistical Communiqué of the People's Republic of China on the 2003 National Economic and Social Development," February 26, 2004; Xiao, Jing Jian, "Chinese Consumer Movement," in *Encyclopedia of the Consumer Movement*, ed. Stephen Brobeck (Santa Barbara, CA: ABC-CLIO, 1997); Yin, Shijie, ed., *Zhongguo "Jiuwu" Shiqi Xiaofei Jiegou Fazhan Qushi Yanjiu* (Research on trends of consumption structures in China during "the 9th five-year plan" period) (Hunan, China: People's Press, 1998).

Jingjian Xiao

Corporate Governance

China's corporate governance structure is neither the Japanese-German style, in which banks have significant control over corporations, nor the Anglo-American style, in which stock and managerial markets function to alleviate principal-agent problems in modern corporations. China's enterprise reform, however, is striving to build a modern enterprise system that resembles the Anglo-American mode of corporate governance. The governance structure concerns primarily the ownership and control structure in China's **state-owned** enterprises (SOEs) that have undergone certain type of share-system reform in four aspects: banking, capital market, government intervention, and employment.

Firms and Banks

The relationship between firms and banks prior to economic reforms was not commercial. Banks functioned as policy banks and performed bookkeeping for enterprises. One enterprise banked with a designated bank that kept the account for the firm's working capital. Fixed investments came primarily from fiscal budget appropriations, and other sources, including loans from financial institutions, self-raised funds (retained earnings and funds raised through issuing bonds and shares), and foreign investments, played a supplementary role.

Economic reforms have changed the role of fixed investment in Chinese enterprises. Fund raising has become the largest source of investment, and among the external sources, government budget appropriations have declined over time, but bank loans have increased. State enterprises rely on budget appropriations and bank loans more than other types of firms, and they have the lowest ratio among domestic firms of self-raised funds.

The extent of the supervising role of banks characterizes different types of governance structures. In China, three major factors limit the supervising role of Chinese banks:

1. Banks are prohibited from directly investing in enterprises, unlike in Japan and Germany. Chinese banks supervise their loan performance through the role of creditors (as in the United States).

2. Since many loans have been and continue to be made according to administrative instructions, loan-making decisions can be loan-performance independent.

3. Chinese banks, being SOEs themselves, had little incentive to efficiently supervise the performance of their loans. As a result, China's state banks have been burdened by nonperforming loans. An important part of China's economic reforms is to promote the role of banks as specialized commercial banks with greater supervising power over their debtors.

Firms and the Capital Market

Bond issuance constitutes an insignificant portion (9.4 percent) of capital investment from financial institutions and capital markets. The majority of the value of total bond issuances comes from government bonds and financial bonds, and bond financing of state enterprise investment is a negligible part of total investment.

Investment financing through stock markets officially began in 1992. By the end of January 2003, 1,229 Chinese firms, almost all state enterprises, had become publicly listed stock companies. Chinese listed company shares are divided into the following by types of investors:

1. Nontradable state shares, held by central and local governments represented by local financial bureaus, state asset management companies, or investment companies.

2. Nontradable legal person shares, held by domestic institutions, such as industrial enterprises, securities companies, trust and investment companies, foundations and funds, banks, construction and real-estate development companies, transportation and power companies, and technology and research institutes. Almost all the largest legal person shareholders are industrial SOEs; thus the state is directly or indirectly in control of listed companies.

3. Tradable A, B, and H shares, held by individuals and institutions.

4. Employee shares, held by management and employees of listed companies. Their issuances have been discontinued since 1998.

China's stock markets affect firms insignificantly for the following reasons:

1. Tradable shares comprise only about one-third of all shares among listed firms.

2. Stock capitalization is insignificant relative to GDP, smaller than in many developing countries, such as Indonesia, Thailand, and Mexico.

3. Stock markets signal limited information to investors because of non-standard accounting practices of firms and the general lack of policy transparency by the government and firms alike.

4. The state has remained the majority shareholder (not necessarily of the tradable shares) of most listed firms, which makes political interference more likely and thus limits the influence of the stock market on firms' incentive structure.

Firms and the Government

In China, the state, or the government, serves on behalf of the people as the owner, or the principal, and firms' managers are the agents. Before the reforms, firms produced according to quotas and prices set and materials allotted by the government. Appointed by the government, the Party secretary of an SOE would have the highest authority in the firm by being in charge of a firm's ideological matters, and the factory director would be in charge of production matters that were of secondary importance. Salary scales of workers and cadres were set by the government, which took differences in job skills, difficulties, and regional conditions into consideration.

The behaviors of the management had to be politically correct. Because there were few market opportunities for cadres, the principal-agent relationship was simpler and was reflected primarily in cadres' quota fulfillment. Since employees, who were the "masters" of the firm and were given "iron rice bowls" (lifelong employment security), had strong incentives to disobey discipline and to shirk, production plans were often carried out with poor quality, if at all. The government then replaced the top management as a way of exercising the right of the principal. Model cadres and workers were often selected to boost morale and work incentives.

Economic reforms have returned autonomies to firms on what to produce, how to produce, and at what prices to sell their products. Because the macro-economic priority has been switched to economic growth, the central government calls for limiting government interference in enterprises, but local governments and their branches may interfere even more if they are in urgent need of revenue. Top managers are still appointed, especially in large enterprises. The government also sets the maximum salary of the top manager as a certain multiple of that of the lowest-paid worker. The Party secretary, no longer the number one boss, is in charge of human resources and public relations, while the factory director makes major decisions.

The autonomy of the management and the emerging market opportunities have led to a more complex principal-agent relationship. The cadres of SOEs have considerable control over remunerations, in-kind benefits, and dealings that maximize the management's interest at the expense of the state.

Among listed companies, an overwhelming feature is that the state remains the controlling shareholder of either tradable shares or nontradable legal person shares. In extreme cases, the state remains the ultimate controller of listed companies through its ownership of the holding company by default. This structure is also called pyramiding corporate hierarchy. At the bottom of the pyramid lies the listed company, in the middle, the holding company that owns the controlling share, and on the top, the state, which owns 100 percent of the holding company but no share at all of the listed company.

Because of the state's controlling share status, Chinese boards, compared with practices in other market economies, have relatively little decision-making power, while government ministries and securities regulatory authorities enjoy substantial decision-making power. However, the state's shares can also be unattended and the state's interest unrepresented. In fact, piracy of state assets has been a common phenomenon and has become a major problem in the new principal-agent relationship.

Firms and Their Employees

Before reforms, a state enterprise functioned as a small society that provided its employees with housing, medical care, day care, retirement benefits, and an "iron rice bowl." While employees were "masters" of the firm and could not be laid off, fired, or fined, they did not join decision making within the firm. Firms' cadres were administratively superior to the employees, who were subordinates. Though there were too few market opportunities to breed corruption, unequal distribution of in-kind remunerations such as housing existed.

Reforms have made employees contract laborers. They can be laid off, fired, or fined. The "iron rice bowl" has melted. The management that now has more autonomy and greater control of the firm also possesses greater power over employees. There is less democracy within the firm in terms of workers' voices being heard, their involvement in decision making, and the atmosphere of camaraderie. In theory, however, workers still have a number of legal rights to protect their interests. First, collective contracting and negotiations typically govern narrow employee interests related to compensation, firing, social benefits, working conditions, and related issues. Second, **workers' congresses** and **trade unions** have extensive rights to consultation and information regarding production plans, use of public welfare funds, and other matters that could affect employee interests.

Among listed companies, employees can be represented on boards of directors and supervisors, as required by the Company Law. In China, the board of supervisors is a mixture of the German-style supervisory committee and China's traditional concept of employees as masters of enterprises. Employees can also participate in corporate governance in their capacity as owners. Employee ownership, by the regulation of the central government, cannot exceed 2.5 percent of total shares.

China's employee-owned firms are mostly small and medium-sized enterprises that are closely held and have few opportunities for going public. Within the firm, the "three new committees" (the conference of shareholding employees, the board of directors, and the board of supervisors) coexist with the "three old committees" (the workers' congress, the Party committee, and the trade unions), which has resulted in conflicts over the functions of the governing bodies and confusion by shareholders in their perception as owners and employees. The current links between legal labor rights and ownership form thus create a bias in favor of the status quo.

See also Banking and Financial System Reform; Business Decision Making in the Public and Private Sectors; Privately Owned Enterprises (POEs).

Bibliography

Chen, Aimin, "Inertia in Reforming China's State-Owned Enterprises: The Case of Chongqing," *World Development* 26, no. 3 (March 1998): 479–495.

Aimin Chen

Correction System

The Chinese correction system is an integral part of the criminal justice system, which also includes the police and the courts. The main mission of the correction system is to enforce the legal punishment imposed on convicted criminals by courts and to reform the criminals.

Philosophies of punishment in the Chinese correction system include retribution, deterrence, rehabilitation, and reform. The Chinese have unique understandings of the terms "correction," "rehabilitation," and "reform." Correction refers to correcting small errors in people's daily lives (e.g., a technical error). It has little to do with changing criminals' mind-set. Rehabilitation refers to rectification and reintegration and is extensively used by the Chinese in dealing with minor offenders (e.g., hooligans) through informal social control. Reform refers to education and remolding of the offender by breaking offenders' past psychological patterns and instilling positive social factors, mainly through mandatory legal measures. The ultimate goal of punishment is reform and reintegration. In extreme cases, the death penalty is used as the final measure of deterrence.

In a broad sense, the Chinese correction system has two interrelated parts. One is an informal correction system that relies on extralegal measures. The other is the formal correction system, which derives its authority from criminal law and the legal system. Programs that embody the informal social control system in areas of corrections include (1) social assistance and education, (2) work-study schools for juvenile delinquents, and (3) reeducation through labor for adult deviants.

Social assistance and education are offered to deviants and minor offenders through informal social control agencies such as neighborhood committees, schools, and the workplace. When the first sign of deviant behavior emerges, the community is expected to respond with education, mediation, and intervention.

Work-study schools are administered by the Bureau of Education and are designed to detain and educate troubled urban youths. These procedures are often administered in consultation with parents, teachers, neighborhood committee members, and local police institutions. Students in these facilities receive normal academic education in addition to vocational training and moral and political education.

Reeducation through labor is one of the best-known and most controversial programs in the Chinese correction system. It is controversial because individuals can be placed in a labor camp for a relatively lengthy period of time (typically from one to three years) without having a legal hearing. It is a mandatory administrative procedure involving offenders who exhibited antisocial behaviors and/or committed minor offenses. The decision of committing an individual to a labor camp is made by a committee composed of representatives from

In this 1981 photo, prisoners in Beijing's Municipal Prison take a break from their work; they are not allowed to talk to one another during the break. © Dean Conger/Corbis.

the civil affairs, local police, and labor departments. Individuals in this type of programs are required to engage in physical labor and receive political and academic education. The purpose of reeducation through labor is to educate as well as rehabilitate deviants and to give them a chance to abandon their criminal behavior.

The available forms of legal punishment, as stipulated in the 1979 and 1997 Criminal Law, include control, short-term detention, fixed-term imprisonment, life imprisonment, and the death penalty. Supplementary punishments include fines, deprivation of political rights, and confiscation of property.

Control is the least severe form of punishment. It is similar to probation in the United States. Control is typically applied to first-time offenders and offenders who committed minor offenses. Offenders are placed in the community under surveillance while being allowed to engage in routine activities such as living with family and going to work.

Short-term detention is a jail sentence with a minimum of fifteen days and a maximum of six months of incarceration. Offenders are allowed to visit home once or twice per month. The public security agencies with the assistance of local communities are in charge of carrying out these minor punishments.

For fixed-term incarceration, separate institutions are designed for juveniles and adult offenders. The juvenile reformatory primarily houses young (between fourteen and eighteen years old) and serious offenders who have committed offenses such as assault, rape, and robbery. It also takes delinquents who recidivate after work-study schools. Intensive academic curricula, moral education, and vocational training characterize the routine for young inmates in these facilities.

Reform-through-labor camps are designed to house nonfelony adult convicts or serious criminals who have served their prison term for a period of time and are deemed to be at low risk by correction officials. Supervised by the judicial system, the camp is run like a military base except that convicts are required to engage in manual labor as the primary activity each day. Depending on the location and nature of the reform-through-labor camps, physical labor can consist of one or a combination of the following tasks: farming, manufacturing production, construction, and service work. While the primary goal of these labor camps is education and reform, daily activities mostly revolve around manual labor.

Prisons, which incarcerate the most violent and dangerous criminals, are typically located in remote areas. Aside from performing simple labor, inmates are required to participate in educational programs and "thought reform." Most prisons provide academic education up to the level of high school. Many prisons offer vocational training, and some offer college-level courses by correspondence and **television**. Besides academic training, political education such as criticism and self-criticism, study of current political affairs and important speeches by political leaders, and group discussions are regarded as essential in the reform of offenders. Another characteristic involves reform through labor, because the Chinese believe that labor is instrumental and critical in altering one's mind-set and habits. Labor is believed to help inmates develop good work habits and cooperative spirits, master essential vocational skills, cultivate their mind, and keep them busy.

Due to the nonpublic nature of the prison system in China, the exact number and the distribution of prisons and inmates are unknown. On the basis of incomplete data published by *Law Yearbook of China (1989–1996)*, it appears that both the number of labor camps and the number of incarcerated people are on the rise. For example, in 1988, there were 674 reform-through-labor camps incarcerating 1,052,743 convicts and 224 education-through-labor camps housing 152,939 individuals. In 1995, the number increased to 703 reform-through-labor camps and 283 education-through-labor camps housing 1,320,947 and 206,888 individuals, respectively. The increasing number of these correction facilities over time is consistent with the rising crime rates in China. During the same years, 1988 and 1995, for example, the total numbers of criminal cases established by the public security bureau were 827,594 and 1,690,407, respectively.

It has been widely reported that the Chinese correction system is highly effective, with an extremely low recidivism rate at an estimated 8 percent each year. More detailed data, such as profiles of recidivists and nonrecidivists, are not available. Although there is a lack of independent sources to verify the accuracy of the recidivism rate revealed by the official account, aftercare programs have historically been emphasized in the continuous reform of the criminal. Probationers and parolees were constantly supervised and assisted (e.g., in finding a job) in the community to prevent them from slipping into the criminal subculture.

The death penalty is reserved for the most serious and dangerous offenders. The 1997 Criminal Law stipulates sixty-eight offense types (e.g., graft, bribery, drug trafficking, and theft) that are subject to the death penalty. The final review authority of the death sentence lies in the Supreme People's Court, unless the Supreme People's Court authorizes provincial high courts to review certain types of cases (e.g., murder, robbery, and the bombing of public places). Execution is carried out soon (typically within a month) after the final review. As stipulated in the 1996 Criminal Procedure Law, executions are publicly announced, but not shown to the public. The methods of execution include shooting and lethal injection.

Under the death penalty sentence, offenders who are deemed to be less than extremely dangerous and/or to have shown good attitude may be given the death penalty with a two-year suspension of execution. After two years, the sentence is commuted to life imprisonment if an offender did not commit an intentional crime and to fifteen to twenty years if an offender had major meritorious service. If an offender committed an intentional crime, the death penalty will be carried out after the review of the Supreme Court.

The Chinese criminal law also stipulates that the death sentence not be applied to individuals under eighteen years old and pregnant women. In capital cases, defendants must have legal representation. If they cannot afford an attorney, an attorney should be appointed for them unless offenders choose to waive their rights.

See also Anticorruption Literature and Television Dramas; Corruption and Fraud, Control of; Crime Prevention; Human Rights Debate.

Bibliography

Law Yearbook of China (various issues) (Beijing: Law Yearbook of China Publishing House, 1987–2003); Luo, Wei, *The Amended Criminal Procedure Law and the Criminal Court Rules of the People's Republic of China* (Buffalo, NY: William S. Hein & Co., 2000); "The 1997 Criminal Law of the People's Republic of China," *Law Yearbook of China* (various issues) (Beijing: Law Yearbook of China Publishing House, 1998); Troyer, R. J., J. P. Clark, and D. J. Rojek, *Social Control in the People's Republic of China* (New York: Praeger, 1989).

Hong Lu

Corruption and Fraud, Control of

Many people consider official corruption in China a systemic crime caused by the one-party system. They think that this is true because "power will intoxicate the best hearts, as wine the strongest heads." "No man is wise enough nor good enough to be trusted with unlimited power," as the saying goes. In China, the Chinese Communist Party is the leading party and controls everything. Corruption is generated from many sources. Two principle sources are greed coupled with abundant opportunities for profit raking and a weak legal environment replete with outdated rules and regulations. It is common to find corruption in all social systems during times of a social transition, because the period a country is under significant changes in economic restructuring and social status is also the time for corruption to grow in officialdom, as in Great Britain in the eighteenth century, the United States in the nineteenth century, and Singapore and Hong Kong in the twentieth century. The United Nations reported after investigation in 109 countries that a country with average personal income between $265 and $1,000 is at its highest social upheaval and unstable stage. This is the time for the biggest changes in social economy and ideological formation.

Since 1982, the first year China fought with crime in the economic sector, China has investigated more than 1 million cases and closed more than 20,000 cases related to leaders at county or division levels. Cases related to officials at city or department levels amounted to more than 1,000, and more than 20 cases involved officials at provincial or state ministry levels. From 1992 to 2002, more than 1.5 million Communist Party members, including ones at state, provincial, municipal, and city levels, were investigated, sentenced, fined, or jailed by the Discipline Commission, the Investigation Bureau, and courts. Some high-ranking officials were sentenced to jail or even the death penalty, and some significant cases were disclosed to the public, with the criminals being punished severely. In July 1998, Chen Xitong, who had been a member of the Politburo and mayor of Beijing, was sentenced to sixteen years in prison for official corruption. In February 2000, Hu Changqing, who was the vice governor of Jiangxi Province, was sentenced to death and was executed in March the same year. Wang Leyi, a former deputy director general of China Customs, was sentenced to twelve years in prison. China has shown its people that the central government has been making continuous efforts to control official corruption. The recent tragedy of severe acute respiratory syndrome (SARS) called much more attention to the social and political problems caused by officialdom. The quick spread of SARS disclosed the inefficiency of the Chinese style of officialdom, hurt badly the people's confidence in the government, and ruined China's international reputation as a country responsible for its people. The lesson learned is that it will only cause panic and distrust among the people if the government tries to hide the truth.

Other forms of official corruption among government officials and conglomerate enterprises and financial institutions also exist that have caused severe damage to the Chinese economy and to people's confidence in dealing with businesses in China. Smuggling and fraud raise the question of social honesty in China. The central government has also made serious efforts to totally destroy such kinds of economic or financial kingdoms. For example, the Yuanhua smuggling case in Fujian Province caught the attention of the central government, which had to send several thousand people to investigate and completely destroy the network Yuanhua Company had operated for years. Other ill-famed cases were Yinguanxia and Lantian, two companies that cheated shareholders with false information and carried on insider trading to skim shareholders' money for their own benefit.

There are several characteristics of the way the government controls official corruption and fraud in China. First, the leadership of the Communist Party remains a crucial force of guidance in fighting corruption; second, the government adopts the traditional approach of fighting a case-by-case war, with emphasis on those cases that have the worst influence; third, the government is seeking people's participation in monitoring state officials; and fourth, new laws are being established to limit officials' powers.

China has a feudal history of several thousand years. Feudalistic thoughts have been rooted in the society and the Party bodies. These thoughts legitimize the absolute power of officials. The economic reforms have opened people's minds and enlightened them about Western systems. China is in an early stage of social transition during which many weaknesses have been revealed. The battle against official corruption and fraud in China is being implemented under a special mix of social conflicts and contradictions inherited from the past. But as time goes by, and following the examples of Western developed countries, China will finally find its own most effective way to control official corruption and fraud.

See also Anticorruption Literature and Television Dramas; Correction System; Crime Prevention.

Bibliography

The Name List of Government Officials Sentenced in Five Years (Beijing: Beijing Youth Daily, 2003); *The Report of Investigation on Anti-Corruption in China* (Beijing: Legal System Daily, 2002).

Mei Zhou and Xiaoxiao Li

Credit Spending, Development of

Consumer credit spending in China has experienced two major periods, thirty years (1949–1978) before the economic reform and more than twenty years (1979–2001) after the reform. The earlier years of the People's Republic of China (PRC) were a difficult time for the Chinese economy, and the people's standard of living was very low. In the mid-1950s, socialist reform activities were conducted in urban areas and **people's communes** were created in rural areas, which constituted the foundations of the centrally planned economic system in China. Under a planned economy, financial institutions offered few consumer credit services. Most consumer goods were in short supply and rationed by the government. Households had neither a channel to get consumer credit nor an ability to repay the credit. Thus there was almost no consumer credit in this time period.

Because of the economic reform and opening to the outside world in the late 1970s, the planned economy was gradually transformed into the market economy, and the consumption level of Chinese households rose rapidly. More and more consumer goods were supplied, and various consumption peaks focusing on certain consumer goods appeared continuously. But real consumer credit appeared in the form of installment payments for housing loans in the late 1980s. Because of the constraints of economic development level, market conditions, and consumer values, consumer credit was developed slowly. By the end of 1997, consumer credit in China accounted for only 17.2 billion RMB yuan.

Since 1998, the situation has changed, and consumer credit has developed rapidly. Consumer credit was 47.2 billion yuan in 1998 and 139.7 billion yuan in 1999. In March 1999, the central bank issued "A Guide to the Personal Consumer Credit" and specified policies to promote consumer credit. The categories allowed for consumer credit were then expanded from housing, cars, and durable goods to housing decorations, furniture, tourism, education, medical care, and other items. Although consumer credit has developed rapidly since 1998, its share of GDP is still very low.

By the end of 2000, the consumer credit balance was 426.5 billion yuan, which was twenty-four times that at the end of 1997. By the end of 2001, the consumer credit balance was 699 billion yuan, which was forty times that in 1997. The share of consumer credit in total credit also rose, from 0.3 percent to 6 percent. The credit instruments include credit cards, deposit mortgages, and state treasury bonds mortgages. The financial institutions issuing consumer credit expanded from state-owned commercial banks to all commercial banks.

According to data of the China People's Bank, more than half of Chinese households have no desire to use consumer credit. The survey shows that middle- and high-income households have higher propensities to apply for consumer credit. For households with a monthly income of more than 1,000 yuan, 60 percent want to apply for consumer credit. For households with monthly income between 300 and 1,000 yuan, 45 percent would like to do so. Among households that apply for consumer credit, the percentage of those who need consumer credit for a housing purchase is the largest (38.8 percent), and the second and third largest are for education (19.2 percent) and for durable goods purchases (11 percent). The percentages of those who need consumer credit for car purchases, house decoration, tourism, and weddings are under 10 percent for each.

Housing Consumer Credit

In recent years, with the reform of China's housing system, the personal housing credit has become a key field for the development of consumer credit. To support and stimulate consumers to buy houses, the government has taken many measures to promote housing credit, such as supporting construction of economical houses, offering favorable interest rates for housing credit, and so on. "The Report on the Development of Consumer Credit in China" shows that in 1998, 1999, and 2000, the personal housing credit balances were 42.7 billion, 135.8 billion, and 337.7 billion yuan, respectively. In 2001, the figure reached 559.8 billion yuan, which was about forty-two times that in 1997 and accounted for about 80 percent of the consumer credit balance.

Educational Loans

In May 1999, China People's Bank, the China Education Department, and the China Finance Department issued the Regulation on Management of Educational Loans. In August 2000, "Circular of State Council on Forwarding China People's Bank's 'Additional Suggestions for the Management of Educational Loans' " and "Measures of China People's Bank on the Management of Educational Loans" were issued. These policies promoted the operation of educational loans. The educational loans include state and general educational loans. From 1999 to 2001, state educational loans provided by the Chinese government accounted for 1.44 billion yuan that supported 139,000 college students. In 2001, the educational loan balance reached 3.2 billion yuan, among which state educational loans were 1.3 billion yuan and general educational loans were 1.9 billion yuan.

Car Consumer Credit

China Construction Bank is the first bank to offer consumer credit for car purchases. In May 1996, the bank issued a circular on Jetta car credit that started consumer credit for car purchases in China. In 1998, China People's Bank issued "Measures on Management of Car Credit," which allows four state-owned banks to offer consumer credit for car purchases. Car credit has developed at a relatively steady speed. By the end of 2001, the car consumer credit balance was 43.6 billion yuan, 6 percent of the consumer credit balance. A survey in cities such as Beijing, Guangzhou, and Shanghai showed that 70 percent of households had a desire to purchase a car in three to eight years. Considering the explosion of car consumption and production in 2002 and 2003 and the huge potential car market, the growth of car consumer credit is relatively low, which will restrain the continuing and rapid development of car consumption in China.

Durable Goods Consumer Credit

Consumer credit for durable goods started in China relatively earlier than other types of credits, but it is not fully developed. China Industrial and Commercial Bank started personal consumer credit for durable goods in Shanghai in 1993. In April 1999, the bank decided to expand the credit to forty-one cities in China. Consumer credit for durable goods is often jointly offered by both banks and sellers. Major products that use the credit are household appliances, furniture, instruments, and the like. It is also often offered in the form of cutting prices by banks and sellers, a move that is welcomed by consumers. The demand for household appliances has already declined in urban areas, but it is in the development period in rural areas. In 1998, the rates of possession of ten major household appliances in urban and rural households were 52.08 percent and 7.47 percent, respectively, which suggests the considerable development potential of consumer credit for household appliances in rural areas.

According to the China People's Bank, reasons for the rise and development of consumer credit in China are as follows: (1) The increasing consumption demand is the microeconomic base. With the rise of household income and consumption level and the upgrade of consumption structures, meeting housing, education, and other high-level consumption needs becomes important for consumers. Their current income cannot meet such needs, so they need consumer credit. (2) The occurrence of a buyer's market is the macroeconomic base. Since the mid-1990s, China's market has changed from a seller's market to a buyer's market, which has resulted in the problem of aggregate demand shortfall. Since 1998, the Chinese government has taken several macroeconomic measures to develop consumer credit so as to expand household consumption demand and promote economic growth, which is an important component of government policies to stimulate domestic aggregate demand. (3) The reform of consumption systems has encouraged the development of consumer credit. In recent years, China reformed consumption systems in housing, medical care, and education. (4) The central bank has adjusted its credit policy for developing consumer credit. For a long time, due to the constraint of the economic system and shortage of funds, the central bank's credit-control policies and the credit fund focused on investments. To adjust for the changes in economic and financial environments, the credit policy changed from inflation control to deflation control, which relies on consumer credit to adjust consumption demand. From 1998 to 2001, the central bank issued eighteen consumer credit policies that allow all commercial banks to offer consumer credit services under the condition of preventing credit risk. (5) The change of management mechanism and the optimization of credit structure in commercial banks are internal reasons for developing consumer credit. Consumer credit became a natural choice for commercial banks to adjust their credit structure, avoid credit risk, and search for new sources of profit growth.

See also Banking and Financial System Reform; Consumption Patterns and Statistics of Living Conditions.

Bibliography

China People's Bank, "Zhongguo Xiaofei Xindai Fazhan Baogao" (Report of consumer credit development in China), *Jingrong Shibao* (Finance times), February 10, 2002; He, Biqing, "Zhongguo Xiaofei Xindai Yu Jiaoyu Chanye de Ke Chixu Fazhan" (The sustainable development of Chinese consumer credit and educational industry), *Yue Gang Ao Jiage* (Pricing news of Guangdong, Hong Kong, and Macao), August 20, 2000.

Qingfei Yin and Jingjian Xiao

Crime Prevention

Crime prevention in China is typically represented by the "comprehensive treatment of public security system." The goal of the comprehensive treatment of public security system is to maintain public order and reduce crime. Its impetus is the Chinese belief that crime is not an individual behavioral problem, but rather grows out of larger social conditions, and crime prevention is not merely a task of the criminal justice system, but a responsibility for all members of the society. Its basic principle has two facets, "strike" and "prevention," with crime prevention taking precedence. Its strategies include resort to both legal and extralegal mechanisms and the involvement of multiple governmental agencies and grassroots organizations, under the leadership of the Communist Party, in the control and prevention of crime.

Before the economic reforms started in 1978, the comprehensive treatment of public security system primarily relied on grassroots organizations such as residents' committees in urban neighborhoods and production brigades in rural areas. These grassroots organizations classified and grouped households of urban neighborhoods and rural communes into teams. These teams of varying sizes from fifteen to forty households were charged with responsibilities of dispute resolution and neighborhood watch. Mediation became the primary mechanism in dispute resolution and violence containment at the grassroots level. This form of popular participation was effective in preventing crime in China primarily because of the strict control of population movement and the close-knit community in the earlier decades of socialist construction in China.

Since the 1980s, the system of comprehensive treatment of public security has become more encompassing. While the basic principle remains intact, new strategies have expanded. The current focus of the comprehensive treatment of public security system is on the following four aspects: (1) management of the transient population; (2) crime prevention through environmental design and management of "hot spots"; (3) "strike-hard" campaigns; and (4) legal education of the general public and "help and education" of ex-offenders.

Since the reforms started in 1978, one of the major challenges for crime prevention is the floating population, which is increasingly blamed for social disorder and crime in their host areas. The Office of the Central Comprehensive Treatment of Public Security has summarized four major strategies in the management of this special population in recent years. The first is the establishment of management agencies led by local government officials. By 1997, with the exception of Zhejiang, Hainan, Tibet, and Qinghai Provinces, all twenty-seven other provinces and autonomous municipalities had established such mechanisms. In provinces where the transient population is dense, local management offices and service centers are also established. For example, in Jiangsu Province, 20,000 such offices have been set up. The second is to consolidate macromanagement of the population movement by creating jobs in township enterprises to absorb peasants nearby. In Sichuan Province alone in 1994, township enterprises employed 11.5 million peasants. The third strategy involves "card" management. In Shanghai, by 1994, 76.5 percent of the transient population was issued the temporary resident card, 71 percent received the health inspection card, and 90 percent of renters registered with the authorities. Last, the management strategy focuses on order maintenance in areas with a high concentration of the transient population. For example, 60,000 transients were forcibly sent back to their hometown due to their lack of identification, residency, and employment in Guangdong Province in 1994.

Urban neighborhoods have increasingly become targets of property crimes such as theft and burglary. Enterprises, especially financial institutions, have also become vulnerable to theft. To prevent these crimes, strategies of reinforcing residential dwellings have been adopted in urban areas across the country. The most representative are six projects developed in Shanghai, which include the "iron door project," the "enclosure wall project," the "lighting project," the "bicycle parking project," the "consolidated safe box project," and the "security alert project." All of these measures were designed to harden potential crime targets and allow more effective responses to crime.

The "strike-hard" campaigns were initiated in the early 1980s and continued into the 1990s. Each wave of strike-hard campaigns focused on different types of crimes depending on the pressing social issues of the time. The common objectives of strike-hard campaigns were to suppress criminal elements through swift and severe enforcement of law and punishment. In 2003, the campaigns focused on striking violent crimes, on property offenses, organized crime, and economic and corruption offenses and prohibiting narcotics, sex offenses, and gambling. For example, in Shanxi Province, to eliminate narcotic drugs, the provincial government took a series of actions. First, the government promulgated the "notice on prohibiting illegally planted poppies" in 1997. In 1998, it organized more than 60,000 cadres to clear 6,000 acres of land, overturn 1,680 acres of land that had plantings of illegal poppies, and destroy 242,813 illegal plants. Meanwhile, law enforcement agencies investigated 7,126 drug-related cases, resulting in the arrest of 9,919 criminals and cracking down on 603 organized criminal groups. In collaboration with law enforcement, the correction system committed 2,179 drug addicts to forced drug rehabilitation centers for treatment and 369 drug addicts to rehabilitation-through-labor camps. In the same year, to consolidate the progress on drug prohibition, the provincial drug-prohibition working group promulgated an implementation plan on 100 days of drug prohibition campaigns, aiming at education, prevention, and treatment of drug addiction through grassroots organizations. By the end of the 100 days of campaigns, a total of 2,400 slogans and 4.3 million copies of drug-education-related materials were disseminated to the public, and 12,219 drug addicts were reported by citizens and committed to rehabilitation centers.

The Legal Education Campaign has always been one of the major strategies for crime prevention. Dissemination of legal knowledge takes a variety of forms, such as through news media, public bulletin boards, town hall meetings, exhibitions, and pamphlets. More recently, legal education has focused on the transient population and ex-offenders.

Crime prevention has increasingly met challenges since the 1980s because of the changing political, economic, and social structures in China. In particular, economic development has precipitated a host of changes in interpersonal relationships, rights consciousness, conceptions of the legal system, social control, and opportunities for crime. Crime rates have skyrocketed in the past two decades, particularly those of newly emerging offenses such as prostitution, drug trafficking, organized crime, and corruption.

Nevertheless, the Chinese comprehensive treatment of public security system has been proven to be one of the most effective crime-prevention systems in the world, as evidenced by its low crime and recidivism rates when compared with other developed nations. In addition, China has actively participated in and contributed to international initiatives by the United Nations on crime prevention and control since 1980.

See also Anticorruption Literature and Television Dramas; Correction System; Corruption and Fraud, Control of; Illegal Drugs, Control of.

Bibliography

Law Yearbook of China (various issues) (Beijing: Law Yearbook of China Publishing House, 1987-2003); *Yearbook of Comprehensive Treatment of Public Security in China, 1997-1998* (Beijing: Law Press China, 2000).

Hong Lu

Cultural Revolution

See Great Cultural Revolution (1966-1976).

Currency

See Renminbi (RMB).

D

Death Rates

See Disease and Death Rates.

Debt

See Domestic Government Debt; Foreign Debt.

Democratic Parties, Political Functions of

The People's Republic of China (PRC) recognizes eight "democratic parties," each of which has a history of alliance with the Chinese Communist Party (CCP) in opposition to the one-party rule of the Kuomintang (KMT) Nationalist regime. Historically these democratic parties constituted a major part of the "Third Forces" that sought to provide alternatives to the political platforms of both the KMT and the CCP. They were born out of opposition politics at a time when the KMT was the ruling party. It was the KMT's tactics of intimidation, persecution, and assassination that continually drove democratic oppositionists into alliance with the Communists.

The eight democratic parties were founded between the 1920s and the 1940s. One of them, the Revolutionary Committee of the Kuomintang, was formed in 1948, but its roots go back to 1927, when Jiang Jieshi (Chiang Kai-shek) (1886–1975) and Wang Jingwei (1883–1944) ousted pro-Communist elements from the Kuomintang. The purged opponents regrouped to set up the Comrades' Union of the Three People's Principles, the China Association of the Kuomintang for Promoting Democracy, and other groups. In November 1948, these organizations were consolidated into one party, the Revolutionary Committee of the Kuomintang.

The China Democratic League evolved from the China Democratic League of Political Bodies that was founded in 1941 and comprised six or more disparate entities, including the China Youth Party, the Chinese People's National Salvation Association, and others. In September 1944, this umbrella organization changed its name to China Democratic League. The close ties of the Democratic League with the CCP prompted the Kuomintang to assassinate its leaders in 1946 and declare it an illegal organization in 1947. Most of the league's leadership withdrew to Hong Kong, where they expressed willingness to enter into an alliance with the Communists.

The Chinese Peasants' and Workers' Democratic Party was established by a small group of defectors from the Kuomintang in 1927. First known as the Provisional Acting Committee of the Kuomintang, it found its leader in Deng Yanda (1895–1931), who favored military opposition and lived in self-imposed exile in Europe. A few months after his return in 1930, Deng was executed by the Nationalists. The party changed its name to the Acting Committee for the Liberation of the Chinese Nation in 1935 and to its current name in 1947.

Established in December 1945, the China Democratic National Construction Association was an outgrowth of the Vocational School Group founded by Huang Yanpei (1878–1965) in 1917. This party first operated within the Democratic League, aspiring to broker peace between the Communists and the Nationalists. However, the Kuomintang drove it underground in 1947. Upon reemergence, it became independent of the Democratic League and focused on working with the business and professional education communities. The other "democratic" parties are the China Association for Promoting Democracy, which was formed in December 1945 with a platform demanding an immediate cessation of the civil war and the establishment of a coalition government, the Jiu San Society, which was named after its founding date (September 3) in 1945 and was composed of politically active engineers, scientists, and scholars, the Chih Kung Party, which was founded by the American Hong Men Society in 1931 and was devoted to mobilizing overseas support for the democratization of Chinese politics, and the Taiwan Democratic Autonomy League, which was formed in 1947 by pro-Communist elements who had survived the Kuomintang's suppression of the February 28 Uprising and escaped to Hong Kong.

The expression "democratic parties" or *minzu dangpai* was first coined by the CCP in a 1948 May Day slogan that urged "all democratic parties, people's organizations, and public personages" to convene a Chinese People's Political Consultative Conference (CPPCC) for the formation of a New China. The democratic parties had been a rallying point for the Chinese who were opposed to dictatorship. Their participation in the 1949 convocation of the CPPCC was instrumental in legitimizing the new regime as one blessed with the mandate of popular support and the vision of a "New Democracy" that stressed the importance of the United Front. All this was included in the CPPCC's "Common Program" that served as a provisional constitution until 1954, when the **National People's Congress** was convened and took over the power of legislation. The CPPCC remained a symbol of the United Front, but it was reduced to a forum for the propagation of Party lines.

The United Front had a honeymoon period during which members of the democratic parties served as ministers and high-ranking functionaries in the coalition government or as vice chairmen on committees of the National People's Congress, but they soon ran into a wall of institutionalized distrust. Important decisions were made without consulting them, information was classified and rendered available only to Party members, their subordinates looked up to Communist bosses for orders, and they themselves did not have the authority to get jobs done. Their number dropped sharply through subseqent purges.

The coalition, however, was not an ad hoc move. As early as 1939, **Mao Zedong** outlined the class base of a broad united front for the Chinese revolution. Basically, the rural and urban poor were allies of the revolution, whereas the landlords were its foes. Between the two extremes was the bourgeoisie. Mao distinguished three strata within it: the compradore bourgeoisie, which was identified with the enemy, and the national and petty bourgeoisie, which were both identified with the allies. But while intellectuals belonged in the petty bourgeoisie, they were "two-faced," as were the national bourgeoisie, a marginal member of the United Front. It followed that they had to overcome their liberal doubts about the revolution before they could serve the people.

What ensued were drives along two lines. One was to put the democratic parties under the control of the CCP so that they were devoid of financial, organizational, and political independence. Some of the democratic parties were run by people who also had Communist Party membership. The other was to remold members of the democratic parties ideologically through the process of "criticism and self-criticism" so that they would shed their liberal ways of thinking. But would the democratic parties not outlive their usefulness once they became copycats of the CCP? In February 1957, Mao responded with the famous line "long-term coexistence and mutual supervision" to affirm that the democratic parties had a role to play under the new historical conditions.

The democratic parties were found to have propaganda value. Their existence served to sustain the argument that the United Front was alive in the politics and government of China, with democracy being practiced in the guise of dictatorship ("people's democratic dictatorship"). Besides, owing to their links with overseas Chinese and people in Taiwan, the democratic parties were seen as an asset when it came to building an international coalition and seeking national reunification. Finally, with their expertise and talent, the democratic parties were in a position to contribute to the promotion of modernization in China.

Mao reiterated the notion of coexistence after the 1957 Anti-Rightist Campaign. The campaign started with Mao calling on intellectuals to speak freely in assisting the rectification of the CCP and ended with the Communists cracking down on outspoken intellectuals as counterrevolutionary "rightists." In most cases, intellectuals had exercised "loyal opposition" with poignant but sincere criticisms, but the Maoist regime viewed this as proof of their "two-faced" audacity. The Anti-Rightist Campaign effectively gagged loyal opposition from the democratic parties and browbeat its members into acceptance of "conformity politics" for the next two decades. The eclipse of the democratic parties continued throughout the **Great Cultural Revolution**.

During the era of economic reforms that began around 1978, the democratic parties seem to have taken on a new life. They are recognized as "comrades-in-arms" of the working class, more respect is accorded to their organizational independence from the CCP, their consultative and supervisory roles in government are better appreciated, the attitude toward their criticisms is more graceful, and members of the democratic parties are allowed to remain patriots rather than forced to become socialists. The services of the democratic parties have made themselves felt in education, consultation, and areas that promote economic development. Their membership has reached a historical high.

But there is no multiparty government. The democratic parties are expected to operate within a "multiparty cooperation system under the leadership of the Communist Party." Indeed, the democratic parties appear to have steered clear of involvement in openly demanding political reforms. The question naturally arises: Are they still relevant to the cause of democracy in China? Obviously not for people who think that they have lost their soul as liberals. Others still see hope in the democratic parties' ability to pave the way for brokering a workable version of democracy that uniquely accommodates the fundamental values of Chinese culture.

See also Administrative Structure of Government; New Party (NP) (Taiwan); Taiwan, Development of Democracy in.

Bibliography

Jeans, Roger B., ed., *Roads Not Taken* (Boulder, CO: Westview Press, 1992); Mao, Zedong, *Selected Works of Mao Tsetung*, vol. 2 (pp. 305–334) and vol. 5 (pp. 384–421) (Beijing: Foreign Languages Press, 1965, 1977); Seymour, James D., *China's Satellite Parties* (Armonk, NY: M. E. Sharpe, 1987).

Zhiming Zhao

Demographic Transition

See Unfinished Demographic Transition.

Deng Xiaoping (1904–1997), Politics of

Deng Xiaoping, the chief leader of the People's Republic of China in the last two decades of the twentieth century, was born to a relatively prosperous farm family in Guangan County, Sichuan Province, in southwestern China. In 1920, at age sixteen, he left China for France, where he spent the next five years, joining the Chinese Communist Party (CCP) there in 1922. Following his period in France, he spent nearly a year in Russia at a Communist training school and returned to China in 1926. By 1929, he had become the Party's leader in Guangxi Province. Deng participated in the Long March (1934–1935) and assumed the position of general secretary of the CCP three times in his life—in 1927, 1934, and 1954. For about twenty years before 1951, Deng served as one of the chief commanders of the People's Liberation Army. From the early 1950s until 1966, Deng remained one of the nation's top seven leaders. During **Mao Zedong**'s **Great Cultural Revolution (1966–1976)**, Deng was politically purged twice, but both times he survived. To cap his career, Deng served as the head, though not

After coming to power in the late 1970s, Deng Xiaoping instituted a host of economic and political reforms. © Bettmann/Corbis.

always with a formal title, of both the CCP and the Chinese government from 1978 to about 1995.

Deng's main political accomplishment was that, following Mao's death, he ended the Cultural Revolution and led China from a period of political turmoil to one of economic development. Upon taking power in 1978, Deng launched a "Movement of Ideological Liberation," pushing a line of "reform and open" (to reform the economy and to open the country up to the external world) while seeking to maintain a stable political and social order. The economic results were impressive. In Deng's era, China's economy quadrupled in total output, and living standards improved significantly. Deng's reform strategy contrasted starkly with that of Mikhail Gorbachev's Soviet Union by focusing primarily on liberal economic reform while discouraging and even stifling political reform. This approach has been followed consistently since Deng's death by his successors, Jiang Zemin and now Hu Jintao.

Deng's style of leadership can be seen in his handling of four political challenges. First, when Lin Biao died in 1971, which shocked Mao, who encouraged Lin's leftist radicalism, Deng sought to regain Mao's trust after having been purged in 1966 during the early Cultural Revolution period. Deng wrote Mao two apologetic letters expressing regret about his own "wrongdoings" prior to the Cultural Revolution. Yet after coming to power in 1974, Deng reversed course, directly "corrected" all of Mao's policies, and was hence purged by Mao once again in 1975. Second, while Deng denounced Mao's Cultural Revolution in 1978 after he returned to power for the third time in his life, he also proclaimed that China would still hold high the banner of Mao's thought. Third, in June 1989, he ruthlessly repressed the pro-Western democratic movement at Tiananmen Square in Beijing, but then continued to push and even intensified the "reform and open" policy that had helped produce the movement in the first place. Finally, in 1992, Deng silenced an inner Party debate over socialism versus capitalism and accelerated market-oriented reforms. At the same time, he insisted on the need for the CCP's exclusive leadership and for Marxism as the official ideology. All of these instances demonstrate Deng's skill in keeping a balance between accepting and rejecting, between continuing and reforming.

Deng summarized the political guideline of his twenty-year leadership as "one focus, two points": the focus is economic construction, and the two points are "reform and open" and **Four Cardinal Principles** (socialism, people's democratic dictatorship, CCP leadership, and Marxism/Mao Zedong Thought). These three elements, in Deng's simplified expression, became "development, reform, and stability." Although he emphasized all three elements at different times, Deng insisted that development was the "highest principle."

Deng believed that before 1978, the CCP's leadership had suffered for more than two decades from a radical leftist or idealist approach. He modified the CCP's strategic calculation concerning future world war, deeming it unlikely, and in the process disarmed 1 million troops in 1985. He also denied the need for any continuous domestic class struggle, the underlying impulse of Mao's Cultural Revolution. Instead, Deng called for a "returning" to the pragmatic methodology of the CCP's leadership, which he intentionally labeled "Mao's own," to replace the reigning Marxist dogmatism. He established an ambitious long-term economic goal: to quadruple the size of China's GDP by 2000 and then quadruple it once again by 2030 or 2050. He launched agricultural reform ahead of industrial reform, then later established four "special economic zones" that were open to foreign investment. (These were subsequently extended to fourteen coastal cities.) Deng sought a more market-oriented economy, though he refused to completely privatize the economy. His concept of "socialist market economy" reserves a central core of state-owned firms, whereas the rest should be all subject to market forces. Deng let the **Open Door policy** and the economic reform policy complement each other and emphasized a balanced relationship among development, reform, and stability. After he initiated the institution of retirement for top leaders by his own example, Deng picked Jiang Zemin and Hu Jintao as the next two succeeding leaders.

In foreign policy, Deng, as leader in the 1970s, considered the USSR the major threat to China and to world peace and sought an alliance with the United States, Japan, and Europe. In 1985, however, he dropped this policy and pushed for a more balanced diplomatic approach, with a multipolar global order as the goal. Deng improved China's relationships with its neighboring countries, emphasizing their common long-term interests rather than ideological similarity. His guideline was that China fears or follows no one. It will not offend anyone, either. China will go its own way, but will be open to learn from and exchange with others. All of these policies serve one single goal: to develop China well. Deng proposed the policy of **one country, two systems** (socialism and capitalism) to gain Hong Kong and Macao back to China. He hoped that Taiwan would eventually accept the same policy and reunify itself with the mainland in the near future. Although Deng's policy seems to have kept the returned Hong

Kong and Macao relatively stable, his main goal, Taiwan, seems not to have been persuaded yet.

Deng shared with Mao a background of working extensively in the military and in the CCP's rural base areas. Deng thus fell victim along with Mao in an early inner Party political conflict with those leaders of the CCP who were based in urban areas (1933). A longtime colleague, Deng was significantly influenced, trusted, and politically supported and promoted by Mao. It was rather ironic, therefore, that soon after entering into the top leadership, with Mao's backing, Deng began to politically disagree with Mao in 1957. Mao's ambivalence toward Deng resulted in Deng being purged twice in the Cultural Revolution, but twice he left Deng with the possibility of political survival. (Mao insisted that Deng not be ousted from the Party.) Deng differed from Mao in having little interest in history, philosophy, poetry, and Marxist theory and less interest in surpassing the great emperors of ancient China in historical fame. The guideline of Deng's career was thus pragmatism, as opposed to Mao's emphasis on ideology. Deng was also more "democratic" than Mao toward their comrades and kept consulting with his colleague Chen Yun, among others, in decision making.

Deng acknowledged late in life that 30 to 40 percent of all his decisions were "mistakes." Among the most controversial ones were the 1957 extension of the Anti-Rightist Campaign that was partly under his leadership; his silent endorsement of Mao's **Great Leap Forward** in 1958; the 1979 war against Vietnam; the heavy-handed way in which he repressed the 1989 pro-Western democratic movement (though many in and out of China now argue that his decision proved to have positive long-term consequences); and, finally, his decision to keep Shanghai City off the list of the special economic zones for ten years. Compared with Mao, who led China to its military and political rising in recent history, Deng put China on track for its economic rising. Both men, however, made little progress in the next rising, China's cultural rising: Mao failed in his Cultural Revolution, and Deng left nearly untouched the task of developing Chinese cultures.

Deng was physically short (barely five feet), but famous in the world. Twice named *Time* magazine's "Man of the Year," he had a profound impact on China's future, and perhaps the world's future as well. His most renowned phrase remains "No matter black or yellow, a cat looks good if it catches mice." Deng married three times; the longest and latest marriage was with Zhuo Lin. She and their two sons and three daughters offered Deng a rich and stable family life, especially in his later years.

See also Deng Xiaoping (1904–1997), Reforms of; Hong Kong, Return of; Sino-American Relations, Conflicts and Common Interests; Sino-American Relations since 1949; Sino-Japanese Relations since 1949; Sino-Russian Relations since 1991.

Bibliography

Deng, Xiaoping, *Selected Works of Deng Xiaoping*, vols. 1–3 (Beijing: People's Publishing House, 1993).

Xiaosi Yang

Deng Xiaoping (1904–1997), Reforms of

If **Mao Zedong** is remembered as the founder of the People's Republic of China (PRC), as well as the source of wave after wave of nerve-wracking political campaigns, Deng Xiaoping is remembered for deprogramming Mao's system and for leading China onto the road of economic prosperity. According to the economic blueprint Deng laid out in 1987, China would modernize itself through three stages: sufficiency, relative affluence, and reaching the living standard of a medium-level developed country. In terms of income figures, the first step was to reach a per capita GNP of $500 by 1990, doubling the 1980 figure of $250. The second step was to reach a per capita GNP of $1,000 and achieve "relative comfort" by the turn of the century. The third step was to quadruple the $1,000 figure of the year 2000 within thirty to fifty years. That will mean a per capita GNP of roughly $4,000, or the living standard of a medium-level developed country. Recent figures have confirmed that the plan is on schedule. The National Bureau of Statistics shows that in 2002 the gross domestic product stood at 10,239.8 billion yuan, about U.S. $1.3 trillion. In the report of the *Work of the Government*, March 5, 2003, Premier **Zhu Rongji** declared that China had reached the goal of achieving the stage of "relative affluence."

In addition to being a daring road finder, one would have to acknowledge that Deng Xiaoping had magic. In the Chinese context, a steady economic recovery depends primarily on favorable government policies. Improvement of production output requires motivation, hard work, effective administration, and, in particular, a market where trade can be conducted freely. None of these would have existed, however, without reform of the state-controlled economic structure. But to touch state dominance, one had to reform the ideological structure first. Hence the very first step under Deng's leadership was an ideological campaign aimed at liberating people's minds from hard-line communism. Deng Xiaoping was no less a political campaign launcher than his boss Mao Zedong. However, Deng launched a different campaign titled "seeking the truth from facts," under which people were encouraged to question Marxism and Mao Zedong's thought from the perspective of China's reality.

One would not have to be a rocket scientist to discern China's reality. Mao left behind a country that had a population passing the billion mark. Years of political campaigns had destroyed the economy and had reduced people's lives to the survival level. All these consequences, without doubt, resulted from mismanagement by the Mao regime. Without revising the governing theory, China would have to repeat the past mistakes. "Our people's living conditions are so hard," admitted Deng, "that if we do not make every effort to develop the economy, how could we demonstrate the superiority of socialism?" Deng was always a straight shooter. He condemned Mao's concept of "poor communism" as "nonsense."

To start deprogramming the 1 billion minds, Deng made every effort to convince people that reality is the only criterion for judging whether a theory represents the truth. For Deng, the truth was in the reality rather than in some ephemeral dreams. Likewise, Deng stressed that Marxism was a century-old theory imported from the West. To expect Marxism to reflect China's reality in the twentieth century would simply be unrealistic. When Deng stepped out to defend the market economy, the whole world listened in awe. Deng insisted that there is no contradiction between the market economy and socialism, because the market system is simply an economic tool that may serve any ideological cause, including the socialist cause. Deng's challenge to what had been the sacred principles opened up people's views, instilled confidence, and gave rise to a broad-based economic recovery.

The debate of "seeking the truth from facts," however, proved to be a challenging endeavor. The Hundred Flowers Campaign of the 1950s and the ensuing Anti-Rightist Campaign were vividly fresh in memory. However, one year after Mao died, Mao's handpicked successor **Hua Guofeng** urged the nation to resolutely uphold whatever policies and decisions Mao had made and to unswervingly follow whatever instructions Mao had given, better known as the "two whatevers." Deng rebutted this by indicating that Mao himself had admitted his own mistakes, and that none of the prominent Communist leaders, including Marx, Lenin, and Stalin, had ever claimed that their words were universally true. Deng stressed that Mao's thought must be taken as a comprehensive system. Hence the "two whatevers" represented dogmatism that was at best an effort of distortion.

Liberating minds is the first step; making minds creative is the next. For the latter, Deng's legacy is one of pragmatism. Deng put economic development before anything else. As long as a strategy worked, it was acceptable. Deng is remembered for his indiscriminate love for the feline—he indicated that whether a cat is black or white is not essential; as long as it is capable of catching mice, it is a good cat. Deng was the first Communist leader to encourage people to get rich. "Some people must be allowed to get rich ahead of others," he is remembered as saying. "Getting rich through hard work is perfectly legitimate. . . . In a word, our work is aimed at building a socialist country with Chinese characteristics; and we must be evaluated according to how much we facilitate people's happiness, their material well-being, and how much we contribute to the nation's prosperity." With his slogan "To be rich is glorious," Deng won people's support. In fact, no economic recovery plan would have been as effective as people's raised expectations. When a nation is determined to improve its economy, improvement happens.

In Deng's system, Marxism and Mao Zedong Thought became means to support the reform rather than ends that the Party must abide by. Under Deng's influence, the Third Plenum of the Eleventh Central Committee of 1978 endorsed the "Four Modernizations" as the party's primary goal in the new era. At this meeting, however, the Chinese Communist Party (CCP) also spelled out the **"Four Cardinal Principles"** that included keeping to the socialist road, upholding the people's democratic dictatorship, sticking to the CCP's leadership, and adhering to Marxism-Leninism and Mao Zedong Thought. In retrospect, these cardinal principles were essentially set up for the purpose of ensuring stability. It was Deng's firm belief, as he argued in an article published in 1987, that while China must keep its door open to the world, stability must be stressed; to guarantee stability, the Party must be in control. Deng made two points clear: (1) China must take the socialist road; (2) without political stability, it would be impossible to modernize. Deng was ready to maintain a stable environment by any means necessary.

To achieve fast economic development and maintain a socialist system at the same time poses many serious challenges. Creatively and courageously meeting these challenges is the hallmark of Deng Xiaoping's theory. Deng introduced capitalist management by establishing the "special economic zones" (SEZs) in 1979. He later expanded the experience to the rest of the country. A rough estimate is that the share of private ownership has mounted to 40 percent of the economy as of today, and private enterprise has become the leading force of productivity. A direct outcome of this change is that the **privately owned enterprises (POEs)** are pushing the **state-owned enterprises (SOEs)** to shape up. The SOEs must either shake off inertia or disintegrate into privately owned companies.

Would a market economy lead to capitalism or, to word it differently, to the change of color of the CCP? Deng did not believe that socialism and the CCP are incompatible with the market economy. The socialist system is ultimately superior, in Deng's opinion, to capitalism. Deng provided a versatile answer by resorting to Marxist terminology: Both planning economy and market economy are ways to "liberate productivity." In a speech given in February 1987 to high-level officials, Deng pointed out that both planning and market mechanisms are instruments to serve economic growth: "if they serve socialism, they are socialist; if they serve capitalism, they are capitalist." Moving a step further, Deng said, "At one time we copied the Soviet model of economic development and had a planned economy. Later we said that in a socialist economy planning must occupy the dominant position. We should not say that any longer."

The concept of "socialist market economy" dates back to 1979. During an interview with Frank B. Gibney of *Encyclopaedia Britannica*, Deng assured the world that China would develop a market economy under socialism. He emphasized that China did not want capitalism, but neither did people want to be poor under socialism. What China needed, in Deng's words, was socialism in which the productive forces were developed and the country was prosperous and powerful. In an interview with *CBS 60 Minutes*, when confronted with the question of the relationship between profit making and socialism, Deng explained that unlike the capitalist society, where individualism prevails, the socialist market economy leads to common prosperity. Although some individuals or regions get rich ahead of others, as Deng pointed out, this will not lead to polarization, because the socialist system has the strength of working effectively for common prosperity. It would be absurd to prefer Communist poverty over capitalist material wealth, in Deng's opinion, because communism is defined from the beginning to be a system whereby a tremendous prosperity of people's lives is finally achieved.

The political structure must be compatible with the economic reform. It must be a propulsive force instead of a dragging force. Deng's reform had a tremendous impact on the political structure and resulted in many changes. The Party's authority over administrative affairs was significantly reduced. At the grassroots level, for example, while both the Party's leadership and the managerial system widely coexist, it is the production manager who has more say in decision making today. The reform also resulted in the elimination of the lifelong tenure of government functionaries. As mentioned earlier, Deng successfully consolidated the administrative structure by encouraging senior leaders to retire. Being deeply aware of the inertia of state planning, Deng implemented a series of measures aimed at decentralizing the government and allocating more responsibility to local management.

The patriarchic style used to be the hallmark of the rusty socialist machine. In a speech given in 1986 titled "On the Reform of the Political Structure," Deng laid out three objectives: (1) leading cadres must be young, preferably in their thirties and forties; (2) bureaucracy as well as overstaffed units must be eliminated; and (3) the initiatives generated by the grassroots levels must be encouraged; they must be trusted with the power of decision making in production. In rank promotion, the traditional practice used to be following the "ladder" or the seniority-based system that often resulted in the suppression of creativity. Deng had the system replaced with civil service examinations, which were cheered as tremendous progress in the direction of fairness and efficiency.

In retrospect, there is no doubt that Deng's magic worked. From liberal thinking to pragmatist footwork, every tidbit contributed to an effective system. Once-dormant China came back to life. However, one must not lose sight of the "real" helmsman—Mao Zedong. Without Mao's systematic failure, there would not have been Deng's systematic reform. In reality, Deng's reform may be understood as following Mao's blueprint in the opposite direction. Hence the way had been paved to recovery, in a sense, long before 1978.

See also Administrative Reforms after 1978; Deng Xiaoping (1904–1997), Politics of; Hong Kong, Return of; Open Door Policy (1978).

Bibliography

Deng, Xiaoping, *Selected Works of Deng Xiaoping (Deng Xiaoping Wenxuan)* (Beijing: People's Publishing House, 1993).

Jing Luo

Diplomacy

See Deng Xiaoping (1904–1997), Politics of; Deng Xiaoping (1904–1997), Reforms of; Independent Foreign Policy (1982); Jiang Zemin (1926–), Diplomacy of; Korean War (1950–1953); Nixon's Visit to China/Shanghai Communiqué; Ping-Pong Diplomacy; Rhetoric in China's Foreign Relations; Sino-American Relations, Conflicts and Common Interests; Sino-American Relations since 1949; Sino-Japanese Relations since 1949; Sino-Russian Relations since 1991; Sino-Soviet Alliance; Taiwan Strait Crisis, Evolution of; Vietnam War.

Disease and Death Rates

The death rate of urban Chinese residents was 0.544 percent in 2001, while that figure for rural residents was 0.594 percent. There was no change in the leading three causes of death in both urban and rural areas in 2001 when compared with the previous year. In urban areas, the number of deaths caused by the leading ten causes represented 92.0 percent of total deaths, and in rural areas, 92.1 percent of total deaths (see Tables 1 and 2).

The disease pattern in China has changed significantly in the past two decades as the living standards of Chinese population have continuously improved. The change of disease patterns in China has been characterized by growing morbidity of chronic diseases and falling incidence of infectious diseases.

TABLE 1
Leading Causes of Death in Urban Area, 2001

Leading causes of death	Death rate (1/100,000)
Cancers	135.59
Cerebrovascular diseases	111.01
Heart diseases	95.77
Respiratory system diseases	72.64
Injury and intoxication	31.92
Endocrinology, nutrition, metabolism, and immunity-related diseases	17.18
Digestive system diseases	17.06
Urinary and reproductive system diseases	8.55
Mental diseases	5.37
Nervous system diseases	5.20

Source: State Drug Administration Yearbook 2003.

TABLE 2
Leading Causes of Death in Rural Areas, 2001

Leading causes of death	Death rate (1/100,000)
Respiratory system diseases	133.42
Cerebrovascular diseases	112.60
Cancers	105.36
Heart diseases	77.72
Injury and intoxication	63.69
Digestive system diseases	24.14
Urinary and reproductive system diseases	9.09
Newborn diseases	791.2 (1/100,000 newborns)
Tuberculosis	7.38
Endocrinology, nutrition, metabolism, and immunity-related diseases	6.84

Source: State Drug Administration Yearbook 2002.

The percentage of vegetable-based food intake among both urban and rural populations has decreased, while that of meat-based food intake has risen continuously since 1982. The result has been a falling incidence of acute infectious diseases, while the morbidity rates of cancers and cardio- and cerebrovascular diseases has continued to rise. Such diseases as hypertension, cancers (see Tables 3 and 4), coronary heart disease, cerebral apoplexy, and diabetes have accounted for 70 percent of the country's deaths in recent years.

An epidemiological survey in the 1990s also showed that China's incidence of mental diseases is growing rapidly and is approaching the level of developed nations. The average morbidity of all types of mental diseases increased from 1.27 percent in the 1980s to 1.35 percent in the 1990s. There are an estimated 16 million mental disease patients in the country.

The incidence of cardiovascular diseases, including stroke, increased sharply in the 1990s in China. Deaths caused by cardiovascular diseases accounted for 37 percent of the total number of disease-related deaths in China in 2001. According to official statistics, the current morbidity of coronary diseases in the country is still below the international average, while that of stroke is above

TABLE 3
Cancer Death Rates in Urban Areas, 2001

Urban area classification	Average death rate (1/100,000)	Male death rate (1/100,000)	Female death rate (1/100,000)
All cancers	135.59	163.77	106.27
Lung cancer	40.31	-	-
Hepatic cancer	20.87	-	-
Gastric cancer	17.00	-	-
Colon, rectal, and anal cancers	10.25	-	-
Esophagal cancer	7.77	-	-

Source: State Drug Administration Yearbook 2002.

TABLE 4
Cancer Death Rates in Rural Areas, 2001

Rural area classification	Average death rate (1/100,000)	Male death rate (1/100,000)	Female death rate (1/100,000)
All cancers	105.36	130.85	78.31
Hepatic cancer	24.58	-	-
Lung cancer	20.23	-	-
Gastric cancer	19.22	-	-
Esophagal cancer	13.08	-	-
Colon, rectal, and anal cancers	6.58	-	-

Source: State Drug Administration Yearbook 2002.

the international average and advancing toward a leading position. The incidence of high blood pressure grew 25 percent in the past twelve years, and China now has more than 100 million such patients.

On the basis of a nationwide survey, Chinese researchers projected that the diabetes morbidities for males and females are both 1.6 percent of the total population. The survey found that newly discovered diabetes patients represent 75 percent of all the diabetes patients in the survey. The survey covered 110,660 people of different social, educational, and economic status.

Currently, China is estimated to have an obese population of 65 million, and this number is growing. Type II diabetes, of which obesity is a major risk factor, is now believed to affect almost 50 million people, though the actual diagnosed population is around 15 million. Data from an annual study by Isis China, a global market research firm, of more than 200 endocrinologists and 4,000 patients in eleven major Chinese cities show that the average number of type II diabetic patients treated per doctor in a normal week increased from 57 in 1997 to 68 in 2000. Closely associated with diabetes are hypertension, hyperlipidemia, and a host of other cardiovascular problems.

Due to spreading problems of prostitution, drugs, and illegal blood sales, the danger that AIDS and HIV infection will become a widespread epidemic disease in the country is real and near. In 1999, the number of reported new HIV infections was 4,677 cases and of new sexually transmitted diseases (STDs) was 836,655 cases. The figures were up by 41.5 percent and 32.0 percent, respectively, over 1998. Experts also believe that the total number of HIV carriers in China exceeded 850,000 by the end of 2001, and the number grew 58 percent compared with 2000. The Chinese government estimates that the actual number of HIV carriers will reach 1.5 million in 2010, even if prevention is implemented effectively and immediately. However, UN experts say that without effective measures, as many as 20 million Chinese could be infected by 2010.

According to the Ministry of Health, the three leading infectious diseases now in China are viral hepatitis, AIDS, and tuberculosis. Official statistics shows that in China there are now 120 million carriers of hepatitis B virus, 30 percent of all carriers in the world; there are 38 million hepatitis C virus carriers, 20 percent of the world total. Viral hepatitis costs China around RMB 30–50 billion yuan each year.

See also AIDS, Prevention of; Health Care Reform; Medical Provision, Structure of; Pharmaceutical Industry, Administrative and Regulatory Structures of; Pharmaceutical Products, Sales and Marketing of.

Bibliography

Editorial Committee, the State Drug Administration, *State Drug Administration Yearbook 2002* (Beijing: State Drug Administration Yearbook Press, 2003); Editorial Committee of the China Health Yearbook, *China Health Yearbook* (Beijing: People's Health Publishing House, 2002 and 2003); Editorial Committee of the China Pharmaceutical Yearbook, *China Pharmaceutical Yearbook* (Beijing: China Publishing House, 2001, 2002, and 2003); Shen, James, *Marketing Pharmaceuticals in China* (Whippany, NJ: Wicon International, 2001).

Jian Shen

Divorce

See Marriage and Divorce.

Domestic Government Debt

Recent years have seen growing concern over the rise of China's domestic government debt. There is a wide range of estimates of China's domestic government debt, with different components and different estimates of each component. China's government debt includes explicit fiscal debt, local government debt, state banks' nonperforming loans, and fiscal subsidies to social security funds.

Explicit fiscal debt refers to the accumulated government bonds issued for financing budget deficits. The fiscal deficit is the difference between government revenue and government expenditure. The government budget deficit has been increasing since 1986. In the 1980s, deficits were relatively small. For example, in 1989 the budget deficit was 15.9 billion yuan. Deficits started to rise after the 1994 tax reform. Also, a law that prohibits the Ministry of Finance from overdrawing money from the People's Bank of China was passed in 1993. The Ministry of Finance began to finance all its budget deficits by issuing bonds. After the 1997 Asian financial crisis, the Chinese government adopted an expansionary fiscal policy. The government budget deficit increased from 58.3 billion yuan in 1997 to 247.3 billion yuan in 2001. The planned budget deficit was 309.8 billion yuan in 2002.

Deficits can be financed by either money or government bonds. Fearing the negative consequence of inflation, the government has relied on bonds issuance to finance the deficit. Bonds were issued in the amount of 19.9 billion yuan in 1991 and 102.9 billion yuan in 1994. The debt issuance every year after 1994 was a record compared with previous years. In 2001, the government issued 460.4 billion yuan of government bonds, and in 2002, the government planned to issue 592.9 billion yuan of government bonds. The ratio of explicit fiscal debt to GDP has been increasing at an astonishing rate, from 5 percent in 1994 to 16.3 percent in 2001.

Unreported local government debt has not gained much attention in the discussion of total government debt. In China, local governments (provincial, prefecture, county, and township governments) do not have the right to issue bonds. Village resident committees, the lowest level of administrative organization (officially not even a level of government), certainly do not have any right to issue bonds. However, over the years, local governments have accumulated a considerable amount of debt.

The 1994 tax reform put local governments in a difficult fiscal position. In all years from 1960 to 1985, local governments had budget surpluses. From 1986 to 1993, local governments had surpluses in some years and deficits in other years. The 1994 tax reform has changed the story completely. Local government budgets jumped from a surplus of 6.1 billion yuan in 1993 to a deficit of 172.7 billion yuan in 1994. Local government deficits increased at an annual rate of 16 percent from 1994 to 2001. On the basis of the 2002 budget, local government debt was projected to reach 363 billion yuan in 2002, a 25 percent increase from 2001. Since 1994, each year every province has had a budget deficit.

It is believed that debt of township governments is widespread and severe. A conservative estimate of township government debt is around 200 billion yuan, accounting for 2.3 percent of GDP. Looking at the ratio of township government debt to national GDP will lead to an underestimation of the severity of the township debt problem since the township GDP is much lower. A survey from Hunan Province in 1999 indicated that 88 percent of about 2,000 township governments had debt outstanding; some had already used up 2003's budget revenues before 1999. A sampling survey of 100 townships in Sichuan Province in 2000 indicated that 82 out of 100 townships had debt outstanding, 46 percent of townships had debt higher than 1 million yuan, and some had debt as high as 12 million yuan. Some township governments have used up the budget revenue of 2015.

The official number of nonperforming loans (NPLs) was about 259 billion yuan by the end of 2001, 27 percent of GDP. If the NPLs held by the state-owned asset management companies through the debt-equity-swap program were included, the NPLs/GDP ratio would have been 41 percent at the end of 2001. Meanwhile, some international rating agencies have estimated China's NPLs at U.S. $600 billion (nearly 5,000 billion Chinese yuan), equivalent to about 50 percent of GDP. Recent data show that NPLs are decreasing at an annual rate of nearly 4 percent. Thus the NPLs appear not to be a long-term problem.

Many people have compared Chinese banks' bad loans with those of other countries such as Japan. It is important to realize that China's major banks are owned by the government, which possesses a huge amount of national assets. Thus China's bad-loan problem at the moment may not be as explosive as depicted. In the worst case, the government may have to issue bonds to repay the NPLs for the **state-owned enterprises (SOEs)**. Of course, continuous efforts should be made to reform the banking system and reduce the NPLs.

The unfunded social security liability (or, more narrowly, implicit pension debt) is another major concern of economists inside and outside China. International experience indicates that pension debt is about twenty to thirty times the current pension payments. In 2000, pensions for retirees (excluding medical payments to retirees) were 273.3 billion yuan. Thus, on the basis of international experience, the pension debt in China would be between 5,466 billion yuan and 8,199 billion yuan. In 2000, China's GDP was 8,819 billion yuan. Therefore, the ratio of pension debt to GDP would be 62 percent to 93 percent of GDP. There are various estimates of China's pension debt. The World Bank estimated that China's pension debt was between 46 percent and 68 percent of GDP in 1994. The figure was estimated at 94 percent of the 1998 GDP by Dorfman and Fan (2000) and 68 percent of the 2000 GDP by Wang et al. (2001).

In estimating government fiscal burden in the **social security system**, it is meaningful to include only the portion of social security debt that must be financed by government fiscal revenues. In 1999, the government transferred 25.7 billion yuan to cover pension shortfalls at the local level and subsidize laid-off SOE workers, 0.32 percent of GDP. In 2000, budgetary subsidies for national pension funds were 30 billion yuan and for local pension funds 10 billion yuan, 0.45 percent of GDP. In 2001, the central government provided a subsidy of 34.9 billion yuan to national pension funds, 0.4 percent of GDP. If the government has to subsidize the pension fund at the same rate for the next thirty years, then the government's fiscal burden for social security would be 12 percent of current GDP.

There is a wide range of estimates of China's fiscal subsidies to social security pension funds. Yi estimated that the fiscal liability for the social security system is 28 percent of GDP, while Ma and Zhai (2001) showed this fiscal liability as 41 percent of GDP. On the other hand, Fan (2002) excluded social security debt from the government's comprehensive liabilities. Reforms in the social security system will change the government's fiscal subsidies to the social security funds. In the short run, the further China moves away from the pay-as-you-go system, the higher the fiscal subsidies to the social security account will be.

China was under a centrally planned economic system in which the government owned almost the entire economy. Comparing China's debt problem with the debt problems of private market economies can be misleading. China is moving toward a market economy through the growth of private enterprises. The ratio of government net assets to GDP is more than 100 percent, higher than the debt/GDP ratio. Also, the government owns a large amount of natural resources in China. Thus, from a purely accounting perspective, China's government debt problem at the moment is serious but still manageable. This does not imply that the Chinese government should continue to run budget deficits and increase its debt.

See also Banking and Financial System Reform; Credit Spending, Development of; Economic Policies and Development (1949–Present); Economic Structure; Foreign Debt; Renminbi (RMB).

Bibliography

Dorfman, Mark C., and Yvonne Sin Fan, "China: Social Security Reform, Technical Analysis of Strategic Options," Human Development Network, World Bank, Washington, DC, 2000; Fan, Gang, "China's NPL and National Comprehensive Liability," manuscript, National Economic Research Institute, China Reform Foundation, 2002; Jia, Kong, and Zhao Quan-Hou, "The Size of China's National Debt," *World Economy and China* 9, no. 1; Ma, Jun, and Fan Zhai, "Financing China's Pension Reform," manuscript, 2002; National Bureau of Statistics of the PRC, *National Labor and Social Security Yearbook 2001* (Beijing: China Statistics Press, 2002); National Bureau of Statistics of the PRC, *Finance Yearbook of China* (Various issues, 1997, 2000, 2001) (Beijing: China Statistics Press).

Shuanglin Lin

"Double-Hundred" Policy

"Double-hundred" is the abbreviation for "letting a hundred flowers bloom and a hundred schools of thought contend." This was a general guiding principle applicable to every field of culture and science in China in the late 1950s. It aimed mainly at advancing China's culture and science as a whole and bringing about a flourishing socialist culture with richer contents and more diverse styles. The "double-hundred" ideas were first set forth by Communist Party chairman **Mao Zedong**. On May 26, 1956, they were officially claimed to be a new policy for China's literature and art.

The origin of the "double-hundred" ideas dates back to the early 1950s. In 1951, to commemorate the founding of the Research Institute of Traditional Chinese Opera, Mao Zedong wrote the short message "Let a hundred flowers bloom; let us weed through the old to bring forth the new." Mao hoped then that people would critically carry forward the rich heritage of traditional Chinese operas and impel the development of various kinds of Chinese operas. Later, in 1953, when he was advising people on how to study Chinese history, Mao said, "Let a hundred schools of thought contend," wishing that people would examine history from different perspectives. On April 28, 1956, Mao summarized his previous ideas and put together these two sayings for the first time. He stated that in the circle of art, the Communist Party should allow a hundred flowers to bloom, and in the field of academic research, let a hundred schools of thought contend. On May 2, 1956, Mao further elaborated his viewpoints and officially announced that the "double-hundred" idea was the guiding principle for advancing work in the realms of culture and science. For Mao, the spring season had already come; therefore it would be wrong to allow only certain types of flowers to bloom while forbidding other sorts of flowers from doing so. He held that as early as in the "Spring and Autumn" and the "Warring States Period" (770–221 B.C.), the Chinese enjoyed the freedom of disputing among different schools of thought, which eventually resulted in a golden era of academic democracy in China. Such freedom or democracy was also needed in the socialist construction era. In literature and art circles, a larger variety of writings should be permitted to exist, and in the sphere of learning, free discussion was necessary; the voicing of different viewpoints, correct or not, should be encouraged.

On May 26, 1956, Lu Dingyi, the minister of the Publicity Ministry, delivered a special speech about the "double-hundred" policy at a meeting that was held for scientists, writers, and artists. He announced that although this policy aimed at developing culture and science as a whole, it was certainly applicable to literature and art. According to Lu, under this policy, writers and artists had the right to think independently, debate freely, express their own opinions, and hold on to them. Writers and artists had the freedom of writing and criticizing others. In academic criticism and discussion, nobody should have "privilege" over others or should put himself or herself in a superior position, stifling differing opinions. Lu believed that China was badly in need of a more prosperous literature and art arena, because such an environment would be capable of better reflecting a wealthy and powerful China. Lu also declared that socialist realism was by no means the only creative method for writing. As long as writers and artists were willing to serve the people, they could write on any subject matter and use any methods they preferred. On June 13, Lu's speech was published in full in the *People's Daily* and immediately attracted wide attention both at home and abroad.

On the surface, the "double-hundred" policy seems not very unique or significant because even the wording of the policy itself—"let a hundred flowers bloom, let a hundred schools of thought contend"—was "old" and familiar-sounding to the Chinese. At the most, the Chinese leaders seemed to hope for another golden era of academic freedom in China by spurring more prosperity in culture and scholarship. But in fact, the policy suggested some significant changes. First, instead of confining people to some new requirements, it encouraged a larger variety of subject matters and creative methods in writing. The Chinese leaders were, therefore, thinking of giving people more freedom by moving the fences and enlarging the domain of literary and artistic creation. They were expecting that writers and artists could expand their field of vision and, more important, speak their minds more freely. Second, the policy gave socialist realism, which was a Soviet doctrine very popular in the Soviet Union during the socialist construction period in Stalin's era and had been declared to be the "highest principle" of Chinese literary and art creation since 1953, a much less preferred status than before. Mao Zedong did not even mention socialist realism in his speeches, and Lu Dingyi claimed very clearly that socialist realism was on no account "the only method." This shift sent out an important message that the Chinese leaders were attempting to reevaluate the Soviet model and to deviate from their previous confidence in the Soviet experience.

The "double-hundred" policy was the most welcomed policy ever issued during the period 1949–1978. It created an unprecedentedly democratic and moderate atmosphere for literary and artistic creation and criticism. It permitted more freedom in choosing subject matter and creative methods and even made it possible for people to criticize the Communist Party of China and some Party officials. For the first time since 1949, people were encouraged to speak their minds freely, and the total number of literary publications increased enormously. Moreover, a large number of works emerged that, because of their "liberal" contents, would otherwise have been considered "poisonous weeds" or banned before 1956.

Unfortunately, the "double-hundred" policy did not remain in effect for as long as expected. Only thirteen months after the policy was announced, the Communist Party launched the Anti-Rightist Campaign (1957–1958). During this nationwide and ultraleft political campaign, many writers and artists—especially those who had criticized the Party before—were labeled "rightists" and punished accordingly. As a result, for various reasons, some people kept quiet or simply ceased writing out of fear; others only wrote something that whitewashed the realities in the country. Since the period of freedom was short, it did not allow the possibility of literary creation reaching an even higher artistic level. Unlike what Mao Zedong hoped in 1956, some "flowers" and "schools" died too soon, and others never got a chance to "bloom" or "contend"; instead, they were stifled or killed even before they could germinate.

See also Intellectuals; Journalism Reform; Literary Policy for the New China; Press Control; Press Freedom.

Bibliography

Dai, Zhixian, *Studies on Mao Zedong's Cultural Thought* (Beijing: People's University Press, 1992); Zhu, Zheng, *Summer of 1957: From Letting One Hundred Schools Contend to Letting Two Schools Contend* (Zhengzhou: Henan People's Publishing House, 1998).

Dela X. Jiao

Drinking in Ethnic Cultures

The consumption of alcoholic beverages plays an important role in the lives of all Chinese ethnic minorities. In a sense, drinking is no longer a simple dietary habit; rather, it has become part of the culture. Since the launch of the economic reforms in the late 1970s, drinking has become a popular component of business protocol everywhere. Nevertheless, ethnic traditions remain the underpinnings of most of the customs. For example, Chinese Muslims drink only moderately, compared with other ethnic groups, because alcohol consumption is restricted in Islamic scriptures.

In most minority cultures, drinking appears to be an enzyme for relationship building, because there are no feasts without wine. This is justified by many traditional sayings, such as "No liquor, no courtesy"; "It cannot be called a feast with only meat but without liquor"; "No drunks, no drinking"; "No wet floor, no drinking" (people spill wine or liquor on the ground when they get drunk); "No

In the Tibetan culture, liquor is offered to guests to show hospitality. This photo shows a Tibetan drinking ceremony that also involves dance.

meat is okay, but no liquor is not agreeable"; and "No wine, no friendship." Apparently, minority people make use of wine or liquor as a way to express their hospitality and friendship.

There is a variety of drinking protocols and preferences. Tibetans, with the exception of religious clergy who do not drink at all, favor the highland barley wine that exists in two forms, barley beer and barley liquor. When a guest is offered barley wine, he should use his ring finger to pick up a bit of the wine and sprinkle it upward three times before he starts to drink to express his respect to nature and the gods. He is required to empty the cup in three mouthfuls. Mongolians make horse-milk wines by storing horse milk in leather bags for a certain period of time to get it fermented. When one is served a bowl of horse-milk wine, one should empty the bowl at a single breath. Any hesitation would be regarded as a lack of respect and politeness. The Yi people in the Liangshan mountain regions of Sichuan Province usually drink liquor by way of "circulating" the wine cup. A typical scene is a group of Yi people squatting on their heels in a circle, with a big jar of liquor in the middle, and without dishes to accompany. They pass a bowl of liquor around, which lasts until the jar is emptied. Several minorities, such as Qiang, Va, Lisu, Lahu, and Buyei, prefer drinking by drawing from a jar placed in the middle of a group using pipes or straws. The Nu people enjoy a unique wine called "meat wine" that is made by boiling a fried chicken in wine. The alcoholic chicken broth is considered a heavenly treat.

Matchmaking, weddings, funerals, burials, laying house foundations, and harvest celebrations are typical drinking opportunities. Many ethnic groups have drinking songs and dances for persuading guests to drink more. The wine-persuading songs and dances of Tibetans, Mongolians, Miao, and Dong are so beautiful and persistent that guests can hardly refuse the wine served.

While wine drinking is ceremonial and sometimes pompous, tea drinking has its charm. The popularity of tea drinking is comparable to that of liquors. The history of planting and drinking tea dates back 3,000 years, and archeologists believe that Yunnan used to be the source of tea cultivation. Simao and Xishuangbanna are two regions where ancient tea utensils have been unearthed. Among ethnic minorities, only those in southern China grow tea, and some ethnic minorities such as Jinuo and De'ang are regarded as the earliest tea farmers. Today, tea farming and processing have become an important industry for many minority economies. The Pu'er tea produced in Simao and Xishuangbanna is a traditional product of Jinuo, Hani, Bulang, Dai, Lahu, and Va ethnic communities. It is highly appreciated in Asian countries.

Tea drinking has the same role as liquors in smoothing social intercourse. Although only ethnic minorities in southern China grow tea, all ethnic-minority people in China drink tea, and all of them have their own tea customs. Dongxiang people call the engagement ceremony *dingcha*, meaning "engagement tea," since tea is the symbol of permanent relationship. In Linxia, Gansu, if a girl's family keeps the tea delivered by the man who proposes the marriage, it means that the girl's family has agreed to the marriage in the future, however long it may take. In Qinghai and Gansu, both the women of the bride's and the bridegroom's villages need to prepare tea for the bride and bridegroom in the name of wedding tea. In Zhejiang, a bride has to have sweet egg tea as soon as she arrives at the bridegroom's home. Lahu people in Yunnan must send tea to the girl's family to confirm the wedding date, which is why Lahu people say, "No tea, no marriage." De'ang people make use of tea as gifts frequently, so they also have the saying "nothing can be done without tea." In **Tibet**, tea is the usual gift when people go to see a sick person, and tea is one of the holy things that a monk offers to pilgrims.

There are many unique ways to drink tea or even eat tea among ethnic minorities. Jinuo people have planted tea for a long time in their history and eat tea as a dish. They make a delicious cool dish of tea by mixing up the sprouts of tea with different sauces and condiments. Tibetan people's butter tea is very famous throughout China and is the drink that Tibetan people must have almost every day. It is made of boiled tea, walnut bits, salt, butter, and boiled milk that are pressed and mixed in a special butter tea tube. Mongolian people's milk tea is also famous and is cooked by mixing prepared tea and milk and boiling them together. Dong people's oil tea has the function of tea as well as food and is made by boiling fried sticky rice, peanuts, and soybeans with tea oil and tea. Some onions, spinach, and other vegetables are added to the cooked oil tea when people eat it. It can be regarded as a kind of drink as well as food. Among Hui, Baoan, Lasa, and Dongxiang people in northwestern China, Sanpaotai tea is popular, which is made by pouring hot water into a mixture of Yunnan tea with dried fruits and sugar in a tea bowl with a cover. Several minutes later, the Sanpaotai tea is ready to drink. It is called Sanpaotai because the tea set includes tea bowl, tea cover, and tea dish (*san* means three).

Baked tea is very popular among many ethnic minorities in Yunnan Province. The tea is baked in a small clay teapot until it releases a baked fragrance. Boiling water is added to it. A baked tea with good smell and taste is made. Among the many kinds of baked tea, Bai people's three-course tea is the most famous. It is usually made and served in three courses, hence the name "three-course tea." When one drinks the three-course tea, the first course is bitter since the tea is predominant; the second course is slightly sweet because sugar, honey, walnuts, Chinese prickly ash, and cheese are added; the third course has a unique aftertaste since ginger and cinnamon are added. The three-course tea is widely known in Dali, where the Bai people serve it to their prestigious guests. Another baked tea is the one prepared by the Naxi people called "tea of fighting between a dragon and a tiger." The serving procedure starts with pouring baked tea into a cup of liquor. It is said that drinking this tea will enable a fast warm-up, which is apparently true.

See also Ethnic Burial Customs; Ethnic Kinships; Ethnic Marriage Customs; Ethnic Minorities, Political Systems of; Ethnicity and Ethnic Policies; Islam; Taiwan, Ethnicity and Ethnic Policies of.

Bibliography

Song Shuhua, ed., *An Introduction to Chinese Ethnic Minorities* (Beijing: Central University for Nationalities Press, 2001); Xu Wanbang, and Qi Qingfu, eds., *An Introduction to Chinese Ethnic Minority Cultures* (Beijing: Central University for Nationalities Press, 1996).

Yinghui Wu

E

Economic Development

See Auto Industry Development; Credit Spending, Development of; Economic Policies and Development (1949–Present); Growth and Development, Trade-offs of; Labor Market Development; Legal Infrastructure Development and Economic Development; Libraries and Development; Regions of China, Uneven Development of; Sustainable Growth and Development; Taiwan, Economic Transition of; Western Region Development Project.

Economic Policies and Development (1949–Present)

Since 1949, China's economic policies have experienced dramatic changes. From 1949 to 1952, **land reform** was introduced, and the government forced landlords to surrender land to tenant farmers. Capitalists, however, were allowed to continue the operation of their enterprises. China's First Five-Year Plan began in 1953 (1953–1957). In this period, capitalists were asked to surrender their enterprises step by step until they became only managers of the enterprises and had to follow government instructions. Farmers were organized into cooperatives. Trade in farm products by private traders soon ceased, and the government became the sole distributor. In 1958, **Mao Zedong** launched the **Great Leap Forward** movement with the purpose of increasing China's output dramatically and developing its economy rapidly. Mao also organized farmers into communes where they worked as a team and ate together in mess halls. Economic mismanagement, natural catastrophes, and ideological disputes with the Soviet Union combined to result in a great disaster. It was estimated that from 1958 to 1962, more than 25 million people died of famine.

In 1966, the **Great Cultural Revolution** occurred after a short period of readjustment (1962–1965). This was a period of revolutionary upheavals, power struggles, and domestic turmoil. The movement lasted for a decade and prevented the proper functioning of the Chinese economy. By comparing time paths, scholars estimated that output and consumption per capita would have been twice as great in 1990 without the Great Leap Forward, 1.2 times as large without the Cultural Revolution, and 2.7 times the actual amounts if none of these deviations had occurred.

In the Maoist planning economy, economic decisions were centralized. A planning authority, the Economic Planning Commission in the State Council, had control over all resources. Directly or indirectly, it controlled all enterprises and farms. It assigned a production target to each farm and each factory. It supplied the inputs required for production. It assigned workers to different factories and controlled labor transfers. The planning authority also controlled consumer goods distributions, mostly by rationing. In addition, it determined wages for all workers and prices for all products. It was responsible for patterns of investment and regional development.

To make decisions for all economic activities, the planning authority had three difficult tasks to perform. The first was to obtain a mass of information on the production conditions of all the enterprises and the demand conditions of millions of consumers. The second was to provide sufficient incentives to each state enterprise to produce economically. The third was to determine the income of farmers and workers and to set prices for all producer and consumer goods. Not surprisingly, the Chinese economy did not perform well under the central command system.

China started its economic reforms in 1978, beginning with the agricultural reform. In 1979, the "household production responsibility system" was established, and communes were dissolved. Under the new system, landownership still belongs to the village collectively, but individual households have the use right, decide what to grow, and own all outputs after paying a fixed rent in the form of an output quota. The system has the economic characteristics of private farming in a market economy and thus greatly improves productivity. The average annual growth rate of agriculture was 2.9 percent in 1952–1978; it increased to 7.7 percent between 1978 and 1984.

After the success of the agricultural reform, China launched various reforms in the 1980s, following the principle of "touch the stone while crossing the river." Reforms include those of **state-owned enterprises**, the banking and financial system, social security, medical care, urban housing, and the fiscal and tax system. The reforms have transformed the Chinese economy from the Maoist ideological-plan into the post-Mao market-regulatory economy and have ushered in a new development strategy that values efficiency over equity, individual creativity over collectivism, and regional comparative advantages over equal and balanced regional development. These reforms have created a miracle. During the past two decades, China's GDP grew at an average annual rate higher than 9 percent. Per capita GDP rose from 379 yuan in 1978 to 7,078 yuan in 2000, increasing by 458.7 percent in real terms. In the same period, the per capita annual net income of rural households rose from 133.6 yuan to 2,253 yuan, a real increase of 384 percent; the per capita annual disposable income of urban households rose from 343 yuan to 6,280 yuan, a real increase of 284 percent.

China also has implemented its **Open Door policy** since the late 1970s and obtained its accession into the World Trade Organization (WTO) in 2001. In 1979, the government set up four special economic zones. In 1984, it designated fourteen coastal open cities. Along with Hainan Province, these cities were given greater autonomy to attract **foreign direct investment (FDI)** and practice free-market principles. The Open Door policy has greatly promoted China's international trade and made China the largest recipient of FDI in the world. Between 1978 and 2002, trade volume increased thirty-fold, from $20.6 billion to $620.8 billion, 9.6 and 50 percent of China's GDP, respectively. In three years, from 1979 to 1982, China attracted $1.2 billion of FDI inflows. In 2002 alone, the amount increased to $52.7 billion, and China became the largest FDI host globally. By the end of 2002, the cumulated FDI reached $446 billion.

Economic reforms, however, have produced some undesirable consequences. For example, the urban-rural divide has been widened; the ratio of urban to rural per capita income increased from 2.6 in 1978 to 2.9 in 2001. Regional disparity has been enlarged; the ratio of per capita GDP between eastern and western regions rose from 1.94 in 1990 to 2.89 in 2000. From 1998 to 2001, state-owned enterprises laid off 25.5 million workers, and the urban unemployment rate rose significantly in the 1990s. China faces many challenges in its further reforms and future economic development.

See also Auto Industry Development; Central Planning; Economic Structure; Growth and Development, Trade-offs of; Legal Infrastructure Development and Economic Development; Libraries and Development; Regions of China, Uneven Development of; Sustainable Growth and Development; Western Region Development Project; World Trade Organization (WTO) China's Accession to.

Bibliography

Chow, Gregory C., *China's Economic Transformation* (Malden, MA: Blackwell, 2002); Kwan, Yum K., and Gregory C. Chow, "Estimating Economic Effects of Political Movements in China," *Journal of Comparative Economics* 23 (1996): 192–208; National Bureau of Statistics of the PRC, *China Foreign Economic Statistical Yearbook* (Beijing: China Statistics Press, 2002); National Bureau, *China Statistical Yearbook* (Beijing: China Statistics Press, 2001).

Shunfeng Song

Economic Structure

Since the 1950s, China's agricultural sector, also known as the primary sector, has declined significantly and the secondary sector (consisting of manufacturing and construction industries) has risen significantly, while the service sector or the tertiary sector's expansion has remained relatively modest. The shares of GDP produced by the three sectors changed from 50.5 percent, 20.9 percent, and 28.6 percent, respectively, in 1952 to 15.2 percent, 51.1 percent, and 33.6 percent in 2001. In terms of employment, the tertiary sector has experienced the greatest expansion, from 9.1 percent in 1952 to 27.7 percent in 2001, and is predicted to become the main source of creating new jobs in the future.

Urban space and urbanized population have also increased rapidly. The number of cities increased from 450 in 1989 to 663 in 2000. Urbanized population also increased, from 17.92 percent in 1978 to 37.66 percent in 2001. This ratio, however, lags behind both the ratio of nonagricultural employment of 50 percent and the 51.1 percent share of the GDP produced by the second sector. This is primarily a consequence of China's household registration or **hukou system**, which prevented rural-to-urban mobility and created dichotomous development of the urban and rural sectors. Although greater mobility has been allowed in recent years and considerable rural-to-urban migration has been taking place, the dichotomous development has continued, primarily because of a faster growth of the urban sector than the rural sector. Urban-rural income disparity measured by the ratio of per capita urban disposable income to per capita rural net income increased from 2.57 in 1978 to 3.00 in 2002.

A balanced growth between the two sectors is essential for China's social stability and **sustainable growth and development**; such growth has thus become an important development priority of the Chinese government. Industrializing the rural sector, raising values of agricultural products, government agricultural support, lowering taxes and fees on farmers, and creating nonfarm jobs through more rapid urbanization are ways to promote rural-sector growth and narrow urban-rural disparity.

With its own vibrant Western-oriented economy, Hong Kong, which was restored to China in 1997, has proved difficult to incorporate into China's economic structure.

Within the urban sector, China's industries have also been undergoing structural and systemic changes. Structurally, industrial policy has shifted away from skewing toward heavy industry and limiting the development of service industries. Systemically, the distribution between the state and nonstate sectors has gone through several stages. At the establishment of the People's Republic of China (PRC) in 1949, enterprises of various ownership types coexisted. The shares of the gross value of industrial output (GVIO) produced by **state-owned enterprises (SOEs)**, collectively owned enterprises (COEs), joint-ownership enterprises, **privately owned enterprises (POEs)**, and proprietors were, respectively, 26.2 percent, 0.5 percent, 1.6 percent, 48.7 percent, and 23.0 percent. The Chinese government started in 1953 to transform the proprietor and private enterprises toward socialism through merging the proprietors into cooperative firms and private enterprises with public enterprises to form joint public-private-ownership enterprises. By 1957, the shares changed to 53.8 percent, 19 percent, 26.3 percent, 0.1 percent, and 0.8 percent. By 1978, all nonpublic industrial enterprises had disappeared, and China's GVIO was produced entirely by SOEs (77.6 percent) and COEs (22.4 percent). China's industrial structure was one of complete dominance by public enterprises when economic reform started in 1978.

Economic reform then changed the systemic structure gradually back toward nonstate enterprises. The number of industrial SOEs declined from 118,000 in 1995 to 46,800 in 2001, while the number of POEs increased to 36,220 in 2001. China's SOEs have been exiting and consolidating through bankruptcy, merger, and regrouping, and the average employment of industrial SOEs increased from 373 persons in 1995 to 528 in 2001. By 2001, the share of GVIO produced by state enterprises of 100 percent state ownership had shrunk to 18.05 percent, though the share of state enterprises and state-holding enterprises together had risen to 44.43 percent. A state-holding enterprise is one of mixed ownership among which the state holds the largest share. By 2002, private enterprises had regained their ground and produced one-third of the nation's GDP. China's World Trade Organization (WTO) accession has especially led to unprecedented entry of nonstate enterprises into sectors that were off-limits to them. The state now has lost not only its dominance in manufacturing, but also its monopoly in banking, insurance, the **telecommunications industry**, the auto industry, foreign trade, and even the public utilities sector.

Regionally, China's eastern and coastal areas have been more economically developed than the hinterland, as is indicated by measures such as higher GDP per capita, higher rate of urbanized population, lower urban-rural income disparity, higher ratios of educational institutions and educated population, lighter state enterprise burden, and more prosperous development of private enterprises. Geography, natural resource endowment, economic history, and policies have all contributed to the developmental disparity. The policy to first open up the eastern and coastal regions for foreign trade and **foreign direct investment (FDI)** is said to have further widened the disparity.

The Chinese administrative divisions include: provinces that are centrally controlled; autonomous regions that are codirected by the central government and elected representatives from the largest indigenous ethnic groups; municipalities that are centrally controlled and independent from provinces;

and Special Administrative Regions that, while under the People's Republic of China's Constitution's umbrella, are routinely operated in accordance with regional constitutions, such as the Basic Law of Hong Kong.

Having realized the importance of balanced development and growth, the government launched a campaign in 1999 to accelerate the development of China's west, including in the project twelve provinces, autonomous regions, and municipality of **Xinjiang**, Gansu, Qinghai, Ningxia, Shaanxi, **Tibet**, Sichuan, Yunnan, Guizhou, Guangxi, Inner Mongolia, and Chongqing. Under the "go west" project, billions of yuan have been dedicated to infrastructure construction and improvement in the area, in addition to favorable policies granted to attract domestic and foreign direct investment into the region.

Internationally, the economy has become more open, as indicated by a rapidly growing foreign sector relative to GDP. In 1978, total imports and exports were valued at $20.64 billion, with a trade deficit of $1.14 billion; in 2001, the value increased to $509.76 billion dollars, with a surplus of $22.54 billion. The ratio of foreign trade to GDP increased from 9.8 percent in 1978 to 44.7 percent in 2001. China experienced trade surpluses in the entire period 1990–2002 except in 1993. Since its WTO entry on December 11, 2001, China's exports, especially manufacturing goods, have become increasingly competitive in the world market, and their market shares are rapidly expanding. Moreover, according to the National Bureau of Statistics, China attracted total foreign direct investment of $55 billion in 2002, surpassing the United States and becoming the world's number one country in hosting FDI.

See also Administrative Reforms (1949–1978); Administrative Reforms after 1978; Auto Industry Development; Central Planning; Deng Xiaoping (1904–1997), Reforms of; Economic Policies and Development (1949–Present); Great Leap Forward (GLF); Growth and Development, Trade-offs of; Legal Infrastructure Development and Economic Development; Libraries and Development; Open Door Policy (1978); Regions of China, Uneven Development of; Rural-Urban Divide, Regional Disparity, and Income Inequality; Western Region Development Project; World Trade Organization (WTO), China's Accession to.

Bibliography

Book of Chinese Economic Events on Reforming and Opening, vol. 1 (Beijing: Beijing Industrial University Press, 1993); Chen, Aimin, "The Impact of China's WTO Entry: An Analysis *ex ante* and *ex post*," American Review of China Studies, fall 2003; Chen, "The Structure of Chinese Industry and the Impact from China's WTO Entry," *Comparative Economic Studies*, spring 2002, 72–98; Chen, "Urbanization and Disparities in China: Challenges of Growth and Development," *China Economic Review* 13, no. 4 (2002): 407–411; National Bureau of Statistics of the PRC, *China Statistical Yearbook* (various issues) (Beijing: China Statistics Press, 1981–2004).

Aimin Chen

Education

See Character Education in Primary and Secondary Schools; Education Media and Technology; Educational Administration; Educational System;

Education Media and Technology

Chinese educational technology first started with college audiovisual programs in the 1920s in the School of Agriculture of Jinling University (now Nanjing University). In 1922, the School of Agriculture of Jinling University tried to use an audiovisual approach, that is, using slides and films with oral explanations recorded on a phonograph to teach scientific methods for cotton planting. While the audiovisual approach continued to enjoy a role in classrooms, other media were explored as alternative venues for instructional delivery. Following correspondence education in the 1950s, radio and **television** universities were successively established in major cities in China such as Beijing, Shanghai, and Shenyang. By the end of the 1970s, radio and television universities and colleges were widespread all over the country. In the meantime, a net of satellite education took shape that led to a much faster development of distance education in China. With the spread of information technology in 1990s, new learning technologies such as multimedia and hypermedia have found their way into elementary, secondary, and postsecondary education.

The **Internet** has become an effective instructional medium for both regular classrooms and distance education. Currently, more than thirty higher-education institutions offer educational technology specialties to promote the development of educational technology. About ten institutions offer master's programs, and three offer doctoral programs. Educational technology has supplemented, much-needed instructors, particularly in higher education. The use of media and technology takes several formats: (1) the audiovisual approach, (2) distance learning, (3) multimedia and hypermedia learning, and (4) Internet implementation.

Audiovisual Approach

The audiovisual approach was a dominant means of instruction until the mid-1980s. Universities, especially departments of foreign languages, had fully equipped language labs for teaching and learning. Some key high schools in major cities and provinces were also equipped with audiovisual systems to assist language instruction. A drawback of the audiovisual approach was that the instructor was overwhelmingly preoccupied with the complicated technical maneuvering. It was inconvenient for the teacher to adapt teaching to differences in individual learners. This was evident in material selection and content design. Yet, as an instructional method, the audiovisual approach made teachers aware of the benefit of multiple learning cues to the learner, that is, the auditory and visual learning cues in the information process.

Distance Learning

Distance education started from correspondence education in the 1950s, followed by a more aggressive approach through a national broadcast network in the 1960s, which was known as radio and television education. From the mid- to the late 1970s, the radio and television universities boomed as a result of societal needs and a surging quest for knowledge. Through their twenty years' efforts, the radio and television universities formed a system that was headed by the Central Radio Television University (CRTVU) and included 44 provincial radio and television universities, 831 municipal-level radio and television universities and branches, and 1,699 county-level branches. According to 1997 statistics, the total number of graduates of three-year radio and television colleges had reached more than 2.3 million.

Satellite communication technology presents special advantages and vitality. Its use in education brings new vigor to distance education. Satellite technology widens the teaching scale and contents of radio and television universities, improves the development of training for secondary and primary teachers and teachers of vocational education, and pushes forward educational reform and economic development in outlying regions.

Multimedia and Hypermedia Learning

Multimedia and hypermedia as means of instruction have gained recognition in classrooms. The Decision on Strengthening Educational Reform and Boosting Education of Overall Qualification (1999) emphasized that "computer and information technology education should be spread in senior secondary schools and some qualified junior secondary and elementary schools. All the higher education institutions and key secondary vocational schools should establish the educational science and research net, and secondary and elementary schools will establish it step by step." The advancement of information technology makes new learning technologies such as multimedia and hypermedia available for both teachers and students. In recent years, multimedia computers and regional nets on campus have been increasingly used and established in schools in the developed cities. Teaching slides, projective films, and audios and videos for all disciplines have formed a complete series in secondary and elementary schools. The Ministry of Education decided in 1997 to set up 1,000 experimental schools for modern educational technology. All of them are required to make full use of modern educational technology to promote the development and reform of basic education.

Internet Implementation

The instructional use of the Internet in China has undergone ups and downs. A 2001 study by China Internet Network Information Center (CNNIC) indicates that Internet growth in education has been slow in recent years. Nevertheless, the Internet has gradually entered classrooms at all levels. In colleges and universities, the Internet is used in several different ways. In general, it is used as (1) a tool for information search and communication, through which the instructor uses e-mail, browser, and threaded discussion to engage students in various types of learning; (2) an alternative to traditional course delivery, in which instructional Web sites are created as an alternative way of teaching and learning; and (3) a way to facilitate intercollege collaboration, where universities use the Internet to collaborate in research and information sharing.

As in higher education, elementary and secondary schools in China use the Internet as a tool for information search and communication. The Internet is essentially used as an extension of the school library. Although there is a demand from teachers who prefer to have their own instructional Web sites, few teachers know how to build them. Some provinces have started pilot programs by establishing a centralized technology hub that provides technical support to local schools.

Nonetheless, the instructional use of the Internet in China is uneven in terms of distribution, accessibility, and transmission quality. Geographically, the coastal cities and provinces are well developed and have the resources to build the infrastructure, whereas the inland cities and provinces do not have the resources to develop the technology. A CNNIC January 2001 report showed that the nine coastal cities and provinces account for 70 percent of the 265,405 Web sites in China. Accessibility is another issue. The CNNIC study indicated that universities and colleges have a better access rate (65 percent) of using the Internet than that in secondary (23 percent) and elementary schools (6.4 percent). Digital equity is also one of the major concerns in the instructional use of the Internet in China. Statistics showed that males (69.56 percent) accessed the Internet more than females (30.44 percent). The digital equity issue is addressed more at a societal level than within the educational area alone. The changing of the Chinese market economy invited competition into the Internet business, resulting in numerous Internet cafés that provide access to people who do not have computers at home. However, efforts to make the Internet available for more people were curbed by the government. The data of CNNIC indicated that the number of Internet cafés shrank dramatically from 21 percent in 2000 to 15 percent in 2001, which serves as an indicator of the uneven development.

See also Character Education in Primary and Secondary Schools; Educational Administration; Educational System; Foreign-Language Teaching Methodology; Foreign Language Training; Higher-Education Reform; Management Education; Primary Education; Private Education; School Enrollment and Employment; Secondary Education; Taiwan, Education Reform in; Teacher Education; Telecommunications Industry; Television Institute and Self-Learning; United States, Chinese Education in; Vocational and Technical Training.

Bibliography

Central Committee of the Communist Party of the People's Republic of China, *The Decision on Strengthening Educational Reform and Boosting Education of Overall Qualification*, 1999, http://www.moe.edu.cn/wenxian/index.htm, accessed on April 1, 2003; China Internet Network Information Center (CNNIC), *Semiannual Survey Report on the Development of China's Internet*, 2001, http://www.cnnic.net.cn/develst/cnnic200101.shtml, accessed on April 1, 2003; Zheng, R., J.R. Ouyang, and R. Feng,

"Instructional Use of the Internet in China," *Educational Technology Research and Development* 50, no. 1 (2002): 88–92.

Robert Zheng and Ronghua Ouyang

Educational Administration

Finance

The Chinese government presently has established a two-stream channel for financing education. In addition to allocating funds to schools and programs, the government also encourages local businesses and administrative organizations to be funding partners. In general, the central government is responsible for allocating funds to higher-education institutions, whereas the local governments appropriate funds to schools run by local authorities. Subsidies are also made available by the government to support schools operated by counties, villages, and business enterprises. In addition, donations from organizations and prominent businesses/persons have contributed substantially to support of school operations and educational projects.

Since the 1980s, the central government has appropriated special funds to develop primary and vocational education in poor remote areas. In 1995, the State Education Commission and the Ministry of Finance initiated a special project for the implementation of compulsory education in deprived areas. Local government supporting funds also contribute to this project.

In 2001, the central and local governments allocated 463.7 billion yuan for education, an increase of 20.49 percent over the previous year. The growth rate exceeds that of revenues. Educational spending represents 14.31 percent of the total national budget, compared with 13.8 percent in 2000. Education investment as a percentage of the 2001 gross national product (9,593.3 billion yuan) was 3.19 percent, an increase of .32 percent over the previous year. In 2002, the total government educational budget was 548 billion yuan, representing an 18.16 percent increase over the figure of 2001, which was 463.7 billion. In general, educational budgets have increased year after year as stipulated by the Education Law, except for a few deprived provinces and autonomous regions.

Policies

Educational policies are typically modified in response to political, social, and economic climates of different periods. Until the end of the **Great Cultural Revolution (1966–1976)**, educational policies were initiated from the central government and issued to the provincial and local governments for implementation. These policies were instructions from the central government and were not made into law.

As reflected in the Common Guidelines of the First Chinese People's Political Consultative Conference in 1949, the educational mission of China was to enhance people's cultural level, to prepare needed personnel to support China's reconstruction, and to develop ideological education guidelines, the core concept of which is to serve the people. The general educational curriculum was organized for the major areas such as early childhood education, **primary educa-tion, secondary education**, higher education, and political education. A signifi-cant aspect of the educational policy of this time was the effort toward helping the undereducated workers, peasants, and general public learn through alterna-tive educational channels, such as workshops and accelerated programs. In the first fifteen years from 1950 to 1965, educators in China were directed to re-form Chinese education by following the Russian model. This was fully reflected in school organization, teaching materials, instructional process, and manage-ment approach.

In response to the **Great Leap Forward** movement in 1957–1958, directions were given by the central government to align the educational programs with the purpose of serving the proletariat. To achieve this purpose, programs were redesigned to incorporate labor and production modules into the education process. Instructions were also directed toward achieving quantity, quality, speed, and savings. In the implementation process, educational systems exper-imented with different formats of operation, with the Communist Party repre-sentative heading the school reform committee. Confusion was caused by the government's ambition to try many directions of managing education business in a short time. A clear theme of the policy at this time was to install Commu-nist Party leadership in the education arena.

During the Great Cultural Revolution, the policy was to examine totally the function of the old education system and to reform the traditional teaching methodology to reflect social needs. Universities and schools were either closed or operated under the leadership of the workers' propaganda teams. Schools underwent reforms in organization, curriculum, and instructional ap-proach. Students were programmed to learn the essence of communism and Chairman **Mao Zedong**'s doctrine and also to learn from the workers, the peas-ants, and the soldiers by participating in trips to Beijing, a show of loyalty. In this period that was characterized by "destroying the old," reckless educational reforms were implemented in the name of "criticizing the guidelines of the capitalistic educational system."

After the Cultural Revolution, pragmatic educational policies were formu-lated to support the modernization movement in China. It was recognized that education was the backbone of agricultural, industrial, military, and technol-ogy modernization. In 1985, a resolution was made to establish the State Edu-cation Commission to assume leadership of education in China. Priorities were given to the implementation of nine-year compulsory education, development of secondary vocational education, and the independent operation of higher-education institutions. An important policy document released by the Office of State Affairs in 1992 outlined a blueprint of educational development of China in the twenty-first century. Guidelines of this policy document were in-troduced through legal procedures into laws that laid the foundation for edu-cational progress in subsequent years.

Laws

The State Education Commission is charged with the responsibility of en-forcing laws, policies, and principles in education. Since 1978, laws made in education have had a profound impact on educational development in modern China. To implement these educational laws, more than 200 administrative regulations on education have been issued by the State Education Commission.

Regulations on Academic Degrees passed by the Fifth **National People's Congress** in 1980 recognize the academic achievements of scholars by awarding levels of degrees in higher-education institutions. These regulations, followed by subsequent guidelines and criteria for implementation, are the first set of educational regulations approved by the National People's Congress since 1949.

The Law on Compulsory Education passed by the Sixth National People's Congress in 1986 mandates the enforcement of nine years of basic education for all children reaching school age. It serves as a protection of the right of Chinese people to free guaranteed educational opportunities. The law specifies the nature, the age limits, the organization, the funding sources, the human resources, and the implementation processes of compulsory education. Goals were set per individual schedule by different regions to meet their educational needs.

The Law on Protection of Juveniles passed by the Seventh National People's Congress in 1991 provides the legal basis to protect the right of the youngsters to physiological, psychological, and intellectual development as human beings. Education is specifically cited as a significant aspect of intellectual development of the juveniles under protection. Many subsequent educational regulations were made referencing the Law on Protection of Juveniles as a legal basis.

The Teachers' Law was passed by the Eighth National People's Congress in 1993. It recognizes the significant roles that teachers play in the construction of a modern socialistic China. It specifically elaborates on upgrading the conditions relating to the rights, responsibilities, qualifications, appointment, evaluation, classification, and professional development of those in the teaching profession.

In 1995, the Eighth National People's Congress passed the Law on Education. It is generally considered to be a landmark piece of legislation on education because this is the first educational law in the history of the Republic to solidify the importance of education to social and economic development of the country. In the legislative process of the country, the law places education as a priority item to be considered in legislative decision making. It is a significant piece of legislation because it provides the legal basis for organizational reforms of education in later years.

The Law on Vocational Education was passed by the Eighth National People's Congress in 1996. It promotes the development of vocational education by confirming its importance in supporting China's thriving economy. It provides guidelines for essential perspectives of vocational education such as organization, implementation, and evaluation issues. The law also classifies the type of vocational education institutions by level of administrative area and urges businesses and industries to collaborate with educational institutions for the development of vocational education. The sources of funding and guaranteed budgetary increases in support of vocational education are stipulated by the law.

The Law on Higher Education was passed by the Ninth National People's Congress in 1998 and provides general guidelines for the operation of higher-education institutions in China. Right after the Cultural Revolution, many higher-education institutions were established at different levels to respond to the desperate need of the time. Many of these institutions were substandard and cost ineffective. The law of 1998 is specific about rules and regulations in regard to the establishment and organization of institutions and imposes stringent restrictions on minimum standards. Other essential aspects of the law cover areas of national interest, educational investment, funding protection, faculty qualifications, facility requirements, and student rights and responsibilities.

Educational laws passed in the National People's Congress in the 1980s and 1990s have placed the Chinese educational system on solid legal ground. The implementation of these education laws has been supplemented by many regulations established by the State Council. These educational laws and regulations are significant because they serve as models for educational legislation at the provincial and county levels.

See also Character Education in Primary and Secondary Schools; Education Media and Technology; Educational System; Higher-Education Reform; Management Education; Private Education; School Enrollment and Employment; Taiwan, Education Reform in; Teacher Education; United States, Chinese Education in; Vocational and Technical Training.

Bibliography

A Statistical Report on the National Educational Expenditures in 2001 (Beijing: Department of Education, National Statistics Bureau, and Department of Finance, 2002); Du, Zuo Y., *Education System of the People's Republic of China* (Hong Kong: Joint Publishing Company, 1999); Ministry of Education, National Bureau of Statics, and the Ministry of Finance, *Reports on the Spending of 2002 Education Budget*, December 26, 2003, http://www.moe.edu.cn/edoas/website18/info5404.htm, accessed on November 15, 2004.

Tak Cheung Chan

Educational System

Since 1949, the year of the founding of the People's Republic of China (PRC), the Chinese government has set up a comprehensive and complete educational system. It is the biggest educational system in the world, with 701,097 schools at different levels and a total enrollment of 242,637,200 students (Ministry of Education 2002). The Chinese educational system consists of basic preschool education (before the age of six); **primary education** (six years of schooling; five years in rural areas); lower secondary (junior middle) school education (three years or four years of schooling); upper secondary (senior high) school education (three years of schooling); higher education (four years for bachelor's degrees and two to three years for nondegree specialized courses); and postgraduate education (two to three years for the master's degree; two to three years for doctorates).

Preschool Education

Preschool education in China is carried out in kindergartens that provide education for children of three years of age and over. Although the length of preschool education varies, it generally lasts from one to three years, or between the ages of three and six; however, in rural areas, preschool education rarely exceeds one year. By the mid-1980s, only 6.4 percent of the kindergarten schools were run by local departments of education; the majority were operated by factories, mines, business units, collective enterprises, neighborhoods, and even college and universities to serve the children of their own employees. Some schools run a full-day program, some are half day, and some are boarding schools. Due to the one-child-per-family policy, early childhood education has become increasingly emphasized and challenged in China. In the late 1980s, private kindergarten schools merged into preschool education. According to statistics, the number of kindergarten schools increased from 1,300 in 1956 to 111,706 in 1999; the total enrollment of children in school also grew from 130,000 in 1956 to 20,218,400 in 1999 (Ministry of Education 2002; Zhao 2000). Following the Kindergarten Education Guidelines issued by the Ministry of Education, Chinese preschools have currently adopted two models for the curriculum: a five-subject-area model and a six-subject-area model. The five-subject-area model includes language arts, music and painting, social and moral development, health, and science and math. The six-subject-area model covers language, mathematics, social studies, music, physical education, and arts.

Primary and Lower Secondary School Education

As stipulated in the Compulsory Education Law of the People's Republic of China, all children who have reached the age of six should be enrolled in school and receive compulsory education, regardless of sex, race, or class. Compulsory education starts with primary education, which varies in using a five-year model or a six-year model and continues with lower secondary schooling that lasts four or three years accordingly. In the nine-year compulsory education, the "6 + 3 system," the "5 + 4 system," and the "1 to 9 system" exist side by side, with the "6 + 3 system" predominating in most places. The entry age of primary schools is six or seven, while that of lower secondary schools is twelve or thirteen. According to statistics provided by the Ministry of Education in 2002, China has 491,300 primary schools with a total enrollment of 125,434,700 and 66,000 lower secondary schools with an enrollment of 65,143,800. The enrollment ratio of primary school–age children reached 99.1 percent, and the ratio for lower secondary school–age students reached 88.7 percent. According to the Tenth Five-Year Plan (2001–2005) of national development in the twenty-first century, the Chinese government will place great emphasis on the reinforcement and improvement of nine-year compulsory education to generalize quality-oriented education. By 2005, the objective is to reach a total enrollment rate in the lower secondary schools of 90 percent.

Upper Secondary School Education

Upper secondary school (senior high school) education in China is divided into regular upper secondary schools (formal high school) and specialized upper secondary schools (technical schools, normal schools, vocational schools, and specialized subject-oriented schools). By 2001, there were 14,900 upper secondary schools with a total enrollment of 14,049,100 students. Besides regular upper secondary schools, there were also 21,800 specialized upper secondary schools. The gross enrollment rate of special education enrollment in the upper secondary school age group was 42.8 percent, and 78.8 percent of upper secondary school graduates sought further schooling in colleges and universities (Ministry of Education 2002). The entry age of regular upper secondary schools is fifteen or sixteen. The length of schooling is three years. Schooling in specialized upper secondary schools usually lasts four years, although some lasts three years because of subject specialty. Some specialized upper secondary schools also admit upper secondary school graduates. These programs usually last only two years. Upper secondary school education in China will be more emphasized in large and middle-sized cities and economically developed areas. By 2005, it is projected that the gross enrollment rate of upper secondary school education in China will be increased from 42.8 percent to 60 percent.

Higher Education

Higher education plays an extremely important role in China. It offers undergraduate programs that span four to five years as well as special two- or three-year programs. Some medical programs last as long as seven to eight years. Students who have completed a first degree may apply to graduate schools that consist of two levels: master's and doctoral. The entry age of applicants for master's degree programs may not exceed forty, and the program of study lasts two to three years. The entry age of applicants for doctoral programs may not exceed forty-five, and the program usually lasts three years. However, with the **Open Door policy**, higher education has started admitting candidates of all ages to meet lifelong learning needs since 2002. In the late 1990s, China started Project 211, which aims at establishing about 100 key universities to lead the reform of higher education and strengthen a number of key disciplinary areas as a national priority for the twenty-first century. Higher education in China is very competitive because of its huge population. In the early 1980s, only 4 percent of upper secondary school students could be enrolled in colleges and universities. The goal of the Tenth Five-Year Plan (2001–2005) is to raise the gross enrollment rate of higher education to 15 percent.

See also Character Education in Primary and Secondary Schools; Education Media and Technology; Educational Administration; Higher-Education Reform; Management Education; Private Education; School Enrollment and Employment; Secondary Education; Taiwan, Education Reform in; Teacher Education; United States, Chinese Education in; Vocational and Technical Training.

Bibliography

Ministry of Education, *Education in China* (Beijing: Ministry of Education, 2002); Zhao, Jishi, *On Preschool Education* (Jiangsu, China: Nanjing Normal University Press, 2000).

Rongbua Ouyang and Dan Ouyang

Employment

See Labor Market; Labor-Market Development; Labor Policy, Employment, and Unemployment; Labor Relations; Labor Rights; Reemployment of Laid-off Workers; Unemployment.

Energy Industries

The strong growth of the Chinese economy during the past twenty-five years has driven a rapid growth of energy demand. In 2002, China became the second-largest country in energy consumption, following the United States and moving ahead of Japan. By 1994, China was energy self-sufficient by consuming about 10 percent of the world's energy while it accounted for about 10 percent of world energy production. However, China has become a net oil importer since 1993 and a net energy importer since 1995. The rapid growth of energy demand and lagging growth of energy production have become increased concerns in a number of policy areas, including the structural change in energy consumption, availability and cost of energy supplies, and the prospect of further adverse effects on the environment.

On the demand side, utility fuel (fuel used in the generation of electricity and heat) is the largest use of primary energy in China, followed by residential/commercial, industrial, and transportation uses. The growing demand for utility fuel, such as coal, natural gas, or liquefied natural gas, to be used for power plants and heating systems, for example, is important because it is tied directly to the growth in electricity demand, which itself is the fastest-growing component of final energy consumption that each of the other ends use.

Residential and commercial demand, currently China's second-largest energy end use, which accounts for close to one-third of energy consumption, has always been driven more by population, urbanization, and the availability of commercial energy (as distinguished from traditional energy such as wood and crop waste) than by industrial activity. It is projected that future residential and commercial buildings in China will continue to consume about one-third of the total energy.

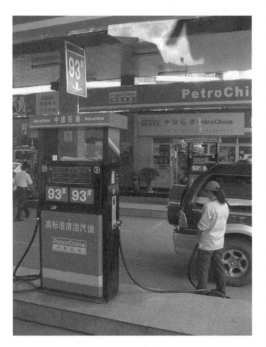

As more cars appear on Chinese streets, the demand for gasoline and the Chinese energy industry have grown.

Industrial demand, currently the third-largest energy use, would seem to be the use most directly related to aggregate economic activity. Two major changes have taken place since the early 1980s in industrial energy demand. One is that the use of energy in most industries, especially heavy industry, was very high historically in relation to output, and this has been gradually improved over time as new facilities have come on line to replace inefficient existing facilities. The other change is a major shift in industrial activities from heavy industry, which required large amounts of furnace fuels, including coal and heavy fuels, toward lighter industries—electrical machinery and appliances—which require primarily electricity and more specialized fuels such as liquefied petroleum gas and natural gas and are mostly less energy intensive.

Transportation demand is currently China's fourth-largest energy end use. Until recently, most transportation energy was associated with industrial uses. As of 2002, increases in transportation energy were mainly associated with industrial uses, an increased reliance on freight (trucking and to some extent air) for industrial shipments, and growing amounts of personal transportation, which increasingly involves cars.

On the supply side, coal makes up the bulk of China's primary energy consumption, and China is both the largest consumer and producer of coal in the world. It accounted for 69 percent of China's energy production in 2002. However, the growth potential in coal production has become questionable in recent years. China's Ninth Five-Year Plan (1996–2000) set a goal of coal production of 1.4 billion short tons by 2000; however, China's actual coal production for that year was 1.27 billion short tons. By 2002, the shortage was more than 200 million tons, and it is expected that the shortage will continue in the future. The diminishing growth of coal production will threaten China's sustainable economic growth. In addition, coal, as the major energy resource, creates a severe pollution problem. Coal burning remains the leading cause of pollution in urban areas. In recent years, the government has attempted to control air pollution in cities by making a major effort to replace coal with cleaner fuels, including natural gas, liquefied petroleum gas, and electricity in **cities** for both residential and commercial uses.

China currently is the world's third-largest oil consumer, behind the United States and Japan. Consumption of petroleum products was 5.56 million barrels per day (bbl/d) in 2003. China is expected to surpass Japan as the second-largest world oil consumer within the next decade and reach a consumption level of 12.8 million bbl/d by 2025, making it a major factor in the world oil market. Like the production of coal, China's oil production has remained basically steady at the level of 2.5–3.0 million bbl/d in recent years. The gap between domestic oil output and China's needs has been widening. Practically, the difference must be made up by imports, which may create much uncertainty about China's energy supply and subsequently about its economic growth.

Natural gas has not been a major fuel in China. Given China's domestic reserves of natural gas, which stood at 48.3 trillion cubic feet at the beginning of 2002, and the environmental benefits of using gas, China has embarked on a major expansion of its gas infrastructure. Natural gas accounted for less than

3 percent of total energy consumption in China in 2003, but consumption is expected to be more than tripled by 2010. This will involve increases in domestic production and imports by pipeline and in the form of liquefied natural gas. The increase program includes the ongoing gas-line project, the West-to-East Pipeline, from gas deposits in the desert in northwestern China to Shanghai. It also includes joint-venture projects of drilling offshore natural gas and importing liquefied natural gas supplies from Australia, Indonesia, Russia, and the Middle East.

As for hydroelectric energy, by far the largest project under construction is the Three Gorges Dam. When fully completed in 2009, it will include twenty-six separate 700 megawatt generators for a total of 18.2 gigawatts. Several other major hydroelectric projects are under construction or will be constructed in China's southwestern region. These projects will significantly increase the electricity supply and improve its distribution.

Nuclear power in China is in its early stage of development and provided only 1 percent of China's total electric power in 2003. Several nuclear projects are under construction with the participation of Russian, French, and Canadian firms. Two 1 gigawatt generating units of Daya Bay nuclear power plant in Guangdong Province and two 600 megawatt generating units at the Qinshan nuclear power plant in Zhejiang Province began to operate in 2002 and 2003. When new plants are brought into operation, China will have a nuclear power capacity of 8.7 gigawatts that will provide 3 percent of total electrical power by 2005.

See also Auto Industry Development.

Bibliography

Energy Information Administration (EIA), Department of Energy, *China Country Analysis Brief* (2004), http://eia.doe.gov/emeu/cabs/china.html, accessed on November 15, 2004; Energy Information Administration (EIA), Department of Energy, *Privatization and Globalization of Energy Markets* (2004), http://www.eia.doe.gov/emeu/pgem/ch4d.html, accessed on November 15, 2004; Gates, David F., and Jason Z. Yin, "Urbanization and Energy in China," in *Urbanization and Social Welfare in China*, eds. Aimin Chen, Gordon Liu, and Kevin Zhang (Burlington, VT: Ashgate Publishing, 2004); International Energy Agency (IEA), *World Energy Outlook 2003*, http://www.worldenergyoutlook.org, accessed on November 15, 2004; Yin, Jason Z., and David Gates, "Automobile and Fuel Industries," in *The Globalization of the Chinese Economy*, eds. Shang-jin Wei, James G. Wen, and Huizhong Zhou, pp. 82–99 (Northampton, MA: Edward Elgar, 2002).

Jason Z. Yin

English Proficiency Levels

Because of ongoing economic globalization, the demand for more professionals who are proficient in English is increasing in today's China. The study of English is booming, especially since China joined the World Trade Organization (WTO) in 2001 and won the bid to host the 2008 Summer Olympic Games in Beijing. Chinese in all age groups are engaged in English learning. Civil servants at various government institutions are taking part in English-language training programs with the goal of improving their English proficiency.

English is tested in the nationwide university entrance examinations as an academic subject. In the past, it was a common phenomenon that a Chinese student who received a satisfactory mark in an English examination could not communicate with a native English speaker because all he/she had learned were reading and translation skills. In Chinese, this type of bookish English proficiency is called "deaf and mute" English.

Nowadays, at four-year colleges, English is being offered throughout the entire curriculum. ESP (English for special purposes) courses are also added to the English curriculum. The goal of these courses is to ensure that students with different specializations can make good use of English in their special areas of work after they graduate.

Since the start of the economic reforms, Chinese-language educators and administrators have started to realize the importance of a more pragmatic approach to foreign-language acquisition. Through cooperation with Western universities and institutions, English teaching in China has shifted from formalism to functionalism, which has also influenced the criteria of English proficiency tests. Thus the focus of foreign-language teaching and testing has shifted from testing and evaluating the learners' linguistic knowledge in the areas of grammar and vocabulary to the learners' communicative competence.

As a result, foreign-language teaching is going beyond the linguistic aspect; practicing the communicative skills of listening and speaking is emphasized by instructors. Further, more stress is laid on the cultural dimension in foreign-language acquisition. A prominent change in reforming the English-language testing system is that listening comprehension and writing skills are now being included in some of the most important English tests.

There are numerous types of tests and level assessments. Most are locally developed; some are imported. Because these tests are often found to overlap or to be unrelated to one another, which results in inconsistencies, the Chinese Ministry of Education established the PETS (Public English Test System) proficiency standard in 1999. PETS was a cooperative project in the educational sector between the Chinese and British governments and is considered the national English proficiency test system of China. PETS is designed and administered by the National Education Examinations Authority (NEEA) under the Ministry of Education.

Foreign-language proficiency levels for learners are defined by the Chinese Ministry of Education. The five-level PETS covers all standards of English, ranging from the completion of junior level three in middle school to the English-major level after two years of university study. The test is divided into several levels, with level one being the lowest and level five the highest. The five-level PETS has become the most widely used system across higher education. It aims to evaluate the examinees' four skills, listening, speaking, reading, and writing, with emphasis on the listening and speaking skills. PETS does not include any specifications about the age, occupation, on educational background of examinees, and anyone is admitted to the tests.

TOPE (Test of Professional English) is a new nationwide test system that was introduced in China in March 2003. This is an English-language proficiency test developed by the Educational Testing Service (ETS) of the United States. It is considered a standard examination of practical English, designed for business and government professionals. TOPE aims to assess reading, writing, listening, and speaking skills in one integrated test.

There are other English proficiency tests designed for students who plan to study abroad or want to qualify for certain jobs in China. Many students are taking the Test of English as a Foreign Language (TOEFL) or the Graduate Record Examination (GRE) to prove their level of proficiency. Students need to pass the TOEFL test to study abroad, especially to attend universities in the United States and Canada. The GRE is acknowledged as a general examination for students to enter graduate programs.

Other English proficiency tests for Chinese who plan to go abroad are the International English Language Testing System (IELTS) and the Graduate Management Admission Test (GMAT). The IELTS is used and acknowledged by universities in England, Australia, New Zealand, Canada, and many other countries. Immigration offices in Canada, Australia, and New Zealand also use the IELTS as the only standard test to evaluate the English proficiency of technical and other professional immigrants. The GMAT is a proficiency test specifically designed for students planning to enroll in MBA programs abroad.

During the past few decades, there have been significant developments in the theory and practice of English teaching throughout the world that have influenced the definition of proficiency in China. More emphasis has been placed on the use of the language for purposeful communication. Strongly influenced by the new trend, China is making progress in standardizing and implementing pragmatically oriented language proficiency tests.

In the field of foreign-language teaching, China is undertaking an overall reform of English testing, teaching methods, and teacher training. The traditional emphasis on gaining a large vocabulary through recitation and through rote learning activities is being replaced by a more integrated approach to English writing, listening, reading, and speaking. Chinese schools are adapting to Western open teaching methods and modern instructional technology. The educational reform in the area of foreign-language acquisition in China is creating business opportunities for Western enterprises that want to enter the Chinese market. English-language proficiency testing accordingly reflects this trend of training English learners to communicate in real-world settings.

See also Foreign-Language Teaching Methodology; Foreign-Language Training; Putonghua, Promotion of; United States, Chinese Education in; World Trade Organization (WTO), China's Accession to.

Bibliography

Ministry of Education, "The Curriculum for Fourth through Sixth Levels of College English Will Include Aural/Oral Tests," March 30, 2004, http://www.moe.edu.cn/edoas/website18/info3771.htm, accessed on November 15, 2004; Luo, Jing, and Dengming Zhao, "Three Models of Foreign Language Reading Comprehension and Their Application in the Instruction of College Level English," *Journal of the Northwest Normal University of China* 36, no. 5 (1999): 98–102.

Senquan Zhang

Entrance Examination System for Colleges and Universities

The entrance examination for colleges and universities can be considered a sensitive indicator of China's educational reform in the second half of the twentieth century. It reflects educational reforms during different periods of time. In the early 1950s, the People's Republic of China (PRC), following the Soviet Union's model, pushed a centralized education system and introduced a unified national entrance examination system for college and university admissions. The subjects that were examined included politics (current issues and history of the Chinese Communist Party), Chinese, mathematics, history, geography, chemistry, physics, and foreign language. The examination required candidates throughout the nation to take the examination on the same day, at the same time, and in the same sequence. Examination scores were then used to allocate all first-year students in accordance with the unified enrollment plans, which were coordinated and carefully balanced between the national and regional levels.

In the late 1950s, the unified entrance examination came under scrutiny. Following the Soviet Union's reform practice, a new form of college admissions was adopted in 1958. Instead of a nationally unified entrance examination, institutions of higher education gave their own examinations either individually or jointly, as had been practiced before 1952. Recommendations and referring components were introduced into the admission process. A new trend of the

College admission is based on scores of college entrance exams. During examination season, streets are lined with tutoring service stands to help candidates with their test preparations.

entrance examination was initially modeled in the newly opened Communist Labor University of Jiangxi Province in 1958. Candidates of worker-peasant origin and cadres who had participated in revolutionary work were granted priority in admission. These people could be admitted based only on the recommendations without taking any written entrance examination. This system then prevailed nationally with the slogan "To make intellectuals of the laboring people and laborers of intellectuals." As a result of the renewed emphasis on political and class background, those from "good" worker-peasant backgrounds in China's colleges and universities increased from 36 percent of all students in 1957 to 48 percent in 1958 and 51 percent in 1959 (Pepper 1996). This reform of admission obviously had a negative impact. Candidates were primarily judged by their backgrounds, and many young people found themselves subjected to different levels of discrimination. Those candidates with so-called problematic backgrounds, such as having in their immediate family relatives in Taiwan or abroad, could be prevented from entering any colleges and universities.

The **Great Cultural Revolution (1966–1976)** further radically reformed guidelines for the entrance examination. The entire body of rules, regulations, precedents, and traditional supports of the old education system was overthrown. Higher education lost its normal function. All graduates from upper secondary schools were ordered to go to the countryside first and perform some practical work for two or more years before being admitted to higher-education institutions. All candidates for higher-education institutions were to be selected from workers and peasants with practical experience, and they should return to production after a few years' study in colleges. Although the college enrollment plans were still drawn up nationally and by province, the unified national college entrance examination was completely abolished. Instead, higher-education institutions started selecting entrants from the pool of candidates recommended by their own work units in the early 1970s. National unified curricula were also abolished, and each institute was left to rebuild its own curriculum base using radical principles like shorter courses, less classroom learning, and more practice of laboring and involvement in political struggle. The criteria for the candidates' recommendation were simple: (1) about twenty years old, (2) junior or above graduates, and (3) a good two-year laboring record. The last requirement certainly forced graduates of lower and upper secondary schools to work in the countryside if they ever wanted to become college students. This reform did not bring any positive impact on higher education and resulted in a corruption of the admission process, since all sons, daughters, or close relatives of those who were in positions of power were recommended. The abolishment of the college entrance examination ruined the complete academic arena and damaged a whole generation of excellent and talented youths.

In 1977, after ten years of radical reform, the decision to restore national college entrance examinations was officially announced. The saying "Respect knowledge, respect science, and respect talent" sparked the complete restoration of entrance examinations. All youths, no matter what their residency was, were highly encouraged and motivated toward taking the national centralized college entrance examination. The entrance examination included three major tracks: liberal arts, science, and foreign language (mainly English). The subjects of politics, Chinese, mathematics, and foreign language were required for all candidates; history and geography were added for the candidates in the liberal arts track, and chemistry and physics for those in the science track. The score for foreign language was counted as a reference for the candidates in the liberal arts and science tracks, and the score for mathematics for the candidates in the foreign-language track. Both foreign language and mathematics became required subjects in the entrance examination after 1978.

The restoration of national centralized college entrance examinations in 1977 stimulated Chinese education. The reversal was swift and complete and changed almost everything in education. Because of the increasingly developed market economics, the flaws of the national centralized college entrance examination, such as favoritism, better known as "special treatment," became the blockade in educational reform. In 2000, a series of reforms was implemented in the Chinese educational system for the college entrance examinations. The reforms addressed mainly greater access to higher education and the age limit for examination registration. The examination styles of "3 + 2" and "3 + comprehensive" were implemented, in which "3" stands for Chinese, mathematics, and foreign language, while "2" refers to history and geography for students intending to study liberal arts and physics and chemistry for students intending to study science. The comprehensive examination covers the subjects in liberal arts or in science.

See also Educational System; Higher-Education Reform.

Bibliography

Ministry of Education, *Reform Trends of Education in China from 1998–1999* (Beijing: Department of International Cooperation and Exchanges, Ministry of Education, PRC, 2000); Pepper, Suzanne, *Radicalism and Education Reform in 20th-Century China: The Search for an Ideal Development Model* (New York: Cambridge University Press, 1996); Yang, Dongping, *2000 Educational Evolution in China*, 2001, http://www.edu.cn/20010101/22290.shtml, accessed on April 3, 2003.

Ronghua Ouyang and Dan Ouyang

Environmental Protection, Policies and Practices

Environmental protection is one of the greatest challenges in our time, and the magnitude of problems that confronts China is daunting. Some of the problems are related to population pressure: China has about 22 percent of the world's population but only 7 percent of its arable land. During the 1990s alone, its population increased by some 125 million, for whom the nation had to produce an additional 45 million tons of grain each year, equivalent to the 1990 grain output of Canada. Unrelenting population pressure puts natural resources under intense strain. China's forest coverage, for instance, is barely half of the world average, which is above 30 percent; the amount of water per capita averages 2,380 cubic meters a year in China, only one-fifth of the world average. Other problems are inherited from the past, such as **Mao Zedong**'s era, during which environmental degradation was dismissed as a phenomenon of capitalism, and people were told to follow the lead of revolutionary fervor rather than science and technology. This attitude wreaked havoc on China's resources and ecology, as in the 1958–1960 **Great Leap Forward** and the 1966–1976 **Great Cultural Revolution**. Still other problems are generated by the spectacular growth of China's economy since 1978, which has taken a considerable toll on the environment.

Habitat destruction, deforestation, soil erosion, and pollution are only a few of the dilemmas that have resulted from disregard of environmental protection in China. A case in point is the Maoist policy that stressed grain production as the key to economic growth (*yi liang wei gang*). The countryside was ordered to increase grain acreage by reclaiming land from forests, hillsides, and lake bottoms, thus causing massive damage to China's natural habitat. Soil erosion can easily arise from deforestation, denuded land, and construction of new development projects. In the late 1990s, soil erosion affected more than one-third of China's land and ranked among its most pressing environmental problems. A major source of pollution in China is industrialization, which produces a huge volume of wastes that pollute the air, water, and soil. Air pollution was found to account for some 300,000 premature deaths a year, and water pollution from chemical, fertilizer, and pesticide runoff made more than 50 percent of the monitored rivers too contaminated to provide drinkable water. According to a 1997 World Bank report (Ma & Ortolano, 2000), the combined annual economic cost of air and water pollution totaled some 11.2 percent of China's GDP.

The notion of environmental protection did not register with China's national agenda until after the 1972 United Nations Conference on Human Environment. In 1973, Beijing held the first national conference on environmental protection. In May 1974, the Environmental Protection Leading Group of the State Council was formed that consisted of representatives from various ministries and departments potentially related to environmental protection. Parallel to this belated start was a remedial approach to issues of environmental protection. In the spring of 1974, peasants on the outskirts of Tianjin irrigated their fields with polluted water from the Ji Canal, only to find that more than half of their 3,000-hectare fields failed to grow a single ear of grain. The State Council intervened; a separate pipeline was laid to collect most of the fouled water and drain it into the sea away from the Ji Canal. The Tianjin Chemical Plant, a major source of pollution, was made to build fifty-eight pollution-control units. In this case, environmental protection was pursued post hoc and took a back seat to production.

Article II of the new constitution of the People's Republic of China (PRC) (1978) provided a legal basis for environmental protection. The promulgation of the Environmental Protection Law of the PRC for Trial Implementation in 1979 marked the beginning of a more proactive official commitment to environmental protection. What had started as an office under the Leading Group of the State Council expanded into a bureau in the Ministry of Construction in 1982 and became the State Environmental Protection Administration (SEPA) with full ministerial rank in 1998. The SEPA is in charge of designing environmental policies and programs. With a staff of a few hundred, its role in the implementation of environmental regulations is confined to the national level.

A vast network of environmental protection bureaus (EPBs) and offices (EPOs) has been established to enforce the regulations at the local levels. Like other government departments, EPBs, which operate at the provincial and municipal levels, report to both their national superior SEPA and local governments. Indeed, each EPB is an organ of local government, as is an EPO, which operates at the county level or below.

With environmental concerns coming into the national spotlight, China developed eight national pollution-control programs in addition to a robust set of laws and policies. At the core of these programs are environmental impact assessments, pollutant discharge fees, and three synchronizations, known as the "three magical weapons." These three programs are based on the idea that environmental protection should be pursued in tandem with economic development. They involve assessing the impact of a project on the local community or habitat against environmental and zoning laws, synchronizing environmental protection with the design, construction, and operation of waste treatment facilities, and setting waste discharge standards to curb pollution. Together the eight programs constitute a wholesome responsibility system that vests each level of government with explicit duties of environmental protection and holds culprits of pollution liable for their violations. This system was incorporated into the Environmental Protection Law of the People's Republic of China in 1989, when the trial implementation status of the basic environmental law was removed.

During the 1980s, China promulgated more than twenty special statutes to facilitate the implementation of the eight pollution-control programs. The number of people engaged in environmental protection work doubled. As of 1990, there were close to 2,500 EPBs and EPOs nationally, which employed more than 60,000 staff. Environmental protection is a long-term commitment. China's Action Plan for 1991–2000 highlighted environmental issues that continued to concern officials. The plan focused on "seven priority problems": water pollution, especially contamination by organic waste; urban air pollution, as measured by particulates and sulfur dioxide; hazardous and toxic solid waste in urban areas; water shortages, particularly in northern China; soil erosion; loss of forests and grasslands; and reduction of species and habitats, especially wetlands. Three of the seven concerns pertained to pollution. Another three concerns were linked to the preservation of natural resources: water shortage, soil erosion, and loss of forests and grasslands. The last concern centered on the overall integrity of China's ecosystem.

A number of measures were taken to address the "seven priority problems." Chief among them were treatment of industrial and municipal wastewater to bring it up to discharge standards, reduction of reliance on low-efficiency coal-burning boilers and stoves to cut down on pollutant loads in the air, restriction of farming on slopes, return of farmland to forestry and nature, and afforestation. At least one of these measures is specifically designed to undo what has been done to the natural habitat. In 2000, a total of 398,000 hectares of farmland were returned to forestry and grassland. Some of the other measures are reflective of a new shift in China's strategies to an emphasis on "cleaner production" that came about in the mid-1990s.

In 1996, China started to consider drafting a law on cleaner production for

2002. To this end, a plan was launched to train 10,000 people in the concepts and methods of cleaner production. In preparing China for the challenge of the next century, the **National People's Congress** also approved the Ninth Five-Year Plan (1996–2000), together with its environmental goals and two implementation strategies. One strategy was to control total waste discharges, which involved limiting the mass as well as the concentration of waste discharges. It was reported that the total amounts of twelve main pollutants in waste discharges were reduced by 10 to 15 percent in 2000 compared with 1995. The other strategy was an afforestation campaign called "Trans-Century Green Plan," under which 836 projects were completed by 2000.

China has come a long way in addressing its environmental problems, even though some of its development projects can be environmentally controversial, such as Three Gorges Dam. Indeed, despite all its regulations and programs, China's ecosystem has continued to degrade. It is admitted that environmental degradation has been slowed down rather than stopped in China. Acid rain, sandstorms, soil erosion, and water pollution remain alarming, to name just a few concerns, and they all have a negative impact globally. Looking ahead, China aspires to further reduce environmental pollution and bring its environmental degradation under "preliminary control"—two goals that are incorporated into its Tenth Five-Year Plan (2001–2005).

See also Central Planning; Industrial Structure; United Nations (UN) and China.

Bibliography

Ma, Xiaoying, and Leonard Ortolano, *Environmental Regulation in China* (Lanham, MD: Rowman & Littlefield, 2000); Ross, Lester, *Environmental Policy in China* (Bloomington: Indiana University Press, 1988); Sinkule, Barbara J., and Leonard Ortolano, *Implementing Environmental Policy in China* (Westport, CT: Praeger, 1995); Xie, Zhenhua, *Report on the State of the Environment in China, 2001* (Beijing: Environmental Information Center, 2002).

Zhiming Zhao

Ethnic Burial Customs

Many Chinese ethnic groups believe that while death marks the end of the present life, it also marks the beginning of the next cycle. Since nobody escapes death, the pursuit of eternal life and happiness is all the more fervent, which is reflected in a variety of burial ceremonies. The general process from death to burial that is followed by most ethnic groups that practice burial includes death announcement, corpse laying, corpse bath, soul calling, coffining, mourning, and procession to the cemetery.

The death announcement is the announcement made to relatives, neighbors, and villagers, which is done immediately after the death occurs. The ways to announce death are different from one ethnic culture to another, and even from place to place. Firing fireworks and guns, blowing buffalo horns or bamboo horns, beating a copper drum, and striking gongs, are common forms of announcement. Lahu, Va, Li, Yao, and Jingpo people fire guns toward the sky to announce death, while the Nu people blow bamboo horns. Different numbers of shots, blows on the horn, or drumbeats carry different meanings that may indicate the gender and the social status of the dead person. Usually neighbors of the same village go to the mourning family to offer condolence and volunteer help. Relatives who do not live in the vicinity arrive only on the special day of the burial ceremony.

Normally, after the death is confirmed, the corpse is moved from where the person died to a proper place in the house. For most ethnic minorities, the corpse is laid in the middle of the sitting room. However, for some ethnic groups, if the person died outside the home, the corpse cannot be placed in the house. Usually the head is directed toward the west and the feet toward the east since Buddhist believers deem the west to be the heavenly destination. Other groups have their unique ways. For example, the Lisu people put the head toward some higher place with the corpse close to the fireplace. The Lahu people put pieces of silver in the mouth of the dead, while the Manchu insert coins made in the Qianlong time of the Qing dynasty (1644–1911). After the corpse is laid properly, some foods are served by the living members of the family and a lamp is lit near the corpse.

Corpse bathing symbolizes cleansing. The water and the persons who conduct bathing are carefully selected. Some ethnic minorities, such as Daur, Ewenki, and some other ethnic minorities in northern China, require the use of the water from the family water jar. Several ethnic minorities in the south, such as Molao and Tujia, need to "buy" water from a stream or well nearby. Usually the oldest son or daughter goes to the stream or well and throws several coins into the stream or well before fetching the water. The persons who conduct the bathing are normally descendants of the same gender. After the bathing, the dead person's male descendant clips the nails of the fingers and toes of the dead before dressing him with a new set of "clothes of longevity." Chinese Muslims use white cloth drenched in perfume to bind the corpse.

Many ethnic groups believe that every corpse has a soul that may be separate from the flesh corpse. Hence when a person dies, a sorcerer or sorceress may be invited to climb up to the family roof, where he/she will vocally call the soul of the dead person to return and rejoin the lifeless body.

Coffining the corpse is the farewell ceremony for the family members, relatives, and other people related to the dead person. All relatives must attend the ceremony, and among some ethnic minorities the dead person's male descendants are required to place the corpse into the coffin in person. According to the traditional customs, the articles of daily use, including tools of the dead person, are put into the coffin. In Oroqen customs, for example, cookers, bowls, tobacco pipes, bows and arrows, saddle, knives, and the like are usually coffined with the corpse.

The mourning usually lasts several days. A small mourning hall is set in the house. All kin relatives must wear mourning clothes of appropriate styles. The sons and daughters must keep the wake and weep while relatives file in. Usually it is the daughters and daughters-in-law who sobbingly read the eulogy. Most of the ethnic villages regard the ceremonies as very important affairs of the entire village and usually hold funeral parties with singing and dancing the same night. The Jingpo people, for example, perform three types of dances. The Tujia people perform the so-called falling flower dance, while the Nu people and the Jinuo people hold a bottle of wine while singing and dancing in the dead person's house. The Jinuos mostly sing and dance on the nights of the following days after the burial. In a sense, funeral ceremonies are special feasting and recreational activities as well.

Carrying the coffin to the cemetery is usually the biggest ceremony. Different ethnic peoples have different styles of funeral processions. Normally, firecrackers and guns are fired to scare ghosts, paper money is burned, and food is tossed along the way. The forms of burial that are used today include earth burial, cremation burial, celestial burial, tree burial, water burial, and pagoda burial. These are variants of the traditional forms such as hanging-coffin, boat-coffin, and cliff burial that used to be popular among ethnic minorities in southern China. Earth burial is the most popular form, adopted by about fifty ethnic minorities. The coffins, coffin pits, tombstones, and grave shapes are different according to the ethnic cultures. Ethnic groups such as Yi, Bai, Naxi, Lahu, Hani, Pumi, Qiang, and She practice cremation. However, influenced by the Han people, some ethnic people have changed their cremation custom into earth burial. Nowadays, the Yi people in Daliangshan and Xiaoliangshan areas, the Mosuo people in Ninglang of Lijiang, Lahu, Dai, and Pumi still practice cremation. Cremation is usually done by burning the corpse on a pile of wood in a forest or on the top of a hill. After the corpse is burned, some bones may be collected to put into a cave, to be brought back home for preservation, or simply to be buried where cremation takes place.

Celestial burial is also called bird burial and is popular among Tibetans, Uygurs, and the Menba. First, the corpse is carried to the special celestial site. After some ritual ceremonies, the corpse is cut into small pieces and mixed with butter, fried flour of highland barley, and other popular foods. The mixture is then displayed on a platform to attract vultures. Some ethnic groups light a bonfire and use the smoke to invite the "habitual" birds.

Tree burial is a form in which the coffin is made of natural tree branches that grew close into the shape of a coffin. The practice is popular among the Oroquens and Ewenkis. Water burial involves throwing the corpse into a river so that it can be eaten by fishes or simply washed away. Most of the Menba and some Tibetans adopt water burial. Pagoda burial is only used in Buddhist temples for eminent monks. Either a treated corpse or some bones left from cremation, and sometimes only the used articles of an eminent monk, are buried for people to worship. A variety of burial and funeral forms have been revived since the late 1970s under the economic reforms that gave people more freedom. During the earlier Mao era, cremation became the standard practice, and other forms were considered superstition.

See also Drinking in Ethnic Cultures; Ethnic Kinships; Ethnic Marriage Customs; Ethnic Minorities, Political Systems of; Ethnicity and Ethnic Policies; Mosuo People, Matriarchal Tradition of; Taiwan, Ethnicity and Ethnic Policies of.

Bibliography

Song, Shuhua, ed., *An Introduction to Chinese Ethnic Minorities* (Beijing: Central University for Nationalities Press, 2001); Xu, Wanbang, and Qi Qingfu, eds., *An Introduction to Chinese Ethnic Minority Cultures* (Beijing: Central University for Nationalities Press, 1996).

Yinghui Wu

Ethnic Kinships

Kinship terminology is an important aspect of ethnic culture. In general, kinship relationship is defined as family members within nine generations, which include the generation of oneself, the four earlier generations, and the four later generations. The nine generations of kinship are further divided into two branches: consanguinity and affinity. Consanguinity is divided into two branches: lineal consanguinity and collateral consanguinity. Affinity follows the same categorization, lineal affinity and collateral affinity.

The kinship naming system has two basic functions: categorization and description. Terminologies of categorization identify only generations without distinguishing the matrilineal kinship from the patrilineal kinship, or lineal from collateral, or elder from younger generations. The descriptive category, however, identifies such relations clearly.

Most ethnic groups in the world adopt the categorization function. In English, French, Russian, and Japanese, for example, uncle is the only word used to indicate one's father's and mother's brothers. In the Chinese language, kinship naming is descriptive. For example, one's father's elder brother is called *bai*, and *bai*'s wife is called *baimu*; one's father's younger brother is called *shu*, and *shu*'s wife is called *shenmu*. One's mother's brothers are called *jiu*, and one's mother's sisters are called *yi*; however, if there are more than one, each *jiu* and *yi* will be given ranking order. For instance, *first yi*, *second yi*, *third jiu*, *fourth jiu*, and so on are ways of appellation to identify each kin member.

In the long process of cultural exchange and communication, many minorities adopted kinship terminologies from Han people. However, others still keep their own traditional systems. The kinship terminologies of contemporary Chinese minorities can be categorized into the following forms.

In some minorities' kinship systems, kin members are not differentiated between patrilineal and matrilineal because people do not maintain a lineal record. For example, among the Va, the word *bai* is used to refer to maternal as well as paternal older uncles; the word *genniamu* refers to younger uncles; *matian* refers to older sisters and *manmian* to younger sisters; the word *da* refers to both mother's father and father's father; the word *ya* refers to both mother's mother and father's mother. In addition, some Va people refer to the father's elder brother (uncle) and the father's sister's (aunt's) husband with the same word, *gengding*; both the father's brother's (uncle's) wife and mother's sister are referred to as *maiding*. Mosuo people in Yunnan call both their mother and their mother's brother's wife *aimei* and call both mother's brother and her father *ahwu*.

There are times when the two kinds of kinship terminology systems, categorical and descriptive, are mixed. Some minorities use descriptive terminology to identify only the lineal kin members of the father's sisters and the mother's brothers; they use categorical terminology to identify the rest of the kinship.

Some minorities' kinship terminologies are differentiated on the basis of gender. Among the Dai of Yunnan, for example, the sons of the family call their father *bobu*, while the daughters call him *botao*; the sons call their mother *miya*, while the daughters call her *mitao*. The grandfather is called *bobuman* by grandsons, but *botaoman* by granddaughters. The grandmother is called *miyaman* by grandsons, but *mitaoman* by granddaughters.

Some minorities do not have sufficient kinship terminologies and have to make do with what they have. In the Lahu people's language, there is not a dedicated term for the father's sister's daughter's husband; therefore one has to say "my father's sister's daughter's husband" whenever this occasion comes up.

In naming systems, about forty minorities adopt the Han's system that includes a surname and a name. While some surnames are local to the minorities, others are imported from the Han. Ethnic surnames tend to be related to the tribal totems; foreign surnames come from interethnic marriages. On rare occasions, the surnames were assigned by the Han emperors. The opposite system where surnames are not used seems to be diminishing. Approximately ten minorities are known to be still using such a system. These ethnic groups include Dai, Lisu, Uygur, Tibetan, Menba, Bulang, Lahu, Gaoshan, Miao, and Dulong.

The economic reforms launched in the late 1970s have had some influence on ethnic naming systems. For the naming of the later generation from interethnic marriages, usually in the countryside, ethnic people mostly follow their traditional naming customs. However, in **cities** or towns, they mostly follow Han people's naming custom or give a child two names—an ethnic name and a Han name. This practice has become a new trend. It makes it more convenient for ethnic people to communicate both within their group and with outside communities. For example, many young Jinuo people may have two names; in their own community, they use their traditional names that are connected to their father's name; when working with the Han people, they use their nontraditional names or Han names. As the economic expansion heads toward the hinterland where minorities reside, flexibility in naming systems is a precursor of a wide-scale integration.

See also Drinking in Ethnic Cultures; Ethnic Burial Customs; Ethnic Marriage Customs; Ethnic Minorities, Political Systems of; Ethnicity and Ethnic Policies; Mosuo People, Matriarchal Tradition of; Taiwan, Ethnicity and Ethnic Policies of.

Bibliography

Song, Shuhua, ed., *An Introduction to Chinese Ethnic Minorities* (Beijing: Central University for Nationalities Press, 2001); Xu, Wanbang, and Qi Qingfu, eds., *An Introduction to Chinese Ethnic Minority Cultures* (Beijing: Central University for Nationalities Press, 1996).

Yinghui Wu

Ethnic Marriage Customs

Under the influence of rapid economic expansion since the late 1970s, many ethnic practices are vanishing. Ethnic marriage customs are one such area. Some minorities in southern China, however, continue to maintain their ethnic systems, opening a window to vanishing traditions.

While Confucian tradition has valued virginity of women before marriage for thousands of years, some minorities very much neglect this moral gulag and practice premarital sexual freedom. The custom of *chuanguniang* (knocking on girls' doors) continues among several southwestern minorities, such as Hani and Dai. Usually a girl in the family is given a separate bedroom for herself when she is considered "grown up" (usually around age fourteen). The girl's room is always built with a staircase and a small hole in the wall of planks opening to the outside, because houses are made of wood. According to the system, the interested young man visits the girl in the evenings. He makes the best use of the small hole in the wall to detect whether the girl is willing to accept his visit by poking a stick into the room. If she is willing, she draws the stick slightly inward; if she is not willing, she pushes the stick out. However, if she is angry, she pushes the stick out angrily. The young man makes his decision on whether to persist or give up according to the signals. If she is willing and he is brave enough, he can go into the girl's bedroom. Once inside, he will present small gifts such as a piece of headdress and spend the night there without any interference from the girl's family members. Actually the family members are happy to know this and may feel relieved that their daughter is attractive. In case there are no visitors, the family will worry a lot about the daughter's future marriage prospects. The girl and the young man may get along for some time to see whether they really love one another and will eventually get married. Otherwise, they may stop the relationship peacefully and start to make new friends.

Apparently, marriage customs of contemporary minority people are in transition. Before the founding of the People's Republic of China (PRC) in 1949, monogamy had been adopted among most of the minority people. However, in a highly stratified society, interclass and interethnic marriages were frowned upon. For example, Tibetan people had a strict restriction that a person of the noble class might not marry a person of the commons. The Yi people and the Jingpo people forbade marriages between different classes. Under the Yi customs, the perpetrator from the lower class had to be sentenced to death. The Jingpo's rules dictated that the perpetrator be assessed a high fine, or the "bride price" and "bridegroom price." Such systems have completely disappeared since 1949, although the concept of compatibility remains somewhat strong with parents.

Cultural changes may be a slow process. Some of the following systems are still in practice today, while others stopped in the 1950s.

Ahzhu Marriage

The Ahzhu marriage is a rare marriage custom currently practiced by the Mosuo people who live in an area around Luguhu Lake between northwestern

Yunnan Province and southwestern Sichuan Province. The system is also referred to as walking marriage. According to the system, the woman and the man both belong to their respective mothers' families, because families preserve the matriarchal tradition. The man travels back and forth to the woman's residence daily. The relationship is characterized as partnership, because such relationships may be changed frequently based on the preferences of the parties.

Marriage with Required Stay in the Wife's Family

According to the tradition of the Han people, the daughter is always married out. While most minorities adopt the same system, some do things differently. Naxi, Va, Dulong, Nu, Lahu, Bulang, Li, Miao, Yao, Maonan, Molao, Gelao, Zhuang, Bai, Dai, and Buyi allow the married man to live with the wife's family for a period of time before he takes his wife back to his own home. The time to live with his wife's family may be different from family to family. Some husbands may stay one or two years with the wife's family, while others may stay much longer. The practice may be a remnant of the ancient group marriage.

Marriage Based in the Wife's Family

In rural China, after a woman gets married, it is the rule that the woman moves into the husband's family. However, among Zhuang, Li, Shui, Molao, Maonan, Miao, and Yao, women do not have to relocate after marriage. They may stay with their own families for a prolonged period of time, some for two or three years, and some even live there as long as more than ten years. The wives may pay visits to their husband's family on festivals or on important occasions.

Cross-Cousin Marriage

Cross-cousin marriage is a liaison between uncle's and aunt's sons and daughters. The custom is popular among some minorities such as Yi, Bai, Dong, Buyi, Lisu, Va, Miao, Yao, Jingpo, Dulong, De'ang, and Tujia. It is practiced under three forms: (1) priority is given to cousins when outside competitors are present; (2) priority is given to the uncle's daughters to marry the aunt's sons; (3) priority is given to the aunt's daughters to marry the uncle's sons. The first form is one of equal choice, while the rest are one-way choices.

Marriage between Aunts' Sons and Daughters and with the Wife's Sisters

Marriages between aunts' sons and daughters are normal among Luoba, Uygur, Uzbek, Tajik, and some other peoples. However, among the Dong, Yi, Miao, and Jingpo, this kind of marriage is forbidden.

The custom that allows the husband to continue to marry his wife's sisters as they grew up such that the man may have several sisters as his wives was practiced until the 1950s. This custom was popular in Dulong, Jingpo, Miao, Uygur, Tibetan, and Ewenki communities.

Marriage by Transfer

Marriage by transfer is a system in which a widow has the right and obligation to marry one of her former husband's brothers or other men in her husband's family. The system is practiced by minorities such as Kazakh, Kirghiz, Ewenki, Dulong, Nu, Jingpo, Lisu, Hezhen, Li, Yi, Miao, Zhuang, Hani, Maonan, Molao, Daur, Oroqen, and Buyi.

Marriage by Capture and Marriage by Purchase

Marriage by capture, which ceased in the 1950s, was a custom that allowed a man to "hunt" for a woman to be his wife. This custom was kept among the following ethnic groups: Lisu, Yi, Bai, Buyi, Miao, Li, Gaoshan, Jingpo, Dai, Achang, Shui, Naxi, and Qiang. Apparently this practice was deemed inappropriate according to the Marriage Law (1950), which stipulated that marriage is based on willingness of both parties. Capture was gradually replaced by the process to acquire the marriage license.

The custom of marriage by purchase, which ceased in the 1950s, was based on the concept that a woman must be bought by the man's family to be the man's wife. The woman could also be exchanged for valuable goods such as cattle, goats, or sheep in place of cash. This custom was practiced by minorities such as Mongolian, Manchu, Tibetan, Yi, Qiang, Va, Oroqen, Lisu, and Nu. For example, the cheapest price for a Va woman was three cows in the 1940s.

Polyandrous Marriage, Polygamous Marriage, and Marriage by Service

Polyandrous marriage is rare in the world and lasted until the 1950s in China. The system allowed several brothers or several friends to share one wife. The children usually would call their mother's first husband father and other husbands uncles.

Polygamous marriage was popular before the 1950s among rich people of many minorities. It was particularly popular among the Han.

Marriage by service is also called marriage by labor. According to the custom, in order for a young man to marry a woman, he must work for the woman's family for several years; some had to work for more than ten years. This custom was popular among Lahu, Gaoshan, Dai, Li, and Tajik minorities before the 1950s.

See also Drinking in Ethnic Cultures; Ethnic Burial Customs; Ethnic Kinships; Ethnic Minorities, Political Systems of; Ethnicity and Ethnic Policies; Marriage and Divorce; Mosuo People, Matriarchal Tradition of; Taiwan, Ethnicity and Ethnic Policies of.

Bibliography

Song, Shuhua, ed., *An Introduction to Chinese Ethnic Minorities* (Beijing: Central University for Nationalities Press, 2001); Xu, Wanbang, and Qi Qingfu, eds., *An Introduction to Chinese Ethnic Minority Cultures* (Beijing: Central University for Nationalities Press, 1996).

Yinghui Wu

Ethnic Minorities, Political Systems of

There are fifty-six ethnic groups in China, out of which fifty-five are minority nationalities whose population accounts for about 8.41 percent of the total population of 1.29 billion and who reside in two-thirds of the territory, mostly in the western mountainous regions. The most populous ethnic group, the Han, accounts for 91.59 percent of the total population and resides on approximately one-third of the land, primarily on the plains and in coastal regions. Despite the difference in population size, Chinese ethnic minorities play an important role in the political system of China.

There has been a great change in the contemporary political system of Chinese ethnic minorities since the 1940s. Before 1949, a variety of political systems existed among different ethnic minorities. Particularly, there was a variety of social structures, ranging from somewhat primitive societies, such as slavery and feudal landlord systems, to ones that were more or less westernized. For example, among the ethnic minorities such as Jinuo, Dulong, Lahu, Va, and Lisu, the primitive communal system was still in practice. The Jinuo people remained at the Neolithic stage in their farming technology, using bamboo instruments in tilling and sowing. The slash-and-burn cultivating technique was still very popular. With respect to their social structure, egalitarianism in distribution was still the dominant system; food was primarily distributed equally according to the number of heads in the community. The Yi people in the Daliangshan and Xiaoliangshan area, in southwest Sichuan Province, practiced a version of slavery until the 1940s. Captives from tribal wars were typically used as slaves. The Dai people in Xishuangbanna, near Laos and Myanmar, practiced the feudal lord system, and some Tibetan people in **Tibet** practiced the feudal slavery system in which the lords usually owned the land and the farmers rented land from them. The farmers not only had to pay tribute to the lords but also had to serve the lords without conditions.

After the founding of the People's Republic of China in 1949, the political system of the ethnic minorities changed gradually into the socialist system. Some ethnic minorities such as Jinuo and Dulong "leaped" from a primitive communal system to the socialist system within a very short period, which is called in China the "direct transition."

The regional nationalities' autonomy system has been playing a very important role in the contemporary political system. Leaders of the ethnic regions are elected from the dominant groups. It is necessary to point out that minority townships are not included in the regional minority autonomous regions according to the Law of Regional National Autonomy. There are a total of five autonomous regions, thirty autonomous prefectures, and around one hundred seventeen autonomous counties. Despite the fact that autonomous administrative units must abide by the Constitution and the Party's policies, they do enjoy more power to make decisions for the regions.

Autonomous governing institutions include the people's congress, the people's government, the people's court, and the people's procurators' office. The chairperson of the autonomous region, the chief of the autonomous prefecture, and the magistrate of the autonomous county are responsible for the administration at each level, respectively.

The autonomous administrative institutions have the power of modifying legislation. Their decisions may affect policies (such as those stipulated by the central government), budget making, the use of minority languages, the preservation of minority culture, the deployment of the police force, and rank-promotion prioritics. The people's congress has the power to establish regional autonomous regulations to suit local needs. The regulations established by the autonomous regions, however, must be authorized by the standing committee of the **National People's Congress (NPC)**, and the regulations established by autonomous prefectures and counties must be authorized by the standing committee of the people's congress of the regional level. Autonomous regions may use the local minority languages in conducting their public affairs. The positions of the chairperson of an autonomous region, the chief of an autonomous prefecture, the magistrate of an autonomous county, and the chairpersons and the deputy chairpersons of the people's congress at different levels of an autonomous governing unit must be filled by people of the minority. With respect to representation, a quota system is followed. For example, in places where the autonomous minority's population is more than two-thirds of the total population of the autonomous place, the proportion of government officials of that minority must not be lower than two-thirds. In places where the autonomous minority's population is more than one-third of the total population of the autonomous place, the proportion of government officials must be higher than one-third.

In the minority political system, the essential principle is to implement equality, unity, common prosperity, autonomy, support of the government, freedom of religious beliefs and practices, respect of ethnic customs, the use of minority peoples' own languages, and the training of minority administrators. Equality means that all nationalities are equal, regardless of population sizes. Every minority group has its own representatives in the National People's Congress and in the Chinese People's Political Consultative Conference (CPPCC) at different levels.

Common prosperity means that all nationalities should help one another to develop the economy and improve living standards. The support of government policy has been required since the founding of the People's Republic of China. Each year the central government and governments at local levels evaluate policy implementations to make sure that national policies are carried out. Apparently, having every ethnic group willingly follow the common agenda has not always been successful. By investing in personnel training and ideological promotion campaigns, the government is hoping to achieve unity and solidarity of a diverse nation.

See also Drinking in Ethnic Cultures; Ethnic Burial Customs; Ethnic Kinships; Ethnic Marriage Customs; Ethnicity and Ethnic Policies; Mosuo People, Matriarchal Tradition of; Taiwan, Ethnicity and Ethnic Policies of.

Bibliography

Ministry of Civic Affairs, *Handbook of Administrative Division of the People's Republic of China* (Beijing: Map Publishing House, 2004); Song, Shuhua, ed., *An Introduction to Chinese Ethnic Minorities* (Beijing: Central University for Nationalities Press, 2001);

Xu, Wanbang, and Qi Qingfu, eds., *An Introduction to Chinese Ethnic Minority Cultures* (Beijing: Central University for Nationalities Press, 1996).

Yinghui Wu

Ethnicity and Ethnic Policies

China is a multifaceted and ethnically diverse society with a multitude of ethnic groups. Its population is composed of fifty-six officially recognized nationalities or ethnic groups, with the Han constituting the majority. The people officially classified as Han comprise about 92 percent of the population, while the remaining 8 percent of the population are divided into fifty-five minority groups and are commonly referred to as ethnic minorities or *shaoshuminzu*. In a country with a total population of more than 1.2 billion, the minority groups still form a significant non-Han population of more than 96 million. Although one can find minority peoples in every province, most of the ethnic groups are concentrated in China's border regions, for example, the Mongols and Uygurs in the north and northwest, the Zhuang, Miao, and Yi in southern China adjacent to Southeast Asia, and Tibetans in the southwest. Some other groups, such as the Hui and Manchus, are scattered throughout the country. Moreover, the regions inhabited by such minority ethnic groups as the Mongols, Tibetans, and Turkic-speaking people occupy about 60 percent of the territory, areas that are of strategic, economic, and demographic significance because they buffer international borders, contain rich natural resources, and provide space into which China's surging population can expand.

The Han majority is in fact an immensely diverse group linguistically and culturally, although it is generally viewed as being united by a common history and a written language. However, the Han perception of minority groups is often stereotyped and scapegoating. For instance, an entrenched Han view regarding the southern minorities is that their costumes, dances, songs, and architectures, albeit primitive and exotic, can enrich the Chinese culture, but that they are inferior to Han in terms of sophisticated political, cultural, and economic development and should follow the Han leadership. Descriptions of non-Han peoples in imperial histories of China were also fraught with denigrating stereotypes. These peoples appeared in the imperial Chinese imagination as imperfect and marginal figures with strange tongues and backward customs and social practices. However, they also epitomized cultural and political "others" and accentuated a uniform identity for the Han majority, even though the lifestyles and cultural customs among the Han Chinese varied greatly.

The ethnic policies of the People's Republic of China have not always been consistent. They have vacillated between tolerance/encouragement of cultural and ethnic diversity and repression/punishment of ethnic differences, depending on or reflecting the political climate. The Communist policies toward ethnic minorities have ranged all the way from official recognition, extension of limited autonomy, and support of cultural and economic developments to control of dissident voices and suppression of dissenting activities. However, the principle that has remained consistent throughout the decades of Communist leadership is that national unity and integrity must be maintained at all costs.

Following the Communist victory in China in 1949, the new government devoted much energy to minority issues and adopted a host of policies in order to garner the support of minority groups. These policies included efforts to end the long-standing attitude of "big Han chauvinism" (*da Hanzuzhuyi*), encouragement of Han cadres' sensitivity toward ethnic cultural and social practices, recruitment of promising minority youth and those believed to be imbued with revolutionary spirit for education and political training, and promotion of economic development in the minority-concentrated regions.

Meanwhile, in the early 1950s, the central government also required the minority groups to present the names by which they wished to be officially registered. By 1955, more than 400 ethnic groups had answered the call. To clarify the confusing situation, the government sent out research teams made up of ethnologists, historians, and linguists to conduct field investigations for proper official identification. Scholars evaluated each application group, employing the Soviet minority identification criteria of common language, common territory, common economic life, and common "psychological makeup." The state initially designated only forty-one groups as official minorities. By the late 1950s, fifty-four groups received official recognition. The remaining groups were either categorized as part of the Han or identified with other official minority groups on the basis of certain shared cultural or historical backgrounds or for political reasons. By 1982, the number of officially represented minority ethnic groups was extended to fifty-five, which has remained to this day, although many more ethnic groups have been petitioning the government for minority status.

Another significant official ethnic policy initiated in the 1950s was the granting of the status of autonomy to regions where traditionally the ethnic minorities were the majority. These province-level administrative areas were known as autonomous regions (*zizhiqu*). Although the Constitution guarantees the right of self-government in *zizhiqu* and the ethnic minorities are supposed to exercise significant political power there, in reality these regions have enjoyed only limited autonomy. Minority cadres have often occupied positions of secondary importance, while the locus of power continues to reside with the Han-dominated Chinese Communist Party (CCP). In China today, autonomous areas exist at several different levels. Besides the five autonomous regions (**Xinjiang**, **Tibet**, Inner Mongolia, Ningxia, and Guangxi), there are also thirty autonomous prefectures (*zizhizhou*) and 117 autonomous counties (*zizhixian*). The state penetration in these areas varies. Some receive special stipends from the government because of their overall low living standards; some have bilingual schools; others are exempt from certain state rules, such as the family-planning policy.

The relative tolerance toward ethnic diversity of the 1950s gave way to violent suppression in the **Great Cultural Revolution** between 1966 and 1976 when cultural forms, social practices, and literature that dissented from the mainstream revolutionary themes were condemned as either bourgeois or feudal. Consequently, ethnic differences were ruthlessly curbed, and the study of the histories and cultures of national minorities also ground to a halt.

However, with the advent of the reform era, policy shifted once more. During the politically more relaxed post-Mao period, the official pendulum has swung more toward tolerance and even encouragement of ethnic and cultural diversity. The implementation of several affirmative action programs has allowed minority peoples to enjoy some tangible benefits, including exemption from the one-child-per-family policy (except in the **cities**), entry into colleges with lower-than-average national examination scores, certain tax breaks, and more freedom to worship and practice their religions. The minority population has grown relatively more rapidly in recent years, partially because of the phenomenon of "category shifting" as some people have managed to change their identity from Han to minority in order to enjoy the benefits associated with minority status. Meanwhile, the ethnic-minority groups have also become more vocal and visible in asserting their own identities, cultures, and histories.

Ostensibly the central government has always acknowledged the existence of ethnic diversity within China. It propagates the notion of ethnic harmony and national unity and presents China as a nation in which the Han majority lives harmoniously with the non-Han minority groups. Nevertheless, from the official perspective, ethnic diversity can only exist within the framework of national integrity and unity. In recent decades, however, the official myth of peaceful coexistence of various ethnic groups has often been challenged by the proindependence and separatist elements from the autonomous regions, such as Xinjiang, Inner Mongolia, and especially Tibet. For example, Uygur separatists in Xinjiang have launched several violent incidents since the 1990s in the name of pan-Turkism, wishing to unite with other Turkic-speaking Muslims across the border. Tibet has also witnessed a number of uprisings against the Chinese government. The ethnic tensions emanating from these regions have challenged the official vision of a culturally diverse China united under the Communist leadership. Confronted with ethnic unrest, the government has routinely resorted to violent suppression in the name of upholding national integrity.

In China today, nationalistic sentiment has reemerged as a popular force. The upsurge of **nationalism** corresponds largely with the country's rapid economic development and modernization and its growing prominence in the global economy. Since the 1990s, rapid economic growth has instilled a strong sense of national pride and self-confidence in many articulate Han Chinese, who have made conscious efforts to search and redefine the meaning of Chineseness. The Chinese government and the Han people have come to a broad consensus regarding the definition of an "authentic" China, which is essentially a unified, pluralistic country with different ethnic groups living peacefully under the leadership of the Han people. However, this official, as well as mainstream, Chinese version of a geographically and culturally diverse but politically unified China whitewashes some of the ethnic tensions that characterize Chinese society today.

See also Drinking in Ethnic Cultures; Ethnic Burial Customs; Ethnic Kinships; Ethnic Marriage Customs; Ethnic Minorities, Political Systems of; Mosuo People, Matriarchal Tradition of; Taiwan, Ethnicity and Ethnic Policies of.

Bibliography

Dikotter, Frank, *The Discourse of Race in Modern China* (Stanford, CA: Stanford University Press, 1992); Mackerras, Colin, *China's Minorities: Integration and Modernization in the Twentieth Century* (New York: Oxford University Press, 1994); Ministry of Civil Affairs, *Handbook of Administrative Division of the People's Republic of China* (Beijing: Map Publishing House, 2004).

Hong Zhang

Experimental Fiction

In the 1980s, following the launch of China's reforms and opening-up in 1979, some Chinese writers, such as Wang Meng, Wang Zengqi, and Wang Anyi, tried to break away from the conventions of realism and political eulogy. They experimented with new forms of expression and narrative possibility to give their works individual voices and aesthetic personalities. However, it was not until the end of the 1980s, when Ma Yuan and subsequently younger writers, such as Yu Hua, Su Tong, Ge Fei, and Sun Ganlu, came onto the scene, dazzling readers with their stylistic and narrative energy, that the experimental movement gained momentum and its writers evolved rapidly into some of the most productive and sustained practitioners of literary innovation in post-Mao China. For a few years, almost all literary magazines in China celebrated this new literary movement, calling it the avant-garde of modern literature. Labeled as "pure literature," "experimental fiction," "metanarrative," or "new wave fiction," it was perceived and described as a profane carnival of formal experiments fulfilling its function in the ongoing construction of Chinese modernism. Indeed, the early works of these avant-garde writers, with their sophisticated narrative and fresh language, invigorated contemporary Chinese literature.

These experimentalist writers share their common interest in themes of human existence and individual experiences and, above all, their emphasis on narrative style. The early works of experimentalist writers such as Yu Hua, Ma Yuan, and Ge Fei were heavily influenced by Kafka, Borges, Robbe-Grillet, and Proust in their narrative skills and language. They distinguished themselves from writers of other schools of the time by three characteristics. The first and foremost distinctive characteristic was their sharp attentiveness to the medium itself—language, form, and narrative. In other words, the focus of experimentalist writers was on how to tell a story rather than on what the story was about. Some of them took this writing experiment to an extreme. They seemed to have redefined the field of literary innovation through writing about writing. Their works have therefore been dubbed "metafiction," and some early modernists viewed experimental fiction as only a set of rhetorical strategies that conveyed a new complex of sociocultural relations, giving voice to the subject positions dwelling within this complex.

Second, experimental fiction was distinct in its quiet constitution of social individuality through the language game with strong thematic implications of alienation and isolation. Reacting strongly against the high-minded concern for humanity and social justice characteristic of most scar literature (also known as "wounded literature"), reportage literature, and **root-searching literature**, experimental fiction broke away from the literary establishment and stretched the limits of "taste" with its depictions of various perversions, including sadism and cannibalism, which revealed its own way of exposing the dark side of contemporary China. It did not position itself as an explicit or implicit rebel against the official discourse of the state. The writers seemed completely preoccupied with their radical experiment with the medium, patiently building up the linguistic archives of a new generation and a new community, completely absorbed in their construction of the labyrinth of stories, with journeys that never went right, tantalizing suspensions, and endless unplanned turns, together with a loss of direction tinged with a sense of emancipation that is standard in metafictional works and too comfortably nestled in metafictional architectonics. More often than not, they overwhelmed the reader with games of violence, sexual fantasy, obscure conversations, self-important running accounts of trivial details, and neurotic attention to a certain pattern. All this leads some critics to perceive experimental fiction as a cynical resignation realized through some younger-generation writers' demolishing not only of the way of literature, but also of the means by which the way is carried out. Indeed, experimental fiction is an integration of all kinds of vocabulary, syntax, and styles and an encyclopedia of the stories of the individual encounters and group adventures of the new era. Finally, unlike the mainstream of postrevolutionary Chinese literary styles that dwelt in a restored life experience, experimental fiction was deeply rooted in a radically contemporary sociocultural experience and sought to turn it into a historical expressivity through its formal, that is, metafictional, artifacts.

Can Xue, Ma Yuan, and Yu Hua are some of the most representative writers of the group. Can Xue is known for her technical exercises in narrative fragmentation and antirealism, which make great demands on her readers: images of stagnation and decay and death, crude language, incoherent plot, and inconsistent development of characters. "Yellow Mud Street" (1983) is one of Can Xue's most controversial novellas. It captures the dark experimentalist theme of hopelessness in economical brushstrokes. Some critics have pronounced Can's fiction virtually "unreadable," but she has been a powerful presence on the Chinese literary scene, along with a number of other talented women writers, including Shen Rong, Zhang Jie, and Wang Anyi.

Ma Yuan set his most impressive novels in the **Tibet** Autonomous Region (e.g., *Goddess of the Lhasa River*). The shock and excitement Ma Yuan brought to the literary world by his experiment with narration in the mid-1980s was unforgettable. His "narrative circle," which was embodied by that tasteless sentence "I am that Chinese called Ma Yuan," was considered to have set in motion a spectacular turn to metafiction. Critics almost unanimously agreed that it was Ma's writing that first awoke Chinese writers' consciousness of the narrative. Sun Ganlu, another member of the avant-garde writers, once said, "A whole generation of writers are under Ma Yuan's shadow." Ma Yuan's own words are highly explanatory of his experiment: "My method is to be sporadically logical, to be logical on the surface, and to be generally illogical in the narrative order."

Yu Hua's writing, which often overwhelms the reader by its labyrinth of slanderous sentences, bizarre conspiracies, sinister lanes and rivers, and physical violence, has become the hallmark of avant-garde fiction. His works, especially the early ones, are particularly well known for their graphic descriptions of physical violence and bodily mutilation. Stories such as *1986* (1987), *The Past and the Punishment* (1987), and *One Kind of Reality* (1988) evoke a cold and callous world of death and mutilated limbs. His focus on sounds and surface details—ants crawling in blood, the thud of bodies falling to the ground, bones breaking, and organs rotting—becomes the paradigmatic symbol of avant-garde fiction.

Su Tong's novella *1934 Escapes* (1987) has been hailed as being among the most eloquent examples of the power of fiction over history, style over content, and purity of craftsmanship over naïve obsession with referent meaning. He is best known for his novella *Wives and Concubines* (1987), which was made into the internationally renowned film *Raise the Red Lantern*, directed by Zhang Yimou. His novel *Rice* (1991) and several disturbing short stories involving children are famous for offering his readers detailed depictions of sex and violence.

For the group of overjoyed critics who were anticipating a more sustained and "genuine" notion of literary modernism, the sudden and overwhelming production of Ma Yuan, Ge Fei, Su Tong, Yu Hua, and Sun Ganlu seemed to announce the coming of age of Chinese literature, which, at long last, based itself in a disinterested sphere, that is, in the literary medium itself. However, although early experimental fiction received close attention from literary circles, it did not have much public appeal. This led Yu Hua to break away from this group in the early 1990s. He has achieved enormous success through his novels *Huozhe* (To live) and *Xu Sanguan Maixue Ji* (Xu Sanguan sells blood) since then. Both were written using extremely plain and simple language and a realistic style. The adaptation for film of his work *To Live* by famous Chinese director Zhang Yimou best demonstrates the incorporation of serious literature and commercial culture. Though all the avant-garde writers have said that they would never give up their literary standards to cater to the superficial appetites of the free market, they all think it better to work with the market machinery than to defy it.

See also Anticorruption Literature and Television Dramas; Avant-garde Literature; Great Cultural Revolution, Literature during; Intellectuals, Political Engagement of (1949–1978); Intellectuals, Political Engagement of (1978–Present); Literary Policy for the New China; Literature of the Wounded; Misty Poetry; Modern Pop-Satire; Neorealist Fiction and Modernism; Pre–Cultural Revolution Literature; Revolutionary Realism and Revolutionary Romanticism; Sexual Freedom in Literature.

Bibliography

McDougall, Bonnie S., ed., *Popular Chinese Literature and Performing Arts in the People's Republic of China, 1949–1979* (Berkeley: University of California Press, 1984); Zhang, Xudong, *Chinese Modernism in the Era of Reforms* (Durham, NC: Duke University Press, 1997).

Xiaoling Zhang

F

Family Collectivism

In cultural studies, the dimension of individualism/collectivism (IC) has been used theoretically and empirically to explain and predict similarities and differences across cultures (Matsumoto et al. 1997). The IC concept is "perhaps the most important dimension of cultural difference in social behavior across the diverse cultures of the world" (Triandis 1988). Although definitions of the IC concept have been numerous, one that is concise and to the point is offered by Matsumoto et al. (1997): IC refers to the degree to which a culture encourages, fosters, and facilitates the needs, wishes, desires, and values of an autonomous and unique self over those of a group.

In comparing cultural differences between Chinese and westerners, many researchers have used the IC dimension, although other terms have occasionally been employed. The roots of American individualism and Chinese collectivism might be traced in the histories of religion and thought (Capps and Fenn 1992). With a persecuted background of Christianity, the first pilgrims to the American continent brought to the new nation a religion from Europe: Protestantism. In contrast to Catholics, Protestants believe in glorifying God by getting ahead and making money, and therefore they work harder than Catholics do to get rich (Weber 1958). Meanwhile, the tenet of "showing your left cheek when someone slaps you on your right cheek" is less respected by Protestants than by Catholics. Compared with Catholics, Protestants emphasize more "this world" (hedonism) and overlook "that world" (heaven), and as a consequence, being nice to others and making friends become less important than making money and getting rich for themselves. In short, the Protestant ethic is one of the foundations of American individualism.

During more than 2,000 years of dynasties, China has been governed by numerous rulers, but Confucianism has prevailed throughout. The teachings of Confucius, which emphasize "virtue," including loyalty to one's true nature, reciprocity in human relations, righteousness, and filial piety, have guided Chinese men and women in their daily behaviors. Such social morality, underpinning a collectivist worldview, is also seen in other Eastern religions and philosophies, such as Daoism, Buddhism, Hinduism, and Shintoism. The essence of Confucianism is harmony, and to achieve the universal harmony, one should start from the family. A fundamental Confucian value that ensures the integrity of ritual performance is filial piety to parents and ancestors, which Confucius believed to be the first step toward moral excellence. Further, Confucians have applied the filial piety morality to higher levels of social settings. They are fond of applying the family metaphor to the community, the country, and the universe. They prefer to address the emperor as the Son of Heaven (*Tian Zi*), the king as ruler-father (*fu wang*), and the magistrate as the "father-mother official" (*fu mu guan*) because they assume that implicit in the family-centered nomenclature is a political vision. Because the family is considered to be the basis of harmony in the universe, Confucianism focuses on order in the family. Besides filial piety, Confucianism teaches the Three Cardinal Guides (*san gang*) (ruler guides subject, father guides son, and husband guides wife) and the Five Constant Virtues (*wu chang*) (benevolence, righteousness, propriety, wisdom, and fidelity) as specified in the feudal ethical code. Additionally, there are further guidelines for women: the Three Obediences (*san cong*) (to father before marriage, to husband after marriage, and to son after the death of the husband) and the Four Virtues (*si de*) (morality, proper speech, modest manner, and diligent work), which are spiritual fetters (requirements) imposed on women in traditional Chinese societies. All these teachings are apparently for the benefit of the family as a basic unit of society aimed at a collective harmony. Confucianism is the foundation of Chinese collectivism.

However, the collectivistic spirit does not seem to prevail at all levels of social life in Chinese communities. Instead, Chinese appear to be individualistic in many observed occasions. For example, in the residence community, Chinese are not used to greeting a stranger. If one does, he or she may be considered weird. Further, Chinese are not accustomed to donating to strangers or to public interests. While 45 to 50 percent of American adults regularly participate in donation and voluntary work, a much smaller percent of Chinese are willing to donate or volunteer for the Hope Project, which is currently a nationwide drive to promote elementary education in remote and rural areas in China (Van Patten, Stone, and Chen 1997). In these occasions, Chinese look very individualistic, compared with what has been observed in American culture.

Chinese are collectivistic, but only to a certain extent. While it is desirable to distinguish in-group collectivism from universal collectivism, Chinese collectivism may be better termed family collectivism. As individuals are to American communities, families are to Chinese societies. Indeed, at a higher level of social interactions such as community, township, and even nation, Chinese are generally less collectivistic than Americans. Although America as a nation is built on individuals, "liberty, equality, and brotherhood" constitute the democratic culture of the society. Under this ideology, Americans should be born free, treat every other person equally, and take all humans as children of God and treat them as brothers. For a person who believes in God, the practice of brotherhood is believed to increase the chance to go to heaven after death. In

Confucianism, liberty in the sense of a free man is missing, and individual free-dom should always be controlled by the family. The Confucian brotherhood is confined to the family, extended family, or people one knows well. Since there is no such thing as heaven in Confucian teachings, the Chinese do not think it necessary to be brothers with everyone in the world.

Throughout history, family collectivism brought China to the top of the world as an economic power for several feudal dynasties, when small industry and manual agriculture dominated the economy. Even today, small or family businesses are more likely to be successful than big enterprises in China. For the same reason, the first industrial revolution did not happen in China as pre-dicted by Karl Marx's economic determinism. Max Weber further elaborated on the failure of China to become industrialized with two other views. Literati, with too much emphasis on education and diplomas, have hindered Chinese men from developing practical skills; and filial piety, an unavoidable duty to re-spect and take care of parents and ancestors, has prevented Chinese young men from exploring opportunities outside of the home (Weber 1958). A Con-fucian motto that is passed through generations is "Not go away from home while parents are still alive." As a consequence, Chinese lose the chance to de-velop themselves in another world by staying with parents, and when their parents are no longer alive, they have become too old to move.

Therefore, the traditional Chinese culture is not suitable for large-scale in-dustries. It is not conducive to a socialist economy either, in which people are encouraged to work for the interests of the public instead of one's own or of the family. This may be the reason that *people's communes* that were estab-lished all over rural China soon after the Communist takeover in 1949 eventu-ally collapsed in the early 1980s, and that the public ownership systems in Chinese industries have been gradually giving way to a market economy in the past two decades. Chinese culture offers a better environment for small or family-based endeavors.

Corruption, against which the Chinese Communist Party is fighting, is not a new problem in Chinese history. From the Qing dynasty to the Kuomintang regime, corruption prevailed and finally brought down the government. While absolute power leads to absolute corruption, there might be some cultural mechanism that is associated with Chinese corruption. The majority of Chi-nese corrupt officials have a nice family to take care of, and the interests of the family are above everything else. Almost all corrupt officials are followed by a greedy wife, and encouragements, support, and harboring come first from the family. Therefore, Chinese corruption is different from that in many other cul-tures. In South Africa, for example, a speeding motorist may be able to avoid a heavy fine by bribing the policeman with a few dollars. Chinese bribers do not work with strangers, and they usually make friends through their contacts with the influential officials before the bribery.

Beyond the family structure, Chinese make every effort to create "contacts" (*guanxi*). By playing with *guanxi*, things that are difficult or impossible other-wise can be easily accomplished by trading favors among friends. When things cannot be done through a legal or regular way, people who have influential contacts will "go through the back door" (*zou hou men*). When out of home-town or overseas, Chinese make friends by establishing fellow countrymen associations (*tong xiang hui*), alumni clubs (*xiao you hui*), and the like to enlarge and strengthen the social networks in order to "go through the back door." The more people in a person's network considered to be that person's family members, the better chance for that person to get what he or she wants. As said in another Chinese motto, "One more friend means one more road, and one more enemy is one more obstacle." To get things done in China, people need *guanxi*. To do business in China, many American MBA programs require students to take a course in Chinese *guanxi* skills.

The Chinese reputation of being a "sheet of loose sand" (*yi pan san sa*) may also be traced to family collectivism. Too much in-group cohesiveness leads to extreme individualism at community and national levels (Schwartz 1990). Cooperation and help among non-in-group members are more difficult in the "collectivistic" Chinese societies than in the "individualistic" American societies. If globalization of the economy also indicates a transfer of Western developed economic systems to a less developed country like China, cultural environments must be taken into consideration for any successful transfer.

Using anthropological observational methods, one may deduce that the Chinese culture is simply collectivism in contrast to American individualism. In light of Chinese interactive behaviors at different levels, it is obvious that Chinese collectivism is confined only to the family and the extended family sphere. At the community and higher levels, Chinese tend to be more individualistic than Americans. Chinese family collectivism may account for many social phenomena in China, such as the failure of the people's communes, the norm of "going through the back door" (*zou hou men*), corruption of officials, in-group fighting (*wo li dou*), and the Chinese image of "a sheet of loose sand" (*yi pan san sa*).

See also Confucian Tradition and Christianity; *Hukou* System; People's Communes/Household Responsibility System.

Bibliography

Capps, D., and R. Fenn, *Individualism Reconsidered: Bearing on the Endangered Self in Modern Society*, Center for Religion, Self, and Society, Princeton Theological Seminary Monograph Series, 1 (Princeton, NJ: A & A Printing, 1992); Matsumoto, D., M. D. Weissman, K. Preston, B. R. Brown, and C. Kupperbusch, "Context-Specific Measurement of Individualism-Collectivism on the Individual Level: The Individualism-Collectivism Interpersonal Assessment Inventory," *Journal of Cross-Cultural Psychology* 28, no. 6 (1997): 743–767; Michels, Robert, *Political Parties* (New York: Free Press, 1966); Schwartz, S. H., "Individualism-Collectivism: Critique and Proposed Refinement," *Journal of Cross-Cultural Psychology* 21, no. 2 (1990): 139–157; Triandis, H. C., "Collectivism and Individualism: A Reconceptualization of a Basic Concept in Cross-Cultural Psychology," in *Personality, Attitudes, and Cognitions*, ed. G. K. Verma and C. Bagley, 60–95 (London: Macmillan, 1988); Van Patten, James, George C. Stone, and Ge Chen, *Individual and Collective Contributions toward Humaneness in Our Time* (Lanham, MD: University Press of America, 1997); Weber, Max, *The Protestant Ethic and the Spirit of Capitalism*, translated by Talcott Parsons (New York: Charles Scribner's Sons, 1958).

Jie Zhang

Fast Food (Western Style), Integration of

The development of fast food to overcome the inadequacy of the urban restaurant businesses was among the various economic reform proposals adopted by upper levels of government in the early 1980s. In China's predominantly planned economy, people had to stand in long lines to eat a simple meal in a restaurant. Even Chinese fast-food restaurants that offered noodles, *huntun* (wonton), *jiaozi* (dumplings), steamed buns, and congee were difficult to use at busy meal times. Partly to phase out most low-profit state-owned food enterprises and partly to create employment opportunities for the "educated youths" (*zhishi qingnian*) who had been sent to rural areas for reeducation during the **Great Cultural Revolution (1966–1976)**, the authorities finally decided to take measures.

Suddenly, with relatively little investment, many people started quick-service restaurants, cafeterias, teahouses and other eateries where Chinese fast food was sold. At the same time, large-scale fast-food factories capable of producing hundreds of thousands of lunch boxes daily were under construction. Instant noodles and various fast-food items, both for eat-in and takeout, mushroomed. The Chinese fast-food businesses enjoyed immediate success before the arrival of Western-style fast-food chains. It is interesting to note that while the Chinese embraced Western books, films, and virtually everything else Western at the time, foreign fast food was by no means universally accepted. According to a 1985 survey (*Fast Food*, 2001), 79.8 percent of respondents preferred Chinese-style

McDonald's is the most popular Western-style restaurant chain in modern China.

fast food, whereas only 20.2 percent favored Western dishes. However, the number of those who preferred Western food was nonetheless believed to be growing among younger generations.

The first Western fast-food chains that opened business in China were Kentucky Fried Chicken (KFC) and McDonald's. McDonald's entered Beijing in 1987; its first restaurant opened in Shenzhen in 1990. Eighteen years later, urban Chinese are increasingly used to Western-style fast food. In February 2003, more than 800 KFC, 100 Pizza Hut, and 500 McDonald's outlets had been established in China. Subway, the U.S.-based second-largest fast-food brand in the world, Bonny and Roosters, both from the United States, and the self-styled California Beef Noodles, a company unknown in the Golden State, are flourishing in China. Today, the presence of American fast-food businesses, along with others from Europe and Japan, is conspicuous.

Along with Western-style fast food, Western soft drinks are also booming. Coca-Cola is now the favorite drink among children. Having entered China in 1979 as soon as the country adopted its **Open Door policy**, Coke had seized 33 percent of the market share by May 2003. Pepsi, which followed its rival in 1981, had taken nearly 17 percent and is growing by 10 percent annually. Sprite, 7-Up, and Mountain Dew also have a share of the market. Before 1999, coffee shops were mainly limited to big hotels and Western-style restaurants where consumers were primarily expatriates and Chinese employees working in foreign companies. Since 2000, Starbucks outlets have opened in many cities, and the company has greatly boosted the growth of cafés, where fast-food items are sold as well. While coffee retailers are mostly Western, an increasing number of businesspeople from Hong Kong and Taiwan have invested in the industry. Ice cream outlets from the West are emerging, too. The Swiss food giant Nestlé plans to speed up investment in its Chinese operations in an effort to surpass its rivals.

During the past two and a half decades of economic reforms, the Chinese palate has very much adapted to Western-style fast foods. Consuming Western food and drinks has become a normal part of urban life. Indeed, for professional couples, dining out provides a welcome break from daily home cooking. People of all age groups, especially the young, enjoy nights out on the weekends mixed with shopping and entertainment. Some people certainly believe that you are what you eat and regard Western-style fast food as a symbol of modernity. In addition, Western fast-food chains have aimed their advertising and promotion at schoolchildren. The fact that young children are required to study English, behind which are social and cultural codes, greatly helps to spread American pop culture, including fast food.

Despite their huge success, Western fast-food businesses have not developed without problems. Xi'an, a major tourist city and the capital of Shaanxi Province, was hit by a string of McDonald's bomb scares in 2001 and 2003. Both incidents involved money extortion from the fast-food chain. In another case, a customer sued a KFC outlet for providing English-only receipts. Of all the woes, the most challenging is the competition for customers with the traditional Chinese fast-food restaurants from both mainland China and Taiwan. Yonghe Doujiang, the Taiwan-invested fast-food chain, seduces many customers away from McDonald's by specializing in ordinary people's most common food items: *dabing* (baked pancake with sesame seeds), *youtiao* (fried twisted dough stick), and *doujiang* (soybean drink). Kang Shifu, the giant of instant noodles, has been successful in selling bowl-packaged noodles. Another interesting event in fast-food competition is the rise of companies like Dicos and Can Can Chicken, a joint venture with Taiwan and a local operator emulating Western competitors by devoting greater attention to service and décor. While the number of Chinese fast-food chains is still small and most of them can hardly compete with international giants, some big Chinese companies have adopted Western-style management and have expanded rapidly. Malan Noodles, the largest domestic franchiser, with 361 outlets in mid-2001, has gained a firm footing.

The strategy that most Western fast-food businesses adopt to cope with competition is localization. Chinese knots, red paper cuts, and other traditional decorations have begun to appear in McDonald's outlets. The Colonel, KFC's trademark, is sometimes seen in Chinese costume. To cater to the Chinese preference for rice, KFC has added mushroom rice, chicken porridge, and seafood and vegetable soup to its menu as supplements to its conventional hamburgers and fried chicken. Pizza Hut has added preserved ham to its pizza. All these adjustments seem necessary to help Western-style fast-food businesses attract more customers, particularly by creating a festive Chinese New Year atmosphere at a time when the Chinese usually turn to traditional foods. However, for older people, a Western fast-food restaurant may be the choice only when they are in a hurry. In their leisure time, more elegant restaurants with a more varied menu are preferred.

The impact of Western-style fast food is far-reaching. What such businesses bring to China goes beyond more hygienic and nutritious food, although some argue about the latter given the increase in obesity among urban children. Indeed, they offer a whole new culture of business management. The Chinese government regards Western-style fast food positively, because it expects a long-term win-win situation for both Chinese and Western food-related businesses. Large-scale poultry operations and chicken-processing plants were already established in the 1980s. Western fast-food chains try to purchase as much food as possible in China. For instance, 95 percent of KFC's raw materials, including bread, chicken, and vegetables, are purchased locally. McDonald's gets 97 percent of its raw materials locally. Instead of importing food, these Western fast-food giants import entire systems of agricultural production and, in turn, teach the Chinese how to raise chicken and grow lettuce with seeds specially developed for China's different climatic regions. They have forged joint ventures with powerful partners and created a previously nonexistent supply network. For example, to supply McDonald's, J. R. Simplot began to grow Russet Burbank potatoes in China, opening the nation's first French-fry factory in 1993.

The development of Chinese fast-food chains lags far behind that of the international giants in scale, operation, marketing, and management. It seems that the increasing competition between Western-style fast foods and Chinese fast foods will intensify. Given Western food giants' substantial capital and modern management style, many predict that the fierce competition will sooner or later drive poorly performing Chinese restaurants out of business.

The fast-food industry has enormous potential in China, because the purchasing power of its massive population remains largely untapped, especially in the vast interior. Now that China is a member of the World Trade Organization (WTO), the food industry will become even more globalized, offering opportunities for further development of both Chinese and Western fast-food companies. McDonald's plans to resort to franchises to further its expansion in China, as KFC has done in the last few years. The latter introduced a drive-in restaurant in Beijing, a city with 620,000 private cars, in late 2002. With improvement in the rule of law, it is believed that once the much-awaited franchise law is passed, more Western fast-food chains will expand via franchising. Indeed, the increasing Chinese economic strength, along with the pervasive influence of Western culture, provides a favorable environment for the sustainable development of Western-style fast-food restaurants.

See also Brand-Building Phenomenon; Coca-Cola in China; Commercial Advertising, Policies and Practices of.

Bibliography

Fast Food and Organized Catering in China: A Market Analysis (London: Access Asia, 2001); *Fast Food Market Report* (Shanghai: Friedle Business Information, 2002).

Helen Xiaoyan Wu

FDI

See Foreign Direct Investment (FDI).

Film Production

The development of film in China from 1949 to the present can be divided into three periods. The first was from the foundation of the People's Republic of China (PRC) in 1949 to 1966, up to the beginning of the **Great Cultural Revolution**. During this initial seventeen-year period, art became the tool of the government for disseminating the Communist ideology and for educating the masses to facilitate the implementation of social changes. The second period of film development covered the decade during the Cultural Revolution (1966–1976). The representative group of films in this era for entertaining the masses and at the same time propagating antibourgeois socialist values was known as the Eight Peking Model Operas. The third period stretches from the 1980s to the present. When the Chinese government, soon after the end of the Cultural Revolution, decided to open China's economy to market demand, the film industry began to have an increasingly economic orientation, as well as commercial variety again. Thus the Chinese film industry started to enjoy greater freedom.

During the first period (1949–1966), hundreds of feature films and documentaries were produced under the sponsorship of the newly founded Chinese Communist government. For example, the heroic figure of Lei Feng was set up and became known to every Chinese in the early 1960s. With the support of the Chinese government, a movie named *Lei Feng* was produced, named after the main character. Lei Feng was an exemplary soldier of the Chinese People's Liberation Army who devoted himself to serving the public and helping the needy. The government hoped to advocate the Lei Feng Model in order to encourage the nation to make selfless contributions to the Communist cause.

During the Cultural Revolution (1966–1976), the film industry was severely restricted. Most previous films were banned, and only a few new ones were produced. Often film producers were exiled or forced to work in labor camps, just like thousands of other Chinese **intellectuals**. Artistic liberties during this period were curtailed. The declared aim of the Cultural Revolution was to attack the Four Olds—old ideas, old culture, old customs, and old habits—in order to bring the areas of education, art, and literature in line with a hard-line Communist ideology. Thus anything that was suspected of being feudal or bourgeois was to be destroyed. Therefore, both domestic and foreign films were banned. The world of film in China during the Cultural Revolution was entirely dominated by the state-designated small set of movies known as the Eight Peking Model Operas. In the earlier stage of the Cultural Revolution, these plays were introduced and performed in Beijing and soon were available to the masses in cinemas all over China. These eight revolutionary model plays were the following:

- *Hongdengji* (The red lantern), a story about a Communist railway worker during the Sino-Japanese War.
- *Haigang* (On the docks), a story set on the Shanghai waterfront.
- *Zhiqu weihushan* (Taking Tiger Mountain by strategy).
- *Qixi baihutuan* (Raid on the White Tiger Regiment), a story set during the **Korean War**; the White Tiger Regiment unit commanded by Americans is captured by the "Chinese People's Volunteers."
- *Shajiabang* (Shajiabang), an exemplary theatrical work and motion picture from the early 1950s popularized during the Cultural Revolution by Jiang Qing (**Mao Zedong**'s wife, who was later disgraced).
- *Baimaonu* (The white-haired girl), a story of overthrowing landlords and the role of women after liberation.
- *Hongse niangzijun* (The Red Detachment of Women), a revolutionary opera/ballet/film. The story features a group of women fighters engaged in a fierce struggle against the evil landlords on Hainan Island in 1949–1950.
- *Shajiabang* (The symphony).

The Eight Peking Model Operas were created to heighten the revolutionary zenith during the time of the Cultural Revolution. A few more revolutionary plays, Peking operas, and ballets with political themes were added to the films during this second period, but all these were generally referred to as the Eight Model Plays. The additional works included the following:

- *Dujuanshan* (Azalea Mountain), a story with the central figure of a female political commissar who must confront male chauvinism as well as the Nationalist Chinese armies.

- *Longjiangsong* (Ode to the Dragon River), a story dealing with class struggle, with the central figure of the female Party secretary of a production brigade who fights saboteurs.

- *Píngyuan Zuozhan* (Fighting on the plains), a patriotic story set during the Sino-Japanese War.

- *Panshiwan* (Boulder Bay), a story about the heroic struggle of village militiamen against counterrevolutionary infiltrators.

- *Caoyuan Yingxiong Xiaojiemei* (Heroic sisters on the prairie), a film about the true story of two young sisters in Inner Mongolia who fought a snowstorm to protect and save the collective property of a herd of sheep, but had their limbs frozen off and ended up handicapped.

Most of these model plays were handpicked by Jiang Qing (Mao Zedong's wife) herself as the most operative vehicles for the propagation of revolutionary Communist ideology. The productions were known as "model peking operas" (*yangbanxi*) or "revolutionary model peking operas" (*geming yangbanxi*). Jiang Qing's group of "model" performance pieces also included two revolutionary modern ballets and one symphony. All the model productions were about class struggle and the building of socialism. They were all made into movies, and the films produced at that time had one goal: to spread a revolutionary spirit among the people. In each of the model operas, the cast reflected the hierarchy of the time, with a proletarian hero or heroine as the main character. During the ten-year Cultural Revolution, traditional operas were attacked with unprecedented vehemence, and many of them were removed as "weeds." In these purges, famous actors and actresses were mercilessly reprimanded and were labeled monsters and freaks, forces of evil, or bad elements. In the world of entertainment, the whole country was supposed to rely on the Eight Model Operas, which signified a healthy cultural life. Thus for an entire decade, the model plays monopolized the movie screens in China.

Among the three stages of Chinese film development, the first two periods were characterized by strong political influence from the socialist government. Before the Cultural Revolution, during the period 1949–1966, and during the Cultural Revolution (1966–1976), filmmakers in the politically controlled film industry were not independent and were deprived of their autonomy in production. The Chinese government's policy toward film production emphasized class struggle and political orientation. From the founding of the People's Republic until the end of the Cultural Revolution, film was a major medium of government propaganda. This changed significantly during the era that followed.

The third period of film development began immediately after the Cultural Revolution, when the film industry unfolded with relative freedom and began to flourish as a medium of popular entertainment. Especially since the early 1980s, when the Chinese government decided to implement its **Open Door policy**, film development has experienced significant changes. During Deng

Xiaoping's new era of reforms, the film industry began to have an increasingly economic orientation, as well as commercial variety. There were only a few short-lived setbacks, such as the anti-spiritual-pollution campaign in 1983 and the anti-bourgeois-liberalism campaign from 1987 to 1989. The films of the third period still show a strong tendency to see the village as a microcosm of China and to represent women as strong, independent, and emancipated.

Economic reforms were implemented all over China under the new government policy and extended to the cultural realm and the entertainment industry. The reforms led to the acknowledgment of the differences between artistic work and political propaganda. The reforms further introduced the idea of financial independence into the film industry. Although nowadays art is not directly employed as a political tool, films are produced in the larger context of society and still reflect Chinese sociopolitical, socioeconomic, and sociocultural settings and background. However, the content and themes of the movies produced during the third development stage have a wider and more sophisticated scope.

In recent decades, Chinese films have found success with international audiences. Popular works include those by film director Zhang Yimou, such as *Red Sorghum* (1987), *Ju Dou* (1991), and *Raise the Red Lantern* (1992), to name only a few. Though there was criticism about its boldness in depicting sex and violence that do not fit traditional Chinese taste, the position of *Red Sorghum* as a first-class film became internationally acknowledged. Zhang Yimou has neither been labeled a bad element nor thrown into a labor camp, but has continued his artistic creations unhindered. Zhang is lucky that he lives and works in a more relaxed political atmosphere, during a time favorable to the unfolding of creative minds. The example of this most prominent film director of contemporary China illustrates the contrast between film before and after the Chinese Open Door policy and its political and economic reforms.

See also Deng Xiaoping (1904–1997), Reforms of; Film Production during the Seventeen Years (1949–1966); Films of the 1980s; Films of the 1990s.

Bibliography

Virtual Museum of the Cultural Revolution, China News Digest International, Inc., http://museums.cnd.org-CR/halls.html, accessed on November 16, 2004.

Senquan Zhang

Film Production during the Seventeen Years (1949–1966)

From 1949, the year of the founding of the People's Republic of China (PRC), to the start of the **Great Cultural Revolution** in 1966, the political agenda seeped into the world of film production and gradually gained control. In the field of arts and literature, this period is known as the "Seventeen Years." During these years, there were three waves of film prosperity, 1949–1955, 1956–1958, and 1959–1966.

The first prosperity came with the founding of the PRC. The film industry of the New China actually started as early as 1946 after Japan's surrender. The

Chinese Communist Party (CCP) took over the company named Manchurian Film (Man Ying) that was based in the Northeast and run by the Japanese and the Chinese puppet government. After the takeover, the company was given the new name Northeastern Film Company (Dong Bei Dian Ying Zhi Pian Chang), which was later changed to Chang Chun Film Company (Chang Chun Dian Ying Zhi Pian Chang). By 1951, there were three state-run film companies and seven private companies based in Shanghai. By 1953, these private companies were deprivatized and became part of the **state-owned enterprises (SOEs)**.

The first film products were created under strong support from the central government. In November 1948, the Central Bureau of Propaganda turned on the green light by stating that because the film industry was learning its first steps, standards must be lowered. The bureau further indicated that strict control might result in suffocating the film industry, which consequently would open up room for bad films. The spirit of the government policy was obvious: as long as the films were politically against the enemy and artistically adequate, they should be encouraged. Financial sponsorship from the government was indeed generous, even when the **Korean War** was ongoing.

Films produced from 1949 to 1953 represented four topic categories: (1) the lives of workers, peasants, and soldiers, for example, *Sergeant Guan*; (2) comparisons of the old society and the new society, for example, *Husband and Wife* and *The Story of Wu Xun*; (3) classic novels brought onto the screen, for example, *Singers of the Red Mansion*, adapted from the novel *The Dream of the Red Mansion* by Cao Xueqin of the Qing dynasty (1644–1911); (4) recreation topics, for example, *My Life*. The films mostly sang the praises of the socialist revolution and supported the work of the central government. However, because of tightened ideological control, some of the films triggered suspicion almost immediately after their release. *The Story of Wu Xun*, released in 1950, was one such case.

Wu Xun (1838–1896) was a man who endured poverty and humiliation throughout his life, but dedicated himself to raising funds to build schools for poor children. Wu Xun was born into a poor peasant's family in Shandong Province that was not able to afford his schooling. He became a farmhand at the age of sixteen. Being ashamed of his own illiteracy and in order to help poor children receive education, he raised money by letting himself be punched and kicked by hooligans from rich families. Instead of paying for his own marriage, he loaned the money out to earn a profit from the debt.

Wu Xun's story is one of compassion, self-sacrifice, humility, and generosity, as most people would believe. However, as soon as the film was released, Chairman **Mao Zedong** was personally involved in condemning the film as rendering a disservice to the Communist cause. In his article "Attention Should Be Paid to the Debate on *The Story of Wu Xun*," published on May 20, 1951, Mao indicated that Wu Xun passionately spread feudal culture and, instead of joining the revolution to overthrow feudal power, bent his back and did whatever he could to please the exploiting class. "Accepting such ugly behavior or tolerating any art form praising such deeds would mean to let the peasants' revolution and the Chinese history be humiliated." "This suggests that the domain of culture of our country is faced with a tremendous ideological chaos. The capitalist reactionary thoughts have invaded the brave Communist Party," Mao alerted (1951). Consequently, a nationwide critical campaign was launched during which producers and artists involved were reprimanded. By 1953, only one film, *Combating in the North and in the South* (1952), was produced, reflecting the ingenuity and heroism of the People's Liberation Army in defeating the Nationalists during the civil war (1946–1949). The first wave of film prosperity was called off; meanwhile, a salient precedent of political intervention was established. Nevertheless, the silence was broken by two successful children's films, *The Feathered Letter* (1954) and *The Flowers of the Nation* (1955).

The second wave of film prosperity did not arrive until around 1956. Once again, the political atmosphere was somewhat relaxed after Mao gave an important speech on May 2, 1956, titled "On the Ten Kinds of Relationships." In his speech, Mao brought forward the slogan of "letting 100 flowers bloom, letting 100 schools of thought debate," which led to the Anti-Rightist Campaign later in the year. Nevertheless, eight films were produced in 1953, twenty in 1954, twenty-three in 1955, and forty-two in 1956. These films reached high artistic levels, and almost every single film enjoyed a tremendous success. Some of the well-known titles include *Liangshanpo and Zhuyingtai, The Militia Fighters in the Plains, Family, For Peace*, and *Flowers of the Nation*.

Once again, ideological freedom and artistic prosperity attracted a political crackdown. A December 1956 article written by Zhong Dianfei and published in the *Wenhui Daily* proposed three concepts: (1) While films may serve the working class, they should not be forced to become working-class films. In other words, films must serve the entire people, including workers, peasants, and soldiers, but do not have to limit their content to the lives of the working class only. (2) Film production must not be subjected to political and administrative dictation, because film is primarily a form of art. (3) The Chinese film art needs to develop its own legacy (versus following a political agenda or the Soviet art style). These concepts were immediately targeted during the Anti-Rightist Campaign that started with the article "What Is This For?" published in the *People's Daily* on June 8, 1957. Zhong Dianfei and many artists were labeled "rightists" and were deprived of their political rights. Their products were banned and went into oblivion. The second wave of prosperity was called off as the nation turned hot-headed with promoting the **Great Leap Forward** movement in 1958.

Chinese film artists as well as their audience apparently belonged to the resilient kind. As soon as the zenith of the Great Leap Forward tapered down, seventeen films of excellent artistic quality were produced in 1959, at the beginning of what is known as the third wave of film prosperity. Interestingly, these films were, in part, "ordered" by the government for the celebration of the tenth anniversary of the PRC. Some of the better films include *The Wind Comes from the East*, praising the revolution, *Commissioner Lin Zexu*, commemorating the struggle against the British opium trade, *The Five Golden Flowers*, reflecting the lives of hardworking southern minority women, and *The Lins' Store*, reflecting the difficulty of survival of a small business in the old society. However, the progress of film production was slowed due to the great famine of 1959–1962 that killed 23 million people. The breakup with the Soviet Union in 1960 further contributed to the worsening of the nation's financial situation, because the Soviets withdrew their technical and financial aid. Furthermore, China was isolated in the world on the heels of its withdrawal from the Soviet-led socialist camp. This situation brought about a general sense of insecurity in the political arena within the country. In particular, film production was directly affected when the Soviets cut off their exports of cellular film tapes. However, forty films were produced in 1960, including such masterpieces as *Sister Liu San Jie*, which was a singing opera that depicted the rebelliousness of a southern minority girl in pursuit of true love.

While the situation was unfavorable, Premier **Zhou Enlai** and Deputy Premier Chen Yi saw in the revival of the film industry an opportunity to boost the nation's morale. In March 1962, Zhou and Chen both admitted that the past leftist tendency had posed tremendous barriers to artistic creations, and that the majority of Chinese intellectuals had always sided with the revolutionary workers and peasants and had weathered many storms together with them in the past. Hence the label "capitalist intellectuals" was unfair and must be discarded. Encouraged by these words, film producers released ninety-five films by 1965. Two highly famed films were *Soldiers under the Neon Lights*, which depicted how soldiers guarding streets of Shanghai in the 1950s fought off the temptations of women and money, and *The Heroic Sons and Daughters*, which depicted the fearlessness of Chinese soldiers fighting in the Korean War.

In 1964, Mao was faced with increasing pressure from his opponents inside the Party. He was blamed for mismanaging the economy by launching the Great Leap Forward that had led to the great famine and millions of lives lost. He was also responsible for the leftist Anti-Rightist Campaign that had sent tens of thousands of intellectuals into exile. But Mao was preparing a counterattack. In 1964, Mao launched the campaign of "Four Cleanups" aimed at lower-level officials who mismanaged the distribution of food, supply, and work points, which led to loss of lives. The campaign had another side, that of promoting the Communist consciousness under the slogans of three "isms"— "patriotism," "collectivism," and "socialism." In a speech given on June 27, 1964, Mao criticized the domain of the arts, asserting that artists and their associations had been refusing to learn from workers, peasants, and soldiers; that they had refused to tell their stories; and that they were falling off the revisionist cliffs. Not surprisingly, the ensuing Cultural Revolution (1966–1976) denied artistic creativities, whether in film production or any other artistic field, entirely. The most prominent art form to be staged during the next ten years were the Eight Model Peking Operas created under the supervision of Jiang Qing, Mao's wife. In general, film production during the "seventeen years" was under the shadow of politics. It was relentlessly molded, both in art expression and in contents, by Mao's ideological framework. The political constraint remained firmly in place until after Mao's passing in 1976 and the launch of the economic reforms in 1978.

See also Film Production; Films of the 1980s; Films of the 1990s.

Bibliography

Cheng, Jihua, Li Shaobai, and Xing Zuwen, eds., *Zhongguo Dianying Fazhanshi* (A history of the development of Chinese cinema) 2 vols. (Beijing: China Film Publishing,

1980); Mao, Zedong, "One Must Pay Attention to the Debate on the Story of Wuxun," *The People's Daily* (Beijing), May 20, 1951; Shu, Xiaoming, *Zhongguo Dianying Yishu Shi Jiaocheng* (A course in the history of the Chinese film art) (Beijing: China Film Publication, 1996).

Jing Luo

Films of the 1980s

While Deng Xiaoping's economic reforms have tremendously changed people's material well-being, their primary significance remains that of raising people's expectations in all aspects of life. This is immediately obvious in the field of artistic creation, and China's film industry offers a good example. Before the reform, films were made to serve the Communist Party and the government. Since the reform started in 1978, films have been more and more geared in the direction of reflecting and exploring reality. It is generally recognized that the 1980s were a special period of transition during which the old-fashioned rigidity left the stage and new trends appeared on the screen.

As is the case with all social transitions, people tend to first linger in hesitation before running ahead to embrace the new future. Chinese films in the 1980s started by looking back into history in search of the roots of the Chinese civilization. The urge was to look for answers to "who we are, what we have done, and where we are going," which was a popular question at the time. This effort involved examining ethnic diversity, religious mystery, and impacts of the ancient state philosophy, Confucianism. This process is commonly referred to as "cultural reflection." Apparently, three decades of communism had alienated the Chinese by cutting them off from both tradition and foreign influences and confining them in the Communist vacuum. Yet the Maoist experience must be embedded in the Chinese tradition. Digging into the past constituted the first step toward recovery. A similar cultural process happened in 1919 during the May 4 Movement. "We start from the poorest, the most backward, deserted areas," said film director Chen Kaige, "to look for the nation's source of power and hope" (Chen, 1989). In this guiding spirit, *One vs. Eight*, directed by Zhang Junzhao, was released in 1983. The film explored kindness and generosity from inside evil. It started a new trend where the prominent heroes of the **Mao Zedong** era were phased out, while the typically condemned, lowly, and even "evil" figures rose and shone on the stage. Soon, *Evening Bell* by Wu Ziniu and *The Yellow Earth* by Chen Kaige strengthened the new trend.

By the mid-1980s, the repertoire of products extended its diversity. *The Grand Army Parade* by Chen Kaige, *On the Hunting Ground* by Tian Zhuangzhuang, and *The Perfect Shot* by Zhang Zeming represented a series of dynamic experimentations. By 1988, Chinese films went into a more mature stage both artistically and with respect to depth of content. *The Red Sorghum* by Zhang Yimou is recognized as representing the peak of this time.

On the theme of root-searching, *On the Hunting Ground* looks into life's wilderness and humanness through describing the daily tribal life of the Mongol herdsmen. Wilderness prevails over humanness when it comes to defending the herds; humanness prevails over cruelty when the communal life pulls tribal members together. The film expresses the longing to return to nature, whereby one is finally free to show love, care, and violence—the truthful things in life. Hence, as noneventful as the details of the story may be, the film presents a strong rebelliousness against the Communist alienation that had molded individuals into the same pattern.

Under Mao's reign, moral standards were defined in the Communist theories. Self-sacrifice for the interest of the country was glorious, selfless contribution was laudable, and blind loyalty to Mao and to the Communist Party was the utmost virtue. Certainly, all oppositions to these "good" things must be bad. Therefore, pursuit of profit, individualism, and disturbance of order topped the list of evils. The film *One vs. Eight* looks at the traditional moral grounds with a critical eye. The film is adapted from the long poem by Guo Xiaochuan that carries the same title. Instead of praising a fearless and loyal Communist Party member, the film spotlights a bunch of "evil" figures, including deserters and local bandits, in a word, the lowest of the low. While these figures are dedicated to self-service at all costs and with all measures, the film shows that they do harbor a conscience deep in their soul. The opium smoker who bullies a Communist nurse in captivity is able to heroically stand up against the Japanese soldiers who are about to rape the nurse. Robbers and bandits are capable of taking up guns and fighting on the side of the Communists at the juncture of the nation's crisis.

Similarly, the films of the 1980s no longer sing the praises of the revolutionary martyrs, but transcend the concept of winners and losers to reach the human being behind. *Evening Bell*, for example, treats the Anti-Japanese War from a nonjudgmental angle, leaving out the dominant routine of showing that justice is on the Chinese side. Instead of highlighting the correctness and ingenuity of the great Communist commanders as well as the bravery of the Eighth Route Army, the film stresses the cruelty of war and soldiers' tormented mentality. It was not uncommon for films of this period to be somewhat revengeful by showing antiheroism and despite of almighty leaders. The film industry led the nation, in a sense, in freeing itself from the deeply rooted personality cult of Mao and the authority of the Party.

The films of the 1980s not only went against the traditional Communist doctrine and behavioral patterns, but, more important, adopted an objective attitude in displaying human nature. *Ju Dou* by Zhang Yimou, for example, sympathizes with the young woman who commits adultery, being fed up with her aging husband. Similarly, films on themes of urban life recognized objectively and sometimes approvingly extramarital relationships. Instead of treating this liberty as a runaway immorality, the new films viewed it as naturally human and further as a quest for what used to be forbidden. *Arch Light* by Zhang Junzhao, *Sunny Rain* by Zhang Zeming, *Putting a Bit of Sugar in the Coffee* by Sun Zhou, and *Reincarnation* by Huang Jianxin all reflected the pursuit, the anxiety, and, sometimes, a self-destructive tendency of the younger generation of the post-Mao era.

In reflecting the new content, film directors gave up the traditional hero-centered Soviet style. Instead, they downplayed great deeds and shifted the focus to common human nature and to the impact of the environment. *The Yellow Earth*, for example, presents vast stretches of land, squeezing man to an insignificant corner. This technique is used to imply that man is nothing more than a product of his environment. *The Red Sorghum* adopts a similar approach by constantly presenting a background of vast sorghum fields that are covered with the red crop. Coupled with the bloody butchering of a live human being, the panoramic display of nature casts a terrifying effect. Obviously, by projecting an overwhelming wilderness, the director shows the cruelty of the battle between a small number of villagers and a group of Japanese soldiers. Thus the glorious Anti-Japanese War is described more as a crude tribal conflict than one with a certain pomposity, much fanfare, and the Communist Party's almighty leadership. The film spells out clearly that all wars are uncivilized and inhumane.

There is little doubt that in the 1980s film directors headed by Zhang Yimou and Chen Kaige made giant steps in transforming Chinese film. They revolutionized Chinese film both in content and in technique. Their common ground seems to be that they all embraced the "art-for-art" ideal and were creative in making new films different from the old ones.

See also Deng Xiaoping (1904–1997), Reforms of; Film Production; Film Production during the Seventeen Years (1949–1966); Films of the 1990s; Root-Searching Literature.

Bibliography

Chen, Kaige, "Discussing Film with Dadaozhu," *Dang Dai Dian Ying* (Modern films), no. 6 (Beijing: 1989); Ma, Debo, and Dai Guangxi, *The Art of Directing: A Study of Five Top Directors of the Beijing Film Co.* (Beijing: China Film Publishing, 1994); Shu, Xiaoming, *Zhongguo Dianying Yishu Shi Jiaocheng* (A course in the history of the Chinese film art) (Beijing: China Film Publication, 1996); Zhang Yimou, "Questions and Answers," *Guangming Daily* (Shanghai), March 15, 1988.

Jing Luo

Films of the 1990s

From the 1950s to the 1980s, Chinese films were primarily an "engaging" form of art. The films of the "Seventeen Years" (1949–1966), for example, served to strengthen the New China by spreading the Communist Party's policies. The films of the "Ten Years" (1966–1976) primarily contributed to the personality cult of **Mao Zedong** and to the elevation of revolutionary models. The films of the 1980s engaged in reflection, root-searching, and recovering the lost status of film as an art in its own right. The films of the 1990s represented a new trend. Political engagement and lofty ideals retreated from center stage, although there was a surge of documentary and fictional films on revolutionary history. The spotlight was shone on tidbits of life's reality, whirls of the world of emotions, and functions of entertainment. Apparently, most of the film directors were born in the post-Mao era. They have little memory of the chaotic Communist time and are faced with a new set of issues.

The themes of the 1990s mostly focused on issues of urban life, such as the pursuit of material wealth and sensual pleasure and the spiritual emptiness that accompanies it. The film *The Vanishing Youthhood*, for example, was adapted from a novel, *Thirsty Pigeons* by Fang Jiajun, by film director Hu Xueyang to vividly depict the troubled mentality of the "gold rush" in the 1990s. The background of the story is the booming special economic zones (SEZs) opened in the late 1970s where Western-style management was first tested. The rapid economic prosperity in these regions attracted people from other provinces. The heroine is a beautiful young woman who joined the gold rush by becoming the mistress of a wealthy overseas entrepreneur. Fed up with a life confined to the mansion, she makes the acquaintance of a young man who lives by playing tennis with rich businessmen. The film depicts the anxiety, hopelessness, and loneliness of the two young people who live by entertaining the rich. Along the same thematic line, Hu Xueyang directed *The Guardian Lady*, which depicts the life and emotions of the family members of those who have gone abroad for the gold rush. Li Xin's *Weekend Lovers* tells the story of a young woman who fell in love with two men, but enjoyed watching them engaging in a duel.

Lou Ye's *Suzhou River* analyzes the meaning of love in the gold rush years of the 1990s. Obviously, once moneymaking opportunities became available, love between men and women began to lose its traditional ground. In the traditional moral system, and even endorsed by the Communist value system, the marriage relationship primarily meant care, responsibility, and understanding. When money became the goal and criterion, hormonal urge, multiple partnerships, and divorce prevailed. Similarly, family relationships also suffered from the materialistic tendencies. The film depicts a father who, having made money through illegal trafficking, frequently hangs around bars and prostitutes and distances himself from his daughter. Thus, in the film, the money-centered society, being nothing but a lowly arena where mobs reign, trust is nonexistent, and morality has disappeared, is no better place than Shanghai's heavily polluted Suzhou River.

Parallel to treating social issues, the film industry of the 1990s produced a number of successful entertainment films. On the one hand, these films stress comic effects that inject laughter into people's lives; on the other hand, they nevertheless depict the transitional society. Feng Xiaogang's *Party A and Party B*, for example, tells the story of a group of unemployed young people with film-production expertise. They find their opportunity in helping those who dream of living a different life realize their fantasies. Taking advantage of support from studios, the group of directors guides its customers to play out seven scenarios—military general, man of justice, survivor in poverty, victim of injustice, man of mediocrity, womanizer, and house owner. The comic effect lies in scenarios where the customers pay handsomely to live their fantasies. Some, for example, who are tired of extravagance, want to experience deprivation of good food and wine and to live on cornmeal and in remote areas. Because the customers signed contracts with the project directors promising never to change their mind until the routine is over, the directors are obliged to sternly enforce the plan. By the end of the course, every customer has received a lesson and learned to appreciate life.

Zhang Yimou's *Raise the Red Lantern* (1991) and *To Live* (1993) are powerful products that explore cultural tradition as well as the fate of man. *Raise the Red Lantern* tells the story of a rich man with four wives. While the man never physically shows up, his voice reveals his dominance. Because the prestige of each woman depends on whether she could give birth to a son, a bloody politics is played out, fueled by male dominance. *To Live* contrasts life and death, good luck and bad luck and demonstrates the relativity of things. Fugui, the son of a rich landlord, having lost the family's entire property in gambling to Long Er, turned into a poor peddler. Long Er, boss of a local opera team, became a wealthy man overnight. However, because of his property ownership, Long Er was executed during the Communist **land reform**, while Fugui escaped what could have been his fate had he not lost his property. Both films are brilliantly crafted, and *Raise the Red Lantern* was twice an Oscar nominee in foreign-language films.

While politics-oriented films faded away during the 1980s, there was a sudden rise of such films in the 1990s. The popular ones include *Trilogy: The Grand Finale Battles* (1991), *Zhou Enlai* (1991), *Mao Zedong and His Sons* (1991), *The Story of Mao Zedong* (1992), *The Forty-four Days of Liu Shaoqi* (1992), *The Jinggang Mountain* (1993), and *The Chongqing Negotiation* (1993). These films put the popular Communist leaders back onto the stage, singing the praises of the hard struggle toward liberation. A significant difference from the political films of the past lies in the touch of objectivity. The past films depicted enemies as evils, while the new ones objectively depict the enemy leaders without defamation. Jiang Jieshi (Chiang Kai-shek) is no longer a shortsighted nationalist generalissimo with an origin in a Shanghai mafia and a thunderous temper, but rather a profound Nationalist leader with the nation's interest at heart and capable of appreciating Mao Zedong's literary talent. Similarly, General Lin Biao, Mao's handpicked successor who was accused by Mao of harboring ambitions to usurp Mao's position and who died in a plane crash, is not depicted as an infamous man with ugly looks, but rather as a taciturn general with great determination and military talent.

The return of political films in the 1990s resulted from multiple factors. First, the Party and the government provided an abundance of financial sponsorship. In January 1988, the government invested heavily in the production of documentary and fictional films depicting major historical revolutionary events as well as current events. The Bureau of Film Industry emphasized the principle of "spotlighting the main melody first and foremost, and exploring the variety in the meantime." The "main melody" referred to the Party's leadership and the **Four Cardinal Principles**. Second, the Party's seventieth anniversary and Mao Zedong's hundredth anniversary were celebrated in 1991 and 1993. Habitually, such occasions are decorated with an abundance of films that reminiscal about revolutionary history. Third, the overheating of urban topics and entertainment films in the 1990s, such as martial art films and comedies, generated an adversary effect. People were longing to return to films with an uplifting effect. Finally, traditional revolutionary films typically carry a strong patriotic and sometimes nationalistic tendency. The 1990s embraced several events that triggered the rise of nationalism, such as Taiwan's election in 1996 that led to the election of **Chen Shuibian**, who is a separatist, and the bombing of the Chinese embassy in Yugoslavia by U.S. warplanes in 1999. Events such as these have made and will always make revolutionary films part of the fabric of Chinese films. It is clear, however, that Chinese films, including political films, are being defined more and more artistically than according to political agendas.

See also Film Production; Film Production during the Seventeen Years (1949–1966); Films of the 1980s.

Bibliography

Huang, Xianwen, *Last Night's Stars: Chinese Film History of the 20th Century* (Hunan: Hunan People's Publishing, 2002); Ma, Debo, and Dai Guangxi, *The Art of Directing: A Study of Five Top Directors of the Beijing Film Co.* (Beijing: China Film Publishing, 1994); Shu, Xiaoming, *Zhongguo Dianying Yishu Shi Jiaocheng* (A course in the history of the Chinese film art) (Beijing: China Film Publication, 1996).

Jing Luo

Financial System

See Banking and Financial System Reform; Central Planning; Economic System; Fiscal Policy and Tax Reforms; Great Leap Forward (GLF).

Fiscal Policy and Tax Reforms

Under a centrally planned economic system, China's budgetary principle was collecting revenues and spending them uniformly (*tongshou tongzhi*). **State-owned enterprises** were required to turn in all their profits to the state. Profits from state-owned enterprises were the major source of government revenues. In 1978, China started market-oriented economic reforms. Tax reform is an important part of economic reform, which aims to provide state enterprises production incentives, cut off fiscal dependence of state enterprises on government, equalize tax burdens among enterprises, and promote fair competition. Tax reforms experienced the following stages.

Allowing State Enterprises to Keep Some Profits (Fangquan Rangli)

Major fiscal reforms have occurred since 1979, when three measures were taken by the central government: raising agricultural product prices, which were set by the government, by 20 percent; raising wages and salaries for employees in state enterprises and government agencies; and lowering taxes and allowing state enterprises keep a part of their profits. Experiments in fiscal reform began in 1979 by allowing the state enterprises to keep part of their profits to expand production and to issue bonuses and awards to workers. These three measures that reduced government tax revenues and increased government spending immediately resulted in high government budget deficits in 1979 and 1980.

Substituting Taxes for Profits (Li Gai Shui)

The success of these experiments in promoting production encouraged the government to pursue further fiscal reform in 1983 by making state enterprises subject to income taxes—a reform that is commonly called substituting taxes for profits (*li gai shui*). This reform unfolded in two stages. In the first stage, state enterprises were required to pay taxes and submit a part of after-tax profits to the government. The corporate income tax rate for large enterprises was 55 percent, and it was progressive for small enterprises. The after-tax profits were divided between enterprises and the government. The two main problems were that there was only one tax, the corporate income tax, which did not allow the government to control resource allocation effectively, and enterprises were still required to submit part of their after-tax profits. The second stage of substituting taxes for profit began in October 1984. State enterprises were subjected to eleven different taxes if applicable, but they no longer had an obligation to submit profits to the state. Thus the process of substituting taxes for profits was complete. However, medium and large firms not only needed to pay income tax but also an adjustment tax that was enterprise specific; many state enterprises suffered a loss and had to negotiate with the state for subsidies, just as they had under the profit-remittance system; the tax rate appeared to be high, but actual exemptions were also large, and tax revenues were not as high as expected; and enterprises had strong incentives to expand investment that caused a heavy debt burden, since they could use the before-tax profits from new projects to pay the debt used to finance the projects.

The Contract Responsibility System (Baogan Zhi)

Because of these problems, the Contract Responsibility System (CRS) was introduced on the basis of substituting taxes for profits in December 1986. Under the CRS, enterprises were contracted to pay income tax and adjustment tax on a specific level of profit. If they did not achieve that level of profit, they were supposed to make up the rest of the taxes from their own resources. If they exceeded the contract level of profit, they paid taxes at a lower rate on their additional profits. The contract levels were usually based on the previous year's profits plus some predicted growth. The CRS provided strong incentives for state enterprises to make profits. However, since the contracted profits were not set to grow at a sufficiently high rate, the revenue growth from enterprise contracts did not keep pace with economic growth, and the CRS caused a loss of government budgetary revenues. Also, under contract with the central government, different provinces remitted different percentages of local revenues to the central government, and counties also transferred different percentages of revenues to provincial governments.

Tax Plus Profit System (Li Shui Fenliu)

To increase government revenues, a new tax reform began in 1989. State enterprises were required to pay corporate income taxes first and then submit a portion of their profits to the government. The basic idea was that as the owner of state enterprises, the government should receive profits from state enterprises. Also, state enterprises no longer had the privilege of using before-tax profits to repay debt caused by investment. To increase the firms' ability to repay their debt, the government lowered the income tax rate for small firms. The tax rate for large and medium enterprises was still 55 percent, but for small enterprises the tax rate was set uniformly at 35 percent. After the introduction of the CRS, negotiations between enterprises and the state and between the central government and local governments had become extensive. In addition, over the years, the central government's revenue share in total revenues decreased significantly, down to only 22 percent in 1993. The central government was determined to reverse this trend.

Tax-Sharing System (Fen Shui Zhi)

In 1994, a new tax system, the tax-sharing system, was established. Several significant changes in the tax system took place, including reduction of the types of tax from thirty-seven to twenty-three; unification of the income tax rate for all enterprises to 33 percent (joint ventures preserve their preferential tax rates); division of taxes into three categories, namely, national taxes that are paid to the central government, joint taxes that are shared by the central and local governments, and local taxes that are paid to local governments; establishment of a central tax bureau and local tax bureaus; and the establishment of a central-to-local tax rebate system.

The most important tax is the value-added tax, which is levied on all stages and spheres of industrial processing and is shared by the central and local governments. Currently, there are two rates: for products related to agricultural production and basic consumption goods the tax rate is 13 percent, and for most other goods the rate is 17 percent. The most significant local tax is the business tax. It is levied on the transfer of intangible assets or sale of immovable properties, primarily of "service enterprises," including transportation, communications, financial services, real-estate sales, and entertainment. As a result of the tax reform, the central government's share in total revenue increased from 22 percent in 1993 to 55.7 percent in 1994. The target rate is 60 percent.

In 1993, the government passed a law that prohibited the Ministry of Finance from overdrawing money from the People's Bank. Since then, the Ministry of Finance has had to finance all its budget deficits by issuing bonds. After the Asian financial crisis occurred in 1997, China adopted an expansionary fiscal policy, and budget deficits and government debt increased at an extraordinary rate.

See also Banking and Financial System Reform; Central Planning; Credit Spending, Development of.

Bibliography

Lin, Shuanglin, "China's Government Debt: How Serious?" *China: An International Journal* 1, no. 1 (2003); Lin, "The Decline of China's Budgetary Revenue: Reasons and Consequences," *Contemporary Economic Policy* 18, no. 4 (October 2000): 477–490; Wong, Christine P. W., Christopher Heady, and Wing T. Woo, *Fiscal Management and Economic Reform in the People's Republic of China* (Hong Kong: Oxford University Press, 1995).

Shuanglin Lin

Five Principles of Peaceful Coexistence

Initiated by Premier **Zhou Enlai** in 1953, the Five Principles of Peaceful Co-existence were later written into the declarations of the **Bandung Conference** in 1955. In 1982, these principles were written into the Constitution of the People's Republic of China and became a fundamental set of principles underlying its diplomatic policies. The Five Principles of Peaceful Coexistence are the following:

1. Mutual respect for territorial integrity and sovereignty
2. Mutual nonaggression
3. Noninterference in each other's internal affairs
4. Equality and mutual benefit
5. Peaceful coexistence

Advocating mutual understanding and respect, the Five Principles of Peaceful Coexistence opened up a new way for nations of the world to establish friendly relations. After its founding, the Chinese government searched for ways to win support from other nations. The settlement of border disputes with its neighbors India and Burma (renamed the Union of Myanmar in 1989) in the early 1950s and the launch of **"Ping-Pong diplomacy"** that relaxed tensions between China and the United States in the 1970s, which eventually led to the normalization of relations of the two countries in 1979s, are examples of success. By the end of 2002, China had established diplomatic relations with 165 countries.

China fought on the side of the Allied countries in World War II. However, tensions and hostilities grew between the Western countries headed by the United States and China when China joined the socialist camp. Refusing to recognize the legitimacy of the People's Republic of China, the United States not only blocked China's admission to the United Nations (UN), but also imposed economic sanctions. Meanwhile, the United States provided economic and military aid to the Kuomintang government, which was defeated by the Communists and fled to Taiwan. The patrolling of the U.S. Seventh Fleet in the Taiwan Strait posed a threat to China.

China's visibility in the world significantly improved when Premier Zhou Enlai attended the Geneva Conference in 1954 to settle the Franco-Vietnamese War. The conference was China's initiative. The Soviet Union, France, the United States, and North Vietnam sent delegations to the conference. It provided an opportunity for the Chinese to express their concern about global affairs. Working with different demands and counterproposals, Premier Zhou helped iron out an agreement whereby the Vietnamese obtained independence in the North, and the political parties pledged to hold elections in two years to create a coalition government of a united Vietnamese state. The Geneva Conference of 1954 virtually ended French colonial authority in Indochina. It formed a landmark in China's move toward an independent foreign policy.

In 1955, Premier Zhou reiterated the Five Principles at the first Asian-African Conference (the Bandung Conference) held in Indonesia from April 18 to April

24. Tensions and hostilities mounted in the Pacific region when the United States, Britain, France, Australia, New Zealand, the Philippines, Pakistan, and Thailand signed the SEATO (Southeast Asia Treaty Organization) agreement. Meanwhile, Taiwan and the United States signed a mutual defense treaty. In response to the heightening of the area's tensions, the five countries of India, Burma, Indonesia, Pakistan (also a SEATO member), and Ceylon (Sri Lanka), known as the Colombo Powers, invited China to join them at a spring conference in Bandung, Indonesia, which drew delegates from twenty-nine Asian and African nations. With Zhou's remark that "the people of Asia will never forget that the first atomic bomb exploded on Asian soil," a united front was formed and the conference voiced strong support for peace in the region, the abolition of nuclear weapons, the principle of universal representation in the United Nations, and arms reductions. The Five Principles of Peaceful Coexistence were affirmed and expanded into the Ten Principles, which became known as the Bandung Spirit. Since then, the Five Principles have become the basic principles that guide relations between countries with different social, political, and economic systems. On the basis of these principles, China established friendly and cooperative relations with both socialist and nonsocialist countries.

Since the 1950s, although the government has undergone many changes, China's diplomatic policies have remained relatively stable. China opposes hegemony and has always held its independent foreign policies to protect its sovereignty and dignity. In 1950, China signed the Treaty of Alliance and Mutual Assistance with the Soviet Union to seek security and economic assistance. However, China exerted its independence. In international economic relations China diversified its trade to the utmost degree that the Western embargo allowed, reducing to some extent its dependence on the socialist bloc. Within five years of its breaking away from the Soviets in 1960, China paid off the Soviet loans of $300 million and became free of all foreign debts. China challenged the Soviet monopoly of ideology and opposed the heavy deployment of Soviet troops along its northern border. However, China expressed its sincere wish to strive for improvements in the relationship of the two countries on the basis of the Five Principles.

As a beacon, the Five Principles guided China to negotiate with Great Britain on the issue of the return of Hong Kong. In the early 1980s, China made it clear that in 1997, when the ninety-nine-year lease of the New Territories was due to end, it would expect to resume control over Hong Kong to recover China's sovereignty. Proposed by Deng Xiaoping, the concept of **"one country, two systems"** permitted Hong Kong to continue to operate under a capitalist economy. The solution of the Hong Kong issue owed much to the concept and ensured continued stability and prosperity in the region. It also promoted peace in Asia and the world. Following agreement on Hong Kong's return, the Chinese and Portuguese governments held their first round of discussions in Beijing in June 1986 and worked out a solution to the issue of Macao, which led to the return of Macao in 1999.

The concept of "one country, two systems" also applies to the reunification of Taiwan. The Chinese on both sides of the Taiwan Strait insist that Taiwan is part of China. The majority of people on both sides find peaceful reunification the only way out. The Chinese government initiated the "three exchanges" of mail, trade, and air and shipping services, believing that the contact enhances mutual understanding and creates favorable conditions for reunification.

A significant upgrade in China's diplomatic policy came in the late 1970s. The focus of foreign policy changed from one on national security to pursuing opportunities for international trade and foreign investment, known as the **"Open Door policy."** Economic modernization took center stage. Peaceful co-existence played a major role in the establishment of good relations, replacing the old Communist concept of uncompromising class struggle. In 1978, a peace treaty with Japan was signed. Throughout the 1980s and 1990s, China settled its differences first with India, Myanmar, and Mongolia and then with the Soviet Union, Vietnam, Indonesia, and South Korea.

Since the mid-1980s, China has increased its participation in the world. It first signed several agreements on human rights. Upholding its principle of nonaggression, China signed a nuclear nonproliferation treaty on March 11, 1992. A few years later, on September 24, 1996, it signed the Nuclear Test Ban Treaty. In addition, China decided to cut its military forces by 500,000 in three years, beginning from 1997, after having cut its forces by 1 million in the 1980s. China has been particularly active in international economic activities. Its negotiations toward joining the World Trade Organization (WTO) eventually led it to become a member of this organization in December 2001.

China has shown its great concern about the crisis in the Middle East. On May 29, 2003, the Chinese government proposed five points for a possible peaceful solution to the crisis in this region. It supports the "Road Map" peace plan and hopes that the positive content provides a sound basis for the resumption of talks between Israel and the Palestinian Authority. It hopes that both sides will cooperate with the peacemaking efforts of the international community.

Overall, the Five Principles of Peaceful Coexistence initiated in the 1950s have been the underpinning of China's foreign diplomacy. China has demonstrated a tremendously conservative attitude on the Taiwan issue, as well as on conflicts in other places in the world. In view of its economic focus, China's foreign policy structure is expected to remain stable in decades to come.

See also Cold War and China; Hong Kong, Return of; Independent Foreign Policy (1982); Jiang Zemin (1926–   ), Diplomacy of; Rhetoric in China's Foreign Relations; United Nations (UN) and China; Vietnam War.

Bibliography

Cohen, Warren I., and Akira Iriye, eds., *The Great Powers in East Asia* (New York: Columbia University Press, 1990); Dittmer, Lowell, and Samuel S. Kim, eds., *China's Quest for National Identity* (Ithaca, NY: Cornell University Press, 1993).

Jingyi Song

Folk Music and Songs of New China

Throughout Chinese history, folk music and songs have been a vehicle of people's emotions. The folk music and songs of China have a documented history of

3,000 years. The *Guofeng* (Airs of the states) in the classic *Shijing* (Book of odes) contains folk songs gathered by the feudal rulers of ancient China. After the People's Republic of China (PRC) was established in 1949, folk music and songs played an important part in propagating the message that only the Communist Party could save the Chinese poor class. Folksy performing art became a major tool in the Communists' revolutionary struggle against the class enemy and foreign imperialism. Thus the art forms of folk music and songs were a vehicle for praising the Party and the heroes of New China and served as an efficient way to educate and influence the Chinese people in modern times.

Since China is a country with multiple nationalities spread over a vast land area, there is great diversity in its folk music and songs, which carry different local characteristics and unique graces. Folk art varies greatly among the Han majority and among China's fifty-six ethnic groups. It is different in form, style, and performance according to different geographic regions, social contexts, local customs, and people's living and working circumstances. The different styles of folk music and songs are embodiments of the variety in Chinese culture and art. In folk music and songs, dialects and minority languages are commonly used, in addition to Modern Standard Chinese. Although one does not always understand all the words of the songs, one can clearly tell the differences among them from their melodies and other musical characteristics.

Chinese folk music and songs have always been produced by working people in rural areas, particularly by rural artists. In modern times, they display the diversity of Chinese society with its changes and developments. Regional folk

Folk music is an important segment of modern Chinese arts.

songs with revolutionary lyrics became popular. For example, the regional Shaanbei folk music and songs became well known all over China after 1949, due to the fact that Shaanbei (or northern Shaanxi) was the central Red base in the 1930s.

Shaanbei folk music and songs were politically tied to the struggle for establishing the PRC and thus even before 1949 played an important role in painting the Chinese Communist Party's image as savior of the poor. They are particularly expressive of the peasants' sorrow and misery before the arrival of the Red Army and their gratefulness to the Chinese Communist Party that brought them liberation happiness.

Folk music and songs created at different times display different themes. Since 1949, the development of Chinese folk music and songs has gone through a number of distinct stages that are commonly categorized under "three turning points."

The first turning point was the founding of New China in 1949. In the period between the establishment of the PRC and the **Great Cultural Revolution (1966–1976)**, popular folk music and songs carried a strong political signal. The main themes promoted were praising the Communist Party and the motherland. The message was: socialism is good; without the Communist Party, there would be no New China. The famous Tibetan folk song titled "Song of Praise" and numerous other Chinese folk songs after the Chinese revolution, such as "Honghu River," were very popular during this time. During this initial period after liberation, folk music and songs demonstrated how people enjoyed the new life the Party and Chairman **Mao Zedong** had brought them. They reflected how New China was engaged in the construction of a socialist country; songs like "Socialism Is Good" and "My Motherland" were representative of the musical works of this era.

The second turning point was the beginning of the Cultural Revolution in 1966. One of the goals of the Cultural Revolution was to get rid of the old tradition and build a new world, and this principle also applied to folk music and songs. During this period, which lasted from 1966 to 1976, traditional Chinese music was trashed as one of the Four Olds (old ideas, old culture, old customs, and old habits). Previously existing folk music and songs were banned, and many new songs were created, laden with the radical political ideology of the time. The main theme was the praise of Chairman Mao, as in "The Golden Hill of Beijing," "Never Forget Chairman Mao's Kindness," and the Hunan folk song "Liuyang River." During the ten years of the Cultural Revolution, political activities permeated all aspects of life in China: workers stopped working, students stopped studying, and farmers stopped farming to sing the praises of Chairman Mao, who was worshipped as God. Other popular songs in this era were "The East Is Red," "Sailing the Seas Depends on the Helmsman," "Long Live Chairman Mao!" and "We Are Chairman Mao's Red Guards."

The third era began in 1976, after the end of the Cultural Revolution, which was marked by the downfall of the **Gang of Four**. China started its economic reform and implemented the **"Open Door policy"**; people started to lead a normal life again; and folk music and songs began to show signs of economic revival. In the new folk art, people rerecognized their homeland, the value of Chinese culture, and the natural beauty of their home country. The theme shifted away from class struggle to glorification, patriotism, and devotion to the motherland. Emotional lyrics such as "I love you, China" and "The moon on the fifteenth of the month," the latter of which expresses a wife's longing, were typical of this new trend.

Through the Open Door policy after the Cultural Revolution, Western rock music entered China and gained popularity as a new trend of Chinese music. Chinese rock music emerged in the late 1980s, with young people as its main audience. However, Chinese folk music and songs are still enjoyed by the majority of Chinese. In the 1990s and at the beginning of the new millennium, there has been a trend to return to Chinese folk music and songs from a moment of passion for Western music. Thus folk music and songs have recently regained the appreciation of Chinese mass audiences, and folk musicians and singers are becoming increasingly popular on the stage. They keep their folksy form, but meanwhile they adapt these forms to the taste of modern life rhythms. Electronic effects are commonly applied.

See also Theater in Contemporary China.

Bibliography

Armstrong, M. Jocelyn, R. Warwick Armstrong, and Kent Mulliner, *Chinese Populations in Contemporary Southeast Asian Societies: Identities, Interdependence and International Influence* (London: Curzon Press, 2002); Scharping, Thomas, *Birth Control in China 1949–2000: Population Policy and Demographic Development (Chinese Worlds)* (New York: Routledge, 2002).

Senquan Zhang

Foreign Debt

Developing countries borrow from abroad usually to fill the savings and investment gap and the foreign exchange and capital imports gap, to invest and reap the high marginal product of capital due to abundant labor, and to build infrastructure for facilitating domestic private investment and attracting **foreign direct investment** (FDI). China's savings rate has been extraordinarily high (around 40 percent of GDP), and China does not really need foreign savings to fill the savings and investment gap. In the early period of economic reforms, China needed foreign exchange to purchase foreign equipment and machinery. China borrowed from abroad mainly to take advantage of low-interest loans to build up its infrastructure.

China began to borrow from abroad during the early 1980s. Foreign borrowing was U.S. $4.3 billion in 1981 and U.S. $6.2 billion in 1993 (the highest since 1979). The borrowing declined after 1994, was down to zero in 1999, and climbed to $0.3 billion in 2000. Starting in 2001, foreign borrowing also includes three-month international trade loans, which is why the borrowing figure was higher in 2001.

China's total accumulated foreign debt had been increasing until 1999 and then started to decline. Total debt was U.S. $15.8 billion in 1985, U.S. $52.45 billion in 1990, U.S. $106.59 billion in 1995, U.S. $151.83 billion in 1999, and U.S. $145.73 billion in 2000, which put China as the fourth-largest debtor among developing countries (behind Brazil, Russia, and Mexico). China's foreign debt exceeded U.S. $180 billion in 2003.

The ratio of China's total foreign debt to GDP was 5.2 percent in 1985, 15.2 percent in 1995, and 13.5 percent in 2000. China's debt/GDP ratio is much lower than that for heavily indebted countries. Thus China has been classified as one of the less indebted countries by the World Bank. Most of China's debt is public or public guaranteed. Before 1992, all the debt was publicly guaranteed. Public or public-guaranteed long-term debt was about 98.9 percent of total long-term debt in 1995 and 80 percent in 2000. The remaining debt is private nonguaranteed. During the period 1990–2000, borrowing from commercial banks and other sources decreased from 72 percent to 65 percent, while borrowing from foreign governments and international financial institutions increased from 28 percent to 35 percent.

Most of China's foreign debt is long term. In 1985, about 60 percent of the foreign debt was long term, while in 2000, 91 percent of foreign debt was long-term debt and only 9 percent was short-term debt. Compared with heavily indebted countries, the figure of short-term debt is not high. In 1996, just before the Asian financial crisis, the ratio of short-term debt to total debt was 57.5 percent in Korea, 25 percent in Indonesia, 19.9 percent in the Philippines, and 39.6 percent in Thailand.

Most of China's foreign debt is in U.S. dollars and Japanese yen. In 1985, about 50 percent of the debt was in Japanese yen and 24 percent in U.S. dollars. In 2000, about 15.3 percent of the debt was in Japanese yen and 74 percent in U.S. dollars. Japan has been China's largest creditor, with U.S. $2,404.81 million in 1996; the World Bank was second, with U.S. $1,880 million in 1996; the United States ranked third, with U.S. $1,160.53 million in 1996; the fourth-largest creditor was the Asia Development Bank, with U.S. $1,102 million in 1996. Hong Kong, Taiwan, and Singapore had large amounts of direct investment in China, but did not have much tied to loans.

The risk indicators of foreign debt include the ratio of debt to exports of goods and services (XGS), the debt/GNP ratio, the ratio of total debt service to exports of goods and services, and the ratio of foreign debt to foreign exchange reserves. The lower these measures are, the less risky a country's foreign debt is. The ratio of debt to XGS was 96.5 percent in 1993 (the highest ratio for China) and 52.1 percent in 2000, the debt/GNP ratio was 17.1 percent in 1994 (highest) and 13.5 percent in 2000, and the ratio of total debt service to exports was 15.4 percent (highest) in 1986 and 9.2 percent in 2000. For all developing countries in 2000, the average ratio of debt to XGS was 114.3 percent, the average debt/GNP ratio was 37.4 percent, and the ratio of total debt service to exports was 17 percent. By all measures, the degree of risk exposure of China's foreign debt is lower. Moreover, the ratio of China's foreign debt to foreign exchange reserves declined from 1,190 percent in 1988 to only 88 percent in 2000; that is China's foreign exchange reserves were higher than foreign debt outstanding. This ratio is still decreasing.

Foreign borrowing has been uneven among provinces in China. The largest borrowing provinces include Shanghai, Guangdong, Tianjin, Beijing, Shandong, and Liaoning. Foreign borrowing in Guizhou, **Tibet**, Gansu, Qinghai, and Inner

Mongolia was relatively low. These provinces also have less foreign direct investment. Hainan, Shanghai, and Tianjin were among the provinces with the highest borrowing/GDP ratio. For example, in 1995, the borrowing/GDP ratio was 9.2 percent for Hainan, 6.9 percent for Shanghai, and 5.3 percent for Tianjin, while the borrowing/GDP ratio was negligible for Inner Mongolia, Gansu, and Qinghai.

The reasons for the low foreign debt in China are as follows: First, China has learned painful lessons from its own experience, as well as that of other countries. China borrowed a considerable amount from the Soviet Union in the early 1950s. Later the two countries' relationship was broken, and China was forced to repay the debt and interest in the early 1960s to the Soviet Union with extreme pain. China followed Mao's self-reliance policy thereafter. Also, debt crises in Latin American countries in the early 1980s and 1990s and the recent Asian financial crisis all reminded China to be cautious in foreign borrowing. Second, China's savings rate is extremely high. In 1999, China's savings rate was 42 percent, while the investment rate was 40 percent. Thus China does not have a shortage of funds. In fact, some government officials have recently argued that China has a surplus of capital. Third, China has accumulated a huge amount of foreign exchange reserves. China's foreign exchange reserves have been increasing, from U.S. $0.84 billion in 1979 to U.S. $165.6 billion in 2000, second only to Japan, which had U.S. $354.9 billion in 2000. By the end of June 2003, China's foreign exchange reserves had reached U.S. $346.5 billion. Meanwhile, China's accumulated foreign debt had reached U.S. $182.6 billion. Fourth, China has attracted a large amount of FDI and can obtain foreign advanced technologies through FDI, which have been recognized as a better way of foreign capital utilization. In 2002, FDI to China was $52.74 billion. China has surpassed the United States and become the largest FDI receiver in the world.

In summary, the ratio of China's foreign debt to GDP is low, most foreign debts are long term, all the indicators show that the degree of risk exposure of China's foreign debt is low, and moreover, China's foreign exchange reserves are much larger than the foreign debt outstanding. Thus foreign debt is not a problem for China purely from an accounting perspective.

See also Domestic Government Debt; Foreign Trade; Taiwan, Trade Relations with the Mainland; Trade Relations with the United States.

Bibliography

Lin, Shuanglin, "China's Government Debt: How Serious?" *China: An International Journal* 1, no. 1 (2003): 73–98; National Bureau of Statistics of the PRC, *Finance Yearbook of China* (various issues, 1997, 2000, 2001) (Beijing: China Statistics Press); National Bureau, *National Labor and Social Security Yearbook 2001* (Beijing: China Statistics Press); National Bureau, *China Statistical Yearbook* (various issues, 1997, 2001, 2002) (Beijing: China Statistics Press); National Bureau, *Twenty Years' Regional Statistics after Reforms and Opening-Up* (1997); World Bank, *Global Development Finance, 1997* (Oxford: Oxford University Press, 2002).

Shuanglin Lin

Foreign Direct Investment (FDI)

China has been the most dynamic host country of foreign direct investment (FDI). Since economic reforms were initiated in 1978, China has become the largest recipient of FDI in the developing world and globally the second largest (next only to the United States) since 1993. In 2002, China received $52.7 billion of FDI inflows, and $53.7 billion in 2003, surpassing the United States and becoming the largest FDI host country in the world. By the end of 2002, the cumulated FDI received in China reached $446 billion. The contributions of inward FDI to the Chinese economy have burgeoned in ways that no one anticipated. In 2001, FDI inflows constituted more than 10 percent of gross fixed capital formation; 28.5 percent of industrial output was produced by foreign-invested enterprises (FIEs); and half of China's exports were created by FIEs.

Many observers view China's success in attracting FDI as a puzzle by noting its obvious disadvantages relative to other host countries: China had little legal security, so property rights were not well defined; China's currency was not convertible, so foreign investors had no insured sources of hard-currency earnings; corruption in China has been severe and growing, so foreign investors incur additional costs. These disadvantages, however, have been offset by China's huge market, large FDI flows from Hong Kong and other overseas Chinese, and the liberalized FDI regime. (1) The huge domestic market made China a highly desirable location for investments by multinational firms and hence was extremely strong positive lure for foreign investors. The advantage of market size has been enhanced by China's rapid economic growth in the last twenty years. China's real GDP grew at an average annual rate of 9.5 percent in 1978–2001, the highest in the world in that period. (2) China has a special asset of overseas Chinese, particularly in Hong Kong and Taiwan, who provide most of the FDI received in China. This can be explained by "Chinese connections," which are based on the facts that overseas Chinese share the same language, culture, and family tradition, and that they also have relatives, friends, and former business ties in China. Therefore, the connections make it much easier for overseas Chinese to negotiate and operate joint ventures in China relative to investors elsewhere. (3) China has been systematically liberalizing its FDI regime since 1979. The attitude of the Chinese government toward multinationals is far more liberal than that of most other developing counties, especially those in East Asia such as Japan, South Korea, and Taiwan.

While market size, overseas Chinese, and the FDI regime play a critical role in the FDI boom, the contributions of other factors cannot be ignored. These factors include China's cheap resources (labor, land, and raw materials), improving infrastructure conditions due to rapid economic growth, and the overall expansion of multinationals in the developing world in the 1990s.

The positive impact of FDI on China's economic growth has been recognized in both policy and academic circles. Some indicators may suggest the importance and contributions of FDI to the Chinese economy. In 2001, the ratio of FDI stock to GDP was 36 percent; the share of FDI flows in gross capital formation was 10 percent; FIEs produced 29 percent of total industrial output; and FIEs also contributed 13 percent of the total tax revenue in 1997. The most important benefits from FDI perhaps are its role in exports and its spillover effects on China's market-oriented reforms. Exports by FIEs in China rose almost 50 percent annually in 1979–2002, and the value of their exports in 2001 (mainly manufacturing goods) was $131 billion, 49 percent of China's total exports in that year. FDI has brought extra gains to China in facilitating its transition toward a market system that started in the late 1970s, which in turn have enhanced the income growth.

The factors behind the overall success in utilizing FDI include China's effective FDI strategy, the strong central government, FDI from Hong Kong and Taiwan, and China's rapid economic growth. (1) China has singled out and encouraged two categories of FDI: export-oriented FDI and technologically advanced FDI, to which many incentives are offered. China's demands cluster around performance requirements in two categories: pressuring multinationals to produce more added value domestically, provide more local content in their finished product, and expand linkages into the indigenous economy; and pushing multinationals to use their worldwide marketing networks to export more products and components out of China. (2) China's competent government lends credibility to its bargains and thus contributes to a stable investment environment. The government's monopoly over joint-venture approvals has the potential to allow it to determine the range of terms for FDI contracts. The central government also is positioned to supervise individual bargaining sessions at the firm level, and the state organs and personnel subject to central supervision can control the negotiating process. (3) The benefits from Hong Kong and Taiwan FDI are various: it presents more opportunity for local control, its technology is more labor intensive and consistent with China's comparative advantages, its focus is primarily on cost reduction and price competitiveness, the majority of its output is exported, and the overall expense to the local economy is less. (4) The growing market size due to rapid economic growth in the last two decades is perhaps the greatest strength China has in bargaining with foreign investors, particularly in industries in which international competition to enter the huge market is fierce. This strength especially provides China with the ability to utilize competition among multinationals to play one off against another for better terms.

While the success is impressive, the challenges China faces in using FDI to enhance growth are severe, particularly after China's accession to the World Trade Organization (WTO). China's FDI regime and relevant policies have to adjust to be consistent with the rule of the WTO, resulting in a growing share of FDI by Western multinational corporations (MNCs). Large Western MNCs have great bargaining power relative to developing host countries, including China. This power is greatly strengthened by their predominantly oligopolistic positions in worldwide product markets. With this power, MNCs enjoy the ability to manipulate prices and profits, to collude with other firms in determining areas of control, and generally to restrict the entry of potential competition.

The net impact of FDI on the Chinese economy in the future will depend largely on how China balances technology transfers and domestic market protection. China may take advantage of its large country size in forming its strategy to shape MNC activities. In particular, China may adopt well-defined measures of investment promotion to choose the right FDI projects, to design realistic domestic-content requirements to upgrade domestic industries, and to set up optimal export-performance requirements to create advanced comparative advantages in global markets.

See also Foreign Debt; Foreign Trade; Hong Kong, Return of; Taiwan, Trade Relations with the Mainland; Trade Relations with the United States; World Trade Organization (WTO), China's Accession to.

Bibliography

Hou, Jack, and Kevin H. Zhang, "A Location Analysis of Taiwanese Manufacturing Branch-Plants in China," *International Journal of Business* 6, no. 2, 53–66; Lardy, Nicholas R., "The Role of Foreign Trade and Investment in China's Economic Transformation," *China Quarterly* 144 (1995): 1065–1082; National Bureau of Statistics of the PRC, *China Statistical Yearbook* (various issues, 1992–1999) (Beijing: China Statistics Press); United Nations Conference on Trade and Development, *World Investment Report* (New York: United Nations, 1991–2002); Zhang, Kevin H., "Why Is U.S. Direct Investment in China So Small?" *Contemporary Economic Policy* 18, no. 1 (2000): 82–94; Zhang, Kevin H., "How does FDI Affect Economic Growth in China," *Economics of Transition* 9, no. 3 (2001): 679–693; Zhang, Kevin H., and Shunfeng Song, "Promoting Exports: The Role of Inward FDI in China," *China Economic Review* 11, no. 4 (2000): 385–396.

Kevin Honglin Zhang

Foreign Trade

China's foreign trade has experienced phenomenal growth in volume. In 1978, China's exports and imports accounted for 9.6 percent of GDP—one of the lowest rates in the world—and its rank in world trade was thirty-second. Since then, trade volume has increased by thirty times in twenty-four years, from $20.6 billion in 1978 to $851.2 billion in 2003. China's trade surged to 60 percent of GDP in 2003, and it became the fourth-largest trade nation in the world. Based on the data of the first ten months of 2004, China's trade would be $1,100 billion in that year, and its world ranking would be third. In 1978, China accounted for less than 1 percent of world trade; the share was 5 percent in 2002. It is virtually certain that China will become even more important in the future because of its size, dynamic economic growth, and continuing policy reforms. According to the World Bank's (1997) projection for the next twenty-five years, China's share in world trade would increase to more than 10 percent in ten years, making it a major engine of growth for world trade. China could become the second-largest trading nation in the world, next to the United States. Four noteworthy features characterize China's trade: (1) the significant expansion of trade volume; (2) the critical role of processing trade; (3) the improving trade structure of products; and (4) the concentration of the exporting market in East Asia and the United States.

The trade boom has several causes, including liberalizing trade institutions and policies, the rapid growth of the Chinese economy, the large amount of **foreign direct investment** (FDI) inflows, and devaluations of China's real exchange rate. In the 1980s, China began trade reforms by moving from monopoly to a decentralized system. Special economic zones and open **cities** led to

Shanghai has been China's largest international port city since the nineteenth century.

greater openings for trade. Government direct controls on trade, especially restrictions on imports, have been gradually relaxed. China's GDP grew at a rate of nearly 10 percent in the last twenty-four years, the highest rate in the world during that period, resulting in rising demand for imports and a large supply of exports. FDI, especially export-oriented foreign-invested enterprises (FIEs), contributed to the trade boom significantly. Most of the inward FDI in China is export oriented, coming from Hong Kong and Taiwan. The share of exports by FIEs in total exports was almost 50 percent in 2001. China's official real exchange rate was devalued from RMB 1.6836 per U.S. dollar in 1978 to 8.27 in 2002, which made China's products cheaper in the world market and thus caused its exports to grow.

The processing trade, that is, processing imported materials or imported components into exports, has become a main source of trade growth. The share of processing exports in total exports rose from 18 percent in 1986 to 55 percent in 2000, and the share of processing imports in the total imports went up from 16 percent to 41 percent. Two factors contributed to the growth of processing trade. First, China's export-oriented FDI strategy encourages foreign firms (mainly from Hong Kong and Taiwan) to engage in processing trade. Along with China's cheap resources (e.g., labor and land), a variety of incentive policies also have been offered to attract FDI for export production. The share of trade by FIEs in total processing trade tripled in ten years from 21 percent in 1988 to 64 percent in 1997. Another factor is related to the classification method of processing trade. Due to growing globalization, more exports involve imported foreign contents, rather than traditional exports that have complete domestic contents only. This causes a rise of trade volume in statistics.

Due to industrial upgrading and rapid economic growth, China's exports have been experiencing two shifts: one from primary to manufacturing products, and the other from labor-intensive to capital-intensive manufacturing products. In 1978, more than half of China's exports (63 percent) were primary products. The share fell to 30 percent in 1988 and then continually shrank to less than 10 percent in 2001, while manufacturing products became dominant in exports (more than 90 percent of the total exports). The largest item in manufacturing exports is machinery and electrical equipment (32 percent of the total in 2001). Exports of machinery and electrical equipment (relatively more capital intensive) increased faster than exports of textiles (relatively more labor intensive) in the 1990s.

Finally, China's exporting markets have been biased toward East Asia and the United States. While China has pursued a policy of diversifying export markets for many years, the destination of China's exports is mainly Asia and the United States; the potential for exports to the European Union has been much less explored. In 1997, exports to Asia (mainly Hong Kong, Japan, South Korea, Singapore, and Taiwan) made up 60 percent of total exports, and to the United States, 18 percent. In 2000, the basic pattern did not change much, except for an increase in the share of the U.S. market, and the share of exports to Asia and the United States together still constituted about 70 percent, although the share fell by 8 percentage points.

While China's achievements in expanding trade are real, some indicators or raw figures about trade are somewhat misleading or deceptive. Three aspects are noteworthy: openness index, booming trade volume, and trade structure of commodity. The index of openness, defined as a ratio of a country's trade volume to its GDP, is usually used to measure the degree of the country's economic integration with the outside world. The rapid growth of China's trade pushed the ratio of trade to GDP from 10 percent in 1978 to 50 percent in 2002, much higher than that for other large countries, such as the United States (21 percent) and Brazil (19 percent). Is China more open than the United States? The question may be addressed by using purchasing-power-parity-adjusted estimates of GDP, which correct for undervaluation of nontradables. When this adjustment is applied to China, it brings the ratio of trade to GDP down to 11 percent, instead of 50 percent, in 2002.

The indication of China's trade volume may not reflect corresponding benefits from trade. Since the main source of China's trade boom is processing trade, the value added has been small relative to ordinary trade. The processing trade does not create as much gain as ordinary trade with China, since it has little connection with domestic firms and the domestic economy does not adjust both to accommodate and to benefit from this expanding volume of processing trade.

By 2001, 90 percent of China's exports and 81 percent of imports were manufacturing goods. The largest item in both exports and imports is machinery and electrical equipment. This structure does not suggest that China has shifted its comparative advantage from labor-intensive products to capital-intensive products. Most of the manufacturing goods China exports are either labor intensive or low-value-added processing exports, and almost all imports of manufacturing goods are capital intensive. For example, more than 75 percent of exports in machinery and electrical equipment are imports processed for exports. Therefore, China's trade basically still is interindustry, not intraindustry.

See also Foreign Debt; Hong Kong, Return of; One Country, Two Systems; Taiwan, Trade Relations with the Mainland; Trade Relations with the United States.

Bibliography

Lardy, Nicholas R., "Chinese Foreign Trade," *China Quarterly* 131 (1992): 691–720; Naughton, Barry, "China's Emergence and Prospects as a Trading Nation," *Brookings Papers on Economic Activity* 2 (1996): 273–344; National State Statistical Bureau of the PRC, *China Statistical Yearbook* (various issues) (Beijing: China Statistics Press, 1992–2002); World Bank, *China: Foreign Trade Reform* (Washington, DC: World Bank, 1994); Zhang, Kevin H., "China as a New Power in World Trade," in *China's Access WTO and Global Economy*, ed. Fung Pei and Johnson, 32–48 (Beijing: Yuhang Publishing House, 2003); Zhang, Kevin H., ed., *China as the World Factory?* (London: Routledge, 2005); Zhang, Kevin H., and Shunfeng Song, "Promoting Exports: The Role of Inward FDI in China," *China Economic Review* 11 (2000): 385–396.

Kevin Honglin Zhang

Foreign-Language Teaching Methodology

Foreign-language education in modern China has come a long way since 1949. In the 1950s, for more than a decade, the Russian language was taught in Chinese secondary and higher-education institutions as the predominant foreign language. At that time, foreign-language teaching was concerned with problems more basic than methodology: the shortage of teaching materials and qualified teachers, and the excessive enrollment of Russian-language majors. When Sino-Soviet relations broke up in the late 1950s and early 1960s, foreign-language teaching in school and university curricula in China shifted from Russian to English, which emerged as the dominant foreign language in Chinese foreign-language education. However, soon the development of - English-language teaching was interrupted by the **Great Cultural Revolution**, which began in 1966. Foreign-language teaching was considered introducing capitalist cultures.

After the Cultural Revolution, which lasted for a decade (1966–1976), China opened its doors to the Western world. Foreign-language education resumed and since then has developed substantially. Although the teaching and learning of English were encouraged and became popular in Chinese schools, language-teaching methodology in China remained formalistic. The teaching of English as a foreign language followed the traditional teaching methods, mainly emphasizing vocabulary and grammatical rules.

In the 1960s and 1970s, English instruction in China was teacher centered, and students assumed a passive role in classroom activities. Language students took notes in English classes, rather than paying attention to the real use of the target language. Practicing the target language in group work was ignored in the classrooms. Foreign languages and the learning of a foreign language were taken as an object of scientific study, rather than training in communication. The only practice of the language was through reading. During this period, students were asked to read their textbooks aloud for fluency practice. In a typical English-language class, students would learn new words and read them aloud, read pattern drills, read English texts and translate them into Chinese, and do exercises on grammar and the usage of words. Students were not encouraged to speak to one another in English; their sole opportunity to listen to English was listening to their teachers and classmates reading textbook passages aloud. The emphasis on grammar and translation resulted in a situation where many foreign-language learners in China found it difficult to communicate with native speakers or participate in discussions.

With the gradual introduction of language labs, exercises in listening comprehension in the foreign language were added to the range of learning activities, but even when listening to recordings, the students still had to complete written exercises that would be checked and corrected by the instructor. This approach hindered the students in their listening comprehension for the purpose of understanding the meaning of the message; it did not offer training in listening strategies and also did not enhance communicative competence. The focus was on the students' attention to individual words, which prevented them from becoming effective listeners. Further, they were not trained to make contextual inferences about unknown words and discard information irrelevant for their listening purposes.

In the 1970s and 1980s, new developments in language-teaching theory and practice in the West had a great impact on the teaching of English as a second language (ESL) in China. In Western Europe and North America, the notion of communicative competence was introduced into language-teaching methodology. Communicative instruction methods were developed in China through cooperative efforts between Chinese institutions and schools from Western countries, and new ideas have taken shape since then. Foreign language is no longer understood merely as a linguistic code, but also as a matter of behavior. Language learners in China are now required to develop not only language skills and knowledge, but also communicative knowledge such as when, where, and how to use the language in social contexts. This includes knowing what to say to certain people and the appropriateness of making certain statements in a certain situation.

In modern China, language educators have become aware that knowledge about a foreign language and the ability to use it are two different things, and that the use of the language should be the ultimate goal of teaching/learning. To achieve this goal, the foreign language has to be taught in communicative situations. For this reason, modern English courses always present the language in a meaningful context, so learners can later use it for the purpose of communication in real-life situations. The teaching content is no longer arranged merely according to vocabulary and grammatical structures. The modern foreign-language courses in Chinese schools highlight the need for communication and take into account functions, notions, and phonetics; they also consider lexical and grammatical items and dynamically integrate and combine all these factors into an organic whole. The teaching materials relate to real situations and thus reflect the learners' communicative needs.

Before communicative language instruction was introduced, whenever learners made a mistake, the teacher would interrupt them and correct their mistake. Consequently, students would feel discouraged from communicating and soon lose their interest and confidence. This teacher-centered instruction method could lead neither to accuracy nor to fluency in using the foreign language. Under functional or sociolinguistic influence and through training, language teachers are now aware that mastering a foreign language means more than acquiring accuracy alone. Thus successful communication is presently the declared goal of foreign-language education. The new teaching methodology adds the sociocultural factor as another important dimension to language-teaching theory. Under the new approach, language instructors tolerate minor mistakes that do not impair conveying the meaning of the message. Thus modern language teaching is more pragmatic and reality oriented, with more emphasis on listening and speaking skills. Learners can concentrate more on communicating ideas and learning to use the foreign language for a social or academic purpose.

See also English Proficiency Levels; Foreign-Language Training.

Bibliography

Savignon, S. J., *Communicative Competence: Theory and Classroom Practice, Texts and Contexts in Second Language Learning* (New York: McGraw-Hill, 1997); Strong, G., "Curriculum Implementation in China," paper presented at the Annual Meeting of the Teachers of English to Speakers of Other Languages, Vancouver, British Columbia, 1992.

Senquan Zhang

Foreign-Language Training

Foreign language in the People's Republic of China (PRC) includes any language other than the native language, Chinese. However, according to public understanding, foreign languages mainly indicate English, Russian, Japanese, Spanish, French, and German, with English being by far the most popular. To a majority of students, the concept of learning a foreign language is linked simultaneously to taking English, so nowadays in China, foreign-language training is often considered English training.

Foreign-language training has experienced fluctuating periods of implementation in China since 1949, the year of the founding of the People's Republic of China. Before 1949, China had a long history of deliberately closing doors to any foreign languages in order to prevent "cultural invasion." After the Communist Party took power in 1949, China adopted Russian as the dominant foreign language to be taught in schools because the Soviet Union was considered a "big brother" to follow. English learning was condemned as unpatriotic because of a national campaign against American imperialism and British colonialism. However, this did not last long. A few years later, in the middle of the 1950s, the relationship between China and the Soviet Union deteriorated. English was gradually accepted as one of the foreign languages that were allowed to be taught in Chinese schools, but in a highly monitored manner. This new allowance was banned once again during the **Great Cultural Revolution (1966–1976)**. The Cultural Revolution brought disaster to Chinese education and resulted in abolishing any foreign-language training in China. The teaching and learning of foreign languages were severely criticized and forbidden. Those who did not discontinue their study were jailed and sometimes even punished with the death penalty under charges of being a suspected traitor of the country and/or espionage. The substantial changes in foreign-language training and the favoritism of English did not reappear until late 1978, when Deng Xiaoping came to the leading position. After the restoration of the higher-education system in 1977, colleges and universities started to recruit students to be foreign-language majors. It was not long after this that foreign language became a required subject in the national college entrance examination for all college candidates.

Since 1978, more attention has been paid to foreign-language training than ever before. The state Ministry of Education has issued guidelines for the curriculum and textbooks, requiring that foreign-language training include listening, speaking, reading, and writing. The college entrance examination requires all foreign-language candidates to take both oral and written examinations. All colleges and universities have adopted both listening and written formats in the foreign-language testing system to assess the effectiveness of instruction and learning. Foreign-language training is not only implemented in the curriculum and testing system at the college and university level, but is also required in China's compulsory education (primary and lower secondary school education). Students start to learn foreign language in lower secondary school, continue the learning in upper secondary school, and minimally study it for two years in colleges and universities. At least 1,600 instructional hours in foreign-language training are accumulated by a college graduate in China.

Due to China's market economic reform and **Open Door policy**, foreign-language training has prevailed nationwide. Quite a number of scholars and students go abroad to receive further education. English is therefore considered one of the most practical foreign languages and a vehicle for success. Besides the training in regular schools, foreign-language learning also occurs in self-accessed language labs, short-term training classes, individual tutoring, programmed **television** courses, and various learning environments. The Web-based self-study language-learning lab of Tsinghua University is open to all students from 8:00 A.M. to 10:00 P.M. seven days a week. Eleven foreign-language training centers directly affiliated with the International Cooperation Bureau of the Ministry of Education provide intensive foreign-language courses to state-funded individuals or groups who are scheduled to study abroad. The training curriculum usually encompasses eighteen-week English or thirty-six-week French and German programs. Short-term intensive trainings for taking standardized foreign-language tests, such as the Test of English as a Foreign Language (TOEFL), also attract thousands of foreign-language learners. More and more Chinese parents provide their children with opportunities to learn foreign languages by hiring tutors, purchasing language audio and video tapes, and subscribing to television programs at home. **Internet** and bilingual Web sites are also becoming resources for English learning. Millions of Internet users are forced to rely heavily on English to communicate each other, and thousands of bilingual Web sites have become available not only for academic scholars but also for students at different levels.

In the 1990s, much more progress was made in foreign-language training, and more children started to learn English in elementary schools; some of them even started learning in kindergarten. In 2000, the government officially mandated that all public schools start offering English courses in the third grade at the elementary-school level. The construction of an English-language teaching system from elementary school (third grade) to the college level is under way. An increasing number of private schools have been implementing English teaching and learning in the curriculum earlier than the third grade. China's entry into the World Trade Organization (WTO) and successful bid for the 2008 Olympic Games have boosted even more the fervor for foreign-language teaching and learning in Chinese schools. It is estimated that the number of people studying English in China is much larger than that of all native English speakers around the world today.

See also English Proficiency Levels; Foreign-Language Teaching Methodology; Primary Education; Secondary Education; World Trade Organization (WTO), China's Accession to.

Bibliography

Hill, Clifford, *English in China: Educating for a Global Future*, 1998, http://www.columbia.edu/~cah34/EIC/EnglishInChina.htm, accessed on November 18, 2004; Ji, Shaobin, "English as a Global Language in China," *Weekly Column*, article 99, May 2002.

Ronghua Ouyang and Dan Ouyang

Four Cardinal Principles, Implementation of

The fundamental political guideline for the Chinese Communist Party (CCP) in running China from 1980 to 2000 was proposed by Deng Xiaoping. The three parts of the guideline are One Focus (to Concentrate on Economic Construction), Two Basic Points ("Open Door and Reform"), and "Four Cardinal Principles and Implementation," (hereafter the Four Principles). These three items are related parts of a whole; the understanding of each requires a reference to the other two. The Four Principles are (1) socialism; (2) people's democratic dictatorship; (3) the CCP's exclusive leadership; and (4) Marxism–**Mao Zedong** Thought as the official ideology.

According to Deng Xiaoping's own interpretations, "One Focus, Two Basic Points" may be simplified into three words. "The Focus on Economic Construction" may be simplified to "development"; the Two Basic Points may otherwise appear as "reform" and "stability." The Four Principles stand for "stability," and the relationship among the "One Focus" and the "Two Policies" can be seen as the one among "stability," "development," and "reform." Only within this framework can one properly understand the Four Principles. At times when Deng needed to emphasize stability, he claimed that the Four Principles are as important as "One Focus" and the "reform" policy. Nevertheless, as only the concepts of "development" and "reform" were newly proposed in Deng's era, the Four Principles were inherited from Mao's time. Deng's order of the priority of the three concepts was "development, reform, and stability."

Before 1978 and especially during the **Great Cultural Revolution (1966–1976)**, the CCP's official ideology always contained the Four Principles. After 1978, however, China's political agenda and ideology became very different from, if not directly opposed to, those in the past, so Deng's Four Principles could not be the same as they had been previously. Though Deng believed in some aspects of the Four Principles, he revised them to a certain extent. For example, in Deng's understanding of the Four Principles, no position was left for Mao's theory of class and class struggle, along with Mao's "Doctrine of Continuous Revolution under the Proletarian Dictatorship." Deng's revision followed two rules: (1) theory needs to fit, and serve the need of, practice, or, in other words, a pragmatic attitude toward theories; and (2) the Four Principles must help, not undermine, his major goal to develop and reform China.

Deng indicated that the nature of socialism remains unclear and exploratory. Furthermore, Deng claimed that socialism does not have a fixed pattern, that it is a dynamic self-improving process. In particular, Deng filled a theoretical void of classical communism, which insists on equality on the basis of public ownership. He claimed that market economy and personal wealth are both compatible with communism. According to Deng, communism is all about improving people's life rather than reducing it to poverty; hence, the pursuit of profit and being rich are glorious rather than shameful.

On the principle of "People's Democratic Dictatorship," Deng said, "China now has no clear-cut classes, so we stopped all class-struggle." The former "Proletarian Dictatorship" should hence be changed into "People's Democratic Dictatorship." The term "dictatorship," now less class based in Deng Xiaoping's context, means to utterly denounce the Western type of tripower distribution (executive, legislative, and judicial). It denies the lawful status of any political rivals in the form of political parties or other organizations, including religious ones, in China. It oppresses all those who violate the law, undermine the political or social order, or work for "foreign hostile forces."

On the principle of the CCP's exclusive leadership, Deng expressed the following view: China has its unique culture and does not fit a multiparty political system; China has eight "democratic parties" that must be led by and maintained in solidarity with the CCP. However, the CCP is no longer a working-class-based party. It recruits "all the Chinese that excel in their fields," so the CCP is more for all the people rather than for one single class, more a party for various kinds of elites than an ideology-oriented party.

On the exclusive official ideology of Marxism and Mao Zedong Thought, Deng emphasized two points. One is to keep people's thoughts and their ways of thinking stable. The other is to unify ideas within the CCP and among all Chinese people. This unification aims "to oppose the ideological pluralism, decrease the unnecessary debates or obstacles on our way, and so we waste no time." However, Deng's talk on Marxism and Mao's Thought was not merely lip service. From Marxism, Deng held high the part on the importance of developing productivity. From Mao's Thought, Deng called for a "restoration" of Mao's pragmatic tradition and the tradition of working hard under difficult situations.

Deng's policy of upholding the Four Cardinal Principles has kept China relatively stabilized since 1978 in key ways. First, politically, the Party reached an agreement about where and how far it should go. In 1978, for example, Deng launched an "ideological liberation" campaign against all the popular ideas in the Cultural Revolution, such as class struggle and leftist, radical revolution. The Four Cardinal Principles served as the brake, or the boundaries to liberalization, in this campaign. The result was that, to a certain extent, people's thinking was liberated even though the country did not lose the common agreements on economic construction. Second, there is historical continuity. The Four Cardinal Principles were known in both Mao's and Deng's eras. This offered the older generations a sense of security that the same history they knew continued. This sense of security based on a stabilized ideology and a continuous history has strengthened the stability of China's political authority. The latter then guaranteed the credibility of all laws, policies, and, to some extent, all kinds of commerce-related credentials.

Another way to summarize the Four Principles is "antipluralism." Deng often used the phrase "antibourgeois liberalism." The pluralisms that were oppressed in Deng's era include ideological pluralism, social institutional pluralism, and plural political authority and/or a plural party system. The CCP's antipluralism aims at several goals, for example, to simplify the process by which a nationwide common recognition on what to do and how to achieve it is formed, to concentrate the whole nation's limited resources and manpower on strategic projects, to make the society relatively stable in a rapidly transforming period, and to have a huge population relatively unified. The ultimate goal of this unification or concentration was, in Deng's opinion, to benefit from a strategic advantage that a socialist country may concentrate all of its sources to solve big problems in a short time.

Deng's implementation of the Four Principles has been one of the most controversial, or even unacceptable, practices in the West. The Chinese antipluralism in the social, political, and ideological spheres directly conflicts with some of the most treasured values of the West, such as democracy and equality. Deng thus has been strongly criticized or denounced by liberal intellectuals, of Chinese or other background, throughout the world. But one thing that has become clear is that it is exactly Deng's emphasis on the mechanism of keeping China stable that has made his enterprise distinguished. The former USSR and Eastern Europeans all tried "development" and "reform." What they did not do, however, was to put forth enough effort to maintain the stability of their countries. Only Deng's China did that, which then led China to its long-term and rapid economic growth. This has been an incredible surprise to many people in the world.

However, Deng's implementation of the Four Principles has its own ironic side. If the meaning of socialism was not clear twenty years ago, it now looks even more vague in China. Although Deng hoped to eliminate exploitation, the reality has been the opposite. Millions of Chinese farmer-workers are now being heavily exploited in the capitalist businesses along the coastal cities of China. If this indicates the disappearance of the Four Principles from "real" life, their theoretical disappearance occurred when Jiang Zemin's new theory, "Three Representations," replaced Deng's Four Principles in 2001.

See also Deng Xiaoping (1904–1997), Politics of; Deng Xiaoping (1904–1997), Reforms of; Open Door Policy (1978).

Bibliography

Deng, Xiaoping, *Selected Works of Deng Xiaoping,* vol. 3 (Beijing: People's Publishing House, 1993); Office of the Document of the CCP Central Commission, *Key Documents of the Thirteenth Congress of CCP* (Beijing: People's Publishing House, 1993).

Xiaosi Yang

Fraud

See Corruption and Fraud, Control of.

Freedom of the Press

See Press Control; Press Freedom.

Fulbright Scholars in China (1979–1989)

In the late 1970s, the Beijing government realized that to attain its Four Modernizations in science and technology, industry, agriculture, and defense, China had to open its educational system to developments in the outside world. The year 1979 saw China opening its doors to foreigners, especially teachers from the West. Universities and colleges all over China invited American, Canadian, British, French, German, and other European teachers into their classrooms, mostly to teach basic foreign-language courses.

In the fall of 1979, the Chinese government officially called for American assistance in the recruitment and support of between twenty and thirty specialists in English-language teaching during a three-year period. The Council for International Exchange of Scholars (CIES), a private agency cooperating with the U.S. government in the administration of Fulbright scholar grants for advanced research and university teaching, chose four teaching English as a second language (TESL) specialists and assigned them to Beijing University in March 1980. For the first time since 1949, American scholars selected solely on the basis of their academic qualifications taught regularly enrolled Chinese university students. After 1980, the number of American Fulbrighters teaching on Chinese campuses increased substantially, and by 1989, the China Fulbright program was one of the largest in the world, with twenty-four American professors teaching on Chinese campuses and a like number of Chinese graduate students and scholars studying at U.S. universities.

When China opened its doors to the West, its primary intention was to use Western scientific technological experience for China's modernization goals. China needed Western teachers in the natural sciences and technology to help the Chinese understand recent scientific and technological developments and to enable China to catch up with the economic achievements of the Western countries. Because it was carrying out social experimentation and being reintegrated into the global economy, China also urgently needed scholars who could understand Western society and culture, as well as Western social science techniques in such areas as economics, law, and management. Chinese leaders, however, wanted their students to reject the dross of Western ideology while absorbing useful techniques from the West.

The U.S. government's educational exchange program, better known as the Fulbright program, is administered by the U.S. Information Agency (USIA). It was created to promote mutual understanding and contribute to scholarly intercultural knowledge. Using educational exchange as a tool of its China policy, the U.S. government has been trying to influence a generation of Chinese youth since the Chinese Communists came to power in 1949. In the 1980s, the U.S. government supported the China Fulbright program for theoretical work in the social sciences to promote an understanding of U.S. scholarship and the American way of life and to offset the strong focus on the sciences of Chinese students and scholars in the United States who were supported by the Chinese government. American professors in China saw the importance of teaching Western culture, as well as their academic subjects, and expected that the Chinese would not only learn technology but also understand U.S. culture and ideology.

The first four Fulbrighters began to teach English at Beijing University in 1980, and by 1989 the number of American Fulbrighters lecturing in China increased to twenty-four. From 1980 to 1989, they taught courses in a broad spectrum of American studies: history, literature, economics, journalism, law, and political science. Half of the grantees were teaching in Beijing and Shanghai, and the rest in other cities. The Tiananmen Square uprising occurred in the summer of 1989. After the suppression of the student movement, the Chinese government announced in July that it would withdraw its invitation to Fulbright professors to teach in Chinese universities. Finding the announcement unacceptable, the USIA made it public in a news release on August 16, 1989, that Beijing would not permit any American Fulbright professors to teach in China. The U.S. government deeply regretted the Chinese decision to suspend the program, which the U.S. government had believed to be of mutual benefit. Beijing, however, decided in March 1990 to restore the Fulbright program on a limited scale later.

From 1979 to 1989, the China Fulbright program was strongly urban based, with 56 percent of Fulbright professors teaching in Beijing and Shanghai, while others taught in such big cities as Tianjin, Nanjing, Wuhan, Guangzhou, Jinan, Changchun, Chengdu, and Lanzhou. In addition to teaching journalism, library science, linguistics, philosophy, political science, sociology, U.S. history, and U.S. literature, the Fulbrighters taught law and economics in the late 1980s, and these programs grew year by year. During this time period, a total of 170 American Fulbright scholars taught on Chinese campuses. They had political and ideological influence on their Chinese students, although they had no intention of imposing Western ideology and values. That unavoidable side effect of inviting American lecturers to China was especially significant on the Beijing and Shanghai campuses.

The majority of the Chinese students were shockingly ignorant about the West when China opened its doors to Western society. They lacked basic knowledge of Americans and their legal system, federalism, Constitution, welfare system, working and living conditions, and social reality. Under the influence of powerful official propaganda, many Chinese still had negative perceptions of American culture and society when the Americans went to the Chinese campuses. Their stereotype of Americans was of a hedonistic, violence-prone, and restless people who indulged themselves in all their desires and neglected their family responsibilities. They thought that Americans were haunted by the specter of joblessness and enjoyed no social security; students had heard plenty about the genocide of the Indians and discrimination against blacks, and they identified American women's liberation with divorce and sexual people.

Most Chinese students were ignorant of, and biased against, Americans, but they were eager to learn and were fully capable of absorbing virtually all the ideas that American professors provided in the classroom. They heartily welcomed the courses the Americans taught. The American professors noted the Chinese students' eagerness and enthusiasm for learning, despite the problems involved in attending classes taught in English and in a very different teaching style. The Chinese enthusiasm impressed the Americans, many of whom reported that their students were the best they had ever encountered. Most American lecturers were happy that they were able to offer new courses, introduce new theories, and use new methods while teaching in the Chinese classrooms. They offered new courses in Western social sciences and humanities, which had not been taught in China since 1949. American scholars also used novel teaching methods that usually stressed individual-centered learning, the kind of individualism discouraged by Chinese professors. These methods helped students develop independent thinking, which was far removed from the traditional Chinese education method of rote memorization of classical texts. In addition, outside the classroom, most American professors gave lectures to other students and various audiences on the campuses and elsewhere. Lectures were principally about the United States.

Trained by Americans in the politically sensitive disciplines of the social sciences and humanities, the Chinese students began to develop positive perspectives on the United States, to understand some political concepts, to criticize Marxism and China's political system, and even to advocate political reforms in China because American professors promoted a better understanding of American society and culture to the Chinese students. Some Fulbrighters believed that they played an important role as confidants or counselors to their Chinese students and fellow teachers. That role manifested itself in discussions about sensitive political issues. Students began to reject blind acceptance of customs and tradition, to question and challenge the official ideology, and to criticize their own political and economic system. Some Chinese students became frustrated with their own country and began to demand democratic reform. In general, American lecturers had a great political and ideological impact on the Chinese students.

When Americans went to the campuses in China, the Chinese students anticipated not only Western knowledge and methods for handling the practical problems of China but Western ideas and values. Having no sense of selectivity and critical perspective when they first came into contact with Western ideas, cultures, practices, and institutions, the Chinese were eager to absorb whatever they saw as useful. Thus Americans played an important role in helping the Chinese students understand American culture and values. They shared with the Chinese students films, tapes, and books borrowed from the U.S. embassy and consulates and gave lectures to students outside their courses. Due to American influences to some extent, Western ideology was rising and official orthodox ideology was declining on the Chinese campuses throughout the 1980s. Therefore, it is not surprising that after the Tiananmen incident of June 1989, Beijing immediately suspended the China Fulbright program.

The influence of the Fulbrighters showed that Chinese leaders in the 1980s were facing the same problems that previous Chinese governments had since the end of the nineteenth century. To the Chinese leaders, Western ideology posed a threat to the hierarchical and authoritarian political system in China. They therefore tried to reject the ideology while adopting Western technology and to maintain traditional Confucian virtue. That has proved impossible. The introduction of Western technology and knowledge has continued to create contradictions within Chinese modernization movements. The 1980s influx of American professors of the social sciences and humanities appeared to worsen political and cultural contradictions within China. Like preceding Chinese governments, Beijing nowadays still has the problem of reconciling the demand for Western teachers with the rejection of Western ideology.

See also Intellectuals; Open Door Policy (1978); Sino-American Relations, Conflicts and Common Interests; Sino-American Relations since 1949; United States, Chinese Education in.

Bibliography

Porter, Edgar, *Foreign Teachers in China: Old Problems for a New Generation, 1979-1989* (Westport, CT: Greenwood Press, 1990); Spence, Jonathan, *To Change China: Western Advisers in China, 1620-1960* (Boston: Little, Brown, 1969); Xu Guangqiu, "The Ideological and Political Impact of U.S. Fulbrighters on Chinese Students, 1979-1989," *Asian Affairs* 26, no. 3 (fall 1999): 139-158.

Guangqiu Xu

G

Gang of Four

The Gang of Four represents the last stand of Maoist radicalism. Promoted by **Mao Zedong** as a guarantee of revolutionary continuity, it wound up signifying the end of the Maoist vision. With the fall of Lin Biao, Mao's handpicked successor, Mao was once again faced with the problem of succession, and it was this question of who would keep the revolution going that provided the context for the rise and fall of the Gang of Four.

Originally there were three: Jiang Qing, Mao's wife; Yao Wenyuan, the literary polemicist whose criticism of Wu Han had touched off the **Great Cultural Revolution**; and Zhang Chunqiao, who had been director of the Propaganda Department in Shanghai and became the head of the Shanghai Commune. Though all were members of the Politburo, it was clear that none of these three could succeed him. Jiang was despised by the old Communist Party leadership and would have faced almost insurmountable difficulties in assuming control. Powerful women also had a negative image in Chinese history. Zhang was associated with the excessive violence that had occurred in Shanghai, while Yao was simply a theorist. Out of relative obscurity, Mao chose Wang Hongwen, the political commissar of the People's Liberation Army (PLA) unit in Shanghai, to lead the left. He promoted Wang to the third position in the Standing Committee in the Politburo, where only Mao and Premier **Zhou Enlai** ranked higher.

Wang, who was thirty-seven, was supposed to appeal to those groups that were key to the continuity of the leftist ideals: youth and workers. Though he was clearly allied with the faction of the other three, Mao's assumption was that he would be politically astute enough to act independently.

Wang's promotion was part of a political movement leftward that had occurred after the Tenth Party Congress in 1973. The Politburo had been expanded from five to nine members to include those whose careers had benefited from the Cultural Revolution. These newly appointed officials, men such as **Hua Guofeng**, the first secretary of Hunan, and Wu De, the Beijing first secretary, represented a group of higher and middle cadres who careers were tied to the rise of the left. These cadres were at least initially the factional allies of the Gang of Four.

It must be noted that the Gang's influence was basically restricted to the ideological sphere. They dominated the newspapers and the journals, but they never controlled either the Party or the army. In addition, the cadres on whom they thought they could rely were in the end bureaucrats who had negotiated the vicissitudes of Chinese politics. Their allegiance could not be taken for granted.

Soon after the changes in the leadership, the Gang launched an attack on its primary enemy, Zhou Enlai. Characteristically, this occurred in the ideological realm, in the campaign to criticize Lin Biao and Confucius (*Pi Lin, Pi Kong*). The attack on Zhou was done through analogy. As Confucius was to be criticized for advocating a return to power for those who had previously been disgraced—"call to office those who have retired to obscurity"—so Zhou Enlai was to be denounced for restoring to the Party those "rightists" who had been purged during the Cultural Revolution. The issue of restoration

Jiang Qing, the widow of Mao Zedong and a member of the Gang of Four, listens to the proceedings during her trial in January 1981. © Bettmann/Corbis.

was taken by this radical left as signifying whether China was to go forward with other cultural revolutions or retreat to a prerevolutionary stage. This contrast was strengthened through the left's celebration of legalism with its stress on discipline, as opposed to the moral laxity of Confucianism. This sense that authoritarianism was central to revolutionary continuity foreshowed its later campaign to learn from the dictatorship of the proletariat.

The four traveled all over the country, "lighting fires" to stir up criticism of Zhou Enlai, and they were at first successful. But this was short lived because Zhou began to retire from public work after being diagnosed with cancer. Mao was once again faced with the question of replacement.

For reasons that are not entirely clear, Mao chose Deng Xiaoping. This choice was certainly connected to Mao's disappointment with Wang Hongwen's failure to establish a more independent persona. In this choice, Mao also distanced himself from the radical group of four, calling them the Gang of Four. He went so far as to denounce his wife for having the "wild ambition" to become Party chairman. Roderick MacFarquhar suggests that Deng's return was designed to move the military out of politics. The argument is that a military reshuffle could only be accomplished by someone whom the generals respected, such as Deng. In this regard, he agrees with later Chinese historians who see Mao's criticism of the Gang as a ruse, with a very different short-term goal in mind.

Deng's reemergence does seem initially to have represented a movement toward the right. Following along the lines of Zhou's speech at the Fourth

National Party Congress in 1975 on the need for modernization in agriculture, industry, defense, and science and technology ("the Four Modernizations"), Deng promoted three major policy documents relating to industry, education, and the need for foreign technology. At the same time he sharply criticized the Gang of Four. This was most evident in his report on the Party's work style. There he argued that efficiency and expertise were the criteria for economic success, and that it was "nonsense" to assume that ideological purity could increase industrial production. Advocating a more traditional system of agricultural organization, he sought to limit the applicability of the Dazhai commune model while restoring commodity relationships throughout the countryside.

Jiang labeled his program "three poisonous weeds" and said that it would lead to the restoration of capitalism. At this point, with Mao's approval, the Gang of Four began an ideological counteroffensive that was the last great factional battle of the Maoist era. Its argument was that this was now a conflict between the reaffirmation of the principle of the dictatorship of the proletariat and the assertion of the "bourgeois right." This is why it launched the movement to learn from the dictatorship of the proletariat. The "bourgeois right" was understood as that which would provide the material basis for the creation of a new bourgeoisie. This was to be seen, for example, in China's commodity economy, in the differential wage system, and in the various types of semi-collective and collective forms of ownership. All of this it saw as part of a movement to destroy efforts toward equality and to reaffirm the differences between town and country, mental and manual labor, and workers and peasants. In two major articles, Zhang and Yao stressed the need for endless class struggle and for a vigilant and authoritarian dictatorship of the proletariat. Praising the idea of "revolutionary violence," they emphasized that there could be no tolerance of class enemies.

This campaign went on through the end of 1975. It was briefly interrupted by another of the Gang's campaigns, this to learn from the novel *The Water Margin*, where the lesson was that leaders—Deng—could not always be trusted. But no one seems to have paid any attention.

In January 1976, Zhou Enlai died. His burial coincided with the traditional Qing Ming festival at which ancestors are venerated. Though the leftists in the Party attempted to suppress the festival as superstition, the people turned the occasion into an outpouring of support for Zhou personally and all that he stood for. As the mourners-protesters were removed from Tiananmen Square, there were some incidents. In the midst of all the criticism of Deng, and fearful of this expression of support for the right, the left blamed Deng for the disorder and had him removed from all official posts. He remained in the Party.

In early April, Mao appointed Hua Guofeng premier and first deputy chairman. At this point, all the factions began to maneuver, waiting for the death of Mao, who died soon afterwards. The generals conspired with Deng, while the left was split, with the Gang of Four intent upon seizing power for itself. Its plan apparently was to cloak itself in the mantle of Mao while it expelled Deng from the Party. In the end, though, isolated and reviled by every other faction, the Gang's members were arrested by the military in conjunction with Hua and accused of conspiring to seize state power. With this, the Jacobin moment in Chinese politics came to an end.

See also Deng Xiaoping (1904–1997), Politics of; Deng Xiaoping (1904–1997), Reforms of.

Bibliography

Chang, Ch'un-ch'iao, *On Exercising All-around Dictatorship over the Bourgeoisie* (Beijing: Foreign Languages Press, 1975); Domes, Jürgen, *The Government and Politics of the PRC: A Time of Transition* (Boulder, CO: Westview Press, 1985); MacFarquhar, Roderick, "The Succession to Mao and the End of Maoism, 1969–82," in *The Politics of China, 1949–1989* ed. Roderick MacFarquhar (Cambridge: Cambridge University Press, 1993); Meisner, Maurice, *Mao's China and After*, 3rd ed. (New York: Free Press, 1999); Yao, Wen-yuan, *On the Social Basis of the Lin Piao Anti-Party Clique* (Beijing: Foreign Languages Press, 1975).

James M. Falkin

GLF

See Great Leap Forward (GLF).

Grassroots Democracy

Since the launch of the economic reforms in 1978, China has gained economic prosperity at lightning speed. In the early 1980s, Deng Xiaoping urged the nation to reach a per capita income of $800 and a total GDP of 200 percent greater than the level of 1980. These goals have been achieved. The next goal is to build a "comprehensively well-off society" in which per capita GDP will reach $3,000 by the end of the twentieth century; meanwhile, polarization between the rich and the poor will be maximally avoided. This means that structural democratization must continue, because growth and sustainability cannot occur without a more open system.

In fact, since the early 1980s, the Chinese government has been quietly pushing democratization at the grassroots level, particularly in rural areas, in an effort to educate its large farming population of 900 million. This has been done through the establishment of directly elected villager committees (VCs), which are viewed as the world's largest grassroots democratic education process. This may also be the best example of how Deng Xiaoping's bottom-up reform differs from Russia's top-down transition.

The 1998 Organic Law on Villager Committees (VC Law) requires VCs to implement democratic administration and subjects them to fiscal accountability. The higher-level township governments guide, support, and assist—rather than lead—the VCs. The VCs, in turn, assist the township governments in their official work, such as tax and grain collection, family planning, and military conscription. Typical VC work plans might include raising funds for and constructing a new schoolhouse, installing cable **television** in the village, or persuading the neighboring village to help build a better road.

The VC is normally composed of three to seven members, including a chair, one or more vice chairs, and ordinary members, all of whom serve three-year terms. It is a common practice for VCs to include an "appropriate number" of national minorities and women, although the proportion of female VC members nationwide is still very low due to the perception among villagers of the "low quality" of the education and experience of rural women. VC membership is not a full-time or salaried occupation, although members generally receive some compensation for the time they spend on VC work.

Supervised by the Ministry of Civil Affairs, VCs constitute the lowest level of civil administration in China. Under the VC Law, peasants learn their rights, responsibilities, and accountabilities. For the first time, peasants are learning to participate in the political process. They can vote VC members out of office or even, in extreme cases, recall them. Their enthusiasm and seriousness in electing accountable leaders are not to be underestimated.

Experience gained at the grassroots level spread at a fast rate. The success of the VC Law is also influencing elections and democratic governance in urban communities, in higher-level township governments, and even within the Chinese Communist Party, among other political arenas. Moreover, the themes the government articulated in justifying the introduction of village democracy—including the complementary nature of political and economic reforms and the intimate relationship between democracy and the rule of law—are now being repeated in a national context, a pattern that suggests a shift toward more openness and pluralism.

The predecessor of village self-governance ironically can be traced back to the **people's communes** during the decade-long **Great Cultural Revolution (1966–1976)**. On the one hand, commune leaders' legitimacy had to feature Party approval first of all; on the other hand, the leaders were elected from the masses based on their hard work and their outstanding political consciousness. This practice guaranteed a close tie between the Party and the masses and resulted in an uninterrupted connectivity between the government and the localities.

After the Cultural Revolution, China's 1982 Constitution provided for villager committees, elected by village residents, to handle public affairs and social services, mediate civil disputes, help maintain public order, and convey residents' requests and opinions to the people's government. In 1987, the **National People's Congress** adopted a provisional law that was made permanent as the VC Law in November 1998, after a decade's experience and debate over issues such as the degree of autonomy villager committees should enjoy. The 1998 VC Law now incorporates important democratic elements designed to ensure that the villagers enjoy a real right to select their leaders. These democratic elements include open, direct nominations by individuals rather than groups, multiple candidates in place of the Party's appointees, secret ballots rather than a show of hands, the mandatory use of secret voting booths to ensure the integrity of the individual vote, a public count of the votes, immediate announcement of election results, and recall procedures.

In a sense, the VC Law satisfies the traditionally valued farmers' ideal of equality, yet adds to it a dynamic sense of responsibility. For example, it introduces the so-called four democracies: democratic election, democratic decision making, democratic management, and democratic supervision. This involves publicizing financial matters, all decisions on important community-related matters, including family planning, disaster relief, payment of electricity and water bills, and announcing the salaries and stipends of Party cadres and VC members.

A far-reaching impact of the VC Law experience is that on the Party's own reform. In fact, the Party is now experimenting locally with a "two-ballot system" for electing local branch secretaries, the first ballot involving a popular vote on potential candidates and the second ballot restricted to Party members. All village-level Party secretaries in Fujian, for example, were elected in May 2000 in a process that involved an initial "confidence vote" of candidates, in which all village voters participated, followed by a Party-members-only vote on the final candidates. In 1999, Sichuan implemented a similar "public recommendation, direct Party member election" system of electing its village Party branch secretaries, and similar multistage Party elections have been tried at the village level in other places, including Anhui, Henan, and Shenzhen of the Guangdong province. Optimistic opinion holds that the grassroots democratic processes will eventually lead to the rule of law as the election and governance procedures are duplicated at each level. At the conclusion of the Fifth Plenum of the Fifteenth Central Committee of the Chinese Communist Party in October 2000, the Party explicitly recognized that restructuring the political system must catch up with the ongoing economic reforms and "socialist" modernization drive. The Party's next goal is to develop a democratic political system by promoting "scientific and democratic" decision making and expanding citizens' participation in political affairs in an "orderly way." The Plenum further endorsed broader implementation of the "four democracies" that were developed in the context of VC elections. Recently, citing the Fifth Plenum's call for greater citizen participation in political affairs, the Chinese government for the first time invited public input on the Tenth Five-Year Plan.

While China's democratization has progressed by leaps and bounds, critical examinations reveal some shortfalls. Some observers point out that the democratic expansion is rather limited at local levels in rural China. Little progress toward participatory democracy has been made. There is yet no clear path to an institutionalized democracy because the impetus toward greater democracy has come primarily from below, from peasants' desires and demands for greater input and accountability. In the leadership, it has emerged mostly under the protection of lower- and middle-level officials. According to this view, higher-level administration has been relatively conservative or even hypocritical in that it persists in a high degree of Party control of electoral processes and sees elections as part of a strategy to induce, with responsibility and accountability, the masses to willingly serve the Party's interests.

Other opinions hold that there has not been enough pressure on further democratic expansion, because the majority of the people are generally content with the substantial increases, compared with prereform baselines, in civil liberties other than democratic participation. The Party's continuing dominance of organized politics also remains a severe constraint on democracy. A third opinion holds that in a larger context, the Chinese-flavored democracy will probably never adapt itself to the Western style. A good example is the long-touted democratic system in Taiwan. In the 2004 presidential election, it was obvious that the Constitution revealed significant weaknesses, including an ambiguous allocation of power among the branches (particularly between the president and the legislature) and a resulting tendency to produce political stalemate and paralyzing partisan politics. Apparently, the sense of rule of law has yet to be deeply rooted in the Chinese mentality, and this may take time.

See also Central Planning; Democratic Parties, Political Functions of; Deng Xiaoping (1904–1997), Reforms of; Jiang Zemin (1926–   ), Populism of; One Country, Two Systems; Open Door Policy (1978); Rural Administrative Organizations; Taiwan, Development of Democracy in.

Bibliography

DeLisle, Jacques, "Democracy and Its Limits in Greater China: A Conference Report," May 27 2004, http://www.fpri.org/enotes/20040527.asia.delisle.democracygreaterchina.html, accessed on June 3, 2004; Horsley, Jamie P., "Village Election—Training Ground for Democracy," *China Business Review* (March–April 2001): 44–52.

Jing Luo

Great Cultural Revolution (1966–1976)

In August 1966, Communist leader **Mao Zedong** and his radical followers launched the Great Cultural Revolution, a violent and destructive campaign that severely shook the Chinese Communist Party (CCP) and Chinese society. The virulent phase of the Cultural Revolution lasted from 1966 and 1969. However, the movement was not officially declared over until after Mao's death in 1976. Profoundly ideological and political, the Cultural Revolution can be broadly defined as cultural only in the sense that it represented an attempt to remold Chinese society into a truly revolutionary one with a genuine commitment to communism.

The causes of the Cultural Revolution can be partially traced back to the **Great Leap Forward** initiated by Mao and the Central Committee of the CCP in 1958, an ambitious endeavor to economically transform China in a short period of time essentially through mass enthusiasm and revolutionary fervor. The Great Leap Forward turned out to be a huge disaster. In its aftermath, Mao voluntarily stepped down as chairman of the state, a position then filled by **Liu Shaoqi**. Mao, however, retained the more powerful position of chairman of the CCP, and the Chinese people continued to revere him as the incarnation of the Communist revolution.

In the early 1960s, Mao held essentially a supervising role and was not as visible as before. On many issues, especially those concerning the economy, Liu Shaoqi and his followers, such as General Secretary Deng Xiaoping, were the major policy makers. Mao, however, became increasingly disturbed by the direction in which China was moving. Enthusiastic about mass-based revolutionary movement, Mao believed in the necessity of continuing revolution and class struggle to achieve a truly egalitarian society where workers and peasants would serve as masters of the country. This vision of Mao's clashed with that of Liu Shaoqi and his supporters, who downplayed ideological campaigns and emphasized instead centralized, planned economic development essentially through utilizing technological knowledge and expertise. Mao deemed that

In August 1966, students and teachers march through Beijing's Tiananmen
Square in support of Mao Zedong's Great Cultural Revolution.
© Bettmann/Corbis.

the revolutionary movement would be made irrelevant if its only outcome was
to have the educated elite in positions of influence. Mao never truly trusted the
intellectuals. The distrust was intensified as a result of the Hundred Flowers
movement, during which intellectuals produced an avalanche of criticisms of
the CCP. In the early 1960s, some prominent scholars published articles and
plays in major newspapers that made veiled attacks on Mao's policies during
the Great Leap Forward, which further deepened Mao's misgivings about the
intellectuals.

Meanwhile, the bureaucrats within the CCP also made Mao uneasy. He saw
them as becoming increasingly ossified, forming a new ruling class divorced
from the masses and lacking in revolutionary enthusiasm. Looking at the relatively high status held by intellectuals and privileges enjoyed by high-ranking
Party members, Mao believed that some fundamental goals of the revolution
had been compromised.

At the age of seventy-three in 1966, Mao wished to leave a permanent stamp
upon China's revolution, to prevent the emergence of Soviet-style revisionism
in China, and to reassert his own effective leadership. Relying on his personal
prestige and political authority and on the support of his wife Jiang Qing, who
would soon emerge as a fierce political force in the cultural arena, and the People's Liberation Army under Minister of Defense Lin Biao, who had been un-
remittingly promoting the cult of Mao in the armed forces, Mao and the Central
Committee initiated the Cultural Revolution with a call for an open attack on
all remnants of the old society, including the so-called Four Olds: old customs,
old habits, old culture, and old ideas.

To jump-start the new movement and to cut down the power and prestige
of China's new elites, Mao turned to those from outside the elites. His main
weapon in the initial stage of the campaign was the Red Guards, who turned

out to be the most colorful and destructive aspect of the Cultural Revolution. The Red Guards consisted essentially of urban youths from high schools and universities. Truly excited that Mao called upon them to continue the revolution and encouraged by such proclamations of Mao as "Rebellion Is Justified" and "Bombard the Headquarters," the Chinese youths immediately answered Mao's call by forming and joining the Red Guards. Enjoying enormous power, they rebelled against the establishment. They engaged in putting up wall posters and condemning, beating, torturing, and even killing those in authority, including Party leaders, teachers, and professors, who were perceived to be lacking in revolutionary commitment or to be following the so-called capitalist road. Meanwhile, largely left alone to interpret the meanings of the Four Olds, Red Guards raided homes at will to search for items from the "old" categories, which were then confiscated, smashed, or burned. They destroyed thousands of temples, statues, and monuments and created havoc within society.

Those people who had previously been assigned the "black" class labels also suffered much during the heat of the Cultural Revolution since they were viewed as class enemies who had exploited the working-class people in the past and who now had to be resisted to prevent them from ever again attempting to harm the new socialist system. They were often paraded through the streets wearing cone-shaped hats as a sign of shame and humiliation.

Chinese youths of high schools and colleges experienced a great moment of excitement in the 1960s. With classes suspended during the peak years of the Cultural Revolution, Red Guards traveled throughout China to share information and experiences and to learn more about revolution, and to Beijing to be received by Mao standing on top of Tiananmen Square and waving to them. When the Cultural Revolution was in full swing, Mao worship became almost hysterical. The "Little Red Books," quotations from Mao, were printed in millions of copies. Red Guards wore green army outfits equipped with bright red armbands emblazoned in yellow with the words "Red Guard." They shouted, "Long Live Chairman Mao," and danced the loyalty dance. Their gatherings in Beijing became scenes of great outbursts of emotions involving waving Little Red Books, singing, and often crying. About 11 million Red Guards visited Beijing in the hope of seeing Mao in person and expressing their great love for him. Meanwhile, there began a nationwide craze for Mao buttons. People pinned at least one such button on their clothes.

In 1967, encouraged by Mao and other radical leaders, Red Guards began a direct attack on government officials at various levels. They demanded that all Party officials accused of being counterrevolutionaries and capitalist roaders be removed from their positions. Because most of these officials had been in office for almost twenty years since the founding of the Communist regime, it was not difficult to find people who were ready to level charges against them. The Party purge also reached the very top, including Chief of State Liu Shaoqi and Secretary General Deng Xiaoping. Condemned as the biggest capitalist roader, Liu was arrested and thrown into prison and died a miserable death a few years later. Deng was sent to a remote town and made to work in a tractor factory.

Meanwhile, the movement became increasingly factionalized. In schools and on campuses, conflicts were developing among the various Red Guard factions. Competing Red Guard headquarters were set up, each proclaiming to be the true follower of Mao's thought. Debate and arguments among the various groups often led to bloody fights. Some even fought with machine guns. Utter confusion and chaos prevailed throughout the country. Mao then used the army to reestablish control. In late 1967, the army moved into every organization. Under Mao's instructions, "revolutionary committees," composed of workers, solders, and some old Party cadres who had escaped the purge, were established to replace the old structures of authority. Mao and the other radical leaders who had supported the young rebels now turned away from them. Beginning in late 1968, following Mao's slogan that "young people should be sent down to the countryside to be reeducated by peasants," millions of urban youths, mostly the former Red Guards, were sent to the countryside to toughen themselves through hard physical labor. Many stayed in the countryside for as long as ten years before they were able to trek back to the cities. This generation of Chinese young people was later referred to as the "lost generation."

The Cultural Revolution resulted in a total breakdown of law and order, especially in urban China. The wanton attack on elder members of the society and the destruction of artworks were huge human and cultural disasters. In the meantime, many factories stopped functioning for a long period. The educational system was in a shambles. All institutions of higher learning were closed down for a few years, because school administrations and teachers were being attacked and students were busy being Red Guards. Most were reopened in the early 1970s, but the academic standard was far inferior to that prior to 1966 because student bodies were not selected based on their academic records, but were chosen mainly among politically active workers, peasants, and soldiers.

After Mao died in 1976, the new leadership soon arrested the **Gang of Four**, the radical supporters of the Cultural Revolution, and the movement came to an official end. The government subsequently referred to the Cultural Revolution as "ten lost years" in China's modern development. Radical ideologies lost steam, and the Chinese people became tired of political struggles and campaigns. In the late 1970s, the pragmatically minded Deng Xiaoping reemerged triumphantly and resumed political power. China entered the era of economic reforms.

See also Great Cultural Revolution, Impact of on Women's Social Status; Great Cultural Revolution, Literature during.

Bibliography

Liang, Heng, and Judith Shapiro, *Son of the Revolution* (New York: Knopf, 1983); Schoenhal, Michael, ed., *China's Cultural Revolution, 1966–1969: Not a Dinner Party* (Armonk, NY: M. E. Sharpe, 1996); White, Lynn, *Policies of Chaos: The Organizational Causes of Violence in China's Cultural Revolution* (Princeton, NJ: Princeton University Press, 1989).

Hong Zhang

Great Cultural Revolution, Impact of Women's Social Status

During the **Great Cultural Revolution (1966–1976)**, women in China were treated the same as male workers and professionals. They were depicted in dynamic poses as workers, peasants, soldiers, and educated youths in literature, plays, and posters produced during this period. Before the Cultural Revolution, the New China had already started advocating equality between men and women. The issue of women's social status had been a main focus of the Chinese Communist Party ever since its birth in 1921. Thus the emphasis on women's role as working people during the Cultural Revolution did not come out of the blue. The political movements that took place before had laid the basis for women's new social status and their further emancipation.

When the New China was founded in 1949, the Chinese authorities were determined to clean up the feudal oppression of women inherited from a history of thousands of years. Women's emancipation was implemented in all aspects of political, economic, cultural, social, and family life. The development of women's rights went through a series of mass movements that had nationwide impacts. The political movements rapidly changed the backward economic and cultural concepts of old China that had fettered and humiliated women. Thus in the 1950s and early 1960s, China had already undergone an earth-shaking historic change in the social position of women.

One of the first campaigns to change women's life was the illiteracy-eradication campaign the new government started in the 1950s. This movement helped women become literate and get rid of the image of inferiority and backwardness. During another campaign, the **Great Leap Forward** in the late 1950s, more and more women started to enter the workforce in both rural and urban areas. Along with the general economic development, there was a nationwide surge of women stepping out of their homes to take part in production, which established the new image of the financially independent working

In March 1974, women, members of the Xiangyang Commune's amateur art troop perform a ballad criticizing Confucius, whose denigration is part of the current ideological campaign of the Great Cultural Revolution. © Bettman/Corbis.

woman. In still another movement, the newly promulgated marriage law of the New China abolished the feudal marriage system that had been characterized by arranged and forced marriage, male superiority, and female obedience. The new Chinese government further outlawed prostitution, guided prostitutes toward a decent lifestyle through education and health care, and helped the victims of exploitation support themselves by proper work.

These movements prepared the masculine image of women and their rise in social status during the Cultural Revolution, a political movement that lasted for ten years (1966–1976) and was initiated by **Mao Zedong**. Mao organized boys and girls from middle and high schools into the Red Guards. The youths were encouraged to spread the ideology of Mao and Marxist theory all over the country. During this ten-year period, female Red Guards, female workers, and female peasants were encouraged to work like men. Political propaganda during the Cultural Revolution emphasized women's productive role in all walks of life. Mao supported and praised women's ability in building the country by saying that women could hold up half the sky. Such slogans made it possible for women to engage in the tough work traditionally done by men in the fields and in factories. The image of women being capable of doing hard work was also represented in the medical area in their role as barefoot doctors. These women were medical workers responsible for treating patients with basic medicine in the backward countryside. The female barefoot doctors were praised as one of the "new things" that the Cultural Revolution had created.

During the Cultural Revolution, the equality of men and women was further emphasized. The women's strong and masculine image led to the fashion of women dressed in men's clothes—clothes designed for women such as dresses and skirts were considered bourgeois and were denied. In line with the egalitarian character of Maoist culture and ideology, gender distinctions regarding social status were mostly erased, and women achieved independence in their work and finances. Many posters created during the Cultural Revolution showed women to be equally as physically strong as men. Women during this period preferred being dressed plainly in gray, army-green, or worker-blue men-style clothes; it was popular for women to look plain and simple, with short hair, or two short pigtails for young girls and young women.

As a result of the Cultural Revolution and political and social changes, Chinese women today are less traditional compared with the older generations. After the Cultural Revolution ended in 1976, China underwent political and economic reforms that further changed Chinese women's social status. Women nowadays are not only respected as equal in the workforce, but also admired in the areas of science, business, fashion designing, and even homemaking. However, gender boundaries were redrawn in the 1980s, a process that continued in the 1990s. Women were urged to return to their traditional supportive role in their families, and government officials no longer feel compelled to call on women to break through the traditional assumptions of gender inferiority.

The recent tendency for women to stay at home is not considered a drawback, but an added dimension in women's choices in life. Some of them have acknowledged and recognized the gender difference, and they think that they can contribute more to their families and society and do not have to behave like men. Playing a more supportive role in their own family does not diminish women's status in society, because they stand equally as tall as before when they held up half the sky.

The recent economic reform has also changed women's opinion about their appearance. Today's women turn away from manly clothes and appreciate fashionable clothing, accessories, cosmetics, and hairstyling. They enjoy better living, education, and health services. The Chinese government wants to continue in this direction and is planning to provide sufficient budgetary support for the development of women and children.

See also Great Cultural Revolution, Literature during; Women, Role as Mothers; Women, Social Status of.

Bibliography

Stefan Landsberger's Chinese Propaganda Poster Pages, http://www.iisg.nl/~landsberger/iron2.html, accessed on October 15, 2003; Watson, J. L. (1991), "The Renegotiation of Chinese Cultural Identity in the Post-Mao Era: An Anthropological Perspective," in *Perspectives on Modern China. Four Anniversaries*, ed. K. Lieberthal, J. Kallgren, R. MacFarquhar, and F. Wakeman, Jr. (Armonk, NY and London: M. E. Sharpe, 1991).

Senquan Zhang

Great Cultural Revolution, Literature during

During the **Great Cultural Revolution (1966–1976),** the Yan'an talks of **Mao Zedong,** which declared that art and literature should serve the cause of the Party, continued to serve as the basic guide to literary works. His principle that literature and art should serve politics and promote socialism was very rigidly adhered to. At the height of the Cultural Revolution, publication of literary works almost came to a standstill. Literary organizations were closed down, and writers and artists were sent to the countryside to be "reformed." New guidelines such as the principle of "**three prominences**," which stressed positive character, heroism, and leadership (unfailingly, Party members), were put forward by Jiang Qing (Mao's wife) and her associates and were imposed on all literary works. Chinese literature during the Cultural Revolution is seen by many as very boring.

Theater

Due to its public nature and its great potential as the best medium of propaganda for Communist ideology, theater became the focus of attention from Jiang Qing and her associates. They organized new performing troupes while banning all dramas deemed ideologically counterrevolutionary, dismantling cultural institutions of all kinds, closing training schools and research institutes, and ruthlessly persecuting writers, playwrights, and theater professionals.

Like all other traditional forms of performing arts, Beijing opera suffered as a major target of political attack and censorship during the Cultural Revolution. It was accused of being feudalistic and vulgar and of having kept the major forces of socialist China—workers, peasants, and soldiers—off its stage. However, unlike other forms of performance, Beijing opera did not disappear.

Instead, it became the most dominant performing form during this unusual period—it was singled out as a traditional theatrical art to be adapted to fit new ideological contexts so that it could be used as a political tool to promote the agenda of the Cultural Revolution. Great efforts were made to adapt traditional techniques to portray contemporary themes. By late 1966, five Beijing operas emerged on the stages of China: *The Red Lantern, Taking Tiger Mountain by Strategy, Shajiabang, On the Docks,* and *Raid on the White Tiger Regiment.* Joining them were two ballets, *The White Haired Girl* and *The Red Detachment of Women,* and the symphonic suite based on *Shajiabang.* These were known as the Eight Modern Revolutionary Model Theatrical Works (*xiandai geming yangbanxi*), also known as the Eight Peking Model Operas, and became standard-bearers of the Cultural Revolution, which documented Communist activities during the Anti-Japanese War and the civil war with the Nationalists, as well as the class struggle after the founding of the People's Republic. This new form of Beijing opera broke away completely from its tradition and "modernized" itself according to the political requirements defined by Maoist Marxism in costumes, stage setting, music, singing, and performance. Within a couple of years, more new operas were written and many regional versions of the original models were produced throughout the country. The film versions were especially valuable for national standardization. They saturated radio waves and **television** screens on a daily basis, in addition to phonograph records, posters, paintings, and sculptures. For a decade, these so-called model theatrical works monopolized China's theatrical and musical stage, and each one of them was watched by every Chinese man, woman, and child more than twice a year on average.

Fiction

During the Cultural Revolution, fiction was a less favored genre. Most fiction that did get published during that period depicted revolutionary development in the countryside. Military and industrial fiction was also common, but in contrast to previous decades, fiction on urban life, especially the life of students or **intellectuals** in the cities, was rare, as was fiction on the life of overseas Chinese and Ventures abroad. The time setting was normally either during the Anti-Japanese War or the civil war with the Nationalists or after the founding of the People's Republic. In line with innovations in theater, fiction had its focus on the creation of heroic characters as models. All characters, including villains, gave prominence to positive characters, who in turn yielded to heroic characters; heroic characters bowed in turn to the main hero. "Middle characters" did not exist anymore. Villains were totally evil, and heroes were never less than perfect. Representing the Communist Party and being models for the masses, the heroic characters were mostly unmarried young men and women, were invariably from a humble peasant or working-class background, and had limited formal education. They were perfect specimens physically as well: bright big eyes, bronze skin, black swordlike eyebrows, and red lips. They invariably possessed qualities such as generosity, honesty, reasonableness, levelheadedness, and courtesy. They could not be fooled for a minute and never had to learn anything. The stereotyped heroes and heroines, peasants, workers, or soldiers were frequently idealized and romanticized. Their dialogues, contrary to expectation, were full of proverbs and quotations from classical verse, while dialect expressions, slang, and vulgar or abusive terms were conspicuously absent. Whether these characters were true to life or not was of secondary importance; they were created to serve as political models.

Among authors of that period, Hao Ran stood out as the most notable figure. His stories and novels, which sold millions of copies, were extremely and self-consciously political, praising heroic working people for the sacrifices they made for the revolution. In his works, peasant life and values were depicted in a lyrical way. His early short stories followed the Yan'an line in depicting positive heroes in village life and emphasized the increasing prosperity of the countryside. During the Cultural Revolution, the element of class struggle became the main theme of the novels for which he is most famous. In these stories, stereotypical heroes and villains were invariably divided along class lines, and conflicts between people were always explicable in class terms. Hao Ran's choice of female protagonists to receive all the prominence (A Bao in *Sons and Daughters of Xisha*) was very welcome to Jiang Qing for her own agenda for cultural politics.

Yan Yang Tian (Bright sunny sky), Hao Ran's first novel, consisting of three volumes, dealt with "class struggle." It showed the triumph of Party policy that allowed poor peasants, who had worked hard on collective farms, to share equally in profits with the middle-class peasants who contributed private plots of land to the collective. In the story, Hao Ran idealized the peasants and young cadres who directly confronted class privilege, which was a major obstacle to **land reform**, and struggled for a new classless society. His second novel, *Jin Guang Da Dao* (The road of golden light), was concerned with "line struggle," the change from individual labor on farms to mutual-aid teams. These two novels earned Hao Ran fame as a master of characterization. One reason for Hao Ran's success was his ability to convey the familiar details of peasant life in a clear and sympathetic manner, noting the conflicts as well as the achievements of radical structural change in the countryside in the 1950s and 1960s. His third novel, *Sons and Daughters of Xisha*, however, was generally considered nothing but a perfect example of following the "three prominences" principle.

Poetry

Like other literary genres, poetry had to respond fully to the political needs and ideology of the time. The most officially noteworthy trends in poetry during that period were the push toward popularization and classical revival. In the 1970s, an extremely broad cross-section of the general public was encouraged to write poetry as a standard part of their adult daily life. Many poems published in this period were therefore by unknown authors, and amateur writers received great encouragement from the authorities. The latter trend was stimulated by Mao himself, who was generally considered a master of classical verse. Several military generals also wrote and published their verses.

The use of poetry as a vehicle for spontaneous political protest was another phenomenon in that period, as was most vitally demonstrated in the sudden outpouring of poetry on the April 5 Democracy Movement of 1976. Like the event itself, the poems written in memory of **Zhou Enlai** seemed to have been completely spontaneous.

The picture of literature during the Cultural Revolution would be incomplete without mentioning the existence of underground literature. In the 1970s, when openly reading or writing almost anything at all was seen as a sign of dangerous ideological subversion, a group of high-school graduates who were sent down to the countryside to be "reeducated" and who became disillusioned with Chinese society started to use the forms of poetry and fiction to express their desires. Their works were circulated among friends and friends of friends. From this group of young people emerged some poets, such as Bei Dao, Mang Ke, Gu Cheng, and Duo Duo, who were to spearhead literary innovation in the post–Cultural Revolution period. Although the exact amount of underground literature cannot be determined at present, the achievement of what has been seen so far reveals its undeniably great value in literary history.

See also Avant-garde Literature; Experimental Fiction; Great Cultural Revolution, Impact of on Women's Social Status; Literary Policy for the New China; Literature of the Wounded; Misty Poetry; Neorealist Fiction and Modernism; Pre–Cultural Revolution Literature; Root-Searching Literature; Theater in Contemporary China.

Bibliography

McDougall, Bonnie S., ed., *Popular Chinese Literature and Performing Arts in the People's Republic of China, 1949-1979* (Berkeley: University of California Press, 1984); McDougall, Bonnie S., and Kam Louie, *The Literature of China in the Twentieth Century* (London: Hurst & Company, 1997).

Xiaoling Zhang

Great Leap Forward (GLF)

The Great Leap Forward movement (GLF) was started in 1958 as an ambitious economic campaign, but ended in 1959 as an economic bankruptcy accompanied by a famine of a magnitude that was unprecedented not only in China's history, but also throughout world history. About 20 to 30 million people, mostly peasants, died of hunger during the famine. Some put the number at 40 million. The exact death toll may never come to light.

Mao Zedong, then the top leader of China, initiated the GLF. Despite the smooth completion of the First Five-Year Plan in 1957 with help from the Soviet Union, Mao became impatient with the Russian modernization strategy, which emphasized bureaucratic planning, capital accumulation, and the heavy-industry and urban sectors. As a man with a big ego but little knowledge of economics, Mao believed that he could use some of the principles developed during the guerrilla war period, such as mass movement, to better mobilize China's population for economic growth. He put forward a new "General Line for Socialist Construction" that aimed at greatly accelerating economic growth by organizing the people into various kinds of quasi-military units and institutions, such as militias and communes, so that he could easily drive them to fulfill high production quotas.

Mao was able to launch the GLF without much opposition. In 1957, Mao had just cracked down on dissident **intellectuals** in the Anti-Rightist Campaign. In early 1958, he forced some of the top leaders, including then premier **Zhou Enlai**, to make self-criticisms on being too conservative in making production plans. Thus Mao set the stage for the tragedy by silencing all public opinion that disagreed with his radical ideas. Governments at all levels were competing to report one miracle output after another. The greatly inflated outputs were then reported in newspapers or broadcast by radios nationwide, leading the whole nation to believe that China was making a great leap in production and was catching up with the Western developed nations rapidly.

To Mao, the outputs of iron, steel, cotton, and grain were the ultimate symbol of a nation's economic and military prowess. Under his pressure, the Chinese government frequently upwardly revised production quotas. The fulfillment of the iron and steel quotas was viewed as the whole nation's responsibility. Homemade furnaces were erected in school playgrounds, government office compounds, residential backyards, and village open squares across the nation. People were driven either by their blind trust in Mao and the Communist Party or by fear and peer pressure to work day and night without a break. Most of the iron and steel produced by these so-called backyard furnaces was a total waste. In many rural areas, century-old trees were cut down and used as fuel. In many urban areas, steel gates, fences, doors, windows, and other metal framework were taken off buildings and houses as inputs. They became totally useless after being melted, although they were reported as part of the iron and steel outputs. The rural ecology and urban landscaping suffered to a great extent as a result of this mass movement of backyard steel production.

If the GLF movement mainly caused great material losses and disorders in urban areas, in rural areas it resulted in both material and human losses of an unprecedented magnitude. The hard-hit provinces were Sichuan, Henan, Anhui, Shandong, Qinghai, and Gansu. All of these regions except for Shandong are located inland, and little news about the true situation in these remote areas leaked to the outside world.

In the early spring of 1959, Mao learned through classified reports sent to him from various localities that a food shortage was developing in some parts of the country. Realizing that he must do something to control the situation, in early July 1959, Mao convened a summit meeting in Lu Mountain, a summer resort located in northern Jiangxi Province. To be fair, Mao originally intended to cool down the fanatic atmosphere of the GLF by reducing the output quotas and by softening some of the radical economic policies. However, when a number of top leaders, represented by Peng Dehuai, then the defense minister, openly questioned the correctness of Mao's policies, Mao felt that his undisputable authority was seriously threatened. He accused Peng and his supporters of being opportunists and traitors and demanded that all the meeting participants keep their distance from Peng and his supporters. Mao vehemently defended his ideas about the GLF and urged the Party and the nation to adhere even more closely to the goals of the GLF. The meeting ended with the humiliation and demotion of Peng and his supporters. Meanwhile, the famine spread and deepened. China thus lost a good opportunity to control the damage of the GLF at its initial level. Mao's response to Peng's well-grounded criticism clearly revealed the dark side of his personality. He viewed his personal reputation and authority as far more important than the truth and the welfare of the ordinary people. The disaster also clearly revealed the serious flaws in the Chinese political system: there was no accountability, and the most honest and outspoken politicians got weeded out first.

Many factors were listed as possible contributing causes to this disaster: unwieldiness of the huge size of an average commune, reduced areas sown with grain, misleading reports about inflated grain output, the collapse of grain production, overprocurement of grain in rural areas, bad weather, communal dining halls, and physical exhaustion caused by the nonstop mass production movement. The major causes of the famine are still subject to debate.

The Chinese government never officially admitted that a famine took place during the GLF period. However, the government admitted that China was experiencing a food shortage when it became clear that both the summer harvest and the fall harvest of 1959 not only fell far below the planned goals for that year, but also below those of 1958. The culprit first was bad weather, later the main culprit became the Soviet Union when the ideological split between China and its main ally became public in 1961. The Chinese people were told that much of the grain was shipped to Russia because the latter demanded that China pay back its debts immediately.

It has now become clear that bad weather and debt-service obligation could not be the main causes of the famine, nor could the famine have been triggered first by production collapse, as some earlier studies tried to prove. The weather in 1958 was very favorable, and the fall harvest in that year was a record high. It is true that the commune system deprived peasants of incentives to work hard, but during the period 1961–1984, when the commune system was still the dominant rural institution, China never saw any famine again. Heavy procurement could be a factor, but the procurements in 1958 and 1959 were comparable with those of some years in the earlier 1950s. Therefore, procurement alone could not be the main cause of the famine. Since exports came from the pool that was procured by the government, they would not further reduce the grain stock controlled by the communal dining halls. The industrial mass movement was mostly concentrated in urban areas. Given the fact that the abnormal death rate in urban areas was much lower than that in rural areas, physical exhaustion could not be the main cause of the high abnormal death rate that was observed in rural areas. After these factors are excluded as the main factors, the communal dining halls loom large as a more plausible main cause of the famine.

Under the communal dining hall system, food was controlled completely by the communal dining halls. Peasants were not allowed to eat at home. Food distribution in these dining halls was not based on contributions of a commune member to production, but on his or her membership only. At first, these dining halls were popular because they let peasants eat as much as they wanted for free. This policy led to a big demand shock and caused a significant amount of grain stock to be consumed or wasted within a short period of time before the summer harvest of 1959 was ready. When the food shortage developed in the spring of 1959, the egalitarian distribution of food in these dining halls led to rampant shirking and free-riding behavior that in turn led to the collapse of production. As soon as the communal dining halls were abolished in mid-1961, all the food was divided up and allocated directly to individual households. Despite the fact that the level of per capita grain consumption was still lower at this time than that in 1959, the famine ended.

See also Central Planning; Great Cultural Revolution (1966–1976); People's Communes/Household Responsibility System.

Bibliography

Ashton, Basil, Kenneth Hill, Alan Piazza, and Robin Zeitz, "Famine in China, 1958–1961," *Population and Development Review* 10, no. 4 (December 1984): 613–645; Chang, Gene, and Guangzhong James Wen, "Communal Dining and the Causation of the Chinese Famine of 1958–1961," *Economic Development and Cultural Change*, October 1997, 1–34; Yang, Dali L., *Calamity and Reform in China* (Stanford, CA: Stanford University Press, 1996).

James Wen

Growth and Development, Trade-offs of

Since 1978, China's economy has averaged a nearly 10 percent annual growth of real GDP and more than 8 percent real GDP per capita. It has also achieved remarkably in other areas such as life expectancy and education of the population. However, market reforms and developments in China have also brought changes that are undesirable and can be viewed as trade-offs accompanying, or a price paid for, the growth and development. These trade-offs can be measured by decreased job stability, increased work intensity, a worsened social and ecological environment, and growing disparities among social groups.

First and foremost, the "iron rice bowl," or lifelong tenure, has melted away. Chinese people no longer enjoy the job security they did before 1978. Urban **unemployment** has been rising, especially since the 1990s. Even the officially reported unemployment rate, which is based on the number of registered unemployed persons in urban areas and includes primarily laborers newly entering the market but excludes laid-off workers, increased from around 2 percent in the early 1990s to 3 percent in the late 1990s and further to 3.6 percent in 2001. If unemployment were based on all jobless workers who are actively seeking work, including those registered in the official statistics and those who are laid off and have not found new jobs, the rate would have been around 7 to 8 percent. Furthermore, if unemployment included jobless workers and disguised unemployment (such as reduction of pay and working days), the rates would have been about 25 percent in the urban sector, 26 percent in the rural sector, and 25.7 percent nationwide.

For those who hold jobs, work intensity has also increased. As is well known, the number of hours one must devote to work to earn and maintain a basic living is an important indicator of economic welfare. China has achieved reduction

Although China's recent economic growth has been explosive, some areas of the economy still lag, such as public transportation. Beijing's railway station, shown here, lacks basic comforts and is often clogged with long lines.

of working hours from forty-eight to forty hours per week more rapidly than many developed countries. While this is a remarkable achievement, the Chinese have been working more intensively since 1978. Before the reform, workers in **state-owned enterprises** would go to factories to punch in the clock at around 9:30 A.M. instead of 8:00 A.M. and leave for lunch break at around 11:00 A.M. instead of 12:00 noon, for example. Shirking was a norm before the reforms. Moreover, state enterprises that functioned as small societies also afforded workers who were the masters of the firms a work environment with considerable camaraderie. In other words, people were living materially poorly, but were time rich and free of work-related stresses. The higher salaries and greater material possessions today should therefore be discounted in welfare evaluation because of the higher work intensity and the harsher work environment.

Rapid economic growth is often accompanied by ecological environmental deterioration such as desertification, deforestation, and environmental pollution, and when an economy is at a low level of development, environmental protection often takes a lower priority than growth per se. China seems to have gone through this process and has protected its environment more conscientiously since the first phase of rapid development in early 1985. China's annual investment in pollution treatment has grown at double-digit rates since the mid-1980s, and pollution accidents have decreased since 1990, compared with the period before that. Compared with 1985, waste water discharged in

2001 decreased by 21 percent and industrial solid waste discharged declined to 21.8 percent of that in 1985 as a result of treatment and reutilization, but the emission of industrial waste gas increased by more than 117 percent because of greater difficulty in controlling gas emission. These data show not only China's increased efforts at protecting the environment since the late 1980s but also subsequent achievements from the efforts. The most important change is the penetrating awareness among the masses of the critical importance of preserving the environment—Chinese people have now become environmentally conscious. Consequently, China's ecological environment has experienced mixed changes. On the one hand, the protection efforts have made Chinese **cities** greener and the sky bluer as more grass and trees are planted and more emissions problems are solved. On the other hand, some environmental damage has become very difficult to reverse. Deforestation and desertification, for example, have caused frequent sandstorms in northern Chinese cities. To solve the problem, a longer cycle of restoring forestry is required.

In addition to ecological environmental changes, the social and cultural environment surrounding Chinese people has also changed, though not always for the better. The divorce rate has more than doubled, rising from 0.9 percent in 1985 to 2.0 percent in 2001, and the number of daily divorces in 2001 was 272 percent of that in 1985, for example. Moreover, increasing occurrences of crime, such as burglary, thievery, and drug trafficking, have made Chinese cities increasingly unsafe, in part because of increased population mobility and loosened control of household registration. One of the most important changes in Chinese cities, in addition to bigger apartments and routine traffic jams, is the installation of metal doors by almost every family. The doors not only keep out criminals, but also dampen the warm connections of neighbors and associates and make the social relationship among residents more distant.

Moreover, accompanying China's rapid economic development are growing disparities among China's regions and between the urban and rural sectors, as well as among different population groups within the urban sector. The disparities have grown to such a level that they have become a threat to China's social stability and the sustainability of economic growth.

If the ratio of urban per capita disposable income to rural per capita net income is used as an indicator, urban-rural income disparity worsened from 2.57 in 1978 to 3.0 in 2002 because of the faster growth of urban income in most years than of rural income. Moreover, rural nonagricultural jobs, such as jobs at **township and village enterprises (TVEs)**, provide much less medical coverage, pensions, unemployment insurance, accident insurance, pregnancy/maternity leave benefits, housing subsidies, and vacation days. The urban-rural income disparity would have been greater if these benefits were included in the calculation.

Regionally, China's eastern and coastal provinces and municipalities have developed at a faster pace than their interior counterparts. The ten provinces and municipalities with the highest per capita GDP are mostly from the eastern and coastal region, and those in the bottom ten are mostly from the hinterland region. The severity of disparity is alarming: the highest per capita GDP among the thirty-one provinces, autonomous regions, and provincial municipalities, that in Shanghai, is 9.65 times the lowest level, in Guizhou. Moreover, the disparity has worsened if it is measured by the ratio to the national average of annual per capita income in the twelve western provinces. This ratio in 1990 was 0.92 and became 0.88 in 2001. Geography, natural resource endowment, economic history, and policies have all contributed to the developmental disparity. Meanwhile, within the urban sector, there has emerged a new "urban poor" class. The western region had the highest concentration of urban poverty.

In addition, nonincome disparities have also arisen, resulting from discrimination against women and rural migrants in the labor market. Chinese women have fallen victim to China's transition, in which both enterprise autonomies that enable firms to be less compliant with policy directives and the lack of legal infrastructure that protects the rights of disadvantaged groups work against them. Women have been laid off first when an enterprise downsizes but have been rehired last to fill new positions because of their future maternity leave, child care, and other family responsibilities that bring higher costs. Consequently, female employment in the urban sector has experienced a steady decline annually since 1995 and is now (42.26 million in 2001) smaller than the level in 1985 (45 million). The discrimination against women employed in labor is also severe. Women are paid lower wages and enjoy considerably less social security benefits in terms of medical coverage, pensions, unemployment insurance, accident insurance, housing subsidies, and vacation days.

More severely discriminated against are rural migrants in the urban labor market. While many industries and jobs in the urban sector have been off-limits to rural migrants, research also finds that migrants are paid, on average, 80 percent of the resident workers' wages. Better provision for housing, health care, and retirement further favors urban workers. Government policies toward rural migrants have been primarily regulating, supervising, and restricting in nature. To work and legally continue their residency in the cities, rural migrants must obtain three official documents, an employment permit, a temporary resident certificate, and proof of compliance with the family-planning policy. In addition to entry barriers, rural migrants also enjoy fewer labor rights and welfare provisions and must pay higher fees for the education of their children.

See also Economic Policies and Development (1949–Present); Economic Structure; Migrant Population; Environmental Protection, Policies and Practices; Rural-Urban Divide, Regional Disparity, and Income Inequality; Sustainable Growth and Development; Urbanization and Migration; Women, Social Status of.

Bibliography

Chen, Aimin, "China's Urbanization, Unemployment, and the Integration of the Segmented Labor Markets," in *Urbanization and Social Welfare in China*, ed. A. Chen, G. G. Liu, and K. H. Zhang (London: Ashgate Publishing, 2003); Chen, "Urbanization and Disparities in China: Challenges of Growth and Development," *China Economic Review* 13, no. 4 (2002): 407–411.

Aimin Chen

H

He Jingzhi (1924–)

He Jingzhi is a poet and scriptwriter, as well as a cultural official. Some of the posts he has held include vice minister of the Publicity Ministry of the Communist Party, vice minister of the Culture Ministry, and secretary of the Association of Chinese Writers.

He Jingzhi was born on November 5, 1924, in Yi County, Shandong Province. In 1940, he went to Yan'an. While studying at Lu Xun Institute of Literature and Art, he wrote many free-verse poems about the miserable rural life that he experienced in his childhood. After the Yan'an Forum on Literature and Art was held in 1942, he made great efforts to use folk songs and ballads to praise the new look in the Communist-Liberated Areas. In 1945, with Ding Yi, He wrote the libretto for the opera *White-Haired Girl*, which was based on a true story of a countrywoman. Huang Shiren, a vicious landlord, forced the poor tenant farmer Yang Bailao to pay debts by selling his daughter Xier as a maid to Huang's family. Yang committed suicide because of grief, indignation, and despair. After being beaten and raped by Huang, Xier finally managed to run away. However, in fear of being found by the Huangs, she could not live a normal life, but hid in a cave deep in the mountains like a savage; her black hair turned white. It was only after the Communists liberated her hometown that she was able to return and live like a human being again. *White-Haired Girl* received tremendous attention the moment it was shown to the public, and it is regarded as a milestone in the history of Chinese opera. In the years following its release, the opera was adapted for a feature film as well as a ballet dance drama, both of which were also very influential in the country.

After 1949, most of He's publications were free-verse poems. In "Back to Yan'an" (1956), He skillfully combined history with reality and expressed his sincere feelings for Yan'an. He is best known for his long political lyrics that focus on the historical changes and the main spirit of his time. *Singing Heartily*

(1956) and *Song of Lei Feng* (1963) are his representative works in this genre. The former describes the happiness and pride of the Chinese people for socialist China and their love for the Communist Party. The latter expounds the significance of Lei Feng, who was an ordinary soldier but became a role model for the entire nation because he tried his best to help other people during his short life. The poems He wrote after 1976, such as "October in China" and "The Song of August," show his keen and philosophical insights into many important social issues.

Especially in his long political lyrics, the descriptions of characters, the richly colored social life, and the natural flow of his high-spirited, optimistic emotions are closely interwoven. In his writings, the protagonists are no longer the poet himself or any other individual characters, but rather the voice of the Chinese people, the working class, or the Party members. All these "voices" have added a flavor of politics and class to his writings, making them more like the epics of the times than anything else. However, He sometimes focused too much attention on embodying the political concepts or policies of his time through his work. As a result, the artistic quality of his poems was given short shrift. In most of his post-1949 lyrics, He attempted to critically learn from the heritage of Chinese folk songs and classical poems. He often used the slang and metaphors that are familiar to ordinary people and, in the meantime, cleverly conveyed his ideas through harmonious rhyme schemes.

See also Anticorruption Literature and Television Dramas; Avant-garde Literature; Experimental Fiction; Great Cultural Revolution, Literature during; Intellectuals, Political Engagement of (1949–1978); Intellectuals, Political Engagement of (1978–Present); Literary Policy for the New China; Literature of the Wounded; Misty Poetry; Modern Pop-Satire; Neorealist Fiction and Modernism; Pre–Cultural Revolution Literature; Revolutionary Realism and Revolutionary Romanticism; Root-Searching Literature; Sexual Freedom in Literature.

Bibliography

Zhou, Liangpei, ed., *Selected Works of He Jingzhi* (Beijing: People's Literature Press, 1997).

Dela X. Jiao

Health Care Reform

The health care system in China has been largely segmented between the urban and rural populations. Currently, the total population in China is about 1.29 billion, with an urban/rural population difference of 40.5 percent to 59.5 percent. According to China Statistics Yearbook 2004 (p. 32), the rural population of China has been shrinking while the urban population is on a growing trend. Between 1978 and 2003, the rural population has shrunk from 82.1 percent to 59.5 percent. Meanwhile, the urban population has grown from 17.9 percent to 40.5 percent of the total population. The rural population in China has never been covered through any publicly financed insurance programs. Therefore, health care for the rural population must be paid for either out of

This Swedish doctor (right) has been in China studying acupuncture for three years. She believes that Chinese medicine offers a comprehensive approach, while Western medicine is more local in its approach.

patients' own pockets or through the so-called cooperative medical plans (CMPs) operated through the voluntary contributions of the local residents at the village or township level. CMPs were popular in the 1960s and 1970s and covered most of the rural population. These village-based plans, however, collapsed massively in the early 1980s when the rural collective economy faded away under the economic reform, which instead promoted the individual household responsibility system in the rural economy. This left most of the rural population without any health care protection, a significant health care financing crisis that drew much attention in the early 1990s from the international community, including the World Bank, the World Health Organization (WHO), and the United Nations Children's Fund (UNICEF).

In the last decade, with support from international funding sources, the Chinese government, especially the Ministry of Health, has engaged both Chinese and foreign scholars in various research and training programs to explore possible ways of financing and organizing health care for the rural population. A promising model suggested organizing rural health care much like traditional CMPs but on a larger scale such as a local community or county level in an attempt to better pool the health risk. Yet there have been no formal policies enacted to endorse and implement such insurance schemes nationwide. Therefore, the feasibility and viability of such models remain to be seen in future experiments. Nevertheless, following these studies, along with some local government efforts, some community-based CMPs have emerged in recent

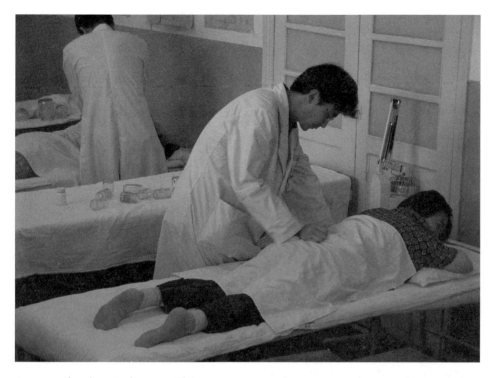

As a cure for chronic diseases, Chinese massage and acupuncture have not lost ground to Western medicine.

years. Various statistics, however, still indicate that nearly 90 percent of the rural population is not under any form of insurance coverage at present. Given the current Chinese economy and population size, it is unlikely that the uninsured status of the rural population can change significantly in the foreseeable future.

In contrast, the urban employed population was served by two major publicly funded insurance programs for nearly four decades from the 1950s through the early 1990s: the Labor Insurance Program (LIP) and the Government Insurance Program (GIP). LIP was a mandated employment-based program primarily paid for by employers for most of the employees working in the **state-owned enterprises.** This program covered about one-third of the urban residents, or 10 percent of the total population. GIP was a government-financed program that served people who worked in the public sectors at various administrative levels and covered less than 5 percent of the total population. Together, the urban health insurance programs covered no more than 15 percent of the total population.

Along with China's market-oriented economic reform, both GIP and LIP were increasingly challenged by some fundamental problems, including inequitable coverage across different working units, poor risk pooling, and the lack of accountability for economic efficiency. This stimulated a series of government-led efforts to reform the existing health care system during the last decade. These initiatives can be characterized in four stages. The initial stage lasted from 1988 through 1994. In this stage, some small-scale and preliminary reforms were explored in a few cities, focusing primarily on the application of some demand-side cost-sharing mechanisms under the existing GIP system. These included linking patient responsibilities and medical payments, imposing some patient cost-sharing policies, employing a social pooling account to pay for health care among the retired population, and implementing catastrophic insurance programs in some cities.

The second stage occurred from 1995 to 1996. This stage began with a pilot experiment initiated by the central government of a newly designed insurance program in the cities of Zhenjiang and Jiujiang. This pilot reform model introduced some fundamental changes in health care financing from the traditional GIP and LIP. The most significant component of the reform model was the socialization of financing: integrating the GIP and LIP to form a citywide insurance pool across all institutions, government agencies, or enterprises. Other innovative features of the pilot model included the three-tier payment system with patient cost-sharing policies, some predetermined payment schedules to providers, and rationing policies such as drug formulary and coverage lists for other medical services.

The third stage started in 1996 when the State Council extended the pilot reform to fifty-seven other cities. In terms of model design, the expanded reform primarily followed the pilot insurance model in Zhenjiang and Jiujiang, although local government insurance agencies were given considerable room to design their own plans with characteristics that would better meet their local needs and socioeconomic conditions. Following the extension to fifty-seven cities, a nationwide effort was pursued in 2000 that required all other remaining regions and cities to begin the reform.

Beginning in late 2000, the fourth stage of the reform efforts extended from the primary insurance policy to hospital institutional reform and the pharmaceutical market. To a large extent, the reforms of the first three stages were mainly in health care financing, whereas the most recent one was on health care organization. It was well understood among researchers and policy makers that China's health care reform could not succeed without the reform of health care institutions, which are dominated by the state-run hospitals. On the pharmaceutical side, because pharmacies are predominantly run by hospitals, sales of drugs have long been the major source of revenues for hospitals in China. This has been widely believed to be a major driving force for the health care utilization pattern observed in China, where pharmaceutical costs account for more than 50 percent of total health care expenditures. This utilization pattern contrasts sharply with that observed in many Western nations, such as the United States, where drug expenditures are often below 10 percent of total health care spending.

Further health care reform in China will have to address several major issues facing the nation. First, for the urban employed population, the ongoing insurance reform so far has been largely focused on the demand side of the market. Future policy efforts will ultimately have to deal with the supply side, a much more difficult and complicated sector to reform, as has been well witnessed from international experiences. Second, the current urban insurance plans are for the employed and leave more than half the total urban population uninsured. While some public welfare programs have been made available to the unemployed, there is clearly a significant and increasing inequality gap in health benefits between the employed and unemployed populations. Third, perhaps the most challenging health care issue in China is the urban-rural inequality in both health care financing and health outcomes. In particular, despite the fact that the rural population is twice as large as the urban population, urban health care expenditures are often more than double those of the rural population. This suggests a highly inequitable allocation or distribution of national health care resources.

See also Medical Provision, Structure of; Pharmaceutical Industry, Administrative and Regulatory Structures of; Pharmaceutical Products, Sales and Marketing of.

Bibliography

Henderson, G., J. Akin, P. M. Hutchinson, S. G. Jin, J. M. Wang, J. Dietrich, and L. M. Mao, "Trends in Health Services Utilization in Eight Provinces in China, 1989–1993," *Social Science and Medicine* 47, no. 12 (1998): 1957–1971; Hu, T., M. Ong, Z. Lin, and E. Li, "The Effects of Economic Reform on Health Insurance and the Financial Burden for Urban Workers in China," *Health Economics* 8, no. 4 (1999): 309–321; Liu, G. G., R. Cai, S. Chao, X. Xiong, Z. Zhao, and Q. Wu, "China's Health Care Insurance Experiment: A Cost and Utilization Analysis," in *Economics of Health Care Reform in Pacific Rim*, ed. T. W. Hu and C. R. Hsieh, 143–158 (London: Edward Elgar, 2001); Liu, G. G., P. Yuen, and T. Hu, "Urban Health Insurance Reform: What Can We Learn from the Pilot Experiments?" in *Urbanization and Social Welfare in China*, ed. A. Chen, G. G. Liu, and K. Zhang (London: Ashgate Publishing, 2003); Liu, G.G., Z. Zhao, and R. Cai, "Equity in Health Care Access: Assessing the Urban Health Care Reform in China," *Social Science and Medicine* 55, no. 10 (2002): 1779–1794; National Bureau of Statistics of the PRC, *China Statistical Yearbook* (Beijing: China Statistics Press, 2004).

Gordon G. Liu

Higher-Education Reform

Modern Chinese higher education started in the late nineteenth century with the establishment of the first Chinese higher-education institution, Jinling University (later merged into Nanjing University) in 1888, followed by Peiyang University (now Tianjin University) in 1895, Nangyang Xue Tang (now Shanghai Jiaotong University) in 1896, Qiushi Academy (now Zhejiang University) in 1897, and Jing Shi Da Xue Tang (now Beijing University) in 1898. For more than half a century, Chinese higher education followed the Western university model in its administration and policies. With the founding of the People's Republic of China in 1949, however, Chinese higher education cut off links to the Western world and turned, for various political reasons, toward the Soviet Union's model for universities.

Higher Education in the 1950s

Chinese higher education in the 1950s was highly centralized. The Ministry of Education (MOE) was the supreme educational administrative body, responsible for administering the colleges and universities and implementing education-related regulations and legislation. Policies regarding admission, job placement, and tenure were made directly by MOE. College students were admitted based on their National College Entrance Examination (NCEE) scores. A college student was guaranteed a "free" higher education, and tuition was paid by the government. In return for a free higher education, university students were asked to take whatever jobs the government assigned them upon graduation. Graduates could not choose their place of work or their jobs.

The promotion system in the 1950s was politically oriented. Faculty promotion was based on one's political performance, collegiality, and academic achievement, which were described as one's political alignment with the Communist Party, relationship with colleagues, and teaching and publication. In China, a university faculty member was guaranteed lifelong tenure from the moment he/she joined the faculty body. However, this situation has begun to change in the recent educational reform.

Higher Education during the Great Cultural Revolution

Chinese higher education was interrupted by the **Great Cultural Revolution (1966–1976)**, a cultural vandalism movement that tried to demolish Chinese tradition, culture, and religions. After three years of a tumultuous political campaign and violence (1966–1969), the government began resuming its college and university recruitment with a dramatic change in its admission policy: qualifying candidates must (*a*) be absolutely aligned with the Communist Party (in fact, most of the candidates admitted were Chinese Communist Party [CCP] members), (*b*) have working experience in either the countryside or manufacture, and (*c*) be recommended by the local CCP secretary. In other words, no high-school graduates could be directly admitted into colleges and universities upon graduation. They first had to become farmers or manufacturing workers before they had a chance to attend colleges and universities.

During this period, university faculty were periodically sent to the countryside to receive what the government called "reeducation by the peasants and workers." Faculty promotion was put to a standstill, and academic research was replaced by political campaigning. Several years later, critics attributed the "knowledge gap" phenomenon in the late 1970s to the Cultural Revolution that demolished all intellectual activities, including teaching and research.

Higher Education in the New Era

Chinese higher education began to recover after the Cultural Revolution. In 1978, China resumed the National College Entrance Examination, a milestone in Chinese higher education after the turmoil of the ten-year Cultural Revolution. The old policies and system were reinstated, including the faculty promotion policy. In the mid- and late 1980s, China launched an economic reform that focused on transforming the socialist planned economy into a market economy. The reform caused a ripple effect in many areas, including Chinese higher education. The old system and its rationale were questioned in regard to higher-education structure, institutional governance, tuition, job placement, and tenure. Colleges and universities began to adapt the market-oriented model to higher education, which has resulted in considerable changes in many areas.

Higher-Education Structure

Chinese higher education in the past consisted only of public colleges and universities. In the mid-1990s, the government began to encourage organizations and individuals to build private schools. By 2001, eighty-nine private institutions of higher education had been accredited by the Ministry of Education to offer degrees and diplomas. Compared with government-controlled colleges and universities, the proportion of private institutions is still quite small. A recent report indicates that proposals regarding the rights of nongovernmental educational institutions and the related laws have been submitted for deliberation to the Standing Committee of the Chinese **National People's Congress**. Experts predict that the future promulgation of the law will serve to enhance private higher education.

Institutional Governance

Like the Chinese economic system, the higher-education system was highly centralized for many years. As the country's economy shifts from a centralized to a market model, however, the governance of Chinese higher education is also undergoing adjustment. One major change in governance has been the introduction of the two-level education provision system, in which the central government (Ministry of Education) shares responsibility for educational governance with local governments (provincial bureaus of education). The reform has brought a positive impact on institutions. Statistics show that the percentage of existing presidents of Chinese universities who hold a master's or doctoral degree has increased considerably. This new generation of higher-education administrators is more knowledgeable and experienced, with a global perspective in understanding China's goals and problems.

Tuition

For four decades following the founding of the People's Republic, Chinese college students did not pay tuition. In the early 1990s, this situation was deemed incompatible with the growth of a market economy, and Chinese universities and colleges began to turn to parents and even students themselves to shoulder some of the costs of education. Studies indicated that the average tuition in a Beijing institute in the year 2002 was between 4,200 and 6,000 yuan ($525–$750) (Duan 2003). Tuition and living expenses put a big stress on Chinese families, especially low-income ones. To help pay for college, many students try to get work-study positions on campus or part-time work on weekends or in the summer.

Job Placement

In the mid-1990s, Chinese higher education began to reform the job-placement system. Instead of government taking the responsibility of assigning jobs to graduates, the graduates will find the jobs themselves. The university job-placement center sponsors job fairs and arranges campus visits by companies. The market economy has also brought changes in salary. Graduates are no longer given the same entry-level salary they used to receive, but are now offered salaries at different entry levels depending on the classification of their job, the region in which they work, and their educational level. Many graduates even seek jobs with better salaries and benefits in branches of top foreign companies in China.

Tenure

For many people, the life-tenure system is a "safe harbor" in higher education. However, it is being challenged by the concept of the market economy. Beijing University, for example, has proposed a new tenure system in which lecturers will be given a contract term of six years, during which they have two opportunities to apply for promotion to associate professor. Associate professors will hold contract terms of nine or twelve years, during which they have two opportunities to apply for a professorship. Anyone who fails twice will be dismissed from the school the next year. The purpose of the tenure reform is to create an academic atmosphere that is more conducive to creative teaching and research. The ongoing reform, as critics observe, might trigger changes across Chinese academia, marking a turning point in the development of China's scholarship.

Challenges

Although Chinese higher-education reform has made considerable progress in the past ten years, there are some issues that need to be addressed seriously. One is overenrollment. The tripling of enrollment over six years and the concomitant financial constraints, for example, have compromised quality since well-trained teaching staff are in short supply and class size has increased substantially. A second is poor strategic planning. The disparity among higher-education institutions between different regions has been intensified in the past ten years. The restructuring of higher education has created a clearly escalating stratification pattern among institutions by geography, source of funding, administrative unit, and functional category. A third is inefficient pedagogy. Pedagogy has failed to encourage critical and creative thinking among students or teachers; a borrowing of the "structure" of foreign models has failed to include an understanding of their purposes; and a high level of political interference has prevented teachers from teaching, students from learning, and educators from educating. A fourth is insufficient funding. Market reforms have ended government underwriting of many colleges in China. Universities face enormous financial shortfalls in their operations, and it is usually only through the use of political connections that they are able to receive funding in the form of bank loans.

Indeed, problems with funding shortfalls, academic quality, and political interference still exist. It should be understood that any significant transformation involves problems. China has a long way to go and a number of problems that need to be solved. Nevertheless, this should not discount the fact that major transformations in Chinese higher education are positive and remarkable in meeting many economic, cultural, and social needs.

See also Character Education in Primary and Secondary Schools; Education Media and Technology; Educational Administration; Educational System; Entrance Examination; Management Education; Primary Education; Private Education; School Enrollment and Employment; Secondary Education; Taiwan, Education Reform in; Teacher Education; United States, Chinese Education in; Vocational and Technical Training.

Bibliography

Duan, X., "Chinese Higher Education Enters a New Era," *Academe* 89, no. 6 (2003): 22–27; Yang, R., "The Debate on Private Higher Education Development in China," *International Higher Education*, fall 1997, 8–9.

Robert Zheng

Hong Kong, Return of

When President Jiang Zemin declared, "July 1 will go down in the annals of history as a day that merits eternal memory," Hong Kong's 156 years of colonial history came to an end. Hong Kong was a British dependent territory until it was handed back to China at midnight, June 30, 1997. Among the many opinions on the impact of Hong Kong's return is the prediction that Hong Kong will be the test case for China's relations with Taiwan. It is widely believed that when Deng Xiaoping brought forward the concept of **"one country, two systems"** as a policy for Hong Kong, he actually had Taiwan's future in mind.

The economic prosperity of Hong Kong is a sheer wonder. With a population of 6 million people and an area six times the size of Washington, D.C., Hong Kong's GDP is approximately 21 percent of that of mainland China, where nearly 1.3 billion people reside. The average per capita income of the island is higher than that of Britain and most Western countries. Hong Kong is the eighth-largest trading economy in the world, as well as the leading financial center in Asia. In fact, it is the third-largest financial center in the world after London and New York.

Hong Kong's history is closely related to the British opium trade in the region. In 1839, the Qing government, witnessing the drain on the nation's wealth from the increasing outflow of silver due to the opium trade, dispatched Commissioner Lin Zexu to Guangzhou, where the commissioner confiscated and torched British opium stock. The event provoked British retaliation in 1840, known as the First Opium War. The island of Hong Kong was subsequently ceded to Great Britain by the Treaty of Nanking in 1842. On the heels of the Second Opium War in 1858, the First Peking Convention was signed which ceded a small area at the tip of Kowloon Peninsula, together with Stonecutter's Island. The Second Convention of Peking, signed in 1898, leased the New Territories (which make up approximately 92 percent of the territory of Hong Kong) to Britain for ninety-nine years. This lease expired on June 30, 1997. Talks aimed at negotiating a settlement on Hong Kong began in July 1983 and were concluded by the signing of the Joint Declaration on December 19, 1984, by the British prime minister, Margaret Thatcher, and her Chinese counterpart, Premier Zhao Ziyang.

The Joint Declaration (officially the Sino-British Declaration on the Question of Hong Kong) set the tone for Hong Kong's new constitution, the Hong Kong Basic Law. The declaration spelled out that Hong Kong would be "restored" to the People's Republic of China with effect from July 1, 1997, and that China would "resume the exercise of sovereignty" from that date. The Joint Declaration will apply for fifty years. Hong Kong will be known as the Hong Kong Special Administrative Region (SAR). The declaration also includes such guarantees as the following: (1) Hong Kong will "enjoy a high degree of autonomy, except in foreign and defense affairs which are the responsibility of the Central People's Government"; and (2) Hong Kong will continue to have a capitalist economy and enjoy existing rights and freedoms, and its basic lifestyle remains unchanged.

The Basic Law for Hong Kong was adopted by China's **National People's Congress** on April 4, 1990. It implemented the provisions of the Joint Declaration and provides a constitutional basis for Hong Kong. In codifying Hong Kong's autonomy, the Basic Law stipulates in Article 3 that the executive authorities and legislature of the SAR "shall be composed of permanent residents of Hong Kong." Moreover, Article 22 forbids any individual department of the Central People's Government, provinces, and autonomous regions from interfering in the affairs of Hong Kong. If there is a need for departments of the central government or for provinces, autonomous regions, or municipalities directly under the central government to set up offices in the Hong Kong Special Administrative Region, the Basic Law stipulates that they must obtain the consent of the government of the region and the approval of the Central People's Government. Article 5 gives Hong Kong the right to run its own system. The article states, "The socialist system and policies shall not be practiced in the Hong Kong Special Administrative Region, and the previous capitalist system and way of life shall remain unchanged for 50 years."

The first test of the new system came in 1989 when Chinese troops opened fire on peaceful democratic demonstrators in Tiananmen Square in Beijing. The bloody crackdown caused worldwide concern over the validity of China's promise to keep Hong Kong free. The British government responded by granting full British passports to 50,000 Hong Kong heads of families and building a new international airport on the island. In 1992, Chris Patten was sworn in as Hong Kong's twenty-eighth and last colonial governor. On October 7, Governor Patten announced proposals for the democratic reform of Hong Kong's institutions for the 1994 local and 1995 legislative elections that outraged the Beijing government. In 1996, the relationship was nevertheless resumed following Dong Jianhua's (Tung Cheehwa) appointment to the position of chief executive–designate of the Special Administrative Region of Hong Kong. Subsequent developments in the legislature favored Beijing's preferences, since the Democratic Party was pushed aside. To demonstrate U.S. concerns over the deterioration of Hong Kong's democracy, President Bill Clinton met with Democratic Party leader Martin Lee in Washington on April 18. The process of the handover of Hong Kong was planned during the next few months, leading to a pompous celebration comparable to the one held in October 1, 1949, when the People's Republic of China was proclaimed. National pride, the success of the Communist Party's leadership, and reminiscence of the historical humiliation were themes of the celebration events.

Hong Kong's destiny is closely related to many interests of the United States. Some 50,000 Americans live and work there. According to the March 2004 testimony given to the Senate by Randall G. Schriver, deputy assistant secretary of state, Hong Kong hosts more than 1,000 American firms, 600 of which have regional operational responsibilities and employ a quarter of a million people. Cumulative American foreign direct investment in Hong Kong totaled more than $35 billion at the end of 2002. Total exports of goods and services amounted to $16.8 billion in 2002, while imports reached approximately $13.3 billion, making Hong Kong the fourteenth-largest trading partner of the United States.

The figure that has caught the world's attention is Dong Jianhua, Hong Kong's chief executive. A skillful politician with broad knowledge and excellent English communication ability, Dong has been able to maintain the stability of Hong Kong's business environment despite the devastating impacts of the Asian financial crisis that started in late 1997. With the backing of the central government, Hong Kong successfully weathered the financial storm, and Dong proudly announced that the "one country, two systems" policy worked. Dong Jianhua was born in Shanghai in 1937 to a privileged background and was educated in China, Hong Kong, and the United Kingdom at Liverpool University, where he read mechanical engineering and watched the Liverpool football club play at Anfield. After living in the United States for almost a decade, working for General Electric, he returned to Hong Kong in 1969 and worked in his father's shipping empire. He eventually became chairman and chief executive officer of Orient Overseas (International) Limited, a Hong Kong–listed investment holding company. His broad business background and his personal relationship with the central government proved to be of tremendous help.

Within a system of special administration, direct elections are among the most difficult things to achieve. On April 24, 2004, China's top legislative panel, the Standing Committee of the National People's Congress (NPC), ruled that the territory could not directly elect its next leader, because such a poll could stir social and economic instability. The NPC committee said that while Hong Kong would be allowed to make changes to its electoral methods, such changes could only happen gradually. On the surface, the central government's decision is lawful, because the Basic Law stipulates in Article 45 that Hong Kong's chief executive shall be "selected by election or through consultations held locally and be appointed by the Central People's Government." The article particularly states that the method of selection must be in accordance with the principle of "gradual and orderly progress." The process of election, the article stipulates, "is the selection of the Chief Executive by universal suffrage upon nomination by a broadly representative nominating committee in accordance with democratic procedures." Clearly, the development of the democratic election process in Hong Kong will be much in the hands of the central government, which is known to be conservative with respect to local choices, particularly given the fact that Taiwan has been threatening to use a referendum to decide Taiwan's fate. The central government has repeatedly expressed warnings against such "separatist" attempts.

However, Hong Kong's economic progress deserves admiration. The 1984 Joint Declaration, the subsequent promulgation of the Basic Law, and Hong

Kong's sustained autonomous management of its day-to-day affairs have laid a foundation for the island's continued economic success. On the 2004 Index of Economic Freedom, a measure that was copublished by the Heritage Foundation and the *Wall Street Journal*, Hong Kong ranks at the top of a list of 155 economies surveyed and has been in the number one spot for ten years.

See also Deng Xiaoping (1904–1997), Reforms of; Special Administrative Region (SAR).

Bibliography

The Basic Law of the Hong Kong Special Administrative Region of the People's Republic of China, http://www.info.gov.hk/basic_law/fulltext/, accessed on November 19, 2004; "Political Rights Essential to Hong Kong's Success," Washington File (EPF404), March 4, 2004, http://www.usembassy-australia.state.gov/hyper/2004/0304/epf404 .htm, accessed on November 18, 2004; "2004 Index of Economic Freedom," Heritage Foundation, 2004, http://www.heritage.org/research/features/index/countries.html, accessed on November 19, 2004.

Jing Luo

Household Responsibility System

See Hukou System; People's Communes/Household Responsibility System.

Housing Reform

After the People's Republic of China (PRC) was founded in 1949, China established a socialist system of urban housing provision. Under the system, the state and public-owned work units took the primary responsibility for housing investment, construction, and allocation. Public housing, together with other benefits, was assigned to workers as in-kind remuneration. It was regarded as a "nonproductive" investment by Chinese planners and thus received declining investment. Between 1949 and 1978, urban per capita living space decreased from 4.3 square meters to 3.6 square meters.

China's urban housing reform started in 1979. The goal of this reform is to establish a new system in which production, distribution, and consumption of urban housing are driven by the market. The reform has involved different strategies and programs. In 1979, China started to reform the urban housing sector by selling newly built public housing to individuals at full construction cost in four designated cities (Xi'an, Liuzhou, Wuzhou, and Nanning). By the end of 1981, housing sales were extended to more than sixty cities in twenty-three provinces. This experiment did not last long because few urban families could afford to buy homes at full-cost rates. Later, in 1982, China carried out another experiment on housing commercialization in four medium-sized **cities** (Changzhou, Shashi, Siping, and Zhengzhou), and the reform strategy became a "three-three" scheme in which the state, work units, and individuals each paid one-third of the sale price. This program was soon stopped because it failed to relieve the government's financial burden and work units were reluctant to share the costs.

In urban areas, residence courtyards like this one have been mostly demolished to make room for modern high-rises and housing developments.

Yet housing reform efforts continued. In February 1986, the State Council formed the first official agency to promote urban housing reform, the Leading Group for Housing Reform. The group immediately recommended a program that aimed to convert hidden in-kind subsidies into open monetary subsidies and change urban housing from a welfare good to a market commodity. Hidden in-kind subsidies refer to low-rent public housing; open monetary subsidies refer to housing vouchers used to pay higher rents. On average, the value of housing vouchers equals the rise in rent. In 1987, the State Council designated three cities (Bengbu, Tangshan, and Yantai) for comprehensive reform programs. This effort took the form of increasing rents and selling houses, increasing rents and issuing housing vouchers. With these changes and the increase in rent, many households were interested in buying a home. By the end of 1988, for example, more than 5,000 families bought homes in Yantai.

Housing reform entered a new stage in 1988 in which the focus of reform shifted from increasing rent to promoting home ownership. Unlike the "three-three" scheme in the early 1980s, which involved only sales of new housing, the new strategy was to sell existing public housing at subsidized rates. The late 1980s were also an important period in terms of lawmaking for the urban housing sector. The State Council held the First National Housing Reform Conference in January 1988, at which the Proposal to Implement Nationwide Urban Housing Reform by Groups and Stages was authorized. The State Council also issued the Opinion on Encouragement to the Staff and Workers to Purchase Old Public Housing Units. In the same year, the **National People's Congress** amended the Land Law, providing better legal protection for urban real estate and thus promoting housing development. With these changes, China began housing reform in all urban areas.

However, urban housing started to grow rapidly only after Deng Xiaoping's southern tour in February 1992. Investment in real estate reached 73 billion yuan in 1992, an increase of 117 percent from the level in 1991. The amount of land developed increased 175 percent, the amount of commodity housing started in 1992 grew 78 percent, and the amount of commodity housing completed in 1992 increased 36 percent. About 43 million square meters of commodity housing were sold in 1992, an increase of 40 percent from the level in 1991.

In mid-1998, the Chinese government decided to end the welfare urban housing system. Reform measures include ending the allocation of welfare housing for employees, promoting mortgage financing, developing the secondary housing market, and liberalizing rental rates. By the end of 1999, all Chinese cities discontinued the practice of employers providing housing for their employees. Thus urban housing in China has been transformed from a redistributive welfare good to a marketized commodity.

With these reforms, China's urban housing has experienced dramatic changes. Housing investment increased more than a hundredfold, from 3.9 billion yuan in 1978 to 431 billion yuan in 1998. As a result, the amount of annual floor space built increased from 37.5 million square meters to 476 million square meters. Urban housing conditions, therefore, have been improved greatly, including a per capita living space increase from 3.6 square meters in 1978 to 9.3 square meters in 1998. The structure of investment has become more decentralized, and the urban housing market has become more market oriented. In 1979, more than 90 percent of total investment came from state and local budgets. This proportion decreased to 0.4 percent in 1999. In 1986, less than 14 percent of newly built commodity housing was sold directly to individuals; this proportion increased to 80 percent in 1999.

Urban housing reform in China, however, has created some undesirable byproducts. Among them is the increasing amount of unsold urban housing. The amount of unsold commodity housing was 38.6 million square meters in 1995. It increased to 61.5 million square meters in 1998. The huge amount of unsold housing is mainly caused by high housing prices relative to incomes, too many taxes and fees imposed by the government, a primitive mortgage market, undeveloped secondary housing markets, and the lack of an effective mechanism to match buyers and sellers.

The experiences of China's urban housing reform suggest that housing reform should be closely linked to reforms in other areas. Without financial reform, real-estate enterprises have no means of obtaining development loans, and individuals cannot purchase houses with mortgages. Without tax reform (especially of property taxes), China does not have much room to lower high housing prices. Without the reform of **state-owned enterprises (SOEs)**, separating housing provision from enterprises is impossible. Without the **Open Door policy**, no foreign funds will enter the housing market to provide capital resources or to construct housing directly. Therefore, China must treat housing reform as an integrated part of its overall economic reform.

See also Rural-Urban Divide, Regional Disparity, and Income Inequality; Urban Households; Urban Housing Privatization.

Bibliography

China Real Estate Market Yearbook Compiling Group, *China Real Estate Market Yearbook* (*CREMY*) (Beijing: China Planning Press [Zhong Guo Ji Hua Chu Ban She], 1997); Liang, Yongping, *Looking Forward Monetary Distribution of Housing* (Beijing: China Price Press [Zhong Guo Wu Jia Chu Ban She], 1998); National Bureau of Statistics, *China Statistical Yearbook* (various issues, 1999 and 2000) (Beijing: China Statistical Press); Song, Shunfeng, "Policy Issues Involving Housing Commercialization in the People's Republic of China," *Socio-economic Planning Science* 26, no. 3 (1992) 213–222; Song, Shunfeng, George S-F Chu, and Rongqing Cao, "Real Estate Tax in Urban China," *Contemporary Economic Policy* 17, no. 4 (1999) 540–551.

Shunfeng Song

HPRS

See Agricultural Reform; People's Communes/Household Responsibility System.

HRM

See Human Resource Management (HRM).

Hua Guofeng (1921–)

Born in Jiaocheng County in a mountainous region in Shanxi Province, a former leader of the highest order who occupied the highest Communist Party and government positions, Hua Guofeng remains a mysterious figure in modern Chinese Communist history. His quick rise and fall and his long absence from public view have aroused much attention.

Hua had hardly been heard of until shortly before he became **Mao Zedong**'s successor in 1976. To promote public awareness, the ailing Mao Zedong had to urge the nation to "promote comrade Hua Guofeng." Mao became acquainted with Hua in the 1950s when the latter was a senior leader of the provincial government of Hunan Province, Mao's home province. Hua subsequently joined the Central Party Committee in 1969 and the Politburo in 1973. By 1975, he had become a vice premier. When **Zhou Enlai** died in January 1976, he replaced Zhou as premier. After Mao died in September the same year, Hua became the successor endorsed by Mao himself, who had allegedly stated, "With you [Hua] in charge, I am at ease." Hua's rise to the top came after an intensive internal feud. It is an eye-catching fact that Mao's two earlier would-be successors, **Liu Shaoqi** and Marshal Lin Biao, both pompous political figures, died miserable deaths. Liu died of torture and starvation during the **Great Cultural Revolution**, and Lin died in a plane crash while trying to escape to Mongolia after his planned coup d'état was leaked.

There are several theories about why Mao Zedong handpicked an almost anonymous political figure to be his successor, in addition to Hua's being a staunch loyalist in charge of the governance of Mao's home province. One theory holds that being aware of the devastation he had done to the nation and not wanting that legacy to continue, Mao picked someone to oppose the **Gang of Four** headed by Mao's wife, Jiang Qing. On the other hand, Nikita Khrushchev's treatment of Joseph Stalin was a fresh lesson that Mao would not want to repeat. Indeed, in this regard, Hua Guofeng accomplished both of Mao's wishes. In October 1976, Hua swiftly detained the Gang of Four and accused them of managing the Cultural Revolution, in which tens of thousands of innocent people had been murdered. The entire nation celebrated the event wholeheartedly. On the heels of the Gang of Four's removal, Hua Guofeng invested handsomely in the construction of Mao Zedong's Memorial Hall. Hua placed the Memorial Hall on the central axis of Beijing along which the Forbidden City, symbol of imperial China, was constructed, and which passes under the throne.

Hua soon collected all prominent positions into his hands. He was chairman of the Party, premier of the State Council, and chairman of the Military Affairs Commission. While he occupied the most important positions, he was clearly incapable of staying on top of things. Hua did not seem to have any vision for China at all. What he did subsequently was in contradiction with the removal of the Gang of Four, but in line with Chairman Mao's wishes. Hua brought forth the theory of the "two whatevers"—whatever Mao had decided was right, and whatever Mao had instructed must be followed. Hua's "whateverism" placed him in the opposite camp to Deng Xiaoping and his reformist force. In Deng's opinion, Mao Zedong had made serious mistakes that must not be repeated. Deng admitted that if the two whatevers had their way, then he himself would never be hopeful of coming back to power in 1977 after having been twice purged by Mao.

To discredit Hua Guofeng and, in particular, to break the rigid Communist ideology that solidly confined people's minds, Deng Xiaoping launched the "Seeking Truth from Facts" debate. In May, the *Guangming Daily* initiated a national debate in an article titled "Practice Is the Sole Criterion for Testing the Truth." The debate was endorsed by high-level leaders, including Ye Jianying, Li Xiannian, Chen Yun, and Hu Yaobang, but was opposed by Hua Guofeng and Wang Dongxing. The debate paved the way to the upcoming pivotal conference of the Third Plenary Session of the Eleventh Party Central Committee that finally put China on the track of economic reforms.

Through the "Seeking Truth from Facts" debate, Deng had three goals to achieve: (1) To remove Mao's personality cult, so that the agenda of the economic reforms could move ahead. To do this, Deng urged the nation to come to the awareness that Mao was not God, that Mao had made mistakes, and that his mistakes must not be repeated. (2) To emancipate people's minds from blind faith in Marxism. He did this by letting people contest the validity of Marxism based on China's reality. He worked to convince people that one must wake up from the Communist utopian dream and set out to develop the economy and get rich. Deng indicated that far from being the "universal truth," as had been touted for decades, Marxism was a century-old theory that must be reexamined against China's reality before it could be useful. (3) To introduce his own pragmatist concepts. These concepts include "to be rich is glorious," "poor communism is nonsense," "socialist market economy," "the market economy serves any system," and so on. The debate lined up the majority of the people on Deng's side.

History shows that to stay in power, one needs at least one of two things: a great vision or strong military backing. Hua Guofeng was clearly not a visionary and had little support from the power class, while his opponent had plenty of both. By 1980, Deng had appointed Hu Yaobang general secretary of the Communist Party and Zhao Ziyang premier of the State Council, both reformists. Hua Guofeng, while still being the chairman of the Party, was actually isolated. In the Twelfth Party Congress held in 1982, Hua Guofeng was ousted, and his position of chairman of the Central Party Committee was also removed. Hua Guofeng returned to his hometown and has vanished from the public ever since.

See also Deng Xiaoping (1904–1997), Politics of; Deng Xiaoping (1904–1997), Reforms of; Jiang Zemin (1926–   ), Diplomacy of; Jiang Zemin (1926–   ), Populism of.

Bibliography

Li, Zhisui, and Anne F. Thurston, *The Private Life of Chairman Mao: The Memoirs of Mao's Personal Physician* (New York: Random House, 1996); Poulin, Richard, *La politique des nationalités de la République populaire de Chine: De Mao Zedong à Hua Guofeng (Documentation du Conseil de la langue française)* (Paris: Conseil de la langue française, 1984); Shi, Dongbing, *Duan Zhan Di Chun Qiu: Hua Guofeng Xia Tai Nei Mu* (The insider story of Hua Guofeng's dismissal) (Hong Kong: Gang Long Chu Ban She, 1993).

Jing Luo

Hukou System

China's *hukou* (household or residential registration) system is a major component of the Chinese sociopolitical structure and a key component of the peculiar Chinese social and cultural characteristics. It performs crucial functions and affects China's political stability, governance, economic growth, social stratification and equality, demography, and internal migration and interregional relations.

The *hukou* system can be traced to the fifth century B.C. during the Warring States period. It was institutionalized and adopted with varying degrees of effectiveness and extensiveness as an important part of the Chinese imperial political system by the dynasties from the Qin (third century B.C.) to the Qing (1644–1911). The Republic of China (ROC) (1911–1949) and the People's Republic of China (PRC) both established a national *hukou* system. However, the *hukou* system achieved an unprecedented level of uniformity, extensiveness, effectiveness, and rigidity only in the PRC, especially after the promulgation of the Regulation on Hukou Registration of the People's Republic of China on January 9, 1958. Twenty-seven years later, on September 6, 1985, Beijing adopted its Regulation on Resident's Personal Identification Card in the People's Republic of China. These two regulations and their implementation procedures are

Like other migrant workers denied equal access to jobs and welfare because of their rural *hukou* registration, this woman, robbed of an entire year's salary by the disappearance of her boss, weeps outside her office in Wuhan in December 2002. © Reuters/Corbis.

the main legal basis for the PRC *hukou* system. Every Chinese citizen knows and is affected by the *hukou* system, yet the system is largely an administrative system and is not even mentioned in the PRC Constitution or the PRC Civil Codes.

The PRC State Council and its ministries and bureaus have issued numerous, often ad hoc regulations, provisional regulations, directives, decrees, and documents that have substantiated and fine-tuned the *hukou* system. The majority of these state documents, estimated to be more than 500 from 1958 to 2002, have concerned the ever-changing criteria and mechanisms of the control of internal migration, especially *qianyi* (permanent migration with *hukou* relocation). The Ministry of Public Security and the local public security bureaus, police stations, and substations are the administrators of the *hukou* system. Specialized *hukou* police officers are assigned to be in charge of *hukou* matters in a neighborhood, a street, a *danwei* (unit), or other kind of community. With the authorization of the central government, provincial and municipal governments can make and have made certain marginal changes and experimental modifications to the *hukou* system in their respective jurisdictions.

The *hukou* system requires every Chinese citizen to be officially and constantly registered with the *hukou* authority (the *hukou* police) from birth. This registration is the legal basis for personal identification of every Chinese citizen. The categories of nonagricultural (urban) or agricultural (rural), the legal address and location, the unit affiliation (employment), and a host of other personal and family information, including religious belief and physical features, are documented and verified to become the person's permanent *hukou* record. A person's *hukou* location and categorization or type were determined by his mother's *hukou* location and type rather than his birthplace until 1998, when a child was allowed to inherit the father's or the mother's *hukou* location and categorization.

One cannot acquire a legal permanent residence and the numerous community-based rights, opportunities, benefits, and privileges in places other than where his or her *hukou* is. Only through proper authorization of the government can one permanently change his or her *hukou* location and especially his or her *hukou* categorization from rural to urban. Travelers, visitors, and temporary migrants must be registered with the *hukou* police for extended stays (longer than three days) in a locality. For longer than a one-month stay and for seeking local employment, one must apply for and be approved to receive a temporary residential permit. Violators are subject to fines, detention, forced repatriation, and even criminal prosecution and even jail sentences. *Hukou* files are routinely used by the police for investigation, social control, and crime-fighting purposes.

Largely operating in secrecy, the PRC *hukou* system performs three leading functions. First, it is the basis for resource allocation and subsidization for selected groups of the population (mainly the residents of the major urban centers). This function has shaped much of the Chinese economic development in the past half century by politically affecting the movement of capital and human resources. The government has traditionally heavily favored the urban centers since the 1950s with investment and subsidies. Second, the *hukou* system allows the government to control and regulate internal migration, especially rural-to-urban migration. The basic principles of the PRC migration control have been to restrict rural-to-urban and small-city-to-large-city migration but to encourage migration in the opposite direction. China's urbanization, as a consequence, is relatively small and slow compared with its economic development level. China's urban slums are also relatively small and less serious compared with those in many other developing nations such as Brazil or India. Third, the *hukou* system has a less well known but powerful role of managing the so-called targeted people (*zhongdian renkou*). Using the *hukou* files, the police maintain a confidential list of the targeted people in each community to be specially monitored and controlled. This focused monitoring and control of selected segments of the population have contributed significantly and effectively to the political stability of China's one-party authoritarian regime.

The *hukou* system may have contributed to China's rapid industrialization and economic growth, which features sectorial and regional unevenness, without serious problems of sociopolitical instability and urban poverty. It has served as a backbone of China's social organization. The *hukou* system, however, also has many negative implications. A major consequence of the *hukou* system has been China's strikingly rigid and clear-cut rural-urban division. For most of the PRC's history, the rural residents, the majority of the Chinese population, have been excluded and openly discriminated against under the *hukou* system. There are only very few and very limited ways (such as entering a state-run college or becoming a state employee or a military officer) for a rural resident to become a privileged urban *hukou* holder. The much smaller urban population (only 14–26 percent of the total population) has had qualitatively much better access to economic and social opportunities, activities, and benefits and has also dominated the PRC's politics. To a lesser extent, urban residents in smaller **cities** and in less developed regions have also been excluded from benefits enjoyed by those living in major urban centers or regions more favored by the government in terms of investment, subsidies, or policy flexibility. Outsiders and temporary residents are treated differently and often openly discriminated against in just about every aspect of their lives. Regional disparities and gaps are therefore created and maintained.

During the reform era that started in 1978, the *hukou* system has demonstrated both significant changes and remarkable continuities. Its basic structure and leading functions remained largely intact by the early 2000s. The system continues to register and identify the 1.3 billion Chinese by their administratively determined location and categories. People with different *hukou* locations and types continue to be treated differently and to have different social status and economic opportunities. However, the administration of the *hukou* system has become more localized and decentralized in recent years. The enforcement of the system has become less intrusive and less offensive as the Chinese sense of civil and individual rights has grown. Forced repatriation and the associated abuses of the *hukou*-less unregistered migrants (mangliu), for example, drew increasing criticism and were discontinued in places like Beijing in 2003. Internal migration, still regulated by the *hukou* system, has been relaxed considerably as the rich and the talented/skilled have acquired substantial nationwide mobility. Temporary residential permits have allowed more than 100 million rural residents to work and live in the cities for extended periods of time that can be as long as a decade. *Hukou*-based biased resource allocation is still important, but many of the old exclusive subsidies for urban consumers have shrunk and even disappeared, thanks to the rapid advance of market forces in the country in the past two decades. Most recently, new reforms since 2001 have relaxed migration controls and obscured the distinctions and divisiveness of the *hukou* system at the level of townships and small cities.

Despite the increased criticisms based on moral grounds and the continuing reform efforts needed by the new market economy, China's *hukou* system is likely to remain omnipresent and powerful, albeit adapting and adjusting, for the foreseeable future. It will continue to be a key element of statecraft for the Chinese government and an important factor in China's sociopolitical organization, population control, economic development, and social and spatial stratification.

See also Migrant Population; People's Communes/Household Responsibility System; Urbanization and Migration.

Bibliography

Wang, Fei-Ling, *China's* Hukou *System: Organization through Division and Exclusion* (Stanford, CA: Stanford University Press, 2004); Wang, "Reformed Migration Control and New List of the Targeted People: China's *Hukou* System in the 2000s," *China Quarterly* (2003–2004): 115–132; Wang, "Stratification and Institutional Exclusion in China and India: Administrative Identification versus Social Barriers," in *Local Governance in China and India: Rural Development and Social Change*, ed. Richard Baum and Manoranjan Mohanty (New York: Sage, 2004).

Fei-Ling Wang

Human Resource Management (HRM)

As a reflection of China's economy, human resource management (HRM) in China has evolved through two stages roughly divided by the year 1978, when the economic reform program began. While the major HRM functions basically remained the same under China's centrally planned economy in the first stage

(1949–1978), they have been undergoing constant, and sometimes dramatic, changes during the past two decades.

Employment

State-owned enterprises (SOEs) were the dominant employer of the Chinese labor force during the first stage. After nine years' "compulsory education" from elementary school (six years) to junior high school (three years), Chinese youth usually faced two paths: joining SOEs as new employees or continuing their education through senior high school (three years) and then college (four years). Junior-high graduates would be assigned jobs by the labor bureaus of local governments and become "workers," while college graduates would be assigned jobs by the Personnel Department of local governments and become government functionaries, better known as "cadres." For both "cadres" and "workers," the government matched the employment demand of SOEs and the supply of graduates from schools and universities according to its central plans at different levels. There was no public labor market because SOEs were not allowed to directly hire new employees by themselves, and graduates were unable to find their own jobs. However, once they were hired, both "workers" and "cadres" would be guaranteed lifelong employment (with a Chinese nickname, "iron rice bowl"). There were no layoffs or downsizing, and even turnover was very rare.

The employment situation in China has changed remarkably in the wake of the economic reform. First, besides the state-owned sector, business established by FDI, and private businesses are also major employers at present. Instead of being assigned jobs by the government, both high-school and college graduates have to seek jobs on their own through the labor market by using such means as job fairs, media ads, and employment agencies. In contrast to the first stage, lifelong employment has now become rare (especially among young employees), and a high turnover rate has become a new problem in SOEs, multinationals, and private businesses alike. The high unemployment rate (as high as two digits in some industrial **cities**) that has resulted from downsizing a redundant labor force by SOEs is a new challenge to the government.

Compensation

During the first stage, the two main compensation tools were structured salary and benefits. Both workers and cadres were paid a monthly salary, but according to two different series of grades, which were composed of rank, seniority, education, and/or skill levels. The pay rates for both series were determined by the government; all SOEs had to follow them rigorously. There were almost no regular pay raises or performance-based pay; the only chance for higher pay would be promotion to a higher-rank position along either the managerial or technical paths. Although the pay rates were very low at that time, SOEs provided full benefits to all employees (including retirees) and their families, workers and cadres alike. All SOE employees lived in company apartments at a nominal rent (approximately 1 percent of monthly pay), enjoyed free medical treatment, sent their children to day-care centers and schools, received up to 80 percent of their pay after retirement, and even saw movies and performances free in company theaters.

During the reform era, pay became more flexible and more closely related to performance. For example, bonuses (monthly, seasonal, or yearly) gradually became a major part of income for all employees and sometimes even exceeded the basic pay. An employee's bonus may be linked not only to his or her individual performance, but also to that of the department or even the organization. The structured salary system is still in effect, but the components have become more diverse and complicated. For example, the system may include various subsidies depending on the payee's job title, position, and even geographic location. Moreover, the pay rates for most employees have been hiked more than tenfold, and pay raises have become more regular, although the range is still stipulated by the government for SOE employees. However, the previous full coverage of benefits has been replaced. Company apartments were sold to employees (though at below market price); company schools and hospitals were either handed over to the government or privatized; medical insurance replaced free treatment; retirees have to rely on their social security annuity and their personal savings; and there are no more free movies and performances. In addition, foreign companies and private businesses usually provide higher pay, which makes the compensation of SOEs look much less attractive to younger employees.

Performance Appraisal

During the first stage, performance appraisal was not a salient HRM function in SOEs—there was little formal annual or semiannual performance evaluation of individual employees. The assumption was that all the employees were "masters of the country" and were expected to work as hard as they could. If someone's performance needed to improve, it would be discussed verbally in one's group through regular seminars, and remedies would be suggested, carried out, and supervised collectively. "Performance race" campaigns between groups as well as between individuals were very popular events, though not on a regular basis. Performance appraisal was highlighted when promotion was being considered or honorable titles were to be awarded. Even in these situations, however, "redness" (political credentials and ideological loyalty) was still considered overwhelmingly superior to "expertise" (technical or managerial skills). Also emphasized was "all-sided evaluation" of candidates by their superiors, colleagues, and subordinates, a concept similar to 360-degree evaluation.

Because employees' pay has become more and more merit oriented since 1978, performance appraisal in SOEs is now more popular than ever before. More quantitative forms and instruments as well as narrative comments have been introduced. Today, with regard to managerial selection, "all-sided evaluation" still prevails. The priority of "redness" or political loyalty has been replaced by a comprehensive set of four criteria—"virtue," "capability," "diligence," and "performance." Some new evaluation systems, such as those used in the United States, have also been implemented in conjunction with the Chinese system, such as the assessment center and various psychological tests.

Training and Development

Given the huge population and abundant labor force in China, training and development have traditionally not been as emphasized in SOEs as they are in American businesses. During the early times, most SOEs trained their new workers through in-house vocational schools, "workers' universities," or experienced "master" workers, while cadres with college degrees mostly worked on their existing knowledge and skills since their professional training was assumed to have been completed in college. Even today, training and development are still given less attention than other HRM functions such as recruitment and compensation. Few companies really take into account their employees' career development. The underlying reason for the underemphasis of training and development might reside in the general attitudes of the Chinese government and organizations toward any type of resources. The most remarkable change in terms of training and development from the first stage to the second was the overwhelming promotion of managerial training by the government since the early 1980s (for more details, see the entry on **management education** in this book).

Labor Relations

Labor relations might be the HRM function most remarkably different between Chinese firms and their counterparts in the United States, and also the one least changed from the first stage to the second. Under the totalitarian polity of China, workers were declared the "masters of the state" and managers "servants of the people." This ideology basically aligned labor and management and denied or outlawed possible interest conflicts between them. Although there was a chapter in every SOE under the National Trade Union Federation, it was considered one of the "five leadership teams" (the other four were the Communist Party Committee, the Administration Team, the Chinese Youth League, and the Women Federation). Most chapters of **trade unions** now act in a consultative manner to shape official policy goals and targets in wages and conditions of work, welfare matters, worker education, and so on. Today, employees in most SOEs are required to sign an employment contract with their employer when hired, which is purely individually based with no collective bargaining at all. Instead, the trade union tries to discipline and ensure the production commitment of the labor force. Although the National Labor Law was enacted as early as 1995, its implementation has been far from satisfactory. Like private businesses, SOEs have been caught violating laws and regulations in the process of downsizing and layoffs of the workforce, hurting employees' interests. Age and gender discrimination in SOEs are also widespread—employees are forced to retire early with no pension and only a nominal amount of severance pay at the age of fifty for men and forty-five for women in some companies. Consequently, more labor disputes or even strikes have been reported since the late 1990s across the country. However, none of them were led by the official trade unions. Nonofficial labor organizations are outlawed.

In sum, human resource management in China has been under transformation as the country carries on its economic reform policy. State control is being phased out, and people enjoy an increased freedom to choose their own jobs, which pushes further reforms in the market economy.

See also Corporate Governance.

Bibliography

Child, J., *Management in China during the Age of Reform* (Cambridge: Cambridge University Press, 1994); Warner, M., *The Management of Human Resources in Chinese Industry* (New York: St. Martin's Press, 1995); Whiteley, A., S. Cheung, and S. Zhang, *Human Resource Strategies in China* (Singapore: World Scientific Publishing Company, 2000).

Wei He

Human Rights Debate

In the West, human rights are generally recognized as the basic rights of mankind regardless of countries and cultural backgrounds. These rights encompass civil, legal, political, economic, social, and cultural rights and freedoms. When the Soviet Union broke up in the early 1990s, the focal point of America's approach to human rights abuses shifted to China. Annual U.S. State Department reports on the subject, along with independent assessments from groups like Amnesty International and Human Rights Watch, denounce China on many levels of human rights implementation and at every turn of time. The issue of human rights has been a major obstacle to closer U.S.-China ties.

The 1948 United Nations (UN) Universal Declaration of Human Rights stipulates that it is governments' responsibility to care for the well-being of their citizens. Later, two covenants (the International Covenant on Civil and Political Rights and the International Covenant on Economic, Social, and Cultural Rights) made this responsibility the obligation of every signatory government, and China is one of the signatory states. Despite all this, the concept of human rights has been the subject of a wide variety of interpretations. China's understanding of human rights is immensely different from that in the United States. Moreover, the Chinese Constitution and several pieces of legislation do incorporate the wording of respecting human rights, but these words do not carry the same meaning as in the United States.

Social and Economic Rights versus Legal and Political Rights

Human rights are typically understood by Chinese to mean being secure in food, shelter, education, job, and peaceful living. Social and economic development and prosperity are the foundation for the full enjoyment of human rights. In the Chinese view, the supremacy of the state assures development and stability, thus guaranteeing the realization of human rights. It is further assumed that the state creates and confers human rights on its citizens; therefore, it can also take them away or even abolish them when necessary.

In contrast, the American notion of human rights is mainly judicial and procedural. It believes that each and every person naturally possesses the right to life, liberty, and property simply because he or she is a person. A person's claim to freedom ultimately supersedes any state-made law unless the state can justify the law otherwise through due process. Furthermore, the government may be held liable for abusing or violating individual rights. To prevent abuse, government must be limited in its exercise of powers and even prohibited from some acts.

The different approaches derive from the sharp distinctions of two cultures and two political systems. Originating in Greco-Roman doctrines, the notion of personal human dignity and worth has been well recognized in the United States. Civil liberties, as they are called, have become the defining feature of the American national heritage to guarantee personal freedoms and safeguard the rights of the accused. All this is alien to Chinese culture because China has never had a tradition of natural law or a custom of due process. To the Chinese, human rights as known in the United States are narrowly construed and procedurally oriented to protect only certain individuals and do so most of the time at the expense of the majority's interest. To the extent that the Chinese Constitution recognizes human rights in general terms, it emphasizes the personal duties to the state more than the individual freedoms from the state. Even for the recognized constitutional human rights, China lacks the enactment of statutory laws or administrative regulations to have them enforced in reality. Another point is that a law must be made known to the people who are to be bound by it. The Chinese government's lack of transparency hinders public awareness of the existence of people's rights and the ways to protect them in practice.

In general, the United States condemns China for its infringement on citizens' private rights, coercive policy of restricting the number of children a family can have, restrictions on freedom of expression and of the press, especially with regard to association and assembly, restricted access to news and information, severely restricted freedom of religion, extrajudicial detention of dissidents, and torture of political prisoners. The U.S. criticisms constantly encounter resistance and denials from China. In response to them, China adopts a tit-for-tat tactic to expose instances of police abuses, racial discrimination, poverty, and homelessness in the United States. Moreover, China insists that improvement needs time and that even in the United States, it took many decades for civil rights such as voting rights for blacks to be fully realized, not to mention a huge and old country like China.

State Rightists versus Human Rightists

The distinction is vivid and real between state rightists and human rightists. State rightists believe that human rights are primarily domestic policy matters, and that how a state treats its people is totally a matter of sovereignty with which other nations have no business, let alone a right to intervention. Theoretically, sovereignty is generally defined as a nation-state being subject to no higher authority and being independent and free to make decisions on matters within its own boundaries. International law upholds state sovereignty. The UN Charter does not allow interference into a state's internal affairs unless that state seeks it voluntarily. As said earlier, in China's view, the right to subsistence or survival is the foremost of human rights. Without national independence, there will be no guarantee for people's lives. According to this reasoning, anything individual or personal can be compromised for the state interest. This genuine belief also stems from China's own suffering from foreign imperialist aggression and colonial occupation throughout much of Chinese contemporary history. To turn an unsympathetic ear to what China has gone through is arrogant at least and vilifying at most.

China also contends that because of differences in history, culture, social system, and stage of economic development, it is very natural for countries to differ in ways, approaches, and processes in realizing human rights. For an outsider like the United States to be critical of others, it has to be inward-looking and self-rectifying first. Furthermore, China is convinced that the U.S. rhetoric of freedom, democracy, and self-determination all too often goes with the practice of imperialism, capitalism, and support for repressive regimes. To make China comply with human rights standards as dictated by the United States is to force China to accept U.S. rhetoric or Western ideas, all the while sacrificing its culture and dignity. This will be a humiliation to China.

Human rightists believe that fundamental moral principles underlie all the legal systems of different nations, and that natural law is the highest law, above any government law. Therefore, human rights should transcend the artificial boundaries of nation-states. When human rights conflict with state rights, human rights should prevail. From that point of universality, any government has an obligation not only to improve its own human rights condition but also to press for other governments to do the same.

Perspective on the Human Rights Debate

The intensity of the debate on human rights has gone through many ups and downs, depending on the U.S. perception of China either as a friend or a foe to U.S. national security and trade interests. Should human rights be promoted with continued vigor to the countries of increasing geopolitical or economic importance such as China? Facing this ever-uncertain world, some Americans advocate taking a pragmatic and reconciliatory approach to China for reasons of the economy and the war on terror. Some still hold to their ideological and sanctional approach in the hope of making China change. This much said, it should be noted that China has made some painstaking progress in improving human rights conditions during the past decades. Overall, the Chinese people are freer in their choices, and the Chinese government is more tolerant of diversity of opinions. It seems that there is a need for any Chinese human rights improvement, as compared with its own past, to be keenly noticed and publicly acknowledged. Too harsh or nagging criticisms of China's failure will be counterproductive because they will do little but incubate more Chinese nationalism.

Thanks to the information age and globalization, nongovernmental organizations (NGOs) like Amnesty International and Human Rights Watch have exerted more influence than ever before in changing human rights practices. In fact, NGO intervention appears more acceptable to China than that of nation-states because an NGO is not perceived as a threat to impose a foreign government's will on a sovereign country. This serves well the dialogue rather than the debate on human rights between the United States and China.

See also Correction System; Crime Prevention; Legislation on China-Related Issues; Rhetoric in China's Foreign Relations; Sino-American Relations, Conflicts and Common Interests; Sino-American Relations since 1949; United Nations (UN) and China.

Bibliography

Chow, Daniel C. K., *The Legal System of the People's Republic of China* (Eagan, MN: Thomson/West, 2003); Genest, Marc, ed., *Stand! Contending Ideas and Opinions in World Politics* (Boulder, CO: Coursewise Publishing, 1999); Information Office of the State Council of the People's Republic of China, *Human Rights in China* (Beijing: Information Office of the State Council of the People's Republic of China, November 1991).

Yan Bai

I

Illegal Drugs, Control of

Of all illegal drugs, narcotic drugs pose the greatest danger to social stability and people's well-being across China. Hence in 1989, shortly after the crackdown on the Beijing student movement, the government began a campaign against what it termed the "six evils" (*liu hai*), of which narcotics were number one, followed by prostitution, pornography, gambling, superstition, and the buying and selling of women.

Historically, China has been plagued by drugs. Widespread opium addiction during the eighteenth and nineteenth centuries crippled its economy. The importing of opium into China by the British sparked two opium wars (1840–1842, 1856–1860) and led to the loss of Hong Kong, which was returned to China in 1997. In the early 1950s, the new government of the People's Republic of China was determined to eliminate illegal drugs. Within three years, China succeeded in wiping out the trafficking of narcotics. What made the government's effort effective until approximately the early 1980s were mass campaigns and China's limited contact with the outside world.

The economic and societal changes of the last two decades have been accompanied by a sharp rise in drug consumption. The most commonly used drugs are heroin, opium, crystal methamphetamine or "ice," cocaine, and marijuana. In recent years, the use of the amphetamine ecstasy, colloquially called *yaotou wan* or "head-shaking pills," has been rising among young people. According to official figures, by the end of 2002, there were 1 million registered drug addicts, up 11 percent from 2001; youths made up 74 percent of this figure. Intravenous injection of drugs was responsible for two-thirds of all HIV/AIDS infection cases, which are estimated to have surpassed 1 million by the end of 2002. Illegal drug use was recorded in 2,148 cities, counties, and districts across China, 97 more than in 2001. In June 2003, Beijing was home to 23,000 registered drug addicts, including unemployed persons, students, private entrepreneurs, lawyers, and government officials. Alongside official statistics, drug use is featured in films and literature.

China legally exports the drug precursor potassium permanganate, which is used to make cocaine, to many countries for medical purposes and has become one of the most vigilant monitors of its use. The ephedra plant, from which the precursor ephedrine is made, grows in the wilds of northern China. China also appears to be the source of "black pearls," the round, black pills that contain varying amounts of the internationally controlled psychotropic benzodiazepine, diazepam. The opening of China's international market sparked a revival of drug smuggling. Indeed, China became a prominent drug transshipment country. **Xinjiang**, Gansu, Heilongjiang, Beijing, Shanghai, Guangdong, and other regions, as well as Hong Kong, Macao, and Taiwan, seemed to have formed a network for the entry, transshipment, and exit of substances produced in Afghanistan or Pakistan.

While illegal drugs are widespread across China, the drug trade is concentrated in Yunnan Province, now the private domain of smugglers and criminals, given its proximity to the Golden Triangle, a narcotics hotbed located on the borders of Laos, Myanmar, and Thailand. Chinese authorities note that more than 90 percent of the heroin that flows through China comes from Myanmar, a major center of heroin production. Yunnan was slow to benefit from the economic reforms that made southeast coastal areas rich during the 1980s and 1990s. Not until the 1990s were southwestern China's borders opened to trade with neighboring countries. As the border trade flourishes, this porous area has become the principal entry point into China for the vast majority of drugs. Chinese manufactured goods pour into Myanmar in exchange for raw materials and rare, high-cost items, including large quantities of heroin. In June 2003, the Yunnan Public Security Bureau acknowledged that drug trafficking had become even more prevalent in the province due to China's intense focus on the outbreak of sudden acute respiratory syndrome (SARS).

China is striking hard at drug crimes. In 1990, the State Council established the National Narcotics Control Commission (NNCC), composed of twenty-five departments, including the Ministry of Public Security, the Ministry of Health, and the General Administration of Customs, in order to strengthen the fight against drugs. In 1998, the Ministry of Public Security set up the Drug Control Bureau, which also serves as an operational agency of the NNCC, and all provinces, autonomous regions, and municipalities, as well as most counties, have set up corresponding drug-control agencies and police antidrug squads. Governments at all levels have included drug-control funds in their budgets. In 1998, the Chinese Narcotics Control Foundation was set up to collect funds from society at large to support drug-control work.

China has also formed an antidrug force backed by governments at all levels. More than thirty national laws and regulations have been promulgated since 1979, including the Regulations on the Control of Transportation Licenses for Ephedrine (2000), the Procedures for the Control of Ephedrine and the Regulations on the Control of the Import and Export of Precursor Chemicals (1999), the Notice on Issues Pertaining to the Strengthened Control of the Export of Ephedrine-Type Products (1998), and the revised Criminal Law (1997), which made important amendments and supplements to the legal regulations on drug-connected crimes. The legislative organs of many provinces have their own bylaws, and the penalties for the possession, use, or trafficking of illegal drugs are steep. The law is strictly enforced, and drug dealers and smugglers are routinely sentenced to death. The constant nationwide antidrug campaigns have resulted in a greater number of arrests and an increased quantity of drugs seized every year.

Meanwhile, about 800 compulsory rehabilitation and drug-treatment reeducation-through-labor centers have been established nationwide. Beijing has experimented with new drug-relief therapy by using adanon, an oral narcotics substitute, to combat drug abuse and the spread of AIDS. As a pilot program to reduce AIDS transmission, Guangdong is providing addicts with clean needles at designated locations. All these measures are seen as evidence of the government's will to curb the fast-growing trade in illegal drugs.

The government has also tried to raise public drug awareness by disseminating information through publications, including the Annual Report on Drug Control beginning in 1998, exhibitions, Web sites, and other mass media. Due to the high percentage of juvenile drug users, the Ministry of Education began antidrug courses in primary and secondary schools in the spring of 2003. In 2000, the All-China Women's Federation launched a three-year program titled "Don't Let Drugs into My Family." All these efforts feature stories on the negative effects of drug addiction and the importance of drug prevention as well as law enforcement vigilance. While borderland checkpoints in inland regions and checkpoints in airports, railway stations, and harbors are still the primary focus for narcotics control, an ongoing nationwide antidrug campaign has also targeted dance halls, nightclubs, and other recreational facilities where drug users and dealers gather. Because drug use is a major source of AIDS transmission, every December 1, World AIDS Day, public health departments organize publicity activities on the theme of "saying no to drugs and preventing AIDS."

Every June 3, the day of commemoration of Lin Zexu's burning of the opium stocks at Humen Beach of Guangdong in 1839, and on June 26, the International Day against Drug Abuse and Illicit Trafficking, Fujian, Guangdong, and several other coastal provinces launch education campaigns. Activities include reminiscing about the opium wars that humiliated the Chinese people. Lin Zexu (1785–1850), born in Fujian Province, a commissioner of the Qing dynasty (1644–1911), is a national hero well known by the Chinese. He ordered the destruction of about 1,000 tons of smuggled opium confiscated from foreign dealers.

Guangzhou, Shenzhen, Zhongshan, Hong Kong, and Macao have also held rallies and sent officials to other cities to demonstrate their firm commitment to a united front in combating the drug problem. The Guangdong, Hong Kong, and Macao Conference on Policy to Tackle Drug Abuse and Trafficking, an annual event organized by the Guangdong Narcotics Control Commission, attempts to strengthen the trilateral cooperation in the fight against cross-boundary drug trafficking. China supports the 1988 UN Drug Convention and has established bilateral cooperation involving mutual legal assistance with many countries, including the United States. This cooperation allows China and the other countries involved to share information concerning transnational crimes, drug control, money laundering, and various drug-related issues.

The increasing amount of drugs confiscated implies that the plague of illegal drugs is still grim. Relying on severe punishment of offenders and many educational programs, China faces a constant uphill battle against narcotics.

See also AIDS, Prevention of; Correction System; Crime Prevention; United Nations (UN) and China.

Bibliography

Narcotics Control in China (Beijing: Information Office of the State Council of the People's Republic of China, 2000); Zhou Yongming, *China's Anti-drug Campaign in the Reform Era*, East Asian Institute Contemporary China Series no. 26 (Singapore: National University of Singapore, 2000).

Helen Xiaoyan Wu

Income Inequality

See Rural-Urban Divide, Regional Disparity, and Income Inequality.

Independent Foreign Policy (1982)

Since 1982, China has been implementing "an independent foreign policy of peace." "Independence" means that China does not align itself with any other major power. China holds that its decisions on foreign policy questions are based on the **Five Principles of Peaceful Coexistence**: mutual respect for sovereignty and territorial integrity, mutual nonaggression, noninterference in each other's internal affairs, equality and mutual benefit, and peaceful coexistence.

Since October 1, 1949, when Chairman **Mao Zedong** declared that the Chinese people had stood up, China's leaders have always conceived of the nation as an independent and major actor in the international system that has felt threatened at times by the United States, at other times by the Soviet Union, and sometimes by both superpowers. But China's leaders never considered themselves to be subordinated to either major power after World War II. Mao remembered the era of unequal treaties all too well, so much so that autonomy and a fierce defense of Chinese sovereignty became the basic tenets of the foreign policy of the People's Republic of China.

A key element of Chinese foreign policy during the Cold War was to participate in the bipolar international system only to the extent necessary to preserve and enhance China's autonomy. China would lean to one side and then to the other and would seek friends in the Third World, but its continual security imperative was the preservation of its sovereignty. Nikita Khrushchev began to acknowledge China's demands for full sovereignty in the middle 1950s when he returned territory and ended economic concessions wrested from Mao by Joseph Stalin. Later, China also achieved U.S. acceptance of the sanctity of China's borders as defined by Beijing. In the Shanghai Communiqué, which was signed when President Richard Nixon visited China in 1972, the United

States acknowledged that the island of Taiwan is a part of China and that unification of the island with the mainland is an internal Chinese affair.

While national security continues to be the highest-priority foreign policy objective of Beijing's leaders, China's approaches to solving its security problems have evolved over time. Mao Zedong's basic inclination was to identify the "main threat" to China at any particular time and to pursue a "united-front" strategy and confrontational tactics to obtain support from other nations to deal with that threat. In the 1950s, China decided to align closely with the Soviet Union. After the Sino-Soviet split occurred in 1960, China adopted a confrontational posture toward both the superpowers during much of the 1960s. In the late 1960s, when Mao decided that the Soviet Union posed the greatest threat to China, he returned to a united-front approach and leaned toward the United States in the hope that Washington would counterbalance the Soviet threat. This continued throughout the 1970s, even under Mao's successors, and, in fact, reached a peak when Deng Xiaoping visited the United States in January 1979 and Beijing tilted strongly toward Washington in the late 1970s. Throughout the 1970s, China's relations with the United States were markedly better than its relations with the Soviet Union.

Deng Xiaoping was the architect of the independent foreign policy of peace. The proximate cause was Washington's April 1979 Taiwan Relations Act (TRA). The passage of the TRA by the U.S. Congress greatly angered Chinese leaders, who felt that the act involved unilateral alteration of a delicate compromise negotiated bilaterally. Beijing was further outraged by U.S. arms sales to Taiwan. Some Chinese analysts concluded that U.S. disregard for Beijing's sensitivities over Taiwan was related to China's seemingly strategic dependence on the United States. If China positioned itself as somewhat more independent of the United States, Washington would be more sensitive to Chinese wishes on the Taiwan issue.

The pro-Soviet faction within the Chinese Communist Party (CCP) complained that Beijing was drawing too close to the United States, in violation of the Chinese principle of nonalignment with a superpower. The most important component of Beijing's independent foreign policy was gradual improvement of relations with the Soviet Union. The leaders who support the independent foreign policy argue that one important reason for its adoption was the fact that any appearance of alignment with either superpower inevitably evokes opposition in China. Thus adoption of a middle position has helped build a broader base of support for China's overall foreign policy.

Soviet military pressure on China had, since the beginning of the 1980s, considerably abated, giving China the option of shifting to a more equidistant stance between the superpowers. Chinese analysts argued in 1982 that the balance of power had shifted again because President Ronald Reagan's defense buildup and more assertive foreign policy had lifted the United States back into a position of rough strategic parity with the Soviets. The rapid buildup of American military strength under Reagan meant that there was less need for China to rally the world's anti-Soviet forces. The Americans had apparently awakened from their slumber, and the Soviets were increasingly on the defensive. Many Chinese strategists also felt that China's relationship with the United States had grown too close, restricting Beijing's diplomatic flexibility.

At a deeper level, the independent foreign policy marked a long-term shift from a confrontational to a conciliatory approach toward the foreign powers, based on the declining influence of Maoist ideology and the increasing importance being given to economic development. Indeed, shifting resources from defense to economic development was a key objective served by China's reduction of tension with Moscow. By the early 1980s, a new leadership consensus had emerged in support of Deng Xiaoping's ambitious program of economic modernization.

By the time Mikhail Gorbachev came to power in March 1985, Sino-Soviet relations were already more cordial than they had been in the late 1950s. Gorbachev proceeded to satisfy Chinese demands to remove "three obstacles" in order to normalize their bilateral relationship. By March 1989, Soviet troops had been withdrawn from Afghanistan. In December 1988, Gorbachev announced a 500,000-man reduction in the Soviet army. Forty percent of this cut was to be in the Soviet military regions east of the Urals. In late 1988, Moscow pressed Hanoi to withdraw its military forces from Cambodia. As a result, Sino-Soviet relations were normalized during Gorbachev's visit to Beijing in May 1989.

In many regards, the 1982 shift was a watershed. Prior to that point, Beijing's approach to the superpowers was essentially confrontational. After 1982, however, China began seeking peaceful, nonconfrontational, cooperative relations with both superpowers. The factors that underlie this transition are a new strategic situation and an overriding emphasis on economic development. China has been able to maintain an independent foreign policy even after the end of the Cold War and the breakup of the Soviet Union.

The independent foreign policy serves Chinese interests well. By not siding with any other power, the Chinese have adopted a posture that gives them greater maneuverability and flexibility in pursuing China's own interests with respect to particular problems and issues. Chinese leaders stress that a peaceful international environment is necessary for China's own development, and China's actions suggest that Chinese leaders are committed to the principle. They are especially sensitive to any issue that they believe involves "sovereignty."

See also Cold War and China; Jiang Zemin (1926–   ), Diplomacy of; Korean War (1950–1953); Nixon's Visit to China/Shanghai Communiqué (1972); Ping-Pong Diplomacy; Rhetoric in China's Foreign Relations; Sino-American Relations, Conflicts and Common Interests; Sino-American Relations since 1949; Sino-Japanese Relations since 1949; Sino-Russian Relations since 1991; Sino-Soviet Alliance; Taiwan Strait Crisis, Evolution of; Vietnam War.

Bibliography

Barnett, Doak A., *The Making of Foreign Policy in China: Structure and Process* (Boulder, CO: Westview Press, 1985); Faust, John R., and Judith F. Fornberg, *China in World Politics* (Boulder, CO: Lynne Rienner, 1995); Nathan, Andrew J., and Robert S. Ross, *The Great Wall and the Empty Fortress: China's Search for Security* (New York: W. W. Norton, 1997).

Guoli Liu

Thanks to an increase in tourism, silk factories, like the one shown here in 2004, were thriving in the early years of the twenty-first century.

Industrial Structure

In the first half of the twentieth century, China's industrial development was limited to a few coastal locations with connections to world shipping routes and to domestic routes. Development, however, was repeatedly interrupted by social turmoil, civil wars, and foreign invasions. When the People's Republic of China (PRC) was founded in 1949, the country had mainly an agricultural economy in which agriculture shared nearly 60 percent of national income and industry shared only 30 percent.

By the twenty-first century, China had made great progress in industrialization, as well as transportation. Industrial production accounted for 44 percent of the GDP in 2000. In 2000, industrial value added was 189.7 times that in 1952 at comparable prices, steel output was more than 800 times that in 1952, and electricity power generation was more than 300 times that in 1952. The country has developed a comprehensive industrial structure and is proud to be the world's number one producer of steel, coal, cement, fertilizer, and **television** sets. As the world's sixth-largest economy and fifth-largest exporter (2002), China is quickly rising as a "world factory" that is flooding the world market with competitively priced industrial goods.

Industrialization of the PRC has taken an unusual path. From 1949 to 1979, for three decades, China followed a Soviet-style development strategy characterized by (1) the Marxist principles of common ownership with the state as trustee and of generalized egalitarianism and (2) the Stalinist practices of **central planning** for resource allocation, suppressing light industries and services in favor of heavy industries, and minimizing trade and financial linkages with the capitalist world. This strategy was supplemented by Mao's principle of regional economic self-sufficiency and by quasi-wartime planning in the 1960s and 1970s. The heavy-industry-biased industrialization was courted by an urbanization policy that controlled the growth of urban population, constrained the growth of central **cities**, and focused on "productive" activities (mining and manufacturing) while it suppressed the "nonproductive" (service and urban infrastructure) sectors.

This unusual industrialization strategy led to investment of a large bulk of state capital in the inland provinces, while the finance of the capital came from heavy "taxation" on coastal cities. Many sets of capital equipment in traditionally coastal industrial bases were relocated to the inland mountains, where basic infrastructure such as transportation and electricity was in short supply, and the markets were far away. Meanwhile, waves of state-sponsored migration moved millions of engineers, technicians, skilled workers, and urban youths from coastal and central cities to the rural areas, inland provinces, and border regions. At the regional and provincial levels, the pursuit of self-sufficiency resulted in a wasteful quest for completeness of local "industrial structure" regardless of economies of scale and comparative advantages.

This industrialization process, already very costly, was disrupted by political campaigns. Both the **Great Leap Forward** (1958–1961) and the **Great Cultural Revolution (1966–1976)** brought chaos and disasters to the economy. It was estimated that 25 million people died of famine after the Great Leap Forward, and both events had the combined effect of reducing China's actual per capita output and consumption by more than 60 percent from what it should have achieved by the early 1990s if these events had not occurred.

From 1953 to 1978, while the gross industrial output increased by 11.4 percent per annum, the output proportion between light industry and heavy industry changed from 64.5 percent versus 35.5 percent to 43.1 percent versus 56.9 percent. The underdevelopment of light industry was a major cause of consumer-good shortages during the prereform years.

Meanwhile, primary industry and the tertiary industries grew by 2.1 percent and 5.5 percent per annum, respectively, well below the GDP annual growth rate of 6.1 percent and the industrial sector's growth rate of 11.5 percent. The value-added proportions among primary, secondary, and tertiary industries changed from 50.5 percent, 20.9 percent, and 28.6 percent in 1952 to 28.1 percent, 48.2 percent, and 23.7 percent in 1978. A number of important service sectors such as real estate, financial services, insurance, accounting and legal services, and tourism and entertainment were substantially suppressed or even totally wiped out. Urban infrastructure was severely underinvested and badly maintained in many cities. By 1978, in the tertiary industries, more than half of value added came from commerce, transportation, post, and telecom services.

After China launched its economic modernization program and embarked on market-oriented reforms in 1978, the government made purposive adjustments to the industrial structure. It reversed Maoist migration policy by allowing millions of previously rusticated urban youth and other former urban employees to return to their city hometowns. The quasi-wartime industrial development plans were abandoned. The autarkic, inward-looking industrialization strategy gave way to an open-trade, export-led growth strategy. Heavy-industry-biased industrial planning gave way to a consumer-oriented industrial policy that encouraged light industry and service sectors. Systematic efforts were made to actively reinvigorate the central role of coastal cities in development. Urban service sectors received favorable official policy support.

Governments at various levels launched hundreds of state-sponsored projects to beef up the bottleneck sectors of energy supply, public utilities, transportation, and telecommunications. From 1978 to 1988, a total of RMB 527.7 billion yuan was invested in capital construction of these basic industries and infrastructure, 1.5 times the amount invested in the previous twenty-five years. Of the amount, 39 percent went into the energy industry, 23 percent into the transport-post-telecom sector, 21 percent into raw-material industry, and 8 percent into urban public utilities. From 1989 to 2001, a total of RMB 6,251.6 billion was invested in these sectors, another tenfold increase from the previous decade. Of the total, 37 percent went into the transport, post, and telecom sector,

35 percent into the energy industry, 12 percent into public utilities, and 8 percent into raw-material industry. For more than a decade, these sectors grew much faster than the whole economy and secondary industry. Their rapid development has effectively improved the physical basis for industrialization.

From the 1980s to the 1990s, thanks to market-oriented reforms, fundamental changes to the decision-making and coordination structure regarding industrial development occurred. As a result of a gradual approach to privatization, the share of (purely) **state-owned enterprises** in total industrial output value declined from 78 percent in 1978 to 24 percent in 2001. Meanwhile, the proportion of limited liability corporations and shareholding companies reached 30 percent, and that of foreign-funded firms rose to 29 percent by 2001. The proliferation of other forms of ownership has substantially reduced the government's direct control over industrial firms. Since the mid-1980s, state intervention in industrial development has gradually moved away from a central planning regime to an industrial policy regime that is similar to that of other newly industrialized economies. Instead of central-planning policy instruments such as direct state financing and planning, administrative intervention, and state manipulation of prices, the government has in the past two decades relied more on measures practiced in other developing countries to carry out industrial policies. These include subsidies (mainly through awarding public projects), preferential tax or tariff rates, favorable financing through the state banking system, trade protection, and restrictions on ownership, business content, and geographic scope for foreign-funded enterprises. The government has also used sequential opening of the economy to implement regional and industrial policies by setting up special zones for certain sectors and in certain regions. In addition, China's investment project approval procedure features a stratified administrative system that oversees the amount and directions of fixed capital investment.

As a consequence of economic transition and accelerated industrialization, China's industrial structure went through substantial changes. From 1979 to 2001, while the GDP grew 9.4 percent per annum, primary, secondary, and tertiary industries grew 4.7 percent, 11.3 percent, and 10.2 percent per annum, respectively, in value added. The shares of value added among the three industries changed from 28.1 percent, 48.2 percent, and 23.7 percent in 1978 to 15.2 percent, 51.1 percent, and 33.6 percent. Meanwhile, of the more than 300 million jobs created in these years, 70 million came from primary industry, 94.5 million from secondary industry, and 140 million from tertiary industry. As a result, the shares of employment of the three industries changed from 70.5 percent, 17.3 percent, and 12.2 percent to 50.1 percent, 22.3 percent, and 27.7 percent.

Within tertiary industry, from 1978 to 2000, the shares of commerce and transportation, post, and telecom services in total value added came down from 30.9 percent and 20.1 percent, respectively, to 24.3 percent and 16.2 percent, respectively. This was largely due to a revival and boom in service sectors such as real estate, financial services, insurance, accounting and legal services, and tourism and entertainment.

In China's rapid industrialization process, secondary industry has been the major growth engine. Of the 9.4 percent annual growth rate of the GDP in

1979–2001, 1.3 percentage points came from primary industry, 5.4 percentage points from secondary industry, and 2.7 percentage points from tertiary industry. Within the manufacturing industry, from 1993 to 2001, the fastest-growing sectors were electronics and telecommunications (increased by 6.92 times); instruments, meters, and cultural and office machinery (5.61 times); electrical equipment and machinery (2.92 times); transportation equipment manufacturing (2.49 times); and medical-pharmaceutical products (2.96 times). Rapid growth has also occurred in new industrial sectors such as microelectronics, computers, nuclear energy, bioengineering, space engineering, communications, new materials and new energy sources, and environmental protection products. Some "sunset sectors" such as textiles, ordinary machinery manufacturing, and special-purpose equipment manufacturing saw their shares in the whole industrial output shrink. Rapid industrialization has brought great changes to China's trade structure. With more than twentyfold rise in foreign trade volume between 1980 and 2000, manufacturing products' share in exports and imports increased from 50 percent to 90 percent and 65 percent to 85 percent, respectively.

Currently, some common structural problems in China's industries are the following: (1) too many firms are operating below their minimum efficiency scale due to domestic (regional) and international trade barriers; (2) many industries have grown by a high-energy-and-raw-material-input and low-technology-input model, resulting in slow or stagnant productivity growth; and (3) weak links in marketing, distribution, and logistic services constrain value-adding capability. To solve these problems, China needs to further open up its market, promote competition, and develop market institutions conducive to industrial restructuring and consolidation.

See also Energy Industries; Labor Market Development; Labor Policy, Employment, and Unemployment; Pharmaceutical Industry, Administrative and Regulatory Structures of; Rural Industrialization; Telecommunications Industry.

Bibliography

Chow, Gregory, *China's Economic Transformation* (Malden, MA: Blackwell, 2002); Lu, Ding, "Revamping the Industrial Policies," in *The Globalization of the Chinese Economy*, ed. Shang-Jin Wei, G. J. Wen, and H. Zhou (Cheltenham, UK: Edward Elgar, 2002); Yu, Yongding, Zheng Bingwen, and Song Hong, eds., *The Research Report on China's Entry into WTO: The Analysis of China's Industries* (Beijing: Social Sciences Documentation Publishing House, 2000).

Ding Lu

Industrialization

See Industrial Structure; Rural Industrialization.

Intellectual Work, Changing Dynamics of

Two important changes in intellectual work since 1978 are the bourgeoisification and professionalization of **intellectuals**. Some intellectuals have felt the need of moneymaking in the market economy. They have decided to leave the public sector and join the private business world as technical experts or advisers or have established moneymaking enterprises in their fields. Most intellectuals, however, have struggled with their professional status, keeping a distance from politics and serving as mere professionals in either the private or the public sector.

Bourgeoisification arrived when slogans such as "to get rich is glorious," "some must get rich first," and "smashing the iron rice bowl" had sanctified acquisitiveness, entrepreneurship, and inequality. Attitudes like these have social and psychological effects on intellectuals as well. One effect is that moneymaking has become a primary concern for intellectuals from all walks of life. Many have felt their livelihood threatened and have decided that they had better forget their scruples and get rich by all means necessary. What used to be nonprofit organizations such as schools and theater groups have established restaurants, clothing stores, or cultural development companies. Journalism has become an entrepreneurial enterprise in which reporters write stories for businesses in exchange for payments. Lawyers are more willing to handle economic cases, where they can earn tens of thousands of yuan, than divorce cases of ordinary people, where they can make little money.

The trend of bourgeoisification was at its peak in the middle of the 1990s and became part of normal intellectual development toward the end of the twentieth century. Knowledge workers seem to have found their niche in the market economy. But intellectual culture has changed dramatically from the previous decades under Communist rule. More are concerned about moneymaking, and fewer people care about traditional intellectual work and ideology. There has been a shift in the social construction of status from *wenren* (the scholar) to *shangren* (the businessperson). Many feel that without money there is no status. The old belief in scholarship as the loftiest ideal of an individual has been torn apart. Corruption in academia has also become a serious issue: plagiarism, vicious attacks on others, huge numbers of errors in printed books, fake study centers set up for profit, sloppy translations, and the like. Intellectuals have tried to turn their knowledge into money, and culture has become a commodity. The humanist spirit is being eroded, as is the sense of equality and innocence people used to have in the revolutionary years. Their value changes include also their views on themselves, their social responsibility, and their sense of mission.

This movement toward bourgeoisification, however, has also afflicted intellectuals with a dual personality. It is not easy for intellectuals to make a complete change of values overnight. Many try to strike a balance between business and intellect, but when they do so, the bourgeoisified intellectuals may experience many built-in stresses. For example, they may spend a good deal of their time doing business. This means that they have less time for their professional and intellectual jobs. Even more important, there is a conflict between morality and the single-minded pursuit of profit. It is true that commerce is not necessarily in contradiction with scholarship and often funds it. But the primary focus of businesses is to make money, and the means to make money can very well be controversial. Even if the goal is to fund scholarship or inform scholarship, as some would argue, the end may not always justify the possibly dubious means. This is a tension that may cause a dual personality, and it is a conflict that Confucian businesspeople have to constantly strive to manage. The more leaning towards business, the less they will be intellectual. But they do have the freedom to move between positions.

Professionalization is the process of achieving professional status, a process through which professions are organized for association, for control, and for work and through which they legitimate their control by attaching their expertise to rationality, efficiency, and science. In essence, professionalization serves to achieve a professional autonomy in selecting the economic terms of work, the location and social organization of work, and the technical content of the work. This professional autonomy is largely a result of negotiations with the state and society in general, since it is the state that licenses the professionals and society that approves or disapproves of their practice. Generally, professional associations conduct the negotiations.

How much professional autonomy Chinese intellectuals have is debatable. To be sure, they have some control over the content of their research, or at least the techniques they use. Professional organizations have also been established for doctors, lawyers, journalists, and engineers, but they tend to be sponsored by the government, and intellectuals still have little control over their own work environment. For example, they may have a great deal of control over how they are going to conduct a class on national politics, but they have little control over what they can say about the Chinese political system. The decisions on issues such as income and housing, conditions of work, promotion, and policies in their work are based not on the professional's authority or recognized expertise, but on the authority of the administrative office. The same applies to journalism. Yet true professionalization requires a certain amount of autonomy in decisions like these. Intellectuals are still constrained by a strong state despite the fragmentation of the propaganda system of control of thought work. Professionals continue to fight for more autonomy, but they constantly meet with resistance from a state that still feels uncomfortable about loosening its grip on professional and intellectual issues.

If professionals want to achieve autonomy, independent professional organizations are needed, professionalism must be promoted, and professions must negotiate with other political forces. Professions, in fact, need to become interest groups that lobby to advance their aims and to protect their interests when policy is being made. In other words, rather than waiting to be given policy, they need to be able to make policy. First and foremost, they need to work with the state, because they need the state. It is the power of government that grants the profession the exclusive right to use or evaluate a certain body of knowledge and skill. Once the profession is granted the exclusive right to use knowledge, it gains power. Thus it is necessary for professions to be intimately connected with the formal political process in the course of professionalization, whether it involves establishing professional associations, setting up professional registration or licensing, or maintaining and improving the profession's position in the marketplace. For all this, professionals have to work with the government.

The current debate on the use of the tenure system in colleges and universities in China is a good example of the struggle over professional autonomy.

From the administrators' point of view, it is important for them to have control over the professionals' work, including their tenure and promotion. But from the professionals' point of view, only they themselves should have control over their work through their own organizations. But if there are no faculty organizations like unions that serve the faculty's own interests, and if faculty involvement is undercounted in faculty evaluation, professional autonomy will inevitably be eroded, if not eliminated. If faculty members have no place to go for their grievances or for a fair hearing if they feel that they are unfairly charged by the administration or by other faculty members, they do not have professional autonomy. In this and other matters concerning professional autonomy, Chinese intellectuals still have a long way to go.

Most professionals' concern about politics probably involves only matters about their own professional development, indicating a "professional model" that is new to the intellectual tradition. They may want the Communist Party to lift its heavy hand on intellectuals. They may eventually want it to pull its Party chiefs from institutions of education, law, health, journalism, and other professional fields. They may want the right to freely organize into unofficial groups. They may welcome a multiparty system. Indeed, some may even want to establish an opposition party. But those who do will become revolutionary or otherwise critical intellectuals, or organic intellectuals, those who participate in a political cause on behalf of their own class. Most, however, will not be active in advocating political or even educational reform. Their involvement in politics is limited to the protection of their personal professional interests. It is in this sense that they differ from organic and critical intellectuals. But that may be what unattached intellectuals, or professionals, are all about. Professionals' interests are fundamentally technical, while critical or organic intellectuals' interests are primarily critical, emancipatory, hermeneutic, and hence often political.

The bourgeoisification and professionalization of intellectuals since 1978 have drastically transformed the nature of the traditional intellectual and the dynamics of intellectual work, but this may be just a continuation of the same processes that began with the demise of the Qing dynasty and the establishment of the Republic of China in the early twentieth century. It is part of the modernization process. But how these dynamic changes will affect the direction of social transformation in China remains to be seen.

See also Fulbright Scholars in China (1979–1989); Intellectuals, Political Engagement of (1949–1978); Intellectuals, Political Engagement of (1978–Present).

Bibliography

Davis, Deborah S., Richard Kraus, Barry Naughton, and Elizabeth J. Perry, eds., *Urban Spaces in Contemporary China: The Potential for Autonomy and Community in Post-Mao China* (Washington, DC: Woodrow Wilson Center Press, 1995); Hao, Zhidong, *Intellectuals at a Crossroads: The Changing Politics of China's Knowledge Workers* (Albany: State University of New York Press, 2003); Lynch, Daniel C., *After the Propaganda State: Media, Politics, and "Thought Work" in Reformed China* (Stanford, CA: Stanford Univeristy Press, 1999); Miller, H. Lyman, *Science and Dissent in Post-Mao China: The Politics of Knowledge* (Seattle: University of Washington Press, 1996); Zhu,

Yong, ed., *Zhishi Fenzi Yinggai Gan Shenme* (What intellectuals should do) (Beijing: Shishi Chubanshe [Current Affairs Press], 1999).

Zhidong Hao

Intellectuals

There is no clear-cut definition of intellectuals. Although some argue that the term should refer only to those who serve as the conscience of society, a broader definition is widely used to include people who have completed at least some postsecondary education and/or who are doing professional work.

There are different ways to classify intellectuals. On the one hand, they can be distinguished in terms of the intrinsic characteristics of their intellectual activity. Hence there are scientists, philosophers, and artists, who tend to create knowledge, and engineers, doctors, lawyers, and journalists, who tend to use knowledge. Professors are supposed to be both creating and divulging knowledge. Government statistics indicate that in state-owned institutions in 1997 there were 405,000 college teachers, 4,186,000 secondary school teachers, and 5,794,000 primary school teachers. Industrial and agricultural engineers numbered 5,719,000 and 611,000, respectively. In addition, there were 303,000 scientists, 3,214,000 medical professionals (including doctors and nurses), and 110,000 lawyers. Altogether, there were 20,342,000 such intellectuals. At the beginning of the 1990s, there were about 50,000 journalists who actually collected, wrote, and edited the news, but since there was an expansion of the mass media later in the 1990s, one would expect journalists to far exceed that number. If those intellectuals who work in government agencies and in the private sector are added to the total, estimates can run up to 33.04 million. Of the 13 million cadres, most can be considered as intellectuals, broadly defined. According to some estimates, then, there were about 45 million intellectuals by the end of the 1990s, about 3.5 percent of the total population. The expansion of higher education since the 1990s implies that the ranks of intellectuals will increase in the long run.

On the other hand, intellectuals can be distinguished in terms of their social relations, which may be a more interesting and useful classification for analytical and expository purposes. In other words, there are what one may call *organic*, *professional*, and *critical* intellectuals. These are ideal types. Whether an intellectual is one or the other depends on the preponderance of the evidence. For example, Wang Shuo is a critical intellectual when he makes fun of anything serious and his writing becomes a gadfly to the official discourse. If he

Frequent targets during the Maoist era, Chinese intellectuals have been rehabilitated since the reforms of the late 1970s. Although their average income remains low, they have regained the respect of society.

writes to make money, he is chiefly a professional. If he becomes an official, he will more likely become an organic intellectual to the Communist Party and the government. Thus intellectuals can be one or the other depending on the circumstances, although one can still describe the ideal typical organic, professional, or critical intellectual.

Typically, organic intellectuals are those who serve the government or a business interest. These include about 13 million Communist Party and government cadres. They are the administrators, administrative assistants, theorists, and spokespersons of the Party and the state and include the cadres from various levels of government: the *Ke*-level cadres, who are heads of various departments at the county level; the *Xiang*, which is administratively lower than the county, and heads of companies and agencies at these same administrative levels; the *Chu*-level cadres (such as department heads in central and provincial governments and heads of counties, cities, and companies and agencies at this level); the *Ting ju*–level cadres (directors of the central and provincial government departments, the Party and government heads of the prefectures, cities at this level, and companies, factories, and agencies at the same level); the ministerial-level cadres (ministers of various central and state government agencies, provincial Party and government heads, directors of companies at this level, and the members of the central secretariat of various other Party-authorized parties and organizations); and the state president- and premier-level cadres (the members of the Politburo, the president and vice presidents, the premier and vice premiers, the members of the state council, the chairperson and vice chairpersons of the standing committee of the **National People's Congress**, and the chairperson and vice chairpersons of the Chinese People's Political Consultative Conference).

The organic intellectuals who serve the Party also include those in government think tanks, such as the academies of social sciences at the national (e.g., the Chinese Academy of Social Sciences), provincial (e.g., the Hebei Academy of Social Sciences), and city levels (e.g., the Shanghai Academy of Social Sciences). Governments at various levels often have their own research institutes. The members of the so-called democratic parties and groups, which also serve as think tanks of the government, are organic intellectuals. So are journalists who work for government-controlled newspapers and magazines. The latter are organic because they largely have to follow the Party and government directions in what they can or cannot report in their work.

As the statistics cited earlier indicate, however, most intellectuals are not administrative functionaries. Rather, they are professionals, that is, scientists, engineers, doctors, professors, and lawyers. Hence the second category of intellectuals is based on their social functions. These are what many call the "professional-managerial class." But if they rise up to the positions of managers in either the public or private sector, that is, they serve either the government or a business interest in some serious manner, one would treat them as organic intellectuals. Hence by definition professionals are mainly those who are "ordinary" knowledge workers, while organic intellectuals are part of the state power. Professionals tend to keep a distance from them one way or another, consciously or not. In fact, they keep a distance from politics in general.

But in the years between 1949 and 1978, it was almost impossible for professionals to keep a distance from politics, since everybody belonged to a work unit organized by the government. The Thought Reform movement, the Hundred Flowers movement, and the **Great Cultural Revolution** carried out in these work units drew all intellectuals into politics, and they were in fact deprofessionalized. In the **Mao Zedong** era, professionals were supposed to be both "red" and "expert," and intellectuals did not achieve much autonomy. They had to conform to the Maoist ideology and serve the Party's political goals. Even in their own technical fields, intellectuals were constrained by the Party's objectives. A Party secretary, with or without a professional background, was installed in each work unit and became the authority over technical issues, dictating what could and could not be done. The laity could become judges, and peasants with little training could become doctors as long as they were socially and politically reliable. Deprofessionalized Chinese intellectuals were stripped of what little professional standing they had enjoyed. This happened despite the Party's efforts in 1952 to restructure the universities and its repeated calls to utilize intellectuals and their expertise during the first decade of the People's Republic.

Since the reform that began in the late 1970s, however, intellectuals have been reprofessionalized. The Party has loosened its political control over intellectuals. The educational system has been reformed to train new professionals, and no one can perform duties in medicine, law, engineering, or teaching without credentials. Professionals carry formal technical and academic titles, and they can even set up private practices in medicine, law, engineering, or education.

The third category of intellectuals is defined on the basis of this group's tendency to challenge the governing power, whether the latter is the Party and government officials or the rich. Since 1949, intellectuals have had a difficult time exercising social criticism: the many government-sponsored political movements have largely stifled intellectual dissent. Nonetheless, criticism persisted. Much of this criticism came from the organic intellectuals to the Party. Examples in the 1950s were Hu Feng, Yu Pingbo, and Feng Xuefeng in literary circles and Chu Anping, Zhang Bojun, and Luo Longji of the democratic parties; in the 1960s, Deng Tuo, Wu Han, and Liao Mosha from the Beijing Party Committee; and in the 1980s, Liu Bingyan, Fang Lizhi, and Wang Ruowang. But criticism also came from intellectuals outside the Party, including Lin Xiling, Yu Luoke, and Gu Zhun in the 1950s, 1960s, and 1970s, as well as those in the Democracy Wall movement at the end of the 1970s. The intellectuals engaged in the democracy movement both in and outside the country since the 1980s are critical intellectuals. So are those public intellectuals who are currently engaged in social criticism in China, however limited it may be. The critical intellectuals, functioning as the conscience of society, constitute a very small number of the intellectual complex compared with professionals and organic intellectuals.

The three categories of intellectuals make up the intellectual landscape in China today, and the various roles they play are instrumental in China's modernization efforts. They remain the most powerful agents of social change.

See also "Double-Hundred" Policy; Fulbright Scholars in China (1979–1989); Intellectual Work, Changing Dynamics of; Intellectuals, Political Engagement of (1949–1978); Intellectuals, Political Engagement of (1978–Present).

Bibliography

Cheek, Timothy, *Propaganda and Culture in Mao's China: Deng Tuo and the Intelligentsia* (New York: Oxford University Press, 1997); Goldman, Merle, *Sowing the Seeds of Democracy in China: Political Reform in the Deng Xiaoping Era* (Cambridge, MA: Harvard University Press, 1994); Hamrin, Carol Lee, and Timothy Cheek, eds., *China's Establishment Intellectuals* (Armonk, NY: M. E. Sharpe, 1986); Hao, Zhidong, *Intellectuals at a Crossroads: The Changing Politics of China's Knowledge Workers* (Albany: State University of New York Press, 2003); Miller, H. Lyman, *Science and Dissent in Post-Mao China: The Politics of Knowledge* (Seattle: University of Washington Press, 1996).

Zhidong Hao

Intellectuals, Political Engagement of (1949–1978)

In the long history of China, there are two main traditions concerning **intellectuals'** engagement in politics. The "calling" of intellectuals in traditional Chinese culture is *xiu qi zhi ping*. That is, in ascending order, a member of the literati must cultivate and perfect oneself, get one's family in order, guide or govern one's country in the right course, and finally, help achieve peace in the world. The tradition also calls on intellectuals to *li de*, *li gong*, and *li yan*, that is, set themselves up as moral examples, perform meritorious services, and write great books. To become an official and engage in politics was thus always one of the most important components of traditional intellectual life. The second tradition in Confucianism was the obligation for any degree holder, official or not, to speak out when the government deviated from Confucian ideals. From this belief in speaking out came the *qing yi* (pure opinion) movements that have run throughout China's intellectual history. Many modern intellectuals, following these traditions, became either "organic," that is, participative or "critical" to influence political change in China.

At the beginning of the twentieth century, intellectuals founded the Nationalist (Kuomintang, or KMT) and Chinese Communist (CCP) Parties, and in the course of the party development, each drew more intellectuals to its ranks. When the KMT was in power, many intellectuals were organic to the government. Others, however, were organic to the Communist movement, which was critical of the KMT. Indeed, many intellectuals supported and participated in the Communist revolution, which contributed to the latter's success in 1949.

In the early 1950s, more intellectuals willingly participated in the Thought Reform movement to become good organic intellectuals to the CCP to serve in the officialdom. Ma Yinchu, the president of Beijing University, had proposed a reeducation movement even before the official Thought Reform movement began. Intellectuals like the editor Chu Anping and the sociologist Fei Xiaotong, who had been strongly critical of the KMT government, wrote about the need for intellectuals' reeducation along CCP lines. Formerly professional intellectuals like Ji Xianlin, a returned student from Germany and an accomplished scholar in Buddhism and Sanskrit, felt sorry that they had not participated in the Communist liberation movement, having focused only on their scholarship. Ji believed that he needed to reform his thinking about his avoidance of politics. He also needed to change his erroneous attitude toward the Soviet Union and its control over the CCP. When the reform movement ended, he was moved to tears when the Party was convinced that he had reformed himself. Along with those who had joined the revolution before 1949, many more intellectuals now plunged into the socialist revolution and construction and became good organic intellectuals, either as cadres or political activists.

But the critical tradition of intellectuals serving as the conscience of society was still very much alive in these and other intellectuals. In the early 1950s, many organic intellectuals already had some second thoughts about the Party's policies on literature and art. Intellectuals like Ding Ling (writer), Liang Sicheng (architect), and Yu Pingbo, Feng Xuefeng, and especially Hu Feng, all literary critics, publicly expressed discontent about the rigid Party policies that stifled artistic creativity. Hu was jailed for his criticism. In the Hundred Flowers movement in 1957 and 1958, many took part in the movement launched by the Party to rectify itself and offered their own political criticisms. Huang Qiuyuan, Qin Zhaoyang, and Zhu Guanqian all supported Hu's criticism of the Party's policies. Liu Bingyan and Wang Meng wrote stories that criticized the Party bureaucrats. Chu Anping even suggested increasing the number of non-Party members in high-level government positions and decreasing the Party's involvement where Party members were not experts. He maintained that while the Party was playing a leading role in the country, non-Party members were also masters of the country and should be allowed to make a contribution. Zhang Bojun, a member of the Democratic League and minister of communications, and Luo Longji, Zhang's colleague from the Democratic League and minister of the timber industry, also held that contradictions came from the privileged position of the CCP as opposed to other parties. Zhang Bojun proposed the establishment of a "political planning council" to help rectify the proletarian dictatorship, that is, the Party's dictatorship. He believed that the democratic parties ought to penetrate the county level—only thus could they fulfill their supervisory role. He believed that the CCP was in a dilemma as to where to go, and his own party had the responsibility to help. Students like Lin Xiling even compared Hu Feng's case to the Dreyfus affair and called for a just trial. Many such intellectuals were dubbed "rightists" and suffered all kinds of disgrace, including prison terms or even execution.

Still other intellectuals, such as Hu Yuzhi and Shi Liang, strove to be organic to the Party and participated actively in the criticism and degrading of critical intellectuals. Some of them, however, tried to be critical at other times, although their criticism might be very limited. Chief among them were members of the Beijing Party Committee: Deng Tuo, secretary of the Secretariat and editor of its theoretical journal, *Qianxian* (Front line); Wu Han, vice mayor of Beijing and a prominent historian; and Liao Mosha, director of the United Front Work Department. Most of their criticisms were published in Deng's essays titled "Evening Chats in Yanshan [another name for Beijing]" or the trio's "Notes from a Three-Family Village," published in *Front Line* from September 1961 to

July 1964. In his essays, Deng, who had been the head of the Xinhua News Agency in the 1940s and editor in chief of the *People's Daily* in the 1950s, criticized **Mao Zedong**, without naming him, for his arrogant, subjective, dogmatic, and arbitrary way of leadership and thus began the demystification of the Party and of Mao himself. Deng also criticized the Party's break with the Soviet Union and called for closer contact with the United States. Wu Han published a historical play titled *The Dismissal of Hai Rui from Office*, implicitly supporting upright officials like Peng Dehuai, the defense minister who had criticized Mao and who was deposed from office in 1959. Wu also called for academic work to be independent of politics. Intellectuals from the Party's propaganda departments, including Zhou Yang, Tian Han, Meng Chao, Yang Hansheng, Xia Yan, Mao Dun, and Shao Quanlin, also criticized Mao's dogmatism. So did intellectuals from academic circles, such as Feng Youlan, Ma Yinchu, Yang Xianzhen, Jian Bozan, and Sun Yefang. During the **Great Cultural Revolution** that began in 1966, all of these intellectuals from within the system were dubbed "capitalist roaders" and criticized, if not imprisoned. Some committed suicide.

Intellectuals from outside the system made their own criticisms. These were typical ideal critical intellectuals. Yu Luoke (1942–1968), a young worker turned intellectual, made a huge impact at the very beginning of the Cultural Revolution. His most famous work is "On One's Family Background." First published in a student newspaper, the article spread all over the country. In it, he questioned the then popular belief that if one's family background is bad (capitalists, landlords, rich peasants, reactionary, rightist, and so on), then one is bad; if one's family background is good (workers, poor peasants, and revolutionary cadres), then one is good. His article spoke to the experience of many youths who were not able to go to college, find a good job, or join the army because their parents or grandparents were from one of the "bad" categories. In a sense, it questioned the prevalent class theory. Yu was also able to publish an article in *Wenhui Daily* that criticized Yao Wenyuan and his article, "Dismissal of Hai Rui." (Yao's article was one of the chief events that started the Cultural Revolution.) By doing so, he was indirectly questioning Mao, for it was Mao who was behind Yao's article. Yu was also directly challenging Mao when he said that it was wrong to be against everything your enemy is for, and for anything your enemy is against. He was executed for his ideas.

Gu Zhun (1915–1974), an economist and former vice director of finance in the East China government, was termed a "rightist" in 1957 and spent the rest of his life laboring in the countryside. Gu's uniqueness lies in his persistence in looking beyond the revolution. He had always believed in the absolute correctness of revolutionary idealism, but when he saw it change to reactionary despotism, he found himself turning to "complete empiricism and diversity." He delved into the study of democracy and wrote *The Greek City System*, which was published posthumously in 1982. In the last two years of his life, he wrote *From Idealism to Empiricism*, also published posthumously. He explored why the revolution became antiprogressive, and how totalitarianism had transformed one-time revolutionaries like Mao into despots. Gu died of illness and in poverty.

Intellectuals' political criticism, however, persevered. In 1976, the April 5 Movement broke out that mourned the death of **Zhou Enlai**, the premier, and protested the so-called **Gang of Four**, the radicals in power: Wang Hongwen, Zhang Chunqiao, Jiang Qing, and Yao Wenyuan. The radicals charged that Zhou, who had died in January, was a capitalist roader. But the people seemed to be grieving for themselves and their country as much as for Zhou. Understandably, the articles and poems at the time were not anti-Party, but anti–Gang of Four.

The ensuing **literature of the wounded** movement depicted the pain, violence, injustices, and destruction of the Great Cultural Revolution. Love, which had been a forbidden zone in literature, was again portrayed as being a human emotion. Individuality was restored. There were also a great many novels that depicted the lives of the educated youths who were sent to the countryside and the negative impact of the ultraleftist lines on every aspect of the young people's lives, as witnessed by the educated youths' depression and perplexity. A new literary genre, "obscure poetry" (*menglong shi*, or **misty poetry**), such as that of Bei Dao, Shu Ting, and Gu Cheng, expressed the poets' critique of the absurdity of the Cultural Revolution, the pain of the transition period, and their anxiety about the future. Overall, literature of the wounded and obscure poetry may be viewed as movements that exposed the follies and tragedies of the Mao era. They make one question the legitimacy and efficacy of the political system. In the reform years that began in 1978, both the organic and critical traditions have continued. Intellectuals have remained politically engaged.

See also Fulbright Scholars in China (1979–1989); Intellectual Work, Changing Dynamics of; Intellectuals, Political Engagement of (1978–Present).

Bibliography

Chen, Minzhi, and Ding Dong, eds., *Gu Zhun Riji* (The diaries of Gu Zhun) (Beijing: Jinji Ribao Chubanshe [Economic Daily Press], 1997); Hamrin, Carol Lee, and Timothy Cheek, eds., *China's Establishment Intellectuals* (Armonk, NY: M. E. Sharpe, 1986); Hao, Zhidong, *Intellectuals at a Crossroads: The Changing Politics of China's Knowledge Workers* (Albany: State University of New York Press, 2003); Ma, Licheng, and Ling Zhijun, *Jiaofeng: Dangdai Zhongguo Sanci Sixiang Jiefang Shilu* (Crossing swords: A truthful report on the three thought liberation campaigns in contemporary China) (Beijing: Jinri Zhongguo Chubanshe [Today's China Press], 1998); Xu, Xiao, Ding Dong, and Xu Youyu, eds., *Yu Luoke Yizuo yu Huiyi* (Yu Luoke's works and recollections) (Beijing: Zhongguo Wenlian Chubanshe [Chinese Literature and Art Association Press], 1999).

Zhidong Hao

Intellectuals, Political Engagement of (1978–Present)

The Third Plenum of the Central Committee of the Party's Eleventh Congress in 1978 shifted its focus from class struggle to the economy. To support the shift, the Communist Party had to liberate its mind. Riding the tide, critical **intellectuals** both in and outside the Party and government again questioned the orthodox Marxist-Maoist beliefs and even practices adopted since the death of **Mao Zedong**. Orthodox organic intellectuals, however, rushed to defend the traditional Party line. At the same time, large numbers of intellectuals were incorporated into the cadre ranks or the ranks of government think tanks and the mass media.

The more critical organic intellectuals in the Party and government answered the Party's call to emancipate the mind and launched the debate on practice criteria in 1978. They argued that reality is the sole criterion for judging the truth, not the words of an authority figure like Mao. Many intellectuals participated in this movement, which was spearheaded by Hu Fuming, a philosophy professor from Nanjing University, Sun Changjiang of the Central Party School, Yang Xiguang, the editor of the *Guangming Daily*, and Wu Jiang, also from the *Guangming Daily*.

Meanwhile, critical intellectuals outside the system organized the Democracy Wall movement. In 1978 and 1979, democratic debates took the form of big-character-posters, mostly written with paint brushes on the walls along Chang'an Street in Xidan Avenue of Beijing. Intellectuals criticized those Party members who believed in whatever Mao said, and they challenged Mao's judgment in using Lin Biao and the **Gang of Four**. Their criticism then moved on to question the system itself. The best-known article is Wei Jingsheng's treatise "The Fifth Modernization," which called for democratizing Chinese politics so as to avoid repeating the tragedies of the Mao era. Underground journals sprang up that called for democratization and for voicing public dissent, including *Beijing Spring*, *April Fourth Forum*, *Enlightenment*, *Exploration*, *Today*, and *Masses' Reference News*. The movement, however, ended after the government's imprisonment of some of its members, such as Wei Jingsheng, Liu Qing, Ren Wanding, and Huang Xiang.

By the 1980s, more intellectuals stood up to voice their critical opinions. After a completely new Electoral Law was adopted in 1979 that provided for competitive elections, a number of students in Beijing University ran for a position in the local district in the early 1980s. Students elsewhere in the country followed suit. The candidates called for freedom of speech, freedom of the press, separation of the Party and the government, and division of power into legislative, executive, and judicial branches. They criticized Mao's role in the Anti-Rightist Movement, the **Great Leap Forward**, the **Great Cultural Revolution**, and various other policies devised after "liberation." Many of these activists, such as Hu Ping, Wang Juntao, Chen Ziming, Fang Zhiyuan (all from Beijing), Fu Shenqi (Shanghai), and Liang Heng (Hunan), later became activists in the democracy movement.

Organic intellectuals (those serving in the government) like Wang Ruoshui, the deputy editor of the *People's Daily*, criticized alienation under Chinese socialism. Liu Bingyan, Hu Jiwei, and others advocated an independent judiciary and press to help the Party resolve its problems more efficiently. Wang Ruowang and Fang Lizhi criticized the Party for stalling on political reform. Su Shaozhi, even after he was purged from his post as director of the Institute of Marxism-Leninism–Mao Zedong Thought at the Chinese Academy of Social Sciences (CASS), condemned the Party for its campaigns against so-called spiritual pollution and bourgeois liberalization. Supporting such campaigns were orthodox organic intellectuals like Hu Qiaomu, Deng Liqun, **Ai Qing**, Zang Kejia, Tian Jian, Liu Shaotang, Ding Ling, Huang Gang, and Liu Baiyu. Su Xiaokang and Wang Luxiang launched the documentary **television** series *River Elegy* (1988), which expressed a sense of concern and anxiety over the present through the critical voices of experts and scholars.

In early 1989, intellectuals took more specific actions, but this time they were joined by intellectuals who were non-Party cadres. Fang Lizhi first wrote to Deng Xiaoping and demanded the release of Wei Jingsheng. Wei's case was viewed by some as China's equivalent of the Dreyfus affair. Then three petitions were signed by intellectuals from various fields, started respectively by Bei Dao, an obscure poet, Xu Liangying, a physicist from CASS, and Dai Qing, a *Guangming Daily* journalist. The signers included not only members of the leaders of the democratic movement, such as Yan Jiaqi (director of the Institute of Political Science at CASS), Su Shaozhi, and Wang Ruoshui, but also well-known writers such as Su Wei and scientists like Wang Gangchang. Some cultural intellectuals who were never interested in politics also put their names on the petitions. They demanded not only the release of political prisoners, but also the basic political rights of citizens. University students also organized salons and invited intellectuals to come and make speeches on these issues as well as issues concerning educational reform: raising the salaries of professors and investing more in education.

The situation was now ripe for a major storm, which occurred when Hu Yaobang, the Party secretary who had been supportive of political reform and had been deposed for his stance, died on April 15, 1989. Intellectuals and students started a series of activities to mourn him and to call for the restoration of his name. These activities, which the Party termed "anti-Party," soon evolved into demonstrations that quickly spread to other big cities all over China. The movement was much like the April 5 Movement in 1976, when intellectuals demanded the restoration of former Premier **Zhou Enlai**'s reputation while expressing their own anxiety over conditions at the time. In the 1989 demonstrations, students and other intellectuals called for freedom of the press, the rule of law, direct elections, and extension of human rights. Newspapers and journals such as the *World Economic Herald*, the *Science and Technology Daily*, and the *New Observer* published extensive and positive reports on these demonstrations. Other newspapers followed their line, including even the *People's Daily*. Journalists staged their own demonstrations calling for political reform.

The ensuing crackdown, however, landed some in prison, like Wang Juntao, Chen Ziming, and Dai Qing. Others escaped from the country, such as Yan Jiaqi, Su Shaozhi, and Su Xiaokang. The crackdown of 1989 has made China's intellectuals rethink and reshape their ties with the state. Intellectuals' political engagement in the 1990s thus varied a great deal. Most intellectuals were firmly professionalized and kept their distance from politics, partly from disillusionment over the events in 1989. Other intellectuals found their own ways of engagement.

Avant-garde artists, such as Fang Lijun, Liu Wei, Li Shan, Zhuang Hua, Wang Luyan, and Xu Bing, opted for cynical realism and political pop after 1989. Wang Luyan built a bicycle that moves backward when the rider peddles forward. Like much of life in China, it defies common sense. Xu Bing placed a female and a male pig in their high breeding season into a pen with scattered books. Printed all over the pig were unreadable English words, and all over the sow, nonsensical Chinese characters. The two pigs mated after a brief courtship. The original title of the underground exhibition was *Rape or Adultery?*, but it was later changed to *A Case Study of Transference*, also known as *Cultural Animals*. According to the artist, he wants the spectators to ponder the relationship between China and the West. Popular musicians such as Cui Jian were subversive in their music with titles such as "The Last Gunshot" and "Saying One Thing but Thinking Another." Movie directors such as Zhang Yimou and Chen Kaige produced works that were critical of the Party's performance since 1949.

Orthodox organic intellectuals like Deng Liqun, Liu Baiyu, and Lin Mohan, who adhered to the Maoist socialist ideologies and were critical of Deng's reform, came to represent the Old Left. They published journals such as *Zhenli De Zhuiqiu* (The pursuit of truth) and *Zhongliu* (In the middle of the current) as their way of making their voices heard. The New Left, represented by younger intellectuals, was critical of the social inequalities between the rich and the poor, but it did not have a political or economic solution to the problem. Supporting the government's capitalist reforms were organic intellectuals of the government think tanks and the so-called neoconservatives, who believed that equality and political reform might have to be sacrificed for a stable environment where the economy could grow. Journalists also reflected these strands of thought in their work.

If these intellectuals' political engagement has remained in the realm of political discourse, other intellectuals have tried political organization. Many of the democratic elites who have escaped or exiled themselves from the country have now become dissidents outside the system, joining the existing movements overseas. The democracy advocates abroad publish journals such as *Beijing Spring*, *China Spring*, and *Democratic China*. They have organized alternative parties as a way to effect change in China from outside the country. Inside China, it has become almost impossible to advocate radical political reforms as critical intellectuals did before the June 4 crackdown, and the organization of opposition parties has met with constant repression. But some have kept trying. Wang Youcai, Qin Yongmin, and Xu Wenli organized the China Democracy Party in 1998, but found themselves arrested and sentenced to prison for eleven to thirteen years. Ding Zilin and Jiang Peikun have continued to organize parents whose sons and daughters died during the 1989 massacre for reassessment of the events in 1989 and restoration of their children's names.

At the beginning of the twenty-first century, intellectuals continue to find ways to engage themselves in politics along the lines they developed in the 1990s. The future of China depends on how they discourse with each other and how they organize themselves, as well as the masses, as intellectual traditions have indicated.

See also Avant-garde Literature; Fulbright Scholars in China (1979–1989); Intellectual Work, Changing Dynamics of; Intellectuals, Political Engagement of (1949–1978).

Bibliography

Barmé, Geremie R., *In the Red: On Contemporary Chinese Culture* (New York: Columbia University Press, 1999); Baum, Richard, *Burying Mao: Chinese Politics in the Age of*

Deng Xiaoping (Princeton, NJ: Princeton University Press, 1994); Goldman, Merle, *Sowing the Seeds of Democracy in China: Political Reform in the Deng Xiaoping Era* (Cambridge, MA: Harvard University Press, 1994); Hao, Zhidong, *Intellectuals at a Crossroads: The Changing Politics of China's Knowledge Workers* (Albany: State University of New York Press, 2003); Li Shitao, ed., *Zhishi Fenzi Lichang: Ziyou Zhuyi zhi Zheng yu Zhongguo Sixiang Jie de Fenhua* (The intellectual stance: The debate on liberalism and the division of Chinese thought) (Changchun, Jilin: Shidai Wenyi Chubanshe [Art and Literature of the Time Press], 2000).

Zhidong Hao

International Migration and Overseas Chinese

The Chinese have a long history of international migration. As a result, today overseas Chinese reside in more than 130 countries in the world. The largest number of them reside in Southeast Asian countries. The estimated number of overseas Chinese was around 37 million by 1990, and the number is likely to increase significantly in the twenty-first century. Given the magnitude of this population, the impact on China and destination countries is undoubtedly very significant. The patterns of emigration in post-1949 China, especially the period after 1978 when China initiated a transition to a market-oriented economy, constitute an interesting research issue. Perhaps more than other issues, patterns of international migration are dictated by the characteristics of both sending and receiving countries. The most important factors are immigration/emigration policies, economic conditions of immigrant-sending and receiving countries, and the larger international political context.

The period 1949–1977 was a time with very limited emigration. This limited emigration was very much reflected in clandestine migration from Guangdong and Fujian Provinces to Hong Kong. Some of the Fujianese migrants used Hong Kong as a stepping-stone to the United States. The emigration pattern during this period was greatly influenced by the larger international context, especially the Cold War. All exchanges with Western countries were highly monitored, particularly emigration to other countries. The breakaway from the shadow of the Soviet Union in the late 1950s further led to China's strong ideology of self-reliance in everything. The restrictive emigration policy does not necessarily mean that the Chinese government entirely ignored the traditional immigrant-sending communities (Guangdong and Fujian). In fact, the main component of the Chinese government policy of the 1950s and early 1960s was to protect the interests of overseas Chinese and their businesses in China. In the 1960s, when Indonesia deported thousands of Chinese immigrants, the Chinese government took the responsibility of helping these returned immigrants with their jobs and their children's education. The most tragic chapter of emigration history in the post-1949 period was the time of the **Great Cultural Revolution (1966–1976)**. During the Great Cultural Revolution, individuals who had relatives abroad were often suspected of spying for foreign countries, and some of them were even put in jail and tortured.

The new pattern of emigration from China began in 1978 when China, under the leadership of Deng Xiaoping, initiated a transition to a market-oriented economy. By then, the Chinese leadership also realized that China could not advance its economy without opening the door to the outside world. In 1978, a decision was made to initiate scholarly exchange with Western countries, especially the United States. As a result, by December 1978, about fifty Chinese students enrolled at several elite American universities.

Sending Chinese students abroad had more implications than the small number of the first group might suggest. It signaled an initial intention that China was ready to join the international community after thirty years of isolation. The "fever of going abroad" came first. It began in earnest on college campuses around the country and then spread into the rest of society. In 1981, China's Ministry of Education issued a "Circular Regarding Self-Supporting Students Going Abroad" that formally summarized the procedures for students who intended to go abroad. As a result, the number of students who went abroad dramatically increased. In 1983, only 1,000 students studied abroad. By 1986, the number soared to 100,000.

During this time, the Chinese government also modified its policies regarding emigration in general, especially for individuals who wanted to reunite with family members. In 1986, the **National People's Congress** of China passed a law on emigration of Chinese citizens. The law essentially stipulates that emigration is a basic right of Chinese citizens. Despite many practical difficulties and complexities in implementing this law, the law clearly sets forth a set of procedures. Furthermore, it was one of the first steps in allowing average Chinese citizens to travel abroad or to emigrate. This law is especially relevant in several Chinese provinces, such as Guangdong and Fujian, which have a long history of sending emigrants. There are roughly four categories of individuals who left China during the post-1978 period. The first category is contract labor. This is often arranged by the government at different levels (province or county level, for example). The typical contract labor is for construction and building roads in foreign countries. Most individuals who work as contract labor return after the expiration of their contract, but some decide to stay. The post-1978 emigration is also characterized by people who join their families/relatives abroad. Often these are people whose family members/relatives emigrated earlier, and the new Chinese emigration policy allows them to join their family members abroad. The third group of emigrants consists of people who went abroad as students or scholars. Although China has a long history of sending students abroad, the magnitude of post-1978 students/scholars who have gone abroad and the number of countries involved are unprecedented in Chinese history. From 1978 to 2002, more than 580,000 Chinese students/scholars went abroad to study and conduct research. Among them, 150,000 have returned to China. The fourth category of emigrants is clandestine immigrants. The two major provinces that send clandestine immigrants are Fujian and Zhejiang. The exact numbers are impossible to know, but some estimates put the number of Fujianese emigrants at 400,000 by 2003 and of emigrants from Zhejiang (mainly from the Wenzhou area) at more than 200,000.

Another feature of recent emigration from China is that the province of origin for emigrants has changed significantly over the years. For example, in the early 1980s, Beijing accounted for nearly 22 percent of China's emigrant population, a reflection of the fact that a large number of students who went abroad were living in Beijing before departure. The pattern changed dramatically by the mid-1990s. In 1995, emigrants from Fujian Province accounted for 28 percent of China's emigrant population. What also distinguishes Fujian from other immigrant-sending provinces in China is the fact that emigrants from Fujian are not as educated as emigrants from other provinces and are more likely to come from rural areas. This implies that most Fujianese immigrants are likely to be involved in low-level occupations in countries of destination. The most recent data from the 2000 Chinese census also reveal a sharp increase in emigrants from some border regions, including the provinces of Yunnan in the southwest and Jilin in the northeast. This is even more striking because in 1995, emigrants from Yunnan accounted for less than 1 percent of China's overall emigrant population. As the economic integration and globalization intensify, the border regions take on a particular significance, and their importance is likely to increase over time.

Because of its size and diversity, the post-1978 emigration from China has had a strong impact on both China and destination countries. The most important groups of emigrants in the post-1978 periods are former Chinese students who decided to remain in the host countries and clandestine migrants. Unlike the earlier wave of Chinese students who primarily concentrated in the science fields, there are significant numbers of the new wave of Chinese students who have received advanced degrees in social sciences and law and who now work in higher-education institutions and government agencies. These Chinese immigrants have an intimate knowledge of Chinese culture and institutions and are well poised to play a bridging role between China and the host societies. They have helped the host society understand China and have helped China understand other countries, and they will continue to do so in the years to come. From the perspective of the host society, they also help change the stereotype that the Chinese are only good in sciences. In the business field (especially high technology and financial services), as foreign investment continues to soar and an increasingly large number of international corporations operate in China, Chinese students who were trained in the West play an indispensable role in facilitating this process of economic integration. The current Chinese leadership is very farsighted in terms of not forcing Chinese students to return but encouraging them to contribute to their motherland in diverse ways. Overall, the role played by the former Chinese students and today's immigrants in the modernization and economic integration of China and in Sino-American relations (in the case of the United States) cannot be overstated.

The large number of clandestine migrants from China also has important implications for both China and host societies. Take the example of recent emigrants from Fujian Province. Most of the Fujianese migrants chose New York City as their destination. These Fujianese immigrants have made an enormous contribution to the revitalization of the Chinatown economy in New York City. Unlike earlier Chinese immigrants, the new Fujianese immigrants, backed by strong financial resources from business leaders, are more active in political participation. As a result, the Fukien [*sic*] American Association is a must stop for most political candidates in New York City. In addition, like earlier Chinese immigrants, the Fujianese immigrants send a large amount of remittances back to their home villages, which have been used in building the local infrastructure, schools, and service centers for the elderly, as well as providing new business opportunities.

See also Adoption, American Families and; Cold War and China; Sino-American Relations, Conflicts and Common Interests; Sino-American Relations since 1949; United States, Chinese Education in; United States, Chinese in.

Bibliography

Liang, Zai, "Demography of Illicit Emigration from China: A Sending Country's Perspective," *Sociological Forum* 16, no. 4 (2001): 677–701; Pan, Lynn, ed., *The Encyclopedia of the Chinese Overseas* (Cambridge, MA: Harvard University Press, 2000); Poston, Dudley L., Jr., Michael Xinxiang Mao, and Mei-Yu Yu, "The Global Distribution of the Overseas Chinese around 1990," *Population and Development Review* 20 (1994): 631–643.

Zai Liang

Internet

Compared with the West, China was a late starter in the development of the Internet. The first Chinese networking with the outside world occurred on September 20, 1987, when a message "Surmounting the Great Wall, walking toward the world" (*yueguo changcheng, zouxiang shijie*) was sent via the

Internet bars are popular with young Chinese. This bar charges 2 yuan per hour or 5 yuan for overnight gaming. Food and drink can also be purchased.

newly established China Academic Network (CANET). The ensuing years saw the planning and development of several networks with limited linkages to research institutes in Europe and the United States, including China Research Network (CRN) in 1990, College Network (CASNET) in 1992, and a direct link to Stanford University by the Institute of High-Energy Physics in 1993. The rapid development of networks appeared after 1995 with the completion and operation of several major "backbones," such as Chinese Education and Research Network (CERNET), Chinese Science and Technology Network (CSTNET), Chinese Telecommunication Network (CHINANET), and National Public Economic Information Network, otherwise known as Golden Bridge Network (GBNET). In 1996, these major networks, also called Internet access providers (IAPs), were the only designated nationwide "interconnecting units" with state permission to have direct linkage with the global computer network. The development of networks continued at a fast pace, and as of early 2003, China had nine IAPs, including two under construction with a bandwidth of 9,380 MB.

The increased demand for Internet services paced the development of the major networks. As a result, the number of Internet service providers (ISPs) increased rapidly. In 1996, there were only about thirty ISPs in China. As of early 2003, major ISPs in the hundreds were operating in the Chinese Internet market and were offering services ranging from e-mail, Web design, news, and business information to employment opportunities. Many Western Internet service providers such as Yahoo, AOL, and others have entered the Chinese market.

At the present time, the Chinese government treats the Internet in the same manner as it used to handle the traditional telecommunications infrastructure. Traditionally, media must be owned and controlled by the state, and no foreign investment is allowed. But almost from the very beginning, the Chinese government encouraged competition among different administrative units to break the monopoly over the Internet. For example, in the early 1990s, when the former Ministry of Posts and Telecommunications, which had always enjoyed a monopoly over Chinese telecommunications, began to prepare for building a national backbone network, the State Council, to encourage competition in the new information industry, approved the proposed Golden Bridge project, which would allow the creation of a second major national backbone consisting of several networks. As a result, the China Golden Bridge Network (GBNET), representing the interests of the former Ministry of Electronics Industry, was created. In the same spirit of competition, CERNET and CSTNET were launched.

These networking experiences were no more than sporadic communication on an experimental basis. In the early 1990s, the computer was seen more as a machine that could store information and less as a technology that would be able to transmit a large amount of data and shape the information flow of the global society. As the Internet began to manifest itself as a powerful and sometimes disruptive force in society, the government responded quickly by making laws and regulations on Internet communication. Since 1994, more than a dozen regulations or provisions on the security of computer information and computer networking have been issued in China. The State Council, the Central Propaganda Department, the Ministry of Public Security, the Ministry of

Information Industry, the Press and Publication Administration, and various other administrative agencies have all issued major laws, regulations, or provisions on the Internet, and their efforts have represented different phases of Internet regulation. In addition to the state effort, individual networks and service providers also make their own guidelines or policies to regulate communication on the Internet in conformity with the state mandates. In general, these laws or regulations spell out rules both for technical standards and for content areas for Internet communication. Whereas standards for technical aspects keep changing in these regulations, responding to the advancement of Internet technology, control of the content of information has been fairly consistent. For instance, the December 1997 Computer Information Networks and the Internet Security, Protection and Management Regulations promulgated by the Ministry of Public Security outlaw nine specific uses of the Internet, including "inciting to overthrow the government or the socialist system," "harming national unification," "destroying the order of society," and "injuring the reputation of state organs." These admonitions have been copied almost verbatim in subsequent regulations, even in the latest effort, jointly made in August 2002 by the Ministry of Information Industry and the Press and Publication Administration.

As part of these regulations, China has formed an Internet police force to check and track Internet communication. The Chinese government has demanded that all its networks at the IAP level build firewalls to block certain Web sites. Chinese domestic networks and ISPs have all been required to make strenuous efforts to filter out undesirable content. Despite a level of flexibility allowed in some prohibited areas such as pornography, information critical of the socialist system and the treatment of the Falun Gong religious sect is strictly prohibited. Western ISPs must comply with the Chinese government's regulations to be able to operate in China. There was an extended debate over the rights of several Western Internet providers, including Yahoo, when they opted to collaborate with the Chinese government by blocking blacklisted Web sites. Many search engines have exercised self-censorship by installing software that can filter out problematic materials. In December 2002, AltaVista was temporarily shut down, apparently by the Chinese government, as a punishment for its reluctance to comply with the state in censoring information.

Individuals who violate laws or policies are prosecuted. China has publicized several cases. One of the earliest cases involved a man named Lin Hai who allegedly provided more than 30,000 e-mail addresses to an overseas antigovernment magazine, which sent its materials to these accounts. Lin was sentenced to several years in prison. In recent years, there have been a number of arrests of people who distribute undesirable materials or set up Web sites to publish articles that campaign for democracy in China and challenge the Communist regime.

The Internet, a new form of communication technology, promises many democratic prospects. Authoritarian countries such as China face a dilemma when they use Internet technology. Can a regime like that in China contain the Internet's democratic potential while gaining economically? Many scholars believe that Internet communication will contribute to democratization in

China. The Internet's potential to undermine authoritarian rule lies not only in the scope and ease of obtaining information on the Web, as well as the communication capabilities available to users, but also in the decentralized nature of the Internet that complicates the task of state control of the medium. So far, Chinese experience with the Internet seems to affirm that view. Despite the fact that the Internet regulations have greatly curtailed freedom of speech in China, these regulations and associated punishments cannot be carried out easily and effectively. Internet communication indeed presents to Chinese society unfathomable potentials in its development of a public sphere for its pursuit of democracy.

See also Press Control; Press Freedom; Telecommunications Industry; Television; Television Institute and Self-Learning.

Bibliography

CNNIC, *Survey Report on Internet Development in China* (Beijing: CNNIC, January 11, 2003); *Regulations on the Security and Management of Computer Information Networks* (Beijing: The Public Security Bureau, December 11, 1997).

Changfu Chang

Islam

Islam was introduced into China in the seventh century. While cultural reciprocity enabled the religion to take root in the soil of China, Islam did not become a dominant religion of China, as Buddhism (also imported) did. Since 1949, the Chinese government has enforced many policies preferential to Muslims. At present, more than ten ethnic minorities of probably 20 million people are followers of Islam. Because the Muslim population is scattered all over China, it has been deeply engaged in Chinese political, religious, and social life.

One legendary story relates the introduction of Islam into China in an unusual way: in 628, Emperor Taizong of the Tang dynasty had a dream in which he met Mohammed and thus allowed Islam to be a Chinese religion. Many Chinese Muslims, however, assume that A.D. 651 was the first year for Islam to have entered China, since an Arab ambassador sent by the third caliph arrived in that year. It is said that the delegation was led by Waqqas, who was a maternal uncle of the Prophet Mohammed. Waqqas died in Guangzhou, and the famous "memorial mosque" (Huaishengsi) was built there to commemorate him.

During the Tang (618–907) and Song (960–1279) dynasties, Arab missions, Muslim merchants, and

Islam has a long history in China; shown here is a Chinese mosque.

Islamic missionaries came to China by land and by sea. The arrivals included Arabs, Persians, and central Asians. Their settlements were erected in Guangzhou, Quanzhou, Yangzhou, Hangzhou, Xi'an, and Kaifeng. They married Chinese women, adapted to the Chinese way of life, and gradually merged into Chinese society. During the Yuan dynasty (1279–1368), Mongolian control of the Eurasian continent gave central and West Asian Muslims a chance to migrate to China. In 1335, an edict of the Yuan emperor officially designated Islam as "the Pure and True Religion" (*Qingzhenjiao*). During the Ming dynasty (1368–1644), widespread intermarriage remolded these foreigners. Ming rulers were generous in appointing Muslims to important official positions. Zheng He, a Muslim eunuch, was assigned as the commander to lead the navigation to West Asia and East Africa. Hai Rui, a Muslim official, became known for his integrity at the royal court. Muslims adopted Chinese surnames of Ma, Mo, and Mu to symbolize Masoud, Mohammed, or Mústafa. However, they kept their religion, which prevented total assimilation.

During the Qing dynasty (1644–1911), Chinese Muslims encountered vicious persecution. The Muslims blame Manchu rulers for their discriminatory policies. However, other factors, such as heavy taxes, new sects, internal strife, and social instability, all led to the conflict. During the Qing dynasty, some emperors commanded troops in person to suppress Muslim rebellions.

The downfall of the Qing dynasty ushered the Muslims into a new epoch. Sun Yat-sen proposed that Chinese Muslims were one of the five great peoples. Sun's ultimate goal, however, was to assimilate the five peoples into one unified Chinese race. During the Republic era (1912–1949), the government recognized Islamic believers as an important religious group. Yet while those Muslims of Turkic, Mongolian, and Iranian origins were designated as ethnic minorities, the Hui, who constituted half of all Chinese Muslims, were seen, in Jiang Jieshi's (Chiang Kai-shek's) words, as "members of the Han clan who embraced Islam." In the following decades, the establishment of Islamic schools, the publication of Islamic literature, and the organization of Islamic societies contributed to the revival of the religion. It was during this period that Muslim warlords appeared in the northwest and southwest, notably Ma Bufang and Ma Hongkui in the northwest and Bai Chongxi in the southwest.

The improvement did not mean that all Muslims were at peace with the Chinese authorities. The Turkic-speaking Muslims of **Xinjiang** in the 1930s and 1940s sought to establish a separate Islamic state. From 1933 to 1934, the Turkic Muslims founded the East Turkestan Republic in Kashgar. This republic was not recognized by the international community and soon failed because of internal factionalism. In 1944, the Uygur in the Ili region established the Uygur East Turkestan Republic, which did not last very long. However, these episodes left a legacy upon present-day Xinjiang that inspires separatists to seek independence.

The establishment of the People's Republic of China by **Mao Zedong** in 1949 opened a new page of Islamic history in China. Mao assured the Muslims that their religious belief would be respected. The Hui were formally recognized as an independent ethnic minority. China created two provincial-level autonomous regions for Muslims in the 1950s: Xinjiang Uygur Autonomous Region and Ningxia Hui Autonomous Region. Many Muslim autonomous prefectures and counties were also established. The Chinese Islamic Association was set up in 1953 to run religious schools, train ahong (imams), and publish Islamic books. The government subsidized Muslims in various ways and allowed them special food companies to produce Qingzhen victuals, that is, Muslim food.

During the **Great Cultural Revolution (1966–1976)**, normal religious services were interrupted and mosques closed. The Red Guards, including those of Muslim background, damaged Islamic facilities. Mao's Little Red Book replaced the Koran, and the Mao Badge became a token for loyalty. Worship of a human being contradicted Islamic theology. Some radicals even called for the abolition of Islam: the Koran was burned, circumcision was prohibited, Islamic holidays were canceled, ahong were sent to work with peasants, and Muslim burial was changed to cremation. Some even forced Muslims to raise pigs and condemned Muslim peddlers as capitalists. This led to conflicts. One serious incident occurred in Shadian, Yunnan Province, an almost homogeneous Hui community. The radicals held meetings in Shadian to criticize ahong and burned their Koran. Later, they even forced some Muslims to eat pork, which provoked resistance. A series of military confrontations culminated in a massacre by troops supported by guns, artillery, and aircraft in July 1975. About 1,000 Muslims were killed and 4,400 houses destroyed. Though the Shadian incident was later officially rehabilitated, the scar it left still hurts local Muslims.

Deng Xiaoping's reform gave Islam a new chance to revive due to a number of favorable policies. Islamic schools were reopened and more were established to train ahong. The Arabic script that once was forbidden now is taught at mosques and religious schools. Muslims enjoy an exemption from the one-child policy, and their children are given privileges to attend ethnic schools and colleges. In areas where Islamic believers make up a majority, pig breeding is prohibited to respect Islamic customs. Muslims' marriages can be consecrated by ahong. Muslims are given the chance to observe their religious holidays and are permitted to maintain their own cemeteries. In the 1980s, Muslims were allowed to travel to Mecca for the hajj (pilgrimage). Since then, more than 40,000 Chinese Muslims have made the trip to the Saudi holy city. By 2003, 3,500 Koran schools were operating, and 45,000 Islamic clergymen were working in 35,000 mosques throughout China. Some Chinese Muslims are permitted to pursue Islamic education at universities in Egypt, Syria, Saudi Arabia, and other Middle Eastern countries. The government constantly invests money in a number of subsidy programs for Islamic believers.

State control of Islamic affairs is largely exercised through the Chinese Islamic Association and its 420 branch organizations. The association's purpose, according to its platform, is "to help the spread of the Koran, to nurture patriotism, to encourage cultural exchange with other Islamic states, and to oppose religious extremists." Hence its political duty is evident. Some famous Muslims, such as Bao Erhan, Da Pusheng, Ma Jian, and Shen Xiaxi, were leaders of the association. The current president, Chen Guangyuan (1932-), is a Chinese-trained imam ordained in 1958. Chen has made the pilgrimage to Mecca fourteen times and has visited many Islamic states. He has published books and articles on Islam. Chen always urges Muslims to be patriotic while holding fast to their beliefs. He lists Muslims' political duties as follows: to support the unity of the motherland, to uphold the consolidation of ethnic unity, and to contribute to the maintenance of social stability. Since September 11, 2001, Chen has consistently condemned terrorism, opposed the use of the Koran for extreme activities, and cried out for the purity of Islam. However, in March 2003, Chen denounced the U.S. military invasion of Iraq and called for a peaceful settlement.

In the past decades, more citizens of Muslim background have become prominent in Chinese society. Hui Liangyu (1944–   ) is currently a vice premier of China. Simayi Aimaiti (1935–   ) is currently a vice president of the Chinese People's Political Consultative Conference. Many others have filled positions in the government. Bai Shouyi (1909–2000), a native of the Kaifeng Islamic community, published a large number of books and articles on Islamic history and was a nationally known historian. Ma Sanli (1914–   ) enjoys popularity as a comic dialogue artist. Li Delun (1917–2001) was a famous conductor of the National Orchestra for decades. Mu Qing (1921–2003), a son of an ahong family, became the head of Xinhua News Agency. Da Shichang (1940–   ), a graduate of an Islamic middle school, became a movie star. Uygur singer Kelimu (1940–   ) enjoys popularity among the Chinese for his ethnic songs.

Among the ten Muslim ethnic groups, six are of Turkic origin (their populations are provided according to the 1990 statistics): Uygur (7,214,431), Kazakh (1,111,718), Kirghiz (141,549), Uzbek (14,502), Tatar (4,873), and Salar (87,697); two are of Mongol origin: Dongxiang (373,872), and Bao'an (12,212); and one is of Iranian origin: Tajik (33,538). The last and largest is of Chinese origin: the Hui (8,602,978). Although widely recognized as of Chinese origin, some Hui, motivated by religious zeal, always highlight their remote ancient roots. Some Hui simply declare that they are the descendants of Arab and Persian immigrants. Early in 1958, a Muslim claimed that China is not the fatherland of the Hui nationality and. . . . Arabic is the language of the Hui people. In recent years, the emphasis on Arab and Persian origins has become even stronger. Hui writer Zhang Chengzhi (1948–   ) has written novels and essays to interpret the issue. According to Zhang, eight million Hui are all descendants of those Mohammedans who entered China from West Asia, North Africa and Central Asia and that the Hui settled in every corner of China, intermarried with locals and gradually became indistinguishable from other Chinese. Zhang argues that the Hui experienced three losses: the first was the loss of their fatherland, the second was the loss of their mother tongues, and the worst is the third: the loss of belief. Zhang laments that many Hui have turned out to be a social group that just avoids eating pork. Defying being criticized as a fundamentalist, Zhang investigates the Manchu persecution and compares it to the Jewish suffering in Europe. Zhang asserts that, for his own purposes, God has chosen the Jews in Europe; yet he chose the Hui in China. Zhang asserts that blood is the seed of religion, implying that Muslims' belief was strengthened after each bloody suppression.

In recent decades, the Chinese government has tended to be lenient to Muslims. The "Chinese Rushdie" case verifies this. Soon after the 1989 publication of *Xing Fengsu* (Sexual customs) by Ke Le and Sang Ya, Muslims in Beijing and other cities burst into protests. The reason for them was that the authors strangely interpreted Islamic culture. The book compares Islamic minarets to phallic symbols and further contends that the Islamic pilgrimage to Mecca was only a special occasion for homosexual contact and an exceptional chance for sodomy with camels. On May 12, 1989, more than 3,000 Muslim students from major colleges in Beijing initiated the protest. They shouted, "Down with China's Salman Rushdie" and "Oppose blasphemy against Islam." The authors apologized, but the case was not resolved until the authors were arrested and 13 million copies of the book were confiscated and burned. The government handling of the students' democracy movement in the next month with a harsh military crackdown showed a striking difference from its tolerant treatment of Muslim demonstrators.

However, the government shows no mercy to Muslim terrorists. Indeed, since the fall of the Soviet Union and the reemergence of central Asian Islamic states, some separatists in Xinjiang have resorted to terrorism to attain their political goals. Before 2001, about a thousand Uygurs, according to the government, were trained by Osama Bin Laden in Afghanistan, and some were sent back to China. As a result of the violence, hundreds were killed or wounded in Xinjiang in about a decade. The government arrested many and executed some, but this movement still poses a headache. The officials identify three evils in Xinjiang: "ethnic separatism is their goal, religious extremism is their garb, and [violent] terrorism is their means." To suppress them, the government even plays the international card: to persuade central Asian states and Pakistan to cooperate. In 2001, several central Asian states pledged to help China suppress those terrorists who tried to use central Asia as their base. On December 23, 2001, Pakistani president Pervez Musharraf, during his visit to China, urged Chinese Muslims to be "very patriotic" and work for the betterment of their country. He also promised that "Pakistan will make full efforts to support China to fight against East Turkestan terrorist forces."

Islam has existed in China for about thirteen centuries and has exerted a significant impact on the shaping of Chinese civilization. It has always been an influential religion in China, though not a dominant belief system. The Chinese endorsement has enabled the religion to flourish; however, occasional religious conflicts made its believers sufferers. Today, Chinese Muslims are mostly Sunni and scattered all over the country. Compared with other Islamic nations, China is always ranked as one of the biggest Islamic countries. In fact, besides Egypt, no other single Arab country has such a huge number of Islamic followers as China does. This sizable population and its dispersal all over Chinese territory will continue to assure that Muslims play an important role in Chinese social, religious, and political life.

See also Confucian Tradition and Christianity; Deng Xiaoping (1904–1997), Reforms of; Jews; Religion and Freedom of Religious Belief; Spiritual Life in the Post-Mao Era.

Bibliography

Bai Shouyi, *Zhongguo Huijiao Xiaoshi* (A brief history of Islam in China) (Yinchuan: Ningxia Renmin Chubanshe, 2000); Fu Tongxian, *Zhongguo Huijiao Shi* (A history of

Islam in China) (Taipei: Taiwan Shangwu Yinshuguan, 1969); Lipman, Jonathan N., *Familiar Strangers: A History of Muslims in Northwest China* (Seattle: University of Washington Press, 1997); Zhang Chengzhi, *Xinling Shi* (A history of the soul) (Guangzhou: Guangdong Huacheng Chubanshe, 1991).

Patrick Fuliang Shan

J

Japan

See Sino-Japanese Relations since 1949.

Jews

Jews have migrated by land and by sea to China since ancient times. Historically, there were two groups of Jews in China. The first were Chinese Jews who came to China over centuries and lived in many parts of the country; by the modern era, however, most of them were absorbed into the larger Chinese population. The second were Jews from the West in the late nineteenth century and the first half of the twentieth century who were fleeing religious and political persecution in Europe and came to China, but most of them departed for other countries after World War II. In recent years, foreign Jews have returned to China and are allowed to practice Judaism there.

The evidence to prove the earliest Jewish existence in China is a Hebrew document written during the Tang dynasty (618–907), though Jews might have come earlier. They settled in Beijing, Dunhuang, Guangzhou, Hangzhou, Kaifeng, Luoyang, Nanjing, Ningpo, Quanzhou, Xi'an, Yangzhou, Yinchuan, and other **cities.** Interaction and intermarriage with the Chinese made many of them totally assimilated, leaving few traces. However, the Kaifeng Jewish community was an exception.

Jews migrated to Kaifeng via the Silk Road during the Song dynasty (960–1279). They presented tribute to a Chinese emperor who in turn granted them land on which to reside and to establish a synagogue. The royal court also bestowed popular Chinese surnames on each Jewish clan; one of them was Zhao, then the royal family name. The synagogue established in Kaifeng was one of the largest Judaic temples in the world. Kaifeng Jews held regular religious services, consolidated an ethnic group, and retained an extraordinary culture. Their population, according to scholarly estimates, varied from hundreds to thousands and even to ten thousands at different times.

Some Kaifeng Jews participated in the examination system and even became Jinshi degree holders, which was the highest degree awarded by the palace. Historical documents show that Kaifeng Jews were appointed as county governors or other high-ranking administrators. Their participation in the examination for a political career itself was a way of cultural assimilation, since a degree holder was more a Confucian than a Jew. Though most Jews were assimilated into Han Chinese, some became Chinese Muslims. Despite gradual assimilation, the fact that the Kaifeng synagogue has been standing for about 800 years is an amazing page in both Chinese history and Jewish annals.

Jewish lineal descendants of Kaifeng Jews, totally no more than 200 in the city today (less than 1,000 in the whole of China), still endeavor to maintain Jewish traditions. Their tenacity at retaining an ethnic identity, their stubborn resistance to other religions, and their practice of residual Judaic customs reflect their zeal for being an officially recognized ethnic minority. All the major original Jewish clans of Kaifeng, the Zhao, Li (Levi), Ai, Zhang, Gao, Jin, and Shi, have their lineal descendants. Their residual practices include avoiding eating pork, smearing blood on doors during festivals, plucking the sinews from beef before cooking, observing the Passover, and safeguarding ancestors' tombs. Many still stick to the Ten Commandments. Scholar Zhang Sui (a non-Jew) sees these practices as signs of an awakening ethnic consciousness, a proud sense of a distinctive ethnicity. Yet this may also be motivated, as Zhang notices, by an effort to obtain preferential governmental policies, such as ethnic subsidies, career promotion, educational benefits, and exemption from the one-child-per-family plan. Jewish descendants now are engaged in various occupations, from governmental officials, scholars, and workers to soldiers. In the past, they underwent vicissitudes of turbulent China: some Jewish descendants were labeled as rightists, and others suffered from the persecution of the **Great Cultural Revolution**.

Chinese Jews have been a focus for historians, anthropologists, and religious scholars. In past decades, Chinese scholars published many articles and books on the topic. Currently, they are debating if the government should grant these descendants an ethnic-minority status. Some argue that this should be done because the Jews lived in Kaifeng for almost a millennium and maintained their traditions well. Some emphasize that New China has long recognized Jews as an ethnic group because two Kaifeng Jews (Shi Fengying and Ai Fengming) were invited in 1952 as ethnic representatives to attend the National Day celebration in Beijing. Some contend that these descendants have a right to call themselves Jews. However, official recognition has been delayed due to a political consideration that the move might annoy the Arab world, with which China has maintained a particular tie. Some argue that the Jews should not be recognized as an ethnic minority since their population is small, but this is rebutted with a justification that other officially recognized ethnic minorities such as the Hezhe and the Eluosi (Russian) are also tiny. Optimistic scholars expect that Chinese Jews will soon be added as the fifty-seventh ethnic group in China. Jewish descendants, however, care more for their heritage than the official status; as Kaifeng descendant Zhang Xingwang stated, "we are patriotic

Chinese. However, in our heart, we also claim ourselves as Jewish. It is impossible for me to relinquish this legacy; neither will my son do it."

Western Jews (including those from the British Empire) in Shanghai and other Chinese cities were a particular phenomenon of modern China. During the late Qing dynasty, the Jews arrived for business, and some amassed great fortunes in Shanghai, notably the Sassoons, the Hardoons, and the Kaddories. Later, Jewish refugees flooded in, including those who fled pogroms and the subsequent Russian Revolution in 1917. Some went to Shanghai, but others settled in Harbin, Dalian, Tianjin, and Beijing. They lived in special residential areas, ran businesses in commercial quarters, organized financial groups, opened schools, published newspapers, built synagogues, ran hospitals, set up radio stations, and even owned private cemeteries. Although a small number of Jews were successful, most Jews were small shopkeepers or members of the working class. They got along well with other nationals. Yet the relations between the Jews and Germans in China suddenly deteriorated after Adolf Hitler came to power in Germany.

The Nazi persecution forced many European Jews to seek refuge in China. Chinese consul-general He Fengshan (Feng-shan Ho) in Vienna issued about 2,000 to 4,000 visas to Austrian Jews from 1938 to 1940. For this reason, He Fengshan was awarded a posthumous title of Righteous among the Nations by the State of Israel in 2001, a title given to those who saved Jewish lives during the Holocaust. The Japanese also allowed Jews to enter their occupied regions of China. However, more Jews simply walked in without a visa. Many went to Shanghai. From 1933 to 1941, Shanghai absorbed about 30,000 Jews from European countries. Some of these left for a third country, but by the end of 1941, about 25,000 Jews still stayed in Shanghai. This number was far more than the total number of Jewish refugees accepted by Canada, Australia, India, South Africa, and New Zealand.

Quite a few Jewish refugees took part in the Chinese revolution. Hans Müller (1915–1994) joined the Eighth Route Army and was a vice president of a Beijing medical school after 1949. Heinz Shippe (1897–1941) joined the New Fourth Army and sacrificed his life on the battlefield in Shandong against the Japanese army. Jakob Rosenfeld (1903–1952) was head of a medical unit within a Communist-led army during the war. These men are still eulogized as heroes in mainland China.

After Pearl Harbor, the Japanese began to assume an anti-Semitic stance. From 1942 to 1943, Colonel Josef Meisinger, the chief of the Gestapo in the Far East, repeatedly requested that the Japanese act against the Jews. Meisinger frequently went to Shanghai to press for the Final Solution. Under this pressure, Japan proclaimed Shanghai Jews stateless refugees and established the Designated Area for Stateless Refugees (ghetto) in the Hongkou District to confine them. The Jews had to get temporary permits to leave during the daytime for jobs outside the ghetto. In 1943, the Japanese established a Stateless Refugees Affairs Bureau and enforced the Baojia system to monitor the Jews. The Baojia system was an ancient neighborhood system in which neighbors policed one another. Anyone who violated the rule was punished, and some were even arrested. Within the one-square-mile ghetto, malnutrition and diseases were widespread. Abusive incidents by the Japanese occurred quite often. Living conditions deteriorated. Yet Shanghai Jews were still grateful to the city and the Chinese people and saw Shanghai as a haven to escape the Holocaust. A former Shanghai Jewish refugee, Eric Goldstaub, stated fifty years later that Jews are grateful to their Chinese friends who helped them survive the most horrible time during World War II (Goldstein, 2000).

After the war, most Shanghai Jews emigrated to Israel, the United States, Canada, on Australia. Some became well-known figures, such as Michael Blumenthal, who was secretary of the Treasury for the Carter administration. Some became officials in Israel. By 1958, no more than 300 foreign Jews still stayed in China. Some of them chose to be naturalized. Some became famous literati of the New China: Israel Epstein has been the general editor for the English journal *China Reconstruction*; Sidney Shapiro, a literary critic; Sam Ginzburg, a professor of English and Russian at Shangdong University; David Crook, a well-known editor of the English language for a number of major reference books; and Ye Hua, who was a German Jew and married the Chinese poet Xiao Shan, a literature scholar. In the 1990s, among the ten members of foreign origin of the Chinese People's Political Consultative Conference, five were of Jewish background.

Ever since Deng Xiaoping opened the Chinese door, foreign Jews have returned to Shanghai to work or run businesses. Most of them are professionals; some are descendants of Shanghai Jewish refugees. Their total population is no more than several hundred, but they endeavor to renovate the old synagogues built decades ago. The renovation has attracted international attention. Hillary Clinton paid a visit to the Ohel Rachel Synagogue of Shanghai in 1998. She was accompanied by Madeleine Albright, then the secretary of state. Clinton praised China for having permitted the restoration of the Jewish church as a "very good example of respect for religious difference." Albright, who is of Jewish origin, cautiously told the Chinese that America's interest in religions and religious freedom does not grow out of some desire to interfere in Chinese affairs or to favor one religion over others . . . rather it comes from their belief and experience that spiritual values are not Western or Eastern, capitalist or socialist, but deeply human.

Ever since the 1980s and especially since China and Israel established diplomatic relations in 1992, "the Jewish fervor" (*Youtai re*) has emerged in China. Both Kaifeng Jews and Shanghai Jews have been important topics in Chinese academia. Jewish study centers have been established in many universities. Many Chinese ardently study Jewish culture, history, and diasporas. In 2002, Nanjing University opened a Hebrew class and invited some Chinese Jewish descendants to learn Hebrew and study Jewish culture. An international symposium on the history of the Jewish diaspora in China was held in Kaifeng and Nanjing in May 2002 for stimulating interest in acquiring knowledge of this distinctive page of Chinese history. Many scholars specifically devote their research to Kaifeng Jews and see them as useful in fostering friendship between China and Jewry. Some scholars reason that Jewish assimilation in China itself symbolizes an affinity between the Chinese people and the Jewish people. The Jewish experience in Shanghai especially arouses good feelings among Jewry toward China and is seen as a bridge that links China and Israel. Without any doubt, the Jews in China, whether Kaifeng Jews or Shanghai Jews, will be an ongoing interest to attract writers as well as audiences.

See also Confucian Tradition and Christianity; Deng Xiaoping (1904–1997), Reforms of; Islam; Religion and Freedom of Religious Belief; Spiritual Life in the Post-Mao Era.

Bibliography

Goldstein, Jonathan, ed., *The Jews of China*, 2 vols. (Armonk, NY: M. E. Sharpe, 2000); Pan, Guandan, *Zhongguo jingnei Youtairen de ruogan lishi wenti* (Some historical issues concerning the Jews in China) (Beijing: Beijing Daxue Chubanshe [Beijing University Press], 1983); Pan, Guang, *Youtairen zai Zhongguo: The Jews in China* (Beijing: Wuzhou Chuanbo Chubanshe [China Intercontinental Press], 2001); Shapiro, Sidney, ed., *Jews in Old China: Studies by Chinese Scholars* (New York: Hippocrene Books, 2001); Xu, Xin, *The Jews of Kaifeng, China: History, Culture and Religion* (Jersey City, NJ: KTAV Publishing House, 2003); Xu, *Legends of the Chinese Jews of Kaifeng* (Hoboken, NJ: KTAV Publishing House, 1995); Zhang, Sui, *Youtaijiao yu Zhongguo Youtairen* (Judaism and Chinese Jews) (Shanghai: Sanlian Shudian [Sanlian Books Shanghai Branch], 1991); Zhang, Xingwang, "The Current Situation of Chinese Jews," Travel.eastday.com, http://travel.eastday.com/epublish/gb/paper262/1/class026200001/hwz897637.htm, accessed on November 22, 2004.

Patrick Fuliang Shan

Jiang Zemin (1926–), Diplomacy of

As the core of Chinese third-generation leaders, Jiang Zemin upheld and developed Deng Xiaoping's **independent foreign policy** and **Open Door policy**. Jiang became the general secretary of the Chinese Communist Party (CCP) and chairman of the Central Military Commission in 1989. In 1993, Jiang was elected president of China by the **National People's Congress**. In addition to upholding Deng's policy of opening and reform, Jiang strongly promoted Chinese foreign policy. Jiang has traveled to more foreign countries and built closer personal relations with foreign leaders than any previous top leader of China. Jiang's success in diplomacy both reflected China's growing status in the world of nations and his statesmanship.

From 1989 to 1991, major changes took place in the international system. They included the unification of Germany, the abandonment of socialism by the former Eastern European satellites of the Soviet Union and their opting for independence, and the disintegration of the Soviet Union. These developments and the impressive victory of the coalition led by the United States in the first Gulf War seemed to indicate that the United States had become the sole superpower in the world. The breakup of the Soviet Union meant that China could no longer exploit the differences between the two superpowers and play one off against the other. At this critical juncture, Deng Xiaoping advised Chinese leaders to watch and analyze the developments calmly, keep a low profile, go beyond ideological considerations, and try to avoid controversy. In Deng's view, the key to success was to develop China's economy.

In striving for a peaceful international environment to realize China's modernization program, Jiang Zemin and other Chinese leaders continued to pursue the independent foreign policy initiated by Deng Xiaoping in 1982. Following the Tiananmen crisis in 1989, the Chinese leaders declared that the policies of reform and opening to the outside world "will continue to be stead-fastly carried out as before" and that China "will never go back to the old closed-door path" (*Beijing Review*, July 3, 1989). It was reaffirmed that China's independent foreign policy of peace would not change, and China would con-tinue to develop friendly relations with other countries. After a decade of close economic ties with the West, the Chinese leadership appreciated foreign in-vestors' contribution to China's modernization.

Jiang Zemin took a series of actions to improve relations with China's neigh-bors and soon was able to break diplomatic isolation. By 1992–1993, Chinese leaders had already become more relaxed on both the domestic and the inter-national front, and China's foreign relations were back in full swing. Jiang reaf-firmed Deng's foreign policy line of avoiding the limelight and keeping a low profile while concentrating on China's own affairs. The basic rationale for this continuity in Chinese foreign policy has been China's demand for a peaceful international environment to concentrate on economic development, because Jiang appreciates that the legitimacy of the Chinese government depends on its ability to improve people's living standards. Along with modernization, na-tionalism has also become a key factor in Chinese foreign policy.

Another aspect of Chinese foreign policy is regionalism. This concept em-phasizes that China has remained a regional power, concentrating its political, economic, and military activities primarily in the Asia-Pacific region. The con-cept also refers to China's effort to participate actively in regional institutions such as Asian-Pacific Economic Cooperation and the Asian Development Bank. China has built close ties to the Association of Southeast Asian Nations.

Chinese leaders are in favor of a multipolar rather than a unipolar world. Jiang established strong ties with Russian presidents Boris Yeltsin and Vladimir Putin. They all advocated a strong strategic partnership between China and Russia. However, the partnership is different from an alliance. Jiang also paid special attention to building close relations with Japan. In dealing with the Japanese, Jiang has always emphasized that both countries should not forget the history of Japanese invasion of China before 1945. But Jiang also appreci-ates Japan as China's most important Asian partner. As an indication of the new flexibility of Chinese diplomacy, China established close and increasing ties with South Korea in the 1990s.

In addition to stressing friendly relations with China's neighbors, Jiang paid special attention to improving relations with the United States. After years of hard work, Sino-American relations were significantly improved. The 1995–1996 crises in the Taiwan Strait taught Beijing and Washington a lesson. Brinkmanship must be avoided, and their cordial relations are essential to stability and pros-perity in the Asia-Pacific region. Jiang's high-level exchanges with U.S. officials have given him a chance to shine on the international stage and indulge his in-terest in American culture and technology. During a visit to the United States in 1997, Jiang gave a speech at Harvard University, played host at a banquet for corporate executives, and even rang the opening bell at the New York Stock Exchange. In June 1998, Jiang took the unprecedented step of holding a live televised debate with U.S. president Bill Clinton in Beijing. Jiang and Clinton talked about building a constructive strategic partnership between China and the United States.

After the September 11 terrorist attack on the United States, President Jiang immediately ordered the Chinese government to issue solemn condolences to the American people and to fully cooperate with the U.S. government's efforts to track down the perpetrators. Jiang activated the hot line to the White House to personally convey condolences to President George W. Bush. China's support of the American war on al-Qaeda and global terrorism has contributed to stability and improvement in Sino-American relations. On the issue of Iraq, China is in favor of supporting a UN resolution for complete disarmament of weapons of mass destruction, but like France and Russia, China is in favor of using UN inspections rather than force. On the North Korean nuclear crisis, Jiang preferred to conduct quiet diplomacy and encouraged a direct dialogue between North Korea and the United States.

Jiang has always been keen on modernizing the Chinese economy. At the Fifteenth Communist Party Congress in 1997, he unveiled a sweeping plan to privatize China's massive and unprofitable **state-owned enterprises**. In order to further integrate China into the global economy, Jiang strongly promoted Chinese membership in the World Trade Organization (WTO). After many years of tough negotiation, China finally joined the WTO in December 2001. This is a great achievement of China's economic reform and Jiang's diplomacy. China's entry into the WTO has profound implications for China and the global community.

In July 2001, in a decision that proved to have domestic and global implications for China, Beijing was selected as the host city for the 2008 Summer Olympics. The Olympics bring a great deal of international prestige and an unparalleled opportunity to showcase Beijing and China to a captive audience around the world. The fact that Beijing failed in its former bid for the 2000 Olympics but won the 2008 bid is an indication of progress in both Beijing's image and Chinese diplomacy.

Jiang presided over the return of Hong Kong to China in 1997 and the return of Macao to China in 1999. He consistently supported the policy of **one country, two systems**, which allows both Hong Kong and Macao to maintain a high degree of autonomy. On the issue of Taiwan, Jiang continued to advocate peaceful unification, but he also made it clear that Beijing would adopt resolute measures if Taiwan were to declare independence.

Chinese foreign policy is becoming less and less a personal arena and one driven increasingly by the interests of the state as a whole. In November 2002, Jiang stepped down as general secretary of the CCP but was reelected as the chairman of the Central Military Commission. In March 2003, Hu Jintao was elected as the new president of China. Jiang retired from the position of chairman of the Central Military Commission in September 2004. He is remembered as a great statesman who made outstanding contributions to China's diplomacy and reform.

See also Deng Xiaoping (1904–1997), Politics of; Deng Xiaoping (1904–1997), Reforms of; Jiang Zemin (1926–), Populism of; Sino-American Relations since 1949; Sino-Japanese Relations since 1949; Sino-Russian Relations since 1991.

Bibliography

Hu, Xiaobo, and Gang Lin, *Transition towards Post-Deng China* (Singapore: National University Press of Singapore, 2001); Lam, Willy Wo-Lap, *The Era of Jiang Zemin* (Singapore: Prentice Hall, 1999); Tien, Hung-mao, and Yun-han Chu. *China under Jiang Zemin* (Boulder, CO: Lynne Rienner, 2000); Zhao, Quansheng, *Interpreting Chinese Foreign Policy* (New York: Oxford University Press, 1996).

Guoli Liu

Jiang Zemin (1926–   ), Populism of

If **Mao Zedong** is remembered as the founder of the People's Republic of China (PRC) as well as the source of wave after wave of nerve-wracking political campaigns, and if Deng Xiaoping is remembered for deprogramming Mao's system and successfully turning China to economic prosperity, then Jiang Zemin is remembered for turning the avant-garde of the working class, the Chinese Communist Party (CCP), into a populist party. While Jiang Zemin remains low profile in the hall of fame, his role in China's transition is one of deep impact. Thanks to Jiang's pushing hands, a vibrant "socialist market economy," or Chinese-style capitalism, is in full swing.

Maintaining stability, staying the course of Deng Xiaoping, and achieving fast economic growth are among the major accomplishments of Jiang Zemin, who was chairman of the CCP for thirteen years and the president of the PRC for ten years. Jiang's theory, known as "the Three Representations," is applauded as a breakthrough in modern Chinese communism.

Jiang Zemin's political career was one of rapid ascension in the 1990s. In March 1993, Jiang was elected president of the PRC and chairman of the Central Military Commission. Five years later, in March 1998, he was reelected president of the PRC. He was also twice elected chairman of the CCP, in 1992 and 1997. On March 15, 2003, Jiang Zemin finished serving his second term as chairman and president, but was reelected chairman of the Central Military Commission of the PRC. In September 2004, Jiang Zemin retired from his last position. The newly elected president, Hu Jintao, succeeded him in all governmental and party functions.

While Jiang may have blasted his way to the top within a decade, he had actually started from the grassroots level earlier. Born on August 17, 1926, into a literati family in Yangzhou, a culturally famous city in eastern China's Jiangsu Province, Jiang received a good education. Both his grandfather and father were noted local scholars. He received higher education at the prestigious Shanghai Jiaotong University, where he majored in electrical engineering.

During his college years, Jiang participated in the CCP-led student movements and joined the CCP in 1946. After the founding of the PRC, Jiang worked his way up the ladder. He started as an associate engineer in the 1950s. In 1955, he went to the Soviet Union and worked in the Stalin Automobile Works as a trainee for one year. After returning, he served as deputy division head, deputy chief power engineer, director of a branch factory, and director of factories and research institutes in Changchun, Shanghai, and Wuhan. In the ensuing years, Jiang served as director of the foreign affairs department of the

No. 1 Ministry of Machine-Building Industry. Jiang speaks English, Russian, and Romanian well and has limited reading knowledge in Japanese and French. Before he became mayor of Shanghai in 1985, Jiang had accumulated much management experience through his service as the minister of the Ministry of the Electronics Industry. The mayor's position was the turning point in his life. During the 1989 Tiananmen demonstrations, Jiang was able to maintain peace in Shanghai, which won Deng Xiaoping's appreciation. With almost no delay, Jiang was summoned to the central government to face greater challenges.

Jiang Zemin's theory represents a significant development along the line of Deng Xiaoping's reformist ideology. On the one hand, Jiang remains a loyal guardian of the **Four Cardinal Principles**; on the other hand, he expanded the Party's representation to a level unseen before. Clearly, Jiang's system reflected a sharpened picture of the classic dilemma of a market economy under the CCP's control.

If the CCP is to remain the helmsman of the market economy, the most important thing to do to qualify for this role of leadership, without doubt, is to maintain an open mind. The "Three Representations" offer a more liberal guidance to the CCP's leadership, compared with Deng Xiaoping's admonition of strictly observing the Four Cardinal Principles. The system includes representing (1) the development trend of China's advanced productive forces, (2) the orientation of China's advanced culture, and (3) the fundamental interests of the overwhelming majority of the people.

The term "advanced productive forces" used to refer primarily to the proletariat or factory workers. Because science and technology are the primary productive forces and represent a hallmark of advanced productive forces today, Jiang's system includes **intellectuals** as an essential part of the "advanced productive forces." With respect to the composition of the working class, the classic line that separates the working class from the "other laboring people" is erased. The purity of the "working class" is no longer maintainable, because "some workers have changed their jobs" and have become materially affluent. Jiang insists, however, that this has not changed the status of the Chinese working class.

"China's advanced culture" may be the hardest concept to define. While stressing the importance of adhering to the Communist cardinal principles, Jiang encourages the development of a healthy, progressive, rich, and colorful socialist culture with Chinese styles and characteristics. He calls upon the nation to continue to uphold lofty ideals, moral integrity, better education, and a good sense of discipline, all of which are copied from Mao's revolutionary theory. To these, however, Jiang added such elements as self-reliance, competition, efficiency, democracy, and the rule of law, as well as a pioneering and innovative spirit to create a new paradigm that meets the demands of the new economy. Here, following the classic pattern, the definition from the positive angle is coupled with its counterpart. Jiang urged cleaning up the old decadent and dying culture, including such elements as superstition, ignorance, and vulgarity. Warnings against material gains and money remain an essential component.

Representing the fundamental interests of the "overwhelming majority" of the people is a new kind of task that Jiang assigned to the CCP for the new era. The theory of broadening representation is obviously the hallmark of Jiang's theory. Instead of representing the working class and the laboring people in exercising the proletarian dictatorship, often in detriment to other social strata, the Party will work for the well-being of all people. To achieve this goal, Jiang made a further step to revise the Party membership requirement. The new membership is now based on whether a person works wholeheartedly for the cause of the country, and this factor alone replaces other backgrounds. Because Marxism must adapt to China's new economic and social reality, Jiang indicated that it is not advisable to judge a person's political integrity simply on the basis of whether one owns property and how much property he or she owns. Clearly, if private property ownership is no longer an adverse factor in the definition of Communist revolution, then the nature of communism has to be redefined. The Sixteenth CCP Congress held in 2003 has practically amended the Party's constitution in this way with respect to its membership. Jiang's theory represents a breakthrough in the redefinition process.

While Jiang Zemin's theory has been promoted far and wide, it has not always been without resistance. In particular, after Jiang retreated to the background, his representations were questioned. Jiang is viewed by many as forgetting the interests of the pillars of the socialist revolution: workers, peasants, and soldiers. There are criticisms that Jiang, as much as he claims to represent the entire people, takes care more of the knowledge and entrepreneurial classes. The pressure keeps building because China's economy has slown down since the late 1990s, and millions of workers have been laid off, not to mention that the entire peasantry still has no health insurance.

China's reality's forcing the next generation of leaders, President Hu Jintao and Premier Wen Jiabao, to gear the government focus to improving social welfare and rural economy. It is obvious that without ramping up the rural economy, the sustainability of the state of "relative affluence" will be questionable, to say nothing of further development. From these perspectives, one may conclude that Jiang Zemin's populist tendency has fostered a new style for the Party, but needs to be fine-tuned. One thing is certain: after Jiang Zemin, the CCP is no longer the Party of Mao Zedong. One would easily accept, given the facts of life, that the name does not always have to reflect the essence.

See also Deng Xiaoping (1904–1997), Politics of; Deng Xiaoping (1904–1997), Reforms of; Jiang Zemin (1926–   ), Diplomacy of; Sino-American Relations since 1949; Sino-Japanese Relations since 1949; Sino-Russian Relations since 1991.

Bibliography

Deng, Xiaoping, *Selected Works of Deng Xiaoping* (Beijing: People's Publishing House, 1993); "Life Story of Jiang Zemin," *People's Daily,* http://english.peopledaily.com.cn/leaders/jzm/jzmhome.htm, accessed on November 21, 2004.

Jing Luo

Journalism Reform

The face and soul of Chinese journalism are transforming rapidly. As part of the larger government experiment and recipe to build socialism with Chinese characteristics prescribed by the late Chinese leader Deng Xiaoping more than two decades ago, the sweeping reform includes upgrading the media "hardware" and reforming the journalism "software." The Chinese government seems to be more, at times even exclusively, interested in "hardware" upgrade, which includes but is not limited to the nation's broadcasting system, telephone system, the postal service, the **Internet**, satellites, and other telecommunication and media hardware upgrades and technological advances. However, it would be mistaken to conclude that the Chinese government is not interested in changing the soul or the operating philosophy of Chinese journalism. Although the priority of the government remains to be able to control the media, it also wants a control different from the past to keep up with the changing times and public. The government's guiding principle in journalism reform seems to be balancing the need for continuous political controls with making the public and journalists feel comfortable with this control.

Changes in China's mass media are among the causes as well as the results of the liberalization of Chinese society. While the Chinese government is often singled out for its heavy-handed approach in high-profile media censorship cases, it should also be recognized for the sweeping social changes that have taken place across China, including changes in its media and information industry, although some changes are not exactly as originally envisioned or intended.

The Chinese leadership and government promote vigorously a market-oriented economy the public desires. This market economy has produced new challenges and dilemmas for the state and its media. Media reform vital to the Chinese economy has been discussed publicly as well as privately in the top hierarchy of China's decision-making body. While the Chinese police control Internet cafés and screen for dissident opinions, other branches of the government are even busier wiring and networking the nation and formulating ways to reform Chinese journalism under the current political environment. While tightening control and suppressing sensitive information flow continue, the state has eased restrictions on certain information when it has been pressured internationally. The government is paying increasing attention to public perception and opinion, as well as political pressure from both domestic and international fronts.

Chinese journalists, taking advantage of the changed and changing society, constantly push for greater freedom of information and speech. The government is well aware of this pressure and tries to formulate strategies to compromise within certain political bottom lines. As a result, the Chinese media change rapidly and dramatically due to the changing mind-sets that run the Chinese media. The government is shifting its ideologically controlling role toward one of administrative function to manage the media.

The state plays an active role in incorporating market-based media reforms and practices into the existing media structure. These reforms introduce market forces into news operations without fundamentally changing the Chinese political system. The state has engineered market campaigns and pushed for media conglomeration aimed at enhancing political control, on the one hand, and facilitating media capitalization, on the other.

Control is no longer the only word that characterizes the Chinese media. Internationalization and profit making are seriously pursued by officials and journalists alike. As China joins more international organizations such as the World Trade Organization (WTO) and hosts more international events such as the 2008 Olympics, the country inevitably opens up more, and this opening affects its media practice and reform. Cooperation and joint ventures between Chinese and foreign media and information institutions are under way. Significant media deals have been signed between Chinese and foreign media companies and agencies.

Reforming the world's second-largest and fastest-growing information and journalism market becomes more important and urgent as the Internet links the Chinese population with the outside world. The Internet empowers Chinese citizens and revolutionizes Chinese society. Providing a unique forum to reach a worldwide audience, the Internet is much more accessible and user friendly than the traditional media. Its nature arguably defies and challenges traditional censorship and transforms Chinese society and its way of communication. Reaching almost anything and anybody with only a click, it lets an individual's voice be heard worldwide instantly.

As new breathing space for public and journalists develops, in-depth investigative journalism tests the government's sincerity in journalism reform. Traditionally a taboo, investigative reporting has become popular in recent years, although reports are often selected not for the seriousness or the merits of the cases, but rather on the basis of ideological conformity. The government gives Chinese journalists more discretionary power over how to cover a story now that the central government wants to bolster the role of the mass media as the social custodian of conscience. By exposing officially denounced problems and drawing attention to the need for specific reforms, investigative or watchdog journalism strengthens the Party's hegemony by smoothing the rough edges of the ongoing Chinese transformation and policing the political, economic, and social boundaries of an emerging authoritarian market society.

Political control over the information and media industry still dominates, but economic forces gradually lessen and erode that control. China's economic liberalization has changed the public and challenged official mind-sets regarding the public's right and need for better and real information. As the Chinese economy and society liberalize further, the public is likely to push for more information and political freedom. China's journalism reform, as well as its information and media industry, is at the mercy of an increasingly sink-or-swim market-oriented Chinese market.

See also Media Bodies, Central and Local; Media Distribution; Media Reform; Press Control; Press Freedom.

Bibliography

Pan, Zhongdang, "Spatial Configuration in Institutional Change: A Case of China's Journalism Reform," *Journalism* 3 (2000): 253–282; Zhao, Yuezhi, "Watchdogs on Party Leashes? Contexts and Implications of Investigative Journalism in Post-Deng China," *Journalism Studies* 4 (2000): 577–598.

Yu Zhang

Judicial Reform

The judiciary system of a society functions to administer justice. The rule of law depends on a properly operating judicial system. To be effective, laws must be supported by a judicial system of **conflict resolution**. In addition to applying the rule of law, the judiciary must also interpret laws set up through the legislative process according to established procedures. To these ends, an independent, efficient, and impartial judicial system is vital.

China is moving rapidly toward a socialist market economy and is increasingly opening to the outside world. Economic growth in recent years has provided the Chinese people with a higher standard of living, and as people engage in more economic activities, they desire even greater participation in decision making and may even demand human rights. As more relationships and rights are defined by law, Chinese people today are increasingly turning to the legal system to seek justice (Xin 2003) and to protect their personal and economic rights. However, to their disappointment, the existing Chinese judicial system seems ill prepared to accommodate them. This is because under the socialist system prior to 1978, private property was nonexistent. The socialist state owned everything, and therefore, all economic activities were state activities. Conflicts were handled through administrative means, and the courts possessed only minimal powers in civil matters.

In December 2001, China became a member of the World Trade Organization (WTO). In order to comply with trade regulations, China has been compelled to change many of its existing laws and institutions. The Chinese government consequently has taken serious steps toward the rule of law. At the Fifteenth National Congress of the Chinese Communist Party (CCP) in 1997, President Jiang Zemin called for "promoting judicial reform and providing systemic guarantees for the judicial organs to exercise independently and openly adjudicatory power and prosecutorial power." Li Peng, chairman of the Standing Committee of the **National People's Congress** and a member of the Standing Committee of the Political Bureau of the CCP Central Committee, reiterated that the Chinese Constitution guarantees independent judicial rights by courts, according to a *People's Daily* report in 2000. Significantly, this was the first time since 1949 that the Party explicitly advocated judicial reform.

Following the government's call, the Chinese Supreme People's Court initiated a five-year reform plan in 1999. According to the chief justice of the Supreme People's Court, the foci of the judicial reform include the improvement of the surveillance system, the lawsuit evidence system, and case-hearing procedures, according to a *People's Daily* report in 2001.

Historically, China's written legal codes can be traced to early imperial times. An incomplete criminal law dating back 1,700 years during the imperial Jin dynasty (265–420) was unearthed in northwest China in 2002. The Tang Code was compiled in 624, the earliest complete Chinese criminal code in existence. There were also efforts to establish legal codes based on European models in the Qing dynasty (1644–1911), but implementing the laws proved to be difficult, given the dominant influence of Confucian thoughts that emphasized social obligations, self-sacrifice, and conflict resolution through compromise.

Hence little formally administered justice based on written laws existed in imperial China (221 B.C.–A.D. 1911).

Although imperial history in China ended in 1911, the ensuing Republic of China was marred by frequent conflicts such as civil wars, a war against the Japanese, and the war between the Nationalist Party and the Communist Party. Between 1912 and 1949, efforts to reform the legal system yielded very limited results.

The development of China's judicial system after 1949 can be divided into several distinct stages. From 1949 to 1953, the priority was to establish a new political, economic, and social system. Although the government abolished all the laws enacted under the previous government and eliminated the legal system, it did not establish new codes to replace the old ones. Instead, Party regulations and directives became the guiding premise of the judicial system. It was evident from the very beginning that no effort was made to separate the Party from the judiciary. Following a long tradition of judicial power during the wars prior to 1949, the Communist Party continued to rely on issuing policies as the basis for the administration of justice.

From 1953 to 1979, China began to establish a more formal legal system. Several important pieces of legislation were approved and enacted. In 1954, the first Constitution of the People's Republic of China was approved. The government also enacted the Organic Law of the People's Courts of the People's Republic of China, the Organic Law of People's Procuratorates of the People's Republic of China, and the Regulations for Arrest and Detention. However, criminal and criminal procedural codes were never developed.

During this period, the resulting judicial system adopted a dual system: a formal and an informal system. The formal justice system included three branches: the public security organ (the police), the people's court, and the people's procuratorates. The informal justice system punished "class enemies" through sanctions and handled "nonantagonistic conflicts" among working classes by "criticism and self-criticism" and mediation. However, the Party clearly favored the rule of Party policy over that of law. As a consequence, the formal judicial system not only was not fully developed, it was compromised through various political campaigns, and the law in general was simply ignored.

After the death of **Mao Zedong** in 1976, the government began its effort to replace the rule of man or Party by the rule of law through reform of the judicial system. Several important legal institutions and systems were established: the Legal System Commission of the Standing Committee of the National People's Congress, which is a legislative institution, the Ministry of Justice, which is the people's procuratorate, the People's Courts, which are a lawyers' system, a notarization system, and legal personnel training institutions.

In 1979, the National People's Congress adopted the People's Republic of China's first code of criminal law and criminal procedure law. It also adopted the Organic Law of the People's Courts of the People's Republic of China (1980) and the Organic Law of the People's Procuratorates of the People's Republic of China (1980). The Organic Law of the Local People's Congresses and the Local People's Governments of the People's Republic of China (1980) was also adopted. In 1982, a new constitution was established. The 1994 Administrative

Procedure Law was adopted to protect citizens from abuse of power by government officials. Overall, since 1979, more than 300 laws and regulations have been promulgated.

Judicial reform has brought about major changes. The most important achievement has been changes in the conception of the judiciary itself—its role and purpose, which is to protect individual citizens' rights and interests. Economic and administrative tribunals have been set up across the country to settle civil disputes and safeguard citizens from abuses of authority by officials. Serious efforts have been made to move from an inquisitorial toward an adversarial mode of adjudication. In criminal proceedings, for example, both prosecution and defendant are granted equal legal status, and judges are no longer responsible for investigating and collecting evidence, but only for reviewing evidence. Improvements in judicial procedures also have been made. In 1995, the Judges' Law further defined the status, responsibilities, duties, and rights of judges.

Further reforms, however, may be difficult because of some inherent contradictions in the judiciary system. For example, judicial reform poses the fundamental question of constitutional review, that is, whether China is willing to move away from a system that has practically no constitutional review to one that regards a constitution, as John Marshall described it in *Marbury v. Madison* (1803), as "a superior paramount law, unchangeable by ordinary means." Without constitutional review, true judicial independence cannot be achieved in China since judicial power is derived from the People's Congress instead of from the Constitution. A possible transitional phase would be that in order to guarantee a more complete judicial reform, there must be an independent, national judicial reform committee to oversee reform. Apparently, achieving an independent, efficient, and respected judiciary in China will require further efforts to move toward a constitutionally based judiciary system.

See also Correction System; Crime Prevention; Legal Infrastructure Development and Economic Development.

Bibliography

The People's Daily, "China's Chief Justice Calls for Court Reform," July 30, 2001, http://english.people.com.cn/english/200107/03/eng20010730_76062.html, accessed on December 20, 2004; The People's Daily, "Judicial Reform Meets WTO Rules," March 19, 2002, http://english.people.com.cn/200203/19/eng20020319_92374.shtml, accessed on December 20, 2004; The People's Daily, "1,700-Year-Old Legal Document Found in NW Province," December 10, 2002, http://english.people.com.cn/200212/10/eng20021210_108225.shtml, accessed on December 20, 2004; Situ, Yingyi, and Weizheng Liu, "The Criminal Justice System of China," in *Comparative and International Criminal Justice Systems*, 2nd ed. Obi N. Ibnatius Ebbe, (Boston: Butterworth-Heinemann, 2000); Terrill, J. Richard, *World Criminal Justice Systems, a Survey*, 4th ed. (Cincinnati: Anderson Publishing Co., 1999); Xin, Chunying, "What Kind of Judicial Power Does China Need?" *International Journal of Constitutional Law* 1, no. 1 (New York: Oxford University Press and New York University School of Law, 2003): 58–78; Xinhua, Net, "Top Lawmaker on Judicial Reform," October 26, 2000, http://www.china.org.cn/english/PMD/3260.htm, accessed on December 20, 2004.

Liying Li

June 4 Movement

Demanding more democracy and less corruption, the student-led June 4 Movement consisted of a series of demonstrations that unfolded in the heart of Beijing from April 15 through June 4 in 1989 and turned the world's largest square, Tiananmen, into a sea of protests against the involution of political reforms in China. In the course of the movement, protests spread to other major cities, such as Shanghai and Chengdu. A bloody crackdown brought this fifty-day movement to an abrupt end. Otherwise known as the "Tiananmen incident of 1989," the movement has gained international recognition as a symbol of outcries for political reform. It took place in a period during which there was a retreat of communism in Europe, and *glasnost* (political liberalization) and *perestroika* (economic restructuring) were changing the face of communism in Russia.

The June 4 Movement was triggered by the death of Hu Yaobang (1917–1989), who had fallen from grace in January 1987 because of his support of political reforms in China. Once the secretary-general of the Chinese Communist Party (CCP), he was accused of being too lenient with student protests for democracy that had swept the campuses of some 117 universities, colleges, and middle schools in December 1986. This charge endeared him to the intelligentsia. Upon learning of his death on April 15, 1989, Beijing students took to the streets to mourn Hu, a man they viewed as a martyr who represented "the Soul of China." White wreaths were laid around Hu's portrait on the marble base of the Monument to the People's Heroes that stood in the middle of

The now-famous image of an unknown demonstrator blocking a tank convoy as it moved along the Avenue of Eternal Peace toward Tiananmen Square on June 5, 1989. © Bettmann/Corbis.

Tiananmen Square. In line with Hu's advocacy of political liberalization, students called for freedom of speech and press, resumption of democratic reforms, a crackdown on corruption, and more state funding for education.

The emotions that led to this vocalization of protests had brewed for years. Politically the rigid orthodoxy of communism was relaxed only enough to justify the pragmatism of Deng Xiaoping's **Open Door policy**, which was attentive to economic reforms only. By steering clear of political reforms, this economics-only approach proved inadequate to meet people's desire to have more say in their own future. To make matters worse, price reforms, which were designed to phase out low, subsidized prices in favor of prices regulated by the principle of supply and demand, had hit an impasse. Inflation was reportedly running at 28.5 percent in 1988, and there were gross inequalities. Professors were paid less than waitresses, and the barber who cut a person's hair earned more than the surgeon who operated on the brain underneath it. Last but not least, corruption became rampant, and official graft and profiteering were burgeoning out of control.

The Communist regime was known to have little tolerance of any direct challenge to its political system, as in the case of Fang Lizhi (1936–   ), a renowned astrophysicist and outspoken dissident. He was purged, demoted, and denounced for "inciting students." Participants in the June 4 Movement were savvy enough to acknowledge the leadership of the CCP and dismiss the practicality of grafting Western-style democracy onto Chinese society. It was stressed that all they wanted was to improve the existing system, not overthrow it. There was also a sense of humility in the way that student representatives petitioned for a dialogue with Premier Li Peng (1929–   ) at the April 22 state funeral in honor of Hu. But they were rejected, because their public display of dissent by marches through Tiananmen and sit-ins around the leadership compound of Zhongnanhai had proved more than irksome to the elderly leaders of the CCP. But opinion concerning how to deal with the students was split.

A power struggle was simmering behind the scenes. The April 26 issue of the *People's Daily* carried a stern editorial condemning the student demonstrations as a "planned conspiracy" to overthrow Communist rule. This hard-line approach backfired. Instead of intimidating the students, it ignited greater protests and an outpouring of support from the general public, which showed a political consciousness never seen before. Students insisted that their action was "patriotic and democratic." In defiance, they started to camp out in Tiananmen Square overnight. Days later, their protests received a renewal of energy from the massive demonstration held to mark the seventieth anniversary of the May 4 Movement, a historic event that championed the pursuit of intellectual and political modernization by China's younger generation of the intellectual elite. Not unlike their predecessors, the participants in the June 4 Movement were seized by a deep sense of obligation to act as the conscience of the nation.

Within the CCP leadership, however, the tide continued to turn against the reformers. Back from a visit to North Korea on April 29, Secretary-General Zhao Ziyang (1919–2005) decided to take exception to the editorial in the *People's Daily*. The rift widened when Zhao adopted a conciliatory stance toward the students, describing their grievances as "reasonable" and their movement as "patriotic" in his speech to an audience of the Asian Development

Bank on May 4. A further controversy arose on May 16 when Zhao told visiting Soviet secretary-general Mikhail S. Gorbachev that by a Politburo resolution of November 1987, all important decisions had to be deferred to Deng for approval. It was an implicit statement that responsibility for what loomed ahead rested with Deng.

Frustrated by the steadfast refusal of the CCP leadership to listen to them, more than 300 students started a hunger strike on May 13. In a matter of days, the number of hunger strikers increased to 3,000. From the students emerged a number of charismatic leaders, including Wang Dan (1965–), Chai Ling (1966–), and Wuer Kaixi (1968–). The citizens who joined the students soon swelled the ranks of demonstrators to more than a million people. Among the civilian demonstrators were journalists, writers, teachers, professors, professionals, and factory workers such as the Federation of Autonomous Workers led by Han Dongfang (1962–), as well as individual intellectuals, such as Wang Juntao (1959–), Liu Xiaobo (1958–), Hou Dejian (1960–), Chen Ziming (1952–), and Wan Runnan (1946–).

In the meantime, the power struggle within the CCP headed for a showdown. Li Peng finally consented to meeting with student representatives on May 18, but he greeted them with a stern-faced tongue-lashing, leaving no room for a dialogue. In Shanghai, Party boss Jiang Zemin (1926–) dismissed Qin Benli (1918–1991), the editor in chief of the *World Economic Herald*, for his prodemocracy stand. Zhao Ziyang was ousted from his post on May 19, and martial law was declared in Beijing on May 20. The erection of a "Goddess of Democracy" statue in Tiananmen on May 30 lifted the spirits of demonstrators, but it was the last straw for a seemingly standoffish Communist government.

On June 3, there were signs of an impending crisis. The government **television** station told the citizens of Beijing to stay away from Tiananmen, warning that the People's Liberation Army (PLA) was about to strike and restore order there. Around 4 p.m. a phone call was made to the demonstrators' command post, urging an immediate evacuation of students to avoid bloodshed. Around 10 p.m., the army struck, only to run into blockades put up by civilians in defense of the demonstrators. Most, if not all, of the carnage occurred during the early hours of June 4 away from Tiananmen. An accurate accounting of the casualties is impossible. While the Chinese government set the death toll at around 200, Western estimates ranged from 400 to several thousand. In the days that followed, there was also a nationwide manhunt for demonstration activists. Again, no exact figures of these arrests are possible, but most of the twenty-one activists wanted by the government were able to flee the country.

In the aftermath of the June 4 Movement, there was an uproar of international condemnation, along with economic and military sanctions. A tacit ostracism of China followed. Relations with Hong Kong and Taiwan suffered severely. Foreign investments and credit were cut back or withheld. In the midst of these repercussions, China returned to the economics-only approach, leaving political reforms on the back burner. After a brief ascendancy, however, hard-liners found that there was no turning back of the clock on economic reforms. Deng managed to rekindle the reforms through his 1992 inspection of southern China. This time, he pushed the reforms all the way to a full market economy. A new generation of bureaucrats was brought up thereafter, 92 percent of whom were college graduates. There seem to have been conspicuous strides toward a professional government. But the ghost of the June 4 Movement continues to haunt China today, and its dilemmas are rooted in a political system whose lack of transparency provides the breeding ground for official corruption.

See also Corruption and Fraud, Control of; Deng Xiaoping (1904–1997), Politics of; Deng Xiaoping (1904–1997), Reforms of; Human Rights Debate; Jiang Zemin (1926–), Populism of; Sino-American Relations, Conflicts and Common Interests; Sino-American Relations since 1949; U.S. Legislation on China-Related Issues.

Bibliography

Barmé, Geremie, and Linda Jaivin, eds., *New Ghosts, Old Dreams: Chinese Rebel Voices* (New York: Random House, 1992); Hsü, Immanuel C. Y., *China without Mao* (New York: Oxford University Press, 1990); Pye, Lucian, and Mary W. Pye, *China: An Introduction*, 3rd ed. (Glenview, IL: Scott Foresman, 1998); Turnley, David C., *Beijing Spring* (New York: Stewart, Tabori & Chang, 1989); Zhang, Liang, *The Tiananmen Papers* (New York: Public Affairs, 2001).

Zhiming Zhao

K

Kinships

See Ethnic Kinships.

Korean War (1950–1953)

The Korean War broke out between North Korea and South Korea on June 25, 1950. On June 27, President Harry Truman authorized U.S. air and naval forces to support South Korea and ordered the U.S. Navy Seventh Fleet to the Taiwan Strait to prevent China from attacking the Nationalist-held offshore islands. On July 7, the United Nations (UN) adopted a resolution to use all possible means to aid South Korea and establish the UN Command for the war. The United States and sixteen other nations sent ground forces to Korea to serve under the UN Command. The Korean War shifted the focal point of the Cold War from Europe to East Asia.

China began to pay great attention to the war situation in early July. On July 7, the Central Military Commission of the Chinese Communist Party (CCP) held the first meeting on national defense and decided to establish the Northeast China Border Defense Army, which included four infantry armies, in case of an emergency situation along the Chinese–North Korean border. On August 4, when North Korea's advance in the South was repelled, **Mao Zedong**, chairman of the CCP, called a Politburo meeting to discuss possible involvement and preparation of Chinese forces for the war. After U.S. troops landed in Inchon on September 15, the war situation changed rapidly. On October 1, the UN forces crossed the thirty-eighth parallel and launched a counteroffensive campaign into North Korea. It became clear to Kim Il Sung, North Korea's leader, that he was going to lose the war as well as his Communist government in North Korea. Kim asked the Soviet Union for help and told Joseph Stalin, the Soviet leader, to ask China to send troops to Korea. Stalin telegraphed Mao on

These Chinese prisoners of war were captured by UN forces in North Korea in November 1950. © Bettmann/Corbis.

the same day and suggested that China should send five to six divisions immediately to the thirty-eighth parallel. Mao held a CCP Central Committee Secretariat meeting on October 2, in which there were divergent views on whether China should send its troops to Korea. On October 4–5, Mao chaired an enlarged Politburo meeting. Marshal Peng Dehuai supported Mao's idea to send Chinese troops to Korea. At the meeting, Mao and the Politburo decided to send Chinese troops to aid North Korea in the name of the Chinese People's Volunteer Force (CPVF). The CPVF was established on October 8, and Peng was appointed its commander in chief and political commissar. The first wave of the Chinese forces crossed the Yalu River and entered Korea on October 19. On October 25, the Chinese government made a public announcement and named its war "Resisting the United States, Aiding Korea, and Defending the Homeland."

The Korean War thereafter became in essence a war between China and the United States. By late November 1950, China had sent 450,000 troops to Korea. Its quick deployment apparently was unexpected by the UN and American generals. The CPVF's superiority in manpower enabled the Chinese to overcome their inferiority in equipment and technology. It seemed rational to the Chinese leaders that a large force should serve as a decisive factor for their victory. From November 1950 to April 1951, Peng launched five offensive campaigns and drove the UN forces back to the thirty-eighth parallel. By mid-April, the Chinese forces in Korea had increased to 950,000 men.

In the summer of 1951, the Korean War reached a stalemate. On July 10, truce negotiations began between the Chinese–North Korean and UN-U.S. delegations. In order to achieve a favorable position at the negotiating table, China sent more troops to Korea. By October, the number of CPVF troops had reached 1,150,000. From the fall of 1951 to the spring of 1953, the Chinese command shifted its focus from eliminating enemy units in mobile warfare to securing lines in positional warfare. By March 1953, the Chinese forces had reached a record high, totaling 1,350,000 men. In a limited war, it was difficult for either side to overpower its opponent completely, in contrast to the situation in the Chinese civil war (1946–1949). By the end of their fifth offensive campaign, the Chinese leaders had changed their goal from driving the UN forces out of Korea to a more modest one of defending China's security and ending the war with a truce agreement.

On July 27, 1953, China, North Korea, and the UN and the United States signed the Korean Armistice Agreement. More than 3 million Chinese volunteers had participated in the Korean War. The Chinese casualties included 152,000 dead, 383,000 wounded, 450,000 hospitalized, 21,300 prisoners of war, and 4,000 missing in action. China spent 10 billion yuan in **Renminbi** (equal to U.S. $3.3 billion according to the exchange rate at that time) on the war. China's intervention in the war had a profound impact on the Chinese military, society, and foreign policy.

The Korean War enhanced the Chinese government's political consolidation in its early years. Mao employed the challenge and the threat brought about by the war to cement Communist control over China's state and society. In February 1951, the CCP launched the "Campaign to Suppress Counterrevolutionaries." The mass movement targeted three layers of counterrevolutionaries, who were, by the Chinese official definition, enemies to the society, to the government, and to the Party. The CCP eradicated any resistance in an effort to consolidate control and order. The Party also disarmed the local masses of their weapons and ammunition that had once been used during the long years of warlord and guerrilla fighting in World War II and the Chinese civil war.

In January 1952, the CCP began its "Three-Anti" and "Five-Anti" Campaigns to regulate China's industry and commerce. The three sets of vices were corruption, waste, and obstructionist bureaucracy, and the targeted groups were CCP members themselves. The five vices were bribery, tax evasion, theft of state property, cheating on government contracts, and stealing state economic information. Chinese business owners were shocked and soon found that cooperation with the new regime was absolutely necessary for their survival.

After the Korean War, the CCP developed an integrated plan similar to the Soviet model for the nation's economic development. The Korean War and the mass campaigns against Western imperialists isolated China from most of the industrial countries. As a result, China's choice of the Soviet model was one way of emphasizing the revolutionary and Communist nature of the new Chinese state. The First Five-Year Plan, covering the years from 1953 to 1957, achieved an increase in production across a broad sector of goods. Soviet support in finance, technology, and education aided China's reconstruction and economic growth. This was the period of closest collaboration between China and the Soviet Union.

The Chinese army began developing into a professional force under the strains of combat. In 1951, China purchased enough weapons from the Soviet Union to arm sixty infantry divisions. Thereafter, the Chinese army's weapons became uniform and standard. After the war, China decided to build its own nuclear bomb. In 1954, Mao asked Nikita Khrushchev, the new Soviet leader after Stalin, for the full support of Soviet technology and materials for China's nuclear research and development. In January 1955, Mao called an enlarged meeting of the CCP Central Secretariat to discuss how to start China's nuclear weapons program, and China's first nuclear weapons plan was approved. The army was placed under a newly established Ministry of Defense, where Marshal Peng became the first defense minister. Peng launched a military reform to deal with inevitable conflicts against the international imperialists in the future and achieve a victory in the next war.

Mao considered China's intervention a victory because the Communist regime in North Korea was saved, a perceived U.S. invasion of China was prevented, more Russian military and economic aid came to China, and Beijing emerged as a new Communist power in the world. The war promoted Communist China's international influence. Thereafter, China became a "frontline soldier" fighting against the U.S. imperialists in the Cold War. However, the war also tested the limits of China's cooperation with both the Soviet Union and North Korea. It sowed the seeds of China's discontent with the Soviet Union. Chinese leaders later vowed that China would never again be drawn into such a conflict in the Korean Peninsula. Perhaps the most important lesson that China learned from its Korean War experience was to avoid or prevent such a war in the future. In America, China's intervention provoked a deep antagonism to communism and was seen as an acute and imminent threat.

See also Sino-American Relations, Conflicts and Common Interests; Sino-American Relations since 1949; Sino-Japanese Relations since 1949; Sino-Soviet Alliance; United Nations (UN) and China.

Bibliography

Chen Jian, *Mao's China and the Cold War* (Chapel Hill: University of North Carolina Press, 2001); Cohen, Warren, *America's Response to China*, 4th ed. (New York: Columbia University Press, 2000); Li, Xiaobing, Allan Millett, and Bin Yu, *Mao's Generals Remember Korea* (Lawrence: University Press of Kansas, 2001); Mao, Zedong, *Mao's Manuscripts since the Founding of the PRC*, vols. 1–4, *1949–1954* (Beijing: CCP Central Archives and Manuscripts Press, 1987–1993); Peters, Richard, and Xiaobing Li, *Voices from the Korean War* (Frankfurt: University Press of Kentucky, 2003).

Xiaobing Li

L

Labor Market

The labor market, as a labor-allocation mechanism or institution, is an integral part of the current Chinese economic system. It emerged in the early 1980s and since has experienced rapid development.

In the period between the mid-1950s and the early 1980s, the labor market was nonexistent in China. Under the command economic system, the government controlled all economic affairs, including labor allocation. It drew up employment plans, made job assignments, and decided on labor transfers. This government-controlled unified labor allocation excluded free labor movement, deprived workers and enterprises of the right to choose each other, and sanctified full employment and lifetime tenure for workers, especially for those fixed workers in **state-owned enterprises**. It suited the regime's need for social control, but contributed to the persistent economic inefficiency. This kind of labor allocation began to crumble in the late 1970s, when market-oriented economic reforms were initiated, and has gradually given way to a new labor-allocation mechanism, the labor market.

The economic reform started in the countryside in the late 1970s with the implementation of the household responsibility system, under which the individual household replaced the collective as the basic unit of production. The reform guaranteed individual peasants economic autonomy and especially allowed them to dispose of their own labor. It also created a surplus of rural labor by greatly enhancing agricultural productivity. These changes made a large scale of agricultural labor movement both necessary and possible. More than 100 million peasants have found jobs in nonagricultural sectors (e.g., rural industries, commerce, construction, and transportation), and another 100 million or more have moved to **cities** and become peasant-workers. Many peasants have even migrated to distant provinces, mostly in coastal regions, and found employment there. This movement of rural labor was initiated by peasants themselves rather than by the government. It was realized largely though the working of market forces—the law of demand and supply of labor in the market. However, the long-existing *hukou* **system** (household registration system) continues to separate them from urban residents and has created some level of discrimination by the urban residents against the "floating population."

Profound changes also have occurred in urban labor allocation since the early 1980s, when economic reforms were extended to cities. An earlier urban reform program was the manager responsibility system, which, among other things, granted the manager a high degree of autonomy over hiring and dismissal of workers. In the mid-1980s, the labor contract system was introduced among newly recruited workers, and in the 1990s it was extended to all workers. Under this system, the worker and management had to sign, in accordance with the principle of "equality, voluntarism, and negotiation," a labor contract on their mutual rights and obligations. The terms of labor contracts ranged from one year to eight years. At the expiration of a contract, the worker and management could either negotiate to renew the contract or simply end their labor relations for good. Even before the expiration of the term, the worker or management could terminate the contract by giving notice in advance. The labor contract system allowed much freedom over employment to management and workers. It also put an end to lifelong job security and left workers subject to **unemployment**. Its implementation severely undermined the government-controlled labor-allocation arrangement.

As the economic reform deepened in the 1990s, many unprofitable state-owned enterprises were forced to go bankrupt, which often caused massive unemployment. Some state-owned enterprises sought to enhance profitability by laying off workers. Others became privatized and thus joined the rank of private businesses. Even prior to this privatization of state-owned enterprises, private businesses, both Chinese and foreign invested, had already been flourishing. To both employers and workers in these enterprises, the government-controlled labor-allocation system simply became obsolete.

The government has shifted its role from a job creator and wage subsidizer to a facilitator of job creation, job training, and employment services. The policy of encouraging the development of private sectors and attraction of foreign investment has made these two sectors the most important job providers. More and more people are now employed in the private- and foreign-owned companies. The Chinese government remains the single largest employer in the country. Nevertheless, the number of employees who work in the public sector has been reduced by half. Labor market training is also a major focus of the labor policy. The government has increased its investment in vocational education. Retraining of displaced workers, especially those displaced en masse because of enterprise/industrial restructuring, is given in the newly established reemployment centers.

With the collapse of the government-dominated labor-allocation system, the labor market has gradually emerged as a major mechanism for labor allocation in cities. The labor market takes diversified forms. Two earlier forms were the personnel exchange service center and the skilled workers exchange agency. The former aimed at promoting mobility of scientific and technological personnel and the latter at helping skilled workers change their careers. Another form of labor market was the job fair, open to all urban job seekers. Job fairs were held at irregular intervals, at different levels (city or district), and on different scales. At the job fair, job seekers and hiring personnel from different enterprises met and made deals on employment. The prevailing norm that governed the job fair was mutual free choices and open competition. Job seekers could freely consult with and submit job applications to any employers, and employers had the freedom to select job candidates.

Since the early 1990s, various employment agencies have emerged and have become the principal form of labor market. They are open to all job seekers and are in operation all year round. By the end of 2000, a total of 29,024 employment agencies had been set up nationwide, 20,262 of which were government sponsored, while the rest were run privately. In the single year of 2000, they registered 19.917 million applicants and succeeded in helping 9.752 million of them find jobs. In 100 cities, government-sponsored employment agencies provided free services to laid-off workers. Since the late 1990s, many employment agencies have equipped themselves with computers. Many cities have set up citywide labor market information networks. Job advertisements in newspapers and magazines, on the **Internet**, and even in street posters can be seen everywhere in China. For-profit employment agencies, though a useful means in the job market, are against the International Labor Organization's Fee-Charging Employment Agencies Convention (C96, 1949). Even though China has not joined this convention, there are clearly some limits on the future development of private employment agencies.

The government has played a critical role in promoting the building of labor markets. In fact, most labor markets in cities were established and run by governmental organizations. The government, especially at the local (city) level, has issued numerous regulations on labor market management and frequently conducts inspections of employment agencies to ensure that they provide good-quality services.

The labor market in China is still immature and succumbing to various constraints. One major constraint is the *hukou* system. First established in the 1950s, this system has forced individuals to register with local authorities to gain residency, thereby determining where they live and work. Although it has been increasingly eroded during the reform, it has kept on functioning. This system especially limits the scope of free movement of rural labor to cities and hence hinders the formation of an integrated rural-urban labor market.

See also Labor Market Development; Labor Policy; Labor Policy, Employment, and Unemployment; Labor Relations; Labor Rights; Migrant Population; People's Commune/Household Responsibility System; Reemployment of Laid-off Workers; Taiwan, Labor and Labor Laws.

Bibliography

Ministry of Labor and Social Security, *Labor Statistics Yearbook 2001* (Beijing: Labor Press, 2001); Wang Aiwen, *An Examination of the Evolution of Social and Labor Relations* (Beijing: Hongqi Chubanshe, 1993); Xin, Meng, *Labor Market Reform in China* (Cambridge: Cambridge University Press, 2000).

Yunqiu Zhang

Labor Market Development

A market is where selling and buying take place. The same logic applies to the **labor market**. Before economic reforms first started in 1978, China had virtually no labor market because the basic elements of market demand and supply were nonexistent. In the urban sector, labor resources were administratively allocated by the government. Enterprises had little autonomy as to whom and how many employees to hire at what wage rates and were required to accommodate the placement quota assigned to them. An urban laborer, once hired in an urban work unit, was promised implicitly an "iron rice bowl" or lifetime employment, along with coverage of housing, medical care, and retirement. No market existed in the rural sector either because production was collectively based on the size of the labor force at the level of the village or production team (*sheng chan dui*). Wages were then determined by the average productivity of the production unit.

The labor market in China emerged as a result of market reforms. **Agricultural reform** first returned production to being private and family based. In the urban sector, the ending of the government's assignment of placement quotas and sending educated youth to the countryside resulted in a large number of "youth looking for jobs" (*dai ye qing nian*), many of whom became self-employed and later formed the first batch of China's proprietors and private entrepreneurs in the **cities**. Meanwhile, many talented and skilled workers left their poorly performing **state-owned enterprises** to "plunge into the sea" (*xia hai*), and they formed the most important part of China's private entrepreneur class. With the supply of these laborers and managerial talents and the demand for laborers by many among them, China's labor market first emerged. As the government further withdrew from administratively allocating new jobs, as more state and collective enterprises had to downsize and lay off workers, and as rural redundant laborers previously tied to their land started to migrate to the cities, the market expanded to almost every area of the economy. China's labor market, therefore, emerged as a result of economic reforms that melted the "iron rice bowl," returned autonomy to enterprises, and ended government allocation of labor resources.

China's labor market remains immature, characterized by disguised **unemployment**, limited services and labor mobility, market segmentation, disequilibrium in wages, and rampant discrimination. Disguised unemployment refers to the situation of those employed whose marginal productivities are lower than their remuneration. Researchers give various estimates of the total surplus workforce. Ballpark figures for 1998 center around 50 million in urban areas and 130 million in rural areas. Comparing these redundant labor forces with the total labor forces of 200 million in urban areas and 500 million in rural areas shows an urban unemployment rate of about 25 percent, a rural rate of 26 percent, and a nationwide unemployment rate of 25.7 percent. Some of the disguised unemployed today may have become either fully employed or released into explicit unemployment.

In this newborn market, the service intermediaries are severely underdeveloped. Job ads in newspapers and broadcasting media are few; local job centers provide services primarily to college graduates and professionals; laid-off workers have been responsible for their own reemployment; and migrant rural labor must rely primarily on relatives and village neighbors to find jobs in the cities. These limitations constrain the speed at which the unemployed can find matching jobs and thus make unemployment unnecessarily higher. Another institution incompatible with labor market development is China's enterprise-linked safety net. Since employee pensions, medical benefits, unemployment compensation, and housing are linked closely to individual enterprises, workers often prefer taking a pay cut or early retirement or, once they are laid off, waiting to be reemployed within the same firm to finding a job elsewhere, thus significantly slowing turnover and labor mobility. Moreover, the lack of home ownership and a private rental market makes it physically difficult for one to relocate to a new place for reemployment.

The most inefficient feature of China's labor market is the segmentation of the market. Within the urban sector, there exist "insider" and "outsider" markets, resulting from entry barriers to existing jobs and selected professions. In the "insider market," there are two types of workers: (1) those employed before 1986 with an implicit promise of the "iron rice bowl," which is a stock part of the labor market and shrinks in size over time; and (2) a small group working in government-protected and monopolized sectors, such as banking, communications, the securities industry, and the utilities industry. These workers, especially the second type, earn the highest salaries and enjoy the most job security and other work-related benefits unresponsive to the market situation. In the "outsider market" are contract workers employed after the mid-1980s who enjoy fewer benefits but are protected by terms in their contract, laid-off workers reentering the market, intra-urban migrants from poorer to richer areas, and, most important, rural-to-urban migrants. While the first type in the "outsider market" results from the ending of the "iron rice bowl" system, the latter three types in the "outsider market" are usually poorly educated, poorly skilled, and not socially connected and enjoy little protection by labor contracts, social security benefits, and laws. The segmentation in the urban market will end when the stock portion of the employment from the traditional system shrinks to a negligible amount, entry barriers to protected state enterprises are broken, and labor market discrimination is outlawed.

Between the urban and the rural markets, the segmentation has resulted from the government's development strategy that favored the urban sector at the expense of the rural sector and the *hukou* **system** (household registration system) that prevented rural residents from entering the cities and sharing the fruits of industrialization with urban counterparts. This problem is, therefore, essentially the problem of rural-urban migration. China's rural-urban migration has been attributed to both "pulling factors" (such as higher income and better job, education, and other opportunities) in the cities and "pushing factors" (such as poorer living, lower income, and poorer job and education opportunities) in the countryside. Among the factors, urban-rural income disparity is the most important driving force.

Widespread restrictions and discrimination against rural-urban migration have existed. Government policies discriminate against rural migrants as they have been primarily regulating, supervising, and restricting in nature. To work and legally continue their residency in the cities, rural migrants must obtain three official documents, including an employment permit, a temporary resident certificate, and proof of compliance with the family-planning policy. During the prereform period, the government had classified thirteen industries and, within them, 203 types of jobs to be off-limits to rural migrant labor, according to a report by *CCTV Report*. Although these job restrictions as a government policy were officially lifted in Beijing, they have been replaced by "qualification" restrictions instead. In addition to entry barriers, rural migrants also enjoy fewer labor rights and welfare provisions and must pay higher fees for the education of their children.

Gender discrimination is widespread in the open market, where there are more migrant workers than jobs. Women have fallen victim to intense competition, and there are not enough laws and policies to protect their rights. Women often find themselves hired last and laid off first. Employers impose strict age limits on positions to be filled by female workers out of concern for maternity leave and other family duties that may lower a woman's productivity. From 1985 to 1995, female employment in both urban and rural nonfarming jobs steadily declined. Female workers suffered from lower pay and inferior benefits, pension, and insurance. The situation has not significantly improved as of the beginning of this century.

China's labor market is developing toward an integrated national market and a more mature one. The central government has recently become especially attentive to the unemployment issue, which can be the main source of social unrest. Reports of job retraining and placement centers springing up all over the country have occupied much of the official news. The urban labor force newly entering the market can track job openings not only through the **Internet** but also through cell phones. Rural migrants, however, still rely more on their relatives and other social connections for locating a job in the city.

Between urban and rural markets, barriers of entry and communication have gradually come down. Provinces and cities with less population pressure have published policies to eliminate discrimination and welcome rural migrants. The issue of discrimination against women has also been more noted and discussed. Establishing laws and regulations that protect the civil rights of women, and especially their implementation, have been called for. Outlawing discrimination in the labor market is necessary not only for equity purposes but also for efficient allocation of resources. In the meantime, China must create more nonfarm jobs in both the urban and rural sectors, which remains the biggest challenge to China's policy makers.

See also Labor Policy; Labor Policy, Employment, and Unemployment; Labor Relations; Labor Rights; Migrant Population; Reemployment of Laid-off Workers; Taiwan, Labor and Labor Laws.

Bibliography

Aimin, Chen, "China's Urbanization, Unemployment, and the Integration of the Segmented Labor Markets," in *Urbanization and Social Welfare in China*, ed. A. Chen, G. G. Liu, and K. H. Zhang (London: Ashgate Publishing, 2003); Wang Yuguo and Aimin

Chen, eds., *China's Labor Market and Problems of Employment* (Chendu, China: Southwestern University of Finance and Economics Press, June 2000).

Aimin Chen

Labor Policy

Labor policy comprises the goals, programs, and laws designed to protect the interests of labor. Generally speaking, it includes policies on employment and training, working conditions and safety protections, and labor-management relations. China's labor policy is strongly influenced by corporatism and communism; therefore, it differs in many ways from liberal or social-democratic labor policies. Prior to the 1980s, the Chinese Communist Party (CCP) and the government dictated labor allocation, working conditions and compensations, and activities of **trade unions**. Labor contracts and collective bargaining were nonexistent. A bipartite relation between labor and the state makes labor relations highly political. The state depends on the loyal support of the working class for political legitimacy, and labor in turn depends on the state for jobs, economic welfare, housing, and medical care.

The economic reform since the 1980s has fundamentally redefined China's political and economic systems. As a new free-market economy is gradually replacing the command economy, the ownership of enterprises has been diversified. The number of privately owned firms has grown rapidly, while the number of state- and collective-owned firms has declined sharply. The employment system, labor allocation, and labor conditions have all undergone major changes. A notable change has taken place in the nature of labor relations. A tripartite labor relation between the state, owner-managers, and labor has emerged. Owners' interest of profit maximization and labor's interest of wage maximization for the first time are recognized by the state as legitimate interests. The state has drastically reduced its intervention in investment and wage decisions. Its role as a peacemaker and mediator has been strengthened. Market instead of state control has become one of the driving forces for labor allocation, labor working conditions, labor compensation and welfare, and labor relations. Terms such as "contract labor," "collective bargaining," "labor disputes," "social security," "minimum wage," and "labor standards" have suddenly become part of the new popular Chinese lexicon. Overall, a soft form of authoritarian corporatist labor policy has replaced the traditional state corporatist policy.

China's new labor policy continues to place national interests above labor interests. It claims that the fundamental interests of the state and labor are the same. However, if there is a conflict between the two, labor must observe the national interest first. This policy is clearly translated into the mission statement of the official trade union, the All-China Federation of Trade Unions (ACFTU). It states that the union must preserve the national interests first but at the same time preserve labor interests. To institutionalize this approach, all unions must accept the leadership of the CCP. All high-ranking union leaders are CCP members and must be approved by the CCP. Only one official union is allowed per workplace. No independent union organization is permitted.

When labor disputes arise, the parties involved must accept state-sponsored mediation before a lawsuit can be filed. Most labor disputes are resolved through the mandatory mediation process. At the national and local levels, the tripartite consultation conference system has gradually been established, but has yet to play a vital role in the country's economic and labor policy. This approach serves very well the state's goal of maintaining political and social stability.

China's policy on protecting labor's social and economic rights is somewhat ambiguous. As a result of the drastic economic reform, labor's political rights, such as the right to participate in the decision-making process and the right to be informed, have been eroded. Labor's social status as masters of the workplace and its self-esteem and pride are in serious question. Labor's economic interests in areas such as job security, social security, and health security are all being challenged without much consultation with workers. Although China's labor laws provide more-than-adequate protections for labors on paper, the implementation of these laws and regulations is a major problem. Local government agencies and officials are reluctant or unable to force private and foreign companies to comply with labor codes and regulations. Violations of labor rights and labor standards are rampant. Practices such as forced labor, child labor, sweatshops, and discrimination against female workers are some of the common complaints. The government has adopted several policies to resolve some of these issues, such as the policy to promote **workers' congresses** in workplaces and a system of democratic evaluation of managers.

Employment policy has become the cornerstone of China's labor policy as the reforms have deepened. Promoting employment and reemployment has become a top policy priority for the government due to the continued rise of a large number of first-time job seekers and the millions of workers who have been laid off as a result of the government's restructuring plans. The Chinese government now considers the creation of more employment opportunities to be a major goal of economic and social development. However, instead of provision of jobs by the government, the new policy relies heavily on the adjustment of industrial structure and market-oriented employment mechanisms. The development of labor-intensive industries such as service enterprises is stressed. The state's efforts to encourage the development of private and individual businesses and to attract **foreign direct investment** (**FDI**) also help create much-needed jobs. More than 60 percent of laid-off workers have found new jobs in the private sector. A new **labor market** is emerging in China thanks to the government's new employment policy of "laborers finding employment on their own initiative, the market adjusting the demand for employment, and the government promoting employment." To help laid-off and unemployed personnel, the government has organized a Reemployment Assistance Action drive to extend prompt and effective services to guarantee their basic livelihood, reemployment, and social insurance through various assistance measures. According to the government's own estimate, between 1998 to 2001, more than 25.5 million people were laid off from state enterprises, of whom more than 16.8 million have been reemployed.

To facilitate the development of a market-based labor policy, the **National People's Congress** (**NPC**) has intensified its legislative effort. The Labor Law of 1994 prescribes the basic legal framework for labor relations and labor standards, including the labor contract and group contract systems, the tripartite coordination mechanism, the labor standards system, the labor dispute-handling system, and the labor protection supervisory system. All enterprises and institutions are now required to sign labor contracts with their employees. Collective bargaining and collective contracts are slowly but steadily expanding to many workplaces. In August 2001, the Ministry of Labor and Social Security, the All-China Federation of Trade Unions, and the China Enterprise Association jointly established the State Tripartite Conference System of Labor Relations Coordination, which set a national operating mechanism for China's labor relations coordination.

The development of a new **social security system** is another major policy initiative taken by the government in the past two decades. The long-term goal of the reform is to establish a unified national social security system independent of enterprises and institutions. Funded by employers, employees, and governments at all levels, the new programs are run with socialized management and services. Currently the system provides mainly basic security, urban coverage, and regional management. It consists of social insurance, social relief, social welfare, social mutual help, and special care for disabled ex-servicemen and women and family members of revolutionary martyrs. The most significant changes have been made to the social insurance programs. A new **old-age insurance** system and an urban basic medical insurance system have been put into place. They had already enrolled more than 100 million people by 2003. Furthermore, unemployment insurance, industrial injury insurance, and the childbirth insurance have also been established or restructured to provide maximum wage protection for the employed and their families. A new minimum living standard security system provides welfare assistance to the urban poor. These programs will help establish a social safety network that is desperately needed in China to ensure the continued development of a market economy and to improve social equality so that the transitional process will be less painful for labor.

One of the weakest areas in China's labor policy is workplace safety. The number of industrial accidents and injuries in China is among the highest in the world. Sixty percent of accidents and deaths took place in coal mines and other excavation job sites, and 5,791 coal miners lost their lives in 2002 alone. The NPC has adopted many new safety laws, such as the Work Safety Law of 2002 and the Mining Safety Act of 1992, but the lack of enforcement and noncompliance at the local level have compromised the laws and efforts made by the central government. Occasionally, the central government has to resort to stern administrative measures, such as the shutdown of more than 60,000 small-scale coal mines in 2001, to assure compliance. China needs to strengthen its labor inspection system and improve labor safety training to lower the labor fatality rate.

China has increased its cooperation with international organizations in recent years. When making changes in its labor laws, China is consciously narrowing the gaps between China's own labor standards and these adopted by the International Labor Organization (ILO). So far China has signed only 23 of the 170 ILO conventions. There are signs that China will join more of these international conventions in the near future.

See also Labor Market Development; Labor Policy, Employment, and Unemployment; Labor Relations; Labor Rights; Migrant Population; Reemployment of Laid-off Workers; Taiwan, Labor and Labor Laws; Unemployment.

Bibliography

Chen Kuo-jun, *Labor Policy and Labor Management (Laogong Zhengce Yu Laogong Xingzheng)* (Taipei: Sanmin Shuju, 1993); Guo, Baogang, "Labor Policies in China and Taiwan: A Comparative Study," *Modern China Studies* 64, no. 1 (1999): 104–124; Information Office of the State Council, People's Republic of China, *Labor and Social Security in China* (Beijing: Information Office of the State Council, People's Republic of China, 2002).

Baogang Guo

Labor Policy, Employment, and Unemployment

At the end of 2001, China's total population was 1.276 billion (not including Hong Kong, Macao, and Taiwan), of which 730.25 million were employed. Out of the total work force, 32.8 percent worked in urban areas. The employment distribution for primary, secondary, and tertiary industries was 50 percent, 22.3 percent, and 27.7 percent, respectively. The share of employment in the state-owned and collective-owned sectors among total urban employees (including self-employed persons) dropped from 99.8 percent in 1978 to 37.3 percent in 2001.

The burgeoning Chinese **labor market** is one of the central elements of China's transition to a market economy. Before China's economic reforms began in 1978, there was no labor market in the country; like other components of its command economy, labor was centrally planned. In this system, the government controlled all aspects of employment and job allocation, including the number of workers to be employed and the wages and benefits to be paid, and individual enterprises did not have a right of decision about their workforces. In addition, labor mobility was also strictly controlled by the government. Administrative approval was the only way for urban workers to move across work units and locations. Rural laborers were not permitted to work in an urban area. Furthermore, workers generally enjoyed the security of lifelong tenure at their jobs, a condition referred to as the "iron rice bowl." Moreover, upon their retirement, their employment status could be passed on to their children. Finally, the government's labor policies were focused on urban areas, and largely ignored the vast rural areas. In addition, rural areas were used as a buffer zone to alleviate urban employment pressure. For example, in the 1960s, the government implemented a reduction of millions of urban workers and asked them to return to rural areas to work in agriculture. Also, during the 1960s and 1970s, millions of educated youths were required to move to rural areas.

The market-oriented labor reforms started with the introduction of changes in the administrative labor-allocation system. In the early 1980s, a new type of non-state-owned employment entity was created: the labor service company. As a collectively owned entity, labor service companies create employment opportunities and offer training to those who are seeking jobs. Not being controlled by central planners, labor service companies have great flexibility in providing products and services.

As China's economic reforms continue, decision-making responsibility about the workforce is gradually being transferred to enterprises. The policy of providing workers with lifelong employment is being phased out. Also, social service provisions such as housing, health insurance, and retirement benefits are being separated from enterprises to facilitate the development of labor markets.

In 1986, the government began phasing in a new labor contract system while phasing out lifelong employment tenure. This system requires workers to sign fixed-term, renewable contracts with the enterprises for which they work. When the contract expires, the employment relationship can be terminated or renewed for a new term. This system was initially applied only to new blue-collar recruits, but was gradually applied to all workers. Also, under this system, it became possible for enterprise managers to terminate unruly or poorly performing workers. In 1992, the government stopped issuing "recruitment plans" altogether for enterprises and granted them autonomy in hiring and in setting employment terms.

In 1994, China passed a comprehensive new labor law that took effect in 1995. As a result, the labor contract system became law and was officially recognized as a basic mechanism to promote an efficient labor market. The new labor law expanded on the contract system by stipulating that employers are permitted to lay off workers when doing so is justified by the current economic situation. The passage of the new labor law marked the end of both the administrative labor-allocation system and the "iron rice bowl" employment regime.

With the enactment of the new labor law, the role of the Chinese government in the labor system changed from complete control to regulatory oversight. For example, the government has set minimum wage requirements for employers. In 1997, China launched a unified social pension system. Also, in 1999, the government implemented the Unemployment Insurance Act, which requires each employer and employee to contribute to an **unemployment** insurance fund. An employer pays 2 percent of the total wage bill, while an employee pays 1 percent of his or her salary. To qualify for unemployment benefits, an employee must have contributed to the unemployment insurance fund for at least one year, must leave the job involuntarily and must continue to look for a job, and must register with the government as being unemployed. The unemployment benefit is set below the minimum wage but above the minimum urban cost of living. Those who are unemployed can receive unemployment benefits for a maximum of twenty-four months. In 2001, 3.12 million people received unemployment benefits.

During the economic restructuring, a large number of workers in **state-owned enterprises** have been laid off. These workers are not considered to be unemployed; instead, they are characterized as being "off-duty" (*xiagang*, stepping down from the post). From 1998 to 2001, state-owned enterprises laid off 25.5 million workers. However, state-owned enterprises are required to establish reemployment service centers for those who have been forced off-duty.

The government has also created a so-called three-line insurance system for those who have been forced off-duty. Under this system, they are eligible to receive compensation for basic living expenses from reemployment service centers for three years; after that, they are then eligible for unemployment benefits from the government for two years; and after that, they can apply for income assistance from the urban living expense assistance program.

In the old labor-allocation system, there was no official unemployment. A large number of redundant workers existed in enterprises, in effect being a form of hidden unemployment. During the transformation of the labor system, unemployment has become common. In 2001, the official unemployment rate for urban workers was 3.6 percent. However, the official unemployment rate is calculated on the basis of the number of workers who are registered as unemployed; because not all unemployed workers are registered with the government, the true unemployment rate is higher. Moreover, the unemployment rate does not include those who are forced off-duty. If this group were included, for example, in 2001, the unemployment rate would be doubled.

As urban labor markets have developed, rural laborers have been encouraged to work in **cities**. Millions of rural people have moved, either permanently or temporarily, to work in urban areas. Yet rural industrialization remains the central mechanism for relieving unemployment and labor migration pressure in the countryside. At the end of 2000, **township and village enterprises** employed 128.2 million workers.

Since the economic reforms started, China has made substantial progress in reforming the administrative labor-allocation system and the lifetime employment regime, developing labor markets, and facilitating the utilization of rural labor. Yet there are still many challenges ahead. In particular, the state-owned sector still employs a large proportion of urban workers, urban and rural employment pressure is still severe, and the **social security system** needs to be improved. Therefore, labor market reforms are still an important part of China's overall economic transformation.

See also Labor Market Development; Labor Policy; Labor Relations; Labor Rights; Migrant Population; Reemployment of Laid-off Workers; Taiwan, Labor and Labor Laws.

Bibliography

China Labor and Social Security Ministry and National Bureau of Statistics, "Labor and Social Security Development Report 2001"; Information Office of the State Council, "White Paper on Labor and Social Security in China," 2002; National Bureau of Statistics of the PRC, *China Statistical Yearbook* (Beijing: China Statistics Press, 2001); *People's Republic of China Labor Law*, 1994.

Haizheng Li

Labor Relations

Labor relations in China are undergoing a major transformation. Prior to the 1980s, the labor relationship was fundamentally between workers and the state, since the latter controlled and managed all economic activities. All businesses were owned either by the state or by collective entities. Managers represented the state, and workers depended on the government for employment, wages and salaries, and pensions, as well as for housing, child care, and health care. Administrative or political means rather than laws and market mechanisms governed this bipartite relation. Labor relations were stable, free of open and serious tensions and conflicts, partly because of the heavy-handed governmental control of the workplace and partly because of the absence of major sources of labor disputes, which was in turn attributable to the implementation of the egalitarian system of distribution and the high degree of job security for workers. Lifetime employment guaranteed workers' job security, and the cradle-to-grave welfare system provided by their work units took care of the well-being of the workers and their families.

Laborers, according to the socialist theories, were masters of society and the factories they worked in, and they shared a common interest with each other. Therefore, the state claimed that there was no need for an adversary relationship. In reality, this was far from the truth. Tensions between workers and factory management never ceased to exist. Labor conditions varied considerably in different types of enterprises. Workers in **state-owned enterprises** enjoyed the best protection and welfare and were considered "aristocrats" of all working classes. Workers in urban and rural collective-owned enterprises had a much tougher labor relationship due to low wages and substandard working conditions.

The market-oriented economic reform has altered labor relations in a fundamental way. The state no longer runs corporations and businesses directly. The modern enterprise reform requires enterprises to make their own business decisions and to be responsible for their own profits or losses. As the government has gradually relinquished its direct control, state-owned enterprises increasingly have become independent economic entities, and their managers have become a distinct social group with managerial autonomy. Many state-owned enterprises have been privatized or changed into shareholding companies. At the same time, a large number of private, joint-stock, and joint-venture companies have mushroomed. These changes in ownership and management have shattered the traditional bipartite labor relations. A new, tripartite relationship among state, labor, and management has been slowly but surely established. Labor no longer enjoys the benefits and protection it used to have under the planned economy. Market forces have redefined almost every aspect of this new labor relationship. The tensions between labor and management today are the worst since the founding of the People's Republic of China (PRC).

After nearly a decade of deliberation and some forty drafts, China finally adopted its first comprehensive Labor Law in 1995. It sets up a legal framework for dealing with the new labor relations. The law stipulates that labor contracts must be concluded for all workers in all types of enterprises; labor arbitration and inspection divisions must be established at all levels to deal with labor disputes; workers in enterprises are permitted to engage in collective bargaining when negotiating labor contracts; unified labor standards comparable to the international standards recommended by the International Labor Organization (ILO) are to be implemented nationwide, regardless of enterprise type; and finally, enterprises are allowed to lay off workers for economic reasons without prior consultation with local governments.

The labor contract system was not entirely new. The government used the system in the 1950s, but decided later to replace it with a lifetime employment system. In the 1980s, in light of the profound economic changes, the labor contract system was again reintroduced and experimented with in many places. Since the 1990s, the system has been promoted throughout the country in all types of work units. As a result, the lifetime employment system or "iron rice bowl" has ended. Workers are now "free laborers" in the marketplace, and their employment is determined by their skills, performance, and market demands. Two types of labor contracts are being used: short term and long term. Most employees who have a long history of employment receive a long-term contract to ease their anxiety over the transition process. New hires are offered a short-term contract. A system of group contracts has also been put into place. The Labor Law stipulates that employees of an enterprise may conduct consultation and sign group contracts with enterprises via representatives of **trade unions** or representatives chosen by employees themselves on an equal and voluntary basis with regard to wages, working hours, rest and vacation time, labor safety, labor hygiene, insurance, welfare, and other matters. Each year more than 200,000 group contracts are registered with the government, but overall the use of group contracts in China is still in its early stage of development.

To promote institutionalized democratic labor participation, several mechanisms have been implemented. At the national level, the Ministry of Labor and Social Security (MOLSS), the All-China Federation of Trade Unions (ACFTU), and the China Enterprises Association jointly established the State Tripartite Conference System of Labor Relations Coordination. Tripartite conferences of the same type have also been established in many provinces and major cities. The system of **workers' congresses** has been established at the enterprise level to facilitate labor participation. By law, all company governing boards must also have labor representatives.

Labor relations now are no longer just cooperative but also adversarial in nature. Labor disputes over wages and working conditions have risen steadily in recent years, partially because of the use of Tayloristic management techniques, such as tougher labor discipline, financial penalties and incentives, and very demanding production quotas. The managers' aggressive management styles and their harsh ways of treating workers have clearly backfired. In response, the government has restored the mediation and arbitration system since 1986. The procedures provide for two levels of arbitration committees and a final appeal to the courts. Chinese law requires that all disputes must go through the mandatory mediation or arbitration process before the parties can resort to legal action in the courts. Each enterprise is required to set up a mediation committee. However, if both parties refuse to have mediation, they must apply to the local labor dispute arbitration committee for arbitration. More than 90 percent of these disputes are settled at this level, and less than 10 percent of cases have to be settled through the litigation process.

Chinese laws are still ambiguous about labor's right to strike. The right to strike was included in China's 1975 and 1978 Constitutions, but was removed from the 1982 Constitution on the ground that the common interests of labor and enterprises under the socialist system have made strikes unnecessary. In reality, reformers like Deng Xiaoping wanted to stabilize the country and to begin the ambitious economic reform. Without political stability, such a reform was considered impossible. The economic reform, however, has drastically increased antagonism in labor relations. Officials in recent year have acknowledged occurrences of labor strikes. There have been many high-profile cases of large-scale labor strikes or work stoppages. It appears that officials still consider strikes to be a nondesirable means of dispute settlement. The government tries to give timely attention to potential labor disputes to prevent them from getting out of control. In fairness, the number of labor strikes is still small in China, and their grievances have been mostly targeted at the enterprise level. One secret behind this is the willingness of the government to use any means to prevent labor strikes, including government subsidies and intimidation.

Many other problems exist in the area of labor relations. The rights of migrant workers from rural areas are a major concern. More than 80 million to 100 million rural laborers have migrated to cities since the reform began in the 1980s. This large labor-force transfer provides urban areas, especially in the coastal areas, an abundant supply of low-cost labor and has sustained a prolonged urban economic growth. Although many farm laborers are better off economically, they are in a very disadvantageous position in the marketplace. The labor standards applied to them have been were significantly lower that what the laws have prescribed with regard to their wages, working hours, safety, insurance, and welfare. Wage arrears and discrimination against them by urban residents have been widespread.

The large number of laid-off workers is another major source of tension in labor relations. The reform of state and collective enterprises has resulted in large numbers of unemployed workers. Many enterprises have been closed, merged, or sold to individual or foreign investors. Unpaid debts in the form of pensions, workers' compensation, and health insurance have angered many workers. Many have fallen into poverty. To deal with these problems, the government has intensified its efforts to set up a **social security system**, including **unemployment** insurance, minimum standard-of-living subsidies, and an urban health insurance system. Many advocates of **labor rights** demand a strong union system to protect labor's interests. Some have even attempted to set up their own independent unions or labor parties openly or underground. These efforts have provoked some arrests since the government does not allow any independent political organization to exist outside its network of corporatist political control.

See also Labor Market; Labor Market Development; Labor Policy; Labor Policy, Employment, and Unemployment; Migrant Population; Reemployment of Laid-off Workers; Taiwan, Labor and Labor Laws.

Bibliography

Information Office of the State Council, People's Republic of China, *Labor and Social Security in China* (Beijing: Information Office of the State Council, People's Republic of China, 2002); Levine, Marvin J., *Worker Rights and Labor Standards in Asia's Four New Tigers: A Comparative Perspective* (New York: Plenum Press, 1997); Ministry of Labor and Social Security, *China Labor and Social Security Yearbook* (Beijing: Labor

Press, 1999); Ministry of Labor and Social Security, *China Labor Statistical Yearbook* (various issues, 1995–1999) (Beijing: Labor Press).

Yunqiu Zhang and Baogang Guo

Labor Rights

Labor rights refer to the basic economic, social, and political rights that workers should legitimately enjoy in areas such as employment (including job training), wages, social security, work hours, and labor protection, as well as unionization and strikes. The International Labor Organization (ILO) has developed a set of core labor rights that include the right of freedom of association, the right to organize and bargain collectively, freedom from discrimination in employment and occupation on the grounds of race, sex, religion, political opinion, and other characteristics, and freedom from forced labor. China has a mixed record of protecting these basic rights.

The situation of labor rights in China varied in different eras and for different strata of workers. In the prereform period (before the late 1970s), labor rights were subject to state power. Monopolizing all political and economic power and especially directly controlling major enterprises, the state determined what rights workers could have. Although it claimed to adhere to egalitarianism, the state treated workers differently, favoring one group while discriminating against another. Generally, the fixed or permanent workers in **state-owned enterprises** were the most privileged working people and enjoyed a variety of special treatments—lifetime job security (the so-called iron rice bowl), guaranteed pensions, free health care and child care, and almost free housing. Their working conditions were fairly good, and their wage incomes were stable, albeit low.

These treatments were denied, in varying degrees, to other groups, including workers in collective-owned enterprises, temporary workers, and rural laborers or peasants. Compared with all other groups of workers, peasants were in the most unfavorable state. Their incomes were low (partly because most of their products were procured by the state at low prices) and insecure (because their harvests were susceptible to changes in weather conditions). Peasants had no access to reliable health plans. Their medical costs were supposed to be covered by the collective (the village-based "production brigade"). In most cases, however, the collective was too poor to provide medical coverage. Retired or aged peasants had to rely on their children for a living, since pension insurance was nonexistent for peasants.

Although workers in the prereform era were treated differently, they did share some common experiences. They generally were unaffected by **unemployment** because of the implementation of the official policy of full employment, and they were equally denied the right of freely choosing careers, organizing labor unions, and holding strikes.

The situation of labor rights has changed since the late 1970s, when the market-oriented economic reforms started. As state power has gradually withdrawn from the economic arena, enterprises have become independent economic entities and have operated according to market principles. Accordingly, workers have become less dependent on the state and more on market forces, especially in terms of employment, wages, work hours, and working conditions.

The impact of economic reforms on labor rights is complex and varied for different groups of workers. In the area of employment, workers have gained the right to choose their careers in the **labor market**, which has become the main mechanism for labor allocation. However, they have lost job security and become vulnerable to unemployment. This is especially true for female workers and for those who are senior, are less educated, or have health problems. According to some conservative estimates, the number of the unemployed in **cities** was 2.50 million in 1992 and increased to 5.64 million in 1995 and 20 million in 1997. Unemployment indeed has posed a major challenge to workers' well-being.

To tackle this problem, the government has set up or sponsored various reemployment-training programs in towns and cities. In 1999 alone, 5.13 million unemployed and laid-off workers participated in these programs, and 3.23 million of them got reemployed through training. Meanwhile, the government promoted the labor preparatory system, which aimed at providing occupational training to urban middle- and high-school graduates who could not go on to further education. Rural people were basically denied access to these programs and were left to take care of themselves.

As far as wages are concerned, many workers, especially those with good education or special expertise, are paid well, and their standard of living has been raised, but for many common workers, wages have increased slowly and have barely matched the growth of prices of life necessities. Worse still, many workers frequently have been subjected to such abuses as wage arrears and arbitrary wage deductions, which have been especially severe in unprofitable state-owned enterprises and small-scale private businesses. A survey conducted in 1997 shows that 30 percent of workers experienced unreasonable wage deductions, and 19 percent experienced wage defaults.

Workers have often found their rights violated in the areas of work hours and labor protection. According to the 1997 survey, a quarter of workers were often required to work overtime. In some enterprises, daily work hours were extended to between twelve and fourteen. Workers sometimes did not receive overtime pay. In many enterprises, especially in labor-intensive private businesses, working conditions were poor and labor protection was ignored—for example, ventilation facilities and dustproof and fireproof equipment were lacking or insufficient. Workers often fell victim to work accidents and occupational diseases. The 1997 survey indicated that up to 10.6 percent of workers suffered various occupational injuries.

With the deepening of economic reforms, the traditional **social security system** (particularly free medical care and state-provided pensions) has broken down. In its place there has emerged a new social security system that includes social insurance, social welfare, and special care programs. The social insurance programs consist of old-Age insurance, basic medical insurance, unemployment insurance, industrial injuries insurance, and childbirth insurance. This social insurance system requires joint contributions of the state, the enterprise, and the individual worker. It has benefited increasing numbers of workers. However, the social security system has remained inadequate and inefficient, covering only one-tenth of the population. It has chronically been handicapped by the shortage of insurance funds, primarily because of some enterprises' defaults of their shares and some insurance institutions' misappropriations. As a result, retirees often could not receive their legitimate pensions fully and on time; many workers could not receive due reimbursements for their medical expenses; and the unemployment premiums were set too low, even lower than minimum wages.

The situation regarding labor's political rights is also mixed. On the one hand, workers are encouraged to participate in enterprise management, in both state and private enterprises, through **trade unions** and **workers' congresses** or through collective bargaining and collective contracts. On the other hand, workers continue to be denied the legal right to organize labor unions of their own and to hold strikes, but they have often ignored this legal restriction and have launched strikes and other protest activities without receiving much reprisal from the state. Since the early 1980s, great arrays of labor laws and regulations have been promulgated, including the Labor Law and the Trade Union Law. All these laws emphasize the protection of workers' rights and thus provide a useful weapon to workers in their confrontation with management. Many workers have proved to be willing and able to use this the legal weapon, but effective enforcement of these laws has always remained difficult.

See also Labor Market Development; Labor Policy; Labor Policy, Employment, and Unemployment; Labor Relations; Migrant Population; Reemployment of Laid-off Workers; Taiwan, Labor and Labor Laws.

Bibliography

Chinese Trade Unions Statistics Yearbook, 2000; Ministry of Labor and Social Security, *China Labor Statistical Yearbook* (Beijing: Labor Press, 2001); *Survey of the Status of Chinese Staff and Workers in 1997* (Beijing: All-China Federation of Trade Unions Policy Research Office, 1999); Zhang, Yunqiu, "State Power and Labor-Capital Relations in Foreign-Invested Enterprises in China," *Issues and Studies: A Journal of Chinese Studies and International Relations* (May/June 2000): 26–60.

Yunqiu Zhang

Laid-off Workers

See Labor Market Development; Labor Policy, Employment, and Unemployment; Reemployment of Laid-off Workers; Unemployment.

Land Policy

With barely more than one-tenth of a hectare of arable land per capita, China is the most land-scarce country in the world. The struggle over land has never stopped throughout Chinese history. Indeed, turbulent changes of the land-tenure system have been one of the most dramatic themes in China's history in the last half century. A thorough **land reform** in the early 1950s made China's small landholding system even more egalitarian. The reform, although violent and in many cases bloody, substantially raised agricultural productivity. However, the subsequent collectivization amid the **Great Leap Forward** in 1958 led China into an unprecedented famine that killed 20 to 40 million people in three years. The rectified commune system remained in place for about twenty years after the great famine. Although the growth of Chinese agriculture in this period did not fall shy of the international average, the commune system failed to improve the living standard of China's rural population but instead seriously deprived rural people of many basic economic and political rights. Therefore, it was not a surprise to find that the economic reform started in the rural areas after the **Great Cultural Revolution** formally ended in 1978.

The initial focal point of the reform was a small village called Xiaogang in Anhui Province. On one cold winter night in 1977, a dozen farmers gathered in the house of the village team leader and signed an agreement with blood fingerprints to give up collective farming. Although later research found that some villages in Wenzhou, Zhejiang Province, had maintained family farming since the early 1960s, the Xiaogang reform triggered a series of events that restored family farming in most of the Chinese villages and finally led to the formal fall of the commune system in 1984. In the period 1979–1984, the gross value of agricultural output reached a real annual growth rate of 7.6 percent, and grain output increased by an annual rate of 4.9 percent. By 1984, China found for the first time in history that it had a large grain surplus. While some people believe that increased agricultural prices played a significant role in bringing the rapid agricultural growth, it is estimated that 60 percent of the growth in the early 1980s can be attributed to the adoption of family farming. By raising the income of the farmers and solving China's food problem, the rural reform perhaps was the only reform that was a win-win game for every side.

The land tenure after the reform was officially called the household responsibility system (HRS). The 1984 Constitution granted the ownership of agricultural land to the village collectives, so the HRS is a mixture of collective ownership and individual farming. After the energy of the initial reform was discharged, agricultural growth was considerably slowed down in the second half of the 1980s, and the urban-rural income gap increased again after it had fallen in the early 1980s. The shortcomings of the HRS drew increasing attention from both policy makers and academic researchers. The following characteristics rendered the HRS economically inefficient in the long run: First, it granted each villager, including newborns and wives married in, an equal right to the village land. Hence periodic reallocation of land was necessary. This practice dampened farmers' incentives to invest in their land and thus hurt long-term efficiency. In addition, it enabled some village cadres to use land reallocations to seek personal gains. Second, farmers' use rights were encumbered. Local governments were frequently found to continue to force farmers to plant certain crops. Third, land sales were prohibited, and inheritance was seriously limited by periodic land reallocations. Land rentals were also banned in the early years but have been increasingly encouraged since the early 1990s.

However, some scholars believe that the mixed land tenure is a second-best choice because of multiple market and institutional failures. Noticeably, social protection in the countryside barely exists. Farmers are not covered by any

unemployment or pension system that urban residents enjoy. The rural cooperative health care system that China was so proud of in the commune era has basically collapsed since the HRS was established; by 2002, less than 10 percent of the rural population was covered by any kind of health care plan. Therefore, egalitarian land distribution is thought of as a device for farm households to pool income risk. This insurance mechanism, rudimentary as it may be, has played an effective role in protecting the poorer end of the population and providing a reservoir for returning migrants when the job market in the **cities** has been hit by adverse shocks such as the Asian financial crisis. Some scholars believe that China's more equal land distribution is the key to its higher achievement of nutrition intakes in the countryside than India has.

Perhaps the low terms of trade of agriculture and the high taxes and fees levied on farm households are more detrimental to farmers' incentives for farming than the adverse effects of land reallocations. While the latter can be at least partly dealt with (by, for example, increasing compensation for land investment, setting aside land for future reallocations, and by only reallocating marginal land), it is the high taxes and fees (which amounted to 20 percent of farm income in some localities) and low agricultural prices that have drawn more attention in Chinese politics, especially after one township Party secretary in Jianli County, Hubei Province, publicized his report *Let Me Tell the Truth to the Premier* to then Premier **Zhu Rongji** in 1999. Elected in 2002, the new government, led by Premier Wen Jiabao, has been determined to reduce the agricultural taxes. The agricultural special-product tax was removed in early 2003, and the other agricultural taxes are scheduled to be removed soon.

In regions with fast industrial development or with a significant number of migrants, villages have invented methods to consolidate land operation. Land rentals between individual households could be quite costly, especially when their gains were compared with low grain prices, high input costs, and, above all, high taxes. In the Pearl River Delta, land shareholding was adopted to overcome high transaction costs. Under this arrangement, households pool together their land, which is then managed by the village in industrial development, as well as agricultural production. A group of households elects one representative to join the shareholder committee to participate in the management. Another innovation that originated in central China is called *fanzu daobao* (inversed renting and reversed contracting), by which the households that do not want to farm rent their land to the village, which in turn rents the land to someone, in many cases, a migrant from a less developed region, who is willing to work with a large farm. Both innovations have effectively combined individual ownership of land and the advantages of the village, namely, authority, information, and scale effect.

The problem with the mixed land tenure is more political than economic in nature, primarily because the collective ownership enables the village cadres to seek personal gains. It is sometimes believed that village cadres use land reallocations as a result of rent-seeking habit, but investigators frequently found that village cadres did not enthusiastically conduct reallocations because they were very costly in terms of organization and in balancing interests among different households. Village cadres are more likely to make personal gains in industrial and recreational land development projects. In many cases, they have sold out the village land to developers by cheating the villagers on the terms of the contract. The severity of the problem led the **National People's Congress (NPC)** to pass a new law, the Agricultural Lease Law, in August 2002 to limit the power of the village cadres. The law took effect on March 1, 2003. Although it was politically motivated, the law also brought some fundamental changes to Chinese land tenure. In particular, it generally forbids land reallocations (with a few exceptions for extreme cases), allows inheritance of land, and allows the transfer of land-use rights. Although farmers' right to the land is defined via the contract between them and the village collective, the law nevertheless has pushed Chinese land tenure to a permanent lease system that grants farmers de facto private ownership of land. The law has far-reaching effects on China's land tenure that are not easy to gauge at the present time. However, judging by the empirical studies carried out on the HRS and the experiences of other countries, the law will not be likely to bring the buoyant output growth brought about by the initial adoption of the HRS. In addition, the law breaks up the insurance mechanism of the HRS, so it is quite possible that new polarization in landholding will arise again. To remedy this problem, basic social protection is needed to protect the poor in the countryside. The central government has announced a plan to reestablish the rural cooperative health care system and has pledged financial resources for it. Although there is still a debate on the nature of the new system, the government's move is widely seen as heading in the right direction to fill the deep gap between the amounts of social protection received by urban and rural residents.

See also Agricultural Reform; People's Communes/Household Responsibility System; Rural-Urban Divide, Regional Disparity, and Income Inequality.

Bibliography

Burgess, Robin, "Access to Land and Hunger: Opening the Black Box in China," working paper, Department of Economics, London School of Economics, 2003; Dong, Xiao-Yuan, "Two-Tier Land Tenure System and Sustained Economic Growth in Post-1978 Rural China," *World Development* 24, no. 5 (1996): 915–928; Kung, James, "Egalitarianism, Subsistence Provision, and Work Incentives in China's Agricultural Collectives," *World Development* 22, no. 2 (1994): 175–187; Lin, Justin Y., "Rural Reforms and Agricultural Growth in China," *American Economic Review* 82, no. 1 (1992): 34–51.

Yao Yang

Land Reform

Land reform was one of the most important policies of the Chinese Communist Party (CCP) from its early stage, and of the Chinese Communist government after the establishment of the People's Republic of China in 1949. In old China, land was distributed extremely unevenly. Landlords and rich peasants who made up less than 10 percent of the rural population owned more than 70 percent of the rural land under cultivation. More than 90 percent of the rural residents, most of them poor and middle peasants, owned less than 30 percent of rural land. Many landless tenants and smallholders relied on small plots of land rented from landlords under unfavorable sharecropping contracts to survive.

The average rent exceeded half the tenants' annual yield. In some places, the rent could be as high as 80 percent of the annual yield of the tenants.

One of the major goals of the revolution led by the CCP was to eliminate the ruling class of landlords and abolish the feudal system through distributing land evenly to the rural population. During the late 1920s to the early 1930s, the CCP undertook a movement to "battle the local tyrants" (large landlords) and redistribute land in its occupied revolutionary base areas. In these areas, land owned by local landlords was confiscated and distributed to poor peasants. This movement attracted many poor and landless peasants to join the Red Army to fight for land. It was the start of the Communist land reform in China. During the Anti-Japanese War period, to persuade more people to join the war against the Japanese invasion, the CCP stopped land confiscation and redistribution and changed its policy to rent reduction and interest reduction. After the end of the Anti-Japanese War, the Central Committee of the CCP passed the Outline Land Law of China in 1947, resumed its land-reform policy, and extended it to newly liberated areas.

Shortly after the proclamation of the People's Republic of China in 1949, to consolidate the power of the new government and to reward the masses of mobilized peasants for their support for the Communist revolution, the central government launched its first major economic campaign in rural China, the nationwide land reform. On June 30, 1950, the Land Reform Law was put into effect. According to the Land Reform Law, the land reform was implemented in three stages. During the first stage, the CCP organized farmers' committees and farmers' assemblies, which later evolved into peasants' associations and became the pillars of the land reform. Members of these organizations were recruited from the classes of poor peasants and agricultural laborers, but middle peasants were also admitted.

The second stage of the land reform comprised the census of local landholdings and landownership. On the basis of the amount of land they owned relative to the average landownership in their area, rural households were categorized into several classes as follows:

- Agricultural laborers: those who had no or limited access to land and hence had to hire out their labor for survival

- Poor peasants: those who had only limited and insecure access to land, that is, smallholders who had to lease additional land or were simply tenants

- Middle peasants: those who owned their land and cultivated it exclusively with family labor

- Rich peasants: those who owned relatively large pieces of land and who cultivated their holdings with the help of hired labor or tenants

- Landlords: those who owned excessively large landholdings according to local standards and cultivated them exclusively through hired labor or tenants

This classification scheme formed the basis for subsequent confiscation and reallocation of land.

During the third stage of the land reform, land, livestock and draught animals, farm tools, agricultural implements, and surplus houses owned by landlords were confiscated. The portion of land owned by rich peasants that exceeded the self-cultivation of their family members and had been leased to tenants was also confiscated. A relatively small part of the confiscated land and other agricultural capital and productive materials was handed to the state and became the property of state-owned farms later on. The remainder was given to local peasants' associations and then reallocated to poor peasants at no cost to them. Land was redistributed according to household population, the quantity and quality of local land, and the location of the plots to be redistributed. The landless tenants and poor peasants who lacked land received land that would make their acreage equivalent to the local average. The land owned by middle peasants was not subject to redistribution and was retained by the households so as not to endanger agricultural production. The landlords and their family members who lost their land to the reform received the same amount of land as other local residents, but likely of inferior quality. However, those landlords or any family members who were identified as working to prevent land reform were deprived of their rights to land.

Rural peasants' associations and peasants' representative assemblies served as the executive organ of the land reform. After the accomplishment of the land reform, the state government issued new title deeds to the landowners. Landowners were entitled to cultivate, trade, and lease their land freely.

By the end of 1952, except for Taiwan and a few minority residential regions, nationwide land reform was completed. About 300 million landless and land-lacking poor peasants received 700 million mu (approximately 117 million acres) of land. The annual land rent equivalent to 35 million tons of grain was eliminated. After the land reform, the former poor and middle peasants owned more than 90 percent of the rural land, while the land owned by former landlords and rich peasants was reduced to about 8 percent.

The land reform provided peasants with well-defined and secure property rights and hence with greater incentives to farm, which resulted in a substantial increase in agricultural production. Compared with 1949, in 1952, the gross product value of agriculture increased by 53.4 percent, grain output increased by 44.8 percent, cotton output increased by 193.4 percent, and oil-crops output increased by 63.6 percent.

The land reform also caused a profound social change in rural China. Almost everywhere, the former ruling class of the villages had been socially and in some cases even physically destroyed. Many landlords were tried publicly in the villages and either executed or sent off to perform hard labor under harsh conditions. It is estimated that land reform resulted in at least 1 million casualties. At the same time, the Communist Party cadres established themselves increasingly as the new ruling class and gained a foothold in the rural areas.

The structure of small-scale farming in rural China was generally maintained after the reform. Actually, the reform caused further dispersion of already scattered smallholdings of land, which was not advantageous to the development of rural infrastructure such as roads and irrigation systems. Furthermore, the redistribution of land fell short of creating a truly equal starting position for all rural people. The former landless agricultural laborers and smallholders had limited knowledge and skills in independent farming management. They also lacked means of agricultural production and capital for the acquisition of such means. Consequently, to cultivate their newly acquired land, they had to borrow money from traders, middle peasants, or other moneylenders. Since the right of disposal of ownership permitted the leasing and selling of land, some poor peasants ended up losing their land again. This situation, as well as the concept of private ownership itself, collided with the Communist Party's objective to implement socialist structures in rural areas. Therefore, only one year after the completion of the land reform, the Communist Party felt it necessary to introduce a total collectivization of the agricultural sector. During the following years, collectivization in rural China transferred all agricultural landownership to the local collectives. Although during the earlier stage of collectivization, the members of the collectives received payment from the collective outputs according to the land they donated, this method of income distribution was soon terminated. From 1955 onwards, the members of the collectives received their payment exclusively according to the labor they performed. In this way, the peasants lost the private land that they had acquired during the land reform and were demoted to agricultural laborers for more than twenty years. Not until China launched its economic reform in 1978 and the nationwide replacement of the commune system by the household responsibility farming system succeeded in the early 1980s did Chinese peasants regain their right of private cultivation on farmlands.

See also Agricultural Reform; Land Policy; People's Communes/Household Responsibility System; Rural-Urban Divide, Regional Disparity, and Income Inequality.

Bibliography

Hinton, William, *Fanshen* (New York: Vintage Books, 1966); Kirsch, Ottfried, Johannes Wörz, and Jürgen Engel, *Agrarian Reform in China* (Berlin: Verlag für Entwicklungspolitik, Breitenbach, 1994).

Hong-yi Chen

Legal Infrastructure Development and Economic Development

The economic reforms that were initiated in 1978 have profoundly changed the economic infrastructure in the past two decades. In the late 1970s and early 1980s, the "household contract responsibility production system" was introduced to the rural economy. Starting in 1984, urban reforms that focused on building a "socialist planned commodity economy" introduced a series of changes in the areas of privatization of **state-owned enterprises**, housing, medical care, employment, and the infusion of foreign capital. The promotion and maintenance of this new economic order lies in a fully operational and stable legal system.

Despite China's long history of civilization, the concept of law and the notion of the rule of law never took center stage in ancient Chinese society. Laws throughout imperial China were largely penal in nature. Even though elaborate administrative laws existed in later dynasties such as the Tang and Qing, these Chinese laws were primarily concerned with individual duties rather than rights and with punishment rather than compensation. Even more devastating were the ten years of the **Great Cultural Revolution**, when the legal system came to a complete halt because of the political campaign and class struggle.

To promote the economic transformation and maintain the new economic order, China has embarked on a series of legal reforms since 1978. The most notable has been the passage of various laws that encompass areas such as the basic rights of citizens (e.g., the 1982, 1988, and 1993 Constitutions, the 1979 and 1997 Criminal Laws, the 1979 and 1996 Criminal Procedural Laws, the 1986 Civil Law, the 1991 Civil Procedural Law, the 1996 Administrative Punishment Law, and the 1997 Administrative Supervision Law), economic- and business-related issues (e.g., the 1985 and 1993 Accounting Laws, the 1995 Advertisement Law, the 1996 and 1997 Antitrust Laws, the 1993 Regulations on the Administration of Issuing and Trading of Stocks, the 1988 Enterprise Bankruptcy Law, the 1982 and 1993 Economic Contract Laws, and the 1988 Sino-Foreign Contractual Joint Venture Law), and administrative matters (the 1989 Administrative Procedural Law and the 1991 Regulations on Administrative Reconsideration).

Legal reform efforts also focused on training legal professionals by providing better access to legal education and opportunities that enhance and formalize their professional qualifications and their capability to improve legal services. According to the *Law Yearbook of China*, the number of licensed attorneys increased fivefold, from 21,546 to 136,884, between 1986 and 2003. Legal professionals' qualifications are stipulated in various newly passed laws such as the Lawyers' Law. For example, the status of lawyers as "legal professionals" replaced the traditional role of a "social worker." Formal legal training and/or practical experience have become essential qualifications for a licensed attorney. For the first time in the history of the People's Republic of China, it is stipulated in law that lawyers and private law firms are protected by law. The number of law firms (including both state-run and private law firms) increased from 3,198 in 1986 to 10,873 in 2002.

Another major legal reform involved the transformation of the legal process. Traditionally, the Chinese legal system was inquisitorial in nature and followed the crime-control and order-maintenance model. Following the Soviet model from the 1950s on, the Chinese socialist legal system closely resembled the civil law tradition, particularly in its legal process. This inquisitorial model required that the truth-finding process be dictated by court officials. Defense attorneys in a criminal case and attorneys representing the plaintiffs and defendants in a civil and/or economic case had traditionally been placed in a subordinate position. Since the reform, the Chinese legal system has been moving away from the inquisitorial model to a more adversarial legal system. Under this system, judges are to remain neutral and remove themselves from inquiring into the facts of the case. Attorneys now take on the responsibilities of gathering evidence, making arguments, and moving the case along in the legal process. These changes are important for the following reasons: First, they reduce the burden of the court to delve into the fact-finding process and thus reduce potential judicial biases. Second, even though the "truth" of the case remains the primary consideration under the current system, individual rights and the rights of the parties can be better achieved through competing facts presented by attorneys. Last, effective legal representation achieved through the adversarial system potentially equalizes the status of parties involved in a lawsuit (e.g., consumer versus large corporation) and the status of parties and court officials.

A legal infrastructure is not complete without clienteles who understand how it works and take advantage of the system. Traditionally, Chinese citizens had very little legal consciousness and avoided litigation at any cost because of the Confucian ideology and the harshness of the legal system. To cultivate legal consciousness among the Chinese populace, several legal educational campaigns have been launched in the past two decades. It appears that the Chinese have become more "litigious," resorting to law for civil, economic, and administrative grievances. Litigation rates in economic disputes such as contracts increased from 322,153 cases in 1986 to 2,266,695 cases in 2002. Similarly, litigation rates in civil cases (e.g., divorce, inheritance, and debts) increased from 64,040 cases in 1986 to 4,420,123 cases in 2002, according to *Law Yearbook of China*.

The most profound reform measure has been the Administrative Procedural Law, passed in 1989. This law permits individuals and private entities to challenge the legality of administrative decisions in court. Since its passage, the number of administrative cases has increased dramatically, from 9,934 cases in 1989 to 80,728 cases in 2002. The types of administrative cases have evolved from primarily land issues and public security issues in 1989 to issues such as urban construction, commercial licensing, public health, transportation, taxation, and family planning.

The effectiveness of the use of law to challenge administrative decisions is mixed. Research suggests that between 1990 and 2002, the percentage of administrative decisions sustained by courts decreased markedly. In particular, significantly fewer administrative decisions on land, public health, forest, and commercial matters were sustained by courts and were thus ruled in favor of the plaintiff in 2002 than in 1990. Nevertheless, a substantial percentage of cases (between 35 and 55 percent) were withdrawn by plaintiffs without going into trial. While the high percentage of withdrawn cases may be indicative of the weak protection of the courts in administrative cases, some argue that litigation in itself may have served the purpose of deterrence. In some cases, the government revised the administrative decision in exchange for a withdrawal.

As the economic reforms deepen, China's legal infrastructure will undoubtedly transform, although several structural and cultural conditions may impede the progress of legal development. These conditions may include symbolism (many of the laws are mere ideological or propagandist statements rather than true representations of social, political, or legal reality), lack of consistency and reliability, insufficiency of enforcement of court judgments (e.g., local protectionism), shortage of knowledge of the law among the Chinese populace, judicial corruption, and lack of judicial independence.

See also Economic Policies and Development (1949–Present); Judicial Reform.

Bibliography

Bodde, Derk, and Clarence Morris, *Law in Imperial China* (Philadelphia: University of Pennsylvania Press, 1973); Chen, Albert H. Y., "The Developing Theory of Law and Market Economy in Contemporary China," in *Legal Developments in China: Market Economy and Law*, ed. Wang Guiguo and Wei Chenying, 3–22 (Hong Kong: Sweet & Maxwell, 1996); *Law Yearbook of China* (various issues) (Beijing: Law Yearbook of China Publishing House, 1987–2001); Pei, Minxin, "Citizens v. Mandarins: Administrative Litigation in China," *China Quarterly* 152 (1997): 831–862; Turner, Karen G., James V. Feinerman, and R. Kent Guy, *The Limits of the Rule of Law in China* (Seattle: University of Washington Press, 2000); Wang, Kui Hua, *Chinese Commercial Law* (Oxford: Oxford University Press, 2000).

Hong Lu

Li Zhun (1928–2000)

Li Zhun was a novelist, screenwriter, and dramatist in modern China. He was born into a family of the Man nationality on May 17, 1928, in Luoyang County, Henan Province. Since his grandfather and several uncles were all teachers, Li learned many Chinese classics during his childhood and acquired a very good foundation of knowledge in classical Chinese literature. From 1943 to 1945, he read many works of European writers. Later, he joined an opera troupe and played a large variety of roles on the stage. This performance experience was of tremendous help to his writings in the years to come.

Li's first work, "Don't Go That Way," established his fame. In this short story, Li urged readers to pay close attention to the phenomenon of dividing into two opposing extremes in the countryside—some peasants intended to take the socialist road, while others wanted to take the capitalist road. He warned people that the peasantry should join forces to take the socialist road rather than splitting. Since Li touched upon the issue of socialist revolution in the countryside, which was one of the most important social contradictions in the early 1950s, the work created strong repercussions among readers. Immediately after "Don't Go That Way" was published in *Henan Daily* on November 20, 1953, it was reprinted by more than thirty newspapers and more than ten literary journals.

In the mid-1950s, Li became more interested in describing the "socialist new man" in the countryside. His short stories and novelettes in this period, such as "White Poplar Trees" and "Rain," focused on the new look of the rapidly changing countryside during the early 1950s. "Biography of Li Shuangshuang" (1960) is generally regarded as his most representative work. This short story is more mature than Li's early writings. The female protagonist, Li Shuangshuang, is a peasant woman in whom one can find both the traditional virtues of working women and some new ideas of the times. She is hardworking, smart, humorous, and vigorous. Compared with her husband Xiwang, who is honest and diligent but sometimes selfish, narrow-minded, and timid, she has more courage to resist outdated conventional ideas. After a feature film was made based on this short story, Li Shuangshuang's name became especially widely known in China.

In 1969, Li moved with his family to a village in Xihua County of Henan Province that is often flooded by the Yellow River. During his four-year stay there, he helped more than 600 families write the history of their families and villages. This experience not only gave him deeper insights into the peasants, but also enabled him to write *The Yellow River Runs Eastwards* (1979–1984). Among the writings published in the post–Cultural Revolution era, this novel is one of the most successful works that reexplore the fate of the peasants from the perspective of the long-standing Chinese culture and history. In this giant two-volume work, Li described in depth how, in order to survive, seven families drifted from place to place, struggled against floods, drought, and locusts, and finally returned to their homeland and rebuilt their houses. For Li, the peasants' indomitable and unyielding attitudes toward natural disasters and hardships are the epitome of the spirit of the whole nation; the peasants represent the strength of a nation across history and into the future. In 1985, the novel won the Maodun Prize for Literature, the highest literary prize in China.

Li was a prolific screenwriter and a gifted dramatist. After 1956, he published about twenty scenarios, most of which have been made into films. The well-known films among them include *Li Shuangshuang*, *The New Biography of Old Soldiers*, *Herdsman*, and *Wreath at the Foot of a Mountain*.

See also Anticorruption Literature and Television Dramas; Avant-garde Literature; Experimental Fiction; Great Cultural Revolution, Literature during; Intellectuals, Political Engagement of (1949–1978); Intellectuals, Political Engagement of (1978–Present); Literary Policy for the New China; Literature of the Wounded; Misty Poetry; Modern Pop-Satire; Neorealist Fiction and Modernism; Pre–Cultural Revolution Literature; Revolutionary Realism and Revolutionary Romanticism; Root-Searching Literature; Sexual Freedom in Literature.

Bibliography

Li Zhun, *Not That Road, and Other Stories* (Beijing: Foreign Languages Press, 1962).

Dela X. Jiao

Libraries and Development

Libraries have played a significant role in the development of China since 1949. Tremendous changes and development have been seen in all aspects of libraries. Library development during the fifty-five year history of the People's Republic of China can be divided into four periods.

Reconstruction Period (1949–1953)

When the New China was established, there were only 392 libraries with 26,000,000 volumes in the country; most of these were in Beijing, Tianjin, Shanghai, and a few coastal **cities**. Among these libraries, there were 50 public libraries at the county level and above, 132 university and college libraries, 17 academy of sciences libraries, 44 labor-union libraries, and 44 private libraries. In the immediate postwar period, full-scale reconstruction was under way in all spheres of libraries. First, library infrastructures were revised to reflect the socialist model, including the change of ownership of all private libraries to that of the state, and new regulations for professional practice and administration were promulgated. Then acquisitions and collection policies were changed, and unacceptable materials (often termed "obsolete" or "pornographic") were discarded on a massive scale. All these efforts were aimed at establishing the leadership of the Chinese Communist Party and placing political requirements at the forefront of development.

Expansion Period (1953–1966)

The government started the First Five-Year Plan in 1953 to approach modernization. Libraries were consistently incorporated as an integral component in the plan. The plan included significant administrative initiatives in the development of libraries and extension of library facilities. Library laws and decrees were issued in this period, such as the Directives of the Ministry of Culture on Enhancing Public Library Work (July 1955), the Rules of Vocational Work for Trade Union Libraries (August 1955), and the Regulations for University and College Libraries of the People's Republic of China (December 1956).

The government initiated its "March toward the Sciences" movement in 1956. Libraries responded to this campaign individually by strengthening their services aimed specifically at scientific research. In order to achieve a more coordinated approach, the State Council at the Fifty-seventh Plenary Session on June 6, 1957, ratified the National Plan for Library Coordination, a document aimed at improving the capacity of libraries to serve scientific research. According to the plan, a Library Section, consisting of representatives of the Ministry of Culture, the Ministry of Education, the Chinese Academy of Sciences, the Ministry of Health, and the National Library of China, was established under the State Science and Technology Commission.

As a result of the plan, two national central library committees were established: the First National Central Library Committee in Beijing and the Second National Central Library Committee in Shanghai. Each of these was composed of several leading libraries in its respective area. In addition, nine regional library network centers were established in Wuhan, Shenyang, Nanjing, Guangzhou, Chengdu, Xi'an, Lanzhou, Tianjin, and Harbin. Further, to encourage and monitor feedback on the use of collections and scientists' demands for services, the National Editorial Board of Union Catalogs was created under the National Central Library Committee, an affiliate of the National Library of China.

Following implementation of the plan, horizontal links and coordination were strengthened among different types of libraries, and considerable progress was achieved in the areas of cooperative acquisitions, shared cataloging, interlibrary loan services, compilation of union catalogs, and personnel training. Thus the plan made a significant contribution to the development of Chinese libraries in the late 1950s and 1960s.

The Soviet influence on Chinese librarianship was another characteristic of this period. The majority of libraries followed the Russian model of organization and professional practice. When relations between China and the Soviet Union began to deteriorate after 1960, this influence was less immediate, but the Soviet legacy remained dominant at least until the end of the 1970s.

Through these and similar endeavors, libraries were kept within the development paradigm and, as a consequence, increased rapidly in number. In 1965, there were 573,434 public libraries and 43,546 other libraries, although many of them were **people's commune** libraries or "street libraries."

Disaster Period (1966–1976)

The disastrous effects of the **Great Cultural Revolution** on Chinese libraries are well documented. The decade from 1966 to 1976 was a period of decline, insularity, and destruction. Everything that had been achieved by libraries during the preceding years was largely negated. In particular, the previous endeavor to serve scientific research or, more specifically, scientists was deemed a reactionary practice incompatible with the prevailing theory of serving the workers, peasants, and soldiers.

At the beginning of the Cultural Revolution, library development was curtailed, but this soon degenerated into disruption followed by destruction at the hands of the Red Guards. For any one of a variety of excuses or supposed offenses, libraries were forced to close; most books were banned because they were deemed "feudal," "capitalist," and "poisonous revisionist weeds." As the economy collapsed, libraries were among the first institutions to suffer from budget constraints, which resulted in the cancellation of foreign orders and subscriptions. Furthermore, many librarians, as members of the intelligentsia, were sent to the May Seventh Cadre Schools to labor as part of their ideological remolding. Confronted by such conditions, many libraries were forced to close. Thus the number of public libraries at the county level and above decreased from 1,093 in 1960 to 323 in 1970, and university and college libraries decreased from 434 in 1965 to 328 in 1971.

Growth Period (1977–Present)

In October 1976, the **Gang of Four** was overthrown, signaling the end of the Cultural Revolution and the start of the Four Modernizations. Efforts were made to restore a semblance of order and to begin rebuilding China's social and cultural institutions, including libraries. In 1978, the Chinese government, determined to reform, adopted the **Open Door policy**. This decision brought fundamental changes throughout the nation. It was under this new political atmosphere that three sets of library regulations were promulgated in 1978, representing the three major types of library services: the Communications on Enhancing Library Work in College and University Libraries, the Temporary Regulations for Library and Information Work of the Chinese Academy of Sciences, and the Regulations Governing the Work of Provincial, Municipal, and Autonomous Regional Libraries. These early post–Cultural Revolution actions demonstrated that the government again attached importance to the development of libraries. In July 1979, the China Society for Library Science was established specifically to revive and direct the fortunes of library services.

One of the most momentous events of this period was the ratification of "The Outline Report on Library Services" by the Secretariat of the Communist Party on May 26, 1980. The report proposed five major changes to libraries: first, a new system of provincial, city, and county libraries was to be created by the end of 1985, and libraries dedicated specifically to the needs of children were to be built in large and medium-sized cities; second, library facilities over-all should be improved; third, priority should be given to the development of a full-fledged National Library of China, especially the construction of a new building; fourth, efforts should be made to improve library science education and research; and finally, control and supervision of libraries should be strengthened. On the basis of the report, the Bureau of Library Administration was established in 1980.

In October 1987, the Inter-ministerial Coordination Committee on Library and Information Services was founded. The committee is cosponsored by the State Science and Technology Commission and the Ministry of Culture, with members from the State Education Commission, the Chinese Academy of Sciences, and other relevant agencies. The committee is in a position to generate considerable change by decree.

Supported by the former State Commission for Education, China launched the "211 Project" in 1995. One of its two goals is to turn 101 universities into hubs for high-level research and specialization to aid national economic development in the twenty-first century in China. In line with the project, China has built two service networks, China Education and Research Network and China Academic Library and Information System, to help a total of ninety-six universities exchange research information.

As China regained its membership in such international organizations as the United Nations Educational, Scientific, and Cultural Organization (UNESCO), the Chinese Society for Library Science returned to the International Federation of Library Associations and Institutions (IFLAI) in 1981, and Chinese librarians have since been very active in the federation. In August 1996, the sixty-second IFLAI conference was held in Beijing, and 800 Chinese delegates and 1,584 overseas participants attended the conference.

Many libraries, including academic and public libraries, have enjoyed increased funds, better-developed collections, and improved facilities. A number of specialized associations, such as the Academic Library Association and the Association of Information Science, were also founded during the early 1980s at both national and provincial levels. More than fifty professional journals, a tenfold increase from the 1960s, were published by these associations, libraries, and information institutions.

Present-day library development is fueled by the reforming movement, which recognizes that libraries can contribute not only to economic and educational development but also to the social and cultural well-being of society. Specifically, the traditional concept of "more attention to storage and less attention to usage" has been abandoned by most major libraries. Many libraries have changed from closed to open stacks and have extended their opening hours to permit greater access. Another improvement has been the adoption of international standards for document processing, with only minor modifications to suit the unique features of Chinese literature. This more open acceptance of new ideas has been further encouraged by improved contact between Chinese and overseas librarians.

Many changes have been made in the management of libraries. The allocation of funds is being modified. In the new system, state funding allocations are based to a large extent on the perceived contribution of an institution to society. Libraries are encouraged to accumulate funds by providing fee-based services such as information retrieval and information analysis and by selling information products. Individual library managers are being given increased decision-making powers, and there are to be more freedom and greater rewards for individual librarians.

Many achievements can be seen in library automation and networking. In 1978, the National Conference of Science designated automation of library and information services at key research centers and national networking as top-priority goals of the modernization plan. Before this period, China was still isolated from the rest of the world. Consequently, library automation efforts involved mainly the examination and translation of library automation literature from Western countries. The concept and function of Machine Readable Cataloging (MARC) was introduced to Chinese professionals. Research groups also conducted computer software research for library automation. There has been considerable progress in the development and installation of library housekeeping systems and the localization of information retrieval systems. Most academic libraries, special research libraries, and mid- or large-size public libraries have adopted integrated library management systems. Hundreds of them are using domestic systems. Others are using foreign systems (customized for Chinese users) such as INNOPAC, UNICORN, and Horizon. Various library systems have become part of national networks at a rapid pace. Several digital library projects have also been launched. Libraries have formed local, regional, national, international, and specialty library networks to improve library cooperation, services, and resource sharing to meet a variety of needs of their users.

To enhance the development of library services, to exercise quality control over libraries, and to determine appropriate funding levels, a centralized activity termed Measurement and Evaluation of Library Work (MELW) has been in operation since the early 1980s. MELW employs qualitative and quantitative methods to determine how effectively a library is achieving its aims and satisfying the needs of users. It is based primarily on a series of criteria applied to all libraries. Most librarians report clear benefits from the MELW process: staff for the most part are motivated to improve their work practices as part of the self-evaluation, and the external assessment establishes guidelines for subsequent improvements in library collections, services, facilities, and management.

Including lower-level public libraries, a new public library has been established, on average, every 3.7 days since 1979. According to 1998 statistics, there were 2,721 public libraries at the county level and above with 376,000,000 volumes and 47,900 staff. The university and college libraries increased to 1,123 with 420,000,000 volumes and 38,000 staff. There were also 400 special research libraries with 40,000,000 volumes, 17,000 school libraries with an average of 80 volumes in each, and 98,000 labor-union libraries. The rapid development of the last fifty-five years since the founding of the People's Republic of China and the reform and opening-up of the last twenty-six years have signified that Chinese libraries are ready to meet new challenges and make greater contributions to world civilization.

See also Library and Information Science (LIS) Education.

Bibliography

Gong, Yitai, and G. E. Gorman, *Libraries and Information Services in China* (Lanham, MD: Scarecrow Press, 2000); Lin, Sharon Chien, *Libraries and Librarianship in China* (Westport, CT: Greenwood Press, 1998); Wu, Jianzhong, and Ruhua Huang, "The Academic Library Development in China," *Journal of Academic Librarianship* 29, no. 4 (July 2003): 249–253; Zhu, Qiang, "China Academic Library and Information System: Current Situation and Future Development," *International Information and Library Review* 35 (2003): 399–405.

Xudong Jin

Library and Information Science (LIS) Education

Education for library and information science (LIS) is an important factor in successful library information services. Many changes and rapid development have occurred in LIS education in the last fifty-five years since the founding of the People's Republic of China, especially during the reform and opening-up since 1978.

The beginning of formal education in librarianship can be traced to 1920, when the first school was established by an American librarian, Mary Elizabeth Wood, as a department of Boone College in Wuhan. In 1949, the new Chinese government began to restructure its social, economic, and educational systems. The Department of Library Science opened in Peking University in 1949. The Boone Library School was expanded and attached to Wuhan University in 1952 as the Department of Library Science. Since 1956, both departments have offered four-year undergraduate programs. Around the same time, several other institutions, including Beijing Cultural College and the University of Science and Technology of China, began to offer two-year special programs. In 1964, the first graduate programs in library science began. These universities and colleges trained more than 4,000 students, including 19 who earned graduate library degrees, 1,542 who earned undergraduate library degrees, and 908 students in two-year special programs, from 1949 to 1966.

Library education was seriously restricted from 1966 to 1976 because of the **Great Cultural Revolution** that destroyed much of what had been achieved. Schools and libraries at all levels were closed, books were either burned or locked away, and **intellectuals** in every profession were condemned. As a result, the library science departments at Wuhan and Beijing universities were suspended. No new students were enrolled between 1966 and 1971. Teaching materials were destroyed, and faculty members were dispersed or reassigned to unrelated positions. These actions were so severe that recovery from them was particularly difficult after the Cultural Revolution. Starting in 1972, students identified as "workers, farmers, and soldiers" were enrolled in three-year programs at Wuhan and Peking universities. However, the academic atmosphere had been so effectively destroyed that it was impossible to conduct meaningful instruction. By 1978, there were only two library science departments in China, one at Peking University and one at Wuhan University.

In the aftermath of the Cultural Revolution, libraries were in a state of complete disorder. On the one hand, there was a dearth of trained librarians, while on the other, every library was overstaffed. High-level senior librarians had aged, and there were few potential successors in sight. Midlevel professionals were widely dispersed and would have to be called back and relocated. The younger library staff had never received any formal training. Therefore, there were huge demands for library school graduates.

The year 1978 was a milestone in the recovery of professional library education. During that year, five universities at the national and provincial levels launched library and information science programs and enrolled 1,700 students. The total number of library and information science students in both formal and informal education programs numbered 28,083. Meanwhile, institutions reporting to ministries other than the Ministry of Education also began to develop LIS programs in such specialized fields as medicine and agriculture. In 1988, forty-six institutions of higher learning in China had departments of, or offered special courses in LIS, and twenty technical secondary schools offered similar courses. By 1991, about sixty higher-education institutions had established standard, full-time courses in LIS. Also, a great many kinds of institutions that provided LIS education, such as **television** universities, night universities, and library schools at the secondary level, had been founded.

The School of Library and Information Science was established at Wuhan University in 1984. It provided four fields of study: library science, information science, archive science, and book trade. The long-standing Library Science Department of Peking University added an information specialty, and its name was changed to Department of Library and Information Science (DLIS) shortly after. This event should be considered a milestone in Chinese professional education, marking the breakdown of the Chinese tradition of an emphasis on the liberal arts and a shift in training objectives for Chinese library education. This trend continued into the 1990s and was the result of theoretical debates carried out during the previous few years in Chinese library journals concerning whether or not library studies could be included within the scope of information science. The changing of department names indicated a positive answer.

The DLIS of Peking University again changed its name to Department of Information Management on October 31, 1992, which marked the beginning of a wave of renaming library science departments in China. In a narrow sense, there was an upsurge in creating information-related specialties in almost all departments of library and information science; some even canceled the library science specialty while dropping the word "library" from the department's name. More than twenty library and information science departments have changed their names to department of information management, department of information resources management, or department of information studies. Many universities with graduate programs have added subprograms with names such as economic information or international economic information management.

In September 1999, some universities in China began to enroll freshmen majoring in a newly created specialty called "information management and information systems" in accordance with the new course catalog issued by the Chinese Ministry of Education in July 1998. The new specialty was formed from the merging of five former separated specialties: economic information management, information studies, scientific information, management information systems, and forestry information management. Due to the fact that the new specialty was merged from five fields of specialties, people from different fields have a different understanding of the new specialty and its meanings, educational objectives, and core courses.

Many universities dropped the traditional model of training professionals for libraries and turned toward education for the professions that have become more involved in society. They adjusted their educational goals as well. For example, the School of Communication and Information Science at Wuhan University proclaimed that it trained qualified professionals who not only were able to deal with information consulting and the management of information systems, but also were capable of performing research work for the information departments of industrial and commercial administration, the press, publishing houses, and the like. The Information Management Department at Peking University stated that library science would train information management professionals who possessed both traditional Chinese culture skills and good skills in modern information technology to meet the demands of the developing market economy in China.

Compared with the old information science specialty, the most important change of curriculum in the new one was that more computer-related courses were added. Many programs emphasized teaching computer skills and modern technology in order to strengthen the integration of library and information science.

The information management education model has its roots in the library and information science education model. It is a four-year college education that leads to the bachelor's degree and can be divided into several different research areas according to individual student interests. There are two new teaching models in China. The first focuses on the teaching of economic information management, which is based in economics and management. The second focuses on the teaching of knowledge management and service, which is based in information technology.

In the new century, the development of China's economy, society, science, and technology not only needs a new type of information management professional, but also provides opportunities for cultivating information professionals. Viewing the fact that there are too many schools that offer information-related specialties, the Ministry of Education stipulated that at the turn of the century, all schools applying for the new specialty must be approved by the ministry rather than by the local provinces. This will assure the quality of professional education, it means that some schools will have no qualification to continue their information-related education. As most of the information science specialty is derived from library science, these schools have to face several challenges, including educational objectives, retraining of faculty, shortage of computers, lack of suitable textbooks, and competition with related schools in universities of economics or technology. If some fail, even though they have been approved at this time, they will have to close in the near future. This is not impossible for some schools in China.

Reform of the specialty of information management and systems is still under way. Every department/school is exploiting effective and efficient educational projects to meet the needs of society for high-quality information professionals. How to deepen the new specialty is a new and critical issue.

Fewer graduates from library and information programs are being employed by academic, public, and special research libraries. Currently, more than half do not work in libraries after graduating. The percentage of librarians with master's and doctoral degrees is quite low. For example, at the end of 2002, there were 203 staff in Peking University Library, among whom only two had doctoral degrees and thirty-one had master's degrees. In some small libraries, no one has an MLS or equivalent degree. Therefore, greater attention needs to be given to library and information science education.

See also Libraries and Development.

Bibliography

Chu, Jingli, "Recent Changes in Information Science Education in Chinese Universities," *Library Review* 50, no. 1 (2001): 34–37; Jin, Xudong, "A Comparison Study on the Confusion and Threat of the United States and Chinese Library Education," *International Information and Library Review* 31 (1999): 1–18; Lin, Sharon Chien, *Libraries and Librarianship in China* (Westport, CT: Greenwood Press, 1998); Shen, Xiangxing, Xu Lifang, and Xie Hai, "Library and Information Science Education and Laboratory Construction in China," *Journal of Education for Library and Information Science* 42, no. 1 (winter 2001): 63–68; Wu, Jianzhong, and Ruhua Huang, "The Academic Library Development in China," *Journal of Academic Librarianship* 29, no. 4 (July 2003): 249–253.

Xudong Jin

LIS

See Library and Information Science (LIS) Education.

Literary Policy for the New China

The literary policy of the New China was determined at the First National Congress of Writers and Artists that was held in Beijing (then still called Beiping) from July 2 to July 19, 1949. Altogether, ten delegations and more than 800 delegates from all over the country participated in this largest congress of its kind in the New China, and all the top leaders, including Communist Party Chairman **Mao Zedong**, Commander in Chief of the People's Liberation Army Zhu De, and Premier **Zhou Enlai**, delivered speeches. The delegates unanimously agreed to support Mao Zedong's thought on literature and art and to follow the instructions that Mao Zedong put forward in his "Talks at the Yan'an Forum on Literature and Art" as the general policy for literature and art in the coming New China.

Mao Zedong's "Talks at the Yan'an Forum on Literature and Art" include two speeches that he delivered separately at the Yan'an Forum on Literature and Art, which was convened from May 2 to May 23, 1942, in Yan'an, Shaanxi Province. The forum was held primarily to promote the Rectification movement, a partywide campaign started in February 1942 to disseminate Marxist-

Leninist ideology and to eliminate such "nonproletarian" ideas as subjectivism, factionalism, and stereotypical writing. The main purposes of the forum were to exchange views on literature and art, seek unity of thinking about some controversial issues, rectify the "wrong" tendencies among some liberal writers, and, above all, ensure that literature and art would follow the correct track of development and better help the Communist Party achieve its political goal of liberating the entire country. At the forum, Mao Zedong, in his capacity as the Party's highest leader, addressed some issues of fundamental orientation on the literary and art front and expressed his views about the direction in which literature and art should develop and how writers and artists should accomplish this. After the forum, the party attached great importance to Mao's talks by requiring all writers and artists to seriously study them and act in the spirit of Mao's directives. On November 7, 1943, the Party issued an official resolution that announced openly that Mao's talks had set the basic policy for literature and art at the present stage, and it urged all Party members to carry out the policy in every possible field. By July 1949, the Party's efforts at recommending the talks had resulted in many obvious changes, especially in the Communist-controlled Liberated Areas. Hundreds of writers and artists had gone down to the countryside or battlefronts to learn from the peasants and soldiers. More significant, a new "people's literature and art" that was created under Mao's instructions had taken shape, both in content and in form. These consequences made the Party believe even more firmly that the direction in which Mao pointed was the only correct one for Chinese literature and art. Thus, when the Communist Party successfully became the ruling party of China in 1949, it decided to continue implementing Mao's talks and extending their impact to the whole country.

"Talks at the Yan'an Forum on Literature and Art" is the most systematic and comprehensive summary of Mao's thought on literature and art. In these talks, Mao thought that revolutionary literature and art are for the masses of the people, and in the first place for the workers, peasants, and soldiers. In order to serve the people well, writers and artists should be steadfast in their class stance and always take the side of the worker-peasant-soldier masses. They should integrate themselves with the masses, go among them, and learn from them. In writing, one should speak loyally for the masses and use the language and artistic forms loved by the masses. In literary and artistic creation, one must have a clear-cut political orientation. One should extol the people's struggles and progress and expose or criticize the enemy and all the dark forces that harm the people. Mao held that although literature and politics are different in essence, the former should be subordinate to the latter. Revolutionary literature and art should support the proletarian politics, fit well into the Party's work as a whole, and accord with the general tasks set by the Party in a given period of time. Mao believed that in a class society, there is neither human nature above classes nor all-inclusive love applicable to all classes. Therefore, revolutionary literature and art should consider only the interests of the proletariat and embody the human nature and love of the proletariat rather than that of any other classes. Mao also put forward two basic criteria for literary and artistic criticism: the political criterion and the artistic one. According to him, although both of the criteria are essential, the former deserves more attention. He deemed that in evaluating a literary and artistic work, one needs to examine the subjective intent of the writer, as well as the social effect that a work might have on the people.

Mao's talks have exerted a profound influence on modern China and have greatly changed the course of literary and artistic creation and criticism in the country. In fact, the talks not only were adopted in 1949 by the First National Congress of Writers and Artists as the first general policy of literature and art for the New China, but also were esteemed as the theoretic bases for formulating new literary policies in the years to come. Even today, nearly three decades after Mao's death, the talks are still frequently mentioned and quoted. In the history of the Communist Party of China, no other writings or literary and artistic policies have had a more direct, long-standing, and widespread impact on Chinese literature and art.

See also Anticorruption Literature and Television Dramas; Avant-garde Literature; Experimental Fiction; Great Cultural Revolution, Literature during; Intellectuals, Political Engagement of (1949–1978); Intellectuals, Political Engagement of (1978–Present); Literature of the Wounded; Misty Poetry; Modern Pop-Satire; Neorealist Fiction and Modernism; Pre–Cultural Revolution Literature; Revolutionary Realism and Revolutionary Romanticism; Root-Searching Literature; Sexual Freedom in Literature.

Bibliography

Dai, Zhixian, *Studies on Mao Zedong's Cultural Thought* (Beijing: People's University Press, 1992); Mao, Zedong, "Talks at the Yanan Forum on Literature and Art," in *Selected Works of Mao Zedong* (Beijing: People's Publishing House, 1969).

Dela X. Jiao

Literature

See Ai Qing; Anticorruption Literature and Television Dramas; Avant-garde Literature; Chinese Script, Reform of; Experimental Fiction; Great Cultural Revolution, Literature during; He Jingzhi; Intellectuals; Intellectuals, Political Engagement of (1949–1978); Intellectuals, Political Engagement of (1978–Present); Journalism Reform; Li Zhun; Literary Policy for the New China; Literature of the Wounded; Liu Qing; Misty Poetry; Modern Pop-Satire; Neorealist Fiction and Modernism; Pre–Cultural Revolution Literature; Press Control; Press Freedom; Revolutionary Realism and Revolutionary Romanticism; Root-Searching Literature; Sexual Freedom in Literature; Sun Li; Theater in Contemporary China; Wei Wei; Yang Mo; Yang Shuo.

Literature of the Wounded

The **Great Cultural Revolution** came to an official end in 1976. With its end came increased freedom for writers, which, during the subsequent decade, gave rise to a variety of literary movements. The first to emerge was "literature of the wounded" (also translated as "scar literature"), which lasted from the end of 1977 until 1979. It started with the publication of "Ban Zhuren" (The class teacher) by Liu Xinwu in November 1977. Considered to be the first story officially published in China to expose the damage inflicted on young people by the Cultural Revolution, the short story condemned the educational and cultural policies of the previous decade and praised **intellectuals.**

The movement of "the literature of the wounded" gathered momentum in the summer of 1978 when Lu Xinhua, a first-year student at Fudan University in Shanghai, presented a story titled "The Wounded" as a big-character poster on campus walls. It revealed the physical, psychological, and spiritual pain the Chinese people had endured during the Cultural Revolution. The story was soon published in the newspaper *Wenhui Daily* in Shanghai (August 11, 1978), received enthusiastic responses from readers throughout the country, and inspired hundreds of others. The two writers, Liu Xinwu and Lu Xinhua, became overnight celebrities. For several years, story after story poured out the guilt, regret, and pain over lost lives and ruined careers, betrayal of friends and family members, and the need to seek restitution.

It is widely held that the great responses caused by this literature movement throughout the country were largely due to its social and political impact in the aftermath of the Cultural Revolution, rather than its literary merits. Immediately after the nightmarish experiences of the Cultural Revolution, writers were not sure of what to write. In the first year after the members of the **Gang of Four** were put in prison, literary works were not much different from those during the Cultural Revolution. The only difference was the shift from the criticism of the "capitalist roaders" (*zouzipai*) to the Gang of Four. The publication of the two stories, however, signaled the literary thaw of the late 1970s and 1980s. Writers started to seek to expunge the mental or physical scars left by the Cultural Revolution, although their analysis of the causes was considered superficial. "The literature of the wounded" was considered new only in terms of its themes, and few of its writers or works survived the immediate need for fictional denunciations of the recent past. Many of these works were similar, but a few, such as Liu Bingyan's *People or Monsters?* and Wang Ruowang's *Hunger Trilogy*, did stand out as remarkably fresh. Their language was simple and clear, but they penetrated deeply and produced some shocking effects.

Other works that have been considered more mature in writing skills include Zhang Jie's *Cong Senlinli Laide Haizi* (Child from the jungle), Zong Pu's *Xuanshangde Meng* (Dream on the string), and Chen Shixu's *Xiaozhenshangde Jiangjun* (General in a small town). Many of the fictions, such as Gu Hua's *Furong Zhen* (The hibiscus town), were adapted into films, which gave them even greater social impact. Within the "wounded" tradition, though not literature per se, a number of Chinese have written accounts of this tragic period for Western audiences.

The authorities encouraged the literary movement, because it was necessary for the new regime to criticize and discredit the abuses of the Cultural Revolution. However, they were faced with a serious problem: how could the writers be encouraged to criticize and discredit the abuses of the Cultural Revolution without going beyond tolerable limits? Because this literature contained some disquieting views of the Communist Party and the political system, and because these authors were intensely patriotic, writing cynically of the political leadership that gave rise to the extreme chaos and disorder of the Cultural Revolution, some of them extended the blame to the entire generation of leaders and to the political system itself. Shortly after Wang Ruowang's *Hunger Trilogy* appeared, the authorities made a decision that "scar literature" had gone far enough. At a widely publicized conference, Sha Yexin's play *What If I Were for Real?* and two other works were criticized for "failing to consider social effects." Soon a flood of articles appeared in China's press criticizing some writers for "ignoring social effects." Before long, it was claimed that the scars had been healed and writers should now sing of new achievements.

"The Class Teacher"

The short story "The Class Teacher" by Liu Xinwu, published in the literary magazine *People's Literature* in November 1977, takes place in the spring of 1977. Zhang Junshi, the teacher, decides to admit a young hooligan called Song Baoqi who was just been released from the police station into his class. Xie Huimin, the secretary of the Youth League Branch in the class, is strongly opposed to Song's coming to the class. Other girls declare that they will not come to school on the day Song comes. Zhang visits Song's home and discovers that Song's delinquency was caused by parental neglect and ignorance. Song's parents were ordinary workers, and his crime was the stealing of banned books. Among the books in Song's possession was *The Gadfly* (1897) by Ethel Lillian Voynich. Song could not even pronounce the title of the book correctly and yet believed that it was pornographic. Xie Huimin also believes that any book not found in bookshops must be politically unorthodox or even pornographic and condemns *The Gadfly* as a "poisonous weed." Zhang Junshi fails to persuade her to be more flexible, and the story ends with an echo of Lu Xun's appeal "to save the children."

The two main characters in "The Class Teacher," Song Baoqi and Xie Huimin, are both victims of the Cultural Revolution: Song Baoqi refused to accept any form of education and became the victim of ignorance. Both physically and spiritually distorted, he became a hooligan, nearly an outcast of society. Xie Huimin, always regarded as a model student, presented a completely different side of the picture. Her spiritual distortion was even more striking than that of Song: she never wore short sleeves in summer, because this was "bourgeoisie lifestyle" and "was not recommended by the newspaper." She was always on the alert for any "class enemies." She had no sense of judgment but followed blindly what the authorities or the newspapers advocated. To her, any books that were not on sale were bourgeois or "pornographic." The publication of this story, which received enthusiastic responses from readers, struck the keynote for the new literature.

"The Wounded"

In Lu's story, the protagonist is a young girl who was psychologically abused during the Cultural Revolution. She denounced her mother, who was accused of being a traitor to the revolutionary cause during the war, and voluntarily became one of the educated youth sent to the countryside to be reeducated by the poor peasants at the age of sixteen. She refused to read any letters or open any parcels from her mother. However, all her efforts were in vain: she was not accepted as a member of the Youth League and had to leave her boyfriend, whose future she did not want to spoil. When she finally learned that her mother had been wrongly accused and had returned to her work as a middle-school head teacher, she was still hesitant to go and see her mother. When she finally went, it was too late for her to achieve reconciliation with her mother, who had died of a heart attack. The tragedy lies in the mental distortion of Xiao Hua and her generation, who blindly believed in what they were told.

The publication of "The Wounded" opened up the floodgate of exposing the physical and psychological abuses of the Cultural Revolution. Some critics therefore have argued that it is more appropriate to call this movement "the exposé literature."

See also Anticorruption Literature and Television Dramas; Avant-garde Literature; Experimental Fiction; Great Cultural Revolution, Literature during; Intellectuals, Political Engagement of (1949–1978); Intellectuals, Political Engagement of (1978–Present); Literary Policy for the New China; Misty Poetry; Modern Pop-Satire; Neorealist Fiction and Modernism; Pre–Cultural Revolution Literature; Revolutionary Realism and Revolutionary Romanticism; Root-Searching Literature; Sexual Freedom in Literature.

Bibliography

McDougall, Bonnie S., ed., *Popular Chinese Literature and Performing Arts in the People's Republic of China, 1949–1979* (Berkeley: University of California Press, 1984); Zhang, Xudong, *Chinese Modernism in the Era of Reforms* (Durham, NC: Duke University Press, 1997).

Xiaoling Zhang

Liu Qing (1916–1978)

Liu Qing was a novelist who was regarded as a "people's writer." He was born on July 2, 1916, into a peasant's family in Wubao County, Shaanxi Province. He became a Communist Party member in 1936 and arrived in Yan'an in 1938. One year later, he joined the army and served as a journalist. From 1943 to 1945, encouraged by **Mao Zedong**'s "Talks at the Yan'an Forum on Literature and Art," Liu went down to the countryside and worked together with peasants in Mizhi County of Shaanxi Province. This firsthand experience was used as a creative source in his first novel, *Planting Millet* (1949), which marked the real beginning of his writing career. The novel focused on the different attitudes that a group of peasants took toward the issue of growing millet and described the ideological changes of different social strata during their mutual-aid and cooperation campaign. Because of his vivid portrayals of the peasant characters and the local conditions and customs, this work is generally esteemed as a representative novel in the literature of the Communist Liberated Areas in the 1940s. Liu's second novel, *Impregnable Fortress* (1951), displayed more mature writing techniques. This work was devoted to a battle during the War of Liberation (1945–1949). It depicted how the peasants in the northern areas of Shanxi Province made every effort to support the Communist army by protecting grain, and thus the work showed that the real impregnable fortress was the thousands of revolutionary people above anybody else. *Impregnable Fortress* was one of the first works in modern Chinese literature that created a group of heroic characters, all of whom were ordinary people in the new epoch. More significantly, it was the first literary work ever that described Mao Zedong, **Zhou Enlai**, and some other top Party leaders.

In 1952, Liu moved with his family from Beijing to a village in Changan County, Shaanxi Province, where he settled among the peasants for fourteen years. In that village, Liu participated in the whole process of the agricultural cooperation movement and acquired a good knowledge of the movement itself and rich experience of rural life. Beginning in 1959, Liu's third novel, *The History of Pioneers*, was published in serial form in the literary journal *Yanhe*. This monumental work concentrated solely on the agricultural cooperation movement in China. Through a large number of peasant characters, Liu portrayed the peasantry's enthusiasm for taking the socialist road after the **land reform**. Such characters as Liang Shengbao and Old Liang San have become typical characters in modern Chinese literature. Especially Liang Shengbao, one of the male protagonists, can be regarded as the first successful peasant character of the "socialist new man" in Chinese fiction. *The History of Pioneers* has enjoyed high prestige both at home and abroad. Originally, Liu planned to write altogether four volumes for this novel, but he was not able to complete his huge project before his death. Although what can be seen today is only a part of Liu's whole story, *The History of Pioneers* is one of the most significant novels about the socialist revolution and construction in the countryside.

Liu is best known for his lively presentation of various strata of the peasantry, the epiclike grand tableau of social life and the changes of his time, and an exquisite description of details. He was one of the few writers in modern China who devoted tremendous attention to rural life and attempted to express through his novels the hardships, confrontations, frustrations, and progress among the peasantry. Moreover, his writings demonstrate that he was very familiar with the discourse of the peasantry. The impact of Liu's works is apparent. Many of his sayings have been frequently studied and quoted.

See also Anticorruption Literature and Television Dramas; Avant-garde Literature; Experimental Fiction; Great Cultural Revolution, Literature during; Intellectuals, Political Engagement of (1949–1978); Intellectuals, Political Engagement of (1978–Present); Literary Policy for the New China; Literature of the Wounded; Misty Poetry; Modern Pop-Satire; Neorealist Fiction and Modernism; Pre–Cultural Revolution Literature; Revolutionary Realism and Revolutionary Romanticism; Root-Searching Literature; Sexual Freedom in Literature.

Bibliography

Meng, Guanglai, and Yunqing Niu, eds., *Monograph on Liu Qing* (Fuzhou: Fujian People's Publishing House, 1982).

Dela X. Jiao

Liu Shaoqi (1898–1969)

Liu Shaoqi's role in China's Communist history cannot be overestimated. He was **Mao Zedong**'s loyal supporter during the revolution against the Nationalists and the Japanese, but was brought down by Mao during the **Great Cultural Revolution** in the 1960s. Liu's theory, represented in his article "How to Be a Good Communist," while being condemned as a revisionist and corruptive ideology, left a deep impact on Chinese communism. Many believe that Liu's thoughts, in reality, are far apart from Maoist Communist radicalism and, on the contrary, are deeply embedded in traditional Chinese philosophies.

Coming from the same home province as Mao Zedong and even from a similar family background, Liu Shaoqi was born in Hunan Province in 1898, the youngest son of a rich peasant landowner. Some say that, in terms of demeanor and style, Liu seemed to be from a wealthier class than Mao. Liu attended middle school in Changsha, the capital of Hunan, like Mao, who studied at the Changsha First Provincial Normal School. Thereafter, Liu dedicated himself to continued studies, particularly in Russian and possibly in French also, because studying abroad was sought after by many young intellectuals at the time. His future revolutionary partner Mao Zedong went to Beijing, where he accepted Marxism and joined a Marxist study group at Peking University. In 1920, Liu joined a socialist youth group and subsequently went to Moscow to study communism. In Moscow he joined the Chinese Communist Party. After returning to China, Liu became a dedicated labor movement leader and rose rapidly to the Party's Central Committee in 1927. In the 1930s, Liu joined the Long March (1934–1935), assisted Mao in securing the Party's top leading position at the Zunyi Conference (1935), and directed the Party's underground operations later on. In the 1950s and early 1960s, Liu rose rapidly to become head of state of the People's Republic of China (PRC), replacing Mao Zedong, because Mao was blamed for bringing about the failed **Great Leap Forward**, which resulted in a famine that killed more than 23 million people.

However, while Mao Zedong retired from the post of chairman of the PRC, he remained chairman of the Party and in actual control of the country's operations. In 1966, Mao launched his counterattack, known as the Great Cultural Revolution, and directed the spearhead directly at Liu Shaoqi and his supporters. Mao was concerned with Liu Shaoqi's increasing prominence and with his pro-Soviet tendency, characterized by promoting urban development. Such policies could well undermine the **"people's commune"** movement in rural China that Mao had been pushing since the Great Leap Forward. In particular, Liu's gaining of popularity directly threatened Mao's position as the absolute leader. In 1968, Liu was dismissed from his position as head of state. He was denounced by the Red Guards in public as a traitor of the revolution and was physically tortured. Liu died in detention in 1969.

Liu Shaoqi's representative work "How to Be a Good Communist" was published in 1939. In this article, Liu stresses that it is important for a Communist to first better himself before he can hope to set out and represent the people. Concepts such as this already separated Liu from classical Communist theories. The classical theories believe that Communists are the cream of the working class or the most advanced class in the current society and in history.

Hence there could hardly be any better standards for Communists to live up to. Liu argues, however, that Communists are human beings and are hence prone to weaknesses—some may lack courage, others may be immature. Most ironically, Liu resorts to Confucius's and Mencius's admonitions to substantiate his concept that even Communists need to cultivate themselves, Confucius and Mencius being condemned both then and also in the 1960s as the source of feudal thoughts.

Liu expresses his admiration for Confucius by indicating that Confucius was a great teacher who did not consider himself to have been born a sage. Moreover, Liu appreciates Mencius's admonition that a great man "exercises his mind with suffering and toughens his sinews and bones with toil, exposes his body to hunger, subjects himself to extreme poverty, thwarts his undertakings and thereby stimulates his mind, tempers his character and adds to his capacities." Liu's conclusion is clear: since the great philosophers in history valued self-cultivation to the utmost, why should Communists be exempt from bettering themselves? In fact, Liu could not be more straightforward in stating that the Communist Party did not fall from heaven but was born out of Chinese society, and hence self-cultivation is important for every Communist, especially after the seizure of political power. By these words, Liu takes away the aurora from Communist leaders that Mao Zedong himself sought earnestly in the 1960s through measures such as the "Little Red Book" and other means of personality cult.

Particularly troublesome to Mao Zedong would be Liu Shaoqi's remarks on "fake Communists." Liu indicates that certain Party members practice dogmatism; they know absolutely nothing about Marxism-Leninism, and by babbling Marxist-Leninist phraseology, they regard themselves as China's Marx or China's Lenin. Liu expresses cynicism in stating that these fake Communists show the impudence to require others to revere them as Marx and Lenin are revered, support them as "the leaders," and accord them loyalty and devotion. Liu indicates that these people went so far as to appoint themselves "the leaders" without being chosen, climbed into positions of authority, issued orders to the Party like patriarchs, tried to lecture the Party, abused everything in the Party, and willfully attacked and punished Party members and pushed them around. He asserts that these people had no sincere desire to study Marxism-Leninism or fight for the realization of communism—they were just careerists in the Party, termites in the Communist movement. Obviously, Mao Zedong was very sensitive to such powerful comments and found them particularly haunting because he himself was widely suspected of such behavior after he led the country into the Great Leap Forward disaster.

What, then, according to Liu Shaoqi, are the most essential values that a Communist must possess? The first and foremost is the possession of Communist morality, because the Communist cause is one of justice. Liu states that Communists must not be untrue to themselves and to the people. Second, a Communist must always be practical in that he treats Marxism as guidance instead of as dogma. This concept was inherited by Deng Xiaoping, who developed it in the 1980s into what became widely known as the slogan "the reality is the only standard for judging the truth." Third, Communists must be loyal to the Party and must not possess private agendas. The only concern of a real

Communist must be with the people, but not with himself. Once again, Liu refers to the famous chancellor Fan Zhongyan of the Song dynasty, who said he was the first to worry and the last to enjoy himself. Fourth, Liu believes that a Communist must have the greatest self-respect and self-esteem. This does not mean that he has a strong ego; on the contrary, this means that for the sake of the Party and the revolution, a real Communist can be most forbearing and tolerant toward comrades and can suffer wrong in the general interest, even enduring misunderstanding and humiliation without bitterness if the occasion so demands. Moreover, no personal aims lead him to flatter anyone or to desire flattery from others. Finally, Liu urges Communists to be straightforward, a quality very much stressed by Confucius. Liu believes that if a Party member really takes the Communist cause as his own, he should unconditionally subordinate his own interests to the interests of the Party; under no pretense or excuse may he sacrifice the Party's interests by clinging to his own.

In essence, Liu Shaoqi's Communist cultivation is more derived from Confucian principles than from classic Marxist principles. For him, communism is about serving the people and realizing the general happiness. It is not about exercising the proletarian dictatorship, the way Mao firmly pursued, whereby the people are forced into silent slaves. For that reason, Liu was condemned, among many crimes, as a "revisionist" and a "capitalist," which he may well have been in reality.

See also Zhou Enlai.

Bibliography

Dittmer, Lowell, *Liu Shaoqi and the Chinese Cultural Revolution* (Armonk, NY: M. E. Sharpe, 1998); Liu, Aiqin, *My Father Liu Shaoqi* (Liaoning, China-Liaoning People's Publishing House, 2001); Liu, Shaoqi, *Selected Works of Liu Shaoqi* (Beijing: Foreign Languages Press, 1984).

Jing Luo

Living Conditions

See Consumption Patterns and Statistics of Living Conditions; Unfinished Demographic Transition.

Local Media Bodies

See Media Bodies, Central and Local.